COMPARATIVE PSYCHOLOGY
A Modern Survey

COMPARATIVE PSYCHOLOGY
A Modern Survey

Donald A. Dewsbury

Associate Professor of Psychology
University of Florida

Dorothy A. Rethlingshafer

The Late Professor of Psychology
University of Florida

McGraw-Hill Book Company

New York   St. Louis   San Francisco   Düsseldorf
Johannesburg   Kuala Lumpur   London
Mexico   Montreal   New Delhi   Panama
Rio de Janeiro   Singapore   Sydney   Toronto

Library of Congress Cataloging in Publication Data

Dewsbury, Donald A.   1939–
  Comparative psychology.

  Includes bibliographies.
  1.   Animals, Habits and behavior of.
2.   Psychology, Comparative.   I.   Rethlingshafer,
Dorothy, joint author, II. Title. [DNLM: 1.   Behavior, Animal   2.   Psychology, Comparative.   QL
785 D524c   1973]
QL751.D453   156   72–12572
ISBN 0–07–016670–6

COMPARATIVE PSYCHOLOGY:
A Modern Survey

1234567890 KPKP 79876543

This book was set in Times Roman by Holmes Typography, Inc.
The editors were Walter Maytham and Phyllis T. Dulan;
the designer was Nicholas Krenitsky;
and the production supervisor was Joe Campanella.
The drawings were done by Eric G. Hieber.
The printer and binder was Kingsport Press, Inc.

Contents

v

List of Contributors

Norman T. Adler
Department of Psychology
University of Pennsylvania
Philadelphia, Pennsylvania

Colin G. Beer
Institute of Animal Behavior
Rutgers University
Newark, New Jersey

Bradford N. Bunnell
Department of Psychology
University of Georgia
Athens, Georgia

Lynwood G. Clemens
Department of Zoology
Michigan State University
East Lansing, Michigan

Donald A. Dewsbury
Department of Psychology
University of Florida
Gainesville, Florida

John L. Fuller
Department of Psychology
State University of New York
Binghamton, New York

Eckhard H. Hess
Department of Psychology
University of Chicago
Chicago, Illinois

Charles W. Hill
Department of Psychology
Louisiana State University
New Orleans, Louisiana

James A. Horel
Department of Anatomy
Upstate Medical Center
State University of New York
Syracuse, New York

Allan L. Jacobson
Department of Psychology
San Francisco State College
San Francisco, California

James V. McConnell
Mental Health Research Institute
University of Michigan
Ann Arbor, Michigan

Austin H. Riesen
Department of Psychology
University of California
Riverside, California

Arthur J. Riopelle
Department of Psychology
Louisiana State University
Baton Rouge, Louisiana

Kurt Salzinger
Biometrics Research Unit
New York State Department of
Mental Hygiene
Polytechnic Institute of Brooklyn

John Paul Scott
Department of Psychology
Bowling Green State University
Bowling Green, Ohio

J. M. Warren
Animal Behavior Laboratory
Pennsylvania State University
University Park, Pennsylvania

Richard E. Wimer
Division of Neurosciences
City of Hope Medical Center
Duarte, California

Preface

This book is intended for use as a text in courses in the comparative psychology–animal behavior area. It should be appropriate for both advanced undergraduates and graduate students.

Comparative psychology is a multifaceted and active discipline. Few individuals are capable of writing a comprehensive text that is up to date and accurate in all of its various subareas. An alternative to a single author book is the multiauthored book. The problems with multiauthored books lie in consistency in level of presentation and in avoidance of redundancy. In planning this book, we have decided that what may be lost in these areas may be more than compensated for by gains in accuracy and quality. Therefore, the decision was made to produce a multiauthored book.

Work on this book was initiated by Dr. Rethlingshafer in 1965. It was to be a sequel to the book edited by Waters, Rethlingshafer, and Caldwell in 1960.

Dorothy Rethlingshafer died in 1969. With her death, psychology lost a dedicated and outstanding teacher and researcher. Through her writing and teaching, she had earned a national reputation. Her loss was deeply felt by all those who knew her in person or by reputation.

At the time of her death, Dr. Rethlingshafer had contracted for ten chapters of this book and had tentative plans for several more. I was asked to complete the book.

In producing the final book, I have worked within the framework of the ten chapters contracted by Dr. Rethlingshafer. As no two comparative psychologists view the discipline in precisely the same way, I have inevitably imposed my own views on the book. However, I have tried to do so in a manner which is basically consistent with Dr. Rethlingshafer's intentions. The order of appearance of the editors' names was determined on advice from outside neutral sources.

My primary changes from the original outline concern the beginning and end of the book. I have long felt that a text in this area must start with some descriptive material before advancing to various topics more analytic in nature. Much of the material traditionally covered in a chapter on motivation can be treated in such a descriptive context. In addition, I felt that a coverage of ethology was essential. Therefore, two chapters were placed after the introductory chapter to provide some descriptive information about animal behavior and to introduce the methods used in ethology and comparative psychology in the study of behavior. The topic of evolution also merits treatment. I have attempted to provide that in the final chapter. As I believe that evolutionary theory provides the most substantial hope for unification of the various areas of comparative psychology, I have attempted to write the chapter so that it restates and works toward integration of some of the themes mentioned earlier in the book.

The first chapter provides a basic introduction to comparative psychology. The remainder of the book is divided into five parts. The first part, dealing with patterns of behavior, emphasizes descriptive information and contains chapters on ethology and the behavior of nonmammalian species, mammalian behavior, comparative social psychology, and animal communication. The second part deals with the origins of behavior. The third part is concerned with correlates of behavior and contains chapters on the nervous system, hormones, and sensory and perceptual processes. The fourth part deals with the modification of behavior and contains chapters on learning in invertebrates, learning in vertebrates, and complex processes. The final part contains one chapter—that on evolution and behavior.

The book was written mainly by psychologists and is intended primarily as an introduction to comparative psychology. Much of the material in the book is written with a strong biological flavor. This is in keeping with the general development of comparative psychology and the strengthening of its bonds with zoology and anthropology.

Several authors have expressed a wish to list their acknowledgments. Dr. Salzinger wishes to extend his thanks to his wife Suzanne for editing his chapter and to Joseph Zubin for encouraging work in animal communication.

Preparation of Chapter 6, on behavior genetics by Drs. Fuller and Wimer, was aided by Research Grant MH-11327 from the National Institute of Mental

Health, General Research Support Grant #103-839 from the National Institutes of Health, Research Grant HD-02491 from the National Institute of Child Health and Human Development, and Research Grant OEG-9-9-140395-0057(057) from the Office of Education. Preparation of Dr. Warren's chapter on learning in vertebrates was supported by Grants M-04726 from the National Institute of Mental Health, U. S. Public Health Service and GB-15469.

Donald A. Dewsbury

COMPARATIVE PSYCHOLOGY
A Modern Survey

Chapter 1

Introduction

Donald A. Dewsbury

Man is indeed a marvelous creature. Man builds structures and communities of great complexity. Man constructs machines capable of performing tasks thought impossible only a few years ago. Man develops languages and communication networks extraordinarily more complex than those of any other creature. Despite his remarkable accomplishments, we must remember that man is an animal and a part of nature. However remarkable and unique his achievements, man eats, drinks, urinates, defecates, and copulates as do all other vertebrates. He is not a unique antagonist, an external force struggling against the forces of nature, but rather a part of nature. As such, he must learn to live in harmony with the rest of nature.

If this is true, then a full understanding of man and his nature is inconceivable without an understanding of other species. It is only in the context of a broad understanding of the behavior of many species that man can gain essential perspective to understand himself. Is human language unique? Perhaps it is. But how can we know unless we study the communication systems of other species on the same terms as we study our own? How can we fully appreciate the buildings and machines of man until we have studied the shelters and tools of other species? This approach implies no conclusion regarding the uniqueness or lack of uniqueness of man. It merely permits such questions to be raised in as comprehensive a manner as possible. A

1

leading comparative psychologist, F. A. Beach has made this point succinctly:

> ... if we remove man from the central point in a comparative science of behavior, this may, in the long run, prove to be the very best way of reaching a better understanding of his place in nature and of the behavioral characteristics which he shares with other animals as well as those which he possesses alone or which are in him developed to a unique degree [Beach, 1960, p. 17].

The primary goal of a comparative science of behavior is to seek an understanding of the behavior of a broad spectrum of animal species. It is anticipated that such an understanding will be of value in and of itself as a part of a liberal education and an enlightened world view. It also is anticipated that such an understanding will help us to understand ourselves and our place in nature.

WHY STUDY ANIMAL BEHAVIOR?

Although a major reason that humans study behavior as a comparative science relates to understanding themselves and their place in nature, a kindred reason is an interest in the behavior of animals itself. Homo sapiens is among the more curious and inquiring of species. Men live in close association with other species whether they are hunters living with buffalo, deer, turkey, and beaver, or urban dwellers living with cats, dogs, tropical fish, mice, cockroaches, and ants. It is natural that creatures as inquiring as men have sought to understand the behavior of these other creatures as an endeavor worthy of their time and energy.

There are many other reasons that behavioral investigators may adopt a comparative methodology. For some kinds of experiments, the investigator is concerned not so much with the behavior of the species itself as with the accessibility of a given system. Most species possess characteristics which make them good subjects for some kinds of research and poor subjects for others. For example, much of the basic knowledge about the physiology of nerve cells originated with study of the giant axon of squid. Most axons are quite small, and the available technology was insufficient to permit investigators to place sensing devices within them. The squid giant axon, being larger, served as an excellent research preparation. Principles derived from the study of squid axons have proved applicable to the nerve cells of other species. The cardiac pacemaker ganglion of lobsters contains just nine cells. It has provided an excellent preparation for study of the interactions of nerve cells in a system simpler than that of complex vertebrate brains (Maynard, 1955). White rats, a popular choice as subjects in psychology, probably were good subjects for psychologists interested in maze learning. Rats live in mazelike environments in their natural habitats. However, because they have notoriously poor visual acuity (Hess, 1960), they appear to be less ideal subjects for research on visual pattern discrimination.

Sometimes psychologists turn to research on nonhuman subjects for ethical reasons. For example, ethical standards do not permit experimenters to control the breeding of humans. There are no such restrictions on nonhuman subjects. Thus, controlled genetic experiments impossible with humans can be performed with nonhumans. Certain neural interventions are not permissible in humans except in cases of serious disease. Experiments involving such intervention generally are permissible with nonhuman subjects, as long as humane procedures and considerations are carefully regarded.

Comparative psychology is a basic science. As with most such sciences, it produces basic knowledge which may be applicable in situations not anticipated at the time of the research. For example, research in reproductive behavior has provided valuable information helpful in facilitating the breeding of species judged useful to man, such as zoo animals, farm animals, and animals for biomedical research; and in reducing the breeding of species judged as pests, such as certain insects and rodents. Knowledge from the comparative study of instrumental learning has been applied in training zoo animals, circus animals, and pets; in training nonhuman primates to perform in spacecraft; and in developing an improved technology of human education. Various other immediate applications of knowledge of animal behavior, summarized by Waters (1960), have been useful in conservation , education, agriculture, and a variety of other contexts. The frequent applicability of basic research to the solution of everyday problems related to human welfare is one of the important reasons behind its continued support.

Thus, although the primary goal of comparative psychology is a comprehensive knowledge of the behavior of a wide variety of species, including man, many more immediate benefits accrue from its research activity.

WHAT IS COMPARATIVE PSYCHOLOGY?

In its broadest sense, comparative psychology might be defined as the systematic study of everything every species does or is capable of doing. Because of the overwhelming nature of the task of understanding everything every animal does, and because of the activities of colleagues in related disciplines, comparative psychologists have limited the number of different organisms they study and the kinds of questions they ask (Dewsbury, 1968). The result has been the development of a broad, but manageable, science of behavior. The nature of comparative psychology can best be understood by examining the activities of comparative psychologists as they study behavior.

Behavioral Description

The first task of the comparative psychologist in working with behavior is to describe it. Some comparative psychologists work with a single kind of behavioral pattern as displayed in many species, while others try to describe all the behavior of a few species. These two approaches complement each other. Nevertheless, it may surprise you to learn how few behavioral patterns have been adequately described in even a small number of species.

Describing behavior is more difficult than it may at first seem. In undertaking the task, it is incumbent upon us to be as objective and faithful as possible. Even then, human observers inevitably perceive and describe behavior in terms of some preconceived frame of reference. Behavior occurs as a continuous stream, and the observer must decide what to record and just when a change in behavior is only a minor variation on a continuing pattern or a more fundamental change to a different pattern.

At least two ways of describing behavior can be distinguished (Hinde, 1970). In one, an attempt is made to describe behavior in terms of patterns of movements. Patterns of muscle contractions are grouped together according to their similarity in space and time. Such terms as *knee jerk* and *tail wag* are exemplary of this kind of descriptive category.

Alternatively, the observer may describe the behavior in terms of its consequences—its effects on the environment. When the observer reports that the animal "pressed the bar" or "retrieved a pup," he is describing behavior in terms of its consequences.

These two ways of describing behavior overlap to some extent. Many descriptive analyses of behavior contain mixtures of terms drawn from both types of description. Many patterns imply both a specific pattern of muscular activity and a specific effect upon the environment. Most comparative psychologists tend to emphasize description in terms of the effects of behavior on the environment. Often two highly similar or even identical patterns of muscle contraction can serve two very different ends. Often the same end can be served by two very different patterns of muscle contractions. The same movement pattern can be used to strike a nail or to strike another human. A rat can press a bar of an operant conditioning chamber by using his forepaws or by jumping on it. It is the effect of the behavior on the environment in these two examples that generally is more important than the pattern of muscle movement. Categorization in terms of effects on environment sometimes permits automation in recording. For example, the number of bar presses made by an animal in an operant conditioning chamber can be tallied automatically. Where appropriate and where not abused so that much important behavior is ignored, such automated procedures can be a great time-saver and provide a recording of great objectivity.

Wherever possible, comparative psychologists try to record behavior on motion picture film, on videotape, or with still photographs. The only decision required of the observer is that of when to start and stop the camera. The camera is an unbiased recorder. Once such recordings are obtained, the observer can return to them to check his category system with those of others and to reexamine passages to search for characteristics of the behavior missed in the original observations.

When various behavioral patterns are discussed, the patterns frequently are grouped in terms of the role they play in the life of the organism. Thus we refer to ingestive behavior, eliminative behavior, reproductive behavior, social behavior, communicative behavior, and so forth.

Topics for Study

Once behavior has been described, what kinds of questions do comparative psychologists ask about behavior? Tinbergen (1963) has listed four areas for study in animal behavior: development, mechanisms, function, and evolution. While the first two have provided the primary emphasis in comparative psychology, interest in the latter two is increasing as stronger ties are built between comparative psychologists and zoologists studying behavior.

In investigating the development of behavior, we seek to understand the origins of the behavior. Where did it come from and how did it develop? Emphasis is placed on both its genetic determinants and the environmental determinants with which they interact. Given normal development, differences in behavior may be primarily attributable to genetic or environmental factors. Nevertheless, both play some role in the complete expression of the typical pattern.

The second group of questions involves the mechanisms that determine behavior. Some mechanistic questions relate to physiological determinants. Behavior is determined to a great extent by the action of the nervous system, the endocrine system, the sensory and perceptual systems, and related physiological systems. Conversely, these systems are altered as a function of behavior. It is this interaction between behavior and physiological systems that provides an important area for inquiry about the mechanisms that determine behavior.

Another group of questions centers about the modification of behavior. Learning and other sources of behavioral modification are important to the behavior of most species. Many of these processes can be studied with no physiological intervention. Rather, the interaction of the whole organism and the environment is studied. Whether or not physiological manipulations are performed, many questions can be considered as relating to the immediate causal mechanisms underlying behavior.

In asking about the function of a behavioral pattern, we inquire as to the effect of the pattern on the ability of the animals to survive and succeed.

In some cases, the function of a pattern of behavior is evident. The function of eating is to provide nutrients necessary for survival. In other cases, the function is less clear. For example, we do not yet fully understand why male rats attain a series of about ten vaginal intromissions without ejaculation before they attain an intromission with ejaculation. Questions of the function of behavior have been termed *teleonomic questions* (Pittendrigh, 1958; Williams, 1966). When we say that an animal eats because it needs certain nutrients, we in no way imply that the animal anticipates or comprehends this need. To do so would be to inquire as to mechanism, not function. It also would lead to teleology—an undemonstrated inference of "purpose" in behavior. Psychologists frequently have become embroiled in fruitless controversy because they gave teleonomic or even teleological answers to mechanistic questions. The onset of eating probably is caused by changes in blood sugar level, body temperature, or some such variable (mechanistic explanation), but such eating functions to provide needed nutrients (teleonomic explanation). We cannot say that an animal eats because it "knows" it needs food (teleological explanation). Although it may be impossible to be as precise in dealing with teleonomic questions as when considering mechanistic questions, it is apparent that if we seek a comprehensive understanding of behavior, we must understand the *whys* as well as the *hows*. A teleonomic psychology would consider behavior in relation to its functional significance for the species. Both mechanistic and teleonomic explanations are important; and it is essential that they not be confused.

Finally, we may ask about the evolutionary history of a behavioral pattern or capacity. From Aristotle, and probably before, there is a long history of inquiry into the evolution of "intelligence." The evolutionary history of other behavioral patterns is no less important. If we are to understand the evolution of behavior, it is imperative that we begin with comparative analysis. As many species are extinct and as behavior, unlike bone, does not fossilize, we can study only living species. Nevertheless, by studying different species of different degrees of taxonomic and historical relationship, it frequently is possible to develop reasonable hypotheses regarding the evolutionary history of a pattern of behavior.

A HISTORY OF COMPARATIVE PSYCHOLOGY

In order to understand the nature of comparative psychology as it now exists, it is helpful to examine its history—how did the comparative psychology of today come to be?

Current trends in comparative psychology can best be understood as reflecting the interaction of American animal psychology and European ethology. The last twenty years have seen the interaction of these two groups of scientists which had been studying similar phenomena but in relative isolation from each other. Classical European ethology was developed by zoologists interested in the study of animal behavior through careful observation, particularly in the natural habitat. They emphasized *instinctive* behavior, and their primary subjects were birds, fish, and insects. Traditional American comparative psychology, on the other hand, developed among psychologists who studied animal behavior in the controlled environment of the laboratory. The psychologists emphasized *learned* behavior, with their primary subjects being mammals, especially the white rat. It has been the interaction of these two disciplines that has created the revitalized contemporary comparative psychology. With this growing synthesis has come a merging of interests, methods, and even names. It is now necessary to distinguish *classical ethology*, the European brand that developed prior to 1950, from *contemporary ethology*, which can refer to any animal behavior study, including that usually termed *comparative psychology*.

Animal Behavior before 1800

Prior to the nineteenth century, the antecedents of comparative psychology must be sought in what we now regard as philosophy and natural history. The Greek philosopher Heraclitus proposed that there had been two types of creation. Whereas men and gods were the products of rational creation and possessed souls, irrational brutes fell in an entirely separate category and lacked souls. Thus, the groundwork was set for a distinction between men who were rational and possessed souls, and "beasts," which were primarily creatures of instinct. If beasts were viewed as possessing reason or a soul, it was viewed as fundamentally different from that possessed by man. This tradition persisted through Albertus Magnus, St. Thomas Aquinas, René Descartes, and indeed into the twentieth century (Beach, 1955).

In his *Historia Animalium*, Aristotle laid some foundations of a comparative science of behavior. He was an early evolutionist and proposed a *Scala natura*—a linear ordering of species according to their intelligence. Man was at the peak, directly above the Indian elephant (Beach, 1955; Waters, 1960). Aristotle also was a bit of a naturalist. For many centuries, naturalists have provided useful information in the study of animal behavior. For example, in the eighteenth century, Baron Ferdinand Adam von Pernau, a German zoologist, reported one of the most clear-cut examples of a separation of genetic and environmental variables known today. Whereas some species of birds must hear their species-typical song if they are to sing it, in others the song develops independent of such experience (Hess, 1962).

The Early Nineteenth Century

Jaynes (1969) has traced the beginnings of some of the fundamental issues for divergence between traditional comparative psychology and classical ethology to the Cuvier–Geoffroy-Saint-Hilaire debates of the early nineteenth century. Baron Cuvier, one of the most famous scientists of his time, believed in the immutability of species and in the importance of laboratory research. Étienne Geoffroy-Saint-Hilaire was a younger man and an advocate of naturalistic observation and an evolutionary point of view. In their debates, the naturalistic views of the younger Geoffroy-Saint-Hilaire were overwhelmed. However, advocates of these views may be regarded as early founders of ethology, whereas the intellectual descendants of the Cuvier side proceeded to found comparative psychology. Geoffroy-Saint-Hilaire's son, Isidore, laid some foundations for ethology as a study of living animals in their natural habitat in his writings in 1859.

In 1864 Pierre Flourens, a protégé of Cuvier, published a book under the title of *Psychologie Comparée*. This appears to have been the first substantial attempt to found comparative psychology as a new science.

Darwin

It was from Darwin that the comparative study of animal behavior received significant impetus. With the development of the theory of evolution, the importance of comparative study became more apparent. In addition, in 1873, Darwin wrote a book dealing with the comparative study of animal behavior, *Expression of the Emotions in Man and Animals*. In this remarkable book, now republished in paperbound form, Darwin considered behavior as he considered structure—from a phylogenetic viewpoint. Similarities in behavioral patterns of different species were uncovered and their functional significance considered.

After Darwin

In the 1870s, no fewer than five texts with "comparative psychology" as their title appeared (Jaynes, 1969). In addition, Herbert Spencer wrote an article by the same title. However, it was the influence of George John Romanes that had most impact. His 1882 book, *Animal Intelligence,* presented a mass of data which laid groundwork for the conclusion that mental continuity exists in species. A friend of Darwin, Romanes relied heavily on the anecdotal method. Inclusion of unreliable information made interpretation difficult and provoked violent reaction from other scientists.

Meanwhile, ethology lived in the work of a small minority of French zoologists as zoology came to stress comparative anatomy and the study of corpses rather than the behavior of living organisms. Alfred Giard and his student George Bohn were important in this tradition.

Turn of the Century

Around the dawn of the twentieth century, there appeared several important scientists whose impact was felt in the development of comparative psychology

and ethology. An English naturalist, C. Lloyd Morgan, reacted to the anecdotal method of Romanes. He proposed a law which has been variously termed
Occam's razor, the *law of parsimony*, and *Lloyd Morgan's canon*. According
to Morgan (1894), "In no case may we interpret an action as the outcome
of the exercise of a higher psychical faculty, if it can be interpreted as the
outcome of the exercise of one which stands lower in the psychological scale."
Morgan thus sounded a warning against the proposition of explanations that
involved needless complexity. Although there are some difficulties in its
interpretation, Lloyd Morgan's canon seems applicable today. If alternative
explanations appear truly equal, the simpler is to be preferred until data require
postulation of more complex processes.

Jacques Loeb extended the conservative thinking of Morgan when he
proposed the theory of tropisms in 1890. According to this theory, behavior
is explicable in terms of simple physiochemical reactions toward or away from
stimuli.

Herbert Spencer Jennings reacted to Loeb's tropistic theory. He maintained that even the behavior of very simple organisms was the product of
processes more complex than those suggested by Loeb. He proposed that
the organism reacts as a whole and that behavior frequently is spontaneous
rather than a mere reaction to stimuli.

William James, in his *Principles of Psychology* of 1890, described much
research on animal behavior, including such phenomena as imprinting and
critical periods. The work of Douglas Spalding led one writer to call him
"the first experimental behaviorist" (Gray, 1962). Sir John Lubbock, J. Henri
Fabre, Auguste Forel, and W. M. Wheeler conducted important investigations
into the behavior of arthropods.

Thus, at the turn of the century many important scientists had directed
their attention to the study of animal behavior. There was much controversy,
but there also was increasing emphasis upon the accumulation of reliable data,
and it was out of this scientific turmoil that twentieth-century ethology and
comparative psychology developed.

Ethology in the Twentieth Century

Jakob von Uexküll proposed that the entire behavioral repertoire of a species
must be observed before any single pattern can be understood. This became
a recurrent theme in ethology. He also developed the notion of the *Umwelt*
—that each animal has its own sensory world. Different species are responsive
to different stimuli, and the behavior of a species can be understood only
when one understands its own peculiar *Umwelt*. When species see in the
infrared range and hear what we call ultrasonic, man indeed must exercise
care in dealing with effective stimuli for behavior.

C. O. Whitman, an American zoologist, wrote in 1898 that "Instincts
and organs are to be studied from the common viewpoint of phyletic descent

[Hess, 1962, p. 168]." Oskar Heinroth, a German zoologist, found evidence in the behavior of ducks and geese that this was indeed a fruitful endeavor.

Wallace Craig, a student of Whitman, proposed the distinction between appetitive behavior, the variable, searching part of a pattern, and the consummatory act, rigid in form.

It was with Konrad Lorenz and Niko Tinbergen that ethology reached its peak. Both conducted important research on a variety of species and proposed provocative theories with which to explain what they found. It is the Lorenz-Tinbergen tradition that led to the full development of ethology, leading in turn to the emphasis in Chapter 2 of the present book.

Animal Psychology in the Twentieth Century

In the basement of William James's house in Cambridge, E. L. Thorndike began his research on the intelligence of chicks. Thorndike's thesis, "Animal Intelligence: An Experimental Study of the Associative Processes of Animals," was completed in 1898. This research emphasized the *law of effect* in trial-and-error learning as exemplified in animals learning to escape from problem boxes. Thorndike's influence in pointing the way toward reinforcement and the study of learning was to have great impact (Boring, 1957). W. S. Small was the first to study white rats in maze-learning problems.

John B. Watson collected many of the intellectual threads of the early twentieth century into *Behaviorism*. In his classical paper "Psychology as the Behaviorist Views It," and his book *Behavior: An Introduction to Comparative Psychology*, Watson adopted a position of extreme parsimony and environmentalism.

The story of dominant trends for the next three decades is one of increasing emphasis on the study of learning in rats and in the construction of theories to explain the phenomena involved. This line reached its peak in the thirties and forties with such theorists as Hull, Tolman, and Skinner. What had started out as a broadly based comparative psychology had become the theoretical study of rat learning (Beach, 1950). Even physiological study was diminished.

As frequently is the case, a few scientists kept alive an important tradition as the bulk of the discipline marched off to an extreme. Robert M. Yerkes studied many different organisms from crabs to men and became interested in many different kinds of behavior. His interest in anthropoid apes led him to found primate research facilities both at Yale and in Orange Park, Florida. Karl S. Lashley maintained the traditions of physiological psychology through the dark years of the twenties, thirties, and forties. He too was interested in a broad spectrum of behavior. A student of Watson, Lashley was a teacher of several men who became outstanding in the revitalization of comparative and physiological psychology that occurred after World War II. The classical text of N. R. F. Maier and T. C. Schneirla (1935) did much to maintain the tradition of a broadly based comparative psychology.

Comparative Psychology and Ethology after World War II

Following World War II, the work of a number of American comparative psychologists, including F. A. Beach, J. P. Scott, T. C. Schneirla, C. P. Stone, and C. R. Carpenter, became widely known. These were psychologists studying birds and ants, and maternal and sexual behavior, and doing field studies. A broadly based comparative psychology was reemerging. A student of Lashley, D. O. Hebb set the stage for a reappearance of physiological psychology in 1949 with his book *The Organization of Behavior*.

In the 1950s European ethology and American comparative psychology rediscovered each other. As both groups believed that theirs was *the* objective study of animal behavior, considerable friction was generated. It appeared that both had been studying the same behavior and had come to radically different conclusions. D. S. Lehrman (1953) wrote an extensive critique of Lorenz's theory and Eibl-Eibesfeldt and Kramer (1958) rose to its defense. An English translation of several classical ethological papers was published in 1957 under the title *Instinctive Behavior*. It featured an introduction by Lashley and a preface by Tinbergen that began: "Whenever I meet American behaviorists I am struck by the very great difference in approach between them and us [Tinbergen, 1957, p. xv]."

Meetings between European ethologists and psychologists became more frequent. Polemics died down and fruitful interaction started to occur. Comparative psychologists began better to appreciate the importance of evolutionary and functional considerations. They recognized the distortions in behavior that can occur in the laboratory. For their part, ethologists began to appreciate that some behavior could be studied only under controlled conditions and that quantitative methods could lend great precision to their data. Thus, as ethology and comparative psychology became rejoined, each was modified and broadened. Added to this juncture has been an influence from physical anthropology—particularly with respect to field studies of the behavior of nonhuman primates. An ethologist, R. A. Hinde, was one of several to attempt a synthesis, as, for example, in his book *Animal Behaviour, a Synthesis of Ethology and Comparative Psychology* (1970).

Today there still are many comparative psychologists and ethologists who have been minimally touched by the activities of the other group. However, increasing numbers of workers in both areas find much gain in interaction. Most teachers of comparative psychology regard consideration of ethology as an important part of any contemporary course (Bermant, 1965). Ethologists publish papers in the *Journal of Comparative and Physiological Psychology*, and psychologists publish papers in *Behaviour, Animal Behaviour,* and the *Zeitschrift für Tierpsychologie*. Differences in emphasis remain, but communication has broken down barriers and led to more mature investigation of animal behavior.

ANIMAL SPECIES

Without an orderly system of classification of animal species, the enormous array of different organisms would be overwhelming and orderly inquiry would be impossible. Prerequisite to a study of the content matter of comparative psychology is a consideration of the species which are available for study. This consideration should include taxonomy, which deals with the proper naming and classification of species, and phylogeny, which deals with evolutionary history.

Species

The focal step in classification is that of the grouping of organisms as species. A species is defined as "a group of individuals capable of interbreeding under natural conditions and reproductively isolated from other such groups" (Villee, Walker, & Smith, 1958). This definition comes as a surprise to many psychology students. In effect, species are defined according to their reproductive behavior and physiology in the natural habitat. An excellent discussion of the nature of species has been provided by Mayr (1963). In practice, it often is impossible to gather complete information regarding breeding under natural conditions. Fortunately, because of the nature of gene flow and of the natural environment in which species develop, members of a species closely resemble one another structurally and behaviorally. Thus, it is common to identify an organism as a member of a particular species according to its morphology (form and structure) and behavior. Keys are available which enable one to classify an organism on the basis of a variety of morphological characteristics. For example, a scaly tail and a hard palate that extends beyond the last molar are characteristic of the laboratory rat (*Rattus norvegicus*). Behavioral patterns may serve as a guide to identification of species. Some species of fireflies appear highly similar morphologically, but flash in different patterns. As the flash pattern is a part of their reproductive pattern, these different groups do not interbreed and are considered good species despite their close resemblance in appearance.

A species is a category into which many different but highly similar individuals are classified. Despite their many similarities, each individual is a unique product of the interaction of his own genotype with a particular environment. Thus, we must think of populations rather than of types. *Typological thinking*, in contrast to *population thinking*, has repeatedly led to misconceptions in the study of biology and behavior (Hirsch, 1967).

Table 1-1   Classification of Four Species

Common name	Honeybee	Dog	Chimpanzee	Man
Kingdom	Animalia	Animalia	Animalia	Animalia
Phylum	Arthropoda	Chordata	Chordata	Chordata
Class	Insecta	Mammalia	Mammalia	Mammalia
Order	Hymenoptera	Carnivora	Primates	Primates
Family	Apidae	Canidae	Pongidae	Hominidae
Genus	*Apis*	*Canis*	*Pan*	*Homo*
Species	*mellifera*	*familiaris*	*troglodytes*	*sapiens*

Taxonomy

Each species has one name in a binomial Latin system. This name is used universally. The first word in the Latin name refers to a genus. The generic name is italicized and capitalized. The second word in the Latin name identifies the species. It never is capitalized but is italicized. It identifies one and only one species of the genus. The Latin name is less confusing, more specific, and more indicative of evolutionary history than is a common name. For example, the distinction between mice and rats appears to be based primarily on size and general appearance. Laboratory rats (*Rattus norvegicus*) are more closely related to laboratory mice *(Mus musculus)* than to cotton rats *(Sigmodon hispidus)*, rice rats (*Oryzomys palustris*), or wood rats (*Neotoma floridana*). The latter three "rats" are more closely related to old-field mice (*Peromyscus polionotus*) than to laboratory rats.

Generic names usually are used just once in naming. Thus, there is but one genus called *Peromyscus* or *Microtus*. However, specific names may occur quite frequently. Both of the latter genera contain species which are named *californicus*.

A genus contains a number of similar species. The remainder of the taxonomic system consists of an hierarchical arrangement in which each level represents a more comprehensive grouping of divergent organisms. The major levels are those of kingdom, phylum, class, order, family, genus, and species. Various other levels, such as superorders, subfamilies, and even subspecies, may be added. Classification of four species is presented in Table 1-1.

Phylogeny

One of the principal advantages of the taxonomic system developed by biologists is that it provides a good general approximation to the phylogeny, or evolutionary history, of species. This is a difficult task, particularly because many of the important pivotal species in evolutionary history have become extinct and thus are no longer available for study. Even so, data from paleon-tology and comparative morphology can be integrated to produce a probable course of evolution in most cases.

Such considerations have produced the concept of a phylogenetic tree. Each species can be conceptualized as representing a point on the periphery. Each branching represents the divergence of two or more species from a single common ancestor. Thus, evolution is conceptualized as a process of diversifi-cation—of branching. Each of the many evolutionary lines has gone its own route.

From the time of Aristotle it has been common to conceptualize species as falling along a phylogenetic scale, or *Scala natura*. According to such a scale, man generally is placed at the top, with other species in order of decreas-ing rank placed below (Hodos & Campbell, 1969). Terms such as *phylogenetic scale, higher species*, and *subprimates* still are used today. As we have seen, evolutionary history is best conceived as a tree rather than as a unidimensional scale. Thus, the notion of a single phylogenetic scale does not coincide with the apparent course of evolution. While it is possible to classify species on a scale with respect to any continuous variable, there is no single scale that can be regarded as *the* phylogenetic scale. An ordering according to body size would give a scale very different from one in which species were arranged according to the relative size of their brains.

An example of the confusion generated by *Scala naturae* can be seen within the placental mammals. The probable course of the evolution of the mammals is shown in Figure 1-1. It appears that the various eutherian mam-mals have diversified from a common insectivore stock. These are represented in Figure 1–1 as Deltatheridoidea, Tenrecoidea, Chrysochloroidea, Erina-coidea, Soricoidea, and Macroscelidoidea. Common contemporary insec-tivores include moles, shrews, and hedgehogs. Nevertheless, it is common to conceive of shrews, rats, cats, and monkeys, and man as representing a continuum as if they had evolved from one another. While they may represent a continuum in terms of certain criteria, such as complexity of the brain, they do not represent an evolutionary continuum. In no sense may rats be regarded as ancestral to cats or cats to primates. Rather, all appear to have diverged from insectivores.

In Figure 1-2, the evolution of primates is portrayed. This leads to a related point. We rarely are able to study a species and its ancestor. Most mammalian ancestors appear to be extinct. When we study the modern apes, such as chimpanzees *(Pan)*, we are not studying an ancestor of man *(Homo)*. Rather, we study a species with which man shares a comparatively recent common ancestor. Men and chimpanzees both have evolved according to the selective pressures of their respective environments ever since they diverged from a common ancestor within the Hominoidea. There is no reason to think

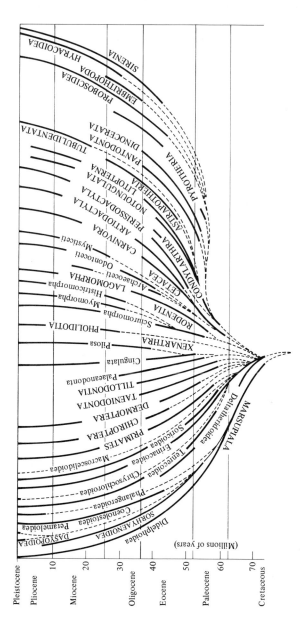

Figure 1–1. Chart showing the probable affinities of the orders of mammals (in capitals) and the lesser divisions of some of the more primitive orders (in lowercase). (From J. Z. Young, *The Life of the Vertebrates*, Oxford: Clarendon Press, 1950.)

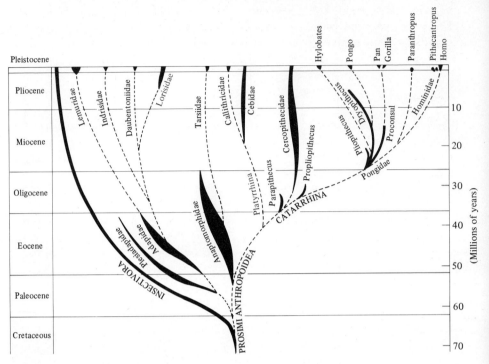

Figure 1–2. Chart showing the evolutionary tree of primates. (From J. Z. Young, *The Life of the Vertebrates,* Oxford: Clarendon Press, 1950.)

that men have necessarily become any more specialized than chimpanzees have.

BEHAVIOR AND EVOLUTION

It should be clear that comparative psychology encompasses a broad range of diverse topics. Because of this breadth and diversity, the comparative psychologist has difficulty in presenting his field and the student has difficulty in comprehending it. The central theme that best unifies comparative psychology is that of evolution. The modern synthetic theory of evolution which binds together many parts of biology provides a means for the systematic integration of the subject matter of comparative psychology. In dealing with behavior in an evolutionary context, the comparative psychologist evaluates the functional significance of the behavioral patterns he describes, or attempts to reconstruct their evolutionary history.

The central theme of evolution and behavior will run through many of the chapters which follow. The final chapter will deal with evolution and behavior as its major topic and serve as a summary to the entire book. The theory of evolution provides the most promising hope of tying together the threads of comparative psychology and of enabling appreciation of the entire field.

SUMMARY

The primary goal of comparative psychology is to seek a comprehensive understanding of the behavior of a broad spectrum of species. Such an understanding will help place human behavior in perspective and also have more immediate and short-term benefits.

The first task of the comparative psychologist is that of describing behavior. After description has been completed, questions regarding development, mechanism, function, and evolutionary history are asked.

The beginnings of contemporary comparative psychology can be traced far back in the history of ideas. With Darwin, the comparative study of animal behavior received a great boost. In the twentieth century, a school of ethology developed among European zoologists, and a comparative psychology was developed in the United States. Contemporary comparative psychology is the product of the interaction of these two areas of thought that has occurred since World War II.

Knowledge of basic taxonomy and phylogeny is essential to the study of comparative psychology. Species are conceived as groups of individuals capable of interbreeding under natural conditions. Morphological and behavioral characteristics are useful in identifying the correct species of an organism. Each species has a unique Latin binomial designation, which generally is more reliable than its common name. The evolutionary history of species is conceived as a phylogenetic tree with species branching apart from each other. There is little support for a unidimensional hierarchy of species.

The modern synthetic theory of evolution provides unification of comparative psychology and is a central theme of this book.

REFERENCES

BEACH, F. A. The snark was a boojum. *American Psychologist,* 1950, **5**, 115–124.

BEACH, F. A. The descent of instinct. *Psychological Review,* 1955, **62**, 401–410.

BEACH, F. A. Experimental investigations of species-specific behavior. *American Psychologist,* 1960, **15**, 1–18.

BERMANT, G. Modern courses in comparative psychology. Paper presented at the meeting of the American Association for the Advancement of Science, Berkeley, Calif., December 1965.

BORING, E. G. *A history of experimental psychology.* (2nd ed.) New York: Appleton-Century-Crofts, 1957.

DEWSBURY, D. A. Comparative psychology and comparative psychologists: An assessment. *Journal of Biological Psychology,* 1968, **10,** 35–38.

EIBL-EIBESFELDT, I., & KRAMER, S. Ethology, the comparative study of animal behavior. *Quarterly Review of Biology,* 1958, **33,** 181–211.

GRAY, P. H. Douglas Alexander Spalding: The first experimental behaviorist. *Journal of General Psychology,* 1962, **67,** 299–307.

HESS, E. H. Sensory process. In Waters, R. H., Rethlingshafter, D. A., & Caldwell, W. E., *Principles of comparative psychology.* New York: McGraw-Hill, 1960. Pp. 74–101.

HESS, E. H. Ethology: An approach toward the complete analysis of behavior. In R. Brown, E. Galanter, E. H. Hess, & G. Mandler (Eds.), *New directions in psychology.* New York: Holt, Rinehart and Winston, 1962. Pp. 157–266.

HINDE, R. A. *Animal behaviour: A synthesis of ethology and comparative psychology.* (2nd ed.) New York: McGraw-Hill, 1970.

HIRSCH, J. Behavior-genetic, or "experimental" analysis: The challenge of science versus the lure of technology. *American Psychologist,* 1967, **22,** 118–130.

HODOS, W., & CAMPBELL, C. B. G. *Scala naturae:* Why there is no theory in comparative psychology. *Psychological Review,* 1969, **76,** 337–350.

JAYNES, J. The historical origins of "ethology" and "comparative psychology." *Animal Behaviour,* 1969, **17,** 601–606.

LEHRMAN, D. S. A critique of Konrad Lorenz's theory of instinctive behaviour. *Quarterly Review of Biology,* 1953, **28,** 337–363.

MAIER, N. R. F., & SCHNEIRLA, T. C. *Principles of animal psychology.* New York: McGraw-Hill, 1935.

MAYNARD, D. M. Activity in a crustacean ganglion: II. Pattern and interaction in burst formation. *Biological Bulletin,* 1955, **109,** 420–436.

MAYR, E. *Animal species and evolution.* Cambridge, Mass.: Harvard University Press, 1963.

MORGAN, C. L. *Introduction to comparative psychology.* New York: Scribner's, 1894.

PITTENDRIGH, C. S. Adaptation, natural selection, and behavior. In A. Roe & G. G. Simpson (Eds.), *Behavior and evolution.* New Haven, Conn.: Yale University Press, 1958. Pp. 390–416.

TINBERGEN, N. Preface. In C. H. Schiller (Ed.), *Instinctive behavior, the development of a modern concept.* New York: International Universities Press, 1957. Pp. xv–xix.

TINBERGEN, N. On aims and methods of ethology. *Zeitschrift für Tierpsychologie,* 1963, **20,** 410–429.

VILLEE, C. A., WALKER, W. F., & SMITH, F. E. *General zoology.* Philadelphia: Saunders, 1958.

WATERS, R. H. The nature of comparative psychology. In R. H. Waters, D. A. Rethlingshafter, & W. E. Caldwell, *Principles of comparative psychology.* New York: McGraw-Hill, 1960. Pp. 1–17.

WILLIAMS, G. C. *Adaptation and natural selection: A critique of some current evolutionary thought.* Princeton, N.J.: Princeton University Press, 1966.

YOUNG, J. Z. *The life of the vertebrates.* Oxford, England: Clarendon Press, 1950.

PART ONE

PATTERNS OF BEHAVIOR

Before analyzing the origins, correlates, modification, and evolution of behavior, one must first describe behavior. The emphasis in Part I is upon the description of animal behavior and the approaches which different scientists use in studying behavior. This is intended to provide a firm foundation in animal behavior, with which the analytical approaches of later chapters can be better understood.

The separate development and subsequent interaction of ethology and comparative psychology were described in Chapter 1. Both disciplines have made important contributions to the study of behavior. In addition, anthropologists have conducted a variety of studies of primate behavior in the field which have made valuable contributions. A number of zoologists other than ethologists have reported significant information about animal behavior gathered in both field and laboratory. Frequently, these have been naturalists, ecologists, or others interested in "whole-animal biology." Finally, the physiologists have added important facts to our knowledge of animal behavior. Some appreciation of the contributions of all these disciplines is important in understanding the contemporary status of the study of animal behavior.

How are we to compartmentalize the continuous stream of behavior into pedagogically useful units for the description of behavior? One might first divide behavior into social behavior and nonsocial behavior. While this distinction is not absolute, it is convenient. Within nonsocial behavior, one might study sleep, exploration, play, orientation, ingestion, thermoregulation, shelter-seeking, elimination, or reproduction. Although all these activities can be social at some times, it frequently is useful to consider them as a separate unit. Social behavior includes aggregative relationships, sexual relationships, leader-follower relationships, dominance-subordination relationships, care-dependency relationships, mutual care relationships, trophallaxis, and so forth. Virtually all social behavior involves communication and all communication involves social behavior.

In Chapter 2, a more complete exposition of ethology than that of Chapter 1 is provided. Major characteristics and topics of study in ethology are described. Examples of behavior generally are drawn from insects, fish, and birds, the primary subjects in much of classical ethology. Mammalian behavior is described in Chapter 3. Data generally have been drawn from comparative psychologists, zoologists, and anthropologists. Much of the information in this chapter might sometimes be discussed under the rubric *motivation*—a construct that increasing numbers of animal behaviorists are finding superfluous. Social interactions are described in Chapters 4 and 5. A broad coverage of social relationships and social organization is provided in Chapter 4. The behavior of wolves and dogs is given particular stress, as man has been close to these species both in mutual relationships and in analogous social organizations. Chapter 5 is focused on animal communication and the evolution of human language.

Together, these four chapters are designed to provide a foundation of descriptions of behavior and of the approaches used in the study of both social and nonsocial behavior.

Chapter 2

Species-Typical Behavior and Ethology

Colin G. Beer

An experienced bird watcher can identify a bird by its call as readily as by its appearance. The tracks an animal leaves may identify it not only because the footprints are those of a paw or hoof of a specific size and shape but also because their spacing and arrangement reflect a pattern of locomotion characteristic of the animal. In general, animals have behavioral as well as morphological features specific to their types.

This point, though commonplace in the lore of gamekeepers, hunters, and amateur naturalists, was long overlooked by scientists. But a little over sixty years ago, it caught the attention of two zoologists: C. O. Whitman in America and O. Heinroth in Germany; and partly through their influence it later became one of the basic propositions of a school of behavioral scientists. "Comparative ethology owes its existence (to the discovery that there are patterns of behavior) which animals of a given species 'have got' exactly in the same manner as they 'have got' claws or teeth of a definite morphological structure [Lorenz, 1950, p. 238]."

This chapter will be concerned with species-typical behavior patterns and ethology, both the ways in which study of such patterns has shaped ethological ideas and the ways in which ethological ideas have influenced study of the patterns.

SOME HISTORICAL PERSPECTIVE

For convenience, the history of ethology can be divided into two phases: the earlier or "classical" work which culminated in Tinbergen's *The Study of Instinct* in 1951, and the more recent work. In this section attention is drawn to some of the sources of classical ethological conceptions about behavior.

Most of the men who shaped classical ethology were naturalists; they enjoyed watching animals in nature or in conditions of captivity that simulated nature. This taste led them to firsthand encounters with a wide variety of behavioral phenomena and also to the large literature of amateur natural history. Natural history thus initially supplied the phenomena that became the topics of ethological study, but zoology provided the conceptual framework within which these phenomena were placed. The classical ethologists were zoologists. They received their training at a time when systematics and comparative morphology still occupied prominent places in zoology, and evolution and ecology were expanding subjects. But the relevance of these subjects to the study of behavior was seen through a complex of beliefs and ideas connoted by the term *instinct*.

Comparative Morphology and Systematics

The study of the anatomy of animals, and the classification of animals on the basis of similarities and differences of form, are the most traditional occupations of zoology. The legacy of their history includes two closely related concepts which have to be understood to appreciate the significance of species-typical behavior for ethology: the concept of shared patterns of organization, and the concept of homology.

An internal axial skeleton divided into articulating segments, a hollow, dorsally situated nerve cord with segmental nerves, and other features are common to all the animals classed together as vertebrates. An external, segmented skeleton, a solid, double, ventrally situated nerve cord with segmental ganglia and nerves, and other features are common to all the animals classed together as arthropods. The notion of shared pattern of structural organization is exemplified in all phyla and the smaller categories into which they are divided.

The wing of a bird, the foreleg of a frog, and the arm of a man are all recognized as corresponding to the same feature of the vertebrate body plan. Even internally, these different structures share the same structural plan, so that their several parts can be put in correspondence, as is implied by the sharing of labels such as humerus, radius, and so forth. Such correspondence between the parts of two or more structures that share a common organization is what is meant by *structural homology*.

Shared patterns of organization and homologies are often far from obvious. Detailed comparative study of anatomy, including fossil and embryological material, may be necessary before correspondence relationships are discerned. Thus, for example, it was established that two of the little bones in the middle ear of mammals are homologous with the two bones that form the articulation between the upper and lower jaws in other vertebrates.

This example also illustrates the point that homologous structures sometimes serve different functions, and have different forms in accordance with these functions. But there are also instances of structures that serve similar functions and are similar in form yet are not regarded as homologous, e.g., the dorsal fins of fish and the dorsal fins of whales.

Whales are classified as mammals, not as fish. This fact illustrates the importance in systematics of the kinds of morphological relationships exemplified by homology, as opposed to similarities and differences associated merely with function. The distinction is not easy to draw, however. Consequently, controversy has frequently attended judgments of taxonomic affinity. Some of the issues are still alive today. They held such a prominent place in the preoccupations of past generations of zoologists that the teaching of zoology used to be dominated to a large extent by comparative morphology and its application in systematics.

The consequence for classical ethology was that most of the men who shaped it were sophisticated in the observation, description, and interpretation of form and formal relationships; they were practiced in the use of the concepts of homology and functional analogy; and they were extensively schooled in the morphology and systematics of animals. However, their applications of this combination of skills, concepts, and knowledge to the study of behavior were imbued with the ideas of evolution and natural selection.

Evolution

The theory of evolution by natural selection transformed thinking about, and interpretation of, the evidence of comparative morphology, the affinities upon which systematics was based, and the relationships between form and function. It also oriented zoologists toward the dynamic interrelationships between organisms and their environments.

The Origin of Species contained two arguments: the argument for evolution, and the argument for natural selection. In summary, the first argument was to the effect that if one accepts the principle that species are related to one another by descent with modification from common ancestors, then a large number of otherwise unconnected facts from diverse sources fit together in a single and extremely plausible pattern: facts from comparative morphology, systematics, the study of fossils, the study of geological strata, the study of geological processes, the geographical distributions of organisms, embryology, and the selective breeding of animals and plants. For Darwin, the combination of evidence made belief in evolution "inescapable." His second argument, that the process that has brought evolution about is natural selection, consisted of deductions from incontrovertible generalizations. It ran thus: As a rule, the number of offspring brought forth in a population of organisms in each generation exceeds the number of parents, yet population size tends to remain more or less stable from generation to generation. It follows that only some of the offspring in each generation succeed in contributing offspring to the next generation. The individuals of a population vary in their characteristics. Those individuals having characteristics better suited to the environment or way of life of the species will have a greater probability of leaving offspring than will other members of the population. Offspring tend to inherit the characteristics of their parents. There thus is preservation of those hereditary characteristics that are most adaptive, at the expense of those less adaptive. And since environments vary in space and time, we thus have the process that brings about evolution: natural selection of heritable variations.

Under the influence of the two arguments in Darwin's book, much of the zoology of the late nineteenth century was directed either to the evolutionary history of animals and its representation in phylogenetic "family trees," or to interpretation of characteristics in terms of adaptation. The ad hoc speculativeness of this work was uncongenial to a tough-minded attitude demanding proof by experiment, however, and when genetics made its entry at about the turn of the century, it was cast in the role of an alternative to Darwinism. But a synthesis of genetics and evolution was eventually effected, emerging in such influential books as *The Genetical Theory of Natural Selection* (Fisher, 1930) and *Evolution, the Modern Synthesis* (Huxley, 1942) to become orthodox zoological doctrine. Complementing this Neo-Darwinism was the science of ecology. The introduction of systematic and quantitative methods to the study of organism/environment interrelationships led to new understanding of such matters as the control of population size and distribution, predator-prey relationships, competition between organisms dependent on similar resources, and in general, enriched conceptions of how various and subtle are the manifestations of evolutionary adaptation.

The classical ethologists were Neo-Darwinians. Indeed, to oversimplify for the purpose of making a point, classical ethology could be described as Neo-Darwinism applied to behavior. At any rate, it brought attention to questions about the evolution and adaptive significance of behavior at a time when most other study of behavior was concerned with other matters. Classical ethology thus echoed Darwin's twofold approach to evolution. It also followed Darwin in construing the study of behavior as the study of instinct.

Instinct

At the beginning of his chapter on instinct in *The Origin of Species*, Darwin acknowledged that there is a problem about the definition of the term. It is used in such a variety of ways, both in everyday speech and in science, that there would seem to be little hope of finding a unifying thread of meaning. "Instinct" and "instinctive" are used to describe a pattern of behavior that is species-typical and stereotyped, a pattern of behavior that is hereditary, unlearned behavior, behavior that is not guided by intelligence or foresight of its consequences, goal-directed behavior expressive of an inner urge or compulsion or of the urge or compulsion itself, and so on.

One way to achieve consistency in the use of these terms would be to stipulate that they apply only where all the different ascriptions can be made of the same thing, i.e., to behavior that is at once species-typical, stereotyped, hereditary, unlearned, internally driven, and so forth. But then it will be an empirical matter whether instinct, construed in this way, has any instances, and, if so, what they are. For neither in logic nor in fact is species-typical behavior necessarily internally driven, or hereditary behavior necessarily unlearned. Nevertheless, many writers have worked under the at least tacit assumption that where behavior is instinctive in one or two of the restricted senses, it must be instinctive in the other senses as well. Darwin thought this way, and so did the classical ethologists.

In *The Study of Instinct* (1951), Tinbergen divided his discussion of behavior between four kinds of problem: immediate causation, ontogeny, adaptive significance, and evolution. In a later publication (Tinbergen, 1963), he reiterated that concern with each and all of these problems characterizes ethology, and he said that " ... it is useful to distinguish between them and to insist that a comparative coherent science of Ethology has to give equal attention to each of them and to their integration [p. 411]." But, by training and theoretical orientation, the classical ethologists were, by and large, inclined more toward the evolutionary aspects of behavior than toward its physiological and developmental aspects. Facts relevant to the evolution and adaptive significance of behavior tended to shape their ideas about proximate causation and ontogeny. This tendency was fostered by instinct rather than by its study.

THE PROXIMATE CAUSATION OF SPECIES-TYPICAL BEHAVIOR

Fixed Action Patterns, Taxes, and Appetitive Behavior

The species-typical behavior, the discovery of which, according to Lorenz (1950), started ethology, comprised patterns that he believed were instinctive in all the senses of the term mentioned here. He regarded these patterns as so distinct from all other kinds of behavior that he proposed that they and they alone should be called instinctive activities. Tinbergen (1951) referred to them as *fixed action patterns*.

Fixed action patterns are stereotyped; they are shown by all members, at least those of the same sex, of a species; they are elicited by simple but specific external stimuli; and they are self-exhausting—their performance reduces for a time the ease with which they can be elicited again. It was also believed that a fixed action pattern, once elicited, does not depend either upon external or peripheral stimulation for its form (i.e., the motor pattern is internally determined) or upon experience for its development.

An example of a fixed action pattern is the tongue flick with which a frog catches flies (Tinbergen, 1951, pp. 87–88). The visual stimulus of a fly in front of a frog's head and within striking distance elicits rapid projection and withdrawal of the tongue, the movement being so inflexible in its timing and direction that if the fly moves quickly enough, the frog will miss it. The social behavior of birds and fish provided Lorenz and Tinbergen with numerous examples of such patterns.

Many of the examples are not pure fixed action patterns, however. In the case of the fly-catching of the frog, the animal first orients itself toward the fly and, in so doing, puts itself into a position in which the fly provides the stimulus that triggers the tongue flick. The behavior as a whole consists of two components—orientation movement and a fixed pattern—which are quite distinct because they do not overlap in time. In other cases, an oriented component may be combined with a fixed pattern component, the two occurring simultaneously. Careful analysis, and perhaps experiment, is necessary to tease apart the two components.

The classic example of such an analysis is the study of egg-rolling in the greylag goose (Lorenz & Tinbergen, 1938). An incubating greylag, like most birds that build shallow nests on the ground, reacts to the presence of an egg at the edge of its nest by stretching toward the egg, placing the underside of its bill against the far surface of the egg, and then bending its neck to bring the bill toward its breast and thus roll the egg into the nest cup (Figure 2-1). If, in its passage over the nest rim, the egg begins to veer to one side or the other, the goose adjusts the position of its bill to counter the deviation. The bending of the neck and head toward the breast, and the side-to-side adjusting movements, have the appearance of a single action. If, however, the egg rolls out of reach of the bill in the course of the action, the side-to-side movements cease abruptly, contact with the egg is lost, but the bending movement is carried through to completion. From this and other observations, Lorenz and Tinbergen concluded that the egg-rolling consists of two components: the bending of neck and head in the vertical plane, which is carried out independently of external stimulation once elicited; and the lateral movements of the bill, which are dependent on moment-to-moment tactile stimulation of the bill.

Figure 2–1. Egg-rolling by a black-billed gull: an action combining a "taxis" and a "fixed pattern."

A similar analysis into a fixed action component and a guided component was made of the food-gaping of nestling thrushes (Tinbergen & Kuenen, 1939). Numerous other examples could be cited. In general, fixed action patterns are coupled, either in succession or simultaneously, with guided reactions to external stimuli.

Guided reactions of the kinds mentioned, and those that determine the direction taken by an animal in locomotion, are referred to collectively as *taxes*. Taxes differ in a variety of respects: the sensory modalities involved, the direction of response with respect to the source of external stimulation, the mode of orientation—e.g., whether it is made on the basis of successive or simultaneous comparison of intensities of stimulation from different directions, or by perception of objects. The most comprehensive review of the subject of orientation in animal behavior is still the book by Fraenkel and Gunn (1961; see also Tinbergen, 1951).

Taxes are included in a broad category that ethologists refer to as *appetitive behavior*: behavior that varies with the circumstances in accordance with goal. The term was taken from a paper by Craig (1918) entitled "Appetites and Aversions as Constituents of Instinct." Craig had observed that many sequences of behavior consist of variable actions that are terminated by performance of a stereotyped, species-typical act of some sort. He concluded that performance of the end act is the goal of the variable behavior and the cause of its coming to an end, not such consequences of the act as intake of food or water, placement of a piece of material in a nest, and so forth. He called the variable behavior *appetitive* and its goal a *consummatory act*.

The classical ethologists adopted Craig's dichotomy and made it the basis of their theories of instinct. They identified consummatory acts with fixed action patterns and thus distinguished the latter from ordinary reflexes. For, while consummatory acts and ordinary reflexes are alike in being stereotyped and species-typical, and are not clearly distinguished by the criterion of self-exhaustion, only of consummatory acts could it be said that they are the goals of appetitive behavior (Lorenz, 1937).

On the assumption that appetitive behavior is compelled by internal motivating forces rather than external agencies, the dependence of consummatory acts on appetitive behavior implies that they too are the expressions of internal compulsions and are hence instinctive in this as well as the other meanings of the term. But for appetitive behavior to reach its culmination in performance of a consummatory act, it normally has to bring the animal into a situation that provides the stimuli necessary to elicit the act.

The Innate Releasing Mechanism

Knowledge of an animal's sensory capacities is necessary to understanding how the outside world affects the animal's behavior. But it can lead to wrong expectations about what the animal is reacting to on a particular occasion. The male European robin reacts with hostility to the intrusion of another male into its territory. In an investigation of the visual stimuli that elicit this hostility, Lack (1943) found that the red breast of the intruder is its most provoking feature; everything else about it is more or less irrelevant. We know that the visual system of the robin provides it with much more information about its rival than the fact that the rival is red, yet this simple feature is sufficient to elicit the species-typical patterns of threat and attack. From experiments using models, Tinbergen (1951) drew a similar conclusion about the red belly of the male three-spined stickleback. There are numerous such cases in which a pattern of species-typical behavior is response to only a single part of what is impinging on the sense organs.

Tinbergen called such simple response-evoking features *sign stimuli*. He used the technique of model presentation to investigate them in a variety of species. In some cases, he found that more than one sign stimulus is included in what elicits a species-typical response. The pecking response of a herring gull chick to its parent's bill provided one of the most complex examples. The adult herring gull has a yellow bill with a red spot near the tip. The pecking response occurs when a parent gull holds its bill down near the head of its chick (Figure 2-2). From a series of experiments in which he used various

Figure 2–2.   Laughing gull chick pecking at its parent's bill: a response ''released'' by ''sign stimuli.''

models, Tinbergen (1953) concluded that the following features affect the strength of the chick's response: the color of the spot (red was superior to all other colors), the degree of contrast between the spot and the rest of the bill (the greater the contrast the stronger the response), the width of the bill (narrow models produced greater response than wide models), the position of the bill (a vertical model was superior to models held at other angles), and the distance of the bill from the chick's head (the closer the model the stronger the response). By combining these features and exaggerating some of them, he contrived a model—a thin red rod with three white bands near its tip—which produced stronger response than a real herring gull's head.

This example of an artificial stimulus that is superior to the natural one in its power to elicit response illustrates what Tinbergen called ''supernormal'' stimulation. Other examples include the supernormal ''eggs'' that incubating ringed plover, oystercatchers, and gulls will choose in preference to their own eggs (Tinbergen, 1951, 1958).

Given a pattern of behavior that occurs in response to several sign stimuli, what is the relationship between the effects of the different stimuli? The first ethologist to study this question was Seitz, a student of Lorenz, who worked on cichlid fishes. He discovered a situation in which the effects of the several stimuli affecting a response are additive. Tinbergen (1951) called this kind of relationship between stimuli ''the phenomenon of heterogeneous summation.'' The best-known example was provided by his own study of the sexual pursuit flight of the male grayling butterfly. The male graylings take off in pursuit of females that fly by them. Tinbergen and his associates used models to investigate what properties of the flying female elicit this response. They found that color and shape were unimportant, but that the darker a model was, the closer it was to a male, and the more it simulated the undulating flight of a female, the more likely it was to elicit response. They also found that deficiency in one of these characteristics could be compensated for by the others. For example, a model that was ''flown''in a straight line, if dark enough and close enough, elicited the same degree of response as an undulating model that was less dark and farther away. The same degree of response could be produced by several combinations of values of the three sign stimuli. This simple additive relationship between the effects of qualitatively different sign stimuli is *heterogeneous summation*.

In some cases, however, the relationships between the different features of a stimulus situation are more complex. Tinbergen and Kuenen (1939) investigated the stimuli that determine why the visually oriented gaping of nestling thrushes is directed at the parent's head. They found that simple models, such as two discs of different sizes attached to one another, were sufficient to elicit and direct the response: the nestlings gaped at the smaller disc, which thus constituted the ''head.'' If the model had two heads differing in size, however, the one at which the nestlings gaped depended upon the size of the ''body'': if the body was large, they gaped at the larger of the two heads; if the body was small, they gaped at the smaller of the two heads (Figure 2-3A). The head was thus not defined by absolute size but by size in relation to the body to which it was attached. This exemplifies what Tinbergen meant by a *configurational stimulus*—a stimulus the effects of which are dependent upon relationships between its elements. Another example was discovered in experiments on the alarm reactions of goslings and ducklings to birds flying overhead. As a rule, such reactions are shown only to short-necked birds like hawks and owls, not to long-necked birds like geese or swans. Tests with models confirmed suspicions that the short-necked feature is a sign stimulus for the alarm reactions. But then Lorenz and Tinbergen designed an ambiguous model: a pair of wings, with edges alike, joined to a body which

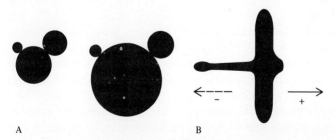

A   B

Figure 2–3. ''Configurational sign stimuli.'' (A) models releasing gaping in nestling thrushes (see text for explanation). (B) the ''hawk-goose'' model (see text for explanation). (After Tinbergen, 1951.)

consisted of a short protuberance in one direction and a long protuberance in the other. This model approximated the shape of a hawk or a goose, depending upon which end of the body was regarded as the head (Figure 2-3B). When the model was "flown" over the young birds, they reacted when the short protuberance was leading but not when the long protuberance was leading. The effective stimulus in this case was not shape alone but shape in relation to the direction of motion (Tinbergen, 1951).

It is characteristic of consummatory acts that they are responses to sign stimuli, many of which have configurational properties or conform to the principle of heterogeneous summation or can be improved upon by supernormal artifacts. That only certain features of an object are reacted to, that their effects are additive, and so forth, are facts pertaining to the animal reacting in a situation, not to the situation. The ethologists argued that there must be an internal neural mechanism controlling each consummatory act—a mechanism which contains "receptive correlates" of the sign stimuli that elicit the act, including correlates of supernormal stimuli, and which makes the summations or integrations that account for the additive or configurational effects of the stimuli. Reception of the sign stimuli activates this mechanism and thus elicits the behavior.

This hypothetical mechanism was not to be thought of, however, as a kind of reflex arc connecting sensory input with motor output in a way that makes the behavior dependent solely on the stimulation. Consummatory acts are self-exhausting: performance makes them refractory to even the most optimal stimulation. This refractoriness is only temporary, however; as time passes, the ease with which the pattern can be elicited progressively increases, i.e., the stimulus threshold of a consummatory act decreases as a function of time after performance. Indeed, Lorenz (1950) and Tinbergen (1951) described cases in which the absence of sign stimuli apparently resulted in the stimulus threshold's dropping to zero: the animals performed consummatory behavior in the absence of any of the stimuli that are normally necessary to elicit it. Such performances were called *vacuum activities*.

Before an animal gets to the point of performing *in vacuo*, however, it usually shows, and persists in, appetitive behavior until sign stimuli sufficient to elicit the consummatory act are encountered. During this appetitive phase, the animal may be continuously ready to perform the consummatory act. It is, in the words of Lorenz and Tinbergen, as though performance of the consummatory act is blocked and that the effect of the sign stimuli is to release the behavior from this blockage. Functionally speaking, therefore, sign stimuli are *releasers*, and the mechanism they activate is a *releasing mechanism*.

Consummatory acts were supposed by the classical ethologists to be instinctive in all senses of the term. In particular, they were assumed to be innate, which implied that the mechanisms underlying them must be innate. The mechanisms that the classical ethologists postulated to explain the facts they had discovered about the stimulation of consummatory acts were called *innate releasing mechanisms* (IRMs).

Action-specific Energy and the Hierarchical Organization of Instinct

To explain the changes in the ease with which consummatory acts can be elicited, Lorenz (1950) postulated that performance of a consummatory act is dependent upon, and effects, the discharge of a quantity of *action-specific energy*. It was supposed that there is a different kind, or a different source, of energy for each kind of consummatory act, and that each is spontaneously and continuously generated within the animal and accumulated between performances of its consummatory acts. Activation of an innate releasing mechanism was thus to be thought of as releasing "dammed up" action-specific energy which is then "drained off" or "used up" in performance of the consummatory act. The consequent depletion of action-specific energy reserves renders the behavior refractory to further stimulation, but, as time goes on, the steady accumulation of the energy builds up "pressure" which makes the behavior more and more easy to elicit; it may even "burst through" or "overflow" the innate releasing mechanism to produce vacuum activity. Accumulation of action-specific energy was also supposed to account for the initiation and persistence of appetitive behavior, but it was thought that only in performance of the motor patterns of the consummatory act can the energy be consumed and hence the behavior sequence terminated. The hydraulic allusions in this account of the theory of action-specific energy are consistent with Lorenz's own description and with the well-known hydraulic model he used to illustrate how it worked (Lorenz, 1950).

Although consummatory behavior is stereotyped in form, performances of it may vary in duration, in the number of repetitions, or in intensity as judged by the particular components or alternatives of the behavior that are included. According to Lorenz's theory, the degree of consummatory response is the resultant of the level of accumulated energy and the sign stimuli available. A principle analogous to the heterogeneous summation of stimuli was thus applied to the internal and external factors governing response. The same degree of response will be forthcoming from various combinations of energy level and stimulation: minimal stimulation can be compensated for by a high level of action-specific energy; optimal stimulation can make up for a low level of action-specific energy.

Perhaps the most elegant illustration of this principle was provided by Baerends (1957; Baerends, Brouwer, & Waterbolk, 1955) in a study of the courtship of male guppies. The external markings of a male guppy vary with its readiness to show courtship. By subjecting fish with the different marking patterns to tests with a standard stimulus, Baerends was able to place the marking patterns on a scale of courtship readiness. In Lorenz's terms, the marking patterns of the fish provided external indicators of their levels of action-specific energy for courtship. The degree to which females stimulate a male's courtship increases with their size. For each of the marking patterns, Baerends and his associates ran a series of tests to find how large a female had to be to stimulate courtship. The results of the tests are summarized in Figure 2-4. For each intensity of courtship, the size of female needed was less the greater the readiness to court, as indicated by the markings. The way in which a male reacts to a female thus depends on both his internal state and the stimulation she provides; but the same behavior can be forthcoming from a range of combinations of these two variables.

Although the results of this study were consistent with Lorenz's theory, Baerends did not use the notion of action-specific energy in his discussion of them. Between the time Lorenz published his theory and the publication of this study, Baerends, working on the nest-provisioning behavior of digger wasps, and Tinbergen, working on reproductive behavior of sticklebacks, had

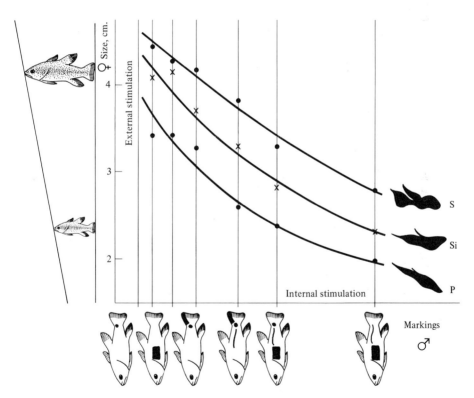

Figure 2–4.   Results of tests of courtship in male guppies: contributions of internal and external factors. (After Baerends, 1957.)

arrived at the idea that instinctive behavior is hierarchically organized. They had observed appetitive behavior consisting of a sequence of stages in which the course of action became progressively narrowed, transition from one stage to the next being brought about by encounter with external stimuli that determined to which of several alternative courses of action the animal proceeded, until the final stage when the sequence terminated in performance of consummatory behavior.

For example, a male stickleback in reproductive condition swims appetitively round its territory until it encounters stimuli that switch it to more narrowly directed actions: aggressive behavior toward a rival male, courtship behavior toward a female, nest-building behavior toward a potential nest site or nest. But still more specific stimuli determine which of the patterns within each of these categories is shown, e.g., the behavior and position of a rival male determine whether it is attacked, threatened, chased, or fled from; the behavior of a female determines which of the several patterns of courtship and mating is shown by the male; the state of the nest determines the kind of nest-building performed (Tinbergen, 1951). A number of functionally related but otherwise quite different action patterns can thus provide alternative consummatory acts for sequences that begin with the same appetitive behavior. Contrary to Lorenz's atomistic conception, according to which each consummatory act has its own supply of energy which is different from, and independent of, the energy for any other, the evidence now suggested that all the behavior serving the same general function (e.g., all behavior having to do with reproduction) depends upon a single source of internal motivation, the expression of which is determined by the kinds and sequence of stimuli that it causes the animal to encounter. The theory that emerged was the hierarchical *theory of instinct* (Tinbergen, 1951).

In this theory, instinct is ''a hierarchically organized nervous mechanism'' that controls activities serving the same general function. The unit of this mechanism is the ''instinctive centre,'' a submechanism that receives and coordinates input from other centers, hormonal influences, and influences of external and internal stimuli, and in consequence is primed to discharge to other centers and to express itself in behavior (Figure 2-5A). Such discharge is prevented, however, by a block which can be removed by the action of sign stimuli on an associated innate releasing mechanism. The centers are arranged in levels, with each center, except the one at the top, receiving input from one of those above it and, except for those at the bottom (those of consummatory acts), feeding into several on the next lower level. At the top of the hierarchy is a single center, the activity of which is endogenous to it or under the influence of hormones and other factors. It is the major source of the excitation that drives the hierarchical mechanism. Tinbergen referred to this excitation as ''motivational impulses.'' Motivational impulses, originating from the top center, load all the centers on the next level and give rise to appetitive behavior, the goal of which is sign stimuli that will activate one of the innate releasing mechanisms of these centers. Once one of the centers has been thus released, all the motivational impulses accumulated at that level "drain away" through it and thus load the centers into which it feeds on the next lower level and change the appetitive behavior accordingly. In this way, the motivational impulses descend from level to level down the hierarchy, being expressed as progressively more narrowly directed activity, until they are finally discharged through the centers of the bottom levels and thus used up in performance of consummatory behavior (Figure 2-5B).

In addition to the evidence from analyses of behavior sequences, sign stimuli, and so forth, Tinbergen drew support for his theory from some of the neurophysiological literature. For example, W. R. Hess had elicited fully coordinated behavior in cats by stimulating them with electrodes placed in the brain. This work was interpreted as evidence for the existence of anatomically localized centers in the central nervous system, some of which are subordinate to others in their activity. The idea of hierarchical organization had also been applied by Weiss (1941) in an analysis of motor coordination. According to Weiss, movement involves six levels of neuromuscular coordination which are integrated hierarchically: the working of individual muscle fibers, coordination of fibers of the same muscle, coordination of the muscles associated with the same joint, coordination of the musculature of a limb as a whole, coordination of the limbs in locomotion, and coordination of the behavior of the animal as a whole. According to Tinbergen (1950 p. 311), the five lower levels of Weiss are those of the consummatory act, but "his highest level is again a complex of several levels, and our system, being an analysis of what Weiss considered the highest level, can be fitted without any trouble into his system" (Figure 2-5B).

Even observations that at first sight might appear to contradict the hierarchy theory were brought within its scope. Tinbergen and others had described behavior which, in the context of its occurrence, was anomalous or irrelevant. During fighting, for example, an oystercatcher or an avocet may briefly adopt the attitude of sleep; many birds show hasty preening movements; sticklebacks show the nest-building pattern of digging, and several species of crabs show fragments of feeding behavior. Such behavior seems to have nothing to do with fighting, yet it is quite ineffectual as far as the function it normally serves is concerned—the feeding movements convey no food to the mouth, the nest-building movements contribute nothing to the building of a nest, and so on. The clue to the causation of the irrelevant, out-of-context behavior was suggested by the fact that it occurs when the ongoing behavior is checked in some way, as when two incompatible tendencies—e.g., attack and fleeing—are stimulated at the same time, or when the sign stimuli for the release of the next response in a sequence are lacking, as in the case of a male whose sexuality is aroused by an uncooperative female. According

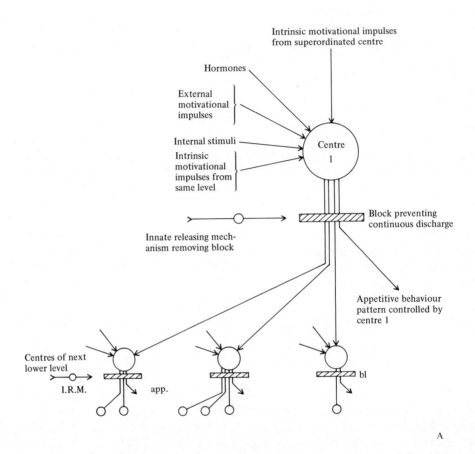

Figure 2–5. Tinbergen's hierarchy theory of instinct. (A) the "instinctive center." (B) the hierarchical organization of connections between centers

to Tinbergen's theory, these are situations in which the motivational impulses of the activated instinct are prevented from further passage down the channels of their own hierarchical system; the accumulated impulses eventually "overflow" or "spark over" into the channels of another instinct and are hence expressed in fragments of the motor patterns of that instinct. This process was called *displacement* and the behavior was called *displacement activity*.

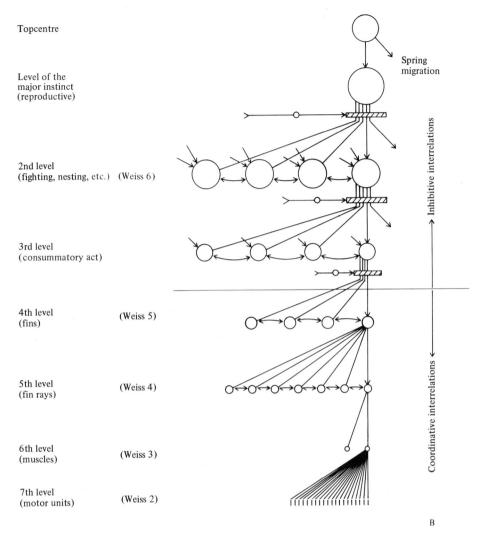

Topcentre

Level of the
major instinct
(reproductive)

Spring
migration

2nd level
(fighting, nesting, etc.)   (Weiss 6)

3rd level
(consummatory act)

4th level
(fins)   (Weiss 5)

5th level
(fin rays)   (Weiss 4)

6th level
(muscles)   (Weiss 3)

7th level
(motor units)   (Weiss 2)

Inhibitive interrelations

Coordinative interrelations

B

as exemplified by the reproductive behaviour of the three-spined stickleback. (After Tinbergen, 1951.)

The hierarchy theory provided a synthesis in which the many traditional meanings of instinct were interlocked, together with a wealth of old and new facts. It exercised a pervasive influence in ethology and attracted the attention of other schools of behavior study. It was the culmination of the development of theory at the heart of classical ethology. However, Tinbergen emphasized that his synthesis was tentative—"a working hypothesis of a type that helps to put our thoughts in order" (1951, p. 127). Later thought and study questioned and tested the assumptions and implications of the theory, and in so doing, carried ethology from its classical period into a period in which theoretical unity gave way to differentiation in theoretical interests and in research.

The Reafference Principle and Feedback

One of the central propositions in the theories of Lorenz and Tinbergen was that it is the using up of energy in performance of the motor patterns of a consummatory act that brings a sequence of instinctive behavior to an end. The effect of performance of a consummatory act on the mechanism underlying it was supposed to be to drain the mechanism of the energy that makes it work. This proposition was called into question by discovery of cases in which it is the stimulation consequent on performance of a movement, not the movement per se, that determines what an animal does next. Such cases were familiar to Lorenz and Tinbergen from their studies of taxis behavior, but it was an investigation by von Holst and Mittelstaedt (1950; von Holst, 1954) that led ethologists to take seriously the possibility that even consummatory acts may produce their effects through the stimuli they provide rather than the energy they consume.

Von Holst and Mittelstaedt experimented on the optomotor reflex of the fly *Eristalis*. A fly confronted with vertical stripes moving horizontally turns in the direction of movement of the stripes. This exemplifies the optomotor reflex. If the stripes are stationary and the fly itself moves, the stimulation to its eyes—bars of light and dark moving across the eyes—is the same as that which causes the optomotor reflex, but the reflex does not occur. Since reflexes are supposed to be fixed stimulus-response connections, it was assumed that the optomotor reflex must be inhibited when a fly moves. Von Holst and Mittelstaedt tested this assumption by rotating a fly's head through 180 degrees and fixing it in place upside down so that the right eye was on the left and the left eye on the right, with the connections to the brain intact. This operation had the effect of reversing the visual consequences of movement. If a normal fly moves toward its left in front of a pattern of vertical stripes, the images of the stripes pass from the left eye to the right eye; for the operated fly, the images passed from the right eye to the left eye. If the optomotor reflex is inhibited when a fly moves, it should fail to appear, whatever the direction in which the world moves across the eyes during locomotion. In fact, switching the position of the eyes caused the response to occur whenever the fly moved. If the fly moved to the left, it began continuous turning toward the left—i.e., in the direction of apparent movement of the stripes—and continued until exhausted. Since this result was inconsistent with inhibition, von Holst and Mittelstaedt offered an alternative. They suggested that when an animal initiates movement, an expectation of the stimulus consequences of the movement is set up in the animal. The change in stimulation actually consequent on the movement is fed back to the central nervous system and compared with the expectation. If the stimulation matches expectation, the animal proceeds to what it was going to do next; but if there is discrepancy between stimulation and expectation, the animal is forced to carry out movement to remove the discrepancy. Thus, in the case of the fly, movement to the left sets up expectation that the world will move to the right across the visual field. In the normal fly, this expectation is realized and so no response to the visual change is made; but in the fly with eyes switched, the consequence of movement was stimulation opposite in direction to that expected, which caused the fly to make correction movements which, in the circumstances, added to the discrepancy and so trapped the fly in a vicious circle. The operation of switching the eyes changed what, in the normal fly, is a negative feedback loop, an effect tending to remove its cause, into a positive feedback loop, an effect tending to add to its cause.

This feedback of the stimulus consequences of movement was called "reafference" by von Holst and Mittelstaedt (1950), and the hypothesis in which they incorporated it is known as the *reafference principle*. In addition to the results of the fly experiment, they applied the principle to some observations on fish and humans. Its influence is to be found in much recent writing on perceptual-motor coordination and perceptual constancy. But we are concerned with its influence on ethological thinking.

The reafference principle and the more general notion of feedback which it introduced to ethology were quickly taken up by ethologists. In 1953 Bastock, Morris, and Moynihan published an important critical paper which included a discussion of displacement activities difficult to accommodate to Tinbergen's theory. Moynihan (1953) had observed that if he took eggs away from the clutch of an incubating gull, the bird performed what he interpreted as displacement nest-building, the amount and intensity of which were greater the more eggs he removed. The gull still performed what was taken to be the consummatory act of incubation (settling on the nest); what seemed to be amiss was the quality of the tactile stimulation from the reduced clutch. Applying the principle of reafference, Bastock et al. suggested that, in cases like this, the concept of *consummatory stimulation* is more appropriate than that of consummatory act to account for termination of instinctive sequences. The importance of tactile feedback for an incubating gull was confirmed by Beer (1961), who also showed that self-exhaustion of the egg-rolling response does not occur when performance of the response fails to replace eggs missing from the nest (Beer, 1962). Hence the consummatory act of egg-rolling can be regarded as appetitive toward the establishment of the consummatory stimulation for incubation! In general, in ethological thinking, the conception of consummatory *act* was replaced by "the conception of a particular neural input as the cause of the drive reduction, and the termination of behaviour [Sevenster-Bol, 1962, p. 231]."

However, the corollary that motivational energy is consumed by stimuli was less plausible than the idea that motivational energy is consumed by movement. The realization that performance of the terminal fixed action pattern is neither necessary nor sufficient to terminate sequences of species-typical behavior withdrew one of the assumptions upon which the ethological notion of motivational energy was based, and thus called the notion into question, together with other postulates of the instinct theories. Even the notion of innate releasing mechanisms was affected; but this was also under pressure from work on the sensory aspects of the causation of species-typical behavior.

Sign Stimuli and Sensory Physiology

The studies of Tinbergen and his associates, in which models were used to investigate the stimuli governing species-typical behavior, inspired further and more sophisticated work of the same sort. For example, Magnus (1955, 1958) constructed an ingenious apparatus for studying the stimuli affecting the sexual pursuit flight of the male fritillary butterfly in a manner similar to, but more precise than, Tinbergen's in his study of this behavior in the grayling. Magnus found that the effectiveness of a model was greatest if it was colored orange like the fritillary female's wings, if it was large in size up to a certain limit, and if it flickered at a rate just short of the limit perceivable by the insect visual system. Knowledge of the structure and physiology of insect visual systems suggested an explanation of these results. The compound eye of an insect consists of numerous unit eyes, called ommatidia, which are shielded from one another and packed together in such a way that each receives only a small and more or less exclusive part of the visual field. For many insect visual responses, it appears to be the number of ommatidia stimulated per unit time, rather than the spatial relations of the ommatidia stimulated, which determines reaction. Hence the fact that insects do not discriminate between some objects that look to us quite different from one another. And hence the greater effectiveness of larger size and higher rate of flicker in evoking such responses as the pursuit flight of the butterfly. For a large moving object (up to the limit where it fills most of the visual field) will stimulate more ommatidia per unit time than will a small object moving in the same way; and similarly, for fast, as opposed to slow, rates of flicker.

These observations reflect on the argument by which Tinbergen (1951) deduced the properties of the innate releasing mechanism underlying the pursuit flight of the grayling. From the results of his investigation, he concluded that pattern of movement, distance away, and depth of shading of an object are the sign stimuli affecting the pursuit response, and that their effects are independent of one another and are "somewhere in the central nervous system, added in a purely quantitative way [Tinbergen, 1951, p. 81]." But if one considers the ways in which these features of the stimulus object affect the visual receptors, one need go no further to explain their additive effects, and it becomes apparent that their effects are not independent in the way Tinbergen implied. For instance, that movement pattern and distance away can be combined in different ways to produce the same degree of response can be explained as a consequence of the two facts that undulating movement stimulates more ommatidia than smooth movement, and that a distant object stimulates fewer ommatidia than a close one. In this case, then, the phenomenon of heterogeneous summation does not necessitate the postulation of a summating mechanism in the central nervous system.

Tinbergen's work on the pecking response of gull chicks was also followed up by others; and again the new studies fostered the view that his results were consequences of properties of the visual receptors and organization of the visual pathways rather than of the operation of a unitary, central nervous, innate releasing mechanism. For example, Hailman (1966, 1967) has found evidence for the belief that the color preferences manifested in the gull chick's pecking response are consequences of the light-filtering effects of oil droplets in the retina. In addition, he has compared some of the other features of the response to features that have been discovered in the visual system of the cat. Hubel and Wiesel (1959; Hubel, 1963) have recorded activity from single cells in a cat's visual cortex while systematically plying the retina with a spot of light. They found that such a cell is affected by light in only a small, elongated area of retina—the receptive field of the cell—which typically consists of an excitatory strip with parallel inhibitory strips on either side. A cell of this sort is maximally stimulated by rodlike shapes oriented in the same direction as the receptive field and covering the excitatory part of the field. Hailman has suggested that such organization in the gull's visual system would account for some of the results of investigation of the pecking response of gull chicks, e.g., the importance of the thickness, orientation, and movement of the stimulus.

Neurophysiological studies of visual systems of other kinds of animals have revealed other types of receptor mechanisms determining selective response to stimuli. Maturana et al. (1960; Lettvin, Maturana, McCulloch, & Pitts, 1959), recording from single fibers in the optic nerve of frogs while presenting various kinds of visual stimuli to the eye, discovered five types of units. The most complex type was the *net convexity detector* which responds to the edge of dark convex or cornered shapes if they are moved into or across the receptive field. The greater the convexity the greater the response. The stimuli to which this type of unit is most responsive are just those presented by the flying insects upon which the frog preys. The unit has therefore been functionally described as a "bug detector."

Another example of complex stimulus selection at the level of the receptor has been provided by neurophysiological and behavioral studies of audition in the bullfrog. Frishkopf and Goldstein (1963) recorded the responses of single neurones in the bullfrog's auditory system when they played sounds of different frequencies to it. They found two groups of neurones responsive to sound: simple units with peak response at 1,500 cycles per second, and complex units with peak response at 400 cycles per second. Frequencies between these two peaks inhibited activity in the complex units. Most of the energy of the vocalizations of bullfrogs is concentrated at the frequencies that excite the auditory units. Capranica (1965) investigated the sounds in reply to which a bullfrog will vocalize, and found the effective stimulus to be a combination of two sounds corresponding to the tuning of the auditory units. When intermediate sounds were added to these combined sounds, they no longer elicited response. Here we have a case in which the properties of the receptor are responsible for species recognition by ear. Detection of predators by an even simpler auditory mechanism has been demonstrated in studies of the responses of auditory neurones of noctuid moths to bat cries (Roeder, 1963).

The details and varieties of sensory mechanisms governing species-typical behavior, with which ethologists have become familiar in recent years, were, for the most part, brought to light by applications of neurophysiological techniques and concepts. The classical ethological work on sign stimuli, on the other hand, relied on inferences from observations of behavior, particularly in experiments using models. Although the classical techniques considerably advanced understanding of communication functions of social displays, nuptial coloration, and so forth, they did not provide the kinds of facts that could settle questions about how the relevant sensory systems work. The concept of the innate releasing mechanism was useful in that it provoked investigation of such questions, but in so doing it led to the realization that, as an explanatory concept, it was too broad and ill-informed to be of further heuristic value.

While the neurophysiological studies have shown that it was a mistake to think of all species-specific behavior as governed by the same type of releasing mechanisms, they have not questioned the assumption that the properties of releasing mechanisms are innate. This assumption has been tested in some behavioral investigations. For example, Schleidt (1961) returned to the question of why the young of ground-nesting birds respond with alarm to a short-necked bird overhead but not to a long-necked bird. It occurred to him that the young birds tested by Lorenz and Tinbergen were raised in a situation in which long-necked birds—geese and swans—were common but short-necked birds rare. He investigated the influence of novelty on the alarm response by giving one group of young birds frequent experience of a hawk silhouette, and another group frequent experience of a goose silhouette, and then testing the reactions of the young to the two silhouettes. The young ignored the familiar shape but showed alarm to the novel shape whether it was a hawk or a goose. In this case, then, reaction to configurational properties is not fixed in the mechanism governing species-typical response but is apparently subject to habituation. Variation in response to repeated stimulation is thus not always in accord with classical ethological theory.

Variation in Response to a Stimulus

In Lorenz's thinking, "specific exhaustibility, a common basic trait of all instinctive behavior, suggests the idea of a reservoir for reaction-specific energy [1939, trans. in Schiller, 1957, p. 247]." Postperformance refractoriness of fixed action patterns was an observation basic to the instinct theories of both Lorenz and Tinbergen. But it was assumed that this refractoriness must be due to the performance of the behavior rather than to other possible effects of the stimulation eliciting the behavior.

This assumption was challenged by observations of refractoriness specific to the stimulus but not to the response. For example, Prechtl (1953) found that the gaping response of a nestling chaffinch could be elicited by vibration of the nest even after the response had waned to auditory stimuli, and vice versa. Clark (1960) similarly found that if the polychaete worm *Nereis pelagica* is repeatedly stimulated with vibration until it ceases to respond by retracting into its tube, the retraction can still be elicited in full strength by visual stimulation, and vice versa. The gobbling call of a turkey can be elicited by various sounds, and Schleidt (1954) found that when response had waned to one sound, it could still be elicited by others.

Other studies have revealed combinations of stimulus-specific and response-specific effects, and both decremental and incremental effects, with repeated stimulation. The chaffinch responds to stationary predators by flying back and forth near them and repeatedly calling "chink." The "mobbing" behavior can be elicited by models and stuffed specimens of owls, dogs, and so forth. Hinde (1954a, b; 1960b) carried out an extensive series of experiments on this behavior. He found, for example, that the rate of chink-calling declined almost to zero after half an hour of continuous exposure to a predator, and that subsequent presentations of the predator never elicited more than about half the initial rate. Response was also reduced to other kinds of predators but not so much as to the original one, the stimulus-specificity of the effect being greatest for long initial exposures. By varying the period of initial exposure, the period between exposures, and the stimuli in different combinations, Hinde obtained results which, on close analysis, revealed both transitory and long-lasting enhancement of response, interacting with transitory and long-lasting decremental effects, i.e., a multiplicity of effects of repeated stimulation of species-typical behavior. The physiological processes underlying this complexity have yet to be elucidated, but it is clear that variation in a single internal factor, such as supply of motivational energy, is inadequate to account for it.

The Concept of Drive

The notions of motivational energy in the instinct theories of Lorenz and Tinbergen were also given trouble by questions of physiological credibility and empirical status. That the principles of neural transmission are different from the principles of a gravity-fed hydraulic system in respects crucial to the instinct theories was already worrisome to ethologists in the early 1950s. And according to the rules of operationism, to which a number of ethologists thought their science should adhere, either the terms of the theories were reducible to observations and measurements, or they were empty of meaning.

At a conference held in Cambridge in 1950, some revisions of ethological concepts were recommended. Action-specific energy was dropped in favor of *specific action potential* (SAP), which referred to whatever it is about the state of an animal that determines its readiness to perform some behavior pattern, without any implications about the nature of this state. Since variation in readiness to perform the behavior in a standard situation is attributable to SAP, quantification of the behavior provides measurement of SAP, which thus meets operational demands. The term *drive* was defined in a similar way. According to Thorpe (1951), a drive is "the complex of internal and external states and stimuli leading to a given behavior [p. 36]." Similar definitions of drive were given by Russell et al. (1954), Baerends et al. (1955). and van Iersel and Bol (1958). The term *tendency* also gained currency to refer to the product of drive—the intensity or probability of occurrence of this or that behavior—which is usually all that the ethologist is in a position to measure.

However, a pattern of behavior may vary quantitatively in a number of respects and hence be measurable in several ways, e.g., frequency of response, duration of response, the number and kinds of components present in response, and the time between stimulus presentation and response (latency). Hence, there may be several alternative measures of drive, or SAP. Although these terms were supposed to imply nothing about physiological mechanisms, they were generally used as though, for a particular kind of behavior, they referred to a single unitary variable: attack drive, escape drive, sexual drive, and so forth. The assumption that drive is unitary implied that alternative measures of it should agree with one another. "We assume that frequency measures and those of duration, latency, etc. are indicators of variation in the same continuous variable Act Tendency . . . [Russell, Mead, & Hayes, 1954, p. 168]."

This assumption has been tested in a number of studies in which several kinds of measures of the behavior have been made and compared. For example, Tugendhat (1960) studied the effects of food deprivation on the feeding behavior of sticklebacks. She found that the longer the period of deprivation the greater the frequency of complete feeding movements, but there was no effect on the amount of time spent feeding. Thus, according to one measure, food deprivation affects feeding drive; according to another, it does not. Similarly, Hinde (1958) found that alternative measures of nest-building activity in canaries did not correlate closely. He commented: "Since the dependent variables are not fully correlated, their use to assess 'drive' would inevitably depend upon arbitrary decisions as to which variable is most suitable [p. 20]."

Drives, like instincts, have been invoked to explain very different aspects of behavior and have been incorporated in a variety of motivational theories. The term is plagued with ambiguity. Its use has frequently led to oversimplification and confusion in discussions of motivation (Hinde, 1956, 1957, 1960a). Many ethologists and psychologists have come to regard the control of behavior as more complex than unitary drive concepts can cope with. Research and theory have diversified, with increasing use of mathematical models (e.g., Wiepkema, 1961; K. Nelson, 1964) and investigation of physiological factors (e.g., Hinde, 1965; von Holst & von St. Paul, 1963; Lehrman, 1961, 1965). Little has survived from the classical instinct theories, apart from a few terms. One of these is displacement activity, but it too has lost its original theoretical connotation.

Displacement and Disinhibition

Tinbergen's theory about displacement activities assumed that when behavior occurs as displacement, its causation is different from what causes it in its true functional context. Doubt was raised about this assumption by discovery of cases in which the kind of displacement performed was influenced by the kind of stimuli present, e.g., fighting turkeys show displacement feeding or displacement drinking, depending upon whether food or water is available (Räber, 1948). Andrew (1956a) and Morris (1956) pointed out that many displacement activities are responses that occur generally to the kinds of autonomic changes that tend to take place during conflict and frustration. For example, grooming movements, which are among the commonest types of displacement activities, are elicited by increase in body temperature, alterations in blood circulation, and disarrangement of feathers or fur, all of which are likely to occur when animals are fighting or courting, i.e., doing the kinds of things that evoke displacement activities.

Another observation was that the kinds of behavior that occur as displacement occupy relatively large amounts of an animal's activity but are readily interrupted whenever the occasion for more urgent behavior arises; e.g., a bird will cease feeding or preening if presented with stimuli provoking flight or aggressive behavior. Since the states and stimuli causing the feeding or preening presumably persist, the arousal of the other behavior must cause inhibition of these less urgent activities. But in situations of conflict, mutually incompatible tendencies—for example, attacking and fleeing—are simultaneously aroused and hence inhibit one another. Andrew (1956a) suggested that such mutual inhibition between conflicting tendencies removes the inhibition of each on the low-priority behavior, which thus appears because its own causal factors have been present all along. In other words, conflict does not *make* an animal perform displacement activity; it *allows* the activity we call displacement in this situation to occur. This explanation is known as the *disinhibition hypothesis*.

The first detailed application of the disinhibition hypothesis to a particular case was by van Iersel and Bol (1958) in a study of displacement preening in terns. They scared incubating terns from their nests and then measured the subsequent changes in approach and withdrawal tendencies. They found that preening occurred when these two tendencies reached equality. They expressed their conclusions in a model according to which incubation drive and fleeing drive inhibit preening drive except when incubation and fleeing drives are equal, in which case they mutually inhibit one another and thus disinhibit preening. That the preening is caused by its own factors was confirmed by the observation that wetting the feathers of the birds (a normal preening stimulus) increased displacement preening. Similar results were obtained in other studies of displacement activities, e.g., Rowell (1961), Sevenster (1961), and Fentress (1968). McFarland (1965, 1966) has employed the concept of attention to extend the disinhibition idea to cases in which only one tendency is obstructed. His thesis was that frustration leads to switch of attention from stimuli relevant to the frustrated behavior to stimuli eliciting displacement activity. He varied the amount of frustration experienced by doves in an operant learning situation and compared the effect of this variation on performance in a task requiring discrimination of stimuli that had been incidentally present in the frustrating situation. The more the birds had been frustrated the more quickly they learned the discrimination, presumably because frustration had caused them to attend to the incidental stimuli in the original situation.

In most of the studies concerned with the disinhibition hypothesis, the observations it is supposed to explain also provide the evidence for it. This presents a difficulty if, as some ethologists insist (e.g., Rowell, 1961), the terms in which the hypothesis is stated are to be understood as operationally defined by observable or manipulated variables. If drive or tendency is reducible to measurements of behavior, then the disinhibition hypothesis provides merely an alternative description of the fact that displacement activities occur when the probabilities of occurrence of incompatible responses are equal. An alternative description is not an explanation unless it refers to something other than the facts to be explained. In this case, the disinhibition model must presumably correspond to a neurophysiological mechanism if it is supposed to account for why displacement activities occur when they do.

Central stimulation of the brain by means of electrodes has provided some support for belief in such a mechanism. Von Holst and von St. Paul (1963) found loci for fleeing and sleep in the brain stem of domestic fowl. Stimulation of the fleeing locus interrupted feeding in a hungry animal, but when the sleep locus was stimulated as well, there was brief recurrence of the feeding behavior. There is also indication that the degree of central nervous arousal might be involved in occurrence of displacement. Delius (1967) has interpreted some of his results from central stimulation of brains of herring gulls as evidence for the idea that displacement occurs when conflict or frustration causes decrease in an arousal system to levels compatible with elicitation of displacement behavior. But the causation of displacement activities is still an unsettled matter. It is not unlikely that the category of displacement activities is causally heterogeneous.

Movements, Actions, and Functions

Displacement activities are recognized as such because they can be described as irrelevant or out of context. So one can ask: Irrelevant to what? Out of what context? In most cases, the answers will be in functional terms. The preening that occurs in the middle of a fight is irrelevant in that it appears to contribute nothing to the beating or avoiding of the rival; and it is out of context because it is unaccompanied by the other movements and conditions that make it an effective means of caring for the plumage.

A functional categorization is not necessarily the best guide to the causal organization of behavior, however. Investigations of incubation and nest-building in gulls illustrate the point. Incubation and nest-building are, obviously, functional terms: they group together patterns of behavior that serve warming of eggs in the one case, construction of the nest in the other. The nest is built before the eggs are laid; incubation can take place only after the eggs are laid. Nest-building movements that occur after laying and during incubation are therefore out of context. This and the fact that such nest-building is associated with conditions in which incubation is hindered or upset led Moynihan (1953) to the conclusion that it is displacement activity caused by frustration of incubation. Implicit in this conclusion was the assumption that corresponding to, and causally underlying, the two functional categories of behavior, there are two drives: an incubation drive and a nest-building drive. If this assumption were correct, then the activities serving incubation should have closer causal affinities to one another than to those serving nest-building, and vice versa. Beer (1963) tested this assumption and found that evidence of causal affinity did not agree with it. For example, "settling" (incubation) proved to be more closely related to "sideways-building" (nest-building) than to "shifting" (incubation); and "collecting" (nest-building) was more closely related to shifting than to sideways-building. Classification of the activities according to the evidence of causal affinity would thus cut across their classification according to function.

The classification of the behavior according to function was also at variance with observations of the forms of the movements. Moynihan (1953) had distinguished two kinds of lowering into the nest: "Scraping," which occurs prior to laying, gives the nest its saucer shape and is hence a nest-building movement; and "settling," which occurs after laying, fits the eggs into the brood patches and is therefore an incubation movement. It was part of his argument for the out-of-context, and hence displacement, character of sideways-building during incubation that, unlike sideways-building prior to laying, it is not associated with scraping. According to Beer, however, the motor patterns of scraping and settling are essentially the same; only on functional grounds can the distinction be made, and even then not sharply. If one regards the prelaying and postlaying forms of lowering into the nest as the same kind of movement, then the out-of-context argument falls, for sideways-building is just as closely associated with lowering into the nest after laying as before.

Beer's conclusion (1963) was that the case for regarding the nest-building of incubating gulls as displacement was based on false assumptions and inappropriate description. The general point illustrated by this example is that behavior can be categorized or described in several different ways: according to functional criteria, causal criteria, the forms of the motor patterns, and in other ways. Items of behavior that are regarded as the same in one description may be regarded as different in another. For instance, the movement with which a great tit pecks at a nut is the same as that with which it pecks at a rival in a fight; functional criteria would distinguish two categories of action where criteria of form would distinguish only one (Blurton Jones, 1968).

An animal in motion on a particular occasion might be described either as running or as fleeing. But not all instances of running are instances of fleeing, and not all instances of fleeing are instances of running. By describing the behavior as running (or trotting, galloping, walking, or a like act), we categorize it by its motor pattern; by describing it as fleeing (or attacking, hunting, avoiding, or a similar act), we categorize it as a directed action. This distinction between describing behavior as movement and describing it as action has been emphasized in some recent writing on the philosophy of mind (e.g., Taylor, 1964). It has been argued that movement and action are concepts of different logical types; that causes can be assigned to movements but not to action, which, instead, implies intentions. The issues here are complex and controversial, but one point emerges clearly: Different kinds of descriptions of behavior raise different kinds of questions, and the answers to one kind of question may be inappropriate to others.

In the instinct theories of Lorenz and Tinbergen, the distinction between appetitive behavior and consummatory acts paralleled that between actions and movements. Appetitive behavior was characterized by the goal aimed at; consummatory acts were fixed motor patterns. The mode of control of appetitive behavior was supposed to be quite different from that of consummatory acts. According to Tinbergen, the hierarchical scheme of Weiss applied to consummatory acts and thus constituted the bottom levels of his own hierarchical model, which was concerned mainly with the organization underlying appetitive behavior. But any instance of appetitive behavior is also an instance of movement of some sort, and Weiss's scheme applied to movement irrespective of whether it be that of consummatory act or appetitive behavior.

Therefore, the fitting of the two hierarchical schemes together posed a more complicated problem than Tinbergen envisaged. These two schemes dealt with quite different categories of behavior, which cut across one another; and they were focused on different kinds of questions: Weiss was concerned with the physiology of the patterning of movement; Tinbergen was concerned with the selection of courses of action.

The fact that the same behavior can be described in different ways—e.g., as movement or action, or in terms of function—can lead to misunderstanding and controversy. If the distinctions are unrecognized, the conclusions of different studies are likely to seem in conflict, and right answers to some questions may lead to wrong conclusions about others. It is therefore important to distinguish between different kinds of descriptions and between different kinds of questions about behavior. Ethological studies of motivation have been hampered by blurred distinctions. So have ethological ideas about the development of behavior.

THE DEVELOPMENT OF SPECIES-TYPICAL BEHAVIOR

Innateness

According to the theories of Lorenz and Tinbergen, instinctive behavior and the mechanisms underlying it are innate: they are genetically determined and their ontogeny does not depend upon the experience of the individual. The ethologists inherited this belief along with the whole legacy of ideas associated with instinct. They claimed support for it from a variety of different kinds of evidence.

Behavioral homologies, discovered by Whitman and Heinroth and later by Lorenz and Tinbergen, provided application for the idea that behavioral characteristics, like morphological characteristics, can be related to one another by descent from a common evolutionary antecedent, and hence, that the genetics of evolution applies to behavior as well as morphology. Agreement between comparative behavior study and systematics argued that species-typical behavior, like species-typical morphology, reflects phylogenetic, and hence genetic, affinities. Behavior patterns possessed by all members of a species were, like species-characteristic morphology, assumed to reflect the genetic heritage that gives a species its integrity.

The adaptedness of species-typical behavior also implied, according to the Neo-Darwinian theory of natural selection, that the behavior has a genetic basis. In some cases, the behavior functions in such a way that the possibility that learning is involved in its development seems to be ruled out. For example, the courtship dance of a male salticid spider must inhibit the female's prey-catching behavior or the male will be caught and eaten before it can mate. The courtship dance is obviously not learned through trial and error, for a single error would end a male's chance of leaving offspring (Lorenz, 1961).

There are also cases of species-typical behavior possessed in absence of conditions that would give it purpose in pursuance of which it might have been learned. The ground-nesting dove (*Nesopelia galapagoensis*) of the Galapagos reacts with a distraction display when someone approaches its nest, yet there are, on these islands, no natural predators against which to protect the nest in this way (Eibl-Eibesfeldt, 1961). The response presumably evolved in the ancestors of the species, in circumstances where it was functional, and has been preserved in the Galapagos doves by heredity.

The results of selective breeding and cross-breeding have also shown that behavioral characteristics can be inherited in much the same way as morphological characteristics. Darwin documented numerous examples from domesticated species. Heinroth (cited in Lorenz, 1937) discovered a behavioral example of what Darwin called "reversion to ancestral type" in hybrids from a mating between a shelduck and an Egyptian goose. Whereas the courtship displays of the two parental species are different and peculiar compared to other species of Anatidae, the displays of the hybrids were of the type most common in this family and presumably close to the ancestral type from which the less common patterns evolved. Similarly, Lorenz (1958) reported that the "down-up" display, which is present in most species of ducks but absent in the pintail and the yellow-billed duck, appears in hybrids from these two species. Cross-breeding between two species of lovebird parrots (*Agapornis*) produced hybrids in which some of the behavior was a mixture of the species-typical patterns of the parents (Dilger, 1960, 1962). In both species the parrots obtain nest material by clipping strips from the edges of leaves, bark, and so on, but they employ different methods of carrying the material to the nest: one tucks the strips amongst the feathers of its back; the other carries the material in its bill. The hybrids showed both patterns: they performed the tucking movement ineffectually and usually ended up carrying the material in their bills. Mixing up the genes thus mixed up the behavior.

Evidence for the irrelevance of experience for the development of species-typical behavior has been claimed from results of what are called "isolation experiments" in which animals are raised in circumstances that exclude experience that might be thought to play a role in the development of some feature of their behavior. Grohmann (1939) raised pigeons in tubes which prevented them from unfolding their wings. When these birds were released, they flew as well as unconfined control birds of the same age almost immediately, thus showing that the wing-flapping performed by nestlings is not necessary for development of normal flight movements. Similarly, Carmichael (1926, 1927) found that tadpoles raised in a solution of an anesthetic drug which inhibited muscle contraction began swimming in the normal way when they were transferred to fresh water at the age when control animals had developed swimming. Drees (1952) raised jumping spiders in isolation from one another and found that the stimuli releasing the courtship dance of the males were those presented by a female, and the stimuli inhibiting prey-catching of the females were those presented by a courting male, even though these animals had not seen another member of the species before. The results of experiments such as these were supplemented by observations of animals performing species-typical patterns the first time they encountered the releasing stimuli and before the functional consequences of the behavior could have been experienced. For example, a newly hatched song sparrow crouches in response to the alarm call of the parents from the first occasion of hearing it (Nice, 1943), and newly hatched cuttlefish strike at prey accurately at the first opportunity (Wells, 1962).

From these various kinds of evidence, the classical ethologists argued that species-typical behavior is the product of growth processes directed by the genes, the environment providing only the conditions in which the potentialities of the genes can be realized. The inflexibility of such processes was exemplified in experiments involving rearrangements of parts of the bodies of developing animals. Weiss (1941, 1950) exchanged the right and left limb buds of larval salamanders so that the animals developed with their limbs reversed with respect to anterior and posterior. These animals moved backward in response to stimuli that normally elicit forward movement (e.g., food), and forward in response to stimuli that normally elicit backward movement (e.g., pain). Even after a year, experience of the inappropriateness of the behavior had made no difference. A similar result was obtained by Sperry (1951) when he rotated the eyes of salamanders 180 degrees. The animals showed reversal of the normal responses to moving visual stimuli: turning the head to the right when the stimuli moved to the left, moving the head up when the stimuli moved down, and so on. This inversion of response occurred even when the optic nerves were severed prior to rotation of the eyes. In these cases, the stimulus-response relationships were apparently fixed by predetermined patterns of neural connections, both in embryology and regeneration.

Lorenz and Tinbergen did not, of course, claim that experience plays no part in behavioral development. But they insisted that the effects of experience are overlaid on innately determined structure and organization and are limited by innate constraints. Tinbergen (1951) illustrated the point with examples of limitations in what an animal can learn and the time when learning can occur. According to his observations, an adult herring gull learns to recognize its own young and its mate on the basis of individual characteristics too subtle for a man to perceive; yet the gull is incapable of distinguishing its eggs from those of another, in spite of differences sufficient to enable a man to tell clutches apart. If a gull is given a choice between its empty nest and its clutch, displaced a meter or so away in another nest, the gull will almost invariably go to its nest and attempt to incubate there. The gull shows itself to be conditioned to the locality of its nest but not to the contents. In more general terms, "it seems to be a property of the innate disposition that it directs the conditioned response to special parts of the receptual field" (Tinbergen, 1951, p. 150). Temporal limitations on when experience can affect behavioral development were exemplified by imprinting.

If the first moving object seen by a newly hatched gosling is something other than a goose, the gosling is liable to become fixated on the object in such a way that it will direct its social behavior to that object or others like it rather than to members of its own species. Lorenz found that this kind of "miscarriage" of behavioral development can occur in a number of bird species, and it has been found in other kinds of animals as well. Lorenz's observations (e.g., 1935, 1937) convinced him that he was dealing with a developmental process different from learning in any conventional sense. He called it *imprinting* and asserted that it differed from ordinary learning in that it can take place during only a short period—the *critical period*—fixed at a particular point in an animal's behavioral development, in that its effects are irreversible, and in that it does not depend upon reinforcement—the effects of reward or punishment. He claimed that critical periods for different patterns of social behavior may be fixed at different stages of development, and hence, that the different patterns can be imprinted on different kinds of objects. He had a jackdaw for which "a human being featured as the parent companion, hooded crows as flight companions, and a young jackdaw as the child companion [Lorenz, 1935, trans. in Schiller, 1957, p. 109]."

In Lorenz's view, the social behavior of an animal is a mosaic of behavior patterns, each of which is controlled independently of the rest. Some are entirely innate, but others can be shaped by experience within limits imposed by the innate constitution. In the case of imprinting, the releasing mechanism for the behavior is not fully determined innately. Experience fills in the details of its stimulus selectivity, but once this process has occurred, the mechanism works like a typical innate releasing mechanism. The objects which provide sign stimuli for innate responses and to which an animal becomes imprinted are normally individuals of the animal's own species. Hence, in spite of its mosaic atomistic character, an animal's social behavior, in the normal case, is appropriately directed and integrated. Lorenz's general position about the role of experience in behavioral development was that experience fills in gaps in otherwise innately determined instinctive mechanisms. As he put it, behavioral development involves "instinct-training interlockings." But he also maintained that the dichotomy of innate behavior and learned behavior is absolute, distinguishing two mutually exclusive and collectively exhaustive categories of behavior.

The Nature of Nurture

The developmental doctrines of classical ethology provoked vigorous criticism, particularly from American psychologists. Beach (1955) pointed out factual and logical objections to the dichotomy of innate and learned behavior. If the dichotomy is between inheritance and learning, then it is not mutually exclusive, for there are examples of behavior that can be affected by selective breeding and yet involve learning in their development. Learning ability itself can be subjected to selective breeding. If, instead, the dichotomy is between learning and its absence, then "innate" is defined negatively in terms of an ill-defined and poorly understood concept. Furthermore, according to Beach, there are factors and processes other than inheritance and learning that enter into behavioral development, and the interactions between a developing organism and its environment are likely to be subtle and complex. Understanding of how behavior develops requires observation and experiment on behavioral development and will not be gained from armchair theorizing. Similar points were made by Lehrman (1953), Hebb (1953), Schnierla (1956), and Jensen (1961). Research on behavioral development has since revealed a diversity that is contrary to expectations consistent with thinking in terms of the innate-learned dichotomy. Diversity can be found even within a single taxonomic group. Birds provide an example.

Marler (e.g., 1967) and his associates have investigated song development in the white-crowned sparrow. They found "dialect" differences between the songs of different populations and carried out experiments to determine when and how a sparrow acquires its song. Young birds raised without any experience of adult song developed a simple song which was recognizably that of a white-crowned sparrow but lacked the detail that distinguishes one dialect from another. Only chicks that had adult song played to them between two weeks and two months of age after hatching developed a full, population-specific version of song, and then the dialect acquired was that of the "tutor" song played to them. However, if the young birds were deafened before they came into full song, they failed to produce anything like a white-crowned sparrow song even if they had been tutored at the appropriate time prior to deafening (Konishi, 1965). Thus experience is involved in song development in this species—both experience of hearing the songs of adult males during the first two months of life, and experience of a bird's hearing its own voice at the time its song is maturing. The song heard in the first two months, however, must be white-crowned sparrow song to have any effect. Tutoring with songs of other species, even species with songs similar to that of the white-crowned sparrow, had no influence on song development in Marler's birds. The learning process here is apparently subject to constraints preventing acquisition of any but the species-specific song type. Once acquired, the song is not subject to change through experience. Even deafening the birds at this stage had little effect on song production. The account that Marler and his associates have given of song development in the white-crowned sparrow is that, during the first two months, the young bird acquires, by hearing songs of conspecific adult males, an auditory template of the population dialect against which it matches its own vocalizations as it comes into breeding condition for the first time. Once full song is established in this way, either template matching is no longer required for its preservation, or the place of auditory feedback can be taken over by proprioceptive feedback.

This account cannot be generalized to other species of songbirds, however. Whitethroats (Sauer, 1954) and European blackbirds (Messmer & Messmer, 1956; Thielke-Poltz & Thielke, 1960) are reported to develop normal species-specific song even when raised alone in isolation from all sounds except those they make themselves. The song of the chaffinch can be influenced by the songs it hears throughout the first year of life (Thorpe, 1958); the songs of European blackbirds (Thielke-Poltz & Thielke, 1960) and canaries (Poulsen, 1959) can be influenced throughout life by heard song. Many species incorporate the songs of other species in their songs (e.g., bullfinches, starlings, mockingbirds), and in some cases a wide range of sounds can be imitated (see reviews by Armstrong, 1963; Thorpe, 1961). Deafening early in life has much less drastic effects on song development in some species than it has on white-crowned sparrows (Konishi, 1964, 1964, 1965). Thus the roles of experience in song development vary from species to species and differ in ways that make it misleading to ask whether song is innate or learned.

Imprinting

Each of Lorenz's propositions about imprinting has been subjected to inquiry, with the consequence that imprinting is now thought to have more in common with other forms of learning than was initially supposed. Investigations of the period during which imprinting can take place have shown that its timing and duration can be influenced by the conditions of rearing. The concept of a brief, predetermined, and fixed critical period has been replaced by the looser concept of *sensitive period*, which refers to a period of indeterminate length during which experience can result in narrowing of the range of stimuli that can elicit such responses as approach and following.

The beginning of the sensitive period for the following responses of birds appears to depend upon growth-determined motor, sensory, and motivational development. Hess (1959) found that it correlated with the development of locomotor ability in domestic chicks and ducklings. He also found that termination of the sensitive period was associated with the development of fear of novelty. He proposed that the peak of the sensitive period is at the intersection of the innately determined rate curves of locomotor development and fear responsiveness to novelty.

But novelty implies familiarity. An object will appear strange only in comparison with what is not strange. Familiarity is a consequence of experience. Chicks raised in social isolation and without experience of moving objects until they were seven days of age—that is, almost a week past the end of the sensitive period, according to Hess—responded to a moving cylinder by approach and "contentment" calling, whereas chicks with 24 hours of experience with other chicks showed fear of the cylinder (Salzen, 1962). When the moving object was painted the same as the surroundings in which the chicks were raised, they showed less persistent fear of it than when the object was painted a different color; and this contrast was the more marked the more conspicuous the visual pattern was in the rearing pen (Bateson, 1964a). These results were paralleled in studies of the effects of experience of visual patterns during the sensitive period on later performance in visual discrimination tests. If one of the patterns to be discriminated was the same as that to which a chick had been exposed, it mastered the problem more quickly than if both patterns were new to it (Bateson, 1964b). From such evidence it has been argued that imprinting is a special case of perceptual learning (Bateson, 1966; Sluckin, 1964).

The supposed irreversibility of imprinting has proved not to be absolute. Moltz (1960) found that habituation to stimuli that initially elicit following in chicks can cause loss of the following response to such stimuli. Hinde, Thorpe, and Vince (1956) found that coots up to at least two months of age will follow a new object if they are tested in familiar surroundings. The concepts of extinction and generalization appear to apply to imprinting as they do to learning in general.

The question of whether reinforcement is involved in imprinting is not a simple one. If, as in Hullian learning theory, reinforcement is supposed to be linked to reduction of one of the primary drives—hunger, thirst, and so on—then imprinting is not peculiar in being independent of such reinforcement. The studies of perceptual learning (e.g., Gibson, Walk, Pick, & Tighe, 1958) have shown that animals can learn from visual experience without their having to be contingent on any specific or conventional rewards or punishments. However, there is now evidence for the view that the stimuli to which an animal becomes imprinted may be reinforcing in themselves, i.e., that an animal will work for the opportunity to experience such stimuli. Day-old chicks and ducklings can be trained to press a pedal if the reward is only the turning on of a flashing light (Bateson & Reese, 1968). The ease with which the young birds can be conditioned in this way decreases as they get older, at the same rate as does the ease with which they can be imprinted. Imprinting apparently narrows the range of stimuli that can be reinforcing.

The subject of imprinting has thus turned out to be more complex than Lorenz envisaged it. Numerous problems remain to be solved, but they no longer appear to be different in kind from problems that have arisen in psychological studies of perception and learning.

The Mischief of Ambiguity

The evidence on which the classical ethologists based their arguments for the innateness of species-typical behavior can be divided into two sorts. On the one hand, there was evidence that the behavior has a genetic basis. On the other, there was evidence that excluded certain forms of experience from a necessary role in development of the behavior. There was more of the former than there was of the latter, and in some cases there was only evidence of genetic inheritance to support the claim that a behavior pattern is innate. But the term *innate* has two meanings corresponding to these two kinds of evidence: it can mean genetically inherited, and it can mean unlearned or acquired without any influence of experience. This ambiguity of the word innate has perhaps been one of the main hindrances to clear thinking on the issue that has divided European ethologists and American psychologists more than any other: the nature-nurture or innate-learned dichotomy.

Both the classical ethologists and some of their opponents on this issue tended to assume that the two senses of innate imply one another: that to assert that a piece of behavior is genetically inherited is ipso facto to assert that the behavior is unlearned. In fact, the question of the extent to which a behavior pattern can be regarded as genetically inherited, and the question of the factors and processes that enter into its development, are two different questions. The evidence relevant to the one may have no bearing on the other, and the kinds of research appropriate to the two kinds of questions are different: comparative ethology and breeding experiments in the one case, developmental study in the other. The findings of ethologists interested in genetic or evolutionary aspects of behavior, and the findings of experimental psychologists interested in the development of behavior, are therefore not incompatible. They do not confront one another on the common ground of a shared question.

That the nature-nurture issue is to a large extent a consequence of conceptual confusion has recently been argued in detail by Lehrman (1970). Nevertheless, the issue is still kept alive by such confusion. In *Evolution and Modification of Behavior,* Lorenz (1965) attempted to muster new arguments for his old dichotomy. His uses of the word innate, and also the word adaptation, perpetuate the mischief of ambiguity, but in such ways that it is clear that Lorenz, as always, was more interested in accounting for the adaptedness of species-typical behavior in evolutionary terms than in understanding how behavior develops.

THE ADAPTEDNESS OF SPECIES-TYPICAL BEHAVIOR
Function and Survival Value

Performance of behavior of some sort may have both immediate and remote consequences of various kinds. For example, the singing of a male bird may have the effects of repelling the approach of other males, of attracting females, of helping to synchronize changes in the reproductive physiological state of the two birds of a pair or of the conspecifics in the vicinity, of spacing out the breeding birds so that the density of the population is commensurate with the food supply, and of preventing interbreeding between individuals of different species. These various effects, supposing them to have been established by observation and experiment, point to the functions served by the behavior: territorial defense, pair formation, reproductive synchronization, control of population density, and reproductive isolation. But one can then ask why these functions need to be served. In the case of pair formation, the answer is obvious, for if the birds did not form pairs, there would be no copulation and hence no reproduction and the species would die out. (Much more would have to be said to give a complete answer, however, for some animals can effect copulation without forming pair bonds, and others effect fertilization without copulation.) The other functions also suggest answers in terms of reproductive success and survival of the species. But it would have to be proved, for instance, that a different degree of dispersion, or lack of reproductive synchronization, would make any difference to reproductive success or species preservation. The hypotheses that might suggest themselves would require investigation in addition to, and different from, that which elucidated the functions of the behavior.

Attempts to understand the adaptedness of behavior can thus be divided into two overlapping categories. On the one hand are investigations of the more or less immediate effects of performance of the behavior. On the other are attempts to find in what ways these effects contribute to survival. Here, the former will be referred to as the study of *biological function*, and the latter, as the study of *survival value*.

Investigation of survival value tends to be practically more difficult and logically less conclusive than investigation of function. The roles of displays in the establishment and maintenance of territories have been analyzed in many species; the contribution of territory to reproductive success has been demonstrated in very few. Ideas about survival value have often been based solely on inferences from observations on function.

Social behavior has offered the richest material and the greatest challenge for explanation in terms of evolutionary adaptation. Tinbergen (1951, 1953) showed how the concept of *social releaser* could illuminate the functional significance of species-typical displays, including the features of structure and coloration shown off by displays. He analyzed the mating behavior of the three-spined stickleback into a chain of different patterns, each of which is a response to the preceding behavior of the partner and a releaser for the next response of the partner, the red belly of the male and the swollen belly of the female being contributory to the releaser effectiveness of the behavior patterns. Thus is achieved the coordination necessary for effective fertilization: meeting of male and female, orientation to the nest, and close timing of egg-laying and sperm ejection there. Such analyses bring out another distinction that can be made about the adaptedness of behavior. In a sequential process like that of mating in sticklebacks, in which each item in the sequence is necessary for its completion, there will be selection pressure intrinsic to the process to preserve each item in the species repertoire, for failure of any item will adversely affect reproduction. However, understanding of such intrinsic selection pressure, implicit in knowledge of *how* a behavior sequence works, may not give much idea of *why* such a sequential pattern was evolved. To get at this kind of question requires understanding of extrinsic selection pressures: pressures that have acted in the past to mold the sequential pattern into its present form, and that act in the present to preserve and adjust it according to how its products fit the environment and way of life of the animal. It might be asked, for example, why courtship behavior is as elaborate as it tends to be, and why it differs in related species. At least a partial answer might be given by showing that there is selection against interspecies hybridization, the hybrid offspring having less chance of surviving or reproducing than the offspring of intraspecies matings, and that the complexity and heterogeneity of the courtship patterns make interspecies hybridization unlikely.

The following parts of this section will be confined to studies of survival value and extrinsic selection pressures. Apart from the inferences based on functions, conclusions about survival value have been sought by ethologists in two ways: search for adaptive correlations, and experimental study.

Adaptive Correlation

The different species of gulls breed in different habitats and differ in features of their breeding behavior. One of the most aberrant species is the kittiwake, which nests on cliff ledges. E. Cullen (1957) compared the breeding behavior of kittiwakes with that of more typical species which nest on the ground in dunes, marshes, and similar spots, and found thirty-two differences that could be related to cliff nesting, namely, either the protection afforded by cliffs against predation, or the limited number, cramped space, and dangerous height of nest sites. For example, kittiwakes use an elaborate nest-building technique whereby they build a deep, cup-shaped nest, strengthened with mud, in which the young remain confined virtually until they are ready to fly. Ground-nesting gulls have a simple nest-building technique with which they construct a shallow nest, without any addition of mud, which the young leave a few days after hatching. It can therefore be argued that the behavioral characteristics that distinguish the breeding behavior of kittiwakes from that of other gulls are evolutionary consequences of the selection pressures peculiar to cliff-nesting and hence show adaptive correlation.

Beer (1966) made a similar comparison of the breeding behavior of black-billed gulls and black-headed gulls and concluded that a number of the special characteristics of black-billed gulls are adaptively correlated with the fact that these gulls breed on river beds that are subject to flooding. J. B. Nelson (1967) studied the breeding behavior of gannets, which, like kittiwakes, nest on cliffs, and found that gannets show many of the behavioral characteristics of kittiwakes even though the two species are not at all closely related taxonomically. There is thus evidence of convergence in behavioral adaptations.

Another example of adaptive convergence is alarm calling of songbirds (Marler, 1959). In response to a flying predator, many songbirds utter a call that signals danger without giving away the locality of the caller. Such a call must have none of the properties that cause the binaural reception differences upon which judgments of the direction from which a sound comes depend. Apparently as a consequence of this constraint, the alarm calls of the several species studied by Marler are remarkably similar (Figure 2–6A); they show adaptive convergence. Where they occur together, the species react to one another's alarm calls, and the survival value of this may also have fostered the convergence. A different kind of call is uttered in the presence of a stationary predator, such as a perching owl, or of a ground predator, such as a weasel (Figure 2–6B). The effect of this call is to attract other birds to the predator so that a crowd builds up and harasses it in a manner that can drive it away. The function of the call is to pinpoint the predator; and, correlated with this function, it possesses, in contrast to the alarm call, all the characteristics that facilitate localization (Marler, 1959). Comparison of these two types of call thus shows adaptive correlation within the behavior typical of a species.

Other examples of adaptive correlation in behavior studies will be found in Crook (e.g., 1964), in Wickler (1958, 1961), and in the writings of numerous other ethologists. But in comparative ethology, as in comparative morphology, the evidence of adaptive correlation and the inferences based on it involve a "best-fit" pattern of argument. Plausible as such argument might be, it is less compelling than argument based on experimental tests of hypotheses and the use of quantitative methods, at least to those who insist that experiment and measurement are the essence of scientific method. In some cases, experiment and measurement have been applied to test hypotheses about the survival value of behavior.

Experiments on Survival Value

In countershaded animals, the surfaces of the body most exposed to the light are more darkly colored than the surfaces of the body shaded from the light. Seen from side on, such an animal looks flat and does not appear to stand out from its background as a solid object. The function that suggests itself for countershading is camouflage. But for countershading to camouflage, the animal must orient itself appropriately to the light: it must position itself with its dark surfaces uppermost. Some animals are dark on the dorsal surface and pale on the ventral surface; others are the reverse. Those that are darker dorsally position themselves with the dorsal surface uppermost; those that are darker ventrally position themselves upside down. There is thus adaptive correlation between the direction of countershading and orientation of the body with respect to light.

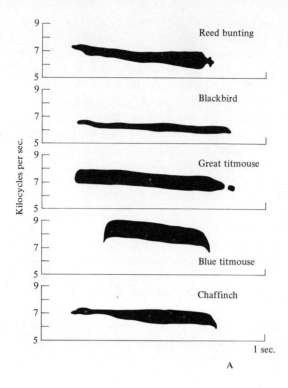

A

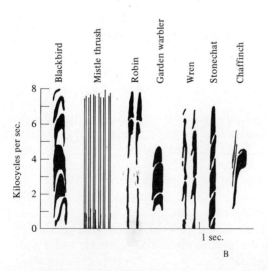

B

Figure 2–6. Sound spectrograms of songbird calls. (A) alarm calls. (B) mobbing calls. (After Marler, 1959.)

De Ruiter (1956) experimentally tested the belief that countershading and the orientation behavior associated with it can have survival value against predator pressure. He chose several species of moths and butterflies in which the caterpillars are reverse countershaded (with pale dorsal and dark ventral surfaces), and normally move about upside down. Caterpillars were killed and fixed to twigs which were then distributed in shrubbery in an aviary containing a number of hungry birds. Half the caterpillars were fixed in the normal position; half were fixed with dorsal surfaces uppermost. The birds found and ate significantly more of the abnormally oriented caterpillars than of the others; and it was observed that the birds usually detected the abnormally oriented caterpillars at greater distances. When de Ruiter painted the caterpillars a uniform green, thus eliminating countershading, there was no difference between the numbers of normally and abnormally oriented caterpillars found, nor in the distances at which the caterpillars were detected. The survival value of the camouflage conferred by countershading and upside-down orientation in these animals was thus demonstrated.

In many species of moths and butterflies, the hind wings of adults carry conspicuous round markings which have the appearance of eyes. When such an insect is at rest, these eyespots are concealed by the forewings; but if it is approached or touched, it suddenly uncovers the eyespots (Figure 2–7A). Blest (1957a) tested the possibility that such displays have survival value because of the intimidating effect they can have on a predator. First, he brushed off the eyespots on a number of individuals and then released them, along with intact individuals, in an aviary containing birds. The displays of the insects lacking the spots were less effective at repelling predatory attention than were the displays of those with the spots. Second, he compared the repelling effectiveness of different visual patterns when they were illuminated on either side of a prey object on an apparatus to which birds had been conditioned to come to feed. In each test, Blest flashed the visual pattern just as a bird alighted to take the prey, and recorded whether the bird ate the prey immediately, hesitated before doing so, or flew away without eating it. The effectiveness of the images at intimidating or preventing prey-catching by the birds was correlated with their similarity to a pair of eyes (Figure 2–7B). Thus, both removal of eyespots from living insects and simulation of the eyespot displays supported the hypothesis that the eyespot displays of butterflies and moths are antipredator adaptations.

In most species of gulls, the parents carry the eggshells from the nest and drop them some distance away shortly after the chicks hatch. That the kittiwake does not do this suggested that it might be an antipredator adaptation, since kittiwakes are subject to little predator pressure, compared to most other gulls. Tinbergen and some associates (Tinbergen, Broekhuysen, Feekes, Houghton, Kruuk, & Szulc, 1962) experimentally analyzed the stimulus characteristics conducive to the carrying response in black-headed gulls and

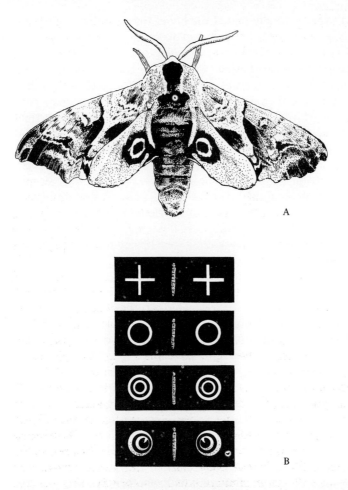

Figure 2–7. (A) the eye-spot display of the eyed hawk moth. (B) images used in Blest's experiment to test the effectiveness of eyelike patterns as stimuli inhibiting prey-catching by birds. The prey object was a meal worm placed between an image pair. The order of the images, reading from top to bottom, is of their increasing effectiveness. (After Tinbergen, 1958.)

found conspicuousness to be one of the most important. This result suggested that eggshell removal is a defense against predators that locate the nest, and hence the brood, by sight. The investigators then constructed nests outside the gullery and compared the survival of conspicuously and inconspicuously colored clutches placed in the nests, and of clutches with and without an eggshell in the nest. The results confirmed that a conspicuous object in a nest increases the likelihood that the nest will be preyed upon. Observation showed that the nest predators were carrion crows, herring gulls, and occasionally the black-headed gulls themselves, i.e., birds that locate food by sight. Later study by Tinbergen's group, involving both observation and experiment, showed that eggshell-carrying is only part of an intricate system of antipredator adaptations in the black-headed gull in which compromise between the influences of opposing selection pressures is to be found (e.g., Kruuk, 1964; Patterson, 1965).

Such applications of experimental methods, although modest in their achievements so far, have brought new and complementary considerations to questions about the adaptive significance of species-typical behavior—one of the central preoccupations of classical ethology. The other aspect of the evolution of behavior has remained almost completely out of reach of experiment, however. Unless one includes the studies on *Drosophila* that have shown that behavior can be changed by selective breeding (see Manning, 1965), and studies in which animals from different phyletic lines have been given the same tests of learning ability (e.g., Bitterman, 1960), the study of the evolutionary history of behavior is still the preserve of the comparative approach of classical ethology.

THE EVOLUTION OF SPECIES-TYPICAL BEHAVIOR

Behavioral Homology

In comparative anatomy, homology between a part of one kind of organism and a part of another is correspondence according to the connections or position of the parts relative to a structural plan common to the two kinds of organisms. It is the *principle of connections* of eighteenth century zoology that still provides the main criterion for recognizing structural homologies, even though they are now thought about in terms of descent from common origins.

Behavioral homology is more difficult to specify. A behavioral counterpart of the principle of connections would imply a common sequential or contextual pattern for behavior regarded as homologous. Sequence and context are utilized in ethological comparisons, but they provide neither necessary nor sufficient criteria for judgments of homology, for it has become apparent that evolution can change both the sequential position and the context of occurrence of a behavior pattern. Assumption of a shared repertoire of patterns is often implicit in judgments of behavioral homology, but it begs, rather than answers, the question of what the criteria of homology are. Correspondence in characteristics of form of the motor patterns provides the most frequently used criterion, but this too is insufficient evidence of homology because similar motor patterns in different species can arise through convergent evolution. Similarity of form is usually backed up, at least implicitly, by independent evidence of common origin, such as morphological evidence of phyletic affinity. For example, turning the head to face away from the other bird is a component of agonistic and courtship behavior in gulls, in some ducks, and in the common crane. The facing-away displays of the different species of gulls (Figure 2-8) are regarded as homologous to one another but not to those of ducks or cranes, since the latter are unrelated taxonomically to gulls (see Tinbergen, 1959).

Figure 2–8.   Facing away in gulls. (A) Black-billed gull. (B) Laughing gull. (C) Black-headed gull. (D) Red-billed gull. (Drawn from photographs.)

Judgments about behavioral homology thus involve several kinds of evidence, and the direction of inference varies from one case to another. Arguments about common origins, and even about taxonomic affinity, have been based on comparisons of forms of behavior; interpretations of similarities and differences of form have been influenced by accepted views about taxonomic affinity. The possibility of circular argument will be obvious, and it has to be admitted that the concept of behavioral homology lacks the precision and rigor that one is accustomed to in science (see Atz, 1970). Nevertheless, its use has led to plausible accounts of behavioral evolution, and it is better represented by its "logic in use" (Kaplan, 1964) than by any attempt at explicit definition. This logic has much of the nature of comparative morphology.

Given a number of behavior patterns regarded as homologous, it may appear that some are more primitive than others—have deviated less from the common ancestral form. From such evidence the comparative ethologist builds arguments about the evolution of behavior in much the same way as a comparative anatomist builds arguments about the evolution of structure. For example, one of the reasons for believing that the whale's flipper evolved from the pentadactyl limb of other mammals, rather than vice versa, is that the pentadactyl limb is the typical mammalian type. Similarly, it has been argued (Lorenz, 1939) that the primitive locomotory pattern in songbirds is hopping, not walking, for hopping is typical of the group and walking occurs in only a small number of species. Moreover, the young in some of the species that show walking pass through a stage during which they move by hopping, which Lorenz interpreted as ontogenetic recapitulation of the phyletically ancestral pattern. In many species of birds, the head-scratching movement involves lowering the wing on one side and extension of the leg on the same side over the wing. This movement, which looks awkward in a bird, is widespread in amphibia, reptiles, and mammals. Some species of birds head-scratch in a less awkward way, bringing the foot up in front of the breast and neck and leaving the wings folded. The restricted occurrence of this pattern suggested that it was more recently evolved than the other. In the sheathbill, head-scratching consists of the round-the-front movement of the leg, together with wing lowering, which looks quite pointless since it does not serve the function it does in other species of making room for the leg to get at the head over the shoulder. The occurrence of wing lowering in the sheathbill has been interpreted as a behavioral vestige, a remnant of an ancestral pattern, just as the pelvic vestiges in whales are regarded as remnants of ancestral structures (Heinroth, cited in Lorenz, 1939).

Such evolutionary interpretations of comparative observations are sometimes difficult to make, however. In a detailed study of antipredator displays in moths, Blest (1957b) distinguished a variety of behavior patterns but found that the distribution of the different types among the various species did not conform in any simple, systematic way to the accepted taxonomic affinities of the species. On the one hand, some taxonomically close species showed quite different patterns; on the other hand, similar or virtually identical patterns were found in taxonomically distant species. The amount of divergence and convergence in the evolution of protective displays of moths has apparently been considerable, and evolutionary interpretation is complicated in consequence. Nevertheless, Blest was able to argue that the displays evolved from flight movements, and to arrange them in a genealogy of evolutionary succession. Such evolutionary change, in which behavior, originally having nothing to do with signaling, has been modified to serve a signal function, is called *ritualization*.

Ritualization

Display is a functional term. However, the stereotyped and species-typical character of display behavior is sufficient for it to be described with reference to motor patterns only. Such description has been one of the major and most fruitful occupations of ethologists. It was the necessary first step in the comparative approach that led to the conception of displays as "derived activities" (Tinbergen, 1952). Ideas about the evolutionary derivation of displays were then forthcoming from interspecific and intraspecific comparison of the forms of movement, the sequences and contexts in which they occur, and the functions they serve.

For example, a display posture called the "upright" has been described in all the species of gulls that have been studied except the kittiwake. A gull in this posture stands with neck stretched vertically, bill horizontal or pointing slightly up or down, carpal joints of the wings held away from the sides of the body, and plumage sleeked (Figure 2-9). The display occurs in agonistic and courtship contexts. The actions most often preceding and following its occurrence are attacking and fleeing. The similarities in form, context, and sequential position of the uprights of the different species argue that they are homologous and hence have a common evolutionary derivation. Analysis of the form of the posture has led to the conclusion that it is made up of "frozen" components of attack behavior: The lifted head corresponds to the first part of the action of pecking down at an opponent, and the lifted carpals correspond to the first part of the action of wing-beating at the opponent. The sleeked plumage is a sign of fleeing tendency. These correspondences between details of the display and components of the behavior that tends to precede and follow its occurrence argue that the display "must have originated as a mosaic of intention movements of attack, inhibited by escape tendencies [Tinbergen, 1959, p. 47]." Further comparison added support to this interpretation. The kittiwake, which lacks an upright, has no downward pecking in its attack behavior. The great skua has a version of the upright which lacks lifting of the carpals, but it does not use wing-beating in fighting either.

Figure 2–9. Upright postures of black-billed gulls.

Intention movements—the initial parts of an action performed without leading into completion of the action—appear to have been one of the main evolutionary sources of displays. Daanje (1950) argued that ritualization of intention movements of taking off to fly has frequently given rise to social displays in birds. Tail-flicking in songbirds presents many examples of such displays. They have been analyzed in fine detail by Andrew (1956b). In some cases intention movements of more than one pattern are combined in one display, either simultaneously, as in the upright of gulls, or in alternation, as in the zigzag dance of the male three-spined stickleback, which has been interpreted as a ritualized combination of intention movements of attack and swimming to the nest (Tinbergen, 1951).

Comparison between species has provided evidence of the stages through which evolution of a display from an intention movement probably passed. Lorenz (1958) has compared the "inciting" movements of different species of ducks. In the shelduck, according to Lorenz, the movement is present in its primitive, unritualized form. When a pair of shelducks encounters another pair, the female often launches an attack on the rival pair. Usually she turns and flees back toward her mate without making contact with the rivals; but before she reaches her mate, she may stop, with her body still oriented toward him, and make intention movements of turning to resume attack: she stretches her neck over her shoulder and points her bill toward the rivals. This behavior can incite her mate to act aggressively toward the other birds, but neither in its form nor in its apparent motivation does it show any evidence of the kinds of modifications that result from ritualization. In the mallard, on the other hand, the pointing of the bill over the shoulder is a quite stereotyped pattern, performed without reference to the position of the rivals and without accompanying attacking and fleeing. The inciting of the mallard has apparently been derived by ritualization of behavior like that of the shelduck.

Displacement activities probably rival intention movements as evolutionary sources of displays. There are numerous examples of displays that show formal resemblance to nest-building, grooming movements, and so forth, and that occur in the kinds of conflict situations in which such movements are made as displacement activities. For example, the territorial threat display of the male three-spined stickleback is little different from a typical displacement, nest-digging movement (Tinbergen, 1951). Again, comparison may suggest the evolutionary source of a display which, taken by itself, would defy interpretation. The form of the threat display of the Manchurian crane would not suggest that it is a ritualized preening movement, but when it was compared with the threat displays of other species of cranes, it was seen to be homologous with patterns that connected it via a more or less continuous series of variations to unritualized displacement preening (Lorenz, 1935; Tinbergen, 1952).

Another evolutionary source of displays or display components has apparently been peripheral manifestations of autonomic changes. Their possible involvement in the causation of displacement activities has already been mentioned. They can also cause changes in the appearance of an animal through effects on peripheral blood circulation, erection or depression of fur or feathers, and so forth. Morris (1956) described how feather posture in birds is affected by temperature in ways that suggest the evolutionary basis of such features of displays as crest-raising, ruffling of breast and back feathers, and sleeking.

Evolution of supporting morphological features has accompanied ritualization in many cases, e.g., the crests, plumes, highly colored and contrasting patches of plumage, and so forth shown off by the display movements and postures in so much of the ritualized behavior of birds. In most species of ducks, the males possess brightly colored secondary feathers on the wings, the colors and patterns varying from species to species. These wing specula are shown off in a courtship display that Lorenz (1941) has concluded to be derived from displacement preening. In some species, such as the mallard, the display is little different from a preening movement and the wing speculum is a relatively modest pattern of contrasting colors. In the mandarin duck, the movement is a highly stereotyped prod behind a feather which is a large, fanlike structure bright orange in color. In the garganey, the display movement points the bill to the outer plumage of the wing precisely at the spot where there is a bright gray-blue patch. Similar examples could be cited from other kinds of animals.

There are also displays in which the movement conceals a morphological characteristic. For example, the facing away of gulls presents the back of the head, and hence hides bill, eyes, and, in those species possessing it, the dark facial mask from the view of the other bird (Figure 2-8). In most of the other aggressive and courtship displays of gulls, these features are presented in full view and appear to enhance threat (Moynihan, 1955; Tinbergen, 1959, 1964). There is also evidence that facing away decreases the probability of attack or flight by the other bird, and does so by removing stimuli tending to elicit such reaction. It has been described as an appeasement display. Interspecies comparison has led to the view that facing away evolved by ritualization of intention movements of turning away and fleeing. In the black-headed gull, the movement is usually performed in the upright and is very stereotyped, but in the common gull (Weidmann, 1955) and the black-billed gull (personal observation) it is more variable in form and often leads into full turning away of the whole body and retreat.

An effective signal is one that gets attention and is unambiguous. Some of the ways in which ritualization has met these requirements are by making behavior conspicuous, by increasing its distinctness from other behavior that might be confused with it, and by giving it constancy of form. Conspicuousness and distinctness have been achieved by such changes as exaggeration of some component of movement, increase or decrease of speed of performance, rhythmic repetition, and loss of components. Stereotyping of motor patterns has been assisted by elimination of variation in response to variation in eliciting factors: whereas unritualized behavior tends to vary in intensity with variation in strength of eliciting factors, its ritualized form shows *typical intensity*—it is constant in form over most of the range of variation in eliciting factors (Morris, 1957). Selection, presumably against interspecies hybridization, has tended to favor interspecies distinctness in homologous reproductive displays, particularly those involved in pair formation. According to Lorenz (1941), the pair formation behavior of ducks consists of a set of displays present in each species, but the homologous displays differ from species to species in details of form, timing, morphological support, and sequential position.

Evolutionary change in the outward form of species-typical behavior implies change in the motor mechanisms underlying the behavior. Ritualization has also effected change in stimulus-response relationships and in deeper motivational control of such behavior. Typical intensity reflects one kind of stimulus-response change. In some cases, it appears that the ritualized behavior has come under the control of causal factors quite different from those governing its nonritualized counterpart. Many of the displays that originated as displacement activities have apparently been divorced from any connection with factors having to do with preening, feeding, and so on, and have been attached to factors governing aggressive or sexual response. Such evolutionary change in the causation of behavior is known as *emancipation* (Tinbergen, 1952).

The concepts of ritualization and emancipation have been widely used by ethologists to give evolutionary interpretations to comparative observations. The arguments in which they are used are, of necessity, indirect, since only the end products of behavioral evolution are available for observation. Blest (1961) went so far as to say that since "there is no fossil record of microevolutionary changes in behavior, ... any statement about specific evolutionary events in a given group ... is never likely to be more than an inspired guess [p. 103]." But the pattern of arguments about behavioral evolution would be no different if there were a fossil record of behavior. As in comparative morphology, so in comparative ethology evolutionary interpretation is persuasive if it fits the facts together in the most plausible and economical manner conceivable. If questions about the evolution of behavior are to be asked at all, then the evolutionary, comparative, and naturalistic traditions in ethology still provide the concepts, methods, and facts most appropriate to investigation of such questions.

The notion of behavioral homology is central to the comparative ethological approach. However, the confidence with which it can be applied decreases with taxonomic distance between the animals compared, and for comparisons between phyla it is virtually of no use at all. The further one goes from the microevolutionary levels—evolution within genera or families—the more uncertain the grounds for evolutionary speculation become and the more warily one must proceed.

CONCLUSION

This chapter has given only a sketch of ethological work and ideas. For fuller treatments, the reader is referred to Thorpe (1963), Marler and Hamilton (1966), Eibl-Eibesfeldt (1970), and Hinde (1970).

The aims of this chapter have been to present and illustrate the following propositions:

1 Ethology has evolved from a unified theoretical approach, with its roots in traditional zoology and natural history, into a diversity of approaches, some of which show convergence with physiology, others with psychology, and still others with ecology.

2 This diversity of approach reflects the diversity of animal behavior and the diversity of questions it poses.

3 Failure to distinguish clearly between the different kinds of questions has caused confusion in the past and could do so again.

The last point needs to be stressed because the current urgency of problems about human aggression and population control has created a demand for an understanding of the biological bases of human behavior which some ethologists have been eager to try to meet (e.g. Lorenz, 1966; Morris, 1970). The relevance of the comparative observations on which these ethologists have drawn to the most pressing problems of human motivation and behavioral development is questionable in ways they tend to ignore. Interpretations of, for instance, the behavior of geese, even if they were correct, may have so little relevance to problems in human behavior that attempts to apply them to such problems could hinder, rather than help, understanding.

REFERENCES

ANDREW, R. J. Some remarks on behaviour in conflict situations, with special reference to *Emberiza* spp. *British Journal of Animal Behaviour,* 1956, **4,** 41–45. (a)

ANDREW, R. J. Intention movements of flight in certain passerines, and their use in systematics. *Behaviour,* 1956, **10,** 179–204. (b)

ARMSTRONG, E. A. *A study of bird song.* London: Oxford University Press, 1963.

ATZ, J. W. The application of the idea of homology to behavior. In L. Aronson, E. Tobach, D. S. Lehrman, & J. S. Rosenblatt (Eds.), *Development and evolution of behavior.* San Francisco: Freeman, 1970. Pp. 53–74.

BAERENDS, G. P. The ethological analysis of fish behavior. In M. E. Brown (Ed.), *The physiology of fishes.* New York: Academic Press, 1957.

BAERENDS, G. P., BROUWER, R., & WATERBOLK, H. Tj. Ethological studies on *Lebistes reticulatus* (Peters): I. An analysis of the male courtship pattern. *Behaviour,* 1955, **8,** 249–334.

BASTOCK, M., MORRIS, D., & MOYNIHAN, M. Some comments on conflict and thwarting in animals. *Behaviour,* 1953, **6,** 66–84.

BATESON, P. P. G. Effect of similarity between rearing and testing conditions on chicks' following and avoiding responses. *Journal of Comparative and Physiological Psychology,* 1964, **57,** 100–103. (a)

BATESON, P. P. G. Relation between conspicuousness of stimuli and their effectiveness in the imprinting situation. *Journal of Comparative and Physiological Psychology,* 1964, **58,** 407–411. (b)

BATESON, P. P. G. The characteristics and context of imprinting. *Biological Review,* 1966, **41,** 177–220.

BATESON, P. P. G., & REESE, E. P. Reinforcing properties of conspicuous objects before imprinting has occurred. *Psychonomic Science,* 1968, **10,** 379–380.

BEACH, F. A. The descent of instinct. *Psychological Review,* 1955, **62,** 401–410.

BEER, C. G. Incubation and nestbuilding behaviour of black-headed gulls: I. Incubation behaviour in the incubation period. *Behaviour,* 1961, **18,** 62–106.

BEER, C. G. The egg-rolling of black-headed gulls *Larus ridibundus. Ibis,* 1962, **104,** 388–398.

BEER, C. G. Incubation and nestbuilding behaviour of black-headed gulls: IV. Nestbuilding in the laying and incubation periods. *Behaviour,* 1963, **21,** 155–176.

BEER, C. G. Adaptations to nesting habitat in the reproductive behaviour of the black-billed gull *Laurus bulleri. Obis,* 1966, **108,** 394–410.

BITTERMAN, M. E. Toward a comparative psychology of learning. *American Psychologist,* 1960, **15,** 704–712.

BLEST, A. D. The function of eyespot patterns in the Lepidotera. *Behaviour,* 1957, **11,** 209–256. (a)

BLEST, A. D. The evolution of protective displays in the Saturnioidea and Sphingidae (Lepidoptera). *Behaviour,* 1957, **11,** 257–309. (b)

BLEST, A. D. The concept of ritualization. In W. H. Thorpe & O. L. Zangwill (Eds.), *Current problems in animal behaviour.* Cambridge, England: Cambridge University Press, 1961. Pp. 102–124.

BLURTON JONES, N. G. Observations and experiments on causation of threat displays of the great tit *(Parus major). Animal Behaviour Monographs,* 1968, **1,** 74–158.

CAPRANICA, R. R. *The evoked vocal response of the bullfrog: A study of communication by sound.* Cambridge, Mass.: M.I.T., 1965.

CARMICHAEL, L. The development of behavior in vertebrates experimentally removed from the influence of external stimulation. *Psychological Review,* 1926, **33,** 51–58.

CARMICHAEL, L. A further study of the development of behavior in vertebrates experimentally removed from the influence of external stimulation. *Psychological Review,* 1927, **34,** 34–37.

CLARK, R. B. Habituation of the polychaete *Nereis* to sudden stimuli: I. General properties of the habituation process. *Animal Behaviour,* 1960, **8,** 82–91.

CRAIG, W. Appetites and aversions as constituents of instincts. *Biological Bulletin,* 1918, **34,** 91–107.

CROOK, J. H. The evolution of social organisation and visual communication in the weaver birds (Ploceinae). *Behaviour Supplement,* 1964, **10,** 1–178.

CULLEN, E. Adaptations in the kittiwake to cliff-nesting. *Ibis,* 1957, **99,** 275–302.

DAANJE, A. On locomotory movements in birds and the intention movements derived from them. *Behaviour,* 1950, **3,** 48–98.

DARWIN, C. *The origin of the species.* New York, Appleton, 1859.

DELIUS, J. D. Displacement activities and arousal. *Nature,* 1967, **214,** 1259–1260.

DILGER, W. C. The comparative ethology of the African parrot genus *Agapornis. Zeitschrift für Tierpsychologie,* 1960, **17,** 649–685.

DILGER, W. C. The behaviour of lovebirds. *Scientific American,* 1962, **206**(1), 68–88.

DREES, O. Untersuchungen über die angeborenen Verhaltensweisen bei Springspinnen (Salticidae). *Zeitschrift für Tierpsychologie,* 1952, **9,** 169–207.

EIBL-EIBESFELDT, I. *Galapagos.* New York: Doubleday, 1961.

EIBL-EIBESFELDT, I. *Ethology, the biology of behavior.* New York: Holt, Rinehart and Winston, 1970.

FENTRESS, J. C. Interrupted ongoing behaviour in two species of vole *(Microtus agrestis* and *Clethrionomys britannicus).* I and II. *Animal Behaviour,* 1968, **16,** 135–167.

FISHER, R. A. *The genetical theory of natural selection.* Oxford, England: Oxford University Press, 1930.

FRAENKEL, G. S., & GUNN, D. L. *The orientation of animals.* New York: Dover, 1961.

FRISHKOPF, L. S., & GOLDSTEIN, M. H. Responses to acoustic stimuli from single units in the eighth nerve of the bullfrog. *Journal of the Acoustical Society of America,* 1963, **35,** 1219–1228.

GIBSON, E. J., WALK, R. D., PICK, H. L., & TIGHE, T. J. The effect of prolonged exposure to visual patterns on learning to discriminate similar and different patterns. *Journal of Comparative and Physiological Psychology,* 1958, **52,** 74–81.

GROHMANN, J. Modifikation oder Functionsreifung? Ein Beitrag zur Klärung der wechselseitigen Beziehungen zwischen Instinkthandlung und Erfahrung. *Zeitschrift für Tierpsychologie*, 1939, **2**, 132–144.

HAILMAN, J. P. Mirror-image color-preference for background and stimulus-object in the gull chick (Larus atricilla) Experientia, 1966, **22**, 1–4.

HAILMAN, J. P. The ontogeny of an instinct. *Behaviour Supplement*, 1967, **15**, 1–159.

HEBB, D. O. Heredity and environment in mammalian behaviour. *British Journal of Animal Behaviour*, 1953, **1**, 43–47.

HESS, E. H. Imprinting. *Science*, 1959, **130**, 133–141.

HINDE, R. A. Factors governing the changes in strength of a partially inborn response, as shown by the mobbing behaviour of the chaffinch *(Fringilla coelebs)*: I. The nature of the response, and an examination of its course. II. The waning of the response. *Proceedings of the Royal Society of London*, Series B, 1954, **142**. Pp. 306–358. (a) (b)

HINDE, R. A. Ethological models and the concept of drive. *British Journal for the Philosophy of Science*, 1956, **6**, 321–331.

HINDE, R. A. The nest-building behaviour of domesticated canaries. *Proceedings of the Zoological Society of London*, 1958, **131**. Pp. 1–48.

HINDE, R. A. Energy models of motivation. *Symposium of the Society of Experimental Biology*, 1960, **14**. Pp. 199–213. (a)

HINDE, R. A. Factors governing the changes in strength of a partially inborn response, as shown by the mobbing behaviour of the chaffinch (*Fringilla coelebs*): III. The interaction of short-term and long-term incremental and decremental effects. *Proceedings of the Royal Society of London*, Series B, 1960, **153**. Pp 398–420. (b)

HINDE, R. A. Interaction of internal and external factors in integration of canary reproduction. In F. A. Beach (Ed.), *Sex and behavior*. New York: Wiley, 1965. Pp. 381–415.

HINDE, R. A. *Animal Behaviour*. (2nd ed.) New York: McGraw-Hill, 1970.

HINDE, R. A., THORPE, W. H., & VINCE, M. A. The following response of young coots and moorhens. *Behaviour*, 1956, **9**, 214–242.

HOLST, E. VON. Relations between the central nervous system and the peripheral organs. *British Journal of Animal Behaviour*, 1954, **2**, 89–94.

HOLST, E. VON, & MITTELSTAEDT, H. *Das Reafferenzprincip. Naturwissenschaften*, 1950, **37**, 464–476.

HOLST, E. VON, & ST. PAUL, U. VON. On the functional organization of drives. *Animal Behaviour*, 1963, **11**, 1–20.

HUBEL, D. H. The visual cortex of the brain. *Scientific American*, 1963, **209**(5), 54–62.

HUBEL, D. H., & WIESEL, T. N. Receptive fields of single neurones in the cat's striate cortex. *Journal of Physiology*, 1959, **148**, 574–591.

HUXLEY, J. S. *Evolution, the modern synthesis*. London: Allen & Unwin, 1942.

IERSEL, J. J. A. VAN, & BOL, A. C. A. Preening of two tern species. A study on displacement activities. *Behaviour*, 1958, **13**, 1–88.

JENSEN, D. D. Operationism and the question "Is this behavior learned or innate?" *Behaviour*, 1961, **17**, 1–8.

KAPLAN, A. *The conduct of inquiry*. San Francisco: Chandler, 1964.

KONISHI, M. The role of auditory feedback in the vocal behavior of the domestic fowl. *Zeitschrift für Tierpsychologie*, 1964, **20**, 349–367.

KONISHI, M. Effects of deafening on song development in two species of juncos. *Condor*, 1964, **66**, 85 102.

KONISHI, M. The role of auditory feedback in the control of vocalization in the white-crowned sparrow. *Zeitschrift für Tierpsychologie*, 1965, **22**, 770–783.

KRUUK, H. Predators and anti-predator behaviour of the black-headed gull *Larus ridibundus*. *Behaviour Supplement*, 1964, **11**, 1–129.

LACK, D. *The life of the robin*. London: Penguin, 1943.

LEHRMAN, D. S. A critique of Konrad Lorenz's theory of instinctive behaviour. *Quarterly Review of Biology*, 1953, **28**, 337–363.

LEHRMAN, D. S. Gonadal hormones and parental behavior in birds and infrahuman mammals. In W. C. Young (Ed.), *Sex and internal secretions*. Baltimore: Williams & Wilkins, 1961. Pp. 1268–1382.

LEHRMAN, D. S. Interaction between internal and external environments in the regulation of the reproductive cycle of the ring dove. In F. A. Beach (Ed.), *Sex and behavior*. New York: Wiley, 1965. Pp. 335–380.

LEHRMAN, D. S. Semantic and conceptual issues in the nature-nurture problem. In L. R. Aronson, E. Tobach, D. S. Lehrman, & J. S. Rosenblatt (Eds.), *Development and evolution of behavior*. San Francisco: Freeman, 1970. Pp. 17–52.

LETTVIN, J. Y., MATURANA, H. R., MCCULLOCH, W. S., & PITTS, W. H. What the frog's eye tells the frog's brain. *Proceedings of the Institute of Radio Engineers*, 1959, **47**. Pp. 1940–1951.

LORENZ, K. Der Kumpan in der Umwelt des Vogels. *Journal für Ornithologie*, 1935, **83**, 137–213.

LORENZ, K. Uber die Bildung des Instinktbegriffes. *Naturwiss enschaften*, 1937, **25**, 289–300.

LORENZ, K. Vergleichende Verhaltensforschung. *Zoologischer Anzeiger Suppl. Bd.*, 1939, **12**, 69–102.

LORENZ, K. Vergleichende Bewegungsstudien an Anatinen. *Journal für Ornithologie Suppl.*, 1941, **89**, 194–294.

LORENZ, K. The comparative method in studying innate behaviour patterns. *Symposium of the Society of Experimental Biology*, 1950, **4**. Pp. 221–268.

LORENZ, K. The evolution of behavior. *Scientific American*, 1958, **199**(6), 67–78.

LORENZ, K. Phylogenetische Anpassung und adaptive Modifikation des Verhaltens. *Zeitschrift für Tierpsychologie*, 1961, **18**, 139–187.

LORENZ, K. *Evolution and modification of behavior*. Chicago: The University of Chicago Press, 1965.

LORENZ, K. *On aggression*. London: Methuen, 1966.

LORENZ, K. & TINBERGEN, N. Taxis und Instinkthandlung in der Eirollbewegung der Grau-gans. *Zeitschrift für Tierpsychologie*, 1938, **2**, 1–29.

MAGNUS, D. Zum Problem der überoptimalen Schlüsselreize. (*Versuche am Kaisermantels* Argynnis paphia L.) *Verhandlungen Zoologish Gesellschaft Tubingen*, 1954 (Zoologischer Anzeiger) *Suppl.*, 1955, **18**, 317–325.

MAGNUS, D. Experimentelle Untersuchungen zur Bionomie und Ethologie des Kaisermantels *Argynnis paphia* L. (Lep. Nymph): I. Uber optische Auslöser von Anfliegereaktinonen und ihre Bedeutung für das Sichfinden det Geschlechter. *Zeitschrift für Tierpsychologie*, 1958, **15**, 397–426.

MANNING, A. *Drosophila* and the evolution of behaviour. In J. D. Carthy & C. L. Duddington (Eds.), *Viewpoints in biologie 4*. London: Butterworth, 1965. Pp. 125–169.

MARLER, P. Developments in the study of animal communication. In P. R. Bell (Ed.), *Darwin's biological work*. Cambridge, England: Cambridge University Press, 1959, 150–206.

MARLER, P., & HAMILTON, W. J. Mechanisms of animal behavior. New York: Wiley, 1966.

MATURANA, H. R., LETTVIN, J. Y., MCCULLOCH, W. S. & PITTS, W. H. Anatomy and physiology of vision in the frog (*Rana pipiens*). *Journal of General Physiology*, 1960, **43** (Supplement 2), 129–175.

MCFARLAND, D. J. Hunger, thirst and displacement pecking in the Barbary dove. *Animal Behaviour*, 1965, **13**, 293–300.

MCFARLAND, D. J. The role of attention in the disinhibition of displacement activities. *Quarterly Journal of Experimental Psychology*, 1966, **18**, 19–30.

MESSMER, E., & MESSMER, I. Die Entwicklung der Lautäusserungen und einiger Verhaltensweisen der Amsel (Turdus merula merula L.) unter natürlichen Bedingungen und nach Einzelaufzucht in schalldichten Räumen. *Zeitschrift für Tierpsychologie*, 1956, **13**, 341–441.

MOLTZ, H. Imprinting: Empirical basis and theoretical significance. *Psychological Bulletin*, 1960, **57**, 291–314.

MORRIS, D. The feather postures of birds and the problem of the origin of social signals. *Behaviour*, 1956, **9**, 75–113.

MORRIS, D. "Typical intensity" and its relation to the problem of ritualisation. *Behaviour*, 1957, **11**, 1–12.

MORRIS, D. *The naked ape*. London: Cape, 1967.

MORRIS, D. *The human zoo*. London: Cape, 1970.

MOYNIHAN, M. Some displacement activities of black-headed gulls. *Behaviour*, 1953, **5**, 58–80.

MOYNIHAN, M. Some aspects of reproductive behavior in the black-headed gull *(Larus ridibundus L.)* and related species. *Behaviour Supplement*, 1955, **4**, 1–201.

NELSON, J. B. Colonial and cliff nesting in the gannet. *Ardea*, 1967, **55**, 60–90.

NELSON, K. The temporal patterning of courtship behaviour in the glandulocaudine fishes (Ostarophysi, Characidae). *Behaviour*, 1964, **24**, 90–146.

NICE, M. M. Studies in the life-history of the song sparrow: II. *Transactions of the Linnaen Society of New York*, 1943, **6**, 1–328.

PATTERSON, I. J. Timing and spacing of broods in the black-headed gull, *Larus ridibundus*. *Ibis*, 1965, **107**, 433–459.

POULSEN, H. Song learning in domestic canary. *Zeitschrift für Tierpsychologie*, 1959, **16**, 173–178.

PRECHTL, H. F. R. Zur Physiologie der angelborenen auslosenden Mechanismen: I. Quantitative Untersuchungen über die Sperrbewegung junger Singvögel. *Behaviour*, 1953, **1**, 32–50.

RABER, H. Analyse des Balzverhaltens eines domestizierten Truthahns (Meleagris). *Behaviour*, 1948, **1**, 237–266.

ROEDER, K. D. *Nerve cells and insect behavior*. Cambridge, Mass.: Harvard University Press, 1963.

ROWELL, C. H. F. Displacement grooming in the chaffinch. *Animal Behaviour*, 1961, **9**, 38–63.

RUITER, L. DE. Countershading in catepillars. *Archives Neerlandaises de Zoologie*, 1956, **11**, 285–341.

RUSSELL, W. M. S., MEAD, A. P., & HAYES, J. S. A basis for the quantitative study of the structure of behaviour. *Behaviour*, 1954, **6**, 153–205.

SALZEN, E. A. Imprinting and fear. *Symposium of the Zoological Society of London*, 1962, **8**. Pp. 199–217.

SAUER, F. Die Entwinklung der Lautäusserungen vom Ei ab schalldicht gehaltener Dorngrasmücken (Sylvia c. communis, Latham) in Vergleich mit später isolierten und mit wildlebenden Artgenossen. *Zeitschrift für Tierpsychologie*, 1954, **11**, 10–93.

SCHILLER, C. H. *Instinctive behavior*. New York: International Universities Press, 1957.

SCHLEIDT, W. Untersuchungen über die Auslösung des Kollerns beim Truthahn (Meleagris gallopavo). *Zeitschrift für Tierpsychologie*, 1954, **11**, 417–435.

SCHLEIDT, W. Reaktionen von Truthühnern auf fliegende Raubvögel und Versuche zur Analyse inher AAM's. *Zeitschrift für Tierpsychologie*, 1961, **18**, 534–560.

SCHNIERLA, T. C. Interrelationships of the "innate" and the "acquired" in instinctive behavior. In *L'Instinct dans le Compartment des Animaux et de L'homme*. Paris: Fondation Singer Polignac, 1956.

SEVENSTER, P. A causal analysis of a displacement activity (Fanning in *Gasterosteus aculeatus* L.). *Behaviour Supplement*, 1961, **9**, 1–170.

SEVENSTER-BOL, A. C. A. On the causation of drive reduction after a consummatory act. *Archives Neerlandaises de Zoologie*, 1962, **15**, 175–236.

SLUCKIN, W. *Imprinting and early learning*. London: Methuen, 1964.

SPERRY, R. W. Mechanisms of neural maturation. In S. S. Stevens (Ed.), *Handbook of experimental psychology*. New York: Wiley, 1951. Pp. 236–280.

TAYLOR, C. *The explanation of behaviour*. New York: Humanities Press, 1964.

THIELKE-POLTZ, H., & THIELKE, G. Akustiches Lernen verschieden alter schallisolierter Amseln (Turdus merula L.) und die Entwicklung erlernter Motive ohne und mit künstlichen Einfluss von Testosteron. *Zeitschrift für Tierpsychologie*, 1960, **17**, 211–244.

THORPE, W. H. The definition of some terms used in animal behaviour studies. *Bulletin of Animal Behaviour*, 1951, **9**, 34–40.

THORPE, W. H. The learning of song patterns by birds, with especial reference to the song of the chaffinch, *Fringilla coelebs*. *Ibis*, 1958, **100**, 535–570.

THORPE, W. H. *Bird-song*. Cambridge, England: Cambridge University Press, 1961.

THORPE, W. H. *Learning and instinct in animals*. (2nd ed.) London: Methuen, 1963.

TINBERGEN, N. The hierarchical organization of nervous mechanisms underlying instinctive behaviour. *Symposium of the Society of Experimental Biology*, 1950, **4**. Pp. 305–312.

TINBERGEN, N. *The study of instinct*. Oxford, England: Oxford University Press, 1951.

TINBERGEN, N. Derived activities: Their causation, biological significance, origin and emancipation during evolution. *Quarterly Review of Biology*, 1952, **27**, 1–32.

TINBERGEN, N. *The herring gull's world*. London: Collins, 1953.

TINBERGEN, N. *Curious naturalists*. London: Country Life, 1958.

TINBERGEN, N. Comparative studies of the behaviour of gulls (Laridae): A progress report. *Behaviour*, 1959, **15**, 1–70.

TINBERGEN, N. On aims and methods of ethology. *Zeitschrift für Tierpsychologie*, 1963, **20**, 410–433.

TINBERGEN, N. On adaptive radiation in gulls (Tribe Larini). *Zoologische Mededelingen*, 1964, **39**, 209–223.

TINBERGEN, N., BROEKHUYSEN, G. J., FEEKES, F., HOUGHTON, J. C. W., KRUUK, H., & SZULC, E. Egg shell removal by the black-headed gull, *Larus ridibundus* L.; a behaviour component of comouflage. *Behaviour*, 1962, **19**, 74–117.

TINBERGEN, N., & KUENEN, D. J. Uber die auslösenden und die richtunggebanden Reizsituationen der Sperrbewegung von jungen Drosseln (*Turdus m. merula* L. und *T. e. ericetorum* Turton). *Zeitschrift für Tierpsychologie*, 1939, **3**, 27–60.

TUGENDHAT, B. The normal feeding behavior of the three-spined stickleback *(Gasterosteus aculeatus)*. *Behaviour,* 1960, **15,** 284–318.

WEIDMANN, U. Some reproductive activities of the common gull, *Larus canus* L. *Ardea,* 1955, **43,** 85–132.

WEISS, P. Self-differentiation of the basic patterns of coordination. *Comparative Psychology Monographs,* 1941, **17,** 1–96.

WEISS, P. Experimental analysis of coordination by disarrangement of central-peripheral relations. *Symposium of the Society of Experimental Biology,* 1950, **4.** Pp. 92–111.

WELLS, M. J. Early learning in *Sepia. Symposia of the Zoological Society of London,* 1962, **8.** Pp. 149–169.

WICKLER, W. *Vergleichende Verhaltensstudien an Grundfischen:* II. *Zeitschrift für Tierpsychologie,* 1958, **15,** 427–446.

WICKLER, W. Okologie und Stammesgeschichte von Verhaltensweisen. *Fortschrift Zoologie,* 1961, **13,** 303–365.

WIEPKEMA, P. R. An ethological analysis of the reproductive behaviour of the bitterling. *Archives Neerlandaises de Zoologie,* 1961, **14,** 103–199.

Chapter 3

Mammalian Behavior Patterns

Bradford N. Bunnell

In this chapter we shall look at some examples of behavior patterns in mammals. Why is there a separate chapter on mammalian behavior patterns? After all, most of the basic problems, approaches, and principles relating to the topic of species-typical behavior can be described and established by reference to invertebrates, fish, and birds, as has been done in the last chapter. There are, however, a number of reasons for placing particular emphasis on mammals.

First, although mammals comprise only 0.005 of all the living animal species, the more advanced mammalian forms represent the apex of vertebrate development. As such, they would be worth special consideration in any case, but because man is a mammal and has always been very curious about his own behavior, the study of mammalian behavior has been of special interest to psychology. Next, mammals, with their relatively complex brains, are particularly well adapted for profiting from previous experience. The problem of describing and analyzing mammalian behavior patterns is especially challenging and interesting when one recognizes the importance of the role of this behavioral plasticity in the adaptations of these animals to their environments. Finally, some of the behaviors that have been studied by ethologists under the general heading of species-typical behavior have been examined in mammals by animal psychologists in their investigation of behaviors traditionally subsumed under motivational concepts and constructs. One objective of this chapter is to put some of the findings from the two fields into the same context.

In this chapter we shall describe some of the things that mammals do that enable them to survive and reproduce. Throughout the chapter, the emphasis will be upon the behavior of the individual animal. The problems of social behavior and communication will be examined in detail in later chapters.

THE INTERRELATEDNESS OF BEHAVIORAL PATTERNS

To facilitate the survey of mammalian behavior patterns, behavior has been subdivided into a number of functional categories (e.g., locomotion, activity rhythms, nesting, feeding, and the like). Where possible, the probable adaptive significance of the behavioral examples is indicated in order to help the reader to understand the role of the behavior in the life of the animal. While this organization allows an appreciation of the range and diversity of the behaviors utilized by different mammals in meeting their requirements, it does not provide a description of the complete behavioral repertoire of any one species. It should be remembered that the ways in which a given animal feeds, nests, travels, protects itself, mates, and cares for its young are all interlocking parts of a whole. In other words, an animal is an adapted organism, and not simply a collection of specialized adaptations.

This point has been emphasized by Bartholomew and Caswell (1951) in their analysis of locomotor behavior in kangaroo rats of the genus *Dipodomys*. The kangaroo rat is a small, burrowing, nocturnal rodent that lives in arid and semiarid regions of western North America. It can survive for long periods without drinking free water. Its needs for water are met by the preformed water contained in its herbivorous diet and from oxidative water produced by the metabolism of its food. Further, water is conserved because of the unusual ability of the kidney to concentrate urine, and by the animal's habit of spending the hottest part of the day in its burrow, so that minimal amounts of water are expended in thermoregulation. *Dipodomys* has cheek pouches used in gathering and transporting food back to the burrow where it is eaten or stored for future use. The two species investigated by Bartholomew and Caswell, *D. merriami* and *D. panamintinius*, are sympatric, that is, they both occupy the same geographic area. Both are aggressive (*D. panamintinius* more so than *D. merriami*), a factor which keeps adults separated except when mating and helps to ensure an adequate food supply for all. Care of the pelage involves sandbathing, a pattern that probably originated from movements used in spreading scent (see Eisenberg, 1964). Scent-marking, in its turn, is a means of advertising the presence of animals within an area.

In appearance, the kangaroo rat is quite unusual. It has long, powerful hind feet and a long tail with a tuft of hairs at the end. Its forelegs are relatively short. The large head has small, weak jaws, and enlarged eyes so placed that it is impossible for the animal to see what it is eating. The auditory bullae are disproportionately large for an animal of its size (see Figure 3-1).

To a casual observer, the most striking thing about the kangaroo rat's behavior is its bipedal, saltatorial (jumping) locomotor pattern. Although these animals may use other gaits when moving slowly, when feeding, or when approaching elevated objects, bipedal leaping is commonly used during moderate and fast straightaway movements, during exploration, and when excited or taking evasive action. These movements are quite spectacular, with the animals reaching an altitude of 2 feet or more during vertical leaping, and covering horizontal distances of at least 5 feet when trying to escape. The long, tufted tail is an integral part of *Dipodomys's* locomotor equipment, being used as a support when the animal is standing erect, and as both a static and a dynamic balancing organ when it is moving. The course and trajectory of the escape behavior are unpredictable, a feature which has obvious survival value in counteracting the predation of foxes, coyotes, snakes, and owls. Despite their erratic appearance, these leaps are beautifully controlled. Bartholomew and Caswell report an instance in which a rapidly escaping kangaroo rat, landing 2 feet beyond a burrow entrance which could not have been seen until the animal passed it, instantly altered its direction on the next leap to dive directly into the hole. M. H. Smith and I have filmed brief, paired encounters between kangaroo rats in small (30" x 12" x 12") cages. In avoiding an aggressor, the animals were very adept at maneuvering without touching the sides of the cage and at changing direction during a leap (through as much as 180 degrees) so that they usually landed in a position facing the opponent.

Figure 3–1. A kangaroo rat *(Dipodomys spectabilis).* By permission from Schmidt-Nielsen, K. *Desert animals.* London: Oxford University Press, 1964.

Bartholomew and Caswell note that the economy of the kangaroo rat is admirably geared to the efficient avoidance of danger in areas where there is a lack of continuous plant cover. The burrow, in addition to reducing the animal's thermoregulatory problems, serves as a refuge from predators. As it rarely forages more than 50 to 70 feet from the home burrow, efficient escape from predators requires quick-starting, evasive locomotion over short distances in open terrain instead of sustained high speed.

For the most part, the need for leaving the burrow has to do with feeding. The presence of cheek pouches reduces the time the animal is exposed by separating foraging from feeding. Although the kangaroo rat cannot see what it is eating, the eyes are admirably situated for detecting danger from above. The forelimbs are not required during rapid locomotion, and are used to assist the foraging process by sifting through the sand and, on occasion, to carry large food objects. Thus, the sensory and motor apparatus used in the detection of danger and the rapid initiation of evasive action are not used during foraging, and are always available for escaping predators. In summary, the kangaroo rat, like every other animal, is an integrated whole composed of mutually supporting adaptations. Its locomotor behavior is only the most obvious of these specializations.

LOCOMOTION
Terrestrial Quadrupeds

For movement on land, the limbs of mammals must provide both support and propulsion for the body. The primitive monotremes, like most of the reptiles, have limbs extending horizontally from the body which are moved back and forth in a horizontal plane. In marsupials and eutherian mammals, the limbs extend below the body and are moved in a vertical, longitudinal plane. The evolution of rapid terrestrial locomotion has involved a shift from a flatfooted posture in which the weight is borne on the plantar surfaces of the extremities (plantigrade habit) to one in which the limbs are raised and straightened so that the animal stands on its phalanges (digitigrade habit). Finally, in the hooved mammals, the contact with the ground is provided by the distal end of the phalanges (unguligrade habit), and the limbs are relatively long and light in weight.

The most primitive four-footed gait, and one which is also seen in amphibians and reptiles, utilizes a movement pattern in which the hindlimb is always moved before the forelimb on the same side, as in the sequence: left forelimb (LF), right hindlimb (RH), right forelimb (RF), left hindlimb (LH), left forelimb (LF), and so on. When the footfalls are spaced about equally in time, the result is a four-beat gait, or single-foot, which is a natural way of walking in horses and cattle. In most mammals, there is a tendency for the footfalls of the forelimbs and hindlimbs on opposite sides of the body to occur closer together in time than movements of the ipsilateral limbs in normal walking. Thus, the usual walking gait combines the lateral sequence of limb movements just described with a "diagonal couplet" of the timing of limb movements (Hildebrand, 1965).

Some mammals, including the camels, giraffe, and some antelopes, large cats, and many canids, while retaining the lateral sequence of moving the hindlimb before the forelimb on the same side, couple the movements of the ipsilateral limbs in time. The lateral sequence–lateral couplet gait includes periods during which support is provided only by two limbs on the same side of the body—a highly unstable condition—and the pattern is not used for slow walking.

Diagonal walking sequences, in which a hindlimb is moved before the forelimb on the opposite side of the body (e.g., LH-RF-RH-LF) are found in many primates, the aardvark, giant armadillo, and kinkajou (Hildebrand, 1965), and in bison and some dogs (Gray, 1968).

A running single-foot is the only fast gait possessed by the elephant. Although it provides maximum support, it is tiring to maintain since it involves four shifts in the center of gravity during each complete stride the animal takes. Other mammals use different gaits when moving rapidly.

In moving from a walk to a trot, the difference in phase between a hindlimb and the contralateral forelimb decreases while the phase difference between the hindlimb and the ipsilateral forelimb increases so that, in a completely synchronized trot, the animal is supported alternately on diagonal pairs of limbs, with intervening periods during which all four limbs are off the ground. This gait is used at moderate speed by most large mammals, at maximum speed by animals such as the bull moose and caribou whose heavy racks or short necks make galloping unsuitable, and at slow tempo, in which two feet are usually in contact with the ground, by clumsy, broad-beamed mammals like the badger and hippopotamus. In the running pace, the phase difference between ipsilateral limbs is decreased so that they are moved together in a lateral sequence–lateral couplet pattern. The pace is used by camels, the giraffe, and some dogs and horses as a natural gait (Hildebrand, 1965; Gray, 1968).

The most rapid gait is the gallop. Here the most distinctive feature is the partial synchronization of the two forelimbs and the two hindlimbs. Animals like the whippet and the cheetah have very supple joints and spines which allow considerable flexion and extension of the limbs and back and produce relatively long strides (see Figure 3–2) (Gray, 1968).

Bipedalism

Movement on the hind feet is not uncommon in mammals, although only man, with his striding, plantigrade gait, and the saltatorial mammals that have long,

Figure 3–2. The transverse gallop of the horse (top) and rotary gallop of the cheetah. Due to the greater flexion and extension of the limbs and back, the length of the cheetah's stride is about twice that of the horse when the relative height of the animals is taken into account. (Gray, 1968, p. 279.) (By permission after M. Hildebrand. Motions of the running cheetah and horse. *Journal of Mammalogy,* 1959, **40,** 481–495.)

powerful hind legs and short forelegs, such as the kangaroos and certain rodents, regularly move in this fashion. Man's bipedal gait is related to a major modification in his pelvis, to the development of powerful musculature on the hips and back of the thighs, and to alterations in the structure of the foot. Although these changes limit his abilities as a running (cursorial) mammal, they free his forelimbs for hunting, carrying, and manipulating.

Arboreal Mammals

Strong, sharp claws, attached to relatively flexible paws, and well-developed visual and vestibular systems enable many small mammals to climb and to move through the trees with essentially the same locomotor patterns they utilize in terrestrial movement. The tail is frequently used to provide balance.

Brachiation, movement through the trees by swinging by the arms, is seen in the gibbons and in the anthropoid apes. Extensive modifications, including elongation of the arms and adaptations enabling rotation, flexion, and abduction of the arm and shoulder, are seen in these animals.

In the wild, chimpanzees are often seen to brachiate, though the maximum distances covered are quite short—about 20 feet (van Lawick-Goodall, 1968). They use quadrupedal terrestrial locomotion when traveling between feeding and resting places. Gorillas, which also are terrestrial in their trekking behavior, climb trees slowly but skillfully and can move through terminal branches in feeding and nesting although they apparently do very little brachiating (Schaller, 1963). However, they are "structural" brachiators and have the typical brachiator movements in their behavioral repertoires (Avis, 1962).

Four New World monkey genera (*Ateles, Logothrix, Alouatta, Brachyteles*) are arm swingers, but their structural modifications are not so extreme as those seen in Pongidae. They are classed as semibrachiators, as are the six genera of Old World monkeys that sometimes use arm swinging. (see Napier & Napier, 1967).

Fossorial Mammals

Many mammals dig burrows which protect them against predators and shelter them from extremes of climatic conditions. Most of these animals are only semifossorial, however, emerging to move about the surface to feed, gather nesting material, and engage in the other activities making up their daily rounds. A few, such as the marsupial "moles" (Notoryctidae), many genera of moles (Talpidae) and golden moles (Chrysocloridae), pocket gophers (Geomyidae), and the mole rats (Bathyergidae and Spalacidae), spend nearly all their lives underground.

The fossorial mammals exhibit many adaptations for a subterranean life. The eyes are greatly reduced in size and may be sealed beneath the eyelids. The pinnae of the ears, which otherwise would impede passage through the burrow, are small or absent. In some species, the nostrils are laterally placed, a location which may help to keep dirt out of the nasal passages. The animal may be nearly naked or as in most cases its fur may be short, soft, and capable of lying forward as well as backward so that the pelage offers little resistance to locomotion (Hamilton, 1939).

Swimming

All mammals, with the possible exception of the great apes, can swim, and a number are specialized for a semiaquatic life. The platypus has webbed feet and uses its paddlelike tail as a stabilizer in swimming and diving. Under water, its eyes and ears are closed by a flap of skin so that it relies on its sensitive muzzle when navigating and feeding submerged (Lyne, 1967).

Webbed feet, fringed toes, tails modified as rudders or for propulsion, streamlining of the body, and the development of efficient heat-retaining mechanisms are among the adaptations exhibited by aquatic and semiaquatic placental mammals. Some, such as otters and cetaceans, use undulatory movements of the body and tail base for thrust; others rely upon movements of the appendages. In some orders, notably the Pinnipedia, the Sirenia, and the Cetacea, specialization for an aquatic life has reached the point where it seriously interferes with terrestrial locomotion (Gray, 1968).

Flight

Among mammals, active flight occurs only in bats. The forelimbs are modified in that the long, thin fingers are joined by a membrane (patagium) which extends to the side of the body and is usually attached to the legs and tail. The movement of the wings in flight is similar to that used by birds, despite the fact that the skeletal structure is completely different (Gray, 1968). The flying foxes, the fruit-eating bats of the genus *Pteropus*, may have a wing span in excess of 5 feet (*P. vampyrus*) and are relatively slow flyers, but the insectivorous free-tailed bats of the family Molossidae may reach speeds as high as 95 kilometers per hour. Most bats are clumsy on the ground; the rear feet are adapted for hanging upside down even during hibernation, and the thumb frequently has a small claw that may be used in clinging. Pteropodids may use their wings for rowing if forced into the water (Koopman & Cockrum, 1967).

All the remaining "flying" mammals are restricted to gravitational gliding. Gliders appear in three genera of one marsupial family (the Phalangeridae) and in approximately thirty species of true squirrels (family Sciuridae) (Gray, 1968). The most impressive performance is given by the Dermopterans. These "flying lemurs" have been reported to travel over 200 feet while losing as little as 1 foot of altitude for each 15 feet of horizontal distance. They have a highly developed patagium and disklike feet, and they are reported to be unable to stand erect and to be so slow-moving as to be virtually helpless if they accidentally reach the ground.

ACTIVITY

Mammals alternate periods of high activity with periods in which they are more or less inactive. In addition, qualitative changes in the character of the animals' behavior take place from time to time. Finally, many of the shifts in the intensity and quality of activity are cyclic; that is, they tend to recur regularly throughout most, or all, of the lifetime of the animal. For example, if a nonpregnant, adult female laboratory rat is placed in an activity wheel and her daily "spontaneous" running is recorded, the amount of running she does reaches a maximum of 10,000 to 20,000 revolutions per day about every 4 days. On the other 3 days in the cycle, she may average only 2,000 to 4,000 revolutions (Figure 3–3). Examination of vaginal smears shows that ovulation occurs just before the peak of running behavior is reached. The time she is most active corresponds with qualitative changes in her behavior toward male rats. She may approach the male and nuzzle him; after the first contact she runs a little way and then stops. The male pursues and mounts her and she adopts the lordosis posture permitting copulation (Barnett, 1963). At other times during the 4-day estrous cycle, she shows little interest in the male and will actively resist his advances. Thus, there is a recurrent 4-day rhythm in which both quantitative and qualitative changes in behavior may be observed.

In this section, we shall concentrate on changes involving the intensity

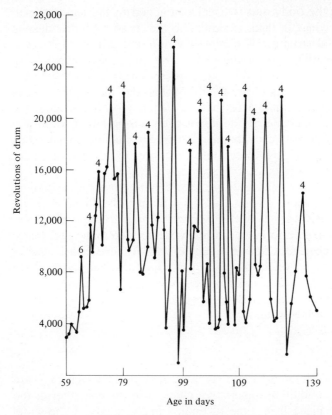

Figure 3–3. In an activity wheel, the activity of an adult female rat shows a peak about every four days. (After Richter, C. P. Biological Foundations of Personality Differences. *American Journal of Orthopsychiatry,* 1932, **2,** 345–354. Copyright ©, the American Orthopsychiatric Association, Inc. Reproduced by permission.

dimension of mammalian activity. Later there will be an opportunity to examine some of the qualitative aspects of the problem, i.e., the different kinds of behavior patterns that mammals exhibit.

Twenty-four-hour Periods

Some insectivores, such as the short-tail shrew, are active almost all the time whereas some bats sleep as much as 20 hours in each 24-hour period (Allison & van Twyver, 1970). Most mammals are somewhere between these two extremes in terms of the amount of time during which they are active each day.

Nocturnal animals are those that are active at night; diurnal animals are active in the daytime. Other mammals are crepuscular, that is, they are active at dawn, or at dusk, or both. Many of the larger herbivores and their predators are nocturnal or crepuscular. This is not a rigid rule, however, and a number of exceptions can be found. Furthermore, while many mammals are exclusively diurnal, nocturnal, or crepuscular, others may modify their habits in response to changes in food supply, the onset of the breeding season, climatic conditions, hunting pressures, and the like. Also, there are a number of species, usually either fossorial or grazing animals, that show active intervals throughout the 24-hour period (Cloudsley-Thompson, 1961).

Laboratory studies of 24-hour activity periods indicate that each species has its own characteristic pattern of activity. Although there are often reliable individual differences between members of a species, the general form of the activity curves produced by each individual reflects the species-typical pattern. Thus the shrew (*Sorex araneus*) alternates brief periods of activity and rest over an entire 24-hour period, but also shows a peak of activity in both the light and the dark phase of the daily cycle. The mouse (*Mus musculus*) is active primarily in the dark, during which time it exhibits two peaks, the first occurring shortly after the lights go out and the second at the end of the dark period. The golden hamster (*Mesocricetus auratus*) exhibits a single rise in activity that begins to build 3 to 4 hours before dark and reaches a maximum just about the time the light-dark shift occurs. Activity in this animal remains high for a few hours, then falls to low levels during the last half of the dark phase (Aschoff & Honma, 1959).

The prosimian *Lorisidae* are all nocturnal. Both the potto (*Perodicticus potto*) and the slow loris (*Nycticebus coucang*) exhibit bimodal activity peaks at night while a third member of the family, the slender loris (*Loris tardigradus*), does not. The slender loris and the potto are most active in the dark phase, whereas the slow loris has major activity peaks early and late at night (Seitz, 1967).

Measures of Activity

In the field, the activity of some species may be observed directly. The study of animals that are nocturnal, cryptic, or fossorial often requires an indirect approach. The frequent checking of traps, artificial feeding stations, or areas specially prepared to record the tracks of animals have all been used to give a rough indication of when animals are active. Godfrey (1954) placed small radioactive rings on the legs of voles and followed their activity with a Geiger counter. More recently, it has been possible to attach small electronic signaling devices which can indicate when an animal is moving about and when it is quiescent. The various indirect methods all have drawbacks. Trapping data are usually incomplete; appearance at feeding stations may not be indicative of the total time the animal is active. Methods used for following animals are not very sensitive to the amount of time the animal is awake and active in the nest or burrow but is not moving about very much.

In the laboratory, two commonly used devices for measuring activity are the activity wheel and the stabilimeter cage (e.g., Richter, 1927). Tilting cages and photocell cages which require movement for a specific distance and/or in a specific direction to produce a record are also used. Many investigators have obtained records of active periods by having animals perform instrumental responses. For example, Kavanau (1963) had his deer mice (*P. maniculatus*) perform such tasks to leave the nest, to gain access to an activity wheel, and to obtain food and water. Although most of these methods are adequate for detecting diurnal rhythms, it has been shown that the correlations between scores obtained with different devices are often very low (e.g., Tapp, Zimmerman, & D'Encarnacao, 1968), indicating that they are not all measuring the same thing. For this reason, direct comparisons between species of data obtained from different methods should be avoided. A device which records movements by recording changes in standing wave patterns in a chamber flooded with ultrasonic noise offers much promise for the measurement of nearly all of an animal's activity (Peacock & Williams, 1962).

Sleep

Mammals spend varying amounts of their inactive periods in sleep. Two qualitatively different stages of sleep are recognized (see Figure 7-2).

Slow-wave Sleep   This stage is so named because the electroencephalograph (EEG) record, as taken from the cerebral cortex, consists primarily of large amplitude waves of relatively low frequency.

Paradoxical Sleep   Here the cortical EEG shows the low-amplitude, high-frequency, "desynchronized" pattern typical of an active waking animal, but the animal is in the deepest stage of sleep, hence the term *paradoxical sleep*. Skeletal muscle tone drops out, and it takes a much stronger stimulus to arouse the animal than in the case of slow-wave sleep. Rapid eye movements appear during paradoxical sleep.

Both stages of sleep may be identified in birds as well as in mammals, but there is considerable doubt as to whether reptiles and amphibians sleep at all. Sleep appears to be a characteristic unique to warm-blooded animals.

On the basis of laboratory studies of mammals, Allison and van Twyver (1970) have identified "good sleepers," that sleep 8 to 20 hours a day and show a high proportion of paradoxical sleep, and "poor sleepers," that sleep fewer hours and exhibit relatively small amounts of paradoxical sleep. The poor sleepers typically require long periods of adaptation to the laboratory situation before they show much, if any, sleep. In the mammals studied to date, good sleepers appear to be either predators or animals that have secure sleeping places, while poor sleepers are subject to predation at all hours (see Table 3-1).

Table 3–1   The Relationship between Sleep, Behavior, and Habitat in Mammals

Animal	Behavior and habitat	Sleep
"Good Sleeper"		
Mole	Carnivore, active day or night. Lives below ground in an extensive network of burrows.	Sleeps 8 hours per day in lab with almost no adaptation. 24 percent paradoxical sleep.
Ground squirrel	Herbivore, hibernates, prey. Lives in extensive burrows of its own making.	Deep sleeper, about 14 hours a day in lab. 25 percent paradoxical sleep.
Cat	Predator. Only the domestic cat has been studied.	Deep sleeper, readily sleeps about 14 hours a day in lab. 27 percent paradoxical sleep.
Macaque	Omnivore, strong fighter. Sleeps in tops of tall trees.	After short adaptation, sleeps 8 hours a day, 15–20 percent paradoxical sleep.
Chimpanzee	Omnivore, most similar to man. Lives in tropical rain forests and shelters in tree nests at night.	After relatively short adaptation, sleeps 11 hours a day. 19 percent paradoxical sleep.
Man	Omnivore. Has mastered defense from other species and the elements. Chief predator is man. Inhabits all ecological ranges.	Deep sleeper. After short adaptation, sleeps 8 hours in lab. 24 percent paradoxical sleep.
"Poor Sleeper"		
Guinea pig	Herbivore; nervous, hyperactive, excitable; prey. Lives in burrows, which it excavates or borrows, in rocky areas, savannas, swamps, and at edges of forests.	After long adaptation will sleep 12 hours per day. 5 percent paradoxical sleep.
Rabbit	Herbivore, prey. Some strains are extremely nervous and easily excited. Usually lives in grass nests on the surface or occasionally in burrows.	Difficult to adapt; sleep is seen only after several months in lab with some strains. Up to 15 percent paradoxical sleep when well adapted.
Sheep	Herbivore; nervous, excitable, prey. Lives in grasslands. (Study includes only domestic species.)	Requires long adaptation. About 4 percent paradoxical sleep.
Goat	Herbivore, excitable, prey. Lives in grasslands or mountains. (Only domestic species studied.)	After two months adaptation, will enter paradoxical sleep but only rarely.
Donkey	Herbivore, excitable, prey. Lives in grasslands. (Only domestic species studied.)	After several months in lab, will sleep about 4 hours a day, but paradoxical sleep apparently not seen.
Baboon	Omnivore. Strong fighter but subject to predation. Lives at edges of forests, in savannas and rocky areas. Sleeps in tops of scrub trees where it is easily visible.	Enters paradoxical sleep phase after extended adaptation. 4–9 percent paradoxical sleep.

Circadian Rhythms and Their Entrainment

In recent years, much has been made of findings which support the idea that the basis for the patterning of 24-hour activity periods is endogenous. That is to say, the occurrence of regular changes in external environmental stimuli, such as light, temperature, and the like, is not required in order for the species-typical alteration of activity and quiescence to appear. While it is not possible to eliminate all possibilities for the existence of external pacemakers (e.g., Brown 1970), activity records of mammals kept under nearly constant conditions of illumination, temperature, humidity, and sound show that the animals continue to exhibit the regular daily pattern characteristic of the species and of the individual animal being studied. An example of such a record is given in Figure 3–4. The activity rhythm fluctuates within fairly narrow limits around a period of 24 hours (hence the term *circadian* rhythm, meaning rhythm of about a day). In addition, under constant experimental conditions, the pattern is seen to drift in a consistent fashion, from day to day. This free-running pattern is a behavioral manifestation of a presumed biological clock, with a period of about 24 hours, that runs continuously

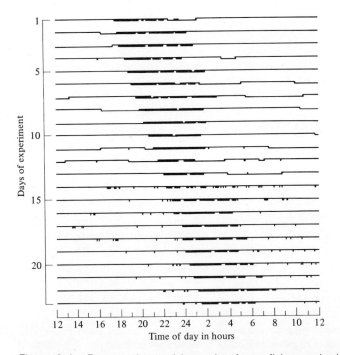

Figure 3–4. Free running activity cycle of one flying squirrel, *Glaucomys volans* in an activity wheel cage. By permission after DeCoursey, P. J. Effect of light on the activity of the flying squirrel, *Glaucomys volans. Zeitschrift für Vergleichende Physiologie,* 1961, **44,** 331–354.

(Aschoff, 1963), even during hibernation (Saint Girons, 1965) and even when the animal is rendered inactive by electroshock convulsions or nitrous oxide anesthesia (Richter, 1965).

The free-running rhythm may be synchronized, or entrained, by a periodic repetition of a stimulus change. Under natural conditions, the primary synchronizing factor *(Zeitgeber)* which entrains the mammalian circadian activity rhythm to a periodicity of exactly 24 hours is the 24-hour light-dark cycle produced by the earth's daily rotation (e.g., Aschoff, 1963).

Photoperiodism

Seasonal changes in quantitative and qualitative aspects of activity, such as those seen in animals which hibernate, migrate, and have breeding periods at particular times of the year, may be, under some conditions, direct responses to environmental factors such as precipitation, temperature, light intensity, and availability of food. In other cases, these factors are not sufficiently consistent in their appearance to provide reliable timing for initiating and regulating changes in the animals' activity. Also, in many instances, it is necessary that the animal anticipate the appearance of climatic changes (Sadlier, 1969).

Many animals are susceptible to seasonal changes in day length, and photoperiodic control is utilized to achieve appropriate timing. For example, it is possible to get some animals to breed, to hoard food, and to show preparations for hibernation during the "wrong" time of year. This is done by exposing them to daily changes in light-dark ratios which imitate the seasonal day-length changes normally associated with naturally occurring seasonal, behavioral, and physiological changes.

SHELTER AND NESTING

Most mammals exhibit behavior patterns which have the effect of altering the microenvironment in such a way as to enhance survival. Such behaviors range from relatively simple orienting responses, through the utilization of natural features of the environment, to the complex sequences employed in making nests, burrow systems, and the like. They may serve one function or many in promoting the welfare of the animal. For example, among the several mechanisms available to the camel in solving the thermoregulatory problem posed by its desert habitat is the response of sitting in such a way that a minimum of its body surface is exposed to the sun. Many canids curl up and protect their faces from the cold by covering them with their tails. Basking in warm sunlight is a common response of mammals in cool weather; it is a particularly prominent behavior in animals that are poor thermoregulators such as the hyrax which undergoes a considerable drop in body temperature while sleeping. Hares and rabbits remain motionless through most of the day in forms—flattened resting places situated in dense vegetation. Many species seek shelters in trees, crevices, and caves, while still others, including a number of bats and rodents, have moved in with man. Beavers build dams, lodges, and canals that ensure access to food, control water levels, protect against predators and climatic extremes, and provide a place to store food.

Shelter may be in the form of a permanent home, as in the case of the burrow systems of wild Norway rats, prairie dog "towns," and the beaver colonies just mentioned. It may be temporary, as in the selection of a shady spot near a handy tree by domestic sheep, the making of a sleeping nest that is normally used only for a single night by the chimpanzee, or the construction of a special "maternal" nest by a pregnant rabbit.

Nest-building in the Great Apes

Chimpanzees, orangutans, and gorillas construct nests. Gorillas are more likely than chimpanzees to omit nest-building or to build ground nests or nests in low vegetation, and they are less likely to line the bottom of the nest. However, all three genera of great apes appear to utilize whatever material is handy, and they use the same basic method of construction by pulling and bending in surrounding foliage toward themselves and using their weight to hold it in place (Schaller, 1963).

The chimpanzees use any well-foliaged tree 20 or more feet high, and readily modify their basic technique to suit the materials at hand. Figure 3–5A illustrates the method used in building a nest in the top of a palm tree.

Captive apes have been tested for nest-building (Bernstein, 1962, 1969). Although there were no trees available, and although most of the materials presented to the apes were not normally found in the wild (e.g., pine straw, newspapers, strips of burlap, lengths of hose, rope and chain), some of the animals constructed cohesive nests which they used for sleeping and resting (Figure 3–5B). The basic method used in nest construction was similar to that seen in the wild. Nest-building is learned early in life, and Bernstein suggests that there may be a critical age for acquiring this behavior. Captive-born adult chimpanzees do little or no nest-building, even though they exhibit all the requisite motor skills.

Nesting in the Norway Rat

The nest-building behavior of wild and domesticated Norway rats has been observed under laboratory conditions (e.g., Barnett, 1963; Eibl-Eibesfeldt, 1957, 1963). Materials are picked up with the mouth (sometimes with an assist from the forepaws, but first contact is always made with the mouth). They are carried to a sheltered spot in the cage if one is available, and piled or pushed with paws and nose into a heap. Paper or cloth may be torn up and thick pieces of straw split lengthwise, providing finer-textured material. A cup is

Figure 3–5. (A) A chimpanzee adapts its basic technique in building a nest in a palm tree. By permission after Lawick-Goodall, J. van, The behaviour of free-living chimpanzees in the Gombe Stream Reserve, *Animal Behaviour Monographs,* 1968, **1,** 161–311. (B) Nest built by captive chimpanzee born in the wild. (Photo courtesy of I. S. Bernstein.)

formed as the rat turns around on the heap, using the forepaws to push and press pieces of material into place, and collecting stray pieces with raking movements of the forepaws or by pulling them in with the teeth. Although all these motions are usually seen, they need not follow a rigid sequence but are adapted to the materials at hand and the moment-to-moment requirements of the situation. Postpartum females may construct hooded maternal nests which are shaped from both the inside and the outside. These nests change in size and shape as the litter becomes larger and more active (Rosenblatt & Lehrman, 1963).

Eibl-Eibesfeldt (1961) raised female rats in a situation in which they were not allowed any experience with carrying and manipulating objects. They were fed powdered food, their fecal bolli dropped through a mesh floor, their tails were amputated, and no nesting material was available. Eibl-Eibesfeldt tested his rats in their home cages, some of which had been fitted with partitions to provide a sheltered corner. He found that thirty-three of thirty-nine females built nests in bare but familiar cages within 5 hours of the introduction of nesting material. All but one of fifty-five females provided with partitioned cages built within 5 hours of the time materials were presented, and forty-five did so in the first hour of testing.

Analysis of the behavior of the inexperienced animals that built nests showed that they performed all the stereotyped movements normally exhibited by experienced rats. However, the movements were sometimes hesitant, the total pattern of behavior was poorly organized, and it often was interrupted by feeding and grooming. Sometimes the component movements were performed without the animal's contacting the nesting materials. With continued exposure to nesting materials, however, a smoother, better-coordinated pattern developed.

Thus, nest-building in the rat appears to be an integration of fixed motor patterns into a relatively stereotyped, but nevertheless adaptable, behavior sequence, with practice playing an important role in achieving a coordinated pattern. We shall find a similar process at work as we examine data from studies of other types of behavior.

Nesting in Peromyscus

The white-footed or deer mice of the genus *Peromyscus* are widely distributed over the North American continent. As many as 57 species and over 200 subspecies have been recognized, and they occupy most of the habitats available below the Arctic Circle. The genus represents an ideal taxon for the study of evolutionary mechanisms, population dynamics, a variety of behaviors, and the like (Blair, 1968). Fortunately, some of its members readily adapt to life as laboratory animals, so that behavior may be studied under controlled conditions and, in many instances, related to behavior that is exhibited in free-living animals.

The nest-building behavior of three forms of *Peromyscus (P. floridanus, P. maniculatus bairdii,* and *P. m. gracilis)* has been compared under laboratory conditions (King, 1963). The mice were tested by measuring the weight of cotton they took from a dispenser each day. Statistically significant differences appeared between each group, and there was a correlation between the natural geographic distribution of the mice and the amount of cotton taken. The most northerly form, *gracilis,* averaged 2.8 grams; the more southerly *bairdii,* 1.8 grams: and the southernmost *floridanus,* 1.0 grams. Nest size was positively related to the amount of material taken. However, climatic differences cannot be said to have produced these taxon-specific differences in nesting behavior. Layne (1969) compared nesting in *floridanus* with that of a sympatric species, *P. gossypinus,* and with a close relative of *gossypinus, P. leucopus,* that was obtained in New York State. *Floridanus* took the least cotton and built the poorest nests. Ratings of nest quality showed that more than half the test animals failed to build even an organized nest pad, and only a few built nests of the hooded type. The northern-dwelling *leucopus* took much more cotton than *floridanus,* all animals had at least a loosely organized pad nest, and 52 percent of the nests were hooded. Interestingly, *gossypinus,* originating from the same place as *floridanus*, was hardly distinguishable from *leucopus* in its performance. It took about the same amount of cotton, and, although a small number of this species built no nests, 53 percent of the nests were hooded.

Layne notes that *floridanus*, a poor nest-builder, is restricted to specialized nest sites in burrows and that the species is limited to a narrow geographic range. Species such as *gossypinus*, however, which are good nest-builders, can and do utilize a wide variety of possible nest sites. According to this interpretation, it is the greater habitat and nest-site diversity of these animals that allows them to adapt to a variety of climatic and other conditions rather than the other way around.

FOOD

In all mammals, the energy required to run the life processes, to provide for the production and maintenance of body tissues, and to enable the animals to engage in behavioral activity comes from the metabolism of the food that is eaten. The energy requirements can be satisfied with foods containing proteins, carbohydrates, and fats, either singly or in combination. In addition, the diet must contain a number of essential amino acids and unsaturated fatty acids as well as certain vitamins and minerals, all of which are necessary for normal growth, maintenance, and activity.

Food habits provide a basis for one kind of classification of mammals. Thus, among the carnivorous, or flesh-eating, mammals, there are the categories of carnivore, insectivore, piscivore, and scavenger, depending upon the kind of flesh that is eaten. Herbivorous, or plant-eating, mammals may be granivores, fructivores, or grazing or browsing herbivores. Mammals that eat both plant and animal matter are classified as omnivores. Although a few mammals have highly specialized diets (e.g., the koala, honey possum, three-toed sloth, baleen whale, and certain anteaters), most will take more than one kind of food either routinely or under special circumstances, so that omnivorousness is more common than the categories listed above imply. Certainly no one should confuse the name of the order, Carnivora, with the food habit of carnivorousness. When available, fruits and berries make up a significant portion of the diet in raccoons, bears, wolves, and foxes. Even commercial dog food often contains a high proportion of cereal grains. In the wild, the giant panda apparently exists exclusively on bamboo, although it will take animal protein in captivity (Morris & Morris, 1966). Similarly, at least some arboreal species of Insectivora eat plant matter. Normally herbivorous cattle, sheep, and giraffe may eat all or a part of the placenta after giving birth. Chital (axis deer) living near the mouth of the Ganges River are reported to eat small crabs (Stanford, 1951).

In this section we shall describe eating behavior in a number of mammals; then we shall look at a few examples of complex behavior patterns used in obtaining and storing food; finally, we shall survey some of the factors involved in controlling food intake and dietary selection.

Prehension

In unguligrade mammals, as well as in certain other forms such as elephants, anteaters, whales, and seals, the limbs usually are not used for grasping and manipulating food. Instead, prehension is accomplished with the tongue, teeth, lips, and, in the elephant, with the trunk formed from the nose and upper lip.

Some good examples of herbivores that do use the forelimbs for the prehension of food are found among the rodents. With a few exceptions, such as the kangaroo rat (discussed earlier), rodents do not pick up or carry food with the paws. Usually the food is picked up by grasping it between the incisors; the paws, if used at all, simply assist in balancing the load or as in the case of pouched rodents like the hamster, in shifting food into and out of the cheek pouches. Also, many rodents will use a paw to steady large, movable food items against the ground while gnawing on them. The primary use of the forepaws is in holding small pieces of food while the animal chews off manageable bites and in cracking nuts and seeds. Usually a rodent sits back on its haunches and grasps and manipulates food with a two-handed grip, although some lean on their forearms and elbows, and the cane rat supports itself on three legs and holds seeds with one paw (Ewer, 1968a).

The methods of holding and manipulating food tend to be constant within a given species. Although it has been suggested that these behavior patterns are acquired as the animal learns by trial and error to make the most efficient use of its inherited motor apparatus, Ewer (1968a) argues that the basic techniques for dealing with food are not developed through practice. She reports that both infant African ground squirrels and giant rats pick up and hold pieces of food in the adult manner the first time they encounter it. They do so even though their motor coordination is so poor that they have such difficulty balancing on their haunches that it would be easier for them to leave the food on the ground and steady it with one paw, the method commonly used when gnawing bites from large pieces of food. She also notes that Petersen (1965) has found that of three species of field mice studied, two *(Apodemus sylvaticus* and *A. flavicollis)* hold nuts well away from their bodies with their relatively long arms. They make a hole, then insert the lower incisors and gnaw from inside to outside. However, the third species *(A. grarius)* holds the nut close to the body, inserts the upper incisors, and works at the near side of the hole despite the fact that the length of its arms make it capable of holding the nut in the same way as *A. sylvaticus* and *A. flavicollis*.

Practice does enter into certain parts of the feeding pattern of herbivorous rodents. For example, Petersen's field mice had to learn the best place to make the initial opening in a shell. Also, most experienced European red squirrels open a nut by using a wedging technique. They gnaw a narrow furrow through the shell from its base to its tip, sometimes making a second furrow on the opposite side. The lower incisors are then placed in this crack and the shell is split open as the head and forepaws are twisted in opposite directions. Eibl-Eibesfeldt (1963) reared red squirrels without allowing them the opportunity to open nuts although they were given objects to gnaw on to ensure that the jaw muscles developed properly. When they were about six months old, nuts were given for the first time. They picked them up and gnawed on them, apparently at random, until the shell broke. The characteristic splitting movement was made, but it was successful only if the furrows were properly placed. With practice, the animals began to make the furrows parallel to the grain of the wood, the path of least resistance, and then they continued to use the prying movement. The animals repeated those actions which led to success, and most of them acquired the wedging technique by the time they had opened twenty to thirty nuts. In this example, the basic movements are assumed to be innate, but the red squirrel must learn the most efficient way of combining gnawing and prying to open nuts. In some cases, the animals develop alternatives to the wedging technique.

In carnivorous mammals, some modification of the teeth and jaws for dealing with skin, meat, and bones is usual. The canine teeth, which many forms use for grasping and killing, tend to be long and pointed, and some groups have well-developed carnassials which they use in cutting and shearing skin and meat.

There is a strong tendency for mammalian carnivores to begin to eat warm-blooded prey at the head end. It has been shown that this may result from a tactile orientation in response to the lie of the hair or feathers of the prey. By using skinned rats, and rat skins stuffed with meat with the head and tail present, absent, or attached to the "wrong" end, Leyhausen (1956) found that the house cat ignores visual cues and orients against the lie of the hair in arriving at the front end. The eating of skinned prey may begin anywhere, but is usually initiated at the soft belly. The large cats, the lions, tigers, cheetah, and the like, usually begin eating large prey at the rump or groin. A recent study of the ontogeny of feeding in lion cubs suggests that they may possess the tactile orienting response (R. L. Eaton, personal communication). If this is indeed the case, the method by which these animals overcome the natural tendency to orient against the lie of the hair and the factors (e.g., learning, other orienting responses) governing the initiation of eating at rump or groin are still unknown.

Very young wolves and gray foxes ignore bloodless rodent carcasses, but readily eat bloody pieces of meat when the carcasses are dissected. Blood is at least one of the triggers of eating by these carnivores (Fox, 1969). This study by Fox is also one of a number of experiments that indicate that, in many carnivores, killing and eating are two different processes that must be linked by experience during the ontogeny of the organism.

In general, specializations for prehension are less extreme in omnivores than in carnivores and herbivores. Although the omnivorous mammal may be somewhat less efficient in dealing with a particular kind of food than a strictly carnivorous or herbivorous animal of the same family or order, its ability to obtain, eat, and digest a variety of foods gives it a considerable advantage for survival in the face of seasonal or other changes in the food supply.

Predation in Cats and Other Carnivores

Solutions to the problem of catching and killing prey, which in many cases is capable of either swift flight, injuring the predator, or both, have resulted in the appearance of some fascinating and complex behavior patterns. Of the terrestrial mammals, the domestic cat has been studied most intensively, but considerable information about other felids, canids, viverrids and mustelids, as well as the dasyurid marsupials and a few insectivores, rodents, and primates, is now available.

The predatory sequence exhibited by the domestic cat has been described by Leyhausen (1956). It is summarized in the following paragraph taken from Ewer.

> Cats stalk their prey, using a series of distinctive movements. When first alerted to the presence of prey at some distance, the cat crouches and then hurries toward it with the body flat to the ground in what Leyhausen graphically calls the slink-run. At a distance determined by the available cover she pauses and "ambushes," crouched low with the whole of the sole of the foot on the ground and the fore paws supporting the body directly under the shoulders, the whiskers spread and the ears turned forwards. For a few moments she watches the prey, her head turning as she follows its every movement, as though her eyes were tied to it by an invisible cord. Depending on distance and cover, a second slink-run and ambush may follow, or she may now stalk the prey, moving forward slowly and cautiously, to the last piece of available cover and here again she ambushes and prepares for the kill. The heels are now raised from the ground, and the hind legs shift back and may make alternating movements, while the tip of the out-stretched tail twitches. From this posture the final attack is launched—not usually as a single leap but as a short run, flat to the ground; the final "spring" too is flat to the ground and is, in fact, a thrust rather than a jump. While the fore quarters are thrust forward to seize the prey, the hind feet do not leave the ground, but remain firmly planted, giving stability for a possible struggle to follow [Ewer, 1968a p. 35].

The prey is pinned to the ground with the forepaws and head, and a "killing bite" is delivered to the nape of the neck. It is then taken to a sheltered place and eaten.

From laboratory observations of many species of viverrids and felids, Leyhausen (1965) has identified several classes of fixed movements in the predatory sequence that are characteristic of most of the animals studied. These behaviors—watching, crouching, stalking, pouncing, seizing, and angling (using the forepaws in a hooking motion to grasp and pull prey toward the animal or to retrieve it from a hole or crevice)—are omitted or modified in some of the more specialized felids. The cheetah does not crouch or ambush, but walks along slowly toward prey, stopping and remaining still if the prey shows signs of alertness. Pouncing is replaced by a swift dash after running prey (Eaton, 1970). Similarly, the ocelot, which feeds primarily on birds, attacks without crouching, and it does not show the ambushing pattern when allowed to attack a rodent even though this behavior would be appropriate to the situation (Leyhausen, 1956).

Leyhausen regards these component behaviors as innate and notes that they may be performed independently of one another, in various combinations with one another, and in combination with nonpredatory movements during play. The components become linked into the predatory sequence only when appetites for killing and eating are dominant. Also, stalking and ambushing movements are often seen in the cat in a bare cage that offers no cover when the cat is presented with a rodent. Leyhausen notes that cats that have not had previous experience are usually unable to kill the first time they encounter prey. He believes that the killing bite has a very high threshold, and initially it is elicited only when the cat becomes very excited. Play with prey, or competition with littermates in the case of the young kitten, produces the excitation necessary. The killing bite is said to "click into place" after only one or a few successful kills—a process which Leyhausen likens to imprinting. Once established, the bite is easy to elicit—it "develops its own appetite," but the threshold will increase again unless the cat is allowed to eat the prey it has killed at least once in a while.

Most canids kill small prey by crushing it in the thoracic region (Fox, 1969), whereas kills of large prey by packs of wolves (Allen & Mech, 1963), African hunting dogs (Kühme, 1965), and spotted hyenas (Kruuk, 1966) result from multiple bites from several animals.

Movement by the prey appears to be an important trigger for initiating chasing and attacking in all species of mammalian predators. Marsupials seem to have difficulty seeing prey that does not move (Ewer, 1969). In canids and felids, immobile or dead prey and even inanimate objects may be poked, prodded, or thrown into motion and then attacked.

Large and potentially dangerous prey cannot usually be killed by a single canid, and wolves, African hunting dogs, and hyenas attack in a group. Wolves occasionally go off alone while foraging, but usually they are within range of one another's calls, and an attack by a lone wolf will bring others to the prey (Scott & Fuller, 1965). When African hunting dogs or spotted hyenas in a pack encounter a herd of prey animals, each apparently chases a different prey until one brings down or slows its victim, whereupon the rest join in the chase and attack (Kruuk, 1966; Kühme, 1965). There is no evidence of organized cooperation although prey, on changing direction, may inadvertently come closer to another predator, so that, between them, the pack members appear to herd the prey.

Hoarding

Food is not equally abundant at all times. This is particularly true for mammals which feed on nuts and grains that may be available in quantity only at certain times of the year, and for predators which, although perhaps having an excess of meat after making a kill, may have to hunt a long time between kills. A number of behaviors have evolved which function to conserve food for varying lengths of time. Several felids conceal uneaten prey by placing it in a sheltered place, and some scratch debris over it or cover it with grass that they bite off. The leopard typically takes the remains of its prey into a tree. Many canids hide prey in dense undergrowth, and their habit of burying food is well known. Some rodents bring food to the homesite and place it in or under the nest or in a special chamber or pit close by *(larder hoarding)*; others bury or otherwise conceal it at scattered sites away from the nest *(scatter hoarding)*. Beavers store branches under water, moles and voles are reported to cache insects in their tunnels, and pikas and some rodents "process" food before storing it.

The European red squirrel buries one nut at a time. Holding a nut in its mouth, it digs a shallow groove with rapid alternating movements of the forepaws. The nut is placed in the bottom of the hole and then rammed down with a series of blows delivered by the upper incisors. The hole is filled in with simultaneous movements of the forepaws, and the squirrel may then camouflage the site by scratching a leaf over it with the paws (Eibl-Eibesfeldt. 1961; 1963). An almost identical pattern of movement is used by the African ground squirrel *(Xerus erythropus),* suggesting that we are dealing with a homologous behavior pattern even though this animal buries only maize seeds, buries several at one time, and burying has only been observed in the female (Ewer, 1965).

The green acouchi *(Myoprocta pratti),* a South American rodent, buries food using a behavior pattern which has the same *functional* components seen in the squirrels, but its pattern involves a very different set of *motor* elements. After a hole is dug, the food is dropped into it and pressed into the bottom by a series of rapid alternations of the forepaws. The hole is filled by pushing loose dirt into it with a forelimb; one leg is used at a time and after making several movements, the animal changes legs. The camouflage, if used, is placed in position with the teeth (D. Morris, 1962). A similar motor pattern has also been observed in the agouti *(Dasyprocta aguti),* another South American hystricomorph (Eibl-Eibesfeldt, 1963).

Red squirrels, when given nuts for the first time, have gone through the complete sequence of "burying" a nut in a wire cage with no earth available (Eibl-Eibesfeldt, 1963), and "vacuum" food burying, including placing an imaginary leaf over the site, has been observed in the acouchi (D. Morris, 1962). No such rigid sequences of behavior are seen in the golden hamster *(Mesocricetus auratus),* which is a larder hoarder. Although the hamster possesses a number of stereotyped movements used in grasping, pouching, carrying, and piling food, these movements are combined in different ways depending upon the situation and past experience of the animal. At least under laboratory conditions, some of the species' typical movements may be abandoned entirely and others not normally utilized (e.g., digging movements) may be incorporated into the hoarding pattern.

The complete set of stimuli controlling hoarding in any species is still not known, and it is likely that different variables will be shown to play different roles across species. Photoperiod is important in controlling nut storage by flying squirrels (Muul, 1970), and it is expected that this will also prove to be true for many other species which depend upon a seasonal abundance of particular kinds of food. Other environmental factors influence the hoarding of at least some species. Increases in hoarding by laboratory rats follow decreases in ambient temperature (McCleary & Morgan, 1946). Hoarding in wild Norway rats is related to social status—subordinate or timid animals take more food under cover than do dominant, bold animals, although low social status is not a prerequisite for inducing storing behavior (Calhoun, 1962). On the other hand, the actual physical presence of a dominant animals inhibits hoarding in subordinate laboratory rats (Denenberg, 1952). Size of the food object also has an effect. The black rat *(Rattus rattus)* may eat small pieces of food where it finds them but carry large pieces to shelter (Ewer, 1968a).

A "security" hypothesis has been used to account for the evolution of food storage at the homesite. Presumably, hoarding evolved out of the tendency of animals to take food, and in particular, large pieces of food which could not be completely consumed at one meal, to the safety of the nest before eating (Ewer, 1965). Food storage at sites away from the nest, on the other hand, is hypothesized to have originated in one of two ways: from *food envy*, i.e., the tendency shown by many mammals to keep food away from conspecifics or from scavengers (Ewer, 1965); or as a modification of *larder hoarding* resulting from selection pressures produced by such factors as parasitization of large food stores or predation of the hoarders which culminated in their giving up a "completely fixed home site" (D. Morris, 1962). As the *scatter hoarding* behavior has evolved independently in several lines of mammals, it is probable that these different factors have all operated to some extent.

Food Preferences and Dietary Selection

Taste, odor, appearance, texture, and size make up one set of variables which influence dietary preference; familiarity, novelty, and the age of the animal comprise another group of factors. Finally, the nutritional consequences of the diet have been shown to influence selection in some species.

Mammals in general exhibit a decided preference for sweet-tasting substances, although species differences in preferences for different substances exist. Calves do not show a preference for saccharin or maltose, although they do respond positively to glucose, fructose, sucrose, and xylose (Kare, 1961). Rats, on the other hand, do show a special liking for saccharin. Saccharin is a nonnutritive substance, yet rats will learn a T maze with saccharin solution as the only reward for a correct response (Sheffield & Roby, 1950), and acquire a bar press response when sated and given saccharin as a reward (Guttman, 1953). Saccharin has also been reported to be more effective as a reinforcing agent than a nutritive, but less sweet, dextrose solution (Sheffield, Roby, & Campbell, 1954). Although some doubt remains as to whether the reinforcing effects of a sweet taste are learned by association with nutritional effects (see Smith & Capretta, 1956), the limited evidence available suggests that aversions to bitter-tasting substances need not be related to an association with nutritional consequences. Guinea pigs, reared on a nonnutritive, bitter solution of sucrose octa-acetate (SOA) that is normally rejected by these animals, later drank SOA and water about equally when given a choice between the solutions. However, the acceptability of SOA disappeared when the animals were retested after 3 to 4 months of being maintained on plain water (Warren & Pfaffmann, 1959). Aversions to food contaminated with offensive odors have also been demonstrated in wild rats (Barnett & Spencer. 1953). In general, while aversions to tastes and smells may be temporarily overcome in hungry or thirsty animals, the change in behavior is not permanent and, given the opportunity, animals will return to the nonaversive choice (e.g., Barnett, 1956).

Different groups of the same species of primates may have different sets of traditional food habits. The same items that are eaten frequently by a group living in one area may be ignored by animals in a different region (see van Lawick-Goodall, 1968, for a brief review). In contrast to cattle, which acquire food habits on their own, young primates learn to eat the food that is eaten by the mother and other members of the group. An instance in which a mother prevented a two-year-old chimpanzee from eating a piece of papaya has been described by van Lawick-Goodall (1968). The acquisition of food habits by imitation and parental guidance also occurs in elephants and at least some of the Carnivora.

In primates, young animals are much more likely to try new food objects than are their elders. For example, the eating of new foods by Japanese macaques was first observed in young animals, and it later spread to other members of the troop so that the entire group came to acquire a new food habit. A young female in this troop also initiated the washing of sweet potatoes which later turned into dipping the potatoes into seawater between each bite, a feeding pattern which has become a tradition in the group. The same female also began separating wheat grains from sand by throwing handfuls of the mixture into the water, a pattern which has now been adopted by many of the other monkeys (Kawamura, 1963).

Wild rats initially avoid or withdraw from any new object, including food, that they encounter in familiar surroundings. However, this neophobia gradually wanes, and a new food will be sampled. If no aversive consequences result, increasing amounts of the new food will be eaten, and it may come to be preferred to what was eaten before (Barnett, 1963). The propensity to sample the entire range of potential foods makes the wild rat extremely adaptable in its food habits and is partially responsible for this animal's ability to establish and maintain itself so widely.

OTHER MAINTENANCE ACTIVITIES

Water

Mammals use water for temperature regulation and for other life processes such as digestion and elimination of waste. Water requirements may be met by drinking free water, by taking advantage of the preformed water present in the food of the animal, and by utilizing metabolic water formed by the breakdown of food.

The actual physical movements involved in ingesting water are different in different mammalian species. Dogs and wolves, for example, stand with their tails down and lap water by scooping it with the tongue (Scott & Fuller, 1965). In cattle, the tongue plays only a passive role as the animals dip their muzzles into the water and suck it into the mouth (Hafez & Schein, 1962). The elephant uses its trunk as a siphon to draw up water which it then expels into the mouth, although baby elephants have been observed to kneel and take water directly into the mouth (Sikes, 1971). Chimpanzees drink by crouching down at the edge of a stream and sucking up water with their lips; they have also been observed to lick raindrops from leaves, which they also may use as sponges to obtain water that has collected in hollows. The leaves are stripped by hand or with the lips and chewed, forming a crumpled mass. The "sponge" is held between the index and second fingers, pushed into the water, and then withdrawn and sucked (van Lawick-Goodall, 1968). Rats normally drink by licking water with their tongues. Laboratory rats that have been on a water-deprivation schedule hoard cotton wads soaked in water (Miller & Vieck, 1944).

Eliminative Behavior

There are various species-specific behavior patterns associated with the elimination of wastes. The odor of feces or urine has social significance in many species, and mammals often have special behavior patterns associated with using feces or urine in scent marking.

Many mammals avoid contaminating the nest or den. Wild rabbits establish latrines near the burrow, and domestic species confine defecation to a specific spot in the cage (Worden & Leahy, 1962). The rock hyrax (*Procavia*) goes outside the communal den to urinate (Sale, 1970). If given sufficient room, swine move away from the nest area to defecate and urinate. This pattern is not seen in pigs reared without their mothers—the elimination pattern in such animals is apparently random (Hafez, Sumption, & Jakway, 1962). Though normally extremely clean animals, swine have been reported to try to wallow in their own urine when environmental temperatures are very high, a behavior which would increase evaporative cooling (Heitman & Hughes, 1949).

In contrast to horses, which typically select a specific part of their pasture for defecation, cattle defecate and urinate anywhere, and do not seem to be able to exert voluntary control over eliminative behavior (Hafez & Schein, 1962). Gorillas frequently foul their sleeping nests with excreta (Schaller, 1963), but healthy chimpanzees do not; the latter defecate and urinate over the edge of the nest (van Lawick-Goodall, 1968).

Care of the Pelage

A variety of behaviors related to care of the fur and skin are present in mammals. As in the case of eliminative behavior, grooming is often done in a social context, an aspect that will be dealt with in the chapter on social behavior.

Sandbathing is used to dress the pelage by a number of rodents. In sandbathing by members of the family Heteromyidae (kangaroo rats and their allies), the pattern is initiated by rapid digging into the sand with the forepaws so that a shallow trench is formed. The animal then lowers its cheek to the sand and extends its body while sliding forward on its side; alternating extension and flexion of the body results in a series of side rubs. In other instances, ventral rubs, in which the extension and flexion of the body are performed with the ventral surface pressed against the sand, are used. Extended sandbathing sequences usually include both side and ventral rubs. Comparative study of several species of Heteromyidae showed that species-typical differences in patterns were related to differences in the coarseness of the pelage and the activity of the sebaceous glands (Eisenberg, 1964).

Some grooming by placental mammals occurs in response to specific external stimuli such as dirt, parasites, or food particles on the face or paws. Such stimuli may be the only triggers for grooming in marsupials (Ewer, 1968b), but placentals seem to exhibit grooming regardless of need. The pattern occurs as a regular part of the round of activities. The animal does not wait for its coat to become dirty, or matted, or parasite-infested (Barnett, 1963). In the rat, face-washing occurs in situations which produce conflict or fear (Thompson & Higgins, 1958), and in animals that have food placed directly into their stomachs the face and paws are not contaminated by it (Baillie & Morrison, 1963). This suggests that changes in internal patterns of stimulation can initiate the behavior. The possibility that some hitherto unsuspected external factor initiates the behavior cannot as yet be ruled out, however, and the possibility that grooming is rewarding, either because of the stimulation it produces or because the execution of the behavior itself is reinforcing, still remains to be investigated.

SEXUAL BEHAVIOR PATTERNS

The basic biological problem resolved by sexual behavior is the same for all mammals: Living male sperm are introduced into the reproductive tract of a fertile female. Despite certain fundamental similarities in the reproductive behavior patterns by which this end is achieved, there is considerable variation in detail.

The laboratory rat   A sexually vigorous male rat will approach and investigate a female. If she is ready to mate, she will allow him to approach and in some cases she solicits his attention. This she does by approaching, sniffing and nudging at his body, and then turning away so that her rump is directed toward his head. The female then runs a little way, using a stiff-legged, hopping gait, and stops. The male pursues her and mounts from the rear, grasping and palpating her flanks with his forepaws. He supports himself on one leg and curves his back to bring his penis into contact with her pudendum. The female, in response to the pressure on her flanks, assumes the lordosis posture with head up and forequarters lowered, and with back arched and tail to one side, exposing her genitalia. Her ears quiver rapidly (Figure 9–2). If the mount is successful, a few rapid pelvic thrusts terminate with a deeper thrust as intromission is achieved. The duration of the intromission is very brief—it lasts about 0.25 seconds (Bermant, 1965). Then the male dismounts with an acrobatic backward leap. He then licks his genital region. Some ten or eleven intromissions precede the first ejaculation. In the ejaculatory pattern, the final pelvic thrust is very pronounced, the forepart of the male's body rises up, and this position is maintained for a second or two. The acrobatic dismount is not present. After dismounting, the male grooms his genitals for a while, then enters a refractory stage during which he pays little or no attention to the female. After 6 or 7 minutes, the male renews his interest in the female and another series of intromissions, terminating in an ejaculation, occurs. In a test with a fully receptive female, a male will engage in about seven of these copulatory series before he apparently loses interest in her.

From this description, it is apparent that mating behavior may be divided into three phases: (1) A preliminary stage of interaction between male and female which precedes actual copulation; (2) the events involved in coitus; and (3) activities associated with the cessation of sexual behavior.

Courtship

The functions of the behaviors which precede copulation are to bring together a male and a female of a species, both of which are in a reproductive condition, and to promote a situation in which there is a high probability that copulation and fertilization·will occur.

In polyestrous species, there is little problem in synchronizing male and female mating potential as, in most cases, the male remains fertile all year. In the seasonal breeders, the availability of a willing, fertile male at the time the female is in season is assured because the male's season precedes and overlaps that of the female. In addition, the female may become sexually attractive to the male before she is fully receptive, so that the likelihood is increased that she will have one or more potential mates interested in her when she is ready for copulation (Ewer, 1968a).

Despite the variability in courtship behavior, it is possible to abstract some general features from the wide range of behaviors exhibited within and across species.

1. Following, Anogenital Investigation, and Urine-testing   Investigation of the female, which helps the male to identify a prospective mate, is common in mammals. In those orders which have well-developed olfactory systems, following, nuzzling, and licking of the anogenital region, and smelling places where the female has urinated are all major features of the courtship period, whether it lasts for only a few minutes, as in the laboratory rat, or for several weeks, as in the porcupine. In most of the ungulates (Suidae are an exception), in the elephant, in carnivores such as the meerkat and the lion, and in at least some bats, a steretyped urine-tasting response is made by the male. The animal, after smelling or licking the urine or anogenital region of the female, holds himself rigid with the neck extended and the upper lip raised. This is the lip curl, or *Flehmen* pattern. It probably aids in bringing olfactory stimuli into contact with the vomeronasal organ via a duct in the anterior portion of the mouth. In many primates, cues as to the receptivity of the female are provided by changes in the tumescence and color of the female sex skin.

2. Invitations by the Female   Solicitation of copulation by the female is common in many mammalian species. One of the behaviors most frequently found is some form of the approaching-followed-by-running response noted earlier in the laboratory rat. In the rat, analysis of the pattern of precopulatory behavior shows that running in the female and pursuit and mounting in the male are interdependent, mutually stimulating activities (Dewsbury, 1967). Females do little running during periods when males do not chase them, and, of course, the male cannot pursue if the female does not run. Studies of the beagle by Beach and his colleagues (e.g., Beach, 1969) indicate that dogs also show this sort of coyness. Estrous bitches would visit caged males and then withdraw. As the males could not chase them, the females returned to the cage, waited a few moments, and again moved off. After this, some females ignored the males, but some sat some distance from the cage and barked at them before finally ignoring the males. Apparently, a male that does not pursue does not interest the bitch, a finding which Beach suggests has considerable generality in mammals (Figure 3–6).

Figure 3–6. Beach's (1969) theoretical model showing why female dogs in heat are not interested in caged males who cannot pursue them. (Drawing by Ton Smits; Copyrighted, 1956, The New Yorker Magazine, Inc.)

In some species, the invitation is a more or less direct assumption of the female mating posture. The female porcupine comes into heat very quickly. She elevates her tail and backs against the male's nose and head (Shadle, 1946). In the golden hamster *(Mesocricetus auratus),* approach followed by withdrawal is often seen in the female, but sometimes she will assume a receptive posture (Figure 7–6) almost immediately after her initial contact with the male. She may hold this position for a minute or more, and if the male does not continue his attentions toward her, she will approach him, touch noses, and sometimes gently pull at his fur before turning away a few steps and resuming the receptive stance; occasionally she attacks vigorously, but then accepts him if he responds by mounting her (Bunnell, Boland, & Dewsbury, in preparation).

Approaching, grooming, and presenting the genitalia to the male are typical of the female rhesus monkey *(Macaca mulata).* She also uses other gestures that are effective in inducing mounting. Michael and Zumpe (1970) found that, of a total of 166 mounts they observed, 76 followed presentations of one form or another, while 90 were preceded by the rather subtle gestures the authors called "hand reaching," "head ducking," and "head bobbing."

3. Attack and Pacification The course of true love is not always smooth, as the male may be highly aggressive toward the female. Attacks on the female are used by wild asses and camelids in forcing her to assume the mating posture; in the meerkat and the striped skunk, fighting may be playful and no injuries are inflicted (Ewer, 1968a).

In some cases, it is the aggressiveness of the female that must be overcome. In some rodents and canids, a call is given by the male which resembles the distress call of the young. This is believed to inhibit aggression by the female. The neck grip is common in Carnivora and is also seen in some rodents and shrews. It appears to have a pacifying effect on the female. The male, by placing his head between the ears of the female and rubbing, has a similar effect in the fat-tailed marsupial mouse *(Sminthopsis crassicaudata)* (Ewer, 1968b). Grooming of the female's head and body is another behavior which seems to quiet the female.

4. Promiscuity and Polygamy There are a variety of kinds of social organization associated with mating. Major systems include temporary pair associations with a return to isolated status after copulation, such as is seen in hamsters; consortships, where animals pair off temporarily within a social group, as in bison and sometimes in rhesus monkeys; pair bonding, in which the pair remains together as a unit after copulation, as has been observed in wolves; and harem formation, where a male associates with, and actively defends, a group of females against other adult males, commonly seen in many hooved mammals and seals. Polygamy and promiscuity are typical of all types of organization except pair bonding (Eisenberg, 1966).

Copulation

The nature of the coital patterns exhibited by mammals is governed in part by general morphological factors. In most mammals, the male covers the female from the rear, with his ventrum next to her dorsal side. This posture is a physical necessity in all but a few mammals, since intromission is not possible in other positions because of the placement of the genitalia.

The great size and weight of the elephant are related to an interesting structural modification. During copulation, the female usually stands with her head braced against a river bank or a tree. The male rises on his hind legs and rests his forelegs on her back. There is no pelvic thrusting by the male; instead, he has an extremely mobile penis that has an S-shaped flexure. When the end of the penis contacts the female's urogenital sinus, the penis is inserted with a series of up and down jerks and ejaculation occurs in less than 8 seconds (Eisenberg, McKay, & Jainudeen, 1971).

Horses and many other mammals, including man, have a vascular penis, which is erected by engorgement with blood. Cattle, sheep, goats, and swine have a fibroelastic penis that is rigid when nonerect and is erected primarily by muscular control. Animals with a fibroelastic penis do not require extensive penile stimulation to achieve intromission, and ejaculation is usually immediate once full intromission has been achieved. An exception is the boar. As in the bull and the ram, ejaculation usually occurs with the first intromission, but copulation averages about 9 minutes, during which time two or three separate waves of semen may be ejaculated (Hafez, 1968; Hafez, Sumption, & Jakway, 1962). Similarly, although long or repeated intromissions prior to ejaculation are common in mammals with vascular penises, some, such as the cat and the rabbit, ejaculate within a few seconds of achieving the first intromission (Table 3–2).

A schema for the behavioral classification of copulatory patterns has been proposed (Dewsbury, 1972). The behavior is classified in terms of (1) whether or not there is a copulatory "lock"; (2) whether or not thrusting takes place during an intromission; (3) single versus multiple intromissions; and (4) single versus multiple ejaculations (Figure 15–2). A description of the copulatory patterns of some common laboratory mammals is given in Table 3–2.

Satiation

The termination of a bout of mating activity is the result of an interaction between cumulative changes in both the male and the female. In the male, satiation rarely, if ever, is due either to general fatigue or to an exhaustion of the supply of semen. This is demonstrated most clearly by the revival of copulatory behavior which occurs when the "exhausted" male is offered a new female for a partner. This phenomenon, called the Coolidge effect, occurs in varying degrees in all the promiscuous mammals studied to date, although there is some doubt as to whether it appears in animals that typically form pair bonds (Dewsbury, 1971; Wilson, Kuehn, & Beach, 1963).

For example, when rams were allowed to copulate with the same female until 20 minutes had elapsed without the male's mounting the ewe, the ten rams in the study averaged 4.6 ejaculations. When a different, previously unmated ewe was then introduced, copulation resumed and the rams achieved a mean of 4.0 ejaculations before once again reaching the satiety criterion. In the control condition, reintroducing the first ewe after the 20-minute criterion had been reached resulted in each ram's making one additional ejaculation (Pepelko & Clegg, 1965).

The rearousal or potentiation of male copulatory behavior is not necessarily restricted to effects produced by introducing new stimulus females. Satiated bulls, like swine and sheep, renew copulatory activity when given a new female. When bulls were allowed one ejaculation per day, always with the same female and always at the same place within the same test room, the latency of their response increased until they consistently took 10 minutes or more to copulate. On subsequent tests, either tethering the stimulus female

Table 3-2 Copulatory Patterns of Common Laboratory Mammals

Species	Characteristics of intromissions	Pre-ejaculatory intromissions	Number of ejaculations per episode	Other characteristics
Hamster (Beach & Rabedeau. 1959)	Fairly brief, with cessation of thrusting	Average = 10	Average = 9	Females hold lordosis between intromissions
Gerbil (Kuehn & Zucker. 1968)	Brief, with cessation of thrusting	Exceptionally high (average = 51)	Average greater than 3	Males show pattern of foot stomping
Mouse (McGill, 1965)	Average 15 to 20 seconds with 1 per second thrust rate	Average 5 to 20	Usually cease after first ejaculation	Large, reliable strain differences
Guinea pig (Young & Grunt, 1951)	Average about 5 seconds, with thrusting	Up to 13; ¼ ejaculate on first intromission	Usually cease after first ejaculation	Female resistance after intromission common
Chinchilla (Bignami & Beach, 1968)	Average less than 10 seconds, with continued thrusting	Up to 18; ⅔ ejaculate on first intromission	Usually cease after first ejaculation	Female resistance after intromission common
Rabbit (Rubin & Azrin, 1967)	Average about 2 seconds, with cessation of thrusting	Ejaculate on first intromission	Multiple ejaculation pattern	Preintromission thrusts average 13 per second
Cat (Whalen, 1963)	Average about 7 seconds, with cessation of thrusting	Ejaculate on first intromission	Average about 7	Distinctive postejaculation display in female
Dog (Fuller & Fox. 1969)	Locks with thrusting. average 20 minutes	None	Frequently multiple locks	Male may dismount during lock
Rhesus macaque (Michael & Saayman, 1967)	Intromissions with thrust rate of 3 per second	Average 11 mounts. most with intromission	1 to 3 in 1 hour	Male mounting varies with menstrual cycle

By permission from D. A. Dewsbury. Copulatory Behavior. In E.S.E. Hafez (Ed.), *Reproduction and Breeding Techniques for Laboratory Animals*. Philadelphia: Lea & Febiger, 1970, 123–136.

in a different place in the test room before bringing the bull into the room, or moving the female about in the presence of the bull, reduced the reaction time from a mean of 10.9 minutes to a mean of 2.2 minutes. Similarly, leaving the stimulus female in the usual location but walking the bull around briefly changed the mean latency of the response from 11.7 to 5.8 minutes (Hale & Almquist, 1960).

These data have been interpreted in terms of a stimulus-specific habituation theory of sexual satiation (Schein & Hale, 1965). Because the male recovers the physiological capacity to ejaculate within a few seconds and because there is no evidence that the semen supply is severely depleted, the waning of male sexual behavior is said to be due to gradual habituation to the stimuli provided by a particular female and a particular situation. The potentiation or rearousal of copulation produced by introducing a new female or by changing the test situation is due to the presence of novel stimuli to which the behavior has not been habituated.

The role of the female in controlling the course of satiety has not been studied very extensively. The female rat does have a period following intromissions and ejaculations by a male during which she will actively avoid attempts to be mounted (Pierce & Nuttall, 1961). However, these refractory periods are generally shorter than the intervals between the male's attempts to copulate, so that it does not appear that her behavior between intromissions and ejaculations has any effect on the usual course of satiation. At least in the hamster, however, copulation shortens the length of time that a female remains behaviorally receptive during her heat period (Carter & Schein, 1971). If this is shown to be true for species other than the hamster, parametric studies of the recent copulatory history of the female should help to resolve some of the existing questions about the course of sexual satiation. In any event, investigations of the termination of copulatory behavior need to study the mutual interaction variables governing male and female behavior more intensively than has been done in the past.

CURIOSITY, EXPLORATION, AND PLAY

During periods when they are awake and active, mammals spend a proportion of their time in activities which are clearly directed toward obtaining food and water, grooming, nest construction, mating, and the like. However, they, as well as other animal forms, including some invertebrates, also exhibit behavior which does not appear to be directed toward the gratification of obvious biological needs. Considerable time may be expended in investigating and manipulating objects in the environment, in exploring the living space, and, at least in some mammalian orders, in playful behavior.

Object Investigation

The reactions of zoo animals to a variety of objects placed in their cages have been investigated by Glickman and Sroges (1966). The objects consisted of pairs of wooden blocks, steel chains, wooden dowels, rubber tubing, and a crumpled paper ball. Two of the findings from this study are illustrated by Figure 3–7.

First, reactivity is at its highest early in the trial and drops off consistently over time. This habituation of responses to novel stimuli, a phenomenon that has been reported many times, is one of the most reliable characteristics of investigatory behavior.

Second, all the mammalian orders represented were more reactive than the reptiles. In general, primates and carnivores made more responses than the rodents and a group of "primitive" mammals (made up by combining the scores of the marsupials, insectivores, edentates, and pholidotes) tested by Glickman and Sroges. These findings provide support for the idea that there is a general tendency for animals with more highly developed nervous systems to exhibit the most investigatory behavior (e.g., Berlyne, 1960).

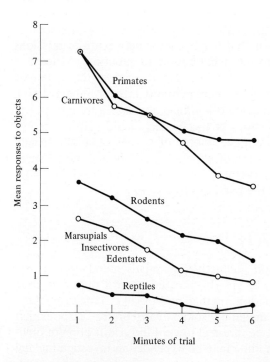

Figure 3–7. Responses to novel objects by different groups of mammals. (See discussion in text.) By permission from Glickman, S. E. & Sroges, R. W. Curiosity in zoo animals. *Behaviour,* 1966, **24,** 151–188, E. J. Brill, Publisher.

Glickman and Sroges suggest that these data can best be understood in terms of the animals' natural habits and environment. Thus, the small, mouselike myomorphs that are very susceptible to predation were very cautious in their approach to novel objects, while the larger hystricomorphs, such as the porcupine, were more bold. Contact responses by representatives of the rodent families consisted largely of gnawing the object, and some hoarding was seen. In the primates, the anthropoids gave more diverse grasping and manipulative responses than did the prosimians.

Of the Old World cercopithecids, the omnivorous, semiterrestrial baboons and macaques that have adapted to a great variety of habitats were much more reactive, and they exhibited more manipulatory behavior than the leaf-eating, tree-dwelling colobus monkeys. The colobus, however, engaged in considerable visual exploration, a finding which Glickman and Sroges felt was consistent with an arboreal existence.

Most carnivores made vigorous, fearless approaches to the test objects. Many of the responses were behaviors commonly associated with the capture and consumption of prey, such as stalking, worrying, swatting, chasing, biting, and tugging at objects held between the forepaws.

Variables Influencing Object Investigation

Novelty   In the laboratory rat, objects which have not previously been encountered evoke approach and investigation. The investigatory behavior wanes over time during a single exposure to a novel stimulus. If presentations of an object are spaced over time, there is some recovery of the response on succeeding presentations, but the reappearance of investigatory behavior is less with each exposure (e.g., Berlyne, 1966). Similarly, the presentation of new manipulable objects to young chimpanzees at first evokes high levels of manipulatory play which decrease rapidly within each session and from session to session (Welker, 1956).

In contrast to the laboratory rat, wild Norway rats tend to avoid new objects that are encountered in familiar surroundings. This neophobia gradually dissipates, and the animals begin to make tentative approaches to the object, stretching toward it, and then withdrawing, and gradually increasing the speed of approach to and duration of contact with the object (Chitty & Shorten, 1946).

Complexity and Manipulability   Stimuli that have a high degree of complexity are usually investigated for longer periods of time than those that are simpler (i.e., vary in fewer dimensions). This has been shown to be the case in laboratory rats (Berlyne, 1955), chimpanzees (Welker, 1956), and humans (e.g., Berlyne, 1966). A variable that appears to be related to complexity is manipulability. In general, nonhuman primates will spend more time with an object that can be handled. If, after interest has waned, some new way of manipulating the object is found, behavior will be reinstated (Voitonis, 1949; cited by Berlyne, 1960).

Age   In discussing the formation of new food habits in groups of primates, we noted that young animals are much more likely to investigate new foods than are their elders. The same relation is found between age and object investigation in laboratory studies. In the chimpanzee, visual-deprivation studies suggest that very young animals fear strange objects from the time they are capable of discriminating them as being novel (Riesen, 1958). When tested at the age of one to two years, they approach and contact objects only after long periods of exposure, and the initial contacts consist of poking with fingers and touching with the lips before the objects are grasped and manipulated. With repeated exposure to novel objects, the initial caution gives way to grasping and manipulatory behavior. Two- to three-year-old animals approach and grasp more quickly, and experienced three- and four-year-olds contact and manipulate novel objects immediately. Seven- and eight-year-old juveniles, while making immediate contact with the objects, satiate much more quickly on a given trial than do the three- and four-year-olds, and they are less responsive to the objects when they are presented in subsequent sessions (Menzel, 1963; Welker, 1956).

Exploration

Mammals also spend considerable time exploring new environments. In rodents, this usually takes the form of locomotor activity in which the animal ranges about the environment, approaching and entering every accessible place. During this time, the animal sniffs and otherwise orients its behavior so that all its sense organs appear to be used as much as possible, suggesting that it is obtaining maximum exposure to the environment. With the passage of time, the duration and intensity of this activity decrease, and the rodent redirects its activities to feeding and other occupations involving the satisfaction of its biological needs. From time to time, however, the animal reexplores the area. These reconnaissance trips are not triggered by any known external stimuli, and they appear to be spatially random. If, however, a novel object or some other change in the familiar environment is encountered, the "new object reaction" described above is evoked and the duration of exploration is prolonged (Barnett, 1958; Shillito, 1963).

Rodents and other small mammals have to move about to obtain information about their environments. Locomotor exploration is less important in animals with well developed visual distance receptors, as is the case in many of the primate orders that can obtain considerable information simply by visual scanning of the surroundings.

A usual approach to the laboratory study of locomotor exploration has been to place a rodent in a strange environment from which it cannot escape, and then to record the distance it travels per unit of time. However, when laboratory rats were given an opportunity to retreat to a small, dark compartment, the amount of time spent exploring a strange, open field apparatus was substantially reduced. This was interpreted as indicating that the high level of exploratory behavior observed during the first minutes of studies employing "forced" exploration was in fact due to attempts of the animal to find a way out of the field. In other words, the behavior was prompted by fear, not by curiosity (Welker, 1957, 1959). Differences between free and forced exploration are also seen in the guinea pig, but not in the chinchilla, hamster, gerbil, albino mouse, and spiny mouse (Glickman & Hartz, 1964).

As in the case of object investigation, exploratory behavior is affected by novelty, complexity, and age.

Play

Play is another kind of behavior that is frequently seen in mammals and that does not appear to be directed toward the gratification of an immediate biological need. Play takes various forms, and a satisfactory universal definition of this behavior is not available. Play sometimes involves the elaboration of new behaviors that are unique to an individual, as in the case of a young badger that learned to turn forward somersaults (Eibl-Eibersfeldt, 1970). In some species, behaviors that are very specific to the play situation appear. This is the case in the "play intention" posture of a cat or dog in which the animal half crouches with the forelegs extended, eyes wide open, and ears pricked forward, and in the "play face" expressions possessed by many primates (Loizos, 1967). Also, elements of the normal behavioral repertoire of the animal that are typically used in aggressive, predatory, and copulatory sequences are often seen in play. The occurrence of these behaviors differs from that seen when the animal is utilizing them in "serious" activity. They are exaggerated and uneconomical when compared with their use in meeting the animal's biological needs. Loizos (1967) has described some of the ways in which motor patterns are altered and elaborated when used in play:

1 The usual sequence of component acts may be reordered.
2 Movements may be exaggerated in intensity.
3 Movements may be repeated over and over again.
4 The sequence may be fragmented; it may be interrupted by the appearance of other acts which normally are not seen in conjunction with it; sometimes, but not always, the sequence may be resumed later on.
5 Movements may be both exaggerated and repeated.
6 Individual movements within a sequence may never be completed.

Adaptive Significance of Play   The two major theories of the function of play are (1) that it allows a young animal to practice the behavior that it will use as an adult, and (2) that it provides the animal with information about the environment and its own capabilities and limits. Although there is evidence that both these functions may occur, animals do not have to play in order to practice, many of the behaviors that are seen in play do not require practice, and animals do not have to play in order to obtain information about the environment. Research in this area of behavior has only just begun, but it appears that when additional information becomes available, it will be found that play serves different functions in different species, and even that it serves more than one function in a given species.

MOTIVATION AND BEHAVIOR

Throughout this chapter, the behavior of mammals has been described and discussed without reference to motivational concepts such as drive, specific energy, arousal, reinforcement, and incentive motivation. This has been deliberate. It can be argued either that reference to such concepts adds very little to our understanding of behavior, or that their use actively interferes with understanding by tempting investigators to ask the wrong questions of their animals.

For example, Leyhausen (1965) has interpreted his data on predation in felids in terms of Lorenz's psychohydraulic model (cf. Chapter 2). Then, noting that cats without previous experience are usually unable to kill when first encountering a prey animal, he says that the threshold for the killing bite is very high and that the cats do not kill because they do not bite strongly enough. Only when a sufficient level of excitement is reached by play with the prey, or by the presence of conspecifics in the case of kittens, are they successful. After only one or a few successful kills, the killing bite clicks into place, and, once established, it " . . . *will continue to develop its own appetite, though this may atrophy unless reinforced by the animal's eating the prey it has killed* [Leyhausen, 1965, pp. 488–489]. (Italics are the author's.) Eating the prey need only be intermittent, however, to keep the killing appetite functional. A psychologist, having made the same behavioral observations, could very easily interpret the data in terms of such concepts as partial reinforcement and incentive motivation. Both the ethological and psychological interpretations are attempts to answer the implied question: *Why* does the cat behave this way?

From one point of view, this is not a relevant question. The answer has already been given: A cat behaves the way it does because it is a cat, a felid, a mammal, a vertebrate, a chordate, a metazoan, an animal, and so on. It behaves the way it does because it is a phylogenetically adapted, living animal. The questions that need to be asked are not of the *why* type; they are *how* type questions, e.g.: "How does a cat behave in a particular situation?" "How is this behavior influenced by its genotype?" "How do its nervous and endocrine systems operate in this behavior pattern?" The list goes on and on.

The point is that we already know something about what a cat is and what it does, and we shall continue to sharpen our description as we continue to study this animal and to develop increased sophistication in our experimental methodology. There is no need for us to replace evolutionary principles with a hypothetical cat full of action-specific energies, or general drive, or activation levels that will give it a purpose in life—to try to develop a new teleology from the objective data base provided by high-speed cameras, activity cages, and T mazes. We don't need a motivational model if motivational models are supposed to tell us *why* an organism behaves the way it does.

Of course, constructs and concepts are important to any science. *Action-specific energy* or *incentive motivation* or *partial reinforcement* may be useful concepts if they enable us to classify a large number of observations into a single descriptive category or if they suggest verifiable hypotheses. We can properly say that the killing behavior of the cat operates in such a way that the animal occasionally must be allowed to eat the prey it has killed in order for the bite to be easily elicited. We can also say that the animal behaves as if it were increasing its capacity to store energy, or in accordance with the principle that greater resistance to extinction follows partial reinforcement. In other words, we can suggest *how* the process underlying the event might function. We cannot say that the killing bite develops its own appetite or that partial reinforcement produces killing behavior that is resistant to extinction.

Because it is so easy to take an idea that purports to tell us something about *how* something functions and use it as if it were the cause of behavior, it can be argued that we are better off without motivational concepts. If we had no genes, no anatomy, no physiology, no ecology, and no past experience, we might need to invent motivation. Since we have all these things, together with a set of evolutionary principles, to guide us, we have all we need in terms of a framework within which to work at the problem of the *how* of behavior.

REFERENCES

ALLEN, D. L., & MECH, L. D. Wolves versus moose on Isle Royale. *National Geographic Magazine,* 1963, **123**, 200–219.

ALLISON, T., & VAN TWYVER, H. The evolution of sleep. *Natural History,* 1970, **79**, 56–65.

ASCHOFF, J. Comparative physiology: Diurnal rhythms. *Annual Review of Physiology,* 1963, **25**, 581–600.

ASCHOFF, J., & HONMA, K. Art- und Individual-Muster der Tages Periodik. *Zeitschrift für Vergleichende Physiologie,* 1959, **42**, 388–392.

AVIS, V. Brachiation: The crucial issue for man's ancestry. *Southwestern Journal of Anthropology,* 1962, **18,** 119–148.

BAILLIE, P., & MORRISON, S. D. The nature of the suppression of food intake by lateral hypothalamic lesions in rats. *Journal of Physiology,* 1963, **165,** 227–245.

BARNETT, S. A. Behavior components in the feeding of wild and laboratory rats. *Behaviour,* 1956, **9,** 24–43.

BARNETT, S. A. Exploratory behaviour. *British Journal of Psychology,* 1958, **49,** 289–310.

BARNETT, S. A. *The rat: A study in behaviour.* London: Methuen, 1963.

BARNETT, S. A., & SPENCER, M. M. Responses of wild rats to offensive smells and tastes. *British Journal of Animal Behaviour,* 1953, **1,** 32–37.

BARTHOLOMEW, G. A., JR., & CASWELL, H. H., JR. Locomotion in kangaroo rats and its adaptive significance. *Journal of Mammalogy,* 1951, **32,** 155–169.

BEACH, F. A. Locks and beagles. *American Psychologist,* 1969, **24,** 971–989.

BEACH, F. A., & RABEDEAU, R. G. Sexual exhaustion and recovery in the male hamster. *Journal of Comparative and Physiological Psychology,* 1959, **52,** 56–66.

BERLYNE, D. E. The arousal and satiation of perceptual curiosity in the rat. *Journal of Comparative and Physiological Psychology,* 1955, **48,** 238–246.

BERLYNE, D. E. *Conflict, arousal, and curiosity.* New York: McGraw-Hill, 1960.

BERLYNE, D. E. Curiosity and exploration. *Science,* 1966, **153,** 25–33.

BERMANT, G. Rat sex behavior: Photographic analysis of the intromission response. *Psychonomic Science,* 1965, **2,** 65–66.

BERNSTEIN, I. S. Response to nesting material of wild born and captive born chimpanzees. *Animal Behaviour,* 1962, **10,** 1–6.

BERNSTEIN, I. S. A comparison of nesting patterns among the three great apes. In *The Chimpanzee.* Vol. 1. New York: Karger, 1969. Pp. 393–402.

BIGNAMI, G., & BEACH, F. A. Mating behavior in the chinchilla. *Animal Behaviour,* 1968, **16,** 45–53.

BLAIR, W. F. Introduction. In J. A. King (Ed.), *Biology of Peromyscus (Rodentia).* American Society of Mammalogists, Serial publication No. 2, 1968. Pp. 1–5.

BROWN, F. A., JR. Hypothesis of environmental timing of the clock. In Brown, F. A., Jr., Hastings, J. W., & Palmer, J. D., *The biological clock: Two views.* New York: Academic Press, 1970. Pp. 13–59.

BUNNELL, B. N., BOLAND, B. D., & DEWSBURY, D. A. Copulatory behavior of golden hamsters *(Mesocricetus auratus).* In preparation.

CALHOUN, J. B. *The ecology and sociology of the Norway rat.* Public Health Service Publication No. 1008. Washington: Government Printing Office, 1962.

CARTER, C. S., & SCHEIN, M. W. Sexual receptivity and exhaustion in the female golden hamster. *Hormones and Behavior,* 1971, **2,** 191–200.

CHITTY, D., & SHORTEN, M. Techniques for the study of the Norway rat *(Rattus norvegicus).* *Journal of Mammalogy,* 1946, **27,** 63–78.

CLOUDSLEY-THOMPSON, J. L. *Rhythmic activity in animal physiology and behaviour.* New York: Academic Press, 1961.

DE COURSEY, P. J. Effect of light on the circadian activity rhythm of the flying squirrel, *Glaucomys volans. Zeitschrift für vergleichende Physiologie,* 1961, **44,** 331–354.

DENENBERG, V. H. Hoarding in the white rat under isolation and group conditions. *Journal of Comparative and Physiological Psychology,* 1952, **45,** 497–503.

DEWSBURY, D. A. A quantitative description of the behavior of rats during copulation. *Behaviour,* 1967, **29,** 154–178.

DEWSBURY, D. A. Copulatory behavior. In E. S. E. Hafez (Ed.), *Reproduction and Breeding techniques for laboratory animals.* Philadelphia: Lea & Febiger, 1970. Pp. 123–136.

DEWSBURY, D. A. Copulatory behavior of old-field mice *(Peromyscus polionotus subgriseus).* *Animal behaviour,* 1971, **19,** 192–204.

DEWSBURY, D. A. Patterns of copulatory behavior in male mammals. *Quarterly Review of Biology,* 1972, **47,** 1–33.

EATON, R. L. The predatory sequence, with emphasis on killing behavior and its ontogeny, in the cheetah *(Acinonys jubatus* Schreber*). Zeitschrift für Tierpsychologie,* 1970, **27,** 492–504.

EIBL-EIBESFELDT, I. *Ausdrucksformen der Saugetiere. Handbuch der Zoologie,* 1957, **8,** (2), 1–26.

EIBL-EIBESFELDT, I. The interactions of unlearned behavior patterns and learning in mammals. In J. F. Delafresnaye (Ed.), *Brain mechanisms and learning.* Oxford, England: Blackwell Scientific Publications, Ltd., 1961. Pp. 53–73.

EIBL-EIBESFELDT, I. Angeborenes und Erworbenes im Verhalten einiger Säuger. *Zeitschrift für Tierpsychologie,* 1963, **20,** 705–754.

EIBL-EIBESFELDT, I. *Ethology, the biology of behavior.* New York: Holt, Rinehart & Winston, 1970.

EISENBERG, J. F. A comparative study of sandbathing behavior in heteromyid rodents. *Behaviour,* 1964, **22,** 16–23.

EISENBERG, J. F. The social organization of mammals. *Handbuch der Zoologie,* 1966, **8,** No. 39, 1–92.

EISENBERG, J. F., MCKAY, G. M., & JAINUDEEN, M. R. Reproductive behavior of the Asiatic elephant *(Elaphas maximus maximus* L.*). Behaviour,* 1971, **38,** 193–225.

EWER, R. F. Food burying in the African ground squirrel, *Xerus erythropus* (E. Geoff). *Zeitschrift für Tierpsychologie,* 1965, **22,** 321–327.

EWER, R. F. *Ethology of mammals.* New York: Plenum Press, 1968. (a)

EWER, R. F. A preliminary survey of the behaviour in captivity of the dasyurid marsupial, *Sminthopsis crassicaudata* (Gould). *Zeitschrift für Tierpsychologie,* 1968, **25,** 319–365. (b)

EWER, R. F. Some observations of the killing and eating of prey by two dasyurid marsupials: The mulgara, *Dasycercus cristicauda,* and the Tasmanian devil, *Sarcophilus harrisi. Zeitschrift für Tierpsychologie,* 1969, **26,** 23–38.

FOX, M. W. Ontogeny of prey-killing behavior in Canidae. *Behaviour,* 1969, **35,** 259–280.

FULLER, J. L., & FOX, M. W. The behaviour of dogs. In E. S. E. Hafez (Ed.), *The behaviour of domestic animals.* (2nd ed.) London: Balliere, Tindall & Cassell, 1969. Pp. 438–481.

GLICKMAN, S. E., & HARTZ, K. E. Exploratory behavior in several species of rodents. *Journal of Comparative and Physiological Psychology,* 1964, **58,** 101–104.

GLICKMAN, S. E., & SROGES, R. W. Curiosity in zoo animals. *Behaviour,* 1966, **24,** 151–188.

GODFREY, G. K. Tracing field voles *(Microtus agrestris)* with a Geiger-Müller counter. *Ecology,* 1954, **35,** 5–10.

GRAY, J. *Animal locomotion.* New York: Norton, 1968.

GUTTMAN, N. Operant conditioning, extinction, and periodic reinforcement in relation to concentration of sucrose used as a reinforcing agent. *Journal of Experimental Psychology,* 1953, **46,** 213–224.

HAFEZ, E. S. E. Sexual behavior. In E. S. E. Hafez (Ed.), *Reproduction in farm animals.* (2nd ed.) Philadelphia: Lea & Febiger, 1968. Pp. 155–172.

HAFEZ, E. S. E., & SCHEIN, M. W. The behaviour of cattle. In E. S. E. Hafez (Ed.), *The behaviour of domestic animals.* Baltimore: Williams & Wilkins. 1962, Pp. 247–296.

HAFEZ, E. S. E., SUMPTION, L. J., & JAKWAY, J. S. The behaviour of swine. In E. S. E. Hafez (Ed.), *The behaviour of domestic animals.* Baltimore: Williams & Wilkins, 1962. Pp. 334–369.

HALE, E. B., & ALMQUIST, J. O. Relation of sexual behavior to germ cell output in farm animals. *Journal of Dairy Science Suppl.,* 1960, **43**, 145–169.

HAMILTON, W. J., JR. *American mammals.* New York: McGraw-Hill, 1939.

HEITMAN, H., JR., & HUGHES, E. H. The effects of air temperature and relative humidity on the physiological well being of swine. *Journal of Animal Science,* 1949, **8**, 171–191.

HILDEBRAND, M. Motions of the running cheetah and horse. *Journal of Mammalogy,* 1959, **40**, 481–495.

HILDEBRAND, M. Symmetrical gaits of horses. *Science,* 1965, **150**, 701–708.

KARE, M. R. Comparative aspects of the sense of taste. In M. R. Kare & B. P. Halpern (Eds.), *The physiological and behavioral aspects of taste.* Chicago: The University of Chicago Press, 1961. Pp. 6–15.

KAVANAU, J. Continuous automatic monitoring of the activities of small captive animals. *Ecology,* 1963, **44**, 95–110.

KAWAMURA, S. The process of sub-cultural propagation among Japanese macaques. In C. H. Southwick (Ed.), *Primate social behavior.* Princeton, N. J.: Van Nostrand, 1963. Pp. 82–90.

KING, J. A. Maternal behavior in *Peromyscus.* In H. L. Rheingold (Ed.), *Maternal behavior in mammals.* New York: Wiley, 1963. Pp. 58–93.

KOOPMAN, K. F., & COCKRUM, E. L. Bats. In S. Anderson & J. K. Jones, Jr. (Eds.), *Recent mammals of the world.* New York: Ronald Press, 1967. Pp. 109–150.

KRUUK, H. Clan-system and feeding habits of spotted hyaenas (*Crocuta crocuta* Erxleben). *Nature,* 1966, **209**, 1257–1258.

KUEHN, R. E., & ZUCKER, I. Reproductive behavior in the Mongolian gerbil *(Meriones unguiculatus).* *Journal of Comparative and Physiological Psychology,* 1968, **66**, 747–752.

KÜHME, W. Communal food distribution and division of labour in African hunting dogs. *Nature,* 1965, **205**, 443–444.

LAWICK-GOODALL, J. VAN. The behavior of free-living chimpanzees in the Gombe Stream Reserve. *Animal Behaviour Monographs,* 1968, 1, 161–311.

LAYNE, J. N. Nest-building behavior in three species of deer mice, *Peromyscus. Behaviour,* 1969, **35**, 288–303.

LEYHAUSEN, P. Verhaltensstudien an Katzen. *Zeitschrift für Tierpsychologie,* 1956, *Beiheft* **2**, 1–120.

LEYHAUSEN, P. Über die Funktion der relativen Stimmungshierarchie (dargestellt am Beispiel der phylogenetischen und ontogenetischen Entwicklung des Beutefangs von Raubtieren). *Zeitschrift für Tierpsychologie,* 1965, **22**, 412–494.

LOIZOS, C. Play behaviour in higher primates: A review. In D. Morris (Ed.), *Primate ethology.* Chicago: Aldine, 1967. Pp. 176–218.

LYNE, G. *Marsupials and monotremes of Australia.* Sydney, Australia: Angus & Robertson, 1967.

MCCLEARY, R. A., & MORGAN, C. T. Food hoarding in rats as a function of environmental temperature. *Journal of Comparative and Physiological Psychology,* 1946, **39**, 371–378.

MCGILL, T. E. Studies of the sexual behavior of male laboratory mice: Effects of genotype, recovery of sex drive, and theory. In F. A. Beach (Ed.), *Sex and behavior*. New York: Wiley, 1965. Pp. 76–88.

MENZEL, E. W. The effects of cumulative experience on responses to novel objects in young isolation reared chimpanzees. *Behaviour*, 1963, **21**, 1–12.

MICHAEL, R. P., & SAAYMAN, G. Sexual performance and timing of ejaculation in male rhesus monkeys *(Macaca mulata)*. *Journal of Comparative and Physiological Psychology*, 1967, **64**, 213–218.

MICHAEL, R. P., & ZUMPE, D. Sexual initiating behavior by female rhesus monkeys *(Macaca mulata)* under laboratory conditions. *Behaviour*, 1970, **36**, 168–186.

MILLER, G. A., & VIEK, P. An analysis of the rat's response to unfamiliar aspects of the hoarding situation. *Journal of Comparative Psychology*, 1944, **37**, 221–231.

MORRIS, D. The behaviour of the green acouchi *(Myoprocta pratti)* with special reference to scatter hoarding. *Proceedings of the Zoological Society of London*, 1962, **139**, 701–732.

MORRIS, R., & MORRIS, D. *Men and pandas*. New York: McGraw-Hill, 1966.

MUUL, I. Day length and food caches. In American Museum of Natural History, *Field Studies in Natural History*. New York: Van Nostrand, 1970. Pp. 78–86.

NAPIER, J. R., & NAPIER, P. H. *A handbook of living primates*. New York: Academic Press, 1967.

PEACOCK, L. J., & WILLIAMS, M. An ultrasonic device for recording activity. *American Journal of Psychology*, 1962, **75**, 648–652.

PEPELKO, W. E., & CLEGG, M. T. Studies of the mating behavior and some factors influencing the sexual response in the male sheep *Ovis aries*. *Animal Behaviour*, 1965, **13**, 249–258.

PETERSEN, E. Biologische Beobachtungen über Verhaltensweisen einiger einheimischer Nager beim Offen von Nüssen und Kernen. *Zeitschrift für Säugetierkunde*, 1965, **30**, 156–162.

PIERCE, J. T., & NUTTALL, R. L. Self-paced sexual behavior in the female rat. *Journal of Comparative and Physiological Psychology*, 1961, **54**, 310–313.

RICHTER, C. P. Animal behavior and internal drives. *Quarterly Review of Biology*, 1927, **2**, 307–434.

RICHTER, C. P. Symposium: Contributions of psychology to the understanding of problems of personality and behavior. IV. Biological foundation of personality differences. *American Journal of Orthopsychiatry*, 1932, **2**, 345–354.

RICHTER, C. P. *Biological clocks in psychiatry and medicine*. Springfield, Ill., Charles C. Thomas, 1965.

RIESEN, A. H. Plasticity of behavior: Psychological aspects. In H. F. Harlow, & C. N. Woolsey (Eds.), *Biological and biochemical bases of behavior*. Madison: The University of Wisconsin Press, 1958. Pp. 425–450.

ROSENBLATT, J. S., & LEHRMAN, D. S. Maternal behavior of the laboratory rat. In H. L. Rheingold (Ed.), *Maternal behavior in mammals*. New York: Wiley, 1963. Pp. 8–57.

RUBIN, H. B. & AZRIN, N. H. Temporal patterns of sexual behavior in rabbits as determined by an automatic recording technique. *Journal of the Experimental Analysis of Behavior*, 1967, **10**, 219–231.

SADLIER, R. M. F. S. *The ecology of reproduction in wild and domestic animals*. London: Methuen, 1969.

SAINT GIRONS, M. C. On the persistence of circadian rhythms in hibernating animals. In J. Aschoff (Ed.), *Circadian clocks*. Amsterdam: North Holland Publishing Company, 1965. Pp. 321–323.

SALE, J. B. The behaviour of the resting rock hyrax in relation to its environment. *Zoologica Africana,* 1970, **5,** 87–99.

SCHALLER, G. B. *The mountain gorilla.* Chicago: The University of Chicago Press, 1963.

SCHEIN, M. W., & HALE, E. B. Stimuli eliciting sexual behavior. In F. A. Beach (Ed.), *Sex and behavior.* New York: Wiley, 1965. Pp. 440–482.

SCHMIDT-NIELSEN, K. *Desert animals.* London: Oxford University Press, 1964.

SCOTT, J. P., & FULLER, J. L. *Genetics and the social behavior of the dog.* Chicago: The University of Chicago Press, 1965.

SEITZ, E. Untersuchungen zur Aktivitätsrhythmik dunkelactiver Halbassen der Unterfamilie *Lorisinae* (Flower et Lydekker, 1891). In D. Storch, R. Schneider, & H. J. Kuhn (Eds.), *Progress in primatology: First Congress of the International Primatology Society.* Stuttgart, Germany: Gustav Fisher, 1967. Pp. 322–326.

SHADLE, A. R. Copulation in the porcupine. *Journal of Wildlife Management,* 1946, **10,** 159–162.

SHEFFIELD, F. D., & ROBY, T. B. Reward value of a non-nutritive sweet taste. *Journal of Comparative and Physiological Psychology,* 1950, **43,** 471–481.

SHEFFIELD, F. D., ROBY, T. B., & CAMPBELL, B. A. Drive reduction versus consummatory behavior as determinants of reinforcement. *Journal of Comparative and Physiological Psychology,* 1954, **47,** 349–355.

SHILLITO, E. E. Exploratory behaviour in the short-tailed vole. *Microtus agrestis. Behaviour,* 1963, **21,** 145–154.

SIKES, S. K. *The natural history of the African elephant.* New York: Elsevier, 1971.

SMITH, M. P., & CAPRETTA, P. J. Effects of drive level and experience on the reward value of saccharine solutions. *Journal of Comparative and Physiological Psychology,* 1956, **49,** 553–557.

STANDFORD, J. Crab-eating chital. *Journal of Bombay Natural History Society,* 1951, **50,** (2), 398–399.

TAPP, J. T., ZIMMERMAN, R. S., & D'ENCARNACAO, P. S. Intercorrelational analysis of some common measures of rat activity. *Psychological Reports,* 1968, **23,** 1047–1050.

THOMPSON, W. R., & HIGGINS, W. H. Emotion and organized behavior. *Canadian Journal of Psychology,* 1958, **12,** 61–68.

VOITONIS, N. I. *Predistoriia intellekta.* Academy of Sciences, Moscow and Leningrad, 1949. Cited by Berlyne, D. E., *Conflict, arousal, and curiosity.* New York: McGraw-Hill, 1960. P. 152.

WARREN, R. P., & PFAFFMAN, C. Early experience and taste aversion. *Journal of Comparative and Physiological Psychology,* 1959, **52,** 263–266.

WELKER, W. I. Some determinants of play and exploration in chimpanzees. *Journal of Comparative and Physiological Psychology,* 1956, **49,** 84–89.

WELKER, W. I. "Free" versus "forced" exploration of a novel situation by rats. *Psychological Reports,* 1957, **3,** 95–108.

WELKER, W. I. Escape, exploratory and food-seeking responses of rats in a novel situation. *Journal of Comparative and Physiological Psychology,* 1959, **52,** 106–111.

WHALEN, R. E. Eexual behavior of cats. *Behaviour,* 1963, **20,** 321–342.

WILSON, J. R., KUEHN, R. E., & BEACH, F. A. Modification in the sexual behavior of male rats produced by changing the stimulus female. *Journal of Comparative and Physiological Psychology,* 1963, **56,** 636–644.

WORDEN, A. N., & LEAHY, J. S. The behaviour of rabbits. In E. S. E. Hafez (Ed.), *The behaviour of domestic animals.* Baltimore: Williams & Wilkins, 1962. Pp. 397–414.

YOUNG, W. C., & GRUNT, J. A. The pattern and measurement of sexual behavior in the male guinea pig. *Journal of Comparative and Physiological Psychology,* 1951, **44,** 492–500.

Chapter 4

Comparative
Social Psychology

John Paul Scott

COMPARATIVE SOCIAL PSYCHOLOGY OF THE DOG AND WOLF

The data and principles of comparative social psychology are best illustrated by a specific example. The dog is an unusually interesting species, because of both its long association with man and the extension of its social relationships to include the human. While the dog lacks the manipulative capacities of primates, its social behavior is elaborately developed, and dogs make far more satisfactory domestic animals than any species of nonhuman primates. Yet, when my colleagues and I first began to study these animals, we found that their social behavior, perhaps because it was so familiar, was almost unknown from a scientific viewpoint (Scott & Fuller, 1965).

Behavioral Repertory of the Dog

One of our first tasks was to describe the behavior of the dog. The natural unit of behavior is the behavior pattern, defined as a segment of behavior having a particular adaptive function. It is a natural unit in the sense that natural selection can act upon behavior only as it is adaptive or nonadaptive. Mapping behavior patterns in the dog presented a unique problem: the possibility that behavior patterns peculiar to the dog-human relationships had been evolved through long human contact. We therefore placed natural groups of dogs, i.e., litters that had grown up together, in large 1-acre fields surrounded by high board fences, where the groups could be observed entirely apart from human contacts. We found that the dogs were reacting to one another with exactly the same behavior patterns that domestic dogs employ in their human contacts. Furthermore, we found that the same behavior patterns were apparent in their presumed wild ancestors, the wolves (Scott 1950). The frequency of certain behavior patterns had been altered in either a positive or a negative direction, but nothing new had been created and very little lost in some 12,000 years or so of domestication.

The social behavior patterns of dogs are organized into nine behavioral systems, each associated with a major adaptive function. The most primitive systems are those of shelter-seeking, investigative, sexual, and ingestive (eating and drinking) behaviors. Behavioral systems having similar functions, although not necessarily homologous, are found in the vast majority of all animals that exhibit behavior, even one-celled animals. More advanced systems, found less generally in the higher phyla of animals, include care-giving (epimeletic) and care-soliciting (et-epimeletic) behavior, both primarily concerned with the care of the young; agonistic behavior, defined as patterns adaptive in conflict between members of the same species; and allelomimetic behavior, defined as doing the same thing as other individuals, with some degree of mutual imitation. This last system is particularly important in cooperative pack activities of dogs and is associated with an internal system of general social motivation (Waller and Fuller, 1961). A more specialized system, which has been modified in part to function in communication, is eliminative behavior. These nine behavioral systems are also found in wolves and (with some modifications) in all members of the family Canidae whose social behavior has been thoroughly studied.

Compared to those of dogs, the social behavior patterns of wolves are more distinct and stereotyped, although not to the extent of many birds, where such patterns will be shown either completely or not at all. In the courtship of turkeys, the male bird goes through a long series of behavior patterns eventually leading to copulation. If this series is interrupted at any point, the bird goes back to the beginning and starts all over again (Schein & Hale, 1961). Dogs may show elaborate courtship behavior, but a male and female pair may also copulate within a few minutes after first meeting, omitting all preliminary behavior.

The Social Behavior and Organization of Wolves

Much of the social behavior of domestic dogs is elicited in relation to human beings. Seen out of its natural context, it may seem mysterious and inexplicable. However, when such behavior is observed in a natural group of wolves, its function is usually obvious.

Ecologically, wolves are hunters of the large herd animals: deer, moose, elk, mountain sheep, and buffalo in the temperate regions of North America, and caribou in the far north. Similarly, the wolves of Eurasia hunt the herd animals of that part of the world. Wolves have never lived in Africa or South America.

The normal social group is a pack composed of several adult males and females. The pack may occasionally be reduced to a single pair, but the "lone wolf" is a rarity, and perhaps does not survive long. Pack size depends on the size of the prey. In the caribou-hunting wolves of the arctic, the usual number is four or five animals, whereas the pack of moose-hunting wolves on Isle Royale in Lake Superior has remained constant for many years at around twenty individuals (Mech, 1966). This pack hunts its large prey as a group, while packs hunting smaller animals may split up and then rejoin after making a kill.

Behavior is organized in relation to daily and seasonal changes in environmental conditions. The daily round of a wolf pack in the summer months starts in the early evening when the pack assembles and often howls in a chorus. After this, its members go off together or singly for the hunt. When one animal is successful, he may sit down and howl, and he is answered by the others. Experimenters (Theberge & Falls, 1967) found that they could easily locate the wolf packs in the dense fir forest of the Algonquin Park in Ontario by mimicking a wolf howl and listening to the replies. Howling, therefore, has the function of keeping wolves in touch with one another, and it also is expressed in the chorus howling of the group preliminary to hunting. In the winter months in northern regions, hunting is more likely to take place during the daylight hours. In summer, the wolves return from the hunt in the early morning and spend most of the day lying around or sleeping.

In addition to these seasonal changes in hunting behavior, wolves have a definite seasonal cycle connected with reproduction. Female wolves may begin to show the preliminary bleeding characteristic of the estrous cycle in canines as early as December, but actual mating takes place in February or March, the young being born in April or May after a 63-day gestation period. Not all the females in the pack have puppies every year. In the wolf pack studied by Rabb and his coworkers (Rabb, Woolpy, & Ginsburg, 1967) in the Brookfield Zoo at Chicago, there is a strict dominance order among females as well as males, and the most dominant female will not allow others to mate, with the result that usually only one litter is born per year. Whether or not this takes place in free wolf packs, there is evidently some sort of social control of numbers. The Isle Royale pack, living in a national park where hunting is forbidden, has neither increased nor divided in several years of observation (Mech, 1966).

The wolves dig out a den, usually by enlarging the hole of some smaller animal, and in this the female has her young. The pack defends the area within a quarter of a mile or so of this den as a territory, both against strange wolves and against potential predators, such as bears. After hunting, members of the pack bring back bones and pieces of meat to the den area and bury them. Thus the mother, who does not hunt for the first few weeks, is able to feed, and eventually the young pups benefit also. All members of the pack, both males and females, will vomit food for the young puppies after they are able to eat it, at approximately three weeks of age. Theberge and Pimlott (1969) say that the Algonquin Park wolves move away from the den when the pups are several weeks old and establish a headquarters in a different sort of place, usually an open, parklike area with adjacent brushy woods in which the half-grown pups can hide while the adults are away. At the same time, they have considerable opportunity for independent exploration in this small area. The pups are apparently able to live on their own and begin to function as adults after they are four or five months of age, when they presumably have developed their permanent teeth. What happens next is not clear. They may join the parent pack, or the litter may go on to form a new pack of its own. In any case, young wolves do not become sexually mature until their second winter, producing their first offspring when approximately two years old.

True leadership is not strongly apparent in a wolf pack, as any animal may initiate its movement. However, the pack is highly cooperative in hunting and in the care of the young. Dominance organization is not strongly apparent in wild wolf packs, but in the captive packs in zoos, where the principal occupation of hunting is made unnecessary by artificial feeding, wolves spend a large amount of their time threatening one another and enforcing dominance. Attachments between members of the same pack are long-lasting, but whether or not there are lasting mating bonds apart from these is not clear. Social interaction in wolves is illustrated in Figure 4–1.

Finally, the behavior of wolves is strongly organized with respect to places. Besides the small territory around the den, a wolf pack occupies a much larger hunting range. As the wolves wander, they mark certain conspicuous objects in the landscape, such as trees or rocks, with urine or feces in the same manner as domestic dogs. There is no evidence that these scent posts are placed at the outer boundaries of the range or that they are responded to as boundaries by other wolf packs. They do, however, form an obvious means of social communication, as will be seen later.

Comparison of Dogs and Wolves

Like the wolf, the typical dog group is the pack rather than a mated pair. This is especially apparent when dogs are used in hunting. Many dogs do not run in packs but are closely associated with human beings, with whom they interact as if with a pack member and with whom they readily learn to cooperate in a variety of activities. House dogs are not allowed to hunt; however, when allowed to run free, they frequently explore an area around their home every day in a regular fashion. For the most part, their daily round of behavior is adjusted to human activity, the dog being active when its human masters are active. Like wolves, dogs may howl when alone, but on the whole they howl less and bark more than wolves. As they wander,

Figure 4–1. Social interaction in wolves. Dogs were presumably domesticated from a small variety of wild wolves, and the descendants of both species show very similar behavior patterns in spite of the great variation of form and appearance in domestic dogs. (Photograph courtesy of Douglas H. Pimlott.)

they mark scent posts in the manner of wolves. If a female in estrus marks such a post the scent alerts the males who also use the post, and they trace her back to her home and attempt to mate.

Some of the ancestral wolf behavior has been lost during domestication. For example, the seasonal cycle of sexual activity has been lost, and most domestic female dogs come into estrus at approximately 6-month intervals at any season of the year. On the other hand, dogs are still territorial. They act as if the owner's home were a territory, and bark at any intruder, whether canine or human, that attempts to cross its boundaries. For this reason, almost any breed of dog is a valuable watchdog. Also, dogs will occasionally bury their food, In laboratory conditions, where the kennel floor is covered with shavings, certain dogs scoop up the bedding with their noses to bury their food pans, and house dogs occasionally bury bones in the yard. Dogs vomit readily, often to the dismay of their masters, and mothers will vomit food for the young. Under domestic conditions, other familiar adult dogs are seldom present in the same household, and hence there is little evidence concerning care of the young except by the mother.

If allowed to grow up together, a group of dogs will develop the same kinds of social organization as wolves, namely a dominance order based on force and threats. (See Table 4–1 comparing the agonistic behavior of the dog, wolf, and fox and Figure 4–2.) Most of the behavior of the dog, however, is organized around a different relationship, that with a human master. Ordinarily, the master is dominant and the dog subordinate, and the exceptional dogs that attempt to dominate their masters are quickly discarded. Furthermore, the master establishes a strong leader-follower relationship with his pet,

Table 4–1 Patterns of Agonistic Behavior in Three Species of Canids

Pattern	Dog	Wolf	Fox
Playful fighting (young animals)			
Pawing, mouthing, gentle biting	x		x
Rolling on back, pawing, extending legs	x	x	x
Serious fighting			
Each animal attempts to seize other by back of neck and force it to ground	x	x	x
Attack			
Chasing, biting	x	x	x
Threat signals			
Snarling (growling, showing teeth, sometimes lunging toward other with extended forelegs)	x	x	
Growling	x	x	x
Barking	x	x	x
Defense and escape reactions			
Sitting	x	x	x
Crouching, tail between legs	x	x	x
Yelping and showing teeth	x	x	
Running away	x	x	x
Attitudes of dominance (tail always erect in dogs and wolves)			
Standing or walking stiff-legged, tail erect	x	x	
Forepaws on back of subordinate, growling, tail erect (may bite neck)	x	x	
Standing over subordinate, growling, tail erect	x	x	
Pinning subordinate to ground by neck	Rare	x	
Head down, back arched, tail down (like cat)			x
Mounting, tail down, neck biting (without pelvic thrusts)			x
Attitudes of subordination (tail always down in dog or wolf)			
Allows dominant animal to place feet on back	x	x	
Tail down, erect posture	x	x	
Tail between legs, crouching, ears depressed	x	x	
Tail down, lies flat	x	x	
Tail between legs, rolls on back, legs extended (may yelp and snap)	x	x	

Note that no patterns of subordination have been observed in the fox, which is not a pack animal. Also, two unique dominance patterns occur in the fox; the dominance patterns of dogs and wolves are missing in the fox.

Figure 4–2. Relationship of mutual threat in the dog. As they compete for the possession of a bone, both the female on the left and male on the right snarl and paw at each other, but do not bite. Raised tail indicates dominance; neither of these dogs is subordinate to the other. These dogs belong to the rare Telomian breed, originating in Malaysia.

partially through the use of food rewards, but mainly through the reward of allowing the dog to enjoy the master's company. This relationship is the one truly new thing which has been established as a result of domestication. It can be best understood from a developmental viewpoint.

THE DEVELOPMENT OF SOCIAL RELATIONSHIPS

Periods of Development in the Dog

The newborn puppy is a very immature animal (see Figure 4–3). It is not only blind but also deaf, and even its olfactory sense is incompletely developed. Its motor behavior consists of a slow crawl, its head being thrown from side to side. When it touches any warm, smooth object, the pattern of nursing is evoked: searching movements with its head, sucking after finding a nipple, pushing with its head, and alternate pushing with its forepaws. In spite of the fact that it cannot hear, it vocalizes in response to pain and discomfort. Its learning capacities are limited, as it requires many more pairings of stimuli

Figure 4–3. Puppy in the neonatal period. Both the eyes and ears are closed, and the animal moves in a slow crawl, turning the head from side to side.

to produce conditioning than do older animals (J. P. Scott, 1968a), although recent evidence indicates that neonatal pups associate nursing and a limited class of stimuli fairly efficiently (Stanley, Bacon, & Fehr, 1970). The principal process that goes on during this period is that of neonatal nutrition, and all the puppy's behavior is adapted for a social environment in which entire care is provided by the mother.

The end of the *neonatal period* comes at approximately two weeks of age, when the eyes open. In less than a week the ears have also opened and all major sense organs are functional. The puppy walks instead of crawling, and there is a sudden change at the end of the week in its ability to be conditioned, the puppy now learning with the same rapidity as an adult animal. During this *transition period*, there is a metamorphosis from behavior that is adapted to neonatal existence to behavior that is adapted to the social life of an adult. By three weeks of age, although still far from being independent, the puppy has become a recognizable young dog. In the transition period, the puppy has undergone a process of *behavioral metamorphosis*.

The phenomenon of metamorphosis is well known in invertebrate animals. The immature dragonfly lives an underwater existence and has a very different form before it emerges as an air-living, flying adult. Development of the dog differs from that of the dragonfly in that in the dog the two phases of existence are related to the social rather than the physical environment.

Behavioral metamorphosis is actually a widespread phenomenon in non-precocial birds and mammals. Its significance is that behavior of the neonatal animal is subject to a different group of selection pressures than is the behavior of the adult. It is therefore possible that much of neonatal behavior does not lead into, or form a foundation for, adult behavior except in the sense that it keeps the infant alive so that later behavior can develop.

One of the patterns of behavior that first appears in the transition period is that of tail-wagging. Along with this, the puppy begins to notice other animals at a distance and develops the ability to rapidly form attachments both to living things and to the particular physical environment in which it lives.

The evidence that such attachments are formed comes from the appearance of a new pattern of behavior (Elliot & Scott, 1961). At the end of the transition period, the puppy will show distress vocalization if it is removed to a strange location. The vocalization rate in most breeds will average 140 per minute and is kept up almost indefinitely, slowing down only when the puppy becomes fatigued. The reaction ceases almost immediately when the puppy is restored to its home environment. Somewhat lower rates of vocalization can be elicited by leaving the puppy in its home room and removing the mother and littermates, showing that the puppy has become attached to other individuals as well as to the physical environment. The reaction first appears at about ten days of age, the puppy apparently noticing changes in the physical environment a little sooner than those in the social environment, but at first the response is weak and quickly disappears. After eight weeks of age the vocalization rate during separation begins to decrease, correlated with the fact that the puppies have been weaned from the breast, but even adult dogs will vocalize when isolated.

The principal process during this *socialization period,* illustrated in Figure 4-4, is therefore the development of social attachments and attachments to particular localities. Up until about twelve weeks of age, the puppy can be readily introduced into new areas and to new individuals. In the same period, the elaboration of social relationships proceeds, particularly in the formation of dominance relationships between puppies brought up together, although these are not completely fixed. The later part of the period, from about eight to twelve weeks, is one in which puppies readily learn new things. This is an ideal time to introduce the puppy to its future adult activity. It probably corresponds to the age in which wolf mothers move their puppies from a den to a new area.

Beginning at twelve weeks, puppies reared in a large area begin to leave the region of the nest and to explore more widely. With this wider activity they enter the *juvenile period,* which lasts until sexual maturity. In this period the principal processes are the development of motor skills that in a more natural environment would be devoted chiefly to hunting.

Figure 4–4. Puppy in the period of socialization. At this age the puppy has gone through a transition period in which behavior is transformed from that adapted for early life in which the mother provides complete care to behavior useful in a more independent existence. It is now a recognizable young dog, with all sense organs functional and greatly improved locomotion. It is in this period that the puppy forms its primary social attachments.

The Dog-Human Relationship

It is a well-known fact that young puppies easily form social relationships with people. A puppy removed from the litter during the early socialization period will show distress for a day or two and then become obviously attached to its human master or masters. Young wolf cubs similarly form close relationships with people, especially if they are acquired early. The problem of how these early relationships are formed has been experimentally attacked in various ways.

In the "wild dog" experiment (Freedman, King, & Elliot, 1961), a pregnant mother is placed in a 1-acre field surrounded by a high board fence. She is provided with a well-constructed nest box and a means whereby she can be fed and watered through the fence without direct human contact. Here the puppies are born, reared only by the mother, and by fourteen weeks of age they have become little wild animals, impossible to approach directly and showing every sign of extreme fear when cornered and caught. Taking such puppies individually out of the field and giving them close human contact for a week produces almost no effect on behavior during the transition period. At three weeks of age, the beginning of the socialization period, there is a moderate effect, and at five weeks, there is maximum effect, both immediately and on later relationships with people. At this age the puppy approaches a passive human without fear, and later tests show that a lasting attachment has been formed. At seven weeks, there begins a gradually increasing fear response. Consequently, the older puppies have less and less contact with people and show a correspondingly reduced attachment to them. By the time a puppy has reached fourteen weeks of age in the field environment, it can become attached to people only after weeks of effort, and even then never shows the complete attachment of a normal dog. Such an animal is well adjusted to other dogs but is always shy and unresponsive with people. At the opposite extreme, if the puppy is taken from the litter at three weeks of age or earlier and kept continuously with people, it becomes an "almost human" dog, very closely attached to people but indifferent or antagonistic to other dogs. The optimum time for adopting a puppy into a human family is therefore somewhere between six and eight weeks of age, although some variation on either side will not produce serious consequences.

Another technique is to place a puppy in visual isolation from other dogs and people at the outset of the period of primary socialization. Such a puppy adapts rapidly to the new situation, grows normally, and appears to behave normally as long as it stays in the isolation quarters. If kept in isolation beyond the end of the socialization period and then allowed to emerge, it shows persistent emotional and behavioral disturbances whose severity increases with the length of the isolation period (Thompson & Melzack, 1956; Fuller, 1967). On the other hand, as little as two 20-minute periods per week outside the isolation box will produce a normal puppy, and if it is removed permanently some time before seven weeks of age, the isolation experience produces no harm (Fuller & Clark, 1966b). These findings further confirm the conclusion that between six and eight weeks of age is an optimum time for forming a strong new relationship.

Another way of attacking this problem is to present an isolated animal with a new companion of some sort and observe the reaction when the companion is taken away. Cairns and Werboff (1967) have shown that such a puppy begins to show distress on being separated from a new companion, such as a rabbit, after being with it only an hour or two, and that it develops a maximum rate of vocalization after being exposed to the new companion for 24 hours. This indicates that during the early part of the critical period, a maximum degree of social attachment may be formed within 24 hours. It is obvious that the puppy will form an emotional attachment to any person, dog, or inanimate object in the environment, provided extended contact is possible (J. P. Scott, 1967).

The following theory will therefore explain the process of primary socialization, i.e., the formation of the first emotional attachments. The puppy's sensory apparatus and learning capacities must be developed to the point where it can immediately discriminate between familiar and unfamiliar objects. At this point, an almost reflex emotional response comes into play: distress vocalization in response to the absence of the familiar. This emotional response acts as an internal reinforcing agent, punishing the puppy when it leaves familiar areas or individuals and rewarding it when it returns. During its early development, the puppy must experience this effect over and over again, with the result that motivation is increased according to the laws of learning. This theory conforms to the facts that socialization occurs most rapidly if a puppy is removed from the litter and the resulting distress is relieved by a human handler, and that long periods of separation increase attachments and dependency (J. P. Scott, 1967). A similar theory has been developed by Moltz (1960) to explain the process of social attachment in young birds. Indeed, the phenomenon of imprinting as described by Lorenz (1935, 1970). Hess (1964), Klinghammer (1967), and others may be considered a special form of the process of primary socialization, the formation of an animal's first social relationships.

The Human-Human Relationship

The general characteristics of the dog-human relationship are that the period of dependency is prolonged throughout the dog's life and that, unlike the relationship formed between littermate puppies of the same age, the human master becomes, under most circumstances, a leader, and the dog a follower. Furthermore, in this relationship the master is almost invariably dominant and the dog subordinate. We can now compare this relationship with the one which normally develops between adult human beings and their own offspring (J. P. Scott, 1963).

In many ways, the periods of development in human beings are quite comparable to those in the dog. The human neonate has better developed sense organs than the newborn puppy but is more poorly developed in a motor fashion. Like the dog, the principal process for the first few weeks of life is that of neonatal nutrition. Behavior is even simpler than that of the dog, consisting almost entirely of nursing and vocalization. However, the next period of human development is not that of transition but of socialization. At about five weeks of age, the human infant shows his first social smile and thereafter smiles at any human face or facelike object. This behavior pattern is similar in function to the tail-wagging of the young puppy, indicating a desire for social contact. For the next few months, from approximately five or six weeks to six or seven months, the baby reacts by smiling at anyone. The period ends with the development of a fear response to strangers. Even in its mother's arms, the six- or seven-month-old baby rarely smiles at strangers and usually cries if they approach it suddenly when its mother is absent.

The period of transition begins with the baby's first crawl, at approximately seven months, and ends when the infant is able to walk, at an average age of fourteen months. There then begins a second transition period not found in the dog—that of transition to the adult form of communication, or speech. Once a baby's language ability is advanced enough so that he can use and understand sentences, usually at a little over 2 years of age, there begins a second process not found in the dog, that of verbal socialization, or training and the development of social relationships involving the use of language.

There are several consequences of the different order of development periods and processes in human beings. Since the socialization process appears before the period of transition, the baby must form its first social attachments to its human caretaker, usually the mother, but also with any other person who may be present and have prolonged contact with it. This contrasts with the socialization of the dog: The mother begins to leave her pups during the period of socialization and their strongest relationships are therefore formed with the littermates. This presumably forms the foundation for the typical canine social group, the pack, whereas in human beings there is a long continued association between adults and young. Human infants, by different rearing, can be made to organize their behavior in a more doglike fashion if they are taken outside the family and raised in peer groups, just as dogs can be modified in a human direction by taking them away from their littermates and allowing them to form a relationship with a human caretaker. It is obvious also that the presence of language in human beings permits the development of far more complex kinds of social relationships than exist among dogs.

The basic emotional mechanisms that underlie the formation of primary social relationships appear to be much the same as in dogs. Like dogs, human infants show distress reactions to the absence of the familiar, first noticeable at about two months of age when the period of primary socialization begins, and very obvious thereafter. One of the easiest and most drastic ways of punishing a young child is to isolate it forcibly; and most of the terrors of the dark arise from forcing a child to sleep alone in its room. Likewise, the young child shows a developing fear response to the strange (known to pediatricians as "eight-month anxiety"), which brings the period of primary socialization to a close by preventing the rapid formation of attachments to strangers.

Attachment experiments with human infants can be readily done, as Fleener & Cairns (1970) have shown. If a mother brings her child to a nursery and leaves it to interact with a strange person, it will begin to show distress when the new person leaves within a very short time, even if the mother is present. Experiments with separation from the familiar have never been deliberately done because of the obvious danger of emotional damage to the infant. However, babies occasionally have to be separated from their parents because of illness requiring hospitalization, and the process of adoption involves the orphan's being separated from familiar places and the individuals who have cared for it since birth. As Schaffer (1958) has shown, hospitalized infants exhibit different emotional reactions before and after seven months of age, the older infants being more drastically affected. Similarly, children who have been adopted after six months of age show a statistical difference in the tendency to develop serious emotional problems later on. Judging from the results with similar experiments with dogs, it is possible that the major symptoms that should be measured in these children are those of increased dependency, which might in turn produce emotional problems, although not necessarily so.

SOCIAL ORGANIZATION AND SOCIAL RELATIONSHIPS

As soon as several individuals come together and react to one another, their behavior is no longer independent but has become organized. The behavior of one becomes related to that of others. The concept of relationship is a basic one to social organization, and a *social relationship* may be defined as the behavior of two or more individuals reacting toward one another in a regular and predictable fashion.

Relationships can be described and analyzed on the basis of the kinds of social behavior involved. Using nine different systems of social behavior as a basis for analysis, we can calculate forty-five different ways in which they can be combined in a relationship between two individuals, each of whom exhibits only one type of behavior. The number of combinations is almost infinite if we consider the possibility that the two individuals may each exhibit more than one major kind of social behavior (J. P. Scott, 1953). Fortunately, only a few of these many theoretical relationships are commonly found among animals. Some of the most important ones are described below.

Aggregative Relationships

During a blizzard the members of a flock of sheep may huddle together for mutual protection and thus exhibit shelter-seeking behavior. This is a very simple type of social relationship and is found widely in the animal kingdom. As Allee (1931) has shown, aggregations occur in any group of animals that have the power of movement, from protozoa to vertebrates, and they usually have the function of providing mutual protection and shelter.

Sexual Relationships

Both individuals in a pair exhibit sexual behavior. Sexual relationships are widespread among animals and vary from the behavior of temporary breeding swarms of midges and similar insects to the long-lasting mating bonds of some birds and mammals

Leader-Follower Relationships

When one individual leads another, the behavior of both is allelomimetic, i.e., both show the same behavior with some degree of mutual stimulation; but there is unequal responsiveness between the two, with the result that one tends to be slightly more independent than the other and becomes a leader. This type of relationship is highly important in flocks of sheep (J. P. Scott, 1945) and other herd mammals, such as deer (Darling, 1937). Lambs develop the habit of following the mother very early in life and continue the habit into maturity. Adult females still follow their mothers after their own lambs are born. Consequently, in a naturally formed flock there is a tendency for the oldest female to be the leader. There is some tendency among male groups to follow older animals but, since the males never reward the younger sheep by allowing them to nurse, no strong system of leadership develops. In packs of dogs or wolves, there is likewise no strong system of leadership. Movement or other activities may be initiated by any member of the group.

Dominance-Subordination Relationship

In this relationship, both individuals exhibit agonistic behavior and, as a result of fighting or force, one individual becomes dominant and the other subordinate. This relationship, with repetition, develops into a strong habit. It may become very important in animal societies that maintain close social groups, such as chickens (Schjelderup-Ebbe, 1922), baboons (DeVore, 1965), and wolves (Rabb et al., 1967). Some sort of dominance relationship is found in all animals that show social fighting (Collias, 1944). It has been described in all major classes of vertebrates and many arthropods.

Care-Dependency Relationships

In this type of relationship, the behavior of one individual is epimeletic (or care-giving), while the other is typically et-epimeletic (or care-soliciting). Such a relationship is well illustrated by the behavior of the mother sheep toward her lamb. Whenever the young lamb is cold, hungry, or isolated from the other sheep, it baas its distress call and the mother comes to its aid with epimeletic behavior. Similar relationships are highly developed in the social insects as well as in birds and mammals, and some trace of care-dependency is found in other arthropods and the lower vertebrates. Its development depends in large part upon the possession of enough manipulative skill so that effective care can be given. Among many species of animals a care-dependency relationship is developed with a male parent, as in many birds, or with an animal which is not a parent at all, as with the workers in social insects.

Mutual Care

In this relationship the behavior of both individuals is care-giving. No good examples are seen in dogs or wolves, but the mutual grooming of monkeys and apes is a good illustration.

Trophallaxis

This is a complex relationship of mutual care involving investigative and ingestive behavior as well as care giving. It is highly developed in the social insects (Wheeler, 1923). When one ant meets another, they first investigate each other with their antennae. Then, if one ant has recently fed, it will regurgitate a drop of honey for the other.

There are many other possible types of social relationships, some of which are probably never exhibited because they serve little useful function. Others, however, may occur and go unrecognized. For example, among mammals which have definite heat periods, there is a regular relationship between males and nonreceptive females which consists of agonistic behavior on the part of the female in response to investigative and sexual behavior on the part of the male.

General and Special Relationships

The usual social group consists of several animals. Each animal has relationships with every other, but not necessarily the same relationships. A young lamb has a tendency to follow any older member of the flock but only nurses from its own mother. In sheep, the leader-follower relationship is therefore a general one, but the care-dependency relationship is a special one developed with only one member of the group, the mother.

THE ANALYSIS OF SOCIAL ORGANIZATION

In addition to the multiple relationships shown by one individal toward others, each pair of animals in a group may develop more than one relationship between them. A male and a female wolf may show between them both a sexual relationship and a dominance relationship, each under different circumstances.

A complete analysis of all sorts of relationships in a group has consequently seldom been attempted. It would involve determining the occurrence of each type of relationship (i.e., dominance-subordination, leader-follower, care-dependency, and so on) between each pair of individuals. The total social organization can therefore be extremely complicated. Some experimenters speak of a dominance-subordination hierarchy as *the* social order, but it is, of course, only one aspect of social organization. In a flock of goats, no correlation was found between leader-follower and dominance-subordination relationships (Stewart & Scott, 1947), and in rhesus monkeys, the dominant male exercises leadership only as a veto power over directions of movement initiated by other members of the troop (Southwick, Beg, & Siddiqui, 1965).

In order to get the complete picture of social organization in a group, the relationships between each pair must be determined by observation or experiment. Since each relationship involves two animals, the total number of relationships in a group of n animals is given by the formula (C. R. Carpenter, 1934):

$$\frac{n\ (n\ -\ 1)}{2}$$

In a group of three, there are three relationships; in a group of four, six; in a group of five, ten; and so on. The result may also be expressed as an arithmetic series: 0, 1, 3, 6, 10, 15..., in which each difference between successive pairs of figures is one greater than the last. It is obvious that a large social group has a very great number of possible social relationships, which makes it hard on the experimenter but not necessarily impossible for the animal. Hens in flocks containing as many as 96 members develop dominance relationships in all possible combinations (Guhl, 1953), as nearly as can be estimated. Each hen develops 95 relationships, making a total of 4,560 in the flock.

The organization of a group can be described either from the viewpoint of the group as a whole or from that of one individual. In either case, there is a complex network of relationships, with many different relationships between the same pairs. While these relationships may have considerable stability, we should remember that the maintenance of a relationship is an ongoing process, constantly forming and developing.

THE FORMING OF SOCIAL RELATIONSHIPS

The Biological Differentiation of Social Relationships

In vertebrate societies, the social behavior of the individual varies according to age and sex. This determines the basic organization of an animal group, and its systematic analysis was first worked out by C. R. Carpenter in his studies of howling monkeys (1934). Social relationships can be developed between males and females, between females and other females, between males and males, and finally, between each of the two sexes and the young.

There are therefore six possible basic relationships. This fact provides a systematic framework for the description of the social organization of a wild population and its comparison with that of other species. For example, howling monkeys show strong allelomimetic behavior in all adult relationships, and the typical group consists of several adult males and females and their offspring. The male-male relationship is unusual among primates in that it includes little or no fighting, which allows adult males to live closely together. The males do not fight over receptive females, and there is no division of the group into pairs on the basis of special sexual relationships. The female-young relationship includes chiefly care and dependency, but very little of this relationship is exhibited between the males and the young.

By contrast, the gibbons studied under natural conditions by C. R. Carpenter (1940) show a great deal of fighting in both the male-male and female-female relationships. The typical gibbon group consists of a single adult male, a single adult female, and their offspring. A strong sexual relationship is developed between the adult pair, and care-dependency relationships are developed between both parents and the young.

It may be concluded from these and many other examples that social behavior determines the type of social organization developed in any particular relationship (J. P. Scott, 1944). Between the two species of primates above, the differences in social behavior and consequently in social relationships seem to be determined almost entirely by heredity, but training can also be a powerful factor in the determination of a social relationship, as in the following example.

Methods for training male mice to fight and not to fight were developed. Mice which had never fought before were taken out, handled roughly, and then replaced in their boxes with a female. After this had been repeated for several days, two males were placed together in the same box. They did not fight at first but lived together for a period of several weeks without fighting and without developing any relationship based on fighting. The next part of the experiment was to teach mice to fight. Helpless mice were dangled in front of and brushed against other males. Within a few days the other males were vigorously attacking the dangled mice. When two individuals which had been treated in this way were brought together, they began to fight almost at once, and as a result, developed a dominance-subordination relationship. The result confirmed the hypothesis that social behavior determines social organization. When no fighting was present, there was no organization based on fighting, but when fighting was present, dominance appeared (J. P. Scott, 1944).

In this last example the difference in social organization was produced by a difference in training rather than by biological factors. The effect of psychological factors on the development of a social relationship merits discussion in further detail.

The Psychological Differentiation of Behavior: The Dominance-Subordination Relationship

The organization of fighting behavior into a definite social relationship has been thoroughly studied in flocks of hens (Guhl, 1953). When two strange hens meet, they usually begin aggressive behavior after a short period of investigation. A fight follows, with the result that one hen wins and the other runs away. Whenever the two individuals meet thereafter, the hen which won tends to attack, while the one which lost stops resisting sooner and sooner. After several encounters, the winning hen has only to threaten the losing one to make it dodge out of the way. The result is a fully developed dominance-subordination relationship.

If a group of several strange hens is thrown together, each pair will go through the same process, so that the new flock becomes organized into a *peck order*. In some cases there is a straight-line peck order, with the dominant hen at the top pecking everyone beneath and so on down the line. In other cases, the order may not be so clear-cut, with triangles and other relationships possible.

From a psychological point of view, the two strange hens present a problem in social adaptation to each other. Each attempts to drive the other away by fighting, but only one can be successful. The hen which wins the fight has its behavior rewarded by success and forms a habit of fighting or attacking. The losing hen is able partially to avoid punishment by remaining passive and avoiding the other, and it forms a habit of escape and nonresistance. Social relationships formed in this way tend to be extremely stable.

Dominance-subordination relationships can be developed both in natural conditions and in the laboratory. In the latter case, artificial competitive situations can stimulate an unusual amount of fighting behavior and develop relationships not seen elsewhere. Goats, which do not compete for natural food, will fight for grain (J. P. Scott, 1948). Dominance relationships can also become complex. Captive chimpanzees reared in the laboratory will compete for food, and the males will usually dominate females. However, when a female is at the height of sexual receptivity, her male cage mate will allow her to dominate the situation and take the food (Yerkes, 1939).

The dominance-subordination relationship has been studied in most detail, but other social relationships are presumably built up in the same way. A well-developed social relationship of any sort always has certain characteristics: (1) There is some sort of mutual stimulation between individuals; (2) each individual is able to discriminate between others, and (3) the behavior between individuals becomes differentiated either by biological or psychological processes or both.

LOCALITY AND TERRITORIALITY

Locality and Homing

In addition to the process of forming primary social attachments, or socialization, young animals show an even more widespread tendency to form attachments to particular physical localities. Except for animals such as jellyfish, which are passively carried by water currents, the tendency seems to be almost universal in free-living animals. Limpets, which are tiny mollusks of the seashore, attach themselves to particular spots on the rocks between the tide marks. When the tide is high, they move away a few inches, grazing on the algae, but always return to the same spot. The shell grows so that it fits the contours of this particular rock (Russell, 1938).

Among fish, salmon lay their eggs in the headwaters of rivers. The young fish go back to the ocean, where they grow up, and several years later they return as adults to the same rivers where they were hatched. The fish are able to identify the water of a particular river by its chemical composition. In order to get salmon to use a new river system, young fish have to be turned loose in that system (Hasler & Wisby, 1951).

Even more remarkable examples are seen in birds which nest in particular localities and return year after year even though they may have migrated thousands of miles in the meantime (Matthews, 1968). The mating spots of the sage grouse of the western plains are used over and over again for many years and may even continue to be used when a public road is laid through the spot (J. W. Scott, 1942). Similar phenomena are found in many mammals. The white-tailed deer spend most of their lives half a mile or so from where they were born and will not move out of the locality even when the food supply is exhausted. Elk have regular migration routes, going to particular spots in the mountains during the summer and returning to lower altitudes in the winter.

We can therefore conclude that, in addition to socialization, most young animals undergo an analogous process of *localization* (the word is used here in a sense different from that of a sensory localization of an object), in which an attachment is formed to a particular locality. As we have seen, young dogs become attached to places during the first few weeks of life at the same time that they form social attachments.

Localization is, in itself, not a social phenomenon, but it does considerably affect the social life of an animal by determining the individuals with which the animal comes into contact and therefore with which it can develop a social organization of some kind. It also has important effects upon the behavior of animals which are artificially moved away from their native environment. These effects deserve greater study. The end result of localization is that an animal has a particular home range or locality in which it spends most of its normal life.

Territoriality

In addition to their attachment to locality, some species of animals show a more highly social phenomenon, the defense of territory against members of the same species. Territory may coincide with the home range, or it may be smaller. That it can be an important phenomenon was first pointed out by Howard in his study of song and territory in bird life (1920). In the English reed bunting, which has habits somewhat like our red-winged blackbird, the males in early spring take command of certain areas in which they sing and from which they drive away all intruders. The territory defended has fairly definite geographical boundaries and nesting takes place within it. The general effect is to divide up the available breeding territory.

Since Howard's studies were made, territoriality has been firmly established as a common phenomenon in birds (Nice, 1941). Even colonial species like the cliff swallows (Emlen, 1954) have a territory which consists of the nest and the area which the birds can reach from the entrance.

Many mammals do not show definite territoriality (Blair, 1953). Most herd animals, such as deer, live in certain localities but make no effort to drive strangers out of them. Many nocturnal rodents will attack strange animals when they see them but have no effective way of patrolling particular environmental boundaries, so that the typical picture of home ranges in these animals shows many overlapping edges. Prairie dogs (King, 1955) form an exceptional case among rodents. These large ground squirrels are active in the daylight and live in immense colonies. The colony is divided up into definite territories, each of which is usually inhabited by one or two males and several females. If any animal from an adjacent territory crosses the invisible line between them, it is immediately attacked and driven back. When the young in a particular territory have been raised to maturity, the adults move out to the edge of the colony, dig new burrows, and set up a new territory. The result is particularly interesting because it not only protects the young animals but provides for a regular method of colonizing new territories, a difficult process if an animal is rigidly localized. Both locality and territoriality have the effect of limiting the movement and social contacts of animals. In addition, territoriality tends to limit population density, which also has an effect on social behavior.

In general, territoriality is not universal but has been evolved in those species for which it has an adaptive function. Among the primate species, territoriality appears sporadically, ranging from definite defense of small territories in the case of a few small monkeys to complete tolerance of groups within the same area, as in gorillas (Schaller, 1963) and in chimpanzees (Goodall, 1965). The most common situation among the highly social primates, such as the rhesus monkey, is a small core area inhabited exclusively by one group, with a larger home range overlapping that of several others. When two groups meet, they threaten each other and one retreats, indicating that one group is dominant over the other, but there is no defense of boundaries by either.

Territoriality is an effective means of social control and organization only where boundaries can be effectively patrolled. Most cases are therefore found in animals which require small living spaces, which live in open rather than wooded areas (or in the air, as birds do), and which are usually diurnal. The lack of generality of territoriality, in contrast to the almost universal occurrence of locality and home range, is of interest in view of man's alleged "instinct for territoriality" as a cause of destructive violence. Actually, there are wide cultural differences in human territoriality, and any well-organized territorial system among other social animals results in the reduction of agonistic behavior. While there may be some biological basis for territoriality in man, the great variety of territorial systems (or their absence) in different cultures indicates that it is by no means an overwhelmingly important factor in human behavior. As with other animals, the phenomenon of attachment to particular localities is much more fundamental.

SOCIAL COMMUNICATION

From the earliest times men have speculated on the possibility that other animals have some sort of language, and scientists have quite properly assumed that such phenomena are not likely unless proved by scientific means. However, improved methods and patient work have produced evidence that remarkably complex types of animal communication actually exist. One of the most interesting of them is the system of communication in bees described by von Frisch (1950).

If a bait of honey is put out at some distance from a hive, it will eventually be discovered by a foraging bee, which feeds and returns to the hive soon after. Shortly thereafter a large number of others arrive at the bait, and as soon as they have gathered food they fly back to the hive in a "beeline." This is the method that enabled the pioneers to locate a bee tree with its colony of wild bees. It is obvious that the bees have powers of communicating the location of food as well as excellent means of directional orientation.

Von Frisch carefully watched marked bees in a special observation hive as they returned from the baits he had set out. When a foraging bee arrives at the hive, it is at first very active, and the other bees nearby cluster around it. When the bait is close to the hive, the returning bee does a "round dance," running in a small circle, reversing itself, and running back again over the exact same path in the opposite direction (Figure 4-5). This goes on for as long as half a minute, and it conveys the information that the food is less than 100 meters from the hive.

If the bait is further away, the returning bee settles on the honeycomb and does a "wagging dance," which conveys more information (Figure 4-5). Clinging to the vertical wall of the comb, it runs in a short, straight line, wagging its tail. It makes a turn to the left, repeats the wagging movements on the same straight line, turns to the right, and repeats the movements again. The resulting track is a figure 8 with a straight crossbar. The closer the food, the more rapidly the turns are made. The dance also indicates direction with reference to the sun (Figure 4-6). If the straight run is upward, the food is toward the sun; if downward, the food is away from the sun. Furthermore, if the bee's path is not directly up or down, the angle with the perpendicular gives the angle at which the bee must turn away from the sun in order to find the food.

Thus a human observer can read signals that indicate what a bee has done and where it has been as effectively as if they were in human language. There has always been some doubt as to how bees could observe these signals in the normal darkness of the hive, and, on the basis of further experiments, Wenner (1968) finds that the actual process of communication is more complex. In the first place, the returning bee produces pulses of sound during the straight run in the figure 8, and the number of pulses is highly correlated with the distance traveled. The bee also carries with it the odor (usually of a flower) from the food source. Wenner proposes that the dancing, sounds, and odor of a returning bee stimulate others in the hive to go out and forage, but that

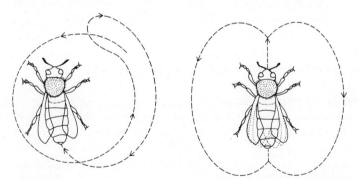

Figure 4–5. The "round dance" (left) and the "wagging dance" (right) of honeybees. The round dance conveys the information that the food is less than 100 meters from the hive. The wagging dance is done when the food is more than 100 meters away. As the bee makes the straight run it wags its abdomen from side to side. (Reprinted from Karl von Frisch: *Bees: Their vision, chemical senses, and language.* Copyright 1950 by Cornell University. Used by permission of Cornell University Press.

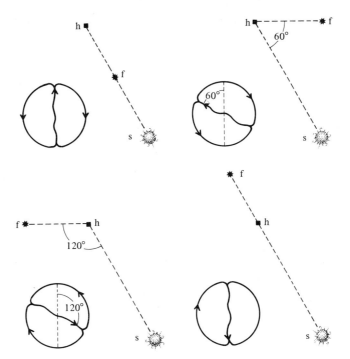

Figure 4–6. This shows how the wagging dance of honeybees indicates the direction of food. Movement straight up means that food is toward the sun; movement straight down means away from the sun. The angle from the vertical, and whether it is to the right or left, indicates the position of the food in relation to the sun. (Reprinted from Karl von Frisch: *Bees: their vision, chemical senses and language.* (Rev. ed.) Copyright 1950, copyright 1971, by Cornell University. Used by permission of Cornell University Press.

the actual method of finding food is to fly downwind from the hive and locate the odor. Furthermore, the experienced foragers (and most of them are experienced at any one time) have a memory of where certain odors occur, and are able to check them after being stimulated. Foraging bees at a particular site leave both their individual and the colony odor, which serves as a further attractant.

This explanation suggests that while animals may produce a great variety of signals, these are not necessarily perceived or understood by their species mates, just as human beings are frequently unable to understand the nonverbal emotional signals of their friends and acquaintances. The test of communication is, of course, to reproduce the signal under experimental conditions and to determine whether an animal responds consistently. This is relatively easy to do with auditory signals. In one of the early studies along these lines, Frings and Jumber (1954) showed that playing a recording of a distress call to starlings would cause flocks to leave the area in apparent fright. Falls (1963) has similarly shown that birds will respond to records of the territorial songs of their neighbors, differentiating between neighboring birds of the same species.

Communication is an essential process for social organization and behavior, since social behavior itself is defined as activity that is either stimulated by, or has an effect upon, another member of the same species. Understanding it is therefore a basic problem in comparative social psychology as well as an interesting phenomenon in its own right.

THE COMPARATIVE STUDY OF ANIMAL SOCIETIES

An animal society may be defined as a group of individuals whose behavior is organized into social relationships. Its form of organization therefore depends upon the kinds of social relationships which receive the most emphasis. These, in turn, depend upon a great many other factors, such as the biological division of labor in the species, the sensory ability to discriminate between different individuals, the psychological capacity to form relationships based on learning, and finally, the motor ability to enter into certain kinds of relationships, particularly those involving the care of offspring. As indicated in previous paragraphs, the kinds of social relationships developed also depend upon the systems of social behavior present in the species.

Aggregations

The vast majority of lower invertebrates have no lasting social groups but frequently come together in temporary aggregations. Most of these groups are based on mutual shelter-seeking behavior which protects the animals from unfavorable conditions. Other temporary aggregations may be based on sexual behavior. In spite of the brief duration and low degree of organization of these groups, they are important in that they probably once provided the basis for evolution of higher degrees of organization (Allee, Park, Emerson, Park, & Schmidt, 1950). Social groups having the function of reproduction develop into groups having highly elaborate social relationships involving the care of the young. Prolonging the period of contact between members of a group provides the basis for the evolution of allelomimetic behavior and the elaborate organization of flocks and herds of higher animals.

Insect Societies

Some degree of social organization is present in many arthropods, but its highest development among invertebrates is seen in insects, whose societies are primarily characterized by great emphasis on care-dependency and mutual-care relationships. The most elaborately organized insect societies occur in the orders Isoptera (termites) and Hymenoptera (ants, bees, and wasps).

The ant may be used as an example (Wheeler, 1923). At the time of the nuptial flight, male and female pairs mate, discard their wings, and dig a small nest. From this time on, the male-female relationship is unimportant. The female can produce two kinds of eggs: fertilized eggs, which develop into females, and unfertilized eggs, which develop into males. The males are produced only at the swarming season. The females are divided into two classes: sterile females, or workers, which establish care-dependency relationships with the developing young, and fertile females, or queens, which are produced only at the time of swarming. The worker females show the complex relationship of trophallaxis, as well as communication through odorous substances, or pheromones (Wilson, 1968). All these relationships seem to be primarily determined by biological means, either heredity or special feeding. However, psychological differentiation is not completely absent, as is shown by the slave-raiding ants. These ants have no workers but steal the young from other species. Developing in the strange nest, the slaves become socialized to their captors, will take care of their offspring, and will drive off members of their own species.

Other types of insects develop more complex social organizations (Allee et al., 1950) with greater differentiation on either a biological or psychological basis. Termites may have several different biologically determined classes of individuals, including soldiers as well as workers, each having a different behavioral function in the nest. In honeybee hives, the worker females do different sorts of tasks in a regular progression as they grow older. However, the insect type of social organization is very different from that in vertebrates, both in the more elaborate biological determination of social relationships and in the greater emphasis on care-dependency relationships at the expense of all others. Furthermore, there is at present no good evidence that either leader-follower or dominance-subordination relationships are important in insect societies.

Vertebrate Societies

There is a great deal of variety in the societies of vertebrates, but all of them show the basic biological differentiation in the behavior of males, females, and young. Among many species of fish, allelomimetic behavior is highly developed and results in the formation of schools. The relationships among different fish in a school are little differentiated, and there is no indication of a leader-follower relationship. A school of fish is very similar to the social group developed by squids, which are marine mollusks and entirely unrelated to fish but which also swim and show allelomimetic behavior. Another social relationship characteristic of many fish is that between the male and the young. Courtship and sexual behavior of a species like the stickleback last but a short time. After this the male remains and guards the nest until the young hatch (Tinbergen, 1953). In this and some other species like the river dogfish (Dean, 1896), the young fish stay with the male for a short period and are guarded by him. The care-dependency relationship in fish is never highly developed, probably because of the poor manipulative abilities of these animals.

Most amphibia show a low degree of social organization. In the breeding season, male frogs sing, attracting the otherwise solitary females, after which the male clasps the female in amplexus, remaining with her until the eggs are laid. Some frogs show mild forms of agonistic behavior and may even guard small territories by jumping on an intruder (Schroeder, 1968; Test, 1954). Among reptiles, the social organization of lizards has been most thoroughly studied (C. C. Carpenter, 1967). These animals, which are the closest living relatives of birds, may develop highly organized territorial systems and, like birds, warn intruders by visual displays and movements, although they have no songs. When forced into groups, they may develop dominance orders. Alligators guard their nests and develop at least some care-dependency relationships. Galapagos tortoises will develop a dominance order when kept in a zoo (Evans & Quaranta, 1949).

A great variety of social organization is found in birds. Like the insect societies, there is a strong emphasis on care-dependency relationships. Unlike the insects, however, birds of both sexes often take part in the care of the young. In a typical society of perching birds, sexual relationships may last over a period of several weeks in the early part of the breeding season, and the same individuals may mate again, year after year. Dominance relationships are important in relation to territory, the resident bird usually being dominant as long as he stays on his home ground. Outside the breeding season, allelomimetic behavior is very important, resulting in the formation of flocks of hundreds and even thousands of individuals.

In many species, flocks show no high degree of differentiation of behavior, but definite leader-follower relationships are found in ducks and geese. There is a strong tendency in most birds to change the type of social organization with the season of the year. During the breeding season, sexual, care-dependency, and dominance relationships are very important. During the rest of the year, these may disappear almost completely, being replaced by a simple allelomimetic relationship in the flocks.

A similar variety of social organization is found among mammals, many of which show seasonal changes similar to those of birds. Rodents emphasize the care-dependency relationship, and a great deal of their social contact takes place within nests. Dominance organization is usually well developed, but as indicated earlier, few species show defense of territory. Aggregations are common in the winter season. The most highly developed rodent societies are found in the ground squirrels, which also show a considerable degree of vocal communication. Rats (Calhoun, 1950) raised under seminatural conditions develop a moderately high degree of organization, emphasizing care-dependency and dominance relationships.

Ruminant animals typically form herds of varying sizes, and there is a great development of social organization based on allelomimetic behavior. In some herds, such as the red deer (Darling, 1937), leader-follower relationships are highly developed. There is some emphasis on the care-dependency relationship between the females and the young, but sexual relationships are of little importance except in the brief breeding season. Dominance organization is important within a herd. These relationships always appear to be individual, and no case of group attacks on an individual has so far been discovered. On the other hand, a mutual defensive relationship is common, and is probably most highly developed in musk oxen.

Those carnivores whose societies have been studied show tendencies toward prolonged sexual relationships, and in some species mating is reported to take place for life. In foxes raised by breeders, it is extremely difficult to get the males to mate with more than one female (Enders, 1945). There is also much greater emphasis on the care-dependency relationship, and many carnivores feed their young for long periods. Capturing prey is a difficult process for a young animal, and in many species, particularly in the cat family, the young seem to learn it from their parents. In any case, there is a long period of dependency. Wolves (Murie, 1944) show much allelomimetic behavior and organization into a pack. The origin of the pack appears to be a litter of several individuals. There is no highly differentiated organization or clear leadership, but members of the group often combine activities, both for attacking prey and for defense against larger predators, such as bears. Dominance relationships are highly developed and are particularly important during feeding.

In recent years our knowledge of primate societies has been broadened out and extended by a number of excellent field studies (DeVore, 1965). The social organization of savanna baboons is of particular interest because their habitat is similar to that of precultural man. These animals travel in permanent groups of twenty-five or thirty individuals, living off grasses and other vegetation and sleeping at night in trees. In the center of the moving group is a dominant male. Spaced out around him are subordinate males, so that the youngest males occupy positions on the outskirts of the group where they are most exposed to danger. When a predator, such as a leopard, is sighted, they give an alarm cry and all the males in the troop rush over and threaten the predator. Females, especially those with young, stay near the center of the group, this being the safest spot. Sexual behavior takes place only when females are in estrus and no permanent consortships are formed. In this species, males do not compete over females, and mating does not necessarily take place only with the dominant male.

The rhesus monkeys of India have a somewhat similar organization that has been extensively studied in groups living under seminatural conditions (Southwick et al., 1965). Females also have a dominance order, which their offspring share. The offspring of any given female tend to associate with her and with their siblings over a period of several years (Sade, 1965), but there are no nuclear family groups of males, females, and young. Social organization in chimpanzees is much looser, with temporary groups being formed and dissolved in the area where the animals live, although there is, of course, a persistent association between mothers and infants. In general, the social organization of primates differs widely from species to species, but where there are large groups including adults of both sexes, the females generally outnumber the males. Contrary to impressions based on zoo animals, sexual and agonistic behavior form only a small proportion of daily activities, with most time being spent in maintenance activities such as finding food and resting (Jay, 1965).

We can conclude that a large variety of social organizations are possible within the same broad taxonomic group. This can be accounted for by various factors, but particularly by the behavior patterns and amounts of social behavior which are determined by the heredity of the species. Equally great variation in social organization is found between broad taxonomic groups. In addition to heredity, the general ecology, or environmental relationships, of a class of animals has strong effects on social organization. The herd mammals typically live under plains conditions and eat vegetable food. There is usually little competition over food, and little skill is required in getting it, so neither dominance nor care-dependency relationships are highly developed, although domestic herds readily develop dominance relations around the feeding trough. The chief problem of these animals is dealing with carnivores, and their highest degree of social organization is centered around escape.

On the other hand, carnivorous mammals depend on a food supply which is widely scattered and often difficult to get, and they are rarely found in large numbers. The nature of their food requires a long period of dependency and learning on the part of the offspring.

Finally, most primates are arboreal and therefore have a special problem of care of the offspring, which are likely to fall out of the trees unless carried and helped. In most species, the young are carried for at least a couple of years, when their motor development has proceeded far enough so that they can move on their own. This care of the young produces a prolonged period of dependency. Some primates are both carnivorous and herbivorous, and they may show tendencies toward group action in both offensive and defensive fighting. In general, primates exhibit greater degrees of social differentiation and variety of social relationships than do other mammals and, hence, develop more complex social organizations.

MAJOR THEORETICAL PROBLEMS

Both descriptive and experimental studies have contributed to the general principles of comparative social psychology. Experimental studies in social psychology are essentially different from those in which the social factor is unimportant. By definition, social behavior involves more than one individual, and in most experiments the basic variable is not individual behavior but the relationship between two or more individuals. This creates many special problems of procedure.

There are two major groups of experimental problems in social behavior. One of them concerns the effects of social behavior upon social organizations, and on a higher level, upon the organization of populations. This type of research has already been illustrated in the studies of peck orders, the processes of socialization, and the phenomena of locality and territoriality. The second kind of investigation concerns the causes of social behavior, which may be hereditary, physiological, and environmental, and includes the process of learning. One basic problem is whether the general principles of learning, which have been developed so largely from experiments with ingestive behavior, will apply to other forms of social behavior as well. A second question relates to the ways in which hereditary factors produce their effects on social behavior. A third consists of tracing the complex network of physiological causes which affect each system of behavior.

A major theoretical problem concerns the origin of social motivation. There are, of course, specific motivations connected with every major system of social behavior. Unfortunately, scientists have rarely studied any but two or three of them—food, fear, and pain, and, to a lesser extent, sexual motivation. An example of a more general type of social motivation arises out of the study of the attachment process in the dog. There is a built-in emotional reinforcement mechanism which has the effect of punishing the young puppy (through the arousal of emotional distress) whenever it is separated from familiar individuals and rewarding it when it rejoins them. This not only produces an attachment but also develops the motivation for the puppy to stay with the object of attachment. This motivation acts reciprocally in a group of dogs and has the effect of producing allelomimetic behavior (J. P. Scott, 1967). In order to stay with the others, each dog has to follow the others' movements. Waller and Fuller (1961) and Stanley and Elliot (1962) have demonstrated that this kind of motivation has the properties of a general social drive.

This kind of motivation is related to the general phenomenon of social facilitation (Simmel, Hoppe, & Milton, 1968). Animals which show allelomimetic behavior, such as monkeys (Harlow & Yudin, 1933), puppies (Ross & Ross, 1949; Compton & Scott, 1971), fish (Welty, 1934), and chickens (Tolman, 1968) will eat more in the presence of others than when fed alone, even when there is no competition. Other factors that may produce social facilitation are stimulation or arousal by other members of the group, and reduction of fear. Either of these may be effective in nonallelomimetic animals as well as in species, like the dog, that are strongly motivated to maintain group contacts and to do as the other animals do (J. P. Scott, 1968b).

Another set of problems concerns the nature of social organization and relationship theory. The only social relationships that have been studied in great detail are those of dominance-subordination, and a great deal more information is needed concerning those of leadership, care-dependency, and the like.

A fascinating theoretical problem is that of the evolution of social behavior and organization. As an example, we may take the problem of the evolution of agonistic behavior. Biologists have long since given up the simplistic notions that either the behavior or the structure of nonhuman animal species represents stages in evolution toward the human condition. Rather, each species evolves independently and has diverged in a multitude of different pathways. The evolution of agonistic behavior is no exception.

One hypothesis, that agonistic behavior has developed from predation (and hence that man kills man because he is a bloodthirsty hunter), must be discarded at the outset. Agonistic behavior is well developed in completely herbivorous animals like deer, sheep, and cattle (Eibl-Eibesfeldt, 1967). In carnivorous predators like wolves, the patterns of behavior exhibited in social fighting are quite different from those employed in killing a prey animal, and they ordinarily result in little harm to the combatants. In most forms of social contact, the inhibited bite is a feature of dog and wolf behavior. In serious fights, each animal tries to seize the other by the back of the neck, a spot ordinarily protected by long hair and a thick skin, and force it to the ground, rather than snap at the legs or other vital parts as it would with a prey animal. In general, agonistic behavior is most likely to have developed from defensive fighting, such as is seen in the fear biting of dogs or cornered rats, since such patterns of behavior are found almost universally and are adaptive against predators as well as against accidental injury by species mates (J. P. Scott, 1970). Furthermore, there is a general tendency for agonistic behavior to evolve toward relatively harmless forms having specific adaptive functions. These functions may differ greatly from species to species as well as in degree of severity. For example, the agonistic behavior of the prairie dog, a highly colonial ground squirrel in the western United States, is organized around a territorial system, and is reduced to chasing, flight, and signaling at the boundaries. On the other hand, the woodchuck, a largely solitary rodent of meadow lands in the eastern part of the country, is highly aggressive. No two woodchucks will tolerate each other's close presence except briefly during the mating season and the rearing of the young. Consequently, the animals are spaced out as widely as possible, and they exert a constant pressure on one another to move into new areas. While there is a high incidence of enlarged adrenals and heart disease in this species, it is still a very successful one and woodchucks are in no danger of extinction (Bronson, 1964).

Related species usually have similar patterns of social behavior. Dogs and wolves show almost identical patterns of behavior, with a few exceptions, and one of the prominent features of the agonistic behavior of these highly social animals is patterns indicating dominance and subordination (Scott & Fuller, 1965). In the more distantly related foxes, whose typical social group is a single mated pair, most of the same patterns of agonistic behavior can be found, with the notable exception of those functioning in dominance and subordination (Tembrock, 1957).

The occurrence of destructive violence involving serious injury or death is rare in a well-organized animal society living under the natural conditions to which it is adapted. Outbreaks of destructive behavior occur principally because of social disorganization through the introduction of strangers or the removal of key individuals by death from accident or disease (J. P. Scott, 1962). Certain kinds of disorganization can result from natural or artificial catastrophes which alter the spatial arrangements of an animal society. This kind of disorganization is one of the major results of keeping wild animals in captivity.

Finally, social selection is a major and powerful part of selection pressure exerted by environmental conditions. Of all environmental factors, the social environment is least likely to change from generation to generation. Hence, social selection tends to produce stability, and because a stable environment is the only one for which a stereotyped pattern of behavior is adaptive, the major examples of fixed action patterns usually labeled as instincts come from social behavior.

SUMMARY

There is still a dearth of factual material regarding the social behavior of animals. This short chapter has surveyed basic methods of study, the kinds of phenomena which occur in social behavior, and the general principles which explain them. Both facts and principles need to be studied in many other species.

The primary method of investigating social behavior and organization is observational, used preferably in a natural environment and in a naturally formed group of animals. Only in this way can the full expression of social capabilities be observed. An essential part of observation is recognition of individuals, and since behavior varies with environmental and internal changes, observations should cover both the daily and seasonal cycles and the development of behavior. Once the basic facts have been obtained in this way, experimental studies can follow. One of the basic experimental methods is the measurement of the reaction of pairs of individuals to each other in various situations.

Observation reveals many sorts of social phenomena. Animals show nine important systems of behavioral adaptation, each of which may have at least some social significance. Each species has characteristic patterns of social behavior through which it meets its problems of adaptation, and these patterns can be used as a systematic method of describing the social life of a species and comparing it with others. A second phenomenon is the social relationship, the tendency for animals to exhibit regular and predictable behavior toward one another. These relationships result from the organization of the basic patterns of social behavior. Each species has a limited number of important relationships; often only one or two of them are emphasized. A third phenomenon is that of socialization. Every social species has certain behavioral mechanisms whereby, early in life, an individual forms attachments with a few members of its own species and is normally prevented from forming such attachments with strange individuals and members of other species. The behavioral mechanisms differ from species to species, and some are much more flexible than others. Finally, almost all animals show an analogous phenomenon, that of localization. Early in life they become attached to particular localities and live in or around them as a home range. Under special conditions which usually include the sensory ability to recognize a boundary and the ability to fight, these localities may be defended as territories.

These phenomena may be explained and defined by several important general principles. One is that the essential differences among animal societies are based on hereditary differences in form and function which limit the kinds of behavior and social organization that are likely to be manifested by the species. This is the genetic basis of social behavior. On the other hand, social behavior is also affected by the kind of environmental situation in which the group of animals is placed and to which its members must adapt. This is the ecological basis of social behavior. Finally, their behavior is modified by previous experiences through the process of learning, and this is the psychological basis of social behavior.

The formation of a social relationship is a process of differentiation involving biological growth on the one hand and the psychological phenomenon of learning on the other. One of the principal classes of determinants of a relationship includes the basic capacities for exhibiting different patterns of social behavior. Another is the process of learning, in which the two individuals adjust to each other's behavior. Some species may have social relationships determined almost entirely by biological factors, but in the higher animals the factor of learning is always an important one. In general, the degree of social organization depends on the degree of differentiation of behavior produced by the combined action of biological and psychological factors.

Each animal society has some characteristic process of socialization whereby primary social relationships are determined. In most societies, this takes place in a limited period early in life, which may be described as a critical period for the formation of social relationships. What happens in this period determines the individuals to which an animal becomes related and, under experimental conditions, even the species with which these relationships are formed.

With all these factors affecting the behavior of individuals, it follows that their behavior can be completely understood only in terms of the animal societies to which they belong. An experiment on animal behavior is not performed in a social vacuum. Even when an animal is completely isolated, its very isolation may contribute to its behavior. In this way many of the hitherto mysterious aspects of animal behavior are now becoming understood.

The study of comparative social behavior involves all the phenomena ordinarily analyzed in psychology: the factors of heredity, sensory abilities, learning, motivation, and so on, which are described in other chapters of this book. Hereditary factors determine an animal's capability of social behavior, and social relationships may be differentiated through learning. Each of the different systems of social behavior presents problems in the origin of motivation. In addition, the fact of social organization results in certain new phenomena, such as social relationships, which in turn affect the behavior of individuals. The phenomenon of socialization affects the behavior of most experimental animals used in the laboratory, and it is obvious that the quality of the social relationships formed during the critical period has an important influence on the rest of the animal's life.

REFERENCES

ALLEE, W. C. *Animal aggregations: A study in general sociology.* Chicago: The University of Chicago Press, 1931.

ALLEE, W. C., PARK, O., EMERSON, A. E., PARK, T., & SCHMIDT, K. P. *Principles of animal ecology.* Philadelphia: Saunders, 1950.

BLAIR, W. F. Population dynamics of rodents and other small mammals. *Recent Advances in Genetics,* 1953, **5,** 1–41.

BRONSON, F. H. Agonistic behavior in woodchucks. *Animal Behaviour,* 1964, **12,** 470–478.

CAIRNS, R. B., & WERBOFF, J. Behavior development in the dog: An interspecific analysis. *Science,* 1967, **158,** 1070–1072.

CALHOUN, J. B. The study of wild animals under controlled conditions. *Annals of the New York Academy of Sciences,* 1950, **51,** 1113–1122.

CARPENTER, C. C. Aggression and social structure in iguanid lizards. In W. W. Milstead (Ed.), *Lizard ecology, a symposium.* Columbia: University of Missouri Press, 1967. Pp. 87–105.

CARPENTER, C. R. A field study of the behavior and social relations of howling monkeys. *Comparative Psychology Monographs*, 1934, **10**(2), 1–168.

CARPENTER, C. R. A field study in Siam of the behavior and social relations of the gibbon *(Hylobates lar)*. *Comparative Psychology Monographs*, 1940, **16**(5), 1–205.

COLLIAS, N. E. Aggressive behavior among vertebrate animals. *Physiological Zoology*, 1944, **17**, 83–123.

COMPTON, J. M., & SCOTT, J. P. Allelomimetic behavior in dogs; distress vocalization and social facilitation of feeding in Telomian dogs. *Journal of Psychology*, 1971, **78**, 165–179.

DARLING. F. F. *A herd of red deer*. London: Oxford University Press, 1937.

DEAN, B. The early development of *Amia. Quarterly Journal of Microscopic Science*, 1896, **38**, 413–444.

DEVORE, I. (Ed.). *Primate behavior*. New York: Holt, Rinehart and Winston, 1965.

EIBL-EIBESFELDT, I. Ontogenetic and maturational studies of aggressive behavior. In C. D. Clemente & D. B. Lindsley (Eds.), *Aggression and defense: Neural mechanisms and social patterns*. Los Angeles: University of California Press, 1967. Pp. 57–94.

ELLIOTT, O., & SCOTT, J. P. The development of emotional distress reactions to separation in puppies. *Journal of Genetic Psychology*, 1961, **99**, 3–22.

EMLEN, J. T. Territory, nest building, and pair formation in the cliff swallow. *Auk*, 1954, **71**, 16–35.

ENDERS, R. K. Induced changes in the breeding habits of foxes. *Sociometry*, 1945, **8**, 53–55.

EVANS, L. T., & QUARANTA, J. Patterns of cooperative behavior in a herd of 14 giant tortoises of the Bronx Zoo. *Anatomical Record*, 1949, **105**, 506.

FALLS, J. B. Properties of bird song eliciting responses from territorial males. *Proceedings of the 13th International Ornithological Congress*, 1963, 259–271.

FLEENER, D. E., & CAIRNS, R. B. Attachment behavior in human infants: Discriminative vocalization on maternal separation. *Developmental Psychology*, 1970, **2**, 215–233.

FREEDMAN, D. G., KING, J. A., & ELLIOT, O. Critical period in the social development of dogs. *Science*, 1961, **133**, 1016–17.

FRINGS, H., & JUMBER, J. Preliminary studies on the use of specific sounds to repel starlings *(Sturnus vulgaris)* from objectionable roosts. *Science*, 1954, **119**, 318–319.

FRISCH, K. VON. *Bees, their vision, chemical senses, and language*. Ithaca, N. Y.: Cornell University Press, 1950.

FULLER, J. L. Experiential deprivation and later behavior. *Science*, 1967, **158**, 1645–1652.

FULLER, J. L., & CLARK, L. D. Genetic and treatment factors modifying the post-isolation syndrome in dogs. *Journal of Comparative and Physiological Psychology*, 1966, **61**, 251–257. (a)

FULLER, J. L., & CLARK, L. D. Effects of rearing with specific stimuli upon post-isolation behavior in dogs. *Journal of Comparative and Physiological Psychology*, 1966, **61**, 258–263. (b)

GOODALL, J. Chimpanzees of the Gombe Stream Reserve. In I. DeVore (Ed.), *Primate behavior*. New York: Holt, Rinehart and Winston, 1965. Pp. 368–424.

GUHL, A. M. Social behavior of the domestic fowl. *Kansas State College Agricultural Experiment Station Technical Bulletin*, 1953, No. 73.

HARLOW, H. F., & YUDIN, H. C. Social behavior of primates. I. Social facilitation of feeding in the monkey and its relation to attitudes of ascendance and submission. *Journal of Comparative Psychology*, 1933, **16**, 171–185.

HASLER, A. D., & WISBY, W. J. Discrimination of stream odors by fishes and its relation to parent stream behavior. *American Naturalist*, 1951, **85**, 223–238.

HESS, E. H. Imprinting in birds. *Science,* 1964, **146,** 1128–1139.

HOWARD, E. *Territory in bird life.* London: J. Murray, 1920.

JAY, P. The common langur of North India. In I. DeVore (Ed.), *Primate behavior.* New York: Holt, Rinehart and Winston, 1965. Pp. 197–249.

KING, J. A. Social behavior, social organization, and population dynamics in a black-tailed prairiedog town in the Black Hills of South Dakota. *Contributions from the Laboratory of Vertebrate Biology.* Ann Arbor: University of Michigan, 1955, No. 67.

KLINGHAMMER, E. Factors influencing choice of mate in altricial birds. In H. W. Stevenson, E. H. Hess, & H. L. Rheingold (Eds.), *Early behavior.* New York: Wiley, 1967. Pp. 5–42.

LORENZ, K. Der Kumpan in der Umwelt des Vogels. *Journal für Ornithologie,* 1935, **83,** 137–213, 289–413.

MATTHEWS, G. V. T. *Bird navigation.* (3rd ed.) London: Cambridge University Press, 1968.

MECH, L. D. The wolves of Isle Royale. *Fauna of the National Parks of the United States, Fauna Series 7.* Washington: Government Printing Office, 1966.

MOLTZ, H. Imprinting: Empirical basis and theoretical significance. *Psychological Bulletin,* 1960, **57,** 291–314.

MURIE, A. The wolves of Mt. McKinley. *U.S. Department of the Interior Fauna Series No. 5.* Washington: Government Printing Office, 1944.

NICE, M. M. The role of territory in bird life. *American Midland Naturalist,* 1941, **26,** 441–487.

RABB, G. B., WOOLPY, J. H., & GINSBURG, B. E. Social relationships in a group of captive wolves. *American Zoologist,* 1967, **7,** 305–312.

ROSS, S., & ROSS, J. G. Social facilitation of feeding behavior of dogs. *Journal of Genetic Psychology,* 1949, **74,** 97–108.

RUSSELL, E. S. *The behaviour of animals.* (2nd ed.) London: E. Arnold, 1938.

SADE, D. S. Some aspects of parent offspring and sibling relations in a group of rhesus monkeys, with a discussion of grooming. *American Journal of Physical Anthropology,* 1965, **23,** 1–18.

SCHAFFER, H. R. Objective observations of personality development in early infancy. *British Journal of Medical Psychology,* 1958, **31,** 174–183.

SCHALLER, G. B. *The mountain gorilla.* Chicago: The University of Chicago Press, 1963.

SCHEIN, M. W., & HALE, E. B. *Meleagris gallopavo* (Meleagridae); Sexual behaviour patterns. *Encyclopedia Cinematographica E359/1961.* Gottingen: Institut für den Wissenschaftlichen Film, 1961.

SCHJELDERUP-EBBE, T. Beitrage zur Sozial-psychologie des Haushuhns. *Zeitschrift für Psychologie,* 1922, **88,** 225–252.

SCHROEDER, E. E. Aggressive behavior in *Rana clamitans. Journal of Herpetology,* 1968, **1,** 95–96.

SCOTT, J. P. An experimental test of the theory that social behavior determines social organization. *Science,* 1944, **99,** 42–43.

SCOTT, J. P. Social behavior, organization, and leadership in a small flock of domestic sheep. *Comparative Psychology Monographs,* 1945, **18**(4), 1–29.

SCOTT, J. P. Dominance and the frustration-aggression hypothesis. *Physiological Zoology,* 1948, **21,** 31–39.

SCOTT, J. P. Implications of infra-human social behavior for problems of human relations, In M. Sherif & M. O. Wilson (Eds.), *Group relations at the crossroads.* New York: Harper, 1953. Chap. 2. Pp. 33–73.

SCOTT, J. P. Hostility and aggression in animals. In E. L. Bliss (Ed.), *Roots of behavior.* New York: Harper & Row, 1962. Pp. 167–178.

SCOTT, J. P. The process of primary socialization in canine and human infants. *Society for Research in Child Development Monographs,* 1963, **28**(1), 1–47.

SCOTT, J. P. The development of social motivation. In D. Levine (Ed.), *Nebraska Symposium on Motivation.* Lincoln: University of Nebraska Press, 1967. Pp. 111–133.

SCOTT, J. P. The process of primary socialization in the dog. In G. Newton & S. Levine (Eds.), *Early experience and behaviour.* Springfield, Ill.: A. H. Thomas, 1968. Chap. 13. Pp. 412–439. (a)

SCOTT, J. P. Social facilitation and allelomimetic behavior. In E. C. Simmel, R. A. Hoppe, & G. A. Milton (Eds.), *Social facilitation and imitative behavior.* Boston: Allyn & Bacon, 1968. Pp. 55–72. (b)

SCOTT, J. P. Biology and human aggression. *Journal of Orthopsychiatry,* 1970, **40**(4), 568–576.

SCOTT, J. P., & FULLER, J. L. *Genetics and the social behavior of the dog.* Chicago: The University of Chicago Press, 1965.

SCOTT, J. W. Mating behavior of the sage grouse. *Auk,* 1942, **59,** 477–498.

SIMMEL, E. C., HOPPE, R. A., & MILTON, G. A. (Eds.). *Social facilitation and imitative behavior.* Boston: Allyn & Bacon, 1968.

SOUTHWICK, C. H., BEG, M. A., & SIDDIQUI, M. R. Rhesus monkeys in North India. In I. DeVore (Ed.), *Primate behavior.* New York: Holt, Rinehart and Winston, 1965. Pp. 111–159.

STANLEY, W. C., BACON, W. E., & FEHR, C. Discriminated instrumental learning in neonatal dogs. *Journal of Comparative and Physiological Psychology,* 1970, **70,** 335–343.

STANLEY, W. C., & ELLIOT, O. Differential human handling as reinforcing events and as treatments influencing later social behavior in basenji puppies. *Psychological Reports,* 1962, **10,** 775–788.

STEWART, J. C., & SCOTT, J. P. Lack of correlation between leadership and dominance relationships in a herd of goats. *Journal of Comparative and Physiological Psychology,* 1947, **40,** 255–264.

TEMBROCK, G. Zur Ethologie des Rotfuchses (*Vulpes vulpes L.*) under besonderer Berücksichtingung der Fortpflanzung. *Zoologischer Garten,* 1957, **23,** 289–532.

TEST, F. H. Social aggressiveness in an amphibian. *Science,* 1954, **120,** 140–141.

THEBERGE, J. B., & FALLS, J. B. Howling as a means of communication in timber wolves. *American Zoologist,* 1967, **7,** 331–338.

THEBERGE, J. B., & PIMLOTT, D. H. Observations of wolves at a rendezvous site in Algonquin Park. *Canadian Field Naturalist,* 1969, **83,** 122–128.

THOMPSON, W. R., & MELZACK, R. Early environment. *Scientific American,* 1956, **194,** 38–42.

TINBERGEN, N. *Social behaviour in animals.* London: Methuen, 1953.

TOLMAN, C. W. The role of the companion in social facilitation of animal behavior. In E. C. Simmel, R. A. Hoppe, & G. A. Milton (Eds.), *Social facilitation and imitative behavior.* Boston: Allyn & Bacon, 1968. Pp. 33–54.

WALLER, M. B., & FULLER, J. L. Preliminary observations on early experience as related to social behavior. *American Journal of Orthopsychiatry,* 1961, **31,** 254–266.

WELTY, J. C. Experiments in group behavior of fishes. *Physiological Zoology,* 1934, **7,** 85–128.

WENNER, A. M. Honey bees. In T. A. Sebeok (Ed.), *Animal communication.* Bloomington: Indiana University Press, 1968. Pp. 217–243.

WHEELER, W. M. *Social life among the insects.* New York: Harcourt, Brace, 1923.

WILSON, E. O. Chemical systems. In T. A. Sebeok (Ed.), *Animal communication.* Bloomington: Indiana University Press, 1968. Pp. 75–102.

YERKES, R. M. Social dominance and sexual status in the chimpanzee. *Quarterly Review of Biology,* 1939, **14,** 115–136.

Chapter 5

Animal Communication

Kurt Salzinger

The object of this chapter is to present a rather brief description of some systems of communication which different animals use, to discuss the current place of animal communication in the relatively new area of psycholinguistics, to describe the contribution which behavior theory can make to the area of animal communication, and finally, to review some experiments in the conditioning of communicative responses in different animals as a basis for a comparative psychology of communication.

DIFFERENT SYSTEMS OF COMMUNICATION

In a description of methods of observation of animal communication, Scott (1968) suggested a convenient way of classifying types of communication by the sense organs involved, namely, visual, auditory, chemical, and tactile. Of these, the last is most restricted in usefulness, but tactile communication is important in the context of social and sexual behavior even among animals that otherwise communicate by way of different modalities. Tactile types of communication are difficult to observe, and therefore we know least about this form of communication.

Visual signals are quite commonplace. They vary from particular behavior patterns, such as running toward another animal or doing a complicated dance as in the bee (von Frisch, 1950), to the adoption of special postures, such as the aggressive display in gulls in which the head is held high, thereby increasing apparent size (Marler, 1968). They also include the special visual signals of the firefly (Alexander, 1968). The male firefly flies around flashing until a female firefly below responds. After one to ten flash exchanges, the flight terminates a few centimeters from the female. Then the male fly approaches the female, exchanging flashes all the while, and ultimately mounts her.

Auditory signals are very well known, since they occur in a variety of species including such diverse animals as fishes, insects, porpoises, rodents, and primates. Among the more interesting types of sound-producing mechanisms are those employed by male spiders of some species as they approach the nearsighted but larger and more aggressive females in the web. In order to avoid being attacked, if not devoured, the male spider must pluck the strings of the web in such a way as to signal that he is friend, not foe (Frings & Frings, 1968). Frings and Frings report mechanical signaling in land leeches; apparently, a male leech approaches a female leech that is tapping on a leaf, sets up a duet with her, and ultimately goes on to copulate.

Although chemical systems of communication in dogs, as mediated through the sense of smell, are well known to us, chemical signals are significant in a great variety of other animals, particularly among insects. Pheromones, which is what the chemical signals are called, serve to attract mates, to alarm other members of the group, to mark territory, to help in the identification of the animal's group and rank, to communicate the location of food, and even to alter the physiology of reproduction (Wilson, 1968). Sex pheromones have been found in crustaceans, fish, salamanders, and mammals. Even barnacles have chemical signals which influence cyprid larvae of the same species. When the larvae are prevented from responding appropriately, the barnacles do not settle.

These descriptions of communicative responses are based on the work of ethologists whose approach is founded mainly on Darwin's principle of adaptation. In other words, a primary question is that of the role a particular pattern of behavior plays in survival. From this point of view, communicative responses were found to be critical for such ends as attracting a mate, finding a food source for the group, and escaping from a potential predator. This kind of research is based chiefly upon observation of the behavior under "natural" conditions. It assumes that the behavior studied is of obvious importance to the animal, since otherwise it would not occur with sufficient frequency to be noticed. On the other hand, the so-called artificial behavior found in the laboratory under experimental conditions may deal with atypical and even trivial behavior and thus lead to no significant results. The disadvantage of the ethological approach, however, lies in the fact that observation without experimental intrusion yields only correlations between events and behaviors, and we know that mere association does not prove causal relation.

An example of the difficulties to which the purely observational approach may lead is described by Wenner (1968) in relation to honeybees. The theory of communication among bees by means of the waggle dance is based on the correlation between measures of selected aspects of the dance and the subsequent behavior of the recruited bees that find their way to the food source. There are two findings which question this theory. The first is that regular visitors to a food site leave a characteristic odor at the site which is recognizable by other members of the hive but not by strangers. The second is that bees are apparently easily conditionable to come to a food site simply on the basis of the characteristic food odor which the foraging bee picked up at the food site. This conditioned stimulus then elicits the flight behavior from those bees who have been exposed to that distinctive food-source odor at an earlier time. Only the inexperienced (not yet conditioned) bees respond both to the dance motions and to the sounds which the experienced bees produce, that is, they leave the hive in response to these *alerting* stimuli, finding their way to the hive by odor stimuli produced by the experienced bees and left at the food site for the inexperienced bees to recognize. Although the results on bee communication are far from all in (an experiment by Gould, Henerey, and MacLeod (1970) showed that, under some conditions, directional information can be communicated by the dance but they failed to rule out the possibility that odor stimuli alone might convey the same information under other conditions), it is obvious that the earlier very interesting studies of bee communication did fall prey to the error of deducing causal conclusions from correlational observations.

WHAT IS COMMUNICATION?

The definition of communication to be used for the purpose of comparative psychology must be broad enough to allow its study not only in accordance with the concept of the homologue (behavioral similarities in animals having a common ancestor) but also in terms of the concept of the analogue (behavioral similarities based upon considerations of commonality of function rather than structure). The tracing of homologues will provide us with information on the evolution of communication. On the other hand, the use of analogues allows us, as pointed out by Nottebohm (1970), to separate the variables associated with communication in a causal manner from those associated in a noncausal manner. From this point of view, it becomes useful to indicate, as Tavolga (1968) did, that communication can be viewed in terms of level. In the first, the *vegetative* level, one organism influences another merely by being there, as is true in the interaction of plants. In the second, the *tonic* level, chemical exudates, as by-products of normal metabolism and basic locomotor and color patterns which occur as episodic processes in the animals, may nevertheless influence other animals. The third level, called *phasic*, consists of discontinuous types of responses such as the emission of odors, dances, and sounds by returning forager bees. The responses which act as stimuli for other bees in this context are typically multichannel. The fourth level of communication, *signal*, consists of single-channel outputs where the signal is biologically determined and produced through specialized structures; examples include the pheromones in some insects, sounds produced by cicadas, and color patterns found in birds. The fifth level is called *symbolic*, and it refers to the types of responses made by nonhuman primates in the form of gestures, facial expressions, and vocalizations. Finally, the sixth level is referred to as *language*, and it is confined by Tavolga to human beings. Tavolga further urges that the use of the word "communication" be restricted to the last three levels only. While this restriction is in fact followed in most cases in this chapter, it is clearly not useful or practical to adhere to it in all cases. In any event, the Tavolga-level classification shows that one can think of a continuum of complexity or sophistication of communication. The more primitive types of communication make possible the investigation of communication with less fear of confounding the variables which abound in the more sophisticated forms.

THE PLACE OF ANIMAL COMMUNICATION IN PSYCHOLINGUISTICS

For many years, psychologists' major interest in communication took the form of doing nonsense-syllable experiments. In their avid pursuit of a single methodology, they appeared to remove themselves ever further from explanation of the variables which control the emission of verbal behavior in communication and even in problem solving. More recently, however, there has been a resurgence of interest, stimulated by Miller's (1962) translation of Chomsky's (1957) generative model of grammar. New journals and many books devoted to the study of language have appeared in response to the new linkage between psychology and linguistics, eventually resulting in the term *psycholinguistics*. The marriage between psychology and linguistics replaced the old bond of behaviorism between the partners, with the "freer theorizing" about such concepts as the *language acquisition device*. This was, of course, an attempt to speculate about the inside of the black box, which had been rejected by both behaviorists and linguists of old. No attempt will be made here to go into the pros and cons of the generative model of grammar, but one aspect of it is very pertinent to our discussion.

In 1965, when George Miller formulated a number of basic principles which he felt had to be adhered to in order to make a contribution to the field of psycholinguistics, he stated that the study of animal language was likely to contribute no more than 1 percent of the knowledge necessary for an understanding of human language. This kind of statement is based upon the contention of investigators, such as Lenneberg (1967), who claim that the processes by which language is realized are "deeply-rooted, species-specific, innate properties of man's biological nature [p. 394].'' Lenneberg goes on, further, to reject as not heuristic the study of communication systems in animals now extant, saying that ''no living animal represents a direct primitive ancestor of our own kind and, therefore, there is no reason to believe that any one of *their* traits is a primitive form of any one of *our* traits [pp. 234-235].'' He rejects the notion that vocalization is very important in the study of communication, contending that it is our cognitive processes, entailing categorization, which are basic for the acquisition of language as man uses it. Animals, he asserts, have languages based upon other considerations, such as territoriality and courting behavior.

Despite this minimizing of the role of vocalizing in language, it is difficult to conceive of any other function besides language that animal vocalization (other than sonar) might have. The antipathy toward examining the forms of communication in animals as precursors to human communication is, oddly enough, paired with a belief that human language is, to a great extent, biologically determined, so that the process of acquisition is given a very minor place in the analysis of language. It is particularly ironic that the depreciation of learning in language comes at a time when the power of learning to analyze and control is increasingly being shown in man and animal. A notion, now current among followers of the generative model approach (e.g., McNeill, 1966), is the aforementioned language acquisition device (LAD). This device is said to contain ''templates,'' the purpose of which is to fiter the speech of parents so as to extract the underlying grammar which the child assays through his innate appreciation of the universal categories of language. From my own much more behavioristic point of view, I sometimes think of this concept as ''LAG,'' that is, a language acquisition gremlin, for the concept appears to have simply moved the problem of the acquisition of language from the child to a little man inside the child. The difference between the child and the gremlin is that the former can behave and his behavior can be monitored, while the latter can only be speculated about.

In contrast to Miller's assertion, the contention here is that the study of communicative behavior in animals can serve to elucidate the problem of language in human beings. The importance of the study of animal language for its own sake is obvious enough to require no special justification here.

The significance of the study of animal language for understanding human language lies in the following:

1. The law of parsimony is more easily followed when examining simple rather than complex behavior. In fact, the reason often given for neglecting animal language, namely, its simplicity, is the very quality which produces testable models for studying human verbal behavior. Furthermore, it tends to minimize subjective elements in the model, since scientists are less likely to anthropomorphize than to emphathize.

2. The theory of evolution, which has, of course, served as a unifying factor for many aspects of biology, including ethology, could help in providing

students of language with the appropriate extrapolatory statements for generalizing correctly from findings in animal communication to hypotheses and data in human verbal behavior. Hockett (1963) has shown the importance of examining animal communication systems for the problem of discovering the universal features in human communication. A better understanding of animal communication can also shed light on the theory of evolution, and although most of the data must obviously come from examination of current species, anatomical examination of the speech mechanisms of current and past animals can shed further light on the problem.

3. Perhaps the most important reason for studying animal communication is the one most often given for using animals generally: the greater degree of experimental control which can be exerted over animals than over man. Such control allows for the utilization of physiological, biochemical, neurosurgical, and genetic intervention, as well as extreme modification of the environmental conditions involved in the acquisition of verbal behavior.

Despite these cogent reasons for studying animal language, its application to the study of human verbal behavior has been retarded by much controversy and philosophical discussion concerning the definition of language, as indicated above. Perhaps the most useful treatment of whether animals are capable of language comes from the fruitful restatement of the problem by Hockett (1959, 1960a, 1960b, 1963) in terms of what (rather than whether) properties of human language are within the capabilities of different animals. These properties are listed here, together with comments on them:

1. *Vocal-auditory channel*   Many animals use channels of communication other than the vocal-auditory one (e.g., bee dancing, ant odor trails, spider "web-plucking"). Furthermore, in some animals (e.g., crickets) the channel is auditory but not vocal. One of the advantages of the vocal-auditory system of communication, however, is that it leaves the primate's hands and other potential communicating parts of the body free for other activities. It is also, of course, an example of remote control, keeping pace with the development of the distance receptors. That this channel of communication is not essential for the definition of human language, however, is obvious, as soon as one assays the other channels used by human beings (writing, for example, or sign language in the deaf and dumb, or the even more extreme constriction of communication channels, as in Helen Keller's case).

2. *Broadcast transmission and directional reception*   These two aspects of communication result directly from the first property but are inherent in any sound-communication system. The fact that sounds are broadcast can, of course, allow enemies to receive messages which are intended for friends. The survival value of this aspect of communication will be referred to again when we discuss the conditionability of vocalization in various animals. The property of directional reception makes it possible for an animal to transmit information about location without having to include it as an explicit part of the message; for example, a food call made by a gibbon merely states

that food is available, while the property of directional reception provides the receiving animal with the information about the location of the food.

3. *Rapid fading*   Sound production has the property of fading in a short time, thus making it possible to send a new message immediately after the old. This property does not exist, of course, in information transmission by trails or spoors, which fade slowly. It also distinguishes auditory from olfactory signals, which have the disadvantage of being propagated slowly over any distance. Finally, the possible disadvantage of fading can be overcome by repetitive transmission.

4. *Interchangeability*   Adult human beings can generally reproduce any message they can understand. Among animals, there are many exceptions to this rule, such as the specialized calls of males and females. Hockett recognizes many exceptions among humans but considers them marginal.

5. *Complete feedback*   The human sender both sends and hears the message. The stickleback's courtship dance, on the other hand, receives feedback only in terms of the other stickleback's actions. The property of complete feedback, along with interchangeability, is the combination necessary for planning future behavior. The importance of feedback to the organism can be demonstrated by delaying it (Yates, 1963), or by observing a deaf person's speech. In the former, speech is disturbed; in the latter, its acquisition is severely attenuated and the resultant speech is often hard to understand. Although auditory feedback during vocalization is supplemented by kinesthetic and proprioceptive feedback, there is no proprioceptive feedback from the larynx, thus augmenting the importance of auditory feedback itself. Orr and Cappannari (1964), in tracing the emergence of language, point out that "there are minimal internal neuroanatomical pathways between speaking and hearing [p. 318]," and that their relationship must be channeled in large part through the environment rather than through the nervous system.

6. *Specialization*   Only especially gifted humans, such as Caruso, and certain animals, such as dolphins and bats, appear able to make direct use of their vocalizations, i.e., to make use of the energy rather than the signal. Caruso is said to have shattered a glass by his voice; some animals use the physical nature of sonic feedback to reveal the presence of obstacles, Hockett (1960a) describes "a communicative act, or a whole communicative system, . . . [as] . . . *specialized* to the extent that its direct energetic consequences are biologically irrelevant [p. 407]." Thus, a dog's panting has a biological function of cooling him, but in addition it provides or transmits information about his identity, location, and state. This communication can be characterized as being unspecialized. As Hockett himself admits, it is not always obvious where to draw the line between specialized and unspecialized communication. To the property of specialization might be added the fact that most human verbal behavior is reinforced secondarily, i.e., the organism influenced by the verbal behavior most often mediates nonbiological reinforcement to the emitter of the verbal responses.

7. *Semanticity*   There is a relationship between words and things, to use Roger Brown's (1958) book title, or, to employ Skinner's (1957) terminology, there are tacts (response classes under the control of the environment). Investigation of animals shows that many have semanticity, e.g., the food call of the gibbon.

8. *Arbitrariness*   The semantic relation is described to be *arbitrary* rather than *iconic,* i.e., the size or loudness of words has no relationship with the objects they normally describe. Thus, both mammalian and avian communication systems appear to be semantic and arbitrary. On the other hand, to the extent that Andrew's notion of stimulus-contrast (1962a, 1963) is valid, the primates' vocalizations can be said to have at least some nonarbitrary, or iconic, features.

9. *Discreteness*   Human language is characterized by discontinuities in the sense that words differ from one another by the presence or absence of phonemes, and not by a change in the value of some continuous parameter, say, loudness. It should be noted that continuous communication systems imply iconicity, as in the dance of the bee, where the rate of dancing is inversely proportional to the target location. On the other hand, a discrete system can be either iconic or arbitrary. Sebeok (1962) has discussed this property in slightly different terms, namely, as digital (discrete) and analog (continuous) coding of information.

10. *Displacement*   In human communication, verbal responses can refer to things remote in time and space, i.e., verbal responses usually evoked by certain stimuli are also emitted at times when these particular stimuli are absent. Hockett notes that the calls of gibbons are never displaced in this manner, while bee dances (which are related to communicating the distance of food sources or a new living place) always are. This is opposed to human language where displacement can, but need not, occur. He also points out that without displacement, no discussion of past or future events or planning would be possible; this property is, therefore, considered to be a very important aspect of human language. He also argues that since displacement implies a delay between the reception of a stimulus and the response, it therefore requires some information storage in the brain. However, he does realize that the storage may be of another kind, as in his hypothetical example of the proto-Hominoid, who, while fleeing a predator, is stimulated to make his danger call, when the predator is no longer present, by release of the odor stimulated by his own fear. Storage, mediated by other responses or with no such apparent mediation, has been demonstrated in experiments with many different animals. The very process of learning, of course, is evidence for storage and displacement. Many of the more complicated schedules of reinforcement (Ferster & Skinner, 1957) require storage and displacement. The DRL schedule (differential reinforcement of low rates), for example, requires the animal to emit responses only after a minimum period of time has elapsed following the previous response—a perfect example of displacing or postponing

a response. Whether animals can do this vocally is simply an experimental question, and it is not, in any case, central to the question of whether animals are capable of displacement. Therefore, it seems necessary to disagree with Hockett's statement that displacement is rare. The point that Hockett could validly make is that DRL performance has not been found in nature as a communication system, but whether a given type of behavior *does* exist hardly seems as important as whether it *can* exist. One can also ask whether respondent conditioning might not be considered an example of displacement as well, since the dog (to take the classical example) salivates in response to the bell (anticipates? plans for?) before the food is placed in its mouth.

One other point needs to be made concerning the property of displacement. Hockett's description implies that human beings are responding to stimuli which are not present at the time of the response. The human being's verbal responses, however, are multiply determined by external stimuli, by other verbal responses, by nonverbal responses, and by the stimuli produced by these responses. When a person makes a response to a stimulus which is apparently not present, he is, in fact, responding to one or more of the other mediating stimuli and to responses which control the emission of that response. It is important to remember that the phenomenon of displacement consists of bridging the stimulus and response in ways which should, at least in principle, be within the capacity of many animals. A more detailed analysis of displacement thus contradicts Hockett's assertion of the rarity of this phenomenon among animals.

11. *Productivity or openness*   New messages are produced in human language, according to linguists, by inserting words, or more precisely, morphemes, into grammatical patterns in ways not utilized before, or by modifying the meaning of old words, as in the coining of new idioms. Thus, while bees are said to have the ability to produce a very special sort of grammatical patterning (and thus to describe distances never described before), they are unable to create new idioms. By the same token, gibbon calls also may be considered to be a closed system of verbal behavior.

This particular property attributes to man alone the ability to be original, that is, to put responses together in a novel way. But so-called insight (which, in at least some experiments, has been reduced to low probability although maintaining real stimulus-response connections) has been demonstrated in animals as well as in man; for example, a monkey may put two sticks together to obtain a banana otherwise out of reach. The notion of making responses that have not been made before can also be illustrated in Harlow's (1949) experiments on reversal learning. A monkey was first reinforced to make one out of two responses, and subsequently reinforced to make the other. This procedure was repeated over a series of different problems such that first one response was correct and then the other. The results of the experiment showed that the monkeys eventually learned to make the "other" response on the trial following the first reversal trial nearly 100 percent of the time.

In other words, they were productive, i.e., they learned to make a new response after some training. I am suggesting that once we separate this property of productivity from that of vocalization, it no longer appears to be unique to man. The concepts of response class (Salzinger, 1967) and unit size (Salzinger, 1973), which are necessary to explain animal behavior, can be utilized to demonstrate the phenomenon of productivity in human language as well. Thus, by selecting concepts for analysis which are applicable to both man and animal, some of the seemingly unique properties of human language can be shown to be present in varying degrees in animals.

12. *Tradition* The conventions of language are learned and taught by members of the same species who have learned the language from other members of the species. For some language conventions in some species, the transmission is genetically determined. For others, it is learned. Hockett reports the existence of short-lived traditions among chimpanzees in captivity, but leaves unspecified the kind of learning and teaching process involved. Its importance will be discussed in the section on language-learning potential.

13. *Duality* Every human language is said to have both phonological and grammatical subsystems, i.e., a very large number of different morphemes can be formed on the basis of a small number of phonemes. Hockett (1963) states that "no animal system known to the writer shows any significant duality [p. 9]." Yet, animals can be conditioned to emit relatively complicated chains of responses (with each response acting as a phoneme and each chain of responses as a morpheme) with both verbal and nonverbal responses, as will be shown below. Under experimental conditions, the emission of a series of responses in one order may signify (since it is followed in the experiment by orange juice) as a communication "Give me orange juice," while the emission of the same responses in a different order may signify as a communication (at least to the experimenter who supplies the banana in response to that pattern), "Give me a banana." Here we see how experimentation can uncover an ability in animals which the customary environment does not call forth.

14. *Prevarication* Verbal responses can be false or logically meaningless. Hockett ascribes the admittedly doubtful property of truthfulness to animals other than man. The implication here, as with the properties of displacement and productivity, appears to be that an organism can will to lie. A more reasonable explanation concerning such response classes (lying) is that the verbal response is controlled by different stimuli and reinforcement contingencies than those expected by the hearer in terms of his own reinforcement history. Thus, whether an organism is lying is not related to the degree of stimulus control over verbal responses but rather to the class of stimuli which do the controlling. The difference between man and animal concerning this characteristic might be better described by noting that displacement or mediation through other stimuli occurs more frequently in man than in aminal. The latter is simply more frequently controlled by more immediate stimuli.

15. *Reflexiveness*   Sometimes called metacommunication, reflexiveness refers to man's ability to talk about his talking, whereas bees are destined never to dance about their dancing. It is another example of the differences which exist in types of stimuli which can control verbal responses in man and animal. Like properties 5, 7, 10, and 14, it makes reference to the fact that man's verbal responses are evoked by a large number of different types of stimuli than animals' responses. How much training would be required to extend the number of types or classes of such stimuli in animals is an interesting empirical question.

16. *Learnability*   A speaker of one language can learn another language. Sebeok has suggested that there is a property of multiple coding potential, which should perhaps be included here. It is "the transmutation of one set of verbal signs (e.g., speech) into another set (e.g., script) [Sebeok, 1962, p. 431 fn.]." Some animals lack this property altogether, but some, Hockett tells us, have probably developed communication systems with this property. Together with property 12, this property suggests that it would be useful to examine the role of learning in the comparative analysis of languages in man and animal, particularly in order to determine the extent to which animal language can be made to resemble human communication. This problem relates to that of conditioning verbal behavior.

CONDITIONING OF VERBAL BEHAVIOR

The importance of conditioning lies in the fact that it allows us to go beyond Hockett's list of the properties of language by characterizing the properties of the speaker.

Comparison of the languages of man and animal is incomplete if restricted to examination of behavior in nature. It is obvious that many animals have the capacity to behave in ways not called forth by their usual environment. The experimental work carried out in the context of behavior theory has supplied us with ample evidence for this. The absence of language development cannot be assumed to mean the absence of the *ability to develop* language. Thus, the first reason for examining the relation between learning and language development is to determine which animals have what kind of language development potential. A number of methods can be used for this investigation, such as the modification techniques of imprinting, respondent conditioning, and operant conditioning. Ginsburg (1963) suggested instrumentality as a property to be added to Hockett's list. Here, instrumentality will be subsumed in what will be called property number 1, *language-learning potential*.

A second reason for examining the learning-language relation is to determine to what extent animals throughout the phylogenetic scale show general learning capacities necessary for the development of language. To give an obvious example, an animal whose behavior is only minimally influenced by the environment could certainly not be expected to develop a language like the human one. Furthermore, if environmental influence is possible, it is reasonable to ask what kind—imprinting, respondent conditioning, or operant conditioning. Finally, conditioning studies can produce information on the complexity of the learning possible for different animals. This I shall label property number 2, *general learning capacity*.

A third reason for scrutinizing the conditioning literature is to examine the general rate of verbal response. It is well known that the operant level of a response (response rate before reinforcement is applied) is of importance for conditioning, even if only for the purpose of making a valid estimate of the probable effect of the reinforcement which is to be applied. Such an estimate is necessary to effect the response differentiation required for language. This will be labeled property number 3, *verbal response availability*.

A fourth reason for utilizing the behavior theory model for language comparisons is to discover the relative conditionability of verbal versus nonverbal behavior. An animal whose nonverbal responses are more efficient than its verbal responses in procuring reinforcement will show less verbal conditionability and will therefore be less likely to develop language. This is property number 4, *relative verbal response conditionability*.

The fifth reason for examining the relationship between learning theory and language is to determine how the verbal response classes affect other verbal and nonverbal response classes. There has been increasing interest in both the Soviet Union and the United States in the regulating function of verbal behavior over nonverbal behavior, a function which appears to increase with age. This is property number 5, the *regulating function*.

Let us now look at the literature with respect to these properties.

Language-Learning Potential

Studies relevant to this property can be divided into two types: those that address themselves directly to the conditioning of human language in animals, and those that are concerned with conditioning vocalization in general. It is hoped that conditioning will eventually be applied to communication systems other than vocal ones, such as the dancing of the bee or the odor trails of fire ants, since the critical problem to investigate is the extent to which different communication systems can be modified by the environment.

Attempts to Condition Human Language in Animals The experimental production of speech, or at least of some words, in primates is tempting because of the resemblance of these animals to man in other characteristics. An early study along these lines was reported by Furness (1916). The first word he taught his orangutan was ''Papa,'' a response which took 6 months of daily training. He selected this particular word because it combined two elements of vocalization not generally used by orangutans, namely the lips and expired vowel sounds. He trained the orangutan by enunciating the word repeatedly for minutes at a stretch, while at the same time bringing the animal's lips together and apart in imitation of his own lip movements. He also practiced the motions together with the ape in front of a mirror, so as to provide more stimuli. Then, when the sound was finally produced, the experimenter "praised and petted her enthusiastically." After that, the animal apparently retained the response. Finally, he was able to train her to make the association between the word "Papa" and himself. The next word which Furness taught the orangutan was "cup." By this time, it had become much easier to train the animal, since she had learned to respond to verbal stimuli such as "Open your mouth" or "stick out your tongue." It is instructive to trace the training procedure for the word "cup" as described by Furness:

> The first move in teaching her to say cup was to push her tongue back in her throat as if she were to make the sound "Ka." This was done by means of a bone spatula with which I pressed lightly on the center of her tongue. When I saw that she had taken a full breath I placed my finger over her nose to make her try to breathe through her mouth. The spatula was then quickly withdrawn and inevitably she made the sound "Ka." All the while facing her I held my mouth open with my tongue in the same position as hers so that her observation, curiosity, and powers of imitation might aid her, and I said *Ka* with her emphatically as I released her tongue. [Furness, 1916, p. 284].

The orangutan eventually learned to draw back her tongue before the spatula touched it; she then learned to place the experimenter's finger over her nose, and to say *Ka* without any use of the spatula; then she placed her own finger over her nose and finally made the *Ka* sound whenever asked to. The final consonant was eventually added by having the experimenter close the animal's lips with his fingers as soon as she made the *Ka* sound. By showing the orangutan the cup she used for drinking as he emitted "cup," Furness was able to make the word "cup" a discriminative response under the control of the S^D (discriminative stimulus) "What is this?" He was even able to obtain evidence for the orangutan's use of the word "cup" as a mand (Skinner, 1957) for water, although apparently the animal had had no special training for it. This particularly well-trained animal was conditioned to emit the "th" sound, but she died before the sound could be incorporated into other sound sequences to produce words.

In discussing the general training procedures he employed, Furness called special attention to the fact that "the enticement of food has never been used as an incentive to actions, and praise and petting have been the only rewards. In other words my object has been to endeavor to make them show signs of thought rather than a perfunctory performance of tricks [Furness, 1916, p. 285]." Today's psychologists might find it somewhat surprising that an experimenter would avoid using such a strong reinforcement as food, and would certainly dispute the claim that verbal behavior reinforced by praise and petting is more closely associated with thought than behavior reinforced by food. Nevertheless, reinforcement by means of the intervention of another organism brings it closer to language as man knows it; in other words, conditioned reinforcement is far more important than primary reinforcement in the control and maintenance of the verbal behavior of humans.

Kellogg and Kellogg (1933) raised a female chimpanzee, beginning at seven and a half months of age, along with their nine and a half months old son for a period of nine months. Although they made no special effort to teach the chimpanzee to talk, she was, of course, exposed to speech in the same situations as the human child. Although she did not learn to say any English words during the first 5 months, she surpassed her human sibling in the number of verbal stimuli to which she could respond appropriately. Furthermore, she demonstrated an ability to communicate even though her communication procedures were not always vocal.

The Hayeses (C. Hayes, 1951; K. J. Hayes, 1950; Hayes & Hayes, 1954) raised their chimpanzee beginning at an earlier age (six weeks) and for a longer time (some six years) than the Kelloggs. They taught her to say three words (mama, papa, cup) under appropriate circumstances, i.e., in response to certain S^D's and to use at least one of them (cup) in the form of a request for something to drink (Skinner's mand). Furthermore, they assigned meanings to certain sounds already within the repertory of the animal by reinforcing these sounds with the delivery of different objects. At one point, they attributed the animal's limited language acquisition to a neurological condition much like aphasia, but later, taking note of the obvious difference in degree of vocal practice between the chimpanzee and the child, they attributed the limited language acquisition to a difference in "motivation" to vocalize. Lilly (1962) has more recently become interested in teaching dolphins to talk. He has reported some success, and plans for further research in this area. And finally, we should note a study by Ginsburg (1963), who reported, in a controlled experiment, the instatement of two discriminative verbal responses, "Hello" and "What's up?" in the mynah bird.

These experiments show that a number of different animals can, with some difficulty, be trained to emit verbal responses similar to those emitted by human beings, and to show some of the same functions as human verbal behavior, namely, external (sight of an object) and internal (dry throat) discriminative control. Although responses to verbal stimuli in the chimpanzees showed more than simply intonational control, new combinations of old words were not as easily understood as by the human child. In most cases, new combinations of old words had to be learned all over again. Not enough controlled research of this kind has been done, however, probably because of the difficulty, certainly in working with chimpanzees, with the process merely of getting them to emit English words in the first place. Experiments which utilize animal sounds already in the animal's repertory, or even nonvocal responses, might serve better to investigate the animal's ability to acquire language. A recent study by Lieberman, Klatt, and Wilson (1969) showed that the articulatory apparatus of the chimpanzee and man are so different as to explain the refractoriness of the former to acquisition of human speech. Furthermore, Russian psychologists have reported, in a comparison of the developing child and ape, that the latter does not have an orienting reflex to sounds, whereas the former does (Ladygina-Kots & Dembovskii, 1969). This suggests still another reason for the failure of the ape to learn to make verbal responses.

Three studies reported using nonvocal response systems with chimpanzees. The first of these is essentially a plan for such an experiment (Premack & Schwartz, 1966). The investigators decided to eschew the use of vocalization in the chimpanzee and substituted, instead, a sound-producing joystick—a lever which can be displaced from its central resting position (vertical) to a maximum of 40 degrees from the vertical in any direction. The side of the stick has a pressure gauge which registers the strength of the animal's grip. The displacement of the stick produces a sound which can be described in terms of the following five different dimensions: degree of tilt (corresponding to the frequency of the sound); displacement in the north-south plane (corresponding to a superimposed white noise); displacement in the east-west plane (corresponding to a vibrato, or pulsing, in the tone); pressure on the stick (corresponding to the amplitude of the sound); and length of time that the stick is away from the resting position (corresponding to the duration of the sound). The training procedure was to be a simulation of the usual mother-father and parent-child interaction in order to teach the chimpanzee child the language. Thus, the chimpanzees would be exposed to the interaction between the mother's and father's joysticks, as well as being involved in their own interactions. Some provision would also be made for monitoring babbling, which would, in this case, consist of the animal's manipulation of the stick.

A second attempt at teaching a chimpanzee how to communicate was also reported by Premack (1970). In this experiment, he made use of pieces of plastic varying in shape, size, and color, with each piece standing for a word. Using primary reinforcement as the means for teaching the meaning of the plastic pieces, he followed the procedure of first simply giving the chimp a fruit, and then putting one of the plastic pieces closer to the chimp than the fruit, requiring her to place the piece on a board, and then giving her the fruit. The chimp was taught the names of different fruits by this procedure; then she was taught to choose the appropriate word (out of two) for the fruit on the table, in order to get it. Following that, she was taught the rudiments of a sentence in that she learned to use the pieces which described not only the name of the fruit in question but also the name of the person who was acting as the experimenter. She was, furthermore, required to put the two classes of words in a particular order (one under the other), that is, the name of the donor first and the name of the fruit second. The chimp was taught prepositions, such as "on," by training her to place cards of different colors on one another according to instructions given by the sentences consisting of the words for the different colors and the word for "on." Having trained the chimp to place "red on green," or "green on red," depending on the sentences given her, the experimenter then tested for generalization by instructing the animal to place "yellow on blue," and "red on yellow," instructions on which she had not been trained (although she had been trained on the individual words). The results were apparently quite clear: The chimp performed as well on the new tasks as on the training tasks, thus demonstrating a considerable amount of generalization. Having been trained to follow the instructions of the sentences to perform the tasks of laying one card on another, the chimp was then given the reverse task, that is, she was shown two different cards lying one on top of another and required to "write" the sentence which would describe their position. Her proficiency (80 percent) was as high on the first ten trials of this task as on tasks which she had fully learned, again showing a substantial amount of transfer.

Premack reported a number of further tasks which he was able to train the chimp to perform, including the construction of compound sentences, such as, "Sarah insert the banana in the pail, and the apple in the dish," corresponding in chimp language to "Sara insert banana pail apple dish." He also found evidence for the generalization of this type of sentence, although further work in this direction is still necessary to confirm this finding. Furthermore, he taught the chimp to use the more abstract words "same" and "not the same," and showed that she learned to use them with respect to new objects. She was also trained to "write" the phrase "is the name of." Her resultant performance was equally good for the generalization stimuli she was tested on and for the material she had been trained on, again showing generalization. Finally, Premack demonstrated that the properties assigned to the piece of plastic signifying apple were the same as the properties assigned to the object, apple, thus giving evidence for the idea that the verbal response represents something other than itself. Although all these experiments have been carried out on one animal, they are indeed most impressive and go a long way to dispel the idea that animals are really so different from man in their ability to learn "language."

A third attempt to teach chimpanzees (B. T. Gardner & R. A. Gardner, 1968, 1969, 1970; R. A. Gardner & B. T. Gardner, 1969) language used American sign language for the deaf. These investigators began working with a female chimpanzee ten and a half months old, raising her in a house trailer situated in a garden with trees and a jungle gym. The animal was always accompanied by human beings who used sign language in communicating both with her and with other human companions in her presence. No voiced communication took place within her presence, with the exception of the imitation of any sound the chimpanzee herself made. The authors have made available a summary of a diary which they kept on the progress made in a number of areas of functioning, including social behavior, imitation, perceptual-motor development, and, of course, gestures. By the time the chimpanzee reached the age of fourteen months, she was able to understand the following nine signs: come, look, goodbye, stay (come down), no-no, scolding, in, swing, hug. At that time she had only one arbitrary sign ("more") which she could emit herself. By the time she had reached the age of eighteen months, she showed the attribute of productivity in the use of the word "more." Thus, while she had been exposed to seeing the sign "more" in the context of continued hairbrushing and countinued tickling, she spontaneously used it to ask for continued whispering in her ear, for continued pillow fighting, and for further listening to the ticking of a watch. Some evidence for the overgeneralization of this response was also shown when she used it for a first cup of formula. At the age of eighteen months she showed that she understood some thirty-two different signs and was able to produce five signs (come, more, goodbye-hi, up, sweet). By the time the chimpanzee was twenty-two months old, she was combining signs, such as "gimme more." At thirty-two months of age, the chimpanzee used some twenty-nine different two-sign combinations and four different three-sign combinations. Later reports have continued to show further vocabulary and word combination acquisition, but the increasing amounts of material have made it increasingly more difficult to keep exact count. Although words have been combined in different orders, Gardner and Gardner are just beginning to analyze their material statistically to determine the degree of preference for some orders. The chimpanzee's vocabulary at forty-four months consisted of seventy-seven different single words.

Finally, the investigators noted that the chimpanzee signed to herself when leafing through a picture book and also when she was up in a tree. These results, especially the combinations of words (signs), the productive use of language, and the rehearsing and talking to oneself are all very reminiscent of the observations made by those who have studied the acquisition of language in the human child. It was the productivity, and the spontaneous combination of words which had been separately taught a speech-deficient boy, which foreshadowed greater progress in his acquisition of language (Salzinger, Feldman, Cowan, & Salzinger, 1965).

Attempts to Condition Vocalization in Animals   Studies on the conditioning of animal vocalization have generally dealt with the modification of sounds the animal already has within its repertoire. Using a somewhat unique approach, Lane and Shinkman (1963) circumvented at least some of the problems of comparability of human and animal (chick) vocal behavior, not, as is usually done, by modifying the animal's response in the direction of the human being, but by modifying the human's response by restricting it to a single sound, /u/. Then, the changes in the physical parameters of the human and the bantam chick responses were compared and found to be quite similar in terms of the relative changes which occurred in response topography as the reinforcement contingency was shifted from one schedule to another. This experiment and Lane's other experiments (1960, 1961) have shown that, contrary to the implication of refractoriness (Skinner, 1957) to operant conditioning, animal vocalizations could indeed be conditioned by operant techniques, being responsive to different reinforcement schedules in much the same way as nonvocal (e.g., pecking) responses. Lane (1960) showed that the increase in chirping behavior was due to the effect of the experimental administration of reinforcement, and was not simply an elicited response, i.e., one which was emotional in character, by demonstrating that a free feeding situation elicited no more chirps than a situation which contained no feeding at all (see Figure 5–1).

Grosslight, Harrison, and Weiser (1962) conditioned vocalization in the mynah bird, demonstrating its operant nature by a yoked arrangement. Specifically, whenever the bird A was reinforced for emitting a vocalization, bird B also received food, the presentation of which was independent of bird B's behavior. Under these circumstances, it was again possible to demonstrate that vocalizations of birds can be conditioned by an operant technique. Furthermore, these investigators also showed that it is possible to establish discriminative control over the vocalizations and that the duration of each response unit can be modified.

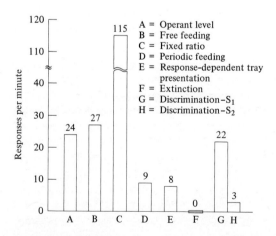

Figure 5–1. Rates of chirping obtained under control and experimental conditions with one bantam chicken. (From Lane, H. L. *Science,* 1960, **132,** 37–38. Copyright 1960 by the American Association for the Advancement of Science.)

Experiments with shell parakeets, undertaken by Ginsburg (1960), demonstrated that the bird's chirp could be conditioned operantly, that it responded differentially to interval and ratio schedules of reinforcement, and that discriminative control could be established over it.

Perhaps the greatest impetus for work with the vocalizations of birds has come from Mowrer (1950). He maintained that the way to train "talking" birds to emit a word was to say the word just before feeding the bird. The animal should then learn the response because the experimenter's emission of the word would become an S^D for the reinforcement; later, the bird's own emission of the word, or initially of sounds similar to it, would also produce the S^D for food and would therefore function as a secondary reinforcer as well. This, in turn, should reinforce the animal's further emission of words.

Mowrer's description of this procedure was an anecdotal one, and the theory was later subjected to a stricter experimental test by Foss (1964). In this experiment, two different kinds of whistle (not originally in the birds' repertory) were played to mynah birds under two different conditions; then their rate of occurrence was compared. One condition consisted of preparing and placing food in the cage of the birds while playing the sounds; the other consisted of playing the sounds only, with nothing else (that is, neither a human being nor food) being shown to the birds at the time. The results revealed that approximately the same number of whistles were reproduced under the two different conditions. Foss concluded that learning theory could not explain the acquisition of the new sounds and that "mynah birds have a tendency to mimic." In another test of Mowrer's theory, Grosslight and Zaynor (1967) found an actual reduction of vocal behavior during the food-speech pairing situation, thereby not supporting the theory. They reviewed a number of the difficulties encountered in trying to work with vocalization in the mynah bird and pointed out that the major problem is that of finding the precise conditions under which mynah birds can reliably be made to talk. According to these investigators, much more needs to be learned about the mynah bird before we extrapolate to man.

The operant conditioning of barking has not enjoyed as much popularity as that of bird vocalization. Nevertheless, Konorski (1948) reported conditioning of barking to the sound of a metronome, and Lawicka (1957) described a procedure in which the latency of response to discriminative stimuli of very short duration was measured. A more complete description of the operant conditioning of barking was given by Salzinger and Waller (1962). In this study, beagles and a wirehaired fox terrier were conditioned operantly on a fixed-ratio reinforcement schedule; discriminative control was demonstrated over the vocal response; control was extended to a multiple-reinforcement schedule consisting of the vocal component and a bar-pushing component; and finally, the multiple schedule was converted to a chain schedule requiring a sequence of ten bar responses followed by ten vocal responses before the administration of reinforcement (see Figures 5-2 and 5-3).

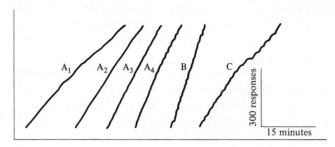

Figure 5–2. Cumulative record of all subjects in fixed-ratio schedules of reinforcement. The letters A₁, A₂, A₃, and A₄ show the progressive increase in fixed ratio from 3:1 to 33:1 for Beagle 1; B shows the 33:1 performance for the wirehaired fox terrier, and C shows it for Beagle 2. (From Salzinger, K. and Waller, M. B. *Journal of the Experimental Analysis of Behavior,* 1962, **5,** 383–389. Copyright 1962 by the Society for the Experimental Analysis of Behavior, Inc.)

Molliver (1963) showed that the cat's meow is as conditionable by means of an operant paradigm as the bark of the dog. More recently, Burnstein and Wolff (1967) used intracranial stimulation to reinforce vocalization in the guinea pig. They were able to show not only that one can modify the rate of vocalization, but also, by reinforcing vocalizations in different frequency ranges, that one can shape the response topography as well.

The operant conditioning paradigm was also extended to marine life. Lilly and Miller (1962) used electrical stimulation of the brain of a dolphin in order to differentially reinforce vocalization of a particular frequency, duration, and amplitude. In a later paper, Lilly (1965) reported mimicking behavior in a dolphin. In this interesting experiment, he reinforced the dolphin for matching the number of its own sonic emissions to the number of nonsense syllables emitted by the experimenter. This was accomplished by first reinforcing any emission of sound, then gradually raising the requirement. Basically, this procedure is a multiple schedule of reinforcement, with each component being characterized as having a different fixed number of responses per reinforcement. Such multiple schedules have been worked on extensively, using nonvocal responses (Ferster & Skinner, 1957), and they have also been applied to vocal responses such as those described above. Lane (1961), as well as Salzinger and Waller (1962), used schedules requiring chains of ten vocal and ten nonvocal responses. In Lilly's experiment, it might have been interesting to compare the rate of acquisition of responses when the discriminative stimuli consisted of the appropriate number of bursts (when the response had to match the stimulus in number) with the acquisition of responses when the discriminative stimuli had no such relationship to the responses required. A more comprehensive review of the dolphin's accomplishments can be found in Lilly (1967). Among Lilly's interesting points is the fact that the sound production need

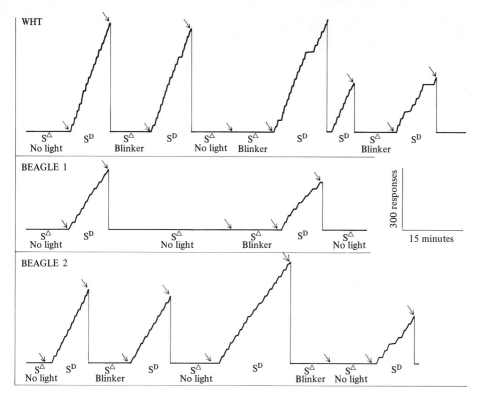

Figure 5–3. Cumulative records of the final performance of all subjects after discrimination training. S^D consisted of a continuous light; while it was on the dogs were reinforced. The two S^Δ conditions consisted of the light being off, or the light flashing on and off at 1 cps; the dogs received no reinforcement during those times. The arrows indicate a change in condition from one stimulus to another. (From Salzinger, K. and Waller, M. B. *Journal of the Experimental Analysis of Behavior,* 1962, **5,** 383–389. Copyright 1962 by the Society for the Experimental Analysis of Behavior Inc.)

not be continuously reinforced by food, some conditioned reinforcement apparently taking over.

The conditionability of the sea lion was demonstrated by Schusterman and Feinstein (1965). These investigators instated a click response in a sea lion that had never emitted such a response in the laboratory, and then brought the response under the control of the size of a circular stimulus. In a more recent experiment Schusterman and Balliet (1970) described conditioned vocalization in sea lions as a way of determining visual-acuity thresholds (see Figure 5-4). Figure 5-5 presents the sound spectrograms of harbor seal vocalizations obtained while the seals were swimming with members of their own species as well as with *Zalophus* and *Eumetopias.*

Figure 5–4. *Zalophus* viewing variable acuity target in air. (From Schusterman, R. J. & Balliet, R. F. *Science,* 1970, **169**, 498–501. Copyright 1970 by the American Association for the Advancement of Science.)

Finally, Leander et al. found it possible to condition vocalizations in jungle-born monkeys on fixed-ratio reinforcement schedules (Leander, Milan, Jasper, & Heaton, 1972).

Thus far, then, it has been shown that a number of different animals' vocalizations can be conditioned by operant techniques. But Mowrer, Palmer, and Sanger (1948) were unable to operantly condition a vocal avoidance response in the rat, although in the same study they were able to condition a running avoidance response.

They utilized an escape-avoidance procedure to condition the two different responses: vocalization in one group, and running in the other. The procedure consisted of the following: A flickering light was turned on, and if the rat did not make the required response in 5 seconds, it received an electric shock which was terminated, along with the flickering light, only when the required response was made. Thus, if the rat made the required response before the end of the 5 seconds, an avoidance response was emitted; if the rat learned to respond after the shock was turned on, an escape response was emitted. It should be noted that electric shock elicits respondent components of the running response (Schoenfeld, 1950), thus amplifying the operant conditioning effect for that response; it also elicits a vocalization response which has been successfully conditioned by respondent, not operant, techniques (Warner, 1932; Schlosberg, 1934; Cowles & Pennington, 1943; Herbert, 1946). On the average,

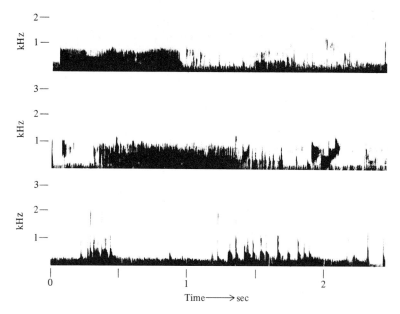

Figure 5–5. Sound spectrograms of underwater growl-type vocalizations from three different harbor seals. Analyzing filter bandwidth, 300 Hz. The sound spectrogram portrays graphically the frequencies present in a sound as a function of time. (From Schusterman, R. J., Balliet, R. F. & St. John, S. *Psychonomic Science,* 1970, **18,** 303–305.)

vocalization responses occurred *after* the shock stimulus went on. By the tenth day of ten trials each, avoidance responses had reached a level of 90 percent for the running response, but only 6 percent for vocalization. Further conditioning at an increased shock intensity for five additional days did not alter the results.

The failure to obtain operant conditioning of the vocal response under the same conditions in which a running response could be conditioned led Mowrer, Palmer, and Sanger to the following inferences: Vocalization in rats must have survival value only if the animal has already been caught (respondent conditioning is generally carried out when the animal's movement is severely curtailed, as it would be if it were caught by a predator); however, when it is only *in danger of being caught* (corresponding in the experiment to the condition where the warning signal is on), vocalization does not have survival value, for it might simply bring the predator to the animal. Therefore they argued that, over many generations, there must have been selection of those rats who would not vocalize under avoidance conditions. Furthermore, Mowrer and his colleagues also maintained that, in many animals, vocalization is a respondent, and not an operant. More recent studies, however, have indicated that both kinds of conditioning paradigm can be applied to many different responses. To determine whether a given vocalization response can be conditioned by an operant or a respondent paradigm, one has to observe whether vocalization can be modified by positive reinforcement; the argument concerning survival value of vocalization would not apply with equal force to nondanger situation, i.e., to situations where vocalization is followed by such *prosurvival* events as food.

Mowrer and his colleagues speculated more generally about the survival value of vocalization in different animals, discussing its greater value in domesticated animals than in those in nature. Finally, they suggested that both man and birds were able to develop vocalization to a higher degree than many other animals because of their sojourn in the trees, which presumably offered them more protection. They accounted for other highly vocal animals by postulating the development, in these animals, of special escape routes or camouflage which enables them to escape the notice their vocalization calls to them. Speculative as this reasoning is, it has suggested the importance of comparing operant and respondent conditioning of vocal responses.

Whether a response class such as vocalization is an operant or a respondent (Salzinger & Waller, 1962) ought to be determined empirically, for vocalization could, in some animals (perhaps the dog, to take one example), be conditionable by both methods.

Further experimentation relevant to the questions raised by Mowrer has recently been performed. Sapon (1965) conditioned vocalization in rats deprived of water by using water as the positive reinforcement. He was able to instate the response of vocalization by two different methods. One consisted of differentially reinforcing ever louder respiratory sounds until the animal vocalized loudly. The other method consisted of piping rat vocalizations into the cage. These were paired with presentation of positive reinforcement. After some two hours of this procedure, which reduced considerably the rats' latency of approach, upon hearing the sound, to the water dipper, the regular shaping procedure was engaged in. It is of interest to note parenthetically the similarity of these shaping procedures to those used in the instatement of barking (Salzinger & Waller, 1962). Two of the dogs that had never been in the experimental enclosure produced a whine, the intensity of which could be slowly increased by reinforcing ever louder sounds until they evolved into barks, which constituted the desired response. Another dog, which had been accustomed to the experimental enclosure, produced no sounds that could be differentially reinforced. Barking was instated in him by the experimenter's barking at him; that, in turn, provoked the dog to bark, at which point he could be reinforced, and eventually his barks were turned into a free operant by increasing the relative number of dog-barks to experimenter-barks before a positive reinforcement was given. Apparently, similar techniques work with different animals in the instatement of vocalization. To get back to Sapon's experiment, however, it is important to note that it was possible to condition vocalization in the rat. What is even more interesting, perhaps, it was found to be relatively difficult to extinguish the vocalization response, although the experiment was, unfortunately, not carried out long enough to assess this completely. Thus, the genetic effect that Mowrer and his colleagues suggested had produced the refractoriness of conditioning of vocalization in the rat would definitely have to be referred only to the avoidance situation.

In a series of experiments, there appeared to be difficulty in conditioning vocalization in rats even by means of a respondent conditioning procedure (Badia, Lewis, & Suter, 1967; Badia, Suter, & Lewis, 1966; Lewis, Suter, & Badia, 1967). The investigators found, contrary to the experiments previously cited, no vocalization to the conditioned stimulus. To complicate the issue further, a paper by Lal (1967) reported conditioned avoidance vocalization in rats, although, to be sure, only four out of ten rats acquired high rates of vocalization, five other rats avoided 20 to 70 percent of the shocks, and one rat, which had learned to escape from practically all shocks by vocalizing, avoided none of the shocks. It turns out that all these seemingly discrepant results can be explained by the variable which Mowrer and his colleagues had pointed out in their original experiment, namely, the variable of confinement. All the experiments which had success in conditioning with an aversive stimulus, whether operant or respondent, had the rats confined in a restraining holder of some sort, while all the experiments which were unable to show conditioning with an aversive stimulus allowed the rats to roam freely in the cage. Thus, the recent experiments by Badia, Lewis, and Suter, which appeared to have shown failure to condition even by means of the respondent paradigm, allowed the rats to roam, whereas the experiment by Lal, which appeared to have shown successful avoidance conditioning, had his rats confined in a rat holder. All these results appear to be in agreement with the hypothesis about the survival value of vocalization under conditions of captivity (when vocalization would be helpful to the survival of other members of the species as a warning of a predator) and the contrasurvival value under conditions of being in danger of being captured by a predator (when vocalizations would lead only to being discovered by the predator). A historical footnote should be added to this discussion, and that is a quotation from Schlosberg (1934), who was examining a variable he called depth of conditioning: "It makes no great difference whether the rat terminates or prevents the shock by its response [escape or avoidance conditioning] or whether, on the contrary, the duration of the shock is held constant [respondent conditioning] [p. 332]." The point is that a careful reading of Schlosberg's old experiment would have shown, even then, that it is not the kind of conditioning paradigm, but the state of confinement, that is the critical factor.

The property of language-learning potential thus reveals a number of interesting aspects of vocalization as a precursor to language in man. Although the extrapolation to man must be cautious indeed, the lawful relations to the environment, both within an experiment and within the much larger context of evolution, make the examination of this variable a promising one.

General Learning Capacity

This property has already been touched on in a number of different ways. Any thorough review of this area would take us too far afield to be useful here. But the reader is invited to inspect the current learning literature, as found in the *Journal of Comparative and Physiological Psychology*, the *Journal of the Experimental Analysis of Behavior*, and the *Journal of Experimental Psychology*, for many experiments requiring different kinds of animals to perform quite complex tasks, many of which reveal the capacity to acquire language. The experiments discussed earlier (Furness, the Kelloggs, and the Hayeses, all of whom were interested in the acquisition of language in primates) agreed on the complexity of verbal behavior to which these primates were able to respond appropriately. Lilly has argued that the dolphin learns easily, although Andrew (1962b) did not appear equally impressed by the dolphin's intelligence. Findley (1962) recently presented some descriptions of what he called "multi-operant behavior repertoires," where animals' training procedures, of increasing complexity, were outlined. Of special interest here is the fact that response chains of greater complexity (with a given response leading to a choice of several responses rather than to one) are more resistant to extinction than simple response chains. Harlow's (1949) reversal learning paradigm revealed that primates could learn what some of the linguistics-influenced psychologists would call a rule, but which can be otherwise described in terms of learning theory as stimulus and response generalization. This particular learning procedure was likened by Brown (1958) to the semantic linguistic process of negation, where the absence of a positive reinforcement could be viewed as an S^D (like the words "not this, the other") for the other response.

Lilly's (1965) experiment, described above, shows the dolphin's ability to match number of responses vocally. It is worthwhile to point out that other animals have acquired what one can loosely call "counting" responses, although this term may not fully describe what the animals were actually doing. Koehler (1956) was interested in birds' ability to count, and he showed that they were able to match numbers of objects as well as to select a given number of objects out of a larger group, depending only on the specific discriminative stimulus (color of the lid) provided by the experimenter.

An experiment by Ferster (1964) produced behavior in chimpanzees which he felt was related to the problem of acquisition of verbal behavior. The chimpanzees went through the following procedures: All their food had to be earned by the behavior in the experiment. Correct responses were reinforced by a brief tone followed, after a given number of successive correct responses, by food. Incorrect responses were followed by "time-out," a short blackout during which time no response on the part of the animal would be positively reinforced. The chimpanzees, incidentally, in contrast to the subjects worked on by the Kelloggs, Hayeses, and Furness, were not handled but were put through automatic stimulus and response devices, working 4 to 5 hours per day (4,000 to 7,000 trials during that time). The chimpanzees were first trained to match colors, i.e., to press a key under that color which matched the color in the window. After they had been trained to make that response, they were trained to match binary numbers, expressed as unlit (0) and lit (1) circles, by selecting which of a pair of three unlit and lit circles matched a standard set. They were also given training in matching number symbols to given numbers of objects. Thus, they were eventually able to match the correct binary number to one through seven objects with an accuracy of better than 95 percent. They were then trained to "write" the binary numbers by being allowed to turn on the lights in such a way as to produce a binary digit number. By the end of the experiment, the chimpanzees had learned to identify from one to seven objects, writing the correct binary number with only 1 to 2 errors per 1,000 trials. The development of this complex behavior required a very large number of trials (hundreds of thousands for the entire repertory), made possible only by the automatic aspects of the experiment.

This brief review indicates that there are indeed experimental techniques available for the study of complex behavior in animals. In order to evaluate the property of general learning capacity, it will be necessary to apply these techniques more widely to a large enough sample of animals up and down the phylogenetic scale to permit useful comparisons among the animals and their language capacity.

Verbal Response Availability

The studies relevant to this property have already been mentioned. Mowrer and his colleagues (1948) have suggested systematic differences in the conditions under which animals are likely to vocalize. Hayes and Hayes (1954) pointed to the utter lack of vocal play in primates. Whether due to lack of motivation, absence of a drive for vocalization, a neurological deficit, or articulatory difficulty, the fact of lack or paucity of vocal behavior might well provide part of the explanation for the difference in conditionability of vocalization between monkey and dolphin, the latter finding vocalization useful for other than communication activities. Finally, we should recall the extensive vocal play found in human children.

From a research point of view, this property requires that a more systematic survey be made of vocal or other potentially communicative responses available in some form of babbling in the early years of animals, since this might well make the difference between the animal which develops verbal behavior and the one which does not. The experiments done on sign language in chimpanzees certainly corroborate this.

Relative Verbal Response Conditionability

Not many studies have been addressed to the problem of *relative* communicative response strength. Little experimental evidence is necessary to buttress the argument for the superior conditionability of verbal over nonverbal behavior in human beings, although at least some such evidence has been collected (Salzinger, Feldman, & Portnoy, 1964). The animal evidence concerning this point has already been mentioned. Both Lane (1961) and Salzinger and Waller (1962) were able to condition vocal as well as nonvocal behavior, obtaining similar results with both response classes, in chick and dog, respectively, while Mowrer, Palmer, & Sanger (1948) found only the nonvocal response class conditionable (under avoidance conditions) in rats. Lilly and Miller (1962) said, in comparing vocal conditioning using electrical stimulation in similar systems of the brain in monkeys and dolphins, that "one cannot induce the monkey to *use* vocalization the way it uses its hands in order to start a desired stimulus. The dolphin apparently uses vocal outputs and may even prefer vocalization to pushing a lever with its beak [p. 76]." Thus, it is important, in tracing the evolution of verbal behavior, not only to gauge the extent of vocalization in infancy but also to examine the extent to which nonvocal behavior exceeds it in probability of occurrence and therefore is more likely to be followed by reinforcement. Vocal behavior is less likely to develop if other competing behaviors are more likely to be followed by positive reinforcement.

The Regulating Function

More explicit attention has been paid to this particular aspect of verbal behavior in Russian work than in work in this country. Pavlov's second signaling system does in fact view verbal behavior as the important regulator of human behavior, a regulator which is presumably absent in animal behavior. Luria (1957, 1961a, 1961b, 1967) has worked extensively on the gradual development of the regulating function of verbal behavior in children. In this country, interest in verbal behavior as a regulator has been more recent. Lovaas (1961, 1964a, 1964b) has been successful in demonstrating this function by way of the operant conditioning paradigm in children.

Little direct evidence on the regulating effect of verbal behavior in animals has so far been found, although Thorndike's theory of the origin of language (1943) did, in fact, suggest that verbal behavior first evolved as a regulator of the speaker's own behavior and only subsequently acquired the function of controlling, or at least stimulating, the behavior of others. The odor trails left behind by an animal, which serve as communication with other animals, can of course also serve that function with respect to communicating with itself. Furthermore, the dolphin and other animals making use of sonar or echo-location have shown a very specialized use of vocalization in guiding or regulating behavior (Griffin, 1958). In addition, the experiments mentioned with respect to the property of general learning capacity give ample evidence for the complex ways in which different response classes can be made to depend on each other's occurrence, the essence of the regulating function. The major difference would seem to lie in the fact that verbal behavior in man is peculiarly suited to this task. The search in animal behavior for such a response class, which, incidentally, need not even function as a communicative system, would be helpful in revealing the steps involved in the evolution of language.

SUMMARY

Beginning with a brief description of some systems of communication and followed by a short discussion of the place of animal communication in the study of psycholinguistics, this chapter has reviewed Hockett's system of describing the similarities and differences in communication in different animals, including man. It then described a list of some five properties of the human speaker which can be fruitfully sought in the communication of animals. These properties, in large part derived from behavior theory, consist of language-learning potential, general learning capacity, verbal response availability, relative verbal response conditionability, and the regulating function of language. Discussion of the five speaker properties included the detailed examination of experiments which have already suggested some dimensions along which one can profitably compare animals up and down the phylogenetic scale.

It seems reasonable to conclude that the study of animal language will figure importantly in the elucidation of the variables which control language in man. Certainly the complexity of the communication process in animals is great enough to occupy many scientists in gaining an understanding of that process. Once we have reached an understanding of animal language, it should be far easier to comprehend the language of man.

REFERENCES

ALEXANDER, R. D. Arthropods. In T. A. Sebeok (Ed.), *Animal communication*. Bloomington: Indiana University Press, 1968. Pp. 167–216.

ANDREW, R. J. The situations that evoke vocalization in primates. *Annals of the New York Academy of Sciences*, 1962, **102**, 296–315. (a)

ANDREW, R. J. Evolution of intelligence and vocal mimicking. *Science*, 1962, **137**, 585–589. (b)

ANDREW, R. J. The origin and evolution of the calls and facial expressions of the primates. *Behaviour*, 1963, **20**, 1–109.

BADIA, P., LEWIS, P., & SUTER, S. Suppression of rat vocalization to shock by an auditory CS. *Psychological Reports*, 1967, **20**, 1063 1067.

BADIA, P., SUTER, S., & LEWIS, P. Rat vocalization to shock with and without a CS. *Psychonomic Science*, 1966, **4**, 117–118.

BROWN, R. *Words and things*. Glencoe, Ill.: Free Press, 1958.

BURNSTEIN, D. D., & WOLFF, P. C. Vocal conditioning in the guinea pig. *Psychonomic Science*, 1967, **8**, 39–40.

CHOMSKY, N. *Syntactic structures*. The Hague: Mouton, 1957.

COWLES, J. T., & PENNINGTON, L. A. An improved conditioning technique for determining auditory acuity of the rat. *Journal of Psychology*, 1943, **15**, 41–47.

FERSTER, C. B. Arithmetic behavior in chimpanzees. *Scientific American*, 1964, **210**, 98–106.

FERSTER, C. B., & SKINNER, B. F. *Schedules of reinforcement*. New York: Appleton-Century-Crofts, 1957.

FINDLEY, J. D. An experimental outline for building and exploring multi-operant behavior repertoires. *Journal of the Experimental Analysis of Behavior*, 1962, **5**, 113–166.

FOSS, B. M. Mimicry in mynas *(Gracula religiosa)*: A test of Mowrer's theory. *British Journal of Psychology*, 1964, **55**, 85–88.

FRINGS, H., & FRINGS, M. Other invertebrates. In T. A. Sebeok (Ed.), *Animal communication*. Bloomington: Indiana University Press, 1968. Pp. 244–270.

FRISCH, K. VON. *Bees: Their vision, chemical senses and language*. Ithaca, N.Y.: Cornell University Press, 1950.

FURNESS, W. H. Observations of the mentality of chimpanzees and orangutans. *Proceedings of the American Philosophical Society*, 1916, **55**, 281–290.

GARDNER, B. T., & GARDNER, R. A. Development of behavior in an infant chimpanzee. Summaries of Washoe's diary. Mimeographed, 1968, 1969, 1970.

GARDNER, R. A., & GARDNER, B. T. Teaching sign language to a chimpanzee. *Science*, 1969, **165**, 664–672.

GINSBURG, N. Conditioned vocalization in the budgerigar. *Journal of Comparative and Physiological Psychology*, 1960, **53**, 183–186.

GINSBURG, N. Conditioned talking in the mynah bird. *Journal of Comparative and Physiological Psychology*, 1963, **56**, 1061–1063.

GOULD, J. E., HENEREY, M., & MACLEOD, M. C. Communication of direction by the honey bee. *Science*, 1970, **169**, 544–554.

GRIFFIN, D. R. *Listening in the dark*. New Haven, Conn.: Yale University Press, 1958.

GROSSLIGHT, J. H., HARRISON, P. C., & WEISER, C. M. Reinforcement control of vocal responses in the mynah bird *(Gracula religiosa)*. *Psychological Record*, 1962, **12**, 193–201.

GROSSLIGHT, J. H., & ZAYNOR, W. C. Verbal behavior and the mynah bird. In K. Salzinger & S. Salzinger (Eds.), *Research in verbal behavior and some neurophysiological implications*. New York: Academic Press, 1967. Pp. 5–20.

HARLOW, H. The formation of learning sets. *Psychological Review*, 1949, **56**, 51–65.

HAYES, C. *The ape in our house*. New York: Harper, 1951.

HAYES, K. J. Vocalization and speech in chimpanzees. *American Psychologist*, 1950, **5**, 275–276.

HAYES, K. J., & HAYES, C. The cultural capacity of chimpanzees. *Human Biology*, 1954, **26**, 288–303.

HERBERT, M. J. An improved technique for studying the conditioned squeak reaction in hooded rats. *Journal of General Psychology*, 1946, **34**, 67–77.

HOCKETT, C. F. Animal "languages" and human language. *Human Biology*, 1959, **31**, 32–39.

HOCKETT, C. F. Logical considerations in the study of animal communication. In W. E. Lanyon

& W. N. Tavolga (Eds.), *Animal sounds and communication.* Washington, D.C., American Institute of Biological Sciences, 1960. Pp. 392–430. (a)

HOCKETT, C. F. The origin of speech. *Scientific American,* 1960, **203,** 89–98. (b)

HOCKETT, C. F. The problem of universals in language. In J. H. Greenberg (Ed.), *Universals of language.* Cambridge, Mass.: M.I.T. Press, 1963. Pp. 1–22.

KELLOGG, W. N., & KELLOGG, L. A. *The ape and the child.* New York: Whittlesey House, 1933.

KOEHLER, O. The ability of birds to "count." In J. R. Newman (Ed.), *The world of mathematics.* Vol. 1. New York: Simon & Schuster, 1956. Pp. 489–496.

KONORSKI, J. *Conditioned reflexes and neurone organization.* Cambridge, England: Cambridge University Press, 1948.

LADYGINA-KOTS, N. N., DEMBOVSKII, Y. N. The psychology of primates. In M. Cole & I. Maltzman (Eds.) *A handbook of contemporary Soviet psychology.* New York: Basic Books, 1969.

LAL, H. Operant control of vocal responding in rats. *Psychonomic Science,* 1967, **8,** 35–36.

LANE, H. Control of vocal responding in chickens. *Science,* 1960, **132,** 37–38.

LANE, H. Operant control of vocalizing in the chicken. *Journal of the Experimental Analysis of Behavior,* 1961, **4,** 171–178.

LANE, H., & SHINKMAN, P. G. Methods and findings in an analysis of a vocal operant. *Journal of the Experimental Analysis of Behavior,* 1963, **6,** 179–188.

LAWICKA, W. The effect of the prefrontal lobectomy on the vocal conditioned reflexes in dogs. *Acta Biologiae Experimentales,* 1957, **17,** 317–325.

LEANDER, J. D., MILAN, M. A., JASPER, K. B., & HEATON, K. L. Schedule control of vocal behavior of cebus monkeys. *Journal of the Experimental Analysis of Behavior,* 1972, **17,** 229–235.

LENNEBERG, E. H. *Biological foundations of language.* New York: Wiley, 1967.

LEWIS, P., SUTER, S., & BADIA, P. Rat vocalizations to shock: With and without a CS; in darkness and in light. *Psychonomic Science,* 1967, **8,** 275–276.

LIEBERMAN, P. H., KLATT, D. H., & WILSON, W. H. Vocal tract limitations on the vowel repertoires of rhesus monkey and other nonhuman primates. *Science,* 1969, **164,** 1185–1187.

LILLY, J. C. Vocal behavior of the bottlenose dolphin. *Proceedings of the American Philosophical Society.* 1962. **106,** 520–529.

LILLY, J. C. Vocal mimicry in tursiops: Ability to match numbers and durations of human vocal bursts. *Science,* 1965, **147,** 300–301.

LILLY, J. C. Dolphin's vocal mimicry as a unique ability and a step toward understanding. In K. Salzinger & S. Salzinger (Eds.), *Research in verbal behavior and some neurophysiological implications.* New York: Academic Press, 1967.

LILLY, J. C., & MILLER, A. M. Operant conditioning of the bottlenose dolphin with electrical stimulation of the brain. *Journal of Comparative and Physiological Psychology,* 1962, **55,** 73–79.

LOVAAS, O. I. Interaction between verbal and nonverbal behavior. *Child Development,* 1961, **32,** 329–336.

LOVAAS, O. I. Cue properties of words: The control of operant responding by rate and content of verbal operants. *Child Development,* 1964, **35,** 245–256. (a)

LOVAAS, O. I. Control of food intake in children by reinforcement of relevant verbal behavior. *Journal of Abnormal and Social Psychology,* 1964, **68,** 672–678. (b)

LURIA, A. R. Experimental analysis of the development of voluntary action in children. *Proceedings of the 50th International Congress of Psychology,* 1957. Pp. 460–461.

LURIA, A. R. The genesis of voluntary movements. In N. O'Connor (Ed.), *Recent Soviet psychology*. New York: Liveright, 1961. Pp. 165–185. (a)

LURIA, A. R. *The role of speech in the regulation of normal and abnormal behavior*. New York: Pergamon, 1961 (b)

LURIA, A. R. The regulative function of speech in its development and dissolution. In K. Salzinger & S. Salzinger (Eds.), *Research in verbal behavior and some neurophysiological implications*. New York: Academic Press, 1967.

MARLER, P. Visual systems. In T. A. Sebeok (Ed.), *Animal communication*. Bloomington: Indiana University Press, 1968. Pp. 103–126.

MCNEILL, D. Developmental psycholinguistics. In F. Smith & G. A. Miller (Eds.), *The genesis of language: A psycholinguistic approach*. Cambridge, Mass.: M.I.T. Press, 1966. Pp. 15–84.

MILLER, G. A. Some psychological studies of grammar. *American Psychologist*, 1962, **17**, 748–762.

MILLER, G. A. Some preliminaries to psycholinguistics. *American Psychologist*, 1965, **20**, 15–20.

MOLLIVER, M. E. Operant control of vocal behavior in the cat. *Journal of the Experimental Analysis of Behavior*, 1963, **6**, 197–202.

MOWRER, O. H. On the psychology of "talking birds"—a contribution to language and personality theory. In O. H. Mowrer (Ed.), *Learning theory and personality dynamics*. New York: Ronald Press, 1950.

MOWRER, O. H., PALMER, F., & SANGER, M. D. Individual learning and "racial experience" in the rat, with special reference to vocalization. *Journal of Genetic Psychology*, 1948, **73**, 29–43.

NOTTEBOHM, F. Ontogeny of bird song. *Science*, 1970, **167**, 950–956.

ORR, W. F., & CAPPANNARI, S. C. The emergence of language. *American Anthropologist*, 1964, **66**, 318–324.

PREMACK, D. A functional analysis of language. *Journal of the Experimental Analysis of Behavior*, 1970, **14**, 107–125.

PREMACK, D., & SCHWARTZ, A. Preparations for discussing behaviorism with chimpanzees. In F. Smith & G. A. Miller (Eds.), *The genesis of language: A psycholinguistic approach*. Cambridge, Mass.: M.I.T., 1966. Pp. 295–336.

SALZINGER, K. The problem of response class in verbal behavior. In K. Salzinger & S. Salzinger (Eds.), *Research in verbal behavior and some neurophysiological implications*. New York: Academic Press, 1967.

SALZINGER, K. Some problems of response measurement in verbal behavior: The response unit and intraresponse relations. In K. Salzinger & R. S. Feldman (Eds.), *Studies in verbal behavior: An empirical approach*. New York: Pergamon, 1973.

SALZINGER, K., FELDMAN, R. S., COWAN, J. E., & SALZINGER, S. Operant conditioning of verbal behavior of two young speech-deficient boys. In L. Krasner & L. P. Ullmann (Eds.), *Research in behavior modification: New developments and their clinical implications*. New York: Holt, Rinehart and Winston, 1965.

SALZINGER, K., FELDMAN, R. S., & PORTNOY, S. The effects of reinforcement on verbal and nonverbal responses. *Journal of General Psychology*, 1964, **70**, 225–234.

SALZINGER, K., & WALLER, M. B. The operant control of vocalization in the dog. *Journal of the Experimental Analysis of Behavior*, 1962, **5**, 383–389.

SAPON, S. M. Conditioning a vocal operant in the laboratory rat. Paper presented at the Meetings of the American Psychological Association, 1965.

SCHLOSBERG, H. Conditioned responses in the white rat. *Journal of Genetic Psychology,* 1934, **45,** 303–335.

SCHOENFELD, W. N. An experimental approach to anxiety, escape, and avoidance behavior. In P. H. Hoch & J. Zubin (Eds.) *Anxiety.* New York: Grune & Stratton, 1950. Pp. 70–99.

SCHUSTERMAN, R. J., & BALLIET, R. F. Conditioned vocalizations as a technique for determining visual acuity thresholds. *Science,* 1970, **169,** 498–501.

SCHUSTERMAN, R. J., BALLIET, R. F., & ST. JOHN, S. Vocal displays under water by the gray seal, the harbor seal and the stellar sea lion. *Psychonomic Science,* 1970, **18,** 303–305.

SCHUSTERMAN, R. J., & FEINSTEIN, S. H. Shaping and discriminative control of underwater click vocalizations in a California sea lion. *Science,* 1965, **150,** 1743–1744.

SCOTT, J. P. Observation. In T. A. Sebeok (Ed.). *Animal communication.* Bloomington: Indiana University Press, 1968. Pp. 17–30.

SEBEOK, T. A. Coding in the evolution of signalling behavior. *Behavioral Science,* 1962, **7,** 430–442.

SKINNER, B. F. *Verbal Behavior.* New York: Appleton-Century-Crofts, 1957.

TAVOLGA, W. N. Fishes. In T. A. Sebeok (Ed.) *Animal communication.* Bloomington: Indiana University Press, 1968. Pp. 271–288.

THORNDIKE, E. L. The origin of language. *Science,* 1943, **98,** 1–6.

WARNER, L. H. An experimental search for the "conditioned response." *Journal of Genetic Psychology,* 1932, **41,** 91–115.

WENNER, A. M. Honey bees. In T. A. Sebeok (Ed.), *Animal communication.* Bloomington: Indiana University Press, 1968. Pp. 75–102.

WILSON, E. O. Chemical systems. In T. A. Sebeok (Ed.), *Animal communication.* Bloomington: Indiana University Press, 1968. Pp. 75–102.

YATES, A. J. Delayed auditory feedback. *Psychological Bulletin,* 1963, **60,** 213–232.

PART TWO

ORIGINS OF BEHAVIOR

In studying the origins of behavior, we examine the factors which influence the development of behavior in individual organisms. It will be recalled that development was the focus of one of the four questions Tinbergen proposes might be asked of behavior. It is in studying the origins of behavior that we see the manner in which the genotype and the environment interact to produce behavior.

All behavior is dependent upon both the genotype and the environment of the organism. Yet, not all organisms behave in identical ways. The reasons for their behavioral differences can be found in the environmental history, the genotype, or both in the individuals themselves. Some of the behavioral differences between normal healthy individuals appear to develop in a manner essentially independent of specific learning, although learned elements may be a necessary part of the total pattern. For the establishment of other behavioral differences, specific events must be experienced in the lifetime of the individual—sometimes at relatively restricted periods in his development. The study of the ways in which genetic and experiential differences between organisms interact to produce behavioral differences has long fascinated scientists of many disciplines.

The extreme environmentalism that characterized behaviorism in psychology during much of the twentieth century retarded the growth of behavior genetics. This environmentalism was epitomized in Watson's 1924 statement: "Give me a dozen healthy infants, well-formed, and my own specified world to bring them up in and I'll guarantee to take any one at random and train him to become any type of specialist I might select—doctor, lawyer, artist, merchant-chief, yes even beggar-man and thief, regardless of his talents, penchants, tendencies, abilities, vocations, and race of his ancestors."* Today, the substantial role of genetics in determining behavior in both humans and nonhumans is recognized by virtually all scientists. The study of genetic determinants of behavior has implications for, and applications to, virtually all areas of behavior. Behavior-genetic variables are important to all psychologists, and not just to those interested in the development of behavior. This is because of substantial individual differences in behavior. These differences, frequently of genetic origin, may result in quite different functional relationships between independent and dependent variables in different individuals. Because of this individuality, the design of the experiments we do and the manner in which we consider variations in the results are undergoing rapid transition. A revolution is taking place in the way animal behaviorists seek to establish the "laws" of behavior.

All behavior has a developmental history, and analysis of the development of any pattern, including those which appear to develop in the absence of specific learning experiences, can shed much light on our understanding of the behavior. Although this has always been appreciated, improved methods are revealing important and sometimes subtle ontogenetic factors essential for behavior.

In Chapter 6, the basic principles of behavior genetics are discussed, and the development of behavior is the topic of Chapter 7. Together, these chapters describe the interaction of genetic and environmental factors in the origination of behavior in individual organisms.

*Watson, J. B. *Behaviorism*. (Rev. ed.) Chicago: The University of Chicago Press, 1924. P. 104.

Chapter 6

Behavior Genetics

J. L. Fuller and R. E. Wimer

Men and mice, chimpanzees and honeybees differ in appearance and in behavior. In a broad sense, these species are distinct because they are genetically different. Viewed in this way, the entire field of comparative psychology is coextensive with behavior genetics. In fact, behavior genetics is often studied for the same reasons that comparative psychology is studied. Nature has produced a tremendous variety of kinds of nervous systems, sense organs, and effectors. Correlations between behavior and these physical substrates lead to a deeper understanding of the links between structure and function. Genetically determined structural variations within a species may have similar value for analytical studies.

Another aspect of behavior genetics is concerned with the distribution and causes of individual differences within populations. In the case of humans, we should like to know how different they are in socially important traits, including intelligence, aggressiveness, response to stress, and the like (Wechsler, 1952). In some situations, the relative contributions of heredity and environment may be of immediate practical interest even though the details of the mechanisms through which genetic and environmental differences produce their psychological effects may presently be obscure.

Behavior genetics is sometimes thought to be a recently emerged division within genetics. But its roots go back to Darwin's (1872) studies of sexual selection as an evolutionary force and to his pioneering studies of domestication and the expression of emotion. In the final quarter of the nineteenth century, Galton (1883) was reporting on the resemblance between relatives in talent and ability. At that time genetics as a scientific discipline was yet to be born. The recognition of Mendel's (1865) work on the genetics of peas stimulated renewed interest in the inheritance of behavioral characteristics in man, particularly of intelligence. Much of this early work suffers because the conceptual tools for a scientific behavior genetics were not available, but the issues of social biology are still alive (Meade & Parkes, 1965; Thoday & Parkes, 1968).

In psychology, genetic ideas became entangled with the theory of instincts, and a belief in genetic influences on behavior became illogically confused with a belief in the nonmodifiability of behavior. Gradually the polarization of psychology into environmentalist and hereditarian camps has moderated. Experience has shown the errors of a nature-nurture dichotomy. Instead, we now see a coaction or synergism between genetic and environmental determinants of psychological development.

GENETIC PRINCIPLES

The distinguishing feature of genetics is the use of biological relationship as an independent variable. All the complex superstructure of modern genetics has its basis in accurate pedigree records and often in planned mating systems utilizing specially bred strains. The genetical approach to biology embraces a broad range of phenomena, as evinced by such descriptive terms as molecular genetics, physiological genetics, population genetics, and behavior genetics. To cover all aspects of genetics which might relate to behavior is impossible within a single chapter. Specialized sources on this subject include Fuller and Thompson (1960), Hirsch (1967a), Parsons (1967), and Lindzey and Thiessen (1970), and there are many treatments of general genetics varying in complexity and viewpoint. The following section is limited to a few fundamentals which are basic to any discussion of the relationships between genes and behavior.

Genotype and Phenotype

A *phenotype* is a category in a classification scheme for assigning living things to different groups on the basis of some observable physical characteristic which they possess, such as color, size, weight, and so on. Schemes vary in complexity and in precision. Thus, all agouti (wild type, gray) mice may be assigned to one phenotype and all albinos to another category. Body weight is a quantitative classification scheme involving assignment to one of a large number of ordered categories.

In behavior genetics the concept of the phenotype is extended to include behavioral processes such as nest-cleaning, learning ability, and alcohol preference. For convenience, we shall divide possible animal phenotypes into two broad categories, using *psychophene* for the behavioral processes studied by behavior geneticists, and reserving *somatophene* for anatomical and chemical characteristics. Psychophenic differences, of course, have physical bases, and genes modify psychophenes through intermediary somatophenes.

Genotype refers to the whole, or a selected portion, of the genetic material of a cell or organism. Regularities in the phenotypic characteristics of related individuals can be explained only by a model which postulates the transmission of discrete bits of information regarding development from parent to offspring. Long before molecular biologists had given substance to the abstract concept of a gene, the reality of this unit of heredity was universally accepted. We now know that the genetic code specifying protein structure is based upon the ordering of a small number of bases in large molecules of DNA (deoxyribonucleic acid), and we expect that the code will prove to be universal in all organisms. Genotypes are named for their more obvious phenotypic effects, and the phenotype of an organism is often, though not always, diagnostic of its genotype (Sinnott, Dunn, & Dobzhansky, 1958).

Transmission Genetics

Among relatives, resemblances and differences in qualitative traits can be explained and predicted by means of a few simple laws originally proposed by Mendel, with certain extensions based upon studies of chromosomes. The Mendelian laws apply to sexually reproducing species and are based on a double (diploid) representation of the genetic material in each body cell. One set of this material comes from the male gamete (special reproductive cell) and one set comes from the female gamete. Each set is composed of a number of chromosomes (N) which is fixed in each species ($N = 23$ in man, $N = 20$ in the mouse, and $N = 4$ in the fruitfly, for example). Since each parent contributes a full set (N), the total number of chromosomes in a body cell is $2N$. The functional units (genes) are arranged linearly along the long axis of the N pairs of chromosomes as houses might be arranged sequentially along streets. Each gene has an address or *locus* on a specific chromosome and can normally be found only at that locus. Since there are pairs of chromosomes in each cell (or two identically laid-out streets, if you will), there are actually two loci for each type of gene. Genes which can occupy the same locus, but which are functionally distinct, are known as *alleles*.

Dominance   Often the phenotypic effect of one type of allele obscures that of the other. For example, *homozygous* (having the same allele at both loci) black mice (genotypic formula, *B/B*), crossed with homozygous brown mice (*b/b*), produce a first filial generation (F$_1$) which is phenotypically black and genotypically *B/b*. Black is said to be *dominant* over *recessive* brown, and the mice are heterozygous (having different alleles at the two loci). Dominance is properly applied to phenotypic effects of genes rather than to the genes themselves, though it is common to speak of dominant genes. When the phenotype is a chemical structure as in blood groups, both alleles are generally functional and are said to be *codominant*.

Segregation   When gametes are produced, chromosome pairs (and thus the alleles located on them) separate so that each egg or sperm contains only one complete set of chromosomes. The process is called *segregation*. Thus, the genes of the F_1 hybrid just described segregate to produce B and b gametes in equal numbers. If an F_1 is crossed with its homozygous brown parent (b/b) (this type of mating is called a backcross), brown and black offspring will be equally probable, assuming that the two phenotypes are equally viable. If F_1 hybrids are bred together, the resultant F_2 generation will on the average contain one-fourth of the recessive phenotypes and three-fourths of the dominant ones. The distribution of phenotypes in segregating backcross and F_2 generations into proportions consistent with these ratios has been considered as evidence that the phenotypic difference is controlled by a single locus, but is is not conclusive, since other genetic systems can simulate Mendelian ratios.

Assortment   Genes which have their addresses on different chromosomes show fully *independent assortment* at the time of gamete production. The intensity of coat color in the mouse is modified by genes at the d locus on a chromosome pair which does not include genes acting at the b locus. Homozygous d/d mice are dilutely pigmented; D/D or D/d are densely pigmented. Breeding dense black (B/B, D/D) by dilute brown (b/b, d/d) yields a dense black F_1 (B/b, D/d). In the F_2, both black and dense have a ¾ probability; brown and dilute a ¼ probability. This means, in everyday terms, that the second generation has a 3 in 4 chance of being black or dense, and a 1 in 4 chance of being brown or dilute. Because the two loci assort independently, dilute black and dense brown animals occur in these hybrids in proportions found by multiplying the probabilities of the two independent components: dense black ($¾ \times ¾ = {}^9/_{16}$); dense brown ($¾ \times ¼ = {}^3/_{16}$); dilute black ($¼ \times ¾ = {}^3/_{16}$) and dilute brown ($¼ \times ¼ = {}^1/_{16}$). Actually, the hypothesis of independent assortment is a deduction from the observation that these ratios occur over and over again within the limits of random variation.

Linkage   If chromosomes were perfectly coherent bodies, they, rather than genes, would be the units of transmission genetics. In fact, homologous chromosomes (the pairs containing addresses for the same genes) exchange material during the process of gamete formation. Genes at the end of a long chromosome, therefore, can be transmitted as independently as though they were on separate chromosomes. But genes close together are *linked* in predictable proportions which are roughly related to their physical closeness. In some cases, it is difficult to distinguish between multiple phenotypic effects from a single gene and phenotypic effects which go together because two or more genes are closely linked.

Quantitative Inheritance

Most psychophenes (and many somatophenes, for that matter) are not classifiable into two or three mutually exclusive classes, but cluster about a central point with a few individuals far above or below the main body. Continuous variation in the phenotype may appear inconsistent with genetic interpretations based upon segregation of two alleles at a single locus. If each of the three possible genotypes (A/A, A/a, a/a) corresponds with a relatively invariant phenotype, there can be only three distinct classes with no organisms between (Figure 6–1A). However, if the genotype has a looser control over development, the three distributions may overlap so much that they appear to form a continuum (Figure 6–1B). The broad curve of Figure 6–1B could also represent the cumulative effects of variation at several independent loci. A simple model postulates two alleles at each locus, one enhancing and one diminishing a particular function. The algebraic sum of these effects determines the phenotype (subject, of course, to environmental effects). Functional equivalence of different genes with the same algebraic sign is not an essential part of this model. Genes acting upon receptors, nerve cells, or endocrine glands could enhance learning ability in different ways while being indistinguishable in terms of effect on error scores.

The methods of quantitative genetics superficially appear to be very different from those of Mendelian genetics, but in fact they are based upon the hypothesis that inheritance is basically similar for all traits (Falconer, 1960). The systems to which these methods are applied are often called polygenic (many genes), implying that effects of individual genes cannot be separated.

Coefficient of Genetic Determination   Variability in behavior can result from either genetic or environmental factors; thus the phenotypic effect of a particular genotype is a function of the environment in which it exists. In symbolic form, one writes:

$$\sigma_P^2 = \sigma_G^2 + \sigma_E^2 + \sigma_{EG}^2$$

in which σ^2 is variance,* and the subscripts refer to phenotype *(P)*, genotype *(G)*, environmental effects *(E)*, and genotype environment interaction *(EG)*.

*Variance is the average of the squared deviations of a set of observations from their mean. The square root of variance is the standard deviation of a distribution. Variances have mathematical properties which are very useful in quantitative genetics.

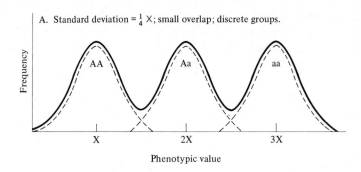

A. Standard deviation = $\frac{1}{4}$ X; small overlap; discrete groups.

Frequency

AA   Aa   aa

X   2X   3X

Phenotypic value

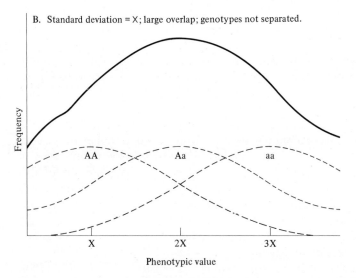

B. Standard deviation = X; large overlap; genotypes not separated.

Frequency

AA   Aa   aa

X   2X   3X

Phenotypic value

Figure 6–1. *(a)* The phenotypic distributions of three genotypes *(AA, Aa, aa)* for a quantitative trait such as weight or intelligence are shown by dashed lines. The trait is assumed to be normally distributed about means *X* units apart with standard deviations of *X*/4. There is relatively little overlap between groups, and a distinct trimodal curve remains when the three are summated (solid line) as would be necessary if the genotypes were not separately identifiable. *(b)* Here the three genotypes have the same means, but the standard deviations are *X*. There is now much overlap and the summated curve is unimodal. In an acutal population its form would vary depending upon the frequency of the two alleles, but the same phenotypic overlapping would occur.

The proportion of phenotypic variance attributable to genetic components σ_G^2/σ_P^2 is called the coefficient of genetic determination which ranges from 0 to 1. Closely related to this coefficient is the coefficient of heritability, σ_A^2/σ_P^2, whose numerator is the variance attributable to additive genetic effects. The point of the difference between the two coefficients is that a part of the total genetic influence is due to dominant genes suppressing their recessive alleles, and part to special interactions between genes at different loci. These effects are not reliably handed down to offspring because of the breaking up of gene combinations during gamete formation. Subtracting them from total genetic variance yields σ^2_A, a measure of heritable phenotypic variation.

Computations of heritability have application only to the population on which they are based. The principle becomes obvious when one considers genetically extreme situations involving only members of the same inbred strain. An inbred strain is so uniform genetically that phenotypic variation within the line is essentially completely environmental in origin so that heritability equals zero. Nevertheless, genes are operating in inbred animals exactly as they are in genetically heterogeneous populations. Zero heritability does not mean absence of genetic effects.

Biometrical Genetics   Because so many of the phenotypes of interest to psychologists do show continuous quantitative variation within an interbreeding population, considerable effort has gone into biometrical analyses of breeding experiments (Broadhurst & Jinks, 1961; Roberts, 1967). A number of methods have been used, the choice depending upon the availability of particular kinds of organisms (parents-offspring, inbred lines and their crosses, specially selected lines, and so forth). Descriptions and evaluations of these methods are beyond the scope of this chapter. The value of the biometrical approach is most evident in population surveys in which one can judge the relative importance of genetics as a contributor to individual variation. From such findings one can predict the efficacy of directed selection in the laboratory or natural selection in the field as applied to behavior. The inability to recognize discrete gene effects in classical biometrical analyses severely restricts their application to problems of physiological behavior genetics, since the full power of genetic analysis requires locus specification. Nevertheless, biometrical genetics continues to play an important role in behavioral studies, and there are signs of convergence of biometrical and Mendelian approaches.

Population Genetics

The principles of genetics have evolved from the results of laboratory studies. In natural populations matings are not arranged to suit an experimenter's convenience. Nevertheless, it has been demonstrated that the distribution of genes in populations is a lawful process, and it is possible to test genetic hypotheses with data from natural groups.

Genetic Equilibrium   The fundamental concept of population genetics is *genetic equilibrium,* an idealized state in which mating is at random and all genotypes are equally viable and fertile. One may visualize a large pool containing eggs and sperm, each of two kinds, A or a, representing the dominant and recessive forms of a gene. A bar over a gene symbol will be used to indicate its frequency, with values ranging from zero to one, and summing to one for all alletic genes $(\bar{A} + \bar{a} = 1)$. By simple algebra it is seen that the frequency of the three possible genotypes is given by the following terms:

Genotype	AA	Aa	aa
Frequency	$\bar{A}^2$	$2\bar{A}\,\bar{a}$	$\bar{a}^2$

It can be shown that gene frequencies remain constant indefinitely provided that mating remains random, all genotypes reproduce equally well, and the genes themselves are stable. This principle is known as the Hardy-Weinberg law. Real populations deviate from these conditions: Individuals may mate preferentially with those of similar phenotype; they may avoid or favor matings with relatives; genes may alter in form, or *mutate;* some genotypes may be incompatible with reproduction or may impair fertility; populations themselves have indefinite limits and can split into subgroups or accept immigrants. All these phenomena occur in nature and also can be deliberately regulated in a laboratory or an animal-breeding operation.

Selection   Differential reproduction of genotypes results in *selection*. If *aa* individuals of one generation contribute less than their share of gametes to the pool, there will be fewer *aa* and *Aa* individuals in the next generation. Continued selection will result in a gradual decrease in $\bar{a}$ and an increase in $\bar{A}$. In actuality, selective forces operate upon phenotypes; hence, the mechanics of selection vary greatly with the degree of dominance of a gene and the degree to which environmental variation influences the selection criterion. All populations, even those sheltered in a laboratory, are exposed to natural selection for viability. Persistence of a dominant lethal gene, for example, is clearly impossible.

In general, selection for behavioral criteria has been successful. Also, genetically distinct lines which have not been deliberately selected for such traits turn out to have a characteristic set of behaviors. In fact, failure to select successfully and absence of strain differences in behavior are so unusual as to merit special attention (Collins, 1969). Seldom are the differences found between selected lines shown to be correlated with segregation at a single specifiable locus. Instead, they seem to be explicable by the summated effects of segregation at numerous loci—each having a small effect on the total phenotypic variation.

Mutation   Mutation, a change in composition of a DNA molecule, is another factor which can alter gene frequencies. Mutations are the raw material of evolutionary change in a species, since those which render an organism less fit to reproduce will disappear, and those which improve chances for reproduction will increase. They are sufficiently rare (frequencies per locus per generation are 10^{-5} to 10^{-6}) that they can usually be omitted from consideration in a population observed through a few generations, but over the long run they will accumulate and cause marked changes.

Most mutations impair the biological efficiency of the individuals in which they are expressed (often called *mutants*). Geneticists, however, go to great trouble to maintain them because of their value as experimental subjects. The use of mutants in behavioral research will be considered later.

Mutation and selection acting in unison upon a population in a stable environment may achieve an equilibrium state in which the introduction of new alleles by mutation is just balanced by their removal through natural selection. Changes in environment which alter the reproductive fitness of one of the alleles (i.e., medical compensation for a genetic deficiency) can change the equilibrium and lead to a new equilibrium. Since most species are exposed to a variety of environments, there appears to be an advantage in genetic diversity which permits a wider range of habitats to be exploited. There is thus no single optimum genotype or phenotype. Variability is as much a part of the species concept as is resemblance to a descriptive prototype.

Testing Genetic Hypotheses

The necessary bases for a genetic study of behavior are phenotypic variation and control of the mating system. An investigator wishing to determine the contribution of genes to individual variation will proceed differently according to the type of genetic material he has available and also according to the nature of the behavioral phenotype. In a general way, four situations can be recognized.

Phenotype Discontinuous; Random-breeding Population   A good example of this situation is the ability in man to taste phenylthiocarbamide. Most people can be clearly designated as tasters or nontasters. Matings are classified by type (taster × taster; taster × nontaster; nontaster × nontaster), and the observed proportions of offspring compared with those predicted from a specified theory. Snyder's solution of this problem is summarized in Fuller and Thompson (1960, p. 99). The analysis is complicated by the fact that the taste gene (T) is dominant; hence, allowance must be made for the fact that tasters can be either T/T or T/t.

Phenotype Discontinuous; Pure Lines or Highly Selected Lines Available   This is the ideal situation for testing simple genetic hypotheses, such as those which account for the coat color of mice. Unfortunately, few psychophenes can be classified readily into one or two classes, normal and abnormal, for example, and those which can are likely to be the functional accompaniment of a well-defined somatophene.

In special situations, however, behavioral differences between lines have been shown probably to be due to gene differences at a single locus. An example is audiogenic seizure susceptibility in mice where a selected susceptible strain differs from a resistant at one locus (Lehmann & Boesiger, 1964).

Phenotype Continuous; Random-breeding Population The inheritance of human intelligence falls in this category, though its solution is complicated by the facts that (1) people seek mates of similar intellectual ability, and (2) environment influences intelligence to a much greater degree than it affects taste sensitivity. The conceptual basis of the methodology for studying such problems is, however, relatively simple. The average proportion of genes held in common (because they have come from common ancestors) is readily calculated for related individuals—for example, it is 1/2 for siblings, 1/8 for first cousins, and 1.0 for one-egg twins. The closeness with which phenotypic correlations parallel these genetic correlations is an indication of the heritability of a trait. This approach has been widely used in human studies (Fuller & Thompson, 1960; Vandenberg, 1965, 1968). It has potential usefulness in animal research as shown by a study of inheritance of avoidance learning in pigs (Willham, Cox, & Karas, 1963).

Another way of determining the heritability of behavioral variation is to see whether a trait of interest can be increased or decreased in a population through selective breeding. Usually, selection for a behavioral character is practiced in order to obtain animals of a desired phenotype—not merely to demonstrate heritability. However, such experiments do yield quantitative estimates of additive genetic variance. Examples are shown in Table 6–1.

Phenotype Continuous; Pure Lines or Highly Selected Lines Available.
Crosses between strains which are unlike in behavior commonly yield offspring (F_1) which are intermediate to their parents. Sometimes the F_1 performs better than either parent and is said to show hybrid vigor or heterosis (Bruell, 1967). Crosses between F_1 individuals yield an F_2, and crosses between the F_1 and the parental type yield backcross generations. Analysis of the means and variances of such Mendelian experiments yield estimates of heritability and sometimes of additive genetic, dominant genetic, and environmental sources of variation (Table 6–1). In many cases, analysis of the means only is highly instructive, as shown in Figure 6–2.

Another frequently used method of genetic analysis is the diallel cross in which a wide array of lines are intercrossed in all possible combinations or in a sample of combinations. Examples of the use of diallel crosses in behavior genetics include Broadhurst's (1960) study of defecation and open field activity in the rat, Collins' (1964) study of avoidance conditioning in mice and Henderson's (1967) experiments on the effect of handling and shock in infancy upon later open field behavior. Estimates of sources of variation

Table 6-1   Heritability Estimates for Psychophenes

Measure	Organism	Method	Reference*	Value (s)	
Open field activity	Mouse	Cross of inbred strains	FT	.60;	.53†
Y-maze activity	Mouse	Cross of inbred strains	FT	.31;	.26†
Wildness	Mouse	Cross wild and tame stocks	D	.55†;	.35‡
Sex behaviors (Various)	Guinea pig	Cross of inbred strains	GJ	.50† to .89	
Aggressiveness	Chicken	Selection	GCM	.22	
Phototaxis	Drosophila	Selection	HB	.57	

*Reference: D, Dawson (1932); FT, Fuller and Thompson (1960); GJ, Goy and Jakway (1959); GCM, Guhl, Craig, and Mueller (1960); HB, Hirsch & Boudreau (1958).
† Heritability calculated by Broadhurst and Jinks (1961).
‡ Heritability calculated by Fuller and Thompson (1960).

are obtained as in the Mendelian experiments, and they may be more representative of the species as a whole than results based upon crosses between two strains.

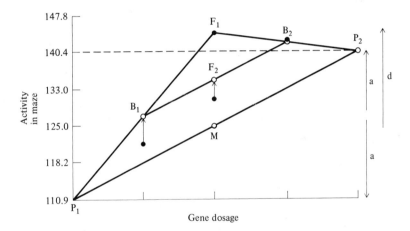

Gene dosage

Figure 6–2.   Observed and expected population means on exploratory activity of mice in a maze. (From Bruell, 1962.) The horizontal axis is scaled to reflect the proportion of genes from P_1 (Strain A) and P_2 (Strain C57BL/10) in each of the tested generations. Thus for both F_1 and F_2 the proportions are equal. The solid circles denote the observed means of the groups; the open circles show values expected in the backcross and F_2 (genetically heterogeneous) given the observations on the parents and F_1 (genetically homogeneous). The distance a on the vertical axis is ½ the range between the parents. If inheritance were strictly additive the F_1 should fall on M, the midparent point. Clearly it does not. The distance between M and the observed F_1 value is the dominance deviation, d. [From J. H. Bruell. Dominance and segregation in the inheritance of quantitative behavior of mice. In E. L. Bliss (Ed.) *Roots of Behavior.* New York: Harper & Row, 1962, Pp. 44–67. By permission of Hoeber Medical Division, Harper Row.]

PHYSIOLOGICAL BEHAVIOR GENETICS

Physiological behavior genetics is concerned with the biological basis and organization of behavior. The primary intent is to understand a behavior by learning more of (1) its biochemical, physiological, and anatomical bases, (2) its adaptive significance, and (3) the relation of its biological bases to those for other behaviors (Hirsch, 1964; Thompson, 1967).

These goals are closely related to those of other physiological or comparative psychologists. However, there is no scalpel to excise tissue or destroy an anatomical connection, no implanted stimulating electrode to elicit heightened activity of a structure, no drug to alter artificially the chemical processes within the organism. Instead, genes acting singly or in combination perform these functions, on occasion resulting in alterations presently obtainable with no other technique and always offering the prospect of observing the consequences of such gene variations on the development and function of an intact nervous system. To understand how genes affect behavior, one must turn to a consideration of the biological processes intervening between primary gene action and behavior.

Pathways from Genes to Behavior

When we speak of the genetics of a behavior, we are using a verbal shorthand as a matter of convenience. Genes never directly determine behavior. Behavior is the product of the activities of populations of cells in muscles and glands of the body. Their activities are coordinated in substantial part by the activities of other remotely located cell groups functioning as sensors and as information-processing systems. Primary gene action is within a cell. There, genes reproduce themselves and make proteins which are enzymes and structural components of the organism. The particular genes activated within a specific cell lead to specialization of that cell into skin, hair, muscle, receptor, neuron, and so on (Caspari, 1958; Sutton, 1965).

But a gene's effects are not restricted to those cells in which the gene is active. Other cells may depend upon the activity of that cell and so be affected by the gene indirectly. Thus, pituitary dwarfism stems from defective gene action in cells in the pituitary which produce growth hormone (Carsner & Rennels, 1960). The result is marked reduction in size of all parts of the body. Neurons deprived of stimulation by other neurons or receptors may fail to develop normally or may degenerate. Thus, genes which operate directly within the retinal rods causing their destruction may indirectly produce failure of normal neuron development in the visual cortex (Gyllensten & Lindberg, 1964). In view of the importance of vision to many tasks, the effects of this gene, whose primary action is restricted to one kind of cell in a specific organ, could be far-reaching.

Since genes have direct and indirect effects, the process by which a gene affects behavior may involve a path consisting of a number of steps stretching from the intracellular site of primary gene action to publicly observable behavior. The pathway can be long or short. It may branch into several distinct routes as a gene's secondary effects become involved in a variety of biological processes. One gene may thus affect several behaviors.

One behavior also necessarily involves many genes. There must be an organism to behave, and each of its essential structures has its own complex genetic determinants (Russell, 1963; Sperry, 1958). A psychophene selected for genetic study may in fact consist of two or more independent components. For example, lines of honeybees vary in their resistance to American foulbrood disease. Studies on crosses between a line of disease-resistant bees and a susceptible line suggest that disease resistance is due to nest-cleaning behavior. When infected larvae and pupae are promptly removed, they do not infect others. This behavior is, in turn, made up of two components: (1) uncapping of cells containing dead larvae, and (2) the removal of the dead larvae. Each component is inherited independently (Rothenbuhler, 1964). A corollary of the complexity of pathways linking genes with psychophenes is that specific genetic hypotheses relate only to differences between individuals or strains. Thus the differences between *uncapping* and *removal* in the two lines studied by Rothenbuhler appear to fit a rather simple genetic pattern, but this does not mean that two genes regulate all the processes which comprise these behaviors.

MUTANT GENES AND BEHAVIOR

The great potential complexities in analyzing the genetics of psychophenes have led some behavior geneticists to concentrate on the effects of gene substitutions at a single locus. This approach has been highly commended (Merrell, 1965) and criticized as leading to mostly trivial results (Wilcock, 1969). The truth is that the method has advantages and limitations which must be understood in appraising results of studies using it.

There are three reasons for studying animals differing systematically at a single genetic locus. They are: (1) Substitution of alleles produces correspondingly precise variations in biological processes and may permit experiments which are obtainable in no other manner; (2) genes may produce abnormalities in experimental animals which closely resemble a human abnormality of medical interest; and (3) genes which are behaviorally neutral can be used to mark chromosomes on which other genes with behavioral effects are located.

No matter what specific strategy the experimenter adopts, there will always be the risk that the nature of the gene action on behavior will be too complex for resolution. It is a risk that must be accepted, but it can be minimized by eliminating from detailed study for at least the present those genes which affect many different and comparatively unrelated behaviors or render the animal ill or seriously incoordinated.

Genic Substitution as a Natural Experiment

There are more than three hundred identified genes producing detectable effects on coat color, morphology, or behavior in the house mouse (M. C. Green, 1966). There is a bias in the detection of single-gene effects favoring phenotypes deviating sharply from the normal. Most neurological mutants run in circles and shake their heads, have convulsions, or show gross motor incoordination (Sidman, Green, & Appel, 1965). Names given to neurological mutants include leaner, reeler, staggerer, weaver, waltzer, whirler, dervish, ataxia, quaking, jimpy, and jittery. An indication of the magnitude of neural involvement which is common is given by other mutant names, such as brain hernia, eyeless, hydrocephalus-1, and cerebral degeneration. Needless to say, many of these mutants would not be appropriate for psychological research, though they might be excellent preparations for the neurochemist or neuroembryologist. Gross behavioral anomaly does not always indicate gross and diffuse alterations within the nervous system, however, for circling behavior can be produced by rather restricted defects in the semicircular canals of the ear.

An example of a gene in the mouse with rather neatly limited effects on a sense organ is retinal degeneration (*rd*). Figure 6-3 shows two retinas. The normal one on the bottom is thicker and has more cell layers than the one on the top, taken from a mouse with a double dose of the *rd* gene. In this condition, the retina in general appears quite normal except that the rods are missing. These cells are located between the outer layers of the eye and the inner layers of the retina. Rods are on the external surface of the retina proper and thus point away from incoming light. They cannot be destroyed surgically without destroying other vital structural and functional components of the eye. A gene, then, has performed an experiment which could be done in no other manner.

Mice with retinal degeneration show some capacity for learning in a Yerkes discrimination box, providing evidence that both brightness and form can be detected by elements other than rods. How this is accomplished is a fascinating problem still open to further experimentation (Bonaventure & Karli, 1969; Fuller & Wimer, 1966, pp. 614–616).

Figure 6-4 shows a mouse with a behavior problem: it eats too much, lies around much of the time, and doesn't do its fair share in procreation of the species. This mouse has a double dose of the *ob* gene for obesity. It is a member of strain C57BL/6-*ob*. The recessive *ob* gene occurred in another stock and was placed on the C57BL/6 genetic background by the

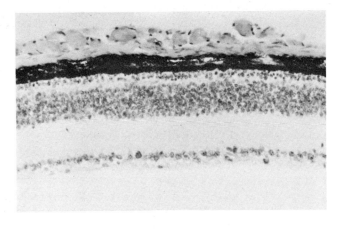

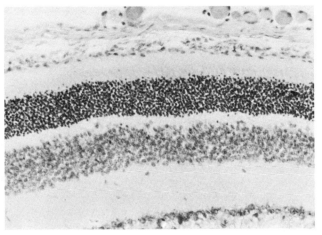

Figure 6–3. On the bottom a normal mouse retina. On the top a retina from a mouse homozygous for the gene for retinal degeneration *(rd/rd)*. The inner cell layer of rods is missing and visual sensitivity is almost completely lost.

cross-intercross breeding system (E. L. Green, 1966, 1968). This mouse is said to be *congenic* with strain C57BL/6 except at the *ob* locus. Reared under typical laboratory conditions with plenty of food always available, *ob/ob* mice end up weighing twice as much as littermate nonobese C57BL/6-*ob*/+ and C57BL/6-+/+ brothers and sisters. When placed on a strict diet, obese mice lose weight and begin to breed (Lane & Dickie, 1954). Normal mice do most of their eating at night, but obese mice eat at a relatively uniform rate throughout the day (Anlikcr & Mayer, 1956).

Figure 6–4. An obese mouse (genotype *ob/ob*) whose metabolic defect impairs regulation of food intake and produces debilitating overweight.

When the caloric content of the diet was altered by diluting it with cellulose or adding fat, normal nonobese mice responded by increasing or decreasing their food intake appropriately to maintain a uniform caloric level. Obese mice altered their food intake patterns in the appropriate direction as well, but palatability seemed to play a greater role than caloric content. When a bitter substance, such as quinine, was put in their food, consumption for both normal and obese mice sharply decreased. Normals slowly increased their food intake toward their standard level over a period of several days, while obese mice continued to eat reduced amounts. The eating defect in the obese mouse, then, appears to involve a defect in central mechanisms which regulate eating as a function of caloric intake (Fuller & Jacoby, 1955).

There are two important points to keep in mind concerning genes and natural experiments. First, the experimenter must invest a great deal of his time and effort defining the experiment which the gene has performed. Since his primary concern is with behavioral consequences of a somatophene, he must know what the mutant gene has done to the organism. Second, the experimenter must evaluate the significance of the gene-produced experiment, applying the same standards he would apply to any other experiment. If it is not one which he would perform were he able to accomplish it in some other manner, it is not worthwhile. For example, a gene whose effects could be approximated by random stabs with a knitting needle into the brain would not be an informative experiment for the neuropsychologist.

Animal Models of Genetic Disease

A number of genes in humans produce inherited diseases or, since a biochemical process must be involved at some step in the pathway, an inborn error of metabolism. Many of these metabolic disorders are associated with mental deficiency (Hsia, 1967; Anderson, 1964). It would be interesting to discover inborn errors of metabolism in animals analogous to human disorders which produce a mental defect. There is good reason to hope that the search will be successful, for two inherited diseases similar to human ones have already been discovered in the mouse. They are diabetes (gene symbol *db*; Coleman & Hummel, 1967) and muscular dystrophy (gene symbol *dy*; Russell & Meier, 1966).

Among the genetically caused forms of mental deficiency, phenylketonuria has attracted particularly great experimental interest. The typical human phenylketonuriac has excessive amounts of phenylalanine and its degradation products in his urine and has a low IQ. The biochemical abnormality is the result of a deficiency of phenylalanine hydroxylase, the enzyme which converts phenylalanine to tyrosine. The nature of the brain defect is not yet known. The degree of mental defect is reduced when affected children are fed a diet low in phenylalanine from an early age, but treatment at a later age does not help. The data are consistent with the view that the unusual products of phenylalanine metabolism interfere with the functional development of neurons. It would obviously be highly desirable to work with the defect in animal populations in the laboratory. There, it might be possible to define the brain defect and to experiment at length with treatments to correct and, ultimately, to repair the metabolic error. Indeed, a gene that reduces phenylalanine hydroxylase level in a manner similar to phenylketonuria has been discovered in animals (Coleman, 1960). Mice with genotypes d/d and d^1/d^1 (dilute lethal) show reduced effective levels of this enzyme. The mechanism is different in the mouse, however, being due to the presence of an enzyme inhibitor rather than to less phenylalanine hydroxylase itself. Considerable effort has been devoted to studying the behavior of dilute mice (dilute lethals survive for only three weeks). They do not have obvious learning deficits nor has a correlation been demonstrated between the d/d genotype and audiogenic seizure susceptibility (Huff & Fuller, 1964; Schlesinger, Elston, & Boggan, 1966). Such an association had been expected because of a high frequency of convulsions in human phenylketonuriacs. Thus the animal model in this case has been less useful than was hoped in the investigation of a medical problem. But we should not expect too close a match between species.

The value of animal models resides not so much in their exact matching with human conditions as in their adaptability to rigorous testing of broadly framed hypotheses.

Mutant Genes as Markers

Paradoxically, one of the potentially important contributions of a mutant gene to experimental behavior genetics depends upon its lack of effect upon behavior. The polygenes which have such an important role in "fine-tuning" behavioral development are undoubtedly operating through chemical pathways. Presumably, if we knew what they were doing, we could detect the physical basis for the overt behavioral variation. But usually we do not know where to look, even though the evidence for an inherited variation in behavior is incontrovertible.

It is possible, however, to locate a gene detectable only by its behavioral effects if these effects can be shown to be linked to a significant degree with another gene, reliably detectable, which does not itself interfere with the behavior being observed. For example, *asp* (audiogenic seizure prone) has been found to lie on the same chromosome as genes affecting coat color, a skeletal malformation, and alternative forms of an enzyme (Collins, 1970). Figure 6-5 illustrates this finding. As data of this kind accumulate, we shall be able to map more genes observable by their psychophenic effects but not by their somatophenic effects. A conceptually similar scheme has been used to allocate the strength of genetic influences upon geotactic response among the three major chromosomes of *Drosophila melanogaster* (Hirsch, 1967b).

Evaluation of Mutants in Behavior Genetics

Studies of behavior in mutant-bearing animals play an important, though not dominant, role in contemporary behavior genetics. If these experiments are to contribute substantially to important psychological issues, they must be well conceived in both their behavioral and genetic aspects. Space does not

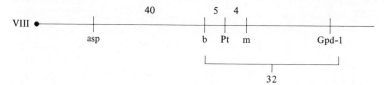

Figure 6–5. A portion of linkage group VIII of the mouse showing the position of audiogenic seizure prone *(asp)*, a gene detectable at present only by its behavioral effects. Other gene loci shown are recognized by their effects upon coat color, brown *(b)* and misty *(m):* upon skeleton, pintail *(Pt):* or upon enzyme structure, glucose-6-phosphate dehydrogenase (Gpd-1). Reprinted by permission of Greenwood Periodicals, Inc. from R. L. Collins in Behavior Genetics, 1(2), May, 1970.

permit consideration of the technical problems involved. Of major importance is the nature of the genetical background on which the mutant gene's effects are observed. Maximum precision is obtained when subjects differ at only one locus. Maximum generality is obtained when a gene's effects are measured in a randomly breeding, heterogeneous population.

Merrell (1965) may be too optimistic and Wilcock (1969) too pessimistic regarding the contribution of mutants to progress in behavior genetics. Under certain circumstances, they have a unique role to play in the search for biological mechanisms underlying behavioral variations. We have not found any dramatic breakthroughs in psychological thinking as a result of their use in experiments, but the basis may have been laid for them in the future.

STRAIN DIFFERENCES IN BEHAVIOR

Often strains or breeds of the same species react differently to identical treatment (Fuller & Thompson, 1960, Manosevitz, Lindzey, & Thiessen, 1969). To understand these studies, particularly those involving inbred strains we must consider inbreeding and its consequences. The genetic similarity of members of a strain is due to a mating system restricted to brother with sister or parent with offspring. In each generation only one pair is chosen to produce all the offspring for the next generation. Genes not present in either of the pair are lost forever to succeeding generations. Gradually, inexorably, all alleles at each locus are lost save one. Thus every animal will eventually be homozygous at nearly all loci. Because of the sex chromosome differences between males and females, highest similarity is achieved only by members of the same sex. When inbreeding has been continued for thirty generations or more, the animals within a strain become virtually as similar genetically as identical twins.

The selection of one male and one female to propagate all offspring for the next generation of an inbred strain results in a kind of random genetic filtering (with deviations caused by differences in viability and fertility). If separate inbreeding programs were begun simultaneously from the same foundation stock, this random filtration would guarantee that the resultant inbred strains would differ from one another. Each would show a characteristic pattern of somatophenes and psychophenes, but the associations within such patterns would not prove a functional relationship. Thus, if a black strain turns out to be a better maze learner than a gray strain, we have absolutely no assurance that the genes affecting pigment have anything to do with learning. On the other hand, we cannot be sure that they do not. Surveys of inbred strains can help to find the answer. If, in a large group of independently derived strains, two traits vary consistently in a similar pattern, the deduction is that they are controlled by a common set of genes.

Genetic Standardization

Inbred strains possess one outstanding advantage to the researcher: genetic reproducibility. As experimental subjects, they may be specified much as one specifies the purity of chemicals. This reproducibility has both spatial and temporal aspects. Two workers using the same inbred strains in different parts of the world can compare their results meaningfully. Temporally, once genetic fixation is attained, variation occurs only by the slow process of mutation. One can work with animals of an inbred strain over many years with reasonable assurance that their biology and behavior have not altered drastically. Finally, the reproducibility of the genotype within an inbred strain enhances flexibility of experimental design. In some instances, it may be unfeasible to take multiple observations on the same animal because of interactions between tasks or technical difficulties. Within an inbred line, it is possible to take different measurements on different animals and proceed inferentially as though they had been taken on the same animal.

Despite these many advantages, some words of warning are in order. Genetic uniformity usually reduces, but does not eliminate, phenotypic variability, and it is the phenotype which is directly observable. In general, inbred lines are less fertile and less vigorous than their hybrids or than random-bred stocks (Bruell, 1967). There is a price for genetic uniformity, and good judgment is needed with inbred strains as with mutants.

Audiogenic Seizures: A Case History of Strain Differences

Some mice, when exposed to high-frequency, high-intensity sound from which they cannot escape, begin to run faster and faster and finally have a convulsion. This convulsion typically involves the animal's falling on its side and kicking rhythmically (clonic phase). Animals may pass on into the more severe tonic phase (limbs extended and no breathing) and die from asphyxiation unless given artificial respiration. Audiogenic seizures are quite dramatic and have aroused considerable scientific interest because they have been conceived as having to do with some general characteristic of nervous-system excitability. A substantial genetic component is involved, for members of some inbred strains are far more likely to show audiogenic seizures than are members of others. In order of increasing incidence (from characteristically very low to very high), they are C57BL/6J, BALB/cJ, CBA/J, SJL/J, AKR/J, RF/J, SWR/J, and DBA/2J (Fuller & Sjursen, 1967).

There are several pieces of information now available concerning the anatomical and chemical bases of the audiogenic seizure phenomenon. We know, for example, that the more peripheral portions of the auditory pathway are likely to be involved and that there are differences between a seizure-prone and a seizure-resistant strain in probable chemical-transmitter substances in brain. We even suspect that only a few genes are involved.

It is possible to increase the incidence of audiogenic seizures in initially nonsusceptible strains by exposing them at a "sensitive age" to the seizure-inducing stimulus (Henry, 1967). When this is done and the animals are tested again two days later, the incidence of seizures is markedly increased. The animals are said to have been sensitized. This sensitization must involve a change in responsiveness in the ear itself, or in portions of the auditory pathway which are involved by stimulation of a single ear, for, when mice are exposed to the sensitizing sound with one ear blocked by glycerol and tested later with that same ear blocked, a high incidence of audiogenic seizures is seen. When only the ear that was blocked at sensitization is open at test, however, very few seizures are observed (Fuller & Collins, 1968).

Difference between strains in chemical activity within the brain could be the basis for the observed strain difference in seizure susceptibility. Schlesinger, Boggan, & Freedman (1965) tested mice of seizure-resistant strain C57BL/6J and seizure-prone strain DBA/2J for levels of the norepinephrine and serotonin in the brain and for audiogenic seizure susceptibility at 14, 21, 28, 35, and 42 days of age. Age of maximum seizure risk was found to be 21 days for strain DBA/2J, and this was also the only age at which a difference in the likely brain neurohumors was found (DBA/2J was lower on both). This result can, of course, prove nothing since only one seizure-prone stock was involved. Nevertheless, the possibility of a functional relation is strengthened by evidence of lower norepinephrine in the brain of a mouse strain selected for audiogenic seizure susceptibility (Lehmann, 1967).

The occurrence of audiogenic seizures in hybrids between susceptible and resistant strains of mice has been widely studied. It might seem to be an easy task to decide whether many or few genes are involved in producing the differences between strains, but in fact a number of conflicting models are still extant (Fuller & Collins, 1970). Viewing the species as a whole, it is safe to say that many genes are potential contributors to susceptibility. When the cumulative effects of those alleles which increase susceptibility surpass some physiological threshold, a convulsion occurs when the animal is appropriately stimulated. But the detailed results of any particular cross depend upon the strains employed and the method of specifying the phenotype. In some instances, a single locus appears responsible for a major difference between strains.

The genetic picture is clarified as we learn more about the environmental determinants of the phenotype. For example, the biological processes involved in first-trial susceptibility to audiogenic seizures and to sensitization-dependent susceptibility must be partially different, since a single locus (*asp*) has been shown to determine whether a mouse has one or the other (Collins & Fuller, 1968). A number of inherited variants of the nervous system which have appeared as the results of mutations in inbred lines are associated with differences in audiogenic seizure susceptibility (Ginsburg, Cowen, Maxon, & Sze,

1967). In this particular area of research, the trend is toward specification of individual gene effects in a polygenic system.

Somatophenic Characteristics of Inbred Strains

The nervous system, in particular the brain, is the great integrative center for behavior. Inbred strains turn out to differ greatly in many aspects of brain anatomy and chemistry. For instance, the gross weight of the brain varies widely in eighteen inbred strains. These differences are not simply proportional to differences in body weight (Figure 6-6). Some strains have brains that average over 20 percent heavier than those of others. Structural differences are not restricted to total weight. The relative volumes of neocortical and hippocampal portions of the brain differ greatly between inbred strains (Wimer, Wimer, & Roderick, 1969). An experimenter interested in the behavioral effects of having a bigger brain could use such data to select strains which are suitable for testing his hypothesis.

Genetic variation in the nervous system is not limited to features which can be ascertained with a balance or a microscope. A sample of five inbred strains of mice differed in the activity of three brain enzymes which are related

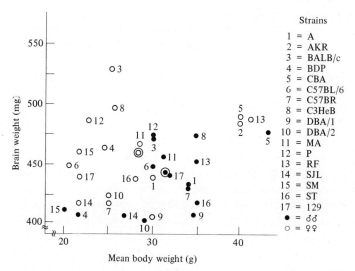

Figure 6–6. The relationship between brain weight and body weight varies greatly among inbred strains of mice. Averages for males are shown by solid circles; females, open circles. Note that some relatively large mice (DBA/1 for example) have small brains, and that the strain with the largest brains (BALB/c) has relatively low body weight. (From Fuller & Wimer, 1966. Based on data from J. B. Storer's article Relation of life span to brain weight, body weight, and metabolic rate among inbred mouse strains. *Experimental Gerontology*, 1967, 2, 173–182 by permission of Pergamon Press.)

to neurotransmitters (acetylcholinesterase, cholinesterase, and aromatic L-aminoacid decarboxylase) (Pryor, Schlesinger, & Calhoun, 1966). Two other enzymes also concerned with metabolism of neurotransmitters did not differ in this particular sample of strains, but a wider search would probably have succeeded in finding some differences. Two strains of mice widely used in behavioral experimentation, BALB/cJ and C57BL/10J, have similar concentrations of brain norepinephrine, but BALB/cJ has significantly more serotonin (Maas, 1962). Three strains of rats reported to be good maze performers had higher activities of L-aminoacid decarboxylase than did three strains considered to be poor performers (Pryor, 1968). The experimenter interested in relationships between brain chemistry and behavior can find strains with extreme somatophenes produced without pharmacological intervention which can be used to test specific hypotheses.

Psychophenic Characteristics of Inbred Strains

Behavioral differences between inbred strains have been reported frequently. Such studies are most useful when the number of strains observed is great enough to justify some confidence in correlations found with other potentially related characteristics. Two major surveys of open field activity in mice found almost identical ordering of the seven strains which were common to the experiments (Southwick & Clark, 1968; Thompson, 1953). From most to least active, the rankings were: C57BR/cdJ, C57BL/6J, DBA/2J (3rd or 4th), AKR/J (4th or 3rd), C3H/HeJ, BALB/cJ, and A/J. It is interesting to note that these two studies were performed in different laboratories 15 years apart, and that Southwick and Clark used males only.

Thompson measured food intake of fifteen strains (including the seven listed above) in an open field and found no correlation with activity, though there was a significant correlation ($-.796$) with defecation. Southwick and Clark rated their sample of strains (fourteen in all) on aggression and found a significant correlation between fighting and open field activity ($r = -.596$), although two strains were striking exceptions.

Another instance of agreement between studies from two laboratories is provided by data on alcohol preference in mice (Fuller, 1964; McClearn & Rodgers, 1959). The two experimenters used different sublines which had been separated for many generations and different methods of rating preference. In order of decreasing intake of alcohol in a choice situation, the four strains ranked: C57BL/6, C3H, A, and DBA/2.

Three studies of active avoidance of shock in a shuttle box have compared inbred strains of mice, but unfortunately the number of strains common to any two of the experiments is too few to permit generalizations (Collins, 1964; Fuller, 1970; Royce & Covington, 1960). There seems to be a tendency for strains which perform well in active avoidance to do poorly in passive avoidance situations, when they must remain quiet to avoid shock (Fuller,

1970). Inbred strains of mice also vary in performance on a one-way shock avoidance test, and it seems that the rank order is different for this task from the order for shuttling (Schlesinger & Wimer, 1967). Again, however, few strains were evaluated under both conditions.

Inbred strains of mice vary in other forms of learning. Five strains were trained to escape from a water maze by distinguishing between a white and a black alley. From best to worst, they ranked: C57BL/6J, DBA/2J, RF/J, AKR/J, and A/HeJ. The last of these essentially learned nothing during the time allowed (Wimer & Weller, 1965).

As more and more data accumulate on the somatophenic and psychophenic characteristics of inbred strains, they will become even more useful to the comparative psychologist. There is need for a behavioral characterization of strains of mice and rats and possibly other species in a manner similar to that which has been used for years in describing chemical compounds. With such characterization, scientists can make more imaginative use of these strains, taking advantage of their individuality and reproducibility.

SELECTED LINES

Selective breeding in the laboratory has two major purposes: (1) to demonstrate the heritability of a trait, and (2) to produce specific phenotypes in large numbers so that biology-behavior relationships can be explored. Selection is basically a technique for making the rare more common, and by producing gene combinations which are highly improbable in nature, it may even "create" new phenotypes. Useful discussion may be found in Lerner (1958) and Falconer (1960).

The efficiency of selection, sometimes called realized heritability, can be measured by the ratio *gain/reach*. Reach is defined as the difference between the mean of the selected parents ($\overline{X}_p$) and that of the base population from which they were taken ($\overline{X}_b$). Gain is the difference between the mean of the offspring of the selected parents ($\overline{X}_o$) and that of the base population. In symbols:

$$\text{Realized heritability} = \frac{\overline{X}_o - \overline{X}_b}{\overline{X}_p - \overline{X}_b}$$

There are several reasons why gain falls short of reach. Part of an animal's phenotypic score is determined by its peculiar life history, and this is not transmitted in gametes. Also part of heredity's effect upon phenotype depends upon specific combinations of genes either at one locus (dominance effects) or at different loci (interaction effects). These critical combinations of genes cannot be passed to the offspring reliably, and their phenotypic effects are thus not fully heritable.

Fortunately, it has been found that genetic selection works in large measure as though individuals contained varying number of *plus* or *minus* genes, and that their phenotypes were related to the algebraic sum of these gene effects. Such additive components are transmitted reliably to offspring according to Mendelian principles, and their magnitude determines the rate of response to selection.

Modes of Selection

Selection for psychological characteristics is usually directional, that is, animals from the high or low end of a distribution are used as parents for the next generation. It is also possible to select from the middle of a distribution, discarding the extremes. This procedure is called stabilizing selection, since it tends to reduce variability. Stabilizing selection is similar to natural selection, for, on the average, extreme phenotypes are not well adapted to normal environments and reproduce less effectively.

In either form of selection, an experimenter can choose the parents of the next generation in two ways. In individual selection he mates similar males and females, for example, high-scoring males with high-scoring females. Parents for later generations are chosen by following the same rules within each selected line. Family selection is used when either (1) heritability is low, or (2) phenotypic measurement destroys or sterilizes the tested animal. Low heritability can be thought of as low reliability of detecting genes with additive effects, when their presence is obscured by environmental influences or by dominance and interactive effects of genes. By establishing an average phenotypic value for all the offspring of a family, the erratic components will be averaged out, and the family as a whole, or individuals chosen randomly from it, can be used for breeding.

Two courses are available when measurement is destructive, as in determining lethal drug dosages. In sib testing, some offspring are used to measure the phenotype and their scores determine whether their brothers and sisters are used as parents. Parent testing simply involves deferring measurement of the phenotype until the potential couple have weaned at least one pair of young. Such offspring are then bred or discarded, depending upon their parents' scores.

Inbreeding is the enemy of selection, for it reduces genetic variability and thus the potential for changes in gene frequency. During a directional selection program, the experimenter must take pains to minimize the rate of inbreeding. Once the desired response has been achieved, brother-sister matings may be used deliberately to stabilize the phenotype.

Psychophenic Selection: A Case History

The best-known behavioral selection study began in 1926 when Robert Tryon initiated a genetic selection study for maze-learning performance. Among the goals cited by Tryon for performing his study were (1) to create a maze-bright and maze-dull line of rats; (2) to determine the nature of the genetic determiners involved; and (3) to identify major biological and psychological correlates of maze ability (Tryon, 1940a).

The maze was a 17-unit T maze carefully designed for objectivity of scoring and reliability. After 8 days of pretraining, rats were given one trial per day in the multiple T maze for 19 consecutive days. Each rat's psychophene was defined as the total number of errors (blind alleys entered) on trials 2 through 19. The selection process involved a combination of individual and family selection mixed with a dash of inbreeding and a pinch of interbreeding between lines.

Tryon clearly achieved his first objective of creating maze-bright and maze-dull lines of rats. The response to selection which he achieved is shown in Figure 6-7. Note that while response to selection was not instantaneous, it did occur quite rapidly and smoothly, and that the distribution of error scores within the high and low lines suggests continuous variation of individual psychophenes about a central value.

Both the gradual nature of the response to selection and the distribution of individual scores within groups suggested a polygenic genetic system determining the trait, a conclusion further substantiated by examination of variability in the maze-learning phenotype in first- and second-generation offspring resulting from a cross of animals in the maze-bright line with animals in the maze-dull line (Tryon, 1940a). This was not surprising, since complexity of genotype was to be expected in view of the complexity of the phenotype which Tryon used.

The factors potentially involved in differences in the learning of a 17-unit T maze are complex indeed. Differences (1) in motivation for food; (2) in fearfulness of the various features of the maze (including curtains, doors which popped up behind the animal as it walked over them and prevented backtracking, treadle switches which depressed and clicked as the animal walked over them, and so on), (3) in sensory acuity (ability to discriminate visual and olfactory cues which might be used to identify the correct path); (4) in ability to utilize kinesthetic cues; (5) in ability to learn and to retain; and (6) in ability to abstract the plan of the maze—these differences and more could have been involved in producing differences in maze performance. Tryon attempted to eliminate differences in sensory acuity by introducing changes in the test situation following learning. Lights were turned out to eliminate visual cues, curtains and choice points were interchanged to alter visual, olfactory, and tactual cues, and maze sections were deleted to eliminate fixed, serial kinesthetic cues (Tryon, 1939). Relatively little disruption occurred, and Tryon concluded that differences in sensory acuity were not a major factor.

Psychological Correlates of Maze Brightness and Dullness From an analysis of the kinds of errors made in the maze, Tryon (1940b) postulated at least

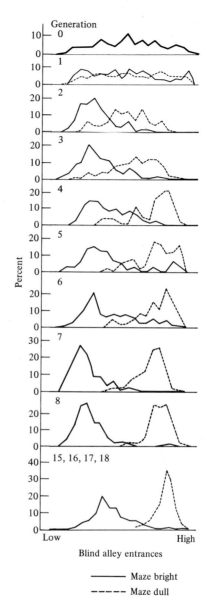

Figure 6–7. Progress of selection for low and high errors in a 17-unit maze. By the seventh generation of selection the lines were well separated, and further selection resulted in no improvement. (After Tryon, 1940b)

ten psychological components involved. He named them direction set; short cut; counter tendency; centrifugal swing; adaptation, or emotional inurement; lassitude; exit gradient; initial inertia gradient; and conflict. From an examination of the error patterns of maze-brights and maze-dulls considered separately, he concluded that the same psychological factors eventually operate in both lines, but that the more abstractive cognitive factors appeared earlier in the series of learning trials for the maze-brights.

Wherry (1941) used Thurstone's centroid factor analyses to analyze the same error data and arrived at three factors which he named forward going (related to Tryon's direction set and centrifugal swing), food pointing, and goal gradient. He disagreed with Tryon's conclusion that the major difference between brights and dulls lay in the speed with which various components were eliminated or emerged during learning. He felt, rather, that food-pointing was more apt to be found in dulls while the forward-going component was stronger in brights. What this implied to Wherry psychologically was that the behavior of dulls appeared to be determined more by external cues, whereas the behavior of brights was influenced more by internalized cues.

Searle (1949) continued the study of these lines, testing the notion that selection had resulted in the creation of two distinctive personality types. He observed groups of brights and dulls on a large variety of tests (open field, Tryon maze, water mazes, elevated runway, 14-unit and 16-unit elevated T mazes, a 6-unit Lashley jumping stand, and an activity cage), and he took a large variety of measures (defecation, urination, rearing, washing, distance, times, errors, and vicarious trial and error). Each rat was assigned a standardized score for each test and measure, and separate correlations were computed for each animal's set of scores with every other animal's. In support of the original notion that the patternings of measures would differ between brights and dulls, the average correlation was .587 among bright animals and .533 among dulls. The average correlation between dulls and brights was −.188 Differences between lines, then, were not simply one of degree. Their behavior profiles differed sharply from a reference group of unselected rats. Brights were above the unselected group median on all food-reward tasks, while dulls were above the unselected median on only the 16-unit elevated T maze. In water-escape situations, brights made more errors. On food-reward tasks, dulls were typically slower; brights took longer in water-escape situations. Both brights and dulls were less active than the reference population. No clear pattern of a difference in emotionality appeared in the open field. However, brights appeared to exhibit more fearfulness on the elevated, unenclosed runway and mazes.

Searle concluded that (1) there was no evidence that maze-dulls were generally inferior in maze-learning performance; (2) maze-dulls were inferior in strength of food drive, but maze-brights were lower in water-escape motivation; and (3) maze-brights and dulls differed in specific fears differentially affecting their performances on different learning tasks.

The problems involved in understanding behavior are complex indeed, or several generations of bright, hard-working psychologists would have established more general principles for behavior by now. What the Tryon rats tell us is that there may be a great deal more specificity in behavior than many of us previously imagined: specificity in fears, in the aversiveness of water, in level of motivation produced by food deprivation, and in the cues and strategies adopted by animals in learning a maze.

Other Selection Studies

Considerable selection for behavior has occurred in domestic animals, most notably in dogs where breeds have become specialized for mode of hunting, aggressiveness, and specialized skills such as sheep herding. That these attributes are not simply the result of human expectations that each breed conforms to a stereotype is shown by the fact that breeds differ when reared and tested under uniform conditions in a laboratory (Scott & Fuller, 1965). Deliberate attempts to modify behavior by genetic selection have been under-taken by several scientists. Maze-bright and maze-dull strains of rats have been produced by Heron (1941), Thompson (1954), and Olson (Pryor, 1968). Rat strains differing in rate of avoidance conditioning have also been obtained (Bignami, 1965).

Selection of rats for emotionality, defined in terms of activity and/or defecation in an open field, has also succeeded (Broadhurst, 1960; Hall, 1938). The Broadhurst strains (known as the Maudsley reactive and Maudsley nonreactive lines) have been extensively studied biologically, pharmacologically, and psychologically. Mice also respond readily to behavioral selection for audiogenic seizure susceptibility (Frings & Frings, 1953; Lehmann & Boesiger, 1964), and aggression (Lagerspetz, 1964).

Behavioral selection is not limited to mammals. Examples of successful programs include social dominance in fowl (Craig, Ortman, & Guhl, 1965), speed of mating in *Drosophila* (Manning, 1961), and geotaxis and phototaxis in *Drosophila* (Erlenmeyer-Kimling, Hirsch, & Weiss, 1962; Hirsch & Ksander, 1969). Experiments with *Drosophila* permit a degree of genetic sophistication which is impossible with mammals and are well worth attention.

Selection for Somatophenes: Correlated Behavioral Changes

It is possible to use genetics as a device for investigating relationships between somatophenes and psychophenes by selecting for a physical trait and noting the correlated behavioral responses. If a true functional relationship exists between a physical and a psychological characteristic, selection for either should cause reciprocal effects in the other. Relatively few experiments of this nature have been reported, but the methodology is potentially powerful.

Rats with high or low cholinesterase activity in the cerebral cortex were produced by selection (Roderick, 1960). The experiment was carried out as a direct test of the hypothesis, based on strain difference studies, that high activity of this enzyme was associated with superior learning. When tested on a Hebb-Williams maze, a Dashiell maze, and a Lashley III maze, however, the Roderick high cholinesterase rats performed less well than the lows (Rosen-zweig, Krech, & Bennett, 1960). This finding does not necessarily mean that neurotransmitters have nothing to do with the physiology of learning, but it disproves any simple linear relationship.

Strains of mice differing in absolute brain weight have also been produced by selection (Wimer, Roderick, and Wimer, 1969). Results for one pair of lines are presented in Figure 6-8. Notable are the gradual change in brain size occurring over a number of generations, indicating a polygenic determination of the phenotype, and the relatively symmetrical changes in response to selection in both high and low lines. The rises and falls in brain weight observed in the unselected line are usually attributed to uncontrolled variations in environment or to variability in measurement techniques. The larger-brained animals seem to be (1) more active in an open field; (2) superior at acquiring a brightness discrimination in an open field; (3) superior at active shock avoidance; and (4) inferior at passive shock avoidance (Elias, 1969; Wimer & Prater, 1966; Wimer, Roderick, & Wimer, 1969).

The somatophenic approach to the gene-behavior complex has not been examined as assiduously as the psychophenic entry as exemplified by studies of the Tryon strains. Both seem equally promising, however, and their basic strategies are similar.

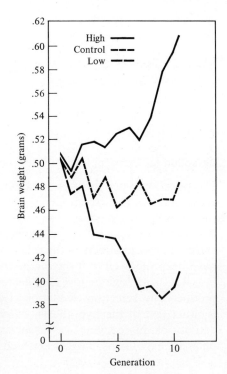

Figure 6–8. Selection for total brain weight in mice from a cross of eight inbred lines. Progress was rapid and approximately equal in both directions. The control unselected line fluctuated randomly, which is good evidence that environmental factors were not responsible for the changes (Roderick, Wimer, & Wimer).

GENE-ENVIRONMENT COACTION

The constant interplay of genetic and environmental factors in the development of behavioral phenotypes has been a major theme of this chapter. In most of the cited studies, however, the major interest has been the demonstration of a genic influence and the mechanisms through which it operates. In this section we are concerned with experiments in which the interplay of the two classes of factors is specifically emphasized.

Although the statistical term *interaction* is commonly used to describe a relationship in which animals of different genotypes react differently to some aspect of their environment, it is conceptually better to think of genes and stimuli as forces which act together (perform in *coaction*) within an organism to determine its phenotype. The genotype of an individual is fixed at fertilization, but the phenotypic consequences of that genotype depend upon its life history in the broadest possible sense.

In mammals, for example, the environment of the fetus varies according to the genotype of its mother. Although the offspring of X-strain females by Y-strain males are genetically similar to those of Y-strain females by X-strain males, their uterine habitat is dissimilar to a generally unknown degree. The possibility that differences in prenatal environment are affecting later behavior must always be considered in experiments which purport to demonstrate effects upon their offspring of stressing pregnant females (Joffe, 1969).

Psychologists have generally been more interested in the differential effects of postnatal manipulations upon unlike genotypes. A sampling of pertinent studies clearly demonstrates that the outcome of an experimental procedure is often greatly influenced by the strain of animal employed. The difficulty in framing broad general principles from experiments with a narrow genetic base is clearly demonstrated by the following examples.

Two strains of rats, selected originally at McGill University for good or poor performance on a Hebb-Williams maze, were exposed either to an enriched environment or to restrictive isolation during early life (Cooper & Zubek, 1958). Comparisons were made with the performance of the same strains reared in a standard, "normal" laboratory environment similar to that used while selection was being performed. Two findings of major interest are presented in Figure 6-9. First, the lines differ on the number of errors only under the environmental rearing condition in which the selection was performed. Second, the effects of enrichment and restriction relative to the normal environment depend upon which selected line is examined. Thus, for McGill brights, enrichment produces no material reduction in error scores, but restriction markedly increases them. Dull rats, on the other hand, show little effect of restriction but are markedly improved by enrichment. Possibly, a more difficult maze task would have detected strain differences in learning even after rearing in a superior environment. Regardless of this possibility, it is clear that the effects of selection in one environment do not transfer directly to another.

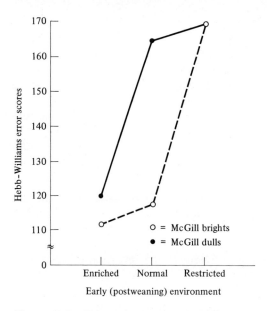

Figure 6–9. The error scores of two strains selected for maze-brightness or maze-dullness differ significantly only when they are reared by procedures similar to those used during the selection process. This is a good example of genotype-environment interaction. (After Cooper & Zubek, 1958.)

A more complex experiment on genotype-environment interaction was reported by Henderson (1967). Four strains of mice and all possible hybrids between them (sixteen groups in all) were subjected to three levels of stimulation in early life and observed later in an open field. Estimates of the effects of exposure to electric shock, of exposure to a buzzer tone, and of remaining undisturbed were made within each of the groups. Using either defecation or locomotion as a measure, Henderson found that almost any of the competing hypotheses for the persistent effects of early stimulation could be supported. In some genetic groups defecation increased with stimulation, in others it decreased. Henderson took the mean defecation score of the twelve hybrid groups as an indication of the response of the "average mouse." Mice shocked in infancy defecated most in the open field; unhandled controls and buzzer-stimulated mice had very similar scores. However, "of the sixteen individual 'experiments' not one showed this effect [Henderson, 1967, p. 374]." The point has often been made that group averages conceal the realities of individual development. In this study, each genetic group can be considered to be comparable to a single individual who is exposed to several life histories. The effects of a life history are predictable only if one knows the genotype of the individual. The implications are as important to developmental psychologists as to behavior geneticists.

Genetic effects upon differences in early experience have been described in another species. Beagle puppies reared for 12 weeks in isolation were less active and interacted less vigorously with objects, persons, and other puppies than did pet-reared beagles (Fuller, 1967). Isolation-reared wirehaired terrier puppies were more active and, after a brief accommodation period, equally interactive with stimuli as compared with pet-reared littermates (Figure 6–10). The direction and duration of the effects of early stimulus deprivation were thus shown to be dependent upon the genotype of the subjects.

Changes over time in heritability and in the relative values of additive and dominant genetic effects are evidence that different genes contribute to individual variation during early and late stages of a developmental sequence. For example, the heritability of rat activity in an open field fell, over 4 days of testing, from 62 percent to 38 percent (Broadhurst & Jinks, 1966). The additive gene effect remained essentially constant, but the influence of dominant genes was much greater on the fourth day. A somewhat different situation was found in a comparison of differences between dog breeds at various stages of learning an overhead maze (Scott & Fuller, 1965, p. 254). The percentage of genetic contribution to variation remained essentially constant during repeated trials although total variation declined sharply as behavior became more uniform. Thus, training does not necessarily decrease, and may even stabilize, the contribution of heredity to behavioral variation.

These examples demonstrate that developmental psychology and behavior genetics are mutually supportive of each other. Instead of regarding genetic variation as a nuisance because it complicates the results of experiments, one can make it a part of an experimental design with a consequent gain in understanding. Eventually, studies of gene-environment interaction can make

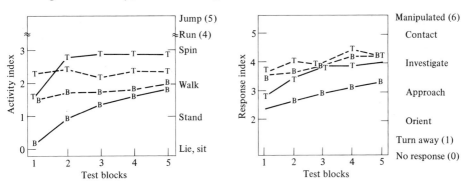

Figure 6–10. Average activity indices (left) and response indices (right) for beagles *(b)* and terriers *(t)* following prolonged isolation during infancy (solid lines) or pet-rearing (dashed lines). Note that isolation increases activity of terriers, but decreases that of beagles. Isolated terriers eventually become as responsive as pet-reared animals of both breeds, but isolated beagles remain below the other groups (From J. L. Fuller. *Science,* 1967, **158**, 1648–1653. Copyright 1967 by the American Association for the Advancement of Science.)

individual variation lawful. This is better than conceiving of individual deviations from idealized laws as errors. Genetic variation within a species in a
sense preadapts some members to perform better in one set of conditions,
other members to excel in different circumstances. Since the environment
of most species includes a rather broad range of habitats and life experiences,
natural selection does not lead to one fixed genotype but to maintenance of
a spectrum of genotypes loosely fitted to a set of most probable environments.
Behavior genetics thus directs the comparative psychologist to think of a
species as a population—not as a collection of uniform, idealized types. Hirsch
(1963) has written forcefully on this point.

GENETICS AND THE SEARCH FOR PSYCHOLOGICAL LAWS

To this point, we have focused on the use of genetically controlled stocks
of animals for either genetic analyses or study of biology-behavior relations.
There is another use of perhaps equal importance, though its significance has
just really begun to be widely appreciated (Vale & Vale, 1969). That is, genetically controlled lines of animals may be of great value in our search for
psychological laws.

A substantial portion of experimental psychology is devoted to the search
for descriptive laws of behavior—statements concerning orderly behavioral
consequences resulting from experimental manipulations. Though psychological constructs with a strong biological flavor (e.g., drive and inhibition) are
sometimes used, the primary concern is not with biology-behavior relationships. Nor is it with individual differences. Indeed, it has been a common
position among experimental psychologists that individual differences can
safely be ignored in the primary phase of the search for general laws, their
effect being the introduction of some additional variability which can be dealt
with later (Hull, 1945). This hypothesis is a sensible, initial, simplifying working assumption insofar as the psychologist's task is made easier (Bitterman,
1960, 1965). It also, of course, represents a statement of our ultimate goal
of achieving a unified set of laws encompassing the behavior of all organisms.
The success which psychologists have experienced in some research areas
would suggest that the simplifying assumption may be justified on occasion.
However, studies have appeared which clearly demonstrate that, under some
circumstances at least, the simplifying assumption is invalid.

Case History: Is There an Optimal Spacing of Training Trials?

Psychologists have long been interested in whether superior learning is
achieved under conditions of massed or distributed practice. The following
experiment demonstrates that there may be no general answer. Two inbred
mouse strains (C57BL/6J and DBA/2J) were taught to escape from an elec-
trified grid floor to a shelf (Wimer, Symington, Farmer, & Schwartzkroin,

1968). Learning trials were either given all closely crowded together in time or at the distributed rate of one trial per day. Results are presented in Figure 6-11. There are two outstanding findings. First, the superiority of one strain relative to the other is clearly dependent upon the practice condition for which the comparison is made. Second, the superiority of one practice condition relative to the other is dependent upon which strain is examined. The Tryon maze-bright and maze-dull rats also differ in the optimal spacing of practice for maze learning (McGaugh, Jennings, & Thompson, 1962).

What do such studies tell us about psychological laws? They indicate that some of the kinds of generalizations we have been seeking (e.g., "Distributed practice is superior to massed practice" may be too far removed in conceptualization, manipulation, and measurement from critical causal processes. Finding a strain difference in the optimal spacing of training trials does not immediately lead to a new generalization, but it does demonstrate a need for rephrasing the question.

Genetic Variables in Behavioral Research

If individual differences can tell us when our approaches are wrong, they can also help us to improve them. By closer examination of the manner in which genetically distinct populations of animals respond differentially to our treatments, we may come to a clearer conception of the more precise biological and psychological processes involved (Pauling, 1968; Verplanck, 1955). The marked individual and strain differences in pattern of response we sometimes have occasion to observe must be lawful, and they can be explained once the more fundamental processes are understood.

The use of a number of distinct genetic stocks of animals in experiments

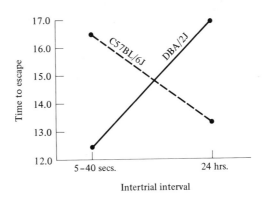

Figure 6-11. Average cumulative escape times in 1/100 minute for two strains of mice under two conditions of practice. The optimal spacing of trials is different for the two strains. Which one should be considered the better learner?

is always advantageous. In instances in which genetic differences are not major sources of variability, their use creates the opportunity to establish that fact. When potent, genetically associated variables are operating and marked individual differences in patterning of response are occurring, the comparative genetic method may be essential for the establishment of orderly psychological relationships.

Bringing genetic variables into research with human beings is more difficult. The chromosomal and genic attributes of man are fundamentally the same as in other mammals. The absence of pure strains (races are far from being genetically homogeneous) and the inability of experimenters to control mating patterns make human behavior genetics observational and analytic rather than experimental. Nevertheless, a considerable body of literature has appeared (Spuhler, 1967; Vandenberg, 1965, 1968). Obviously, the biological, particularly the genetic, basis of human individuality is tremendously important to education and to the treatment of behavioral deviants. Although it is sometimes stated that the heredity-environment controversy is dead, perusal of the literature demonstrates that this is not really true (Glass, 1968; *Harvard Educational Review,* 1969; Jensen, 1969). The point of the view expounded here is that heredity and environment are in constant coaction, and that the relationship between them is not simple. Experimental behavior genetics as practiced with animals makes perhaps its greatest contribution in pointing out the importance of both general laws and specific organisms. In our point of view, individual genetic variation is not just a nuisance; it can be the key to understanding psychological development of man as well as animal.

REFERENCES

ANDERSON, V. E. Genetics in mental retardation. In Stevens & Heber (Eds.), *Mental retardation.* Chicago: The University of Chicago Press, 1964.

ANLIKER, J., & MAYER, J. An operant conditioning technique for studying feeding-fasting patterns in normal and obese mice. *Journal of Applied Physiology,* 1956, **8,** 667–670.

BIGNAMI, G. Selection for high rates and low rates of conditioning in the rat. *Animal Behaviour,* 1965, **13,** 221–227.

BITTERMAN, M. E. Toward a comparative psychology of learning. *American Psychologist,* 1960, **15,** 704–712.

BITTERMAN, M. E. Phyletic differences in learning. *American Psychologist,* 1965, **20,** 396–410.

BONAVENTURE, H., & KARLI, P. Maturation de l'ERG et des potentiels évoqués au niveau du cortex visuel chez la souris atteinte d'une dégénérescence héréditaire du neuroépithelium retinien. *Comptes Rendus de la Société de Biologie,* 1969, **162,** 1421–1424.

BROADHURST, P. L. Experiments in psychogenetics: Applications of biometrical genetics to the inheritance of behavior. In H. J. Eysenck (Ed.), *Experiments in personality.* Vol. I. *Psychogenetics and psychopharmacology.* London: Routledge & Kegan Paul, 1960. Pp. 3–102.

BROADHURST, P. L., & JINKS, J. L. Biometrical genetics and behavior, Reanalysis of published data. *Psychological Bulletin*, 1961, **58**, 337–362.

BROADHURST, P. L., & JINKS, J. L. Stability and change in the inheritance of behaviour in rats. A further analysis of statistics from a diallel cross. *Proceedings of the Royal Society of London*, Series B, 1966, **165**, 450–472.

BRUELL, J. H. Behavioral heterosis. In J. Hirsch (Ed.), *Behavior-genetic analysis*. New York: McGraw-Hill, 1967. Pp. 270–286.

CARSNER, R. L., & RENNELS, E. G. Primary site of gene action in anterior pituitary dwarf mice. *Science*, 1960, **131**, 829.

CASPARI, E. Genetic basis of behavior. In A. Roe & G. C. Simpson (Eds.), *Behavior and evolution*. New Haven, Conn.: Yale University Press, 1958. Pp. 103–127.

COLEMAN, D. L. Phenylalanine hydroxylase activity in dilute and nondilute strains of mice. *Archives of Biochemistry and Biophysics*, 1960, **90**, 300–306.

COLEMAN, D. L., & HUMMEL, K. P. Studies with the mutation, diabetes, in the mouse. *Diabetologia*, 1967, **3**, 238–248.

COLLINS, R. L. Inheritance of avoidance conditioning in mice: A diallel study. *Science*, 1964, **143**, 1188–1190.

COLLINS, R. L. On the inheritance of handedness. II. Selection for sinistrality in mice. *Journal of Heredity*, 1969, **60**, 117–119.

COLLINS, R. L. A new genetic locus mapped from behavioral variation in mice: Audiogenic seizure prone (*asp*). *Behavior Genetics*, 1970, **1**, 99–109.

COLLINS, R. L., & FULLER, J. L. Audiogenic seizure prone (*asp*)—a gene affecting behavior in linkage group VIII of the mouse. *Science*, 1968, **162**, 1137–1139.

COOPER, R. M., & ZUBEK, J. P. Effects of enriched and restricted early environments on the learning ability of bright and dull rats. *Canadian Journal of Psychology*, 1958, **12**, 159–164.

CRAIG, J. V., ORTMAN, L. L., & GUHL, A. M. Genetic selection for social dominance ability in chickens. *Animal Behaviour*, 1965, **13**, 114–131.

DARWIN, C. *On the expression of the emotions in man and animals*. London: J. Murray, 1872.

DAWSON, W. M. Inheritance of wildness and tameness in mice. *Genetics*, 1932, **17**, 296–326.

ELIAS, M. F. Differences in spatial discrimination reversal learning for mice selected for high brain weight and unselected controls. *Perceptual and Motor Skills*, 1969, **28**, 707–712.

ERLENMEYER-KIMLING, L., HIRSCH, J., & WEISS, J. M. Studies in experimental behavior genetics, III. Selection and hybridization analysis of individual differences in the sign of geotaxis. *Journal of Comparative and Physiological Psychology*, 1962, **55**, 722–731.

FALCONER, D. S. *Quantitative genetics*. New York: Ronald Press, 1960.

FRINGS, H., & FRINGS, M. The production of stocks of albino mice with predictable susceptibilities to audiogenic seizures. *Behaviour*, 1953, **5**, 305–319.

FULLER, J. L. Measurement of alcohol preference in genetic experiments. *Journal of Comparative and Physiological Psychology*, 1964, **57**, 85–88.

FULLER, J. L. Experiential deprivation and later behavior. *Science*, 1967, **158**, 1648–1652.

FULLER, J. L. Strain differences in the effects of chlorpromazine and chlordiazepoxide upon active and passive avoidance in mice. *Psychopharmacologia*, 1970, **16**, 261–271.

FULLER, J. L., & COLLINS, R. L. Mice unilaterally sensitized for audiogenic seizures. *Science*, 1968, **162**, 1295.

FULLER, J. L., & COLLINS, R. L. Genetics of audiogenic seizures in mice. A parable for psychiatrists. *Seminars in Psychiatry*, 1970, **2**, 75–88.

FULLER, J. L., & JACOBY, G. A., JR. Central and sensory control of food intake in genetically obese mice. *American Journal of Physiology,* 1955, **183,** 279–283.

FULLER, J. L., & SJURSEN, F. H. Audiogenic seizures in eleven mouse strains. *Journal of Heredity,* 1967, **58,** 135–140.

FULLER, J. L., & THOMPSON, W. R. *Behavior genetics.* New York, Wiley, 1960.

FULLER, J. L., & WIMER, R. E. Neural, sensory and motor functions. In E. L. Green (Ed.), *Biology of the laboratory mouse.* (2nd ed.) New York: McGraw-Hill, 1966. Pp. 609–629.

GALTON, F. *Hereditary genius.* New York: Appleton, 1883.

GINSBURG, B. E., COWEN, J. S., MAXON, S. C., & SZE, P. Neurochemical effects of gene mutations associated with audiogenic seizures. *Proceedings of the 2nd International Congress Neurogenetics and Neuro-ophthalmology.* Montreal, 1967, **1.** Pp. 695–701.

GOY, R. W., & JAKWAY, J. S. The inheritance of patterns of sexual behaviour in female guinea pigs. *Animal Behaviour,* 1959, **7,** 142–149.

GLASS, D. C. (Ed.). *Genetics.* New York: Rockefeller University Press, 1968.

GREEN, E. L. Breeding systems. In E. L. Green (Ed.), *Biology of the laboratory mouse.* (2nd ed.) New York.: McGraw-Hill, 1966. Pp. 11–22.

GREEN, E. L. (Ed.). *Handbook on genetically standardized Jax mice.* (2nd ed.) Bar Harbor, Maine: The Jackson Laboratory, 1968.

GREEN, M. C. Mutant genes and linkages. In E. L. Green (Ed.), *Biology of the laboratory mouse.* (2nd ed.) New York: McGraw-Hill, 1966. Pp. 87–150.

GUHL, A. M., CRAIG, J. V., & MUELLER, C. D. Selective breeding for aggressiveness in chickens. *Poultry Science,* 1960, 970–980.

GYLLENSTEN, L., & LINDBERG, J. Development of the visual cortex in mice with inherited retinal dystrophy. *Journal of Comparative Neurology,* 1964, **122,** 79–90.

HALL, C. S. The inheritance of emotionality. *Sigma Xi Quarterly,* 1938, **26,** 17–27.

HARVARD EDUCATIONAL REVIEW. Science, heritability and IQ. Reprint No. 4, 1969. Authors: Light & Smith, Stinchcombe, Fehr, Cottle, and Deutsch.

HENDERSON, N. D. Prior treatment effects on open field behaviour of mice—a genetic analysis. *Animal Behaviour,* 1967, **15,** 364–376.

HENRY, K. R. Audiogenic seizure susceptibility induced in C57BL/6J mice by prior auditory exposure. *Science,* 1967, **158,** 938–940.

HERON, W. T. The inheritance of brightness and dullness in maze learning ability in the rat. *Journal of Genetic Psychology,* 1941, **59,** 41–49.

HIRSCH, J. Behavior genetics and individuality understood: Behaviorism's counterfactual dogma blinded the behavioral sciences to the significance of meiosis. *Science,* 1963, **142,** 1436–1442.

HIRSCH, J. Breeding analysis of natural units in behavior genetics. *American Zoologist,* 1964, **4,** 139–145.

HIRSCH, J. (Ed.). *Behavior-genetic analysis.* New York: McGraw-Hill, 1967. (a)

HIRSCH, J. Behavior-genetic analysis at the chromosome level of organization. In J. Hirsch (Ed.), *Behavior-genetic analysis.* New York: McGraw-Hill, 1967. Pp. 258–269. (b)

HIRSCH, J., & BOUDREAU, J. C. The heritability of phototaxis in a population of *Drosophila melanogaster. Journal of Comparative and Physiological Psychology,* 1958, **51,** 647–651.

HIRSCH, J., & KSANDER, G. Studies in experimental behavior genetics, V. Negative geotaxis and further chromosome analyses in *Drosophila melanogaster. Journal of Comparative and Physiological Psychology,* 1969, **68,** 118–122.

HSIA, D. Y. The hereditary metabolic disease. In J. Hirsch (Ed.), *Behavior-genetic analysis.* New York: McGraw-Hill, 1967. Pp. 176–193.

HUFF, S. D., & FULLER, J. L. Audiogenic seizures, the dilute locus, and phenylalanine hydroxylase in DBA/1 mice. *Science,* 1964, **144,** 304–305.

HULL, C. L. The place of innate individual and species differences in a natural-science theory of behavior. *Psychological Review,* 1945, **52,** 55–60.

JENSEN, A. R. How much can we boost IQ and scholastic achievement? *Harvard Educational Review,* 1969, **39,** 1–123.

JOFFE, J. M. *Prenatal determinants of behaviour.* New York: Pergamon, 1969.

LAGERSPETZ, K. Studies on the aggressive behaviour of mice. *Annales Academiae Scientarum Fennicae,* 1964, **131,** 1–13.

LANE, P. W., & DICKIE, M. M. Fertile, obese male mice. *Journal of Heredity,* 1954, **45,** 56–58.

LEHMANN, A., & BOESIGER, E. Sur le déterminisme génétique de l'épilepsie acoustique de *Mus musculus domesticus* (Swiss/Rb). *Comptes Rendus de la Société de Biologie,* 1964, **258,**

LEHMANN, A., & BOESIGER, E. *Sur le determinisme genetique de l'epilepsie acoustique de Mus musculus domesticus* (Swiss/Rb). *Comptes Rendus de la Sociéte de Biologie,* 1964, **258,** 4858–4861.

LERNER, I. M. *The genetic basis of selection.* New York: Wiley, 1958.

LINDZEY, G., & THIESSEN, D. D. *Contributions to behavior-genetic analysis: The mouse as a prototype.* New York: Appleton-Century-Crofts, 1970.

MAAS, J. W. Neurochemical differences between two strains of mice. *Science,* 1962, **137,** 621–622.

MANNING, A. The effects of artificial selection for mating speed in *Drosophila melanogaster. Animal Behaviour,* 1961, **9,** 82–92.

MANOSEVITZ, M., LINDZEY, G., & THIESSEN, D. D. *Behavioral genetics: Methods and research.* New York: Appleton-Century-Crofts, 1969.

MCCLEARN, G. E., & RODGERS, D. A. Differences in alcohol preference among inbred strains of mice. *Quarterly Journal of Studies on Alcohol,* 1959, **20,** 691–695.

MCGAUGH, J. L., JENNINGS, R. D., & THOMPSON, C. W. Effect of distribution of practice on the maze learning of descendants of the Tryon maze bright and maze dull strains. *Psychological Reports,* 1962, **10,** 147–150.

MEADE, J. E., & PARKES, A. S. (Eds.). *Biological aspects of social problems.* New York: Plenum, 1965.

MENDEL, G. Experiments in plant hybridization. Trans. in J. A. Peters (Ed.), *Classical papers in genetics.* Englewood Cliffs, N.J.: Prentice-Hall, 1965. Pp. 1–20.

MERRELL, D. J. Methodology in behavior genetics. *Journal of Heredity,* 1965, **56,** 263–266.

PARSONS, P. A. *The genetic analysis of behaviour.* London: Methuen, 1967.

PAULING, L. Orthomolecular psychiatry. *Science,* 1968, **160,** 265–271.

PRYOR, G. T. Neurochemical differences between three pairs of rat strains differing in maze performance. *Comparative Biochemistry and Physiology,* 1968, **26,** 723–729.

PRYOR, G. T., SCHLESINGER, K., & CALHOUN, W. H. Differences in brain enzymes among five inbred strains of mice. *Life Sciences,* 1966, **5,** 2105–2111.

ROBERTS, R. C. Some concepts and methods in quantitative genetics. In J. Hirsch (Ed.), *Behavior-genetic analysis.* New York: McGraw-Hill, 1967. Pp. 214–257.

RODERICK, T. H. Selection for cholinesterase activity in the cerebral cortex of the rat. *Genetics,* 1960, **45,** 1123–1140.

RODERICK, T. H., WIMER, R. E., WIMER, C. C. Genetic studies of brain waves. In preparation.

ROSENZWEIG, M. R., KRECH, D., & BENNETT, E. L. A search for relationship between brain chemistry and behavior. *Psychological Bulletin,* 1960, **57,** 476–492.

ROTHENBUHLER, W. C. Behavior genetics of nest cleaning in honey bees. IV. Responses of F_1 and backcross generations to disease-killed brood. *American Zoologist,* 1964, **4,** 111–123.

ROYCE, J. R., & COVINGTON, M. Genetic differences in the avoidance conditioning of mice. *Journal of Comparative and Physiological Psychology,* 1960, **53,** 197–200.

RUSSELL, E. S. Problems and potentialities in the study of genic action in the mouse. In W. J. Burdette (Ed.), *Methodology in mammalian genetics.* San Francisco: Holden-Day, 1963. Pp. 217–232.

RUSSELL, E. S., & MEIER, H. Constitutional disease. In E. L. Green (Ed.), *Biology of the laboratory mouse.* (2nd ed.) New York, McGraw-Hill, 1966. Pp. 571–588.

SCHLESINGER, K., BOGGAN, W., & FREEDMAN, D. X. Genetics of audiogenic seizures: I. Relation to brain serotonin and norepinephrine in mice. *Life Sciences,* 1965, **4,** 2345–2351.

SCHLESINGER, K., ELSTON, R. C., & BOGGAN, W. The genetics of sound induced seizures in inbred mice. *Genetics,* 1966, **54,** 95–103.

SCHLESINGER, K., & WIMER, R. E. Genotype and conditioned avoidance learning in the mouse. *Journal of Comparative and Physiological Psychology,* 1967, **63,** 139–141.

SCOTT, J. P., & FULLER, J. L. *Genetics and the social behavior of the dog.* Chicago: The University of Chicago Press, 1965.

SEARLE, L. V. The organization of hereditary maze-brightness and maze-dullness. *Genetic Psychology Monographs,* 1949, **39,** 279–325.

SIDMAN, R. L., GREEN, M. C., & APPEL, S. H. *Catalog of the neurological mutants of the mouse.* Cambridge, Mass.: Harvard University Press, 1965.

SINNOTT, E. D., DUNN, L. C., & DOBZHANSKY, T. *Principles of genetics,* (5th ed.) New York: McGraw-Hill, 1958.

SOUTHWICK, C. H., & CLARK, L. H. Interstrain differences in aggressive behavior and exploratory activity of inbred mice. *Communications in Behavioral Biology,* 1968, **1,** 49–59.

SPERRY, R. W. Developmental basis of behavior. In A. Roe and G. C. Simpson (Eds.), *Behavior and evolution.* New Haven, Conn.: Yale University Press, 1958. Pp. 128–139.

SPUHLER, J. N. (Ed.). *Genetic diversity and human behavior.* Chicago: Aldine, 1967.

SUTTON, H. E. Biochemical genetics and gene action. In S. G. Vandenberg (Ed.), *Methods and goals in human behavior genetics.* New York: Academic Press, 1965. Pp. 1–16.

THODAY, J. M., & PARKES, A. S. (Eds.). *Genetic and environmental influences on behaviour.* New York: Plenum, 1968.

THOMPSON, W. R. The inheritance of behavior; behavioral differences in fifteen mouse strains. *Canadian Journal of Psychology,* 1953, **7,** 145–155.

THOMPSON, W. R. The inheritance and development of intelligence. *Proceedings of the Association for Research in Nervous and Mental Disease,* 1954, **33,** 209–231.

THOMPSON, W. R. Some problems in the genetic study of personality and intelligence. In J. Hirsch (Ed.), *Behavior-genetic analysis.* New York: McGraw-Hill, 1967. Pp. 344–365.

TRYON, R. C. Studies in individual differences in maze ability. VI. Disproof of sensory components: Experimental effects of stimulus variation. *Journal of Comparative Psychology,* 1939, **28,** 361–415.

TRYON, R. C. Studies in individual differences in maze ability. VII. The specific components of maze ability, and a general theory of psychological components. *Journal of Comparative Psychology,* 1940, **30,** 283–335. (a)

TRYON, R. C. Genetic differences in maze learning in rats. *National Society for the Study of Education, 39th Yearbook,* Part I, 111–119. Bloomington, Ill.: Public School Publishing Co., 1940. (b)

VALE, J. R., & VALE, C. A. Individual differences and general laws in psychology. *American Psychologist,* 1969, **24,** 1093–1108.

VANDENBERG, S. G. *Methods and goals in human behavior genetics.* New York: Academic Press, 1965.

VANDENBERG, S. G. *Progress in human behavior genetics.* Baltimore: Johns Hopkins, 1968.

VERPLANCK, W. S. Since learned behavior is innate, and vice versa, what now? *Psychological Review,* 1955, **62,** 139–144.

WECHSLER, D. *The range of human capacities.* (2nd ed.) Baltimore: Williams & Wilkins, 1952.

WHERRY, R. J. Determination of the specific components of maze-ability for Tryon's bright and dull rats by means of factorial analysis. *Journal of Comparative Psychology,* 1941, **32,** 237–252.

WILCOCK, J. Gene action and behavior: An evaluation of major gene pleiotropism. *Psychological Bulletin,* 1969, **72,** 1–29.

WILLHAM, R. L., COX, D. F., & KARAS, G. G. Genetic variation in a measure of avoidance learning in swine. *Journal of Comparative and Physiological Psychology,* 1963, **56,** 294–297.

WIMER, C., & PRATER, L. Behavioral differences in mice genetically selected for high and low brain weight. *Psychological Reports,* 1966, **19,** 675–681.

WIMER, C., RODERICK, T. H., & WIMER, R. E. Supplementary report: Behavioral differences in mice genetically selected for brain weight. *Psychological Reports,* 1969, **25,** 363–368.

WIMER, R. E., SYMINGTON, L., FARMER, H., & SCHWARTZKROIN, P. Differences in memory processes between inbred mouse strains C57BL/6J and DBA/2J. *Journal of Comparative and Physiological Psychology,* 1968, **65,** 126–131.

WIMER, R. E., & WELLER, S. Evaluation of a visual discrimination task for the analysis of the genetics of a mouse behavior. *Perceptual and Motor Skills,* 1965, **20,** 203–208.

WIMER, R. E., WIMER, C. C., & RODERICK, T. H. Genetic variability in fore-brain structures between inbred strains of mice. *Brain Research,* 1969, **16,** 257–264.

Chapter 7

Development and Behavior

Lynwood G. Clemens

Behavior does not begin at birth. The chick embryo, for example, starts to behave on about the third day of incubation. Although this initial behavior consists of simple motility movements, it represents the starting point for a behavioral organization and specialization which are often not complete until the organism reaches adulthood.

The objective of this chapter will be to review some of the properties of this organizing process by looking at the characteristics of behavior in the developing organism. Since this process starts during embryonic life, we shall look first at some of the characteristics of behavior in the embryo and then compare these characteristics of the fetus with those of the neonate. Finally, we shall survey the problem of how events early in life may affect adult behavior.

Theoretical Issues

Many of the theoretical issues which have focused research in development and behavior are the same ones which have guided research in other areas of comparative psychology. What are the forces which organize behavior? Is behavior composed of instincts which are released by the appropriate environmental stimuli, or does experience play a role in organization of behavior? If behavior is organized by experience, then at what point does experience have its effect? And so on.

In other contexts, the rationale for studying the developing organism has been that the young organism may provide a simpler model than the adult or yield some insight into why the adult behaves as it does. Although developmental psychologists have not been overwhelmed by the simplicity of the young organism, we are beginning to understand some of the dynamics of behavior in the growing individual.

BEHAVIOR OF THE EMBRYO

Periodicity

Of particular interest to developmental psychologists has been the question of just when do organisms start to behave. Pursuit of this question rapidly carried investigation back into fetal life, since this is when the individual begins to move about. An example of this approach has been the work of Viktor Hamburger (1963), who has studied the ontogeny of motility movements in the chick embryo. The reason for using avian embryos is fairly clear: It is easier to watch embryos through a hole in an eggshell than it is through a hole in the abdomen of another organism.

For much of the chick embryo's life, the main behavior consists of generalized motility responses which are rhythmic or periodic in occurrence. According to Hamburger (1963), the genesis of these periodic bursts of movement is internal or endogenous. That is, these movements do not depend upon external stimulation for their initiation. Several lines of evidence have led to this conclusion. First, these movements start before the sensory-motor systems begin to function, which would suggest an endogenous origin. For example, movement can be observed in the chick embryo from about the third day of incubation (as noted earlier), whereas the earliest responses to tactile stimulation do not occur until around the sixth or seventh day of incubation. Responses to other forms of stimulation occur later as the other sensory-motor systems become functional.

Although the chick embryo can be stimulated to move by external stimuli after day 6, Hamburger still argues that, for the most part, the periodic motility which occurs throughout much of embryonic development has an endogenous origin. Two sets of experiments designed to preclude other interpretations have led to this belief. To exclude the possibility that the periodicity might be induced by external stimuli, an attempt was made to alter the duration of the periods of motility by stimulating the embryo tactually. The embryos were stimulated for a given duration of time during both the active and inactive phases by touching them with fine hair. Other control embryos were left undisturbed. Following stimulation, Hamburger found no difference in the duration of the active-inactive periods between experimentals and controls. Since he could not alter this rhythmicity with external stimulation, he suggested that the duration of these phases of motile movements was under endogenous control.

Another experiment was designed to discount the possibility that such cycles might arise from a periodic buildup of metabolities, or CO_2, in the blood. Hamburger sectioned the spinal cord of the embryo in several places, but he still found cycles of activity and inactivity in each cord segment. However, the cycles were not in phase with one another, thus eliminating a general humoral factor as the stimulus for activity.

While these experiments indicate that motility periodicities may be independent of certain forms of stimulation, they do not necessarily support the conclusion that the embryo is not influenced by sensory stimulation prior to the time when it can give a motor response to that stimulus. As Gottlieb (1968) has pointed out, there is no reason to assume that a sensory system must be connected to a motor system in order for sensory stimuli to affect the development of the individual. The fact that sensory stimuli do not evoke an immediate motor response does not provide grounds for assuming that a stimulus has no effect on development of systems destined to control behavior.

Unlike avian embryos, the mammalian embryo does not become active in advance of responsiveness to external stimulation. Consequently, it is not a simple matter to suggest that the mammalian embryo has an endogenous activity-inactivity cycle, as it was possible to do with the chick embryo. However, in a recent study of the human fetus, it was found that the periodicity of fetal movement was independent of whether the mother was awake or asleep (Sterman & Hoppenbrauiers, 1968). The investigators found the activity was present in the fetus from about the fifth month of pregnancy. The activity became cyclic during the sixth month, with the length of the cycle (the time from the beginning of one active period to the beginning of the next) being about 30 to 60 minutes in duration. This cycle lengthened throughout gestation and reached 40 to 80 minutes by the eighth month.

Thus, in both the avian and the mammalian embryo, we observe a periodicity of movement which so far has not been correlated with immediate environmental stimuli.

Behavioral Selectivity

Even though an embryo has the sensory system to mediate a particular stimulus, this does not necessarily mean it will respond to that stimulus. Responsiveness to external stimuli by the embryo can be highly selective. For example, in the Peking duck embryo, *Anas platyrhynchos* (a domesticated form of the mallard duck), an increase in the rate of oral clicking activity, called *bill clapping*, occurs 12 to 24 hours before hatching (incubation time for the mallard is 27 to 28 days). Bill clapping is a specific response given by the embryo to the call of the mallard mother. The duck embryo also responds to a special brood call of its siblings with an increase in vocalization and heart rate but not with the peculiar bill-clapping activity. The duck embryo then is capable of making a distinctive response to the maternal call and is able to discriminate this form of auditory stimulation from that produced by other unhatched sibling ducks.

Modifiability

This selectivity can be modified by previous experience. For example, if the duck embryos had been placed in auditory isolation by placing each egg in a separate, soundproof chamber from day 23 of incubation until the day of testing, they would not show any increase in bill clapping when exposed to the maternal call. Communally incubated ducklings, on the other hand, do show increased bill clapping to the maternal call. Since Peking duck embryos are capable of vocalizing and do vocalize from day 23, it is likely that such auditory stimulation in communally incubated embryos is necessary if the embryo is to discriminate the maternal call from that of its siblings. This modification of behavior by normally occurring embryonic auditory stimulation may play an important role in regulating the embryo's ability to respond selectively to the maternal call of its species (Gottlieb, 1968). Experiential modification of the avian embryo's behavior has also been shown by conditioning techniques (Gottlieb, 1968).

Although there are several studies demonstrating conditioning in the mammalian fetus, this topic needs much more study. Spelt (1948) seems to have demonstrated conditioned responses in the human fetus, and Sedlacek, Hlavackova, and Svehlova (1964) have obtained conditioning in guinea pig fetuses. In the latter study with guinea pigs, it was found that conditioning did not occur until the fetus was forced to breathe. In this study, the fetuses were freed from the uterus without injury to the fetal-placental circulation, and placed with the mother in a physiological saline bath. If the umbilical circulation remained intact, the fetuses could not be conditioned. If the umbilicus was ligated, thus forcing the fetus to breathe, conditioning could be achieved. Under this latter condition, the performance of the 67-day-old fetus did not differ from that of newborn guinea pigs. The authors attribute the conditionability under the ligated condition to changes in the central nervous system (CNS) as a result of breathing and consequent afferent input.

COMPARISON OF THE FETUS AND THE NEWBORN

Since the behavior of the embryo can be characterized as cyclic, selective, and modifiable through experience, it should come as no great surprise to find that the behavior of the newborn has similar characteristics. This is not to say, however, that the behavior of the neonate is essentially the same as that of the embryo. Observation of the unhatched chick for a short time is sufficient to demonstrate what is missing. If the blunt end of the egg over the air space is removed about 30 hours before the chick is to hatch, the head can be pulled out of the shell and allowed to hang over the edge of the shell (Figure 7-1a). If we observe this embryo, we notice that it continues to show active and inactive periods. During the active phase, the chick will vocalize, open and close its eyes, and periodically raise its head for a brief time. However, if we compare this behavior and posture with those of a chick several hours after hatching would normally have occurred (Figure 7-1b), the behavioral differences between a chick before and after hatching become clear (Balaban & Hill, 1969). Before hatching, muscle tonus is lacking, and to all outward appearances the chick is comatose except for periodic movements. During the active motility periods, the chick remains in this nonvigilant state. If touched or pricked on the wing, it moves the wing but is not aroused. In the hatched chick, however, we find a highly vigilant organism which not only responds vigorously to external stimuli with vocalizations and a high level of muscle tonus but also shows a much higher level of response frequencies. Thus, in characterizing the chick embryo, we must at least also indicate that it is in a nonawake state. During a several-minute period around

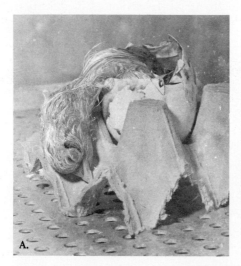 

Figure 7–1. (A) The blunt end of the egg of an unhatched chick has been removed and the chick's head pulled out of the shell. This chick will vocalize and move its head prior to hatching time but does not achieve the state of vigilance seen in (B). (B) One hour after hatching would normally have occurred and the attitude of a chick is entirely different from prehatching. We now have a normal waking chick. (Courtesy, M. Balaban.)

hatching time, the chick embryo moves from a flaccid, spongelike creature to an alert, highly active, awake organism. A good characterization in scientific terms of this difference in state is not available largely because we do not yet understand the properties of the awake, as opposed to the various nonawake, states (Koella, 1967). In mammalian embryos and neonates, rapid changes of state in the organism do occur at birth, but their meaning for behavior is not clear. Levels of vigilance vary widely with the newborn mammal. The young rat, for example, is born after 21 days' gestation and is in a very immature state with its eyes and ears still closed, while the guinea pig, on the other hand, born after 68 days of gestation, has its eyes open, and within a day or so it is able to walk about. Investigations of the prenatal and postnatal states in mammals are not abundant, but the findings of Sedlacek et al. (1964) on conditioning before and after breathing has started suggest that this area may be a very fruitful one for investigation.

BEHAVIOR OF THE YOUNG ORGANISM

If we are to characterize the behavior of young organisms by what they do, then one of the major characteristics of the young organism is sleep. The human newborn, for example, spends 16 to 18 hours a day sleeping. Unfortunately for the parents, these periods of sleep are unevenly distributed throughout each 24-hour period, and only as the infant matures, do they become consolidated into longer ones. In one study, for example, the average duration of single periods of sleep and wakefulness was measured in infants from the first to the sixteenth week of life. The longest sleep period increased from 4.1 to 8.5 hours, or 107 percent, whereas the shorter awake period increased from 2.4 to 3.6 hours, or 50 percent (Kleitman, 1967).

Before discussing the developmental aspects of sleep, a short digression is necessary to review some of the concepts and terminology used in this area of study. For a long time it was thought that activity or wakefulness was maintained by the animal's being bombarded by external stimuli. Sleep was considered a passive process which resulted from the withdrawal or reduction of external stimulation. Several lines of evidence have made this an untenable position. For example, if one electrically stimulates the appropriate region of the brain in a cat, it will go to sleep. In addition to this, it has also been found that transection of the hypothalamus results in insomnia in rats (Koella, 1967). Clemente and Sterman (1967), working with cats, have presented further behavioral evidence that sleep is an active process by showing that when a tone of 2,000 cycles per second is repeatedly paired with electrical brain stimulation which induces sleep, presentation of the tone later by itself will induce sleep in the absence of the brain stimulation. Therefore it would appear that certain brain regions may be actively involved in the induction of sleep.

An apparently passive behavioral state need not necessarily indicate a passive neural state.

Evidence from electrical recordings of single nerve cells in the brain indicates that in some brain regions, cells which are active during waking hours become less active during sleep, whereas other cells increase their gross activity levels during sleep and decrease their firing during waking hours (Evarts, 1967). These kinds of relationships indicate a change or reorganization of brain activity as the organism goes from wakefulness to sleep. Taken together, these sorts of studies suggest that the onset of sleep is an active process and not a simple result of decreased peripheral stimulation.

There appear to be several stages of sleep. For example, the adult cat first goes into a drowsy stage, which is followed by a relaxation of muscle tonus. If one records electrical activity from the surface of the brain, we see that the electroencephalogram (EEG) changes from a low-voltage fast activity (often called a desynchronized EEG), normally associated with the aroused, awake organism, to a pattern of high-voltage slow activity (synchronized) in the asleep animal (see Figure 7–2). Sleep associated with a synchronized EEG pattern is often referred to as slow-wave sleep (SW). After passing into SW sleep, the EEG pattern may again become desynchronized, but behaviorally the cat remains asleep. This phase of sleep is often called paradoxical sleep (PS) because the EEG associated with it is the same as that associated with wakefulness. Often associated with PS are rapid eye movements (REM) in which the eyes move back and forth while the eyelids are still shut. Consequently, this phase of sleep has also been termed REM sleep. REM and PS are often used interchangeably.

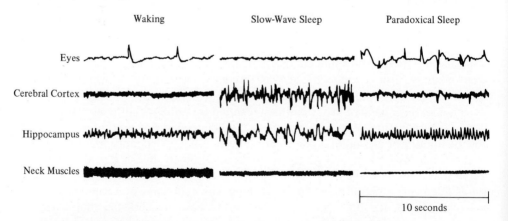

Figure 7–2. Electrical recording from a cat during waking and during Slow Sleep and Paradoxical Sleep. During Paradoxical Sleep the EEG patterns for the cortex and hippocampus look similar to those during the waking period. That the cat is still sleeping would be indicated by its behavior and by the neck muscle recording which shows a loss of muscle tonus. (From Allison and Van Twyver 170b).

The adult human also goes through REM sleep, and if he is awakened during a bout of REM sleep, he will usually report dreaming, whereas, if he is awakened during a period of non-REM sleep, he is less likely to report the occurrence of a dream. Thus, REM sleep appears to be correlated, although not entirely, with dream activity. That this may be so in nonhuman organisms is suggested by the fact that REM sleep occurs in connection with limb movements and other activities which may suggest dream activity in animals.

Returning to the neonate, we can now look at its sleep pattern in more detail. As mentioned earlier, the newborn human spends 16 to 18 hours sleeping within each 24-hour period. Of this time, roughly 50 to 80 percent is spent in REM sleep (Roffwarg, Muzo, & Dement, 1966). If REM activity is associated with dreaming, we may well ask: What does the newborn have to dream about? Obviously, if we consider only the phenomenological and experiential aspects of dreaming, we have little hope of answering this question. However, if dreaming or the state characterized by REM, desynchronized EEG, periodic limb twitches, and so forth is considered as a set of responses, we can explore the possible functions of this behavior and the conditions necessary and sufficient for its occurrence. At present, neither set of questions has an answer, although a set of norms has emerged concerning the

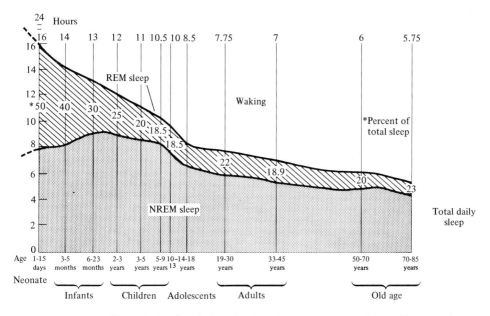

Figure 7–3. Graph showing the change in sleep pattern with increasing age in humans. Explanation in text. (From Roffwarg, H. P., Muzo, J. N. & Dement, W. C. Ontogenetic development of the human sleep-dream cycle. *Science,* 1966, **152,** 604–619. Copyright 1966 by the American Association for the Advancement of Science.)

probability of these responses at various age levels. The graph in Figure 7–3 indicates, first, that as the individual gets older, he spends less time sleeping, and secondly, that he spends a smaller percentage of the sleep period in REM sleep. This trend has also been found in other mammals (Figure 7–4), such as the rat, cat, sheep, and the rhesus monkey (Jouvet-Mounier. Astic, & Lacote, 1970), although it does not appear so marked in the guinea pig and sheep as it does in the other species. Interestingly enough, guinea pigs and sheep do not show much change in the percentage of PS in relation to total sleep time during development. When compared to other species, both these animals are more developed at birth than the other species. Possibly the high levels of PS in most young are in some way a result of their immaturity. Because of the advanced state of development in the guinea pig and sheep at birth, it may be hypothesized that the pattern of PS has already reached its adult form and therefore does not change much during extrauterine development. This is a *post hoc* hypothesis, since it comes after the data have been collected. It will be necessary to test it in order to determine its generality.

The finding that PS is present at birth in some species introduces another interesting question: When does PS begin? Recent work has suggested that

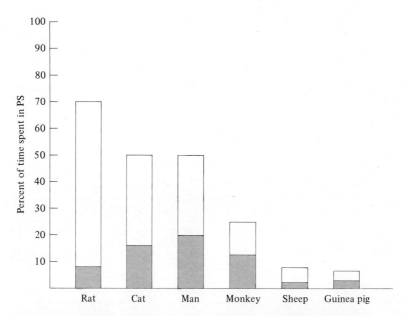

Figure 7–4. Graph showing the percentage of time that infants and adults of 6 species spend in paradoxical sleep (PS). The open portion of each bar indicates the percentage of time for the infant and the hatched portion indicates the percentage of time for the adult. (After Jouvet-Mounier et al., 1970; and Roffwarg et al., 1966.)

in the guinea pig this pattern of brain activity starts around the forty-seventh day of gestation (Astic & Jouvet-Mounier, 1970). Therefore, if PS is indicative of dreaming, we have the interesting possibility of fetal dreams. In other species which are born at a less mature level of development, the onset of PS may occur postnatally. As already mentioned, the rat, at birth, is very immature, and reliable brain recordings from the immature skull are virtually impossible to achieve. Therefore, determination of the state of wakefulness depends entirely upon behavioral criteria. The late Dr. Jouvet-Mounier and her colleagues have described the behavior of the young rat (1970) thus:

> Either it appeared to be awake, with wriggling movement and tonic extensions of the neck, or it lay motionless with a muscular hypotonia interrupted by frequent twitches of the entire body. These twitches were associated with ocular movements from the 5th or 6th day when the behavior became similar to the general pattern of behavior of PS as seen in the adult, the only difference being that the twitches were much more intense in the newborn until about the 10th or 12th day ... episodes of QS [quiet sleep] were very short and very rare at this age.
>
> Near the 12th to the 15th day, when the eyes opened ... the behavior pattern changed. The muscular twitches during PS were less intense; the states of vigilance differentiated, especially QS, as the duration of its episodes lengthened and its percentage increased progressively until the end of the 1st month [p. 218].

Apparently the behavioral evidence of PS cannot be discriminated with any degree of certainty in the rat until around day 5 or 6 of postnatal life. After the first ten to twelve days of life, the amount of time spent in PS decreases and reaches the adult level by the end of the first month. Figure 7-4 shows a comparison of several species in terms of the differences in sleep-wakefulness in the young and the adult of each species.

Why PS sleep decreases with age is not known. In fact, the very function of REM sleep and dreaming is not even clear. One hypothesis has been that the nervous system must receive a certain level of stimulation for proper development to occur. For example, it was proposed that REM provides a mechanism for the establishment of the neuromuscular pathways involved in voluntary, conjugate eye movements. However, if this is so, it is difficult to see why moles show typical levels of PS (Allison & Van Twyver, 1970a). These nearly blind mammals spend most of their lives underground and have degenerate visual systems in which any eye movement is virtually impossible. If PS functions to ensure development of the visual system, then it is without function or success in the mole. It seems likely that the function(s) of PS is of a more general nature than to ensure proper development of a particular sensory function.

This suggestion gains some support from studies in which the subject is deprived of PS by being wakened every time he begins a bout of PS. Specific changes in behavior have been difficult to find, but there appears to be a change in the overall responsiveness to external stimulation. One finding is certain, however: Deprivation of REM sleep by waking the animal up every time it begins REM leads to an increase in REM probability when the animal is permitted to go back to sleep.

Thus, the inactivity phase or sleep phase of the developing organism shows a pattern of change and reorganization during development into what we call the adult sleep pattern: The cycles become longer and the percentage of time spent in REM sleep decreases with age except in those species which show advanced development at birth, such as the guinea pig.

Response Frequency Changes in the Young Awake Organism

There are several varieties of behavioral change which, taken together, seem to characterize the awake behavior of the developing organism: (1) the appearance of new response patterns; (2) the disappearance of a response pattern; and (3) the change in frequency of an existing response over time.

The consecutive appearance of *new response patterns* is highly characteristic of developing organisms. These new responses reflect changes in maturation and in level of experience and practice.

It is necessary to elaborate here on what is meant by new response. The intended meaning is that, given a defined stimulus situation, the organism will reliably respond in a way he has not or could not prior to that time. For example, when an infant takes his first unassisted step, he may be moving his legs and body in a way which he has often done before but never with his total weight on his feet and without holding onto a nearby chair for balance. Under these particular stimulus circumstances this is a "first," and he will continue to repeat this response in this situation. If he had been presented with a similar situation prior to this time, he would have responded by sitting, grabbing a chair, or simply falling over. This response, then, has a boundary within time such that it occurs only after a certain level of development and/or practice has been achieved. Some response patterns are completely bounded by time, and if they do not occur within a given period, they may never occur after that time period. A famous example of this is the following response pattern of the young duckling.

A newly hatched duckling, if left with its mother, will begin to follow the mother duck when she leaves the nest. Ramsey and Hess (1954) placed newly hatched ducklings in a specially constructed runway containing a wooden model of an adult duck. They found that incubator-hatched ducklings were most likely to start following the model between 12 to 20 hours after hatching. However, if ducklings were isolated until approximately 30 hours of age, this following response did not appear. The following phenomenon has come to be known as *imprinting*, and it is a classic example of the fact that certain periods of the organism's life are particularly important or critical for the organization of certain behavior patterns. More will be said about imprinting later.

In addition to the appearance of new responses, development and maturation are also accompanied by the loss or disappearance of some response patterns. For example, if the newborn infant's cheek is stroked lightly, he will move his head toward the stimulus and will form his mouth so as to take in the source of stimulation. This movement toward the source of stimulation is known as the rooting reflex, and its function is to assist the neonate in locating the nipple at feeding time. Within a few months after birth, this response disappears and can no longer be elicited. Similarly, the palmar grasp reflex and the Babinski reflex are also lost during development.

In some cases, these responses reappear in old age following organic brain damage. Teitelbaum (1967) describes a dramatic demonstration of this phenomenon, known as *dissolution*:

> In the course of the examination, while asking the subject various things, Denny-Brown, standing beside and slightly behind the patient, while both were facing the class, lightly touched the side of the patient's cheek, near the mouth. A curious thing occurred. The side of the patient's mouth near the stimulating finger opened and gaped toward the finger. As the stimulation continued, the patient's head turned, his mouth made contact with the finger and sucking movements occurred. If such a patient was asked why he is doing this, he may show surprise and embarrassment, replying that he was not aware of his action, or even denying it, yet he may be unable to stop. These are involuntary automatisms, rooting and sucking reflexes, no longer subject to voluntary control by the patient with frontal-lobe [brain] damage.
>
> Similar approach automatisms can be demonstrated in the hand and foot. Involuntary grasping of the hand is often a diagnostic sign of frontal-lobe damage in human beings. . . . The best way to elicit it is to distract the patient's attention by asking him to look at something on the side wall of the room, or to perform some simple task of mental arithmetic with his eyes closed. While he is thus engaged, the palm of his hand is lightly touched and gently stroked by the examiner's index finger in a movement from the center of the patient's palm outward between the thumb and forefinger. Depending on the amount of damage to the frontal lobes, and also on how much paralysis has been caused by damage simultaneously occurring in the motor areas of the brain, various components of the grasping reflex can be elicited. Deep pressure in the palm elicits strong maintained flexion of the fingers (grasping). Light touch in a stroking movement of the skin elicits closure of the fingers around the stimulating object (trap reaction), in such a way as to prevent it from leaving the palm. Rhythmic flexion and extension of the fingers (forced groping) then occur in a manner which acts to bring the object back to the center of the palm where it can be firmly grasped. If the object is moved out of the palm, the hand and arm follow after it (pursuit reaction), and if the object is moved just slowly enough, the hand and arm follow while just clinging to it (magnet reaction). The same kind of grasping can be seen in the foot in response to pressure or a light touch on the sole.

These actions are very powerful and often not subject to voluntary control. They pervade the frontal-brain-damaged patient's behavior, often to his great embarrassment. Thus, when opening a door, the patient may find himself unable to let go of the doorknob. The grasp reflex is so powerful, that he has to reach over with his other hand and pry his fingers loose. In bed, when he sees a nurse passing by, his hand may automatically reach out and clutch at her dress, an act particularly distressing if she happens to be carrying a tray loaded with food or medicine. The contact approach-reflex of the foot is often so exaggerated that, when walking, the frontal-damage patient is often hampered by the slipping-clutch syndrome: when he starts to walk, his feet seem to be glued to the ground and he has to make several sliding movements on the ground before he can finally free his feet enough to walk forward normally [Teitelbaum, 1967, pp. 110–111].

It is suspected that the disappearance of many responses, such as the rooting and the Babinski reflexes during development results from inhibition by the higher brain centers which develop after birth. The degeneration of these brain areas in old age "releases" these behavior patterns once again.

The appearance of new responses and the disappearance of other responses combine to provide the behavioral picture of a developing organism. But not all changes during development are of this all or none type. Response frequencies may change without the occurrence of a new response or the disappearance of an old one. For example, the frequency of REM sleep appears to decrease as the individual gets older, although it never disappears entirely. Play behavior may occur in greater frequency in the young but not be entirely absent in the adult.

The developing organism presents a behavioral picture of change in concert with a changing physiology. What is important to note is that while many of these behavioral changes may result from events of maturation and growth, the behavior and experience of developing organisms are at the same time affecting the changing physiology.

In a series of experiments carried out at the University of California in Berkeley, rats were reared under different living conditions. While some rats were reared in cages by themselves (isolates), others were reared in large playpenlike cages which had activity wheels, ladders, and a variety of "rat toys." These rats were called the Environmental Complexity Group (EC). As adults, the rats from this group were better maze learners than the isolates. In addition, however, it was found that the EC rats had larger brains and that their brains also had different enzyme ratios from those of the brains of the isolates, indicating that as a result of differential experience, the central nervous system had been modified (Rosenzweig, Krech, Bennett, & Diamond, 1968).

That experience leads to modification and changes in the physiological systems of the developing organism rounds out, so to speak, the dynamic status of development and behavior. Changes in physiology and anatomy in the young provide opportunity for new responses, which result in new experiences, which in turn affect the physiological systems in the individual.

ALTERATION OF ADULT RESPONSE FREQUENCIES BY EARLY EXPERIENCE

As a result of early psychoanalytic writings, such as those of Sigmund Freud, which emphasized the importance of early experience in molding the adult, many animal behaviorists began looking at, and experimenting with, young animals in the hope of gaining insight into the behavior of the adult.

A complete survey of this area is obviously impossible, but an attempt will be made to conceptualize some of the problems of early experience with the goal of providing a structure on which to build with future readings.

An early study in this area by Levy attempted to determine whether deprivation of sucking in a neonatal puppy would increase the probability of later sucking. The problem here stems from theories and notions about thumb sucking in children. Levy (1934) divided a litter of six puppies into three groups. One group remained with the mother, another group was given formula through a bottle with a slow-flowing nipple. The last two puppies were tube-fed for 13 days post partum so they did not have to suck; after day 13, they were fed with rapidly flowing nipples such that they could obtain large amounts of formula with only minimal sucking. The experiment lasted for 20 days, during which time the puppies were observed closely for their tendency to suck. The experimenter tested them by using a nipple to cover his finger, then rated them on the intensity of sucking. In accord with Freudian theory, Levy found that those puppies which did not have to suck so much for their food sucked with greater intensity when tested and were more inclined to mouth parts of their own bodies.

This work provided impetus and promise to the field of behavioral development. From the voluminous number of studies which have been reported since the work by Levy, there appear to be several modes by which early experience can affect adult behavior (Beach & Jaynes, 1954). Early experience or training may result in response patterns which persist into adulthood. Many examples are available for this, such as speech patterns and the development of an accent in the human. Young animals may acquire any number of responses which persist in the adult, such as the family dog that, trained as a puppy to shake hands, will continue to do so upon command. These are examples of responses shown by the young animal and persisting into adulthood. Other response patterns may be acquired as a result of early experience, but the responses themselves may not occur until the animal reaches maturity.

The male chaffinch normally begins to sing its song at around nine months of age. If the male is acoustically isolated from other chaffinches for the first year of life, his adult song will be abnormal. If he is exposed to the adult chaffinch song sometime during the first 12 months, his song will be normal. However, after 12 months of acoustical isolation, he is unable to achieve normal song even if exposed to it (Thorpe, 1961).

The white-crowned sparrow is also dependent upon experience for development of normal song. Like the chaffinch, the white-crowned sparrow develops dialects; Marler found that sparrows captured in Marin County, California, have a different song from those several miles away in Berkeley. If captured sparrows are acoustically isolated from their parents after two or three months of age, they develop normal song. However, if they are isolated after three to fourteen days of age, their song is abnormal and does not achieve the dialect shown by the parent. Exposure to the parent's song for 8 minutes a day from three weeks of age to two months of age is sufficient to permit the development of normal song dialect. (Marler & Tomura, 1962).

For both the chaffinch and the white-crowned sparrow, early experience provides the information or "tuning" necessary for development of the appropriate adult response. It should also be noted, as pointed out earlier, that age, or level of maturation, is also a crucial variable. Since the effects of certain experiences on the developing organisms have time boundaries within which they must occur, it follows that such time variables will play a role in the effects of early experience on adult behavior.

Another means by which early experience can affect adult behavior is through establishment or modification of the stimuli which elicit a response. Earlier, we mentioned that if a duckling is exposed to a moving model of an adult, the duckling will soon begin to follow the model. It is not necessary to use a model of a duck to elicit this following. If exposed at the appropriate age, the duckling can also be induced to follow a purple cube, a green ball, or even a person. Working with turkeys, Schein and Hale (1959) obtained a group of tom turkeys which were imprinted upon their human handlers as a result of extensive early handling. The effects of this early experience were not confined to the following response of young organisms. Later, the tom turkeys had strong attachments to people. When a person entered their pen, the male turkeys would immediately begin courtship of the human (Figure 7–5). They would continue to show the entire courtship pattern to the human even when the hen was present! In the absence of the human, the toms would turn their display to the hens. Unlike the previous example of the chaffinch and the sparrow, the normal response pattern was present in the turkeys, only now it was evoked by stimuli which normally do not elicit it. Apparently as a result of early experience with human handlers, the pattern of courtship was elicited by this unusual set of stimuli.

A similar type of modification may have occurred in the experiment on bill clapping described by Gottlieb (1968). In that experiment, duck embryos which were not allowed to hear the vocalizations of sibling embryos failed to show increases in bill clapping when they were exposed to the maternal

Figure 7–5. Handling of newly hatched turkeys results in a permanent change in the male such that when these turkeys reached adulthood they showed courting responses to human beings even in preference to sexually receptive hen turkeys.

call. Since they did show some bill clapping, it seems clear that the response pattern had developed. The change appears as a modification, in this case an elimination, of the stimulus which normally elicits the response.

Unfortunately, it is not always possible to classify the behavioral changes into one of these two categories: (1) modification of response processes, and (2) modification of stimulus processes. This may be because there are other possibilities we have not considered, because both sets of processes have been modified, or because we need further experimentation. For example, if an adult rat is placed in an open, lighted arena, it will move around and explore the area. A quantitative measure of this activity can easily be achieved if the floor of the arena is marked off in large squares. Each time the rat moves from one square to another, it is given a score of 1. At the end of a 5- or 10-minute period, we have a quantitative measure of its activity. In this same test we can also obtain a measure of autonomic activity if we score the number of times the animal urinates and defecates. Animals which have been handled early in life by being taken out of their nest and placed alone in a small chamber for 3 minutes a day for the first ten days of life will move around more and show lower elimination scores than will rats which have not been handled in this way. How or in what way this form of early experience can affect adult movement in an open area is not clear. It should be recalled that from day 1 through day 10 the rat is very immature; its eyes and ears are closed, and locomotion is achieved through a wriggling type of crawl. Such organisms are, nevertheless, affected by handling in some way which ultimately affects adult behavior (Schaefer, 1968).

In an attempt to ascertain the extent to which certain behavior patterns are innate or develop in the absence of experience, ethologists have often resorted to the deprivation study. In such a study, the experimental animal is isolated from all the stimuli which the experimenter believes are or might be important for the development of the response under investigation. (See Chapter 4 for studies on socialization in the dog.) The experiments with the chaffinches and crowned sparrows are a case in point. Young birds, when isolated from hearing their parents' song, were found not to develop normal song patterns.

Care must be taken in drawing conclusions from these studies. In a study of visual perception, chimpanzees were reared in dark chambers and tested for their ability to solve visual tasks following this isolation. Their inability to perform normally on these tasks was initially interpreted as indicating a lack of visual experience in infancy. Additional study showed, however, that these chimps did not have normal retinas and were partially blind as a result of having spent much of their lives in complete darkness (Riesen, 1966).

The effects of isolation are often dramatic and to some extent pathetic. Young rhesus monkeys reared in isolation develop severe withdrawal symptoms (Harlow, Rowland, & Griffin, 1964) and spend long hours huddling in the corner clutching themselves. As adults they are unable to form normal social bonds and cannot interact sexually. These severe signs of withdrawal can be prevented if the young monkey is allowed some time each day to play with a sibling. It is still too early to offer any explanation for these dramatic behavioral changes, since they undoubtedly involve major psychological changes. As was noted earlier in the discussion of the effects of the rearing condition on brain weight in the rat, early experience can effect physiological modifications. It is, of course, difficult to separate changes in behavior from physiological changes, particularly if one shares the faith that behavior is determined by physiological events as well as external stimuli. That physiological mechanisms are involved in the control of behavior needs little comment. However, one of the implications of that situation is that adult behavior is modified not only by early behavior experience but also by early physiological variations.

EARLY HORMONAL FACTORS WHICH ALTER ADULT RESPONSE FREQUENCIES

One example of the way in which early physiological variables can modify adult behavior comes from studies of the effects of early hormone treatment on adult sexual behavior. In the remainder of the chapter, an attempt will be made to expand this discussion to illustrate how comparative studies can provide the basis for general principles of behavior.

Although there are relatively few behavior patterns shown by the female mammal which cannot also be induced in the male, and vice versa, we still find that male and female mammals behave differently. That is, there are patterns of behavior which occur more frequently in one sex than in the other. For example, a central feature of the mating pattern in the male golden hamster consists of mounting the female. He achieves this by placing his forepaws around the female's flanks while she remains standing with her perineal region elevated so as to permit penile penetration. This mounting behavior shown by the male is a sexually dimorphic trait in that it is seldom, if ever, shown by the female even when she is placed with another sexually receptive female and injected with massive doses of male hormone: testosterone.

A sexual dimorphism also exists for the behavior of the sexually receptive female. For the female, the central response is the postural one shown in Figure 7-6. This response, which permits the male to copulate with her, is called lordosis. While a male hamster will occasionally show lordosis when mounted by another male, his responses are very short even when he has been treated with ovarian hormones. This is in contrast to the female in which

A.

B.

C.

Figure 7-6. Figure showing the mating behavior of the golden hamster. (A) Male grooms female while she maintains a lordosislike posture; (B) male mounts female; (C) after mounting the male grooms himself while the female remains immobile.

lordosis may be maintained for several minutes while the male mounts repeatedly. These clear sex differences exist in the adult mating behavior of the hamster and they cannot be explained in terms of the adult hormones present, since treatment with heterotypical gonadal hormones does not eliminate these differences. However, these sex-specific patterns do depend heavily upon the hormonal events occurring around the time of sex differentiation.

Sex Differentiation and Behavior

The principles which relate early gonadal hormone action to adult mating behavior in the hamster as well as in other rodents are similar to those which relate these early hormones to differentiation of the sex morphology:

> **1** If androgen (male sex hormone) is present during sex differentiation, the individual will develop the sex characteristics of a male, and female sex characteristics will be suppressed.
> **2** If androgen is absent during sex differentiation, the individual will develop the sex characteristics of a female, and male sex characteristics will fail to develop.

For behavior, the presence of *early androgen* (i.e., androgen during sex differentiation) will result in the increased probability of masculine response patterns in the adult. In the absence of early androgen, the probability of feminine response patterns will be increased. Further, in parallel with the sex morphology, early androgen will suppress the development of feminine behavior, whereas male behavior fails to develop in the absence of androgen during sex differentiation.

These principles can be illustrated with experiments carried out on the hamster. Behavioral studies indicate that differentiation of the physiological systems which control mating behavior in the hamster occurs around the time of birth. To determine the importance of androgen at this time, Eaton (1970) castrated male hamsters on the day they were born and studied their patterns of sex behavior when they reached adulthood. The males castrated at birth were divided into several groups. One group received an injection of testosterone following the castration and another group was not given an injection until day 15 of life. Control groups were given an injection of the vehicle in which the hormone was dissolved (sesame oil). When the subjects reached adulthood, they were tested for male sex behavior with a sexually receptive female. Since even in the normal adult male testosterone is needed to sustain mounting behavior, all subjects were given daily injections of this hormone for several weeks prior to testing. Only those males which had received an injection of testosterone on the day of birth showed mounting. If testosterone treatment was delayed until day 15, no mounting occurred in the adult in spite of the adult replacement therapy. These findings indicate that the development of mounting in the adult hamster requires the presence of androgen very early in life.

If androgen during this early stage of development is important for the development of mounting, then it follows that treatment of the neonatal female hamster with androgen should also result in mounting. When female hamsters were treated with testosterone or a control substance shortly after birth and tested for mounting as adults, it was found that only those females treated with testosterone showed mounting when placed with a receptive female. These observations again confirm the hypothesis that androgen very early in life results in an organism which can display masculine behavior characteristics (Swanson & Crossley, 1971).

Not only does this early androgen lead to behavioral masculinization, it also results in suppression of female behavior. In my own laboratory, several groups of female hamsters were treated with testosterone on day 4 and then tested for lordosis as adults. These females showed shorter lordosis responses than control animals even when treated with exogenous ovarian hormones as adults to ensure sufficient ovarian hormone stimulation.

Thus, early androgen has two effects upon the sexual behavior of the hamster, a masculinizing effect in which androgen increases the probability of masculine responses, and a defeminizing effect in which femalelike behaviors are suppressed.

The second principle of differentiation, mentioned earlier, refers to the development of female behavior. Here again, examples from the hamster are illustrative. If the male hamsters which were castrated at birth are treated, as adults, with estrogen and progesterone instead of testosterone, they will show long lordosis responses similar to those seen in the female, indicating that removal of androgen during early development of the genetic male has a behavioral feminizing effect. How general are these principles of sex differentiation?

Species Differences in Sex Differentiation of Behavior

One of the problems encountered in species comparisons is determining when sex differentiation occurs in each species. For example, treatment of the hamster from one to four days of age with androgen resulted in a permanent masculinizing effect, whereas, if treatment was delayed until the tenth day of postnatal life or given prior to birth (Nucci & Beach, 1971), such effects were not noted. This would suggest that for the physiological systems related to this behavior, sex differentiation in the hamster occurs within the first few days of postnatal life. However, if similar treatments are administered to the guinea pig at one to four days of age no permanent masculinizing effect is observed. On the other hand, this comparison may not be too meaningful in view of the differences in length of gestation. The guinea pig, born after a 68-day gestation period, is far more advanced than the hamster, which is born after only a 16-day gestation period. In short, postnatal chronological age does not provide a good basis on which to make developmental comparisons because animals of similar ages may not be at similar points in their development. Another form of chronological age is postcoital age, or the age expressed in days from the time of conception or copulation. Thus, for the hamster, androgen treatment at birth would be at day 17, postcoital age. However, treatment of the guinea pig at this age is ineffective, and only when the guinea pig is treated with androgen at the postcoital age of 30 to 35 days does one observe permanent behavioral masculinization (Goy, Bridson, & Young, 1964).

The problem in using chronological age in development, be it postnatal or postcoital, is that each species has a different set of developmental rates and the stage or period in which a species enters the processes of sex differentiation may vary depending upon the rate of development. What is needed is a point in development, regardless of chronological age, at which we know sex differentiation has begun.

One of the first indications that sex differentiation has started in a fetus is the change in cell structure which takes place in the gonad as it begins to differentiate into a testis. The undifferentiated gonad has an outer layer, or cortex, and an inner core, the medulla. The cortex will develop into an ovary if the individual is a genetic female, whereas the medulla normally develops into a testis if the individual is a genetic male. If the individual is to develop into a male, the onset of testicular differentiation (TD) is characterized by the appearance of elongated cells in the outside layers of the gonad. As differentiation proceeds, these cells come to form the *tunica albuginea*. If we use testicular differentiation as a reference point to indicate when sex differentiation has started, species can be compared at a common stage of development. Such a comparison has been made in Table 7-1 for four rodent species upon which we have sufficient morphological and behavioral data.

The first two columns in Table 7-1 indicate, respectively, the length of gestation and the time at which early androgen suppresses female sexual behavior. It is difficult to see any constancy in the age at which early androgen suppresses female sex behavior. However, if the onset of testicular differentiation is used as a reference point and the effectiveness of early androgen dated from that point, we gain predictive advantage, since each species becomes responsive to early androgen about 4.5 to 5 days after the onset of testicular differentiation.

In the hamster testicular differentiation begins at 11.5 days of postcoital age. Therefore, to affect behavior (mounting or lordosis), androgen must be given or removed around 4.5 days after TD begins (Clemens, unpublished data; Eaton, 1970). In the rat and guinea pig, androgen treatment becomes

Table 7-1 Time Periods When Androgen Treatment Will Suppress Female Mating Behavior (Lordosis) or Facilitate Male Mating Behavior in Four Rodent Species

Species	Length of gestation in days	Androgen suppresses lordosis (postcoital age in days)	Postcoital age for TD* (in days)	Androgen suppresses lordosis (days from TD)	Androgen facilitates mounting (days from TD)	Behavioral references
Hamster	16	16–21	11.5	4.5–7.5	4.5–7.5	Nucci & Beach, 1971; Eaton, 1970; Clemens, unpub. data
Laboratory mouse	19–20	? 20 ?	12.5	? 7.5 ?	— —	Edwards & Burge, 1971
Rat	21–22	18–28	13.0	5.0–14.0	— —	Clemens, Hiroi, & Gorski, 1971; Gerall & Ward, 1966; Nadler, 1969
Guinea pig	68	30–35	25.0	5.0–11.0	5.0–11.0	Goy, Bridson, & Young, 1964

*Onset of testicular differentiation (Price & Ortiz, 1965).

effective in suppressing lordosis if given about 5.0 days after the onset of TD (Clemens, Hiroi, & Gorski, 1969; Goy et al., 1964; Nadler, 1969). The information on the laboratory mouse is not complete, but treatment with androgen 7.5 days after the onset of TD reduced lordosis (Edwards & Burge, 1971).

For the hamster and the guinea pig, the time period for facilitation of mounting by early androgen treatment is the same as it is for suppression of lordosis. In the rat and the mouse, on the other hand, treatment with early androgen does not provide consistent increases in mounting behavior in the adult. In fact, for these latter species it has been suggested that mounting behavior develops independently of early androgens and that the primary action of early androgen for behavior is to defeminize the organism, i.e., to suppress lordosis (Whalen, Edwards, Luttge, & Robertson, 1969: Edwards & Burge, 1971).

Since this conclusion is at variance with the principles outlined earlier, a closer examination of the data is warranted. Three main pieces of evidence point to the idea that mounting in the rat and mouse may be independent of early androgen: (1) The normal female rat (or laboratory mouse), if treated with androgen as an adult, will, unlike the female hamster or guinea pig, achieve mount frequencies which approach the male's. This high level of female mounting in the absence of early androgen treatment might suggest that androgen is not needed for development of this behavior pattern. (2) Early treatment with exogenous androgen fails to consistently facilitate mounting in the female rat. (3) It has been shown that castration of the male rat on the day of birth, while increasing significantly the amount of lordosis he will show as an adult, does not reduce the level of mounting. Thus, neither the exogenous treatment with androgen nor the early removal of androgen sources appears to influence mounting.

However, before accepting these species as exceptions to the rule, alternative views must be examined. While high levels of mounting in normal female rats might suggest behavior independent of early androgen, the same behavior, in light of the principles mentioned earlier, might also be interpreted to suggest that the female is normally exposed to early androgen and consequently shows high levels of mounting as an adult. The source of such androgens is still open to question, but most litters of rats contain eight to fourteen pups per litter, of which half are usually male. The fetal rat testis contains androgen from about day 14 of gestation onward and probably begins secreting androgen before day 18 of gestation (Price & Ortiz, 1965). The extent to which these androgens may influence the female sibs is unknown. In addition, it is not uncommon for the pregnant mammal to secrete some androgen, and this may affect the fetal female. These observations, combined with the indication in Table 7-1 that the period of early androgen action begins prenatally in the rat, suggest that the fetal female may not entirely escape androgen during the process of sex differentiation.

Failure to observe an increase in mounting following early androgen treatment in the rat strongly suggests an insensitivity to androgen, but the reason for this is not clear. It is interesting to note, however, that in none of the rodent species studied does early androgen increase the level of mounting frequency seen in the male. This might indicate that the males normally develop so that they mount at some maximum limit beyond which additional exogenous androgen cannot push them. The effect of exogenous androgen in the female hamster or guinea pig is to increase her level toward that of the male. Since female mice and rats are already near the limit of the male, early androgen would not be expected to have much effect.

Castration of the male rat on the day of birth results in a preparation that achieves high levels of mounting when, as an adult, the rat is given testosterone. On the other hand, if the adult is treated with estrogen and progesterone, he will also show very high levels of lordosis. If castration is delayed until day 3 of life, lordosis will be suppressed in the adult. This set of relations is difficult to interpret. If one argues that mounting is induced by action of androgen prenatally, then why is lordosis not suppressed? The same question can also be applied to the argument that mounting in the female is brought about by prenatal androgen action. Thus we are left with the problem. Does mounting develop independently of androgen in some species, or does mounting indicate the presence of early androgen? If androgen induces mounting, then why does it not also suppress lordosis in those females which mount?

The Role of Early Androgen in Noncoital Behavior

Up to this point, we have discussed the effects of early gonadal hormones upon coital behavior in rodents. Do the principles obtained here have generality beyond these behaviors and beyond these species?

Another pattern of behavior which is sexually dimorphic in many species is aggressive or fighting behavior. Many strains of male laboratory mice, for example, readily fight when placed together. Females, on the other hand, rarely fight. Treatment of the females with androgen around the time of birth results in their increased aggressiveness (Bronson & Desjardins. 1970; Edwards, 1969) indicating that androgens early in life can influence noncoital behavior patterns in the adult.

The generality of early hormone principles is still an empirical matter, but recent work with rhesus monkeys and with several human clinical syndromes indicates that even complex primate behavior has determining factors in the events which occur around the time of sexual differentiation. Robert Goy and his coworkers at the Oregon Regional Primate Research Center isolated infant rhesus monkeys from about 100 days of age (Goy, 1968). At this time, they were housed singly and weaned onto solid food. After that, each subject was placed in age-mate groups of four to six monkeys for 20 to 30 minutes a day, and the behavior of each infant was recorded. Young male monkeys showed a high incidence of rough-and-tumble kinds of play when compared to female infants of similar age. Males also showed higher levels of what is called "threat." This type of behavior is best described as a freezing stare in which the animal looks as though it were about to attack. Male infants also initiated play more often than female infants. These sex differences in the infant rhesus are apparently not due to differences in plasma testosterone levels, because this male hormone is not present in measurable amounts between six and eighteen months of age. Although another form of androgen (androstenedione) is present during this period, it is present in the female infant and juvenile as well. Thus, it is not easy to account for these sex differences as being due to differences in blood hormone levels. In fact, males castrated on the day of birth and tested at ages of three and a half to nine months were found to have response frequencies similar to intact males. The differences between young male and female rhesus monkeys persist throughout the second year of postnatal life.

Goy has suggested that testicular secretions at the time of brain differentiation during fetal development may be in part responsible for these sex differences in the same way that the presence or absence of androgens in rats and guinea pigs affects adult sex behavior. Evidence for this proposal comes from the behavior of infant female monkeys whose mothers were treated with androgen during gestation. Daily injections of testosterone propionate were given to the mothers from about day 39 of gestation to day 64 or day 90. The morphological condition of the female offspring is described by Goy (1968) as:

> characterized by the formation of a well-developed scrotum and a small but apparently complete penis. In addition, the external vaginal orifice was completely obliterated and replaced by a median raphe so that these subjects appeared very much like the normal genetic male [p. 24].

Equally important was the behavior of these young pseudohermaphrodite primates. When compared with normal males and females with regard to rough-and-tumble play and other malelike activities, they showed response frequencies which were intermediate between the normal males and the normal females. The effects of the prenatal androgen were not limited to changes in morphology and play behavior but were also found in mounting behavior. During the first year of life, four of the five pseudohermaphrodites mounted other animals more often than control females did. In the second year of life, only two out of the five displayed more mounting than the controls did.

Since these subjects are still juveniles, we cannot make any statement about the role of prenatal hormones on their adult behavior, but it is apparent that these infant primates are not sexually neutral at birth. Their response probabilities have been affected by prenatal gonadal hormones.

Are there any similarities to be found in human primates? Behavioral differences between boys and girls are clearly established by the age of three years (Sears, 1965). As they mature, their behavioral differences become even more clear, with boys being inclined toward the more energetic forms of play and preferring certain types of so-called boys' toys rather than dolls and the like. Forms of play also differ with boys preferring to take on the man's role during fantasy play while the girls play the mother (Money & Erhardt, 1968).

There are, of course, variations and normal deviations from this. For example, in this culture we normally make allowances for the tomboy. This is the girl who likes energetic sports or play activities and who may not care so much for dolls and playing house. Although this girl is perfectly normal, we recognize a syndrome of behavior here which sets it apart from other complexes of responses which we think of as feminine. The tomboy group appears behaviorally closer to the complex of behaviors we see in boys. Sex differences, then, are not all or none; there are few responses a boy can show that girls do not also show, and vice versa.

Other differences exist on this continuum, such as the fact that females tend to score higher on verbal IQ tests than males, whereas males score higher on mechanical and spatial tests. But again, although this is the trend, there is considerable overlap. What is the nature of these differences? Are they products of our rearing practices, or might prenatal hormones be having some influence, causing differences similar to those seen in the rat, the guinea pig, and the rhesus monkey?

Many of the data which we have on humans and which are relevant to this question come from analysis of clinical material. Four syndromes will be considered here: Turner's syndrome, adrenogential hermaphroditism, progestin-induced hermaphroditism, and testicular feminization.

In our discussion of the nonhuman studies, we noted that in the absence of androgen, development proceeded along the lines of the female. In the case of *Turner's syndrome*, we have an individual who lacks one sex chromosome and is, therefore, referred to as an XO (YO being lethal). Such individuals have no gonads, and as we would expect, they are phenotypically females. In terms of the sex differences we have been discussing, these individuals show a characteristic female behavior patterning. Dr. John Money at Johns Hopkins University has carried out extensive testing and interviews with a group of these individuals. Some of his findings are summarized in Table 7-2, where they have been compared with two other syndromes: *progestin-induced hermaphroditism* and *adrenogential hermaphroditism*. These two syndromes have in common the fact that the genetic female fetus has been exposed to androgenic substances. In the case of the progestin-induced syndrome, these substances were given to the mother during pregnancy (usually to ensure its maintenance). As a result of this treatment, the female fetus is heavily masculinized. Naturally this was soon discovered, and the treatment has been discontinued. In the case of the adrenogenital syndrome, the fetus is exposed to androgens of adrenal origin. This is a hereditary disease in which an enzyme deficiency in the adrenal gland results in secretion of androgen instead of cortisone. In the female, this secretion can lead to a heavy masculinization.

If we look at Table 7-2, we notice very quickly that the individuals who

Table 7–2   Six Indices of Psychosexual Identity in Three Diagnostic Groups

Indices	Progestin-induced hermaphroditism N=10		Adrenogenital hermaphroditism N=12		Turner's syndrome N=15	
	No.	%	No.	%	No.	%
1. (a) Intense outdoor physical and athletic interests	10	100	11	92	0	0
(b) Moderate interest and ability in outdoor activities	0	0	0	0	6	40
2. (a) Known to self and to others as tomboy	9	90	9	75	?1	7
(b) Psychosexual ambivalence but not a tomboy	0	0	1	8	0	0
3. (a) Interest in boys' toys only	6	60	3	25	0	0
(b) Boys' toys preferred and dolls only occasionally	3	30	7	58	0	0
(c) Dolls preferred and no boys' toys	1	10	2	17	13	87
(d) Dolls preferred and boys' toys only occasionally	0	0	0	0	2	13
4. (a) Priority of marriage vs. career	0	0	0	0	4	27
(b) Priority of career vs. marriage	2	20	5	42	1*	7
(c) Marriage and career	6	60	6	50	9	60
(d) No information	2	20	1	8	1	7
5. (a) Slacks, shirts, and shorts strongly preferred	8	80	9	75	0	0
(b) Pretty dresses, plus slacks, shorts, and shirts	2	20	2	17	6	40
(c) Pretty dresses and no slacks, shirts, or shorts	0	0	1	8	9	60
6. Own sex depicted first in draw-a-person test	7	70	7	58	15	100

*Wanted to be a nun.
SOURCE: Money and Ehrhardt (1968, p. 42).

were exposed to early androgens are more inclined to engage in intense outdoor activities, to see themselves as tomboys, to show interest in boys' toys, preferring them to dolls, and to prefer slacks and shirts to dresses. None shows a preference for marriage over a career. With Turner's syndrome, we find quite a different pattern of likes and dislikes, which may be viewed as the more prevalent feminine syndrome. Thus, exposure of genetic females to androgens during prenatal development seems to modify later behavior in a predictable manner.

In relating this work to our earlier discussion, we may still ask: What happens to human genetic males if they do not have early androgen? In practically all cases, they develop into women. Not only that, they also become wives and rear adopted children. Clinically, this syndrome is known as *testicular feminization*. These individuals have testes which secrete male hormones but because of an enzyme deficiency, none of the target tissues can respond to the androgen. Consequently, we have a system which develops in the absence of androgenic stimulation, since the androgen receptors don't work. At birth these individuals are "females" although they lack ovaries, and they are reared as females. The testes remain in an undescended state, and often the true condition of these persons is not discovered until they reach adolescence and fail to begin menstruation. At this time they are usually placed on female hormones and lead relatively normal female lives. Psychosexually, they view themselves as females; they generally prefer the less intense activities, and they look forward to raising a family since most of them love babies; and according to their husbands, they make fine wives.

Now let us return to an earlier question: Are humans psychosexually neutral at birth, or are there prenatal determinants which predispose them to behave later in a certain way? It is still too early to answer this question, but present evidence suggests that there are prenatal biological factors which are involved in what many psychologists have long thought were solely the products of experience.

Therefore, we are faced with another note of caution for future studies. Whenever we make a statement that such and such a behavior is experientially determined, we must assume that we know all the physiological variables which might affect that behavior—an assumption that is becoming more and more difficult to make as we learn more about physiological variables.

One further point should be given consideration. In the last set of examples, we have considered a principle of early hormone action which appears to have relevance across many species, including the human. Obviously, this is not to say that experience is not important. At our present stage of understanding, it appears as though one's sex identity, i.e., whether one regards himself as a male or female, is heavily dependent upon experience and the sex of rearing. For example, in the case of female adrenogenitalism where the newborn is heavily masculinized, mistakes have been made and the child has been designated a boy and reared as one. In such a case the individual takes on the identity of a boy, whereas other children with the same syndrome may be reared as girls and have equal success in establishing a female sexual identity (Money, 1963). Thus, two children, appearing identical at birth, are capable of achieving different sexual identities.

REFERENCES

ALLISON, T., & VAN TWYVER, H. Sleep in the moles, *Scalopus aquaticus* and *Condylura cristata*. *Experimental Neurology*, 1970, **27**, 564–578. (a)

ALLISON, T., & VAN TWYVER, H. The evolution of sleep. *Natural History*, 1970, **79** (2), 57–65. (b)

ASTIC, L., & JOUVET-MOUNIER, D. Etude *in utero* des états de ueille et de sommeil chez le calaye. *Journal of Physiology*, 1970, **62**, 115–116.

BALABAN, M., & HILL, J. Perihatching behavior patterns of chick embryos (*Gallus domesticus*). *Animal Behavior*, 1969, **17**, 430–439.

BEACH, F. A., & JAYNES, J. Effects of early experience upon the behavior of animals. *Psychological Bulletin*, 1954, **51**, 239–263.

BRONSON, F. H., & DESJARDINS, C. Neonatal androgen administration and adult aggressiveness in female mice. *General and Comparative Endocrinology*, 1970, **15**, 320–325.

CARMICHAEL, L. The onset and early development of behavior. In L. Carmichael (Ed.), *Child Psychology*. New York: Wiley, 1954.

CLEMENS, L. G., HIROI, M., & GORSKI, R. A. Induction and facilitation of female mating behavior in rats treated neonatally with low doses of testosterone propionate. *Endocrinology*, 1969, **84**, 1430–1438.

CLEMENTE, C., & STERMAN, M. B. Basal forebrain mechanisms for internal inhibition and sleep. In S. S. Kety, E. V. Evarts, & H. L. Williams (Eds.), *Sleep and altered states of consciousness*. Baltimore: Williams & Wilkins, 1967. Pp. 127–147.

EATON, G. Effect of a single prepuberal injection of testosterone propionate on adult bisexual behavior of male hamsters castrated at birth. *Endocrinology*, 1970, **87**, 934–940.

EDWARDS, D. A. Early androgen stimulation and aggressive behavior in male and female mice. *Physiology and Behavior*, 1969, **4**, 398–403.

EDWARDS, D. A., & BURGE, K. G. Early androgen treatment and male and female sexual behavior in mice. *Hormones and Behavior*, 1971, **2**, 49–58.

EVARTS, E. V. Unit activity in sleep and wakefulness. In G. Quarton, T. Melnechuk, & F. O. Schmitt (Eds.), *The neurosciences*. New York: Rockefeller University Press, 1967. Pp. 545–556.

FANTZ, R. L. The origin of form perception. *Scientific American*, 1961, **204**(5), 66–72.

GERALL, A. A. & WARD, I. The effects of prenatal exogenous androgen on the sexual behavior of the female albino rat. *Journal of Comparative and Physiological Psychology*, 1966, **62**, 370–375.

GOTTLIEB, G. Prenatal behavior of birds. *Quarterly Review of Biology*, 1968, **43**, 148–174.

GOY, R. W. Organizing effects of androgen on the behavior of rhesus monkeys. In R. P. Michael (Ed.), *Endocrinology and human behavior*. London: Oxford University Press, 1968. Pp. 12–31.

GOY, R. W., BRIDSON, W. E., & YOUNG, W. C. Period of maximal susceptibility of the prenatal female guinea pig to masculinizing actions of testosterone propionate. *Journal of Comparative and Physiological Psychology*, 1964, **57**, 166–174.

GRADY, K. L., PHOENIX, C. H., & YOUNG, W. C. Role of the developing rat testis in differentiation of the neural tissues mediating mating behavior. *Journal of Comparative and Physiological Psychology*, 1965, **59**, 176–192.

HAMBURGER, V. Some aspects of the embryology of behavior. *Quarterly Review of Biology*, 1963, **38**, 342–365.

HARLOW, H. R., ROWLAND, G. L., & GRIFFIN, G. A. The effect of total social deprivation on the development of monkey behavior. *Psychiatric Research Report*, 1964, **19**, 116–135.

HOOKER, D. *The prenatal origin of behavior.* Lawrence: University of Kansas Press, 1952.

JOUVET-MOUNIER, D., ASTIC, L., & LACOTE, D. Ontogenesis of the states of sleep in rat, cat, and guinea pig during the first postnatal month. *Developmental Psychobiology*, 1970, **2**, 216–239.

KLEITMAN, N. Phylogenetic, ontogenetic and environmental determinants in the evolution of sleep-wakefulness cycles. In S. S. Kety, E. V. Evarts, & H. L. Williams (Eds.), *Sleep and altered states of consciousness.* Baltimore: Williams & Wilkins, 1967. Pp. 30–38.

KOELLA, W. P. *Sleep, its nature and physiological organization.* Springfield, Ill.: Charles C Thomas, 1967.

LEVY, D. Experiments on the sucking reflex and social behavior of dogs. *American Journal of Orthopsychiatry*, 1934, **4**, 203–244.

MARLER, P., & TAMURA, M. Song "dialects" in three populations of white-crowned sparrows. *Condor*, 1962, **64**, 368–377.

MONEY, J. Cytogenetic and psychosexual incongruities with a note on space-form blindness. *American Journal of Psychiatry*, 1963, **119**, 820–827.

MONEY, J., & EHRHARDT, A. Prenatal hormonal exposure: Possible effects on behavior in man. In R. P. Michael (Ed.), *Endocrinology and human behavior.* London: Oxford University Press, 1968. Pp. 32–48.

NADLER, R. Differentiation of the capacity for male sexual behavior in the rat. *Hormones and Behavior*, 1969, **1**, 53–63.

NUCCI, L. P., & BEACH, F. A. Effects of prenatal androgen treatment on mating behavior in female hamsters. *Endocrinology*, 1971, **88**, 1514–1515.

PHOENIX, C. H., GOY, R. W., GERALL, A. A., & YOUNG, W. C. Organizing action of prenatally administered testosterone propionate on the tissues mediating mating behavior in the female guinea pig. *Endocrinology*, 1959, **65**, 369–382.

PRICE, D., & ORTIZ, E. The role of fetal androgen in sex differentiation in mammals. In R. L. De'Haan & H. Ursprung (Eds.), *Organogenesis.* New York: Holt, Rinehart and Winston, 1965. Pp. 629–652.

RAMSEY, A. O., & HESS, E. A laboratory approach to the study of imprinting. *Wilson Bulletin*, 1954, **66**, 196–206.

RIESEN, A. Sensory deprivation. In E. Stellar & J. Sprague (Eds.), *Progress in physiological psychology.* Vol. 1. New York: Academic Press, 1966. Pp. 117–147.

ROFFWARG, H. P., MUZO, J. N., & DEMENT, W. C. Ontogenetic development of the human sleep-dream cycle. *Science*, 1966, **152**, 604–619.

ROSENZWEIG, M. R., KRECH, D., BENNETT, E. L., & DIAMOND, M. C. Modifying brain chemistry and anatomy by enrichment or impoverishment of experience. In G. Newton & S. Levin (Eds.), *Early experience and behavior*. Springfield, Ill.: Charles C Thomas, 1968. Pp. 258–298.

SCHAEFER, T. Some methodological implications of the research on "early handling" in the rat. In G. Newton & S. Levine (Eds.), *Early experience and behavior*. Springfield, Ill.: Charles C Thomas, 1968. Pp. 102–141.

SCHEIN, M., & HALE, E. B. The effect of early social experience on male sexual behavior of androgen injected turkeys. *Animal Behaviour*, 1959, **7,** 189–200.

SEARS, R. R. Development of gender role. In F. A. Beach (Ed.), *Sex and behavior*. New York: Wiley, 1965. Pp. 133–163.

SEDLACEK, J., HLAVACKOVA, V., & SVEHLOVA, M. New findings on the formation of the temporary connection in the prenatal and perinatal period in the guinea pig. *Physiologia Bohemoslovenica*, 1964, **13,** 268–273.

SPELT, D. K. The conditioning of the human fetus *in utero*. *Journal of Experimental Psychology*, 1948, **38,** 338.

STANLEY, W. C. Feeding behavior and learning in neonatal dogs. In J. F. Bosma (Ed.), *Second symposium on oral sensation and perception*. Springfield, Ill.: Charles C Thomas, 1970.

STERMAN, M. B., & HOPPENBRAUIERS, T. Development of a rest-activity cycle in the human fetus. *Psychophysiology*, 1968, **5**(2), 226.

SWANSON, H. H., & CROSSLEY, D. A. Sexual behavior in the golden hamster and its modification by neonatal administration of testosterone propionate. In M. Hamburgh & E. J. W. Barrington (Eds.), *Hormones in development*. New York: Appleton-Century-Crofts, 1961. Pp. 677–687.

TEITELBAUM, P. *Physiological psychology*. Foundations of Modern Psychology Series. Englewood Cliffs, N.J.: Prentice-Hall, 1967.

THORPE, W. H. *Bird song, The biology of vocal communication and expression in birds*. Cambridge, England: Cambridge University Press, 1961.

WHALEN, R. E., EDWARDS, D. A., LUTTGE, W. G., & ROBERTSON, R. T. Early androgen treatment and male sexual behavior in female rats. *Physiology and Behavior*, 1969, **4,** 33–39.

YOUNG, W. C. Hormones and mating behavior. In W. C. Young (Ed.), *Sex and internal secretions*. Vol. 2. Baltimore: Williams & Wilkins, 1961. Pp. 1173–1239.

PART THREE

CORRELATES
OF BEHAVIOR

Actions of the central nervous system, the endocrine system, and the sensory-perceptual pathways constitute the primary determinants of overt behavior. Thus, these processes might be grouped together as *determinants of behavior*. Yet the relationship is a reciprocal one. Behavior and the environment affect the nervous system just as the nervous system affects behavior. Hormone levels are altered by behavior just as behavior is altered by hormone levels. The structures and functions of tissues mediating sensation and perception are altered by behavior and the environment just as variations in such structures and functions affect overt behavior. Therefore, the four chapters that constitute Part III have been grouped under the heading "Correlates of Behavior" to help emphasize the mutual interaction between behavior and these determinants.

The great variations that are found in the nervous systems of different organisms and the implications of these variations for behavior are discussed in Chapter 8. The exposition of structural and functional changes which have occurred in the evolution of nervous systems provides a basis for appreciating the capabilities and limitations of the behavior of different organisms.

While the relationship between brain and behavior has long been appreciated, appreciation of the relationship between hormones and behavior is just beginning. Yet, the latter relationship is no less important in humans and nonhumans alike. With a rapidly improving technology for working with body chemistry, behavioral endocrinology and neuroendocrinology are developing at a staggering rate. This is typified by the material in Chapter 9. Because particularly swift progress has been made in understanding the relationships between hormones and reproductive behavior, a substantial section on that topic follows the general introduction. It is likely that, in the not too distant future, similar phenomena will be revealed in other behavioral and endocrine systems.

Because of the importance of stimuli in determining responses, one cannot understand the behavior of an organism without understanding its sensory capacities and limitations. Sometimes the range of sensitivity of a species extends to where man cannot detect the stimuli directly with his own sensory equipment. Scientists must develop special apparatus to detect such stimuli and to assess their effect on organisms equipped to react to them. Sensory processes are discussed in comparative perspective in Chapter 10.

From the time of von Uexküll, we have known that each individual perceives the world in a different way. Each has its own inner perceptual world or *Umwelt*. It may seem remarkable to us that an octopus, in lifting weights, can compensate for weight differences but cannot learn a discrimination based on weight differences. An octopus can learn to discriminate the proportion of a surface that has grooves, but cannot detect the pattern of the grooves. Yet, the *Umwelt* of an octopus is different from that of a man, and we must understand how the octopus perceives the world if we are to understand its behavior. The same principle applies to all species.

Together, the four chapters of Part III summarize the mechanisms which are correlated with behavior and the interaction between physiological processes and overt behavior.

Chapter 8

The Brain and Behavior in Phylogenetic Perspective

James A. Horel

There are an enormous variety of animal forms on earth and each group of animals possesses some structural peculiarities that set it off from other groups. Birds have wings, turtles are armored, elephants have an unusual nose, and, as we shall see in the following pages, man has a unique brain. That is not to say that other animals do not possess a brain, nor is a brain the only feature that differentiates man from the rest of the animal kingdom, but if we had to choose one structure that, more than any other, sets man apart, we would probably agree that it is his brain.

The nervous system in animals that possess one regulates and coordinates behavior with respect to conditions of the internal and external environment. Organisms that evolved into more complex animals also evolved a more complex nervous system to handle the increased burden of regulation and coordination. Along with a more complex nervous system came an increased capacity to respond differentially to subtle nuances of the environment. Evolutionary pressures pushed the development of the nervous system to the point that the marvelously complex structure we call a brain was achieved. The brain became a prominent feature of mammals, reached a crescendo of development in primates, attained its ultimate expansion in complexity, versatility, sensitivity, and mystery in man. Where does the story of this achievement begin?

THE ORIGINS OF THE NERVOUS SYSTEM

The brain is made up of glial cells and neurons, the latter forming a vast communication network in complex animals. The glial cells are involved in nutritive and metabolic functions of the brain, but whether they are also a part of the communication network formed by neurons is a matter of debate.

Studies of invertebrates, such as coelenterates and anemones, suggest that neurons probably evolved from epithelial tissue (Horridge, 1968). Epithelium is the tissue that forms the surface covering for the internal and external organs of an animal, such as the skin or the lining of the gastrointestinal tract. All cells are irritable to a degree, and some cells can irritate their neighboring cells through low resistance contacts so that irritation starting at a point of stimulation can spread from cell to cell. In some primitive marine forms, this kind of spread of irritation is seen in sheets of epithelium, and it has been hypothesized (Horridge, 1968) that this is the precursor of the nervous system (Figure 8-1a). Stimulation by some means, such as mechanical deformation, irritates the cells at the point stimulated and causes an electrochemical wave of irritation that passes outward in all directions until it reaches a muscle cell which contracts and produces a simple response. In Figure 8-1b, an arrangement of muscle cells is diagramed where the irritation, and hence the contraction, can spread between these cells. A critical stage in the evolution of the nervous system is diagramed in Figure 8-1d. Epithelial cells are seen to develop processes which bypass large numbers of cells and provide a more direct line of communication to other nerve cells and to muscle. We can probably call these cells neurons and their processes axons. In Figure 8-1e, the neurons connect with muscle cells and in Figure 8-1f, sensory cells make their appearance.

The end result of this evolution is a nervous system with three functional divisions: (1) sensory cells that detect changes in the environment and transmit these changes; (2) neurons that conduct this sensory excitation; and (3) muscle cells which contract in response to stimulation by the neuron, and hence to the environmental change. In Horridge's theory on the evolution of neurons, sensory cells are the last to appear. Earlier views supposed that sensory cells connecting to muscle cells were the first neuronal structures to appear.

The earliest nervous system evolved from a diffuse neural net which, in living coelenterates (hydras, jellyfish, starfish, sea anemones, corals), achieves some degree of specialization. Recent work on mollusks and arthropods reveals a remarkably precise, built-in organization. The delicate control of movement of the crayfish tail, for example, has been found to be accomplished by the intrinsic wiring of the nervous centers in this form (Kennedy, 1967). Stimulation of a single neuron in the nervous system of the crayfish can produce a coordinated motor response that requires reciprocal action of several muscles. Stimulation of different neurons produces different coordinated movements (Kennedy, Evoy, & Hanawalt, 1966).

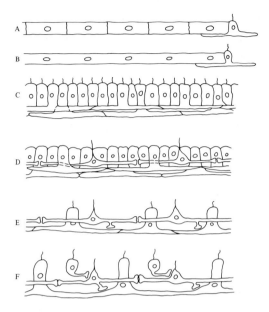

Figure 8–1. The origin of the nerve cell. Hypothetical evolution of nerve nets in epithelial systems of ctenophores and coelenterates. (A) and (B). Conducting epithelium leading to an epithelial muscle cell. (C) Muscle cells connected by their tails. (D) As in (C) but with epithelial cells with processes that connect only with each other and bridge over intervening cells. This is the critical stage of appearance of axons. (E) Connections to muscle cells. (F) Origin of sensory cells, after the appearance of conducting systems. (From *Interneurons—their origin, action, specificity, growth, and plasticity* by G. Adrian Horridge. W. H. Freeman and Company. Copyright © 1968.)

With the evolution of a bilateral body plan, animals became elongated, with a head end and a tail end. This produced an elongation of the nervous system and the development of fiber tracts, conducting systems, and ganglia. Ganglia are clusters of nerve cells found throughout the body. Later, a concentration of these ganglia began to take place in the anterior end in correlation with increased sensory mechanisms that began to develop there. Thus began a line of evolution that resulted in the emergence of the complex clump of nerve cells in the anterior end of many animal forms. It culminated in what man regards as the ultimate evolutionary achievement: the brain of man.

HOW THE NERVE CELLS WORK

Here we shall glance at the basic physiology of transmission in neurons. This glance must be brief and diagrammatic, but most students have probably already studied these processes in other courses.

All cells are irritable to a degree, but nerve cells are extraordinarily sensitive. They come in an enormous variety of shapes, but most often they have one long process that usually branches and that leads information away from the cell. This is called the axon. Dendrites are the processes that carry information toward the cell, and they often (but certainly not always) branch profusely and appear treelike (dendritic) in form.

The discharge that goes down an axon is the result of a change in the nerve-cell membrane that produces an exchange of ions between the inside and the outside of the cell. This exchange of ions produces a momentary change in electrical potential which is measurable with suitable amplification. It has been called the *action potential*. This action potential, omitting some aftereffects, takes only about 0.5 to 2 milliseconds; then the membrane is restored and another action potential can occur.

The action potential moves down the axon, with the activity exciting adjacent inactive parts of the cell membrane in fuselike fashion until the end is reached. The energy for the action potential is contained within the cell and is not supplied by the triggering stimulus. Therefore, the size of the action potential remains the same the full length of the axon and is not dependent upon the intensity of the eliciting stimulus. This unvarying character of the action potential serves to preserve the fidelity of the information that the neuron carries.

With the exception of a few instances of electrical coupling, the junction between nerve cells is bridged by a chemical transmitter. The junction is called a *synapse*, and the action potential, upon arrival at the synapse, initiates the secretion of packets of chemical transmitter substance which cause the excitation or inhibition of the postsynaptic cell. Whether or not the transmitter substance excites or inhibits the postsynaptic cell depends upon the nature of the substance and the characteristics of the postsynaptic cell membrane. The axon may terminate synaptically on the dendrite, cell body, or axon of the postsynaptic cell. This arrangement, with the transmitter substance at the end of the axon and the membrane sensitive to it on the cell where the axon ends, results in one-way conduction across the synapse. Thus the synapse acts as a valve that permits information to go in one direction only.

The excitation produced at the synapse by the chemical transmitter, unlike the action potential, is not independent of its initiating stimulus. In synaptic transmission, the action potential causes a release of chemical transmitter which crosses the tiny gap between the two cells and causes a graded potential change in the postsynaptic cell. The more transmitter substance, the greater is the potential change, and this potential change summates with that produced by surrounding synapses. Inhibitory synapses will subtract from the potential change and excitatory synapses will add to it. If a sufficiently large potential change occurs, it initiates an action potential in the postsynaptic cell that moves down the axon to the next cell.

The number of neurons activated by a stimulus, the pattern in which these neurons are activated, the number and pattern of action potentials that result from this stimulus, all act to encode the environment in the "language" of the nervous system.

The problem of the functioning of individual neurons was solved early in evolution. Much of our information on their physiology was derived from experiments on such animals as crayfish and squid. Little, if anything, was added to the physiology of nerve cells by further evolutionary changes. The complexity in behavior that follows the huge expansion of brain in vertebrates is due to the added number of these units and the consequent increase in complexity of their organization, not in functional changes of the individual neuron.

THE BASIC PLAN OF THE VERTEBRATE BRAIN

In vertebrates, the nervous system achieves a substantial size and a bewildering complexity. The basic parts of the vertebrate nervous system are discernible very early in their phylogenetic development. An understanding of its embryology is helpful in gaining a picture of the basic plan of the generalized vertebrate brain (Figure 8-2).

As in its phylogenetic origins, the nervous system develops embryologically from superficial epithelium. In the embryo, this forms a neural tube, and parts of it expand more rapidly in development than others. The expansions form the three primary embryonic vesicles: the forebrain (prosencephalon), the midbrain (mesencephalon), and the hindbrain (rhombencephalon). The spinal cord is the caudal continuation of this tube. In the following account, we will briefly mention the major divisions of the brain.

The Spinal Cord

The spinal cord is probably a good deal more complex than one might suppose. It receives sensory information from the body, utilizes it in regulating posture and locomotion, and transmits it via long fiber tracts to the brain. In addition, it receives motor-command information from the brain in long, descending pathways that end on cells that either directly or indirectly connect with cells controlling the muscles of the body.

In animals in which the spinal cord is experimentally isolated from the brain by a knife cut, it can be seen that this simplest part of the central nervous system is capable of quite exquisite regulation of the complex musculature of the body. For example, a painful stimulus applied to the toe of a dog whose spinal cord has been cut will cause the limb to withdraw from the stimulus and will cause the leg on the other side of the body to extend to compensate for the support that is lost by the lifted leg. This simultaneously requires excitation of neurons controlling flexor muscles and inhibition of neurons controlling

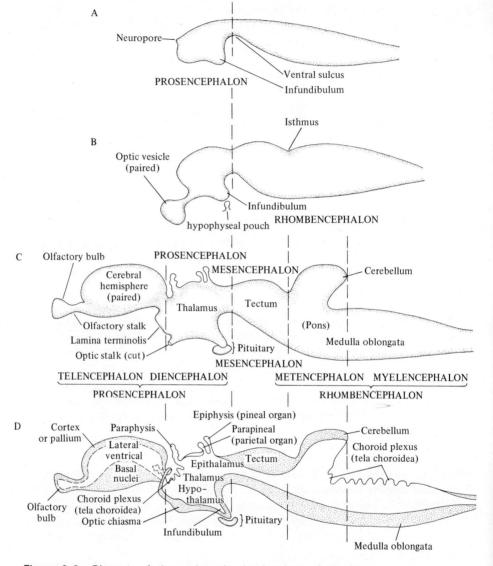

A

Neuropore—

PROSENCEPHALON

Ventral sulcus
Infundibulum

Isthmus

B

Optic vesicle
(paired)

Infundibulum
hypophyseal pouch RHOMBENCEPHALON

C Olfactory bulb PROSENCEPHALON

Cerebral
hemisphere
(paired)

MESENCEPHALON Cerebellum

Thalamus Tectum

Olfactory stalk
Lamina terminolis
Optic stalk (cut)

(Pons)
} Pituitary Medulla oblongata

MESENCEPHALON

TELENCEPHALON DIENCEPHALON METENCEPHALON MYELENCEPHALON

PROSENCEPHALON RHOMBENCEPHALON

Epiphysis (pineal organ)

D Cortex Paraphysis Parapineal Cerebellum
or pallium (parietal organ)
Lateral Choroid plexus
ventrical Tectum (tela choroidea)
Basal Epithalamus
nuclei Thalamus
Hypo-
Olfactory Choroid plexus thalamus
bulb (tela choroidea)
Optic chiasma } Pituitary
Infundibulum
Medulla oblongata

Figure 8–2. Diagram of the embryonic development of the brain. (A) The primitive forebrain is distinct from the remainder of the neural tube. (B) The three main divisions are established. (C) A more mature stage. (D) Mature stage in median view. (From Romer, A. S. *The vertebrate body.* (3rd ed.) Philadelphia: W. B. Saunders, 1962.)

extensor muscles on the side stimulated, together with exactly the opposite excitation and inhibition of flexors and extensors in the opposite leg. A high degree of timing and coordination is required to execute the movement, and all this timing and coordination is controlled by the cells in the isolated spinal cord because the descending control from the brain has been severed. Ordinarily, motor control from the brain is superimposed upon the regulative mechanisms of the spinal cord and this results in the motor behavior we observe in the normal, intact dog.

The Medulla Oblongata

Moving forward in the vertebrate brain, we next encounter the medulla (Figure 8-2), which is the caudal part of the hindbrain. Many important visceral motor centers are in the medulla. For example, the vital vagus nerve (Figure 8-3),

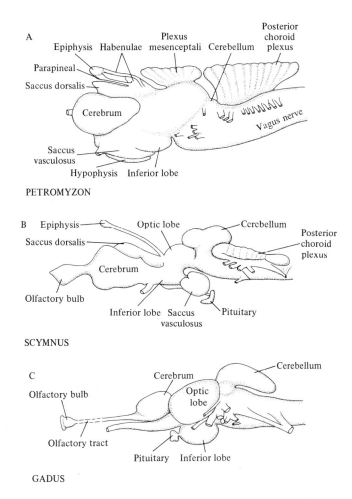

Figure 8–3. Representative vertebrate brains: (A) Lamprey, (B) Shark, (C) Codfish, (D) Frog, (E) Alligator, (F) Insectivore, (G) Goose, (H) Horse, (I) Opossum—medial view, and (J) Man—medial view.

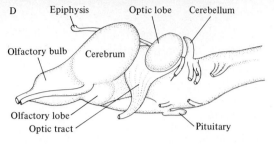

RANA

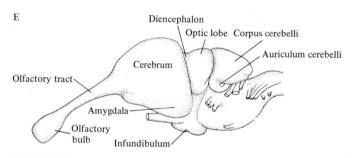

ALLIGATOR

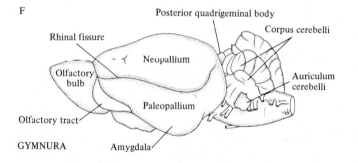

GYMNURA

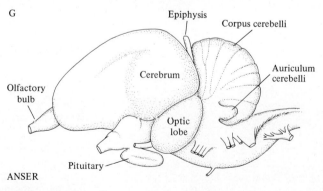

ANSER

278   **Figure 8–3.** *(Continued)*

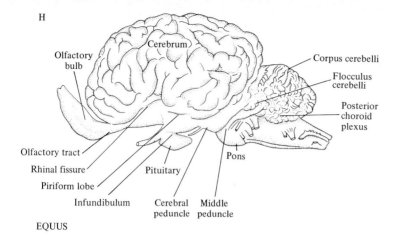

H

Cerebrum

Olfactory bulb

Corpus cerebelli

Flocculus cerebelli

Posterior choroid plexus

Olfactory tract

Rhinal fissure

Piriform lobe

Infundibulum

Pituitary

Pons

Cerebral peduncle

Middle peduncle

EQUUS

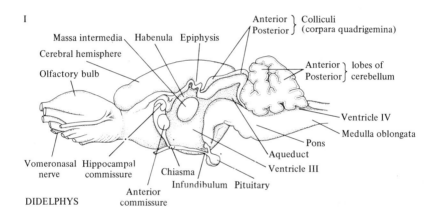

I

Massa intermedia

Habenula

Epiphysis

Anterior } Colliculi
Posterior } (corpara quadrigemina)

Cerebral hemisphere

Olfactory bulb

Anterior } lobes of
Posterior } cerebellum

Ventricle IV

Medulla oblongata

Pons

Aqueduct

Ventricle III

Vomeronasal nerve

Hippocampal commissure

Chiasma

Infundibulum

Pituitary

Anterior commissure

DIDELPHYS

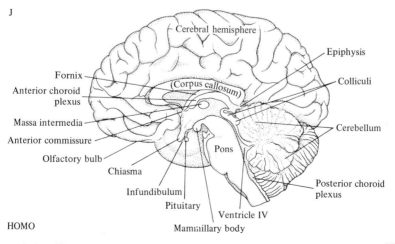

J

Cerebral hemisphere

Epiphysis

Fornix

Colliculi

Anterior choroid plexus

(Corpus callosum)

Massa intermedia

Cerebellum

Anterior commissure

Olfactory bulb

Pons

Chiasma

Posterior choroid plexus

Infundibulum

Pituitary

Ventricle IV

HOMO

Mammillary body

Figure 8–3. *(Continued)*

279

which is involved in nervous control of the heart, stomach, and intestines, takes origin from here. Long motor and sensory pathways to and from the spinal cord pass through the medulla and all rostral structures to the prosencephalon (forebrain). Auditory and vestibular (equilibrium) information enters the brain at the junction of the medulla and the pons.

Cerebellum

The next major structure we encounter moving rostrally is the cerebellum and its associated pons (Figure 8-2c). The cerebellum receives all kinds of sensory information, but its most prominent inputs are vestibular, signaling the position and movements of the head to aid in maintaining equilibrium, and sensory information from muscles and joints indicating the position of limbs and the tension on muscles. Motor-control information from the forebrain destined for the spinal cord is also relayed to the cerebellum via the pons. The cerebellum uses information about muscle tension, limb position, and motor command from the forebrain in regulating and timing locomotion and posture.

The Midbrain (Mesencephalon)

The tectum (Figures 8–2, 8–3) forms the roof of the midbrain, and in mammals it contains the important superior and inferior (or anterior and posterior) colliculi. In nonmammalian vertebrates, the superior colliculus is called an optic lobe (Figure 8-3). It is concerned chiefly with vision and will be discussed later in the chapter. Much of the midbrain ventral to the tectum is part of the reticular formation which extends from the diencephalon in the forebrain through the center of the midbrain and medulla and down into the spinal cord. It is involved with sleep, waking, and general levels of arousal.

The Diencephalon

The forebrain is divided into the diencephalon and telencephalon (Figure 8-2c). We will discuss the telencephalon at length in a separate section of this chapter. Here we will briefly note the parts and functions of the diencephalon. It consists principally of the dorsal thalamus (thalamus, Figure 8-2c) and hypothalamus. The hypothalamus is on the base of the brain and is an important visceral regulative center. It is very much involved in regulating food and water consumption and body temperature. It is also involved in reproductive behavior and attack and flight behavior.

The dorsal thalamus works in concert with the telencephalon. All senses except olfaction terminate on cells in the thalamus which project to the telencephalon. The olfactory system projects to the primitive cortex on the base of the brain (olfactory lobe, paleopallium, Figure 8–3). Some accounts of the evolution of the forebrain suggest that it derives from olfactory structures.

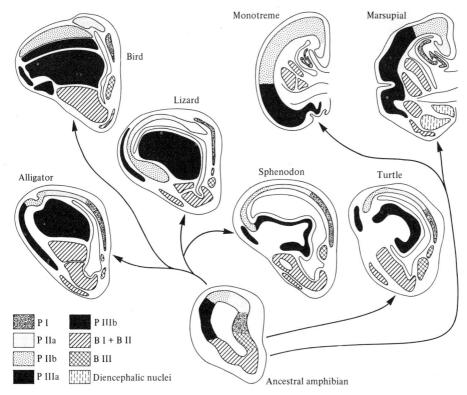

Bird

Lizard

Alligator

Monotreme

Marsupial

Sphenodon

Turtle

P I
P IIa
P IIb
P IIIa
P IIIb
B I + B II
B III
Diencephalic nuclei

Ancestral amphibian

Figure 8–4.   Schematic representation of the evolution of the forebrain from an ancestral amphibian to living animals. (After Northcutt, Encyclopedia of Science and Technology. McGraw-Hill, N.Y.)

In addition to auditory, visual, somatic, and taste sensory information, the thalamus also receives neuronal connections from the cerebellum and motor areas of the forebrain and the hypothalamus. The size of the dorsal thalamus in an animal is closely related to the amount of cerebral cortex it has. The cerebral cortex is the mantle of cells covering the cerebral hemispheres (neopallium, Figure 8–3). However, there is some evidence for the existence of a dorsal thalamus in primitive vertebrates that do not possess a cerebral cortex (Ariëns Kappers, Huber, & Crosby, 1936). The function and structure of the dorsal thalamus are tied in so closely with that of the cerebral cortex that it is difficult to discover what the unique contribution of the dorsal thalamus is to the function of the brain.

THE EVOLUTION OF THE VERTEBRATE FOREBRAIN

It is hard to study the evolution of parts of the brain because they have not been preserved in fossil form except for the general outline on the interior of skulls. Understanding of the evolution of the forebrain is derived, for the most part, from living animals which have all changed in various ways from their common ancestors. Part of the difficulty is in discovering which structures of the various brains of animals are homologous. Homologous organs in different species are those which have been derived from the same organ in their common ancestor and transmitted genetically to living animals. The transmission process may produce moderate or radical changes in the structure and function of the organ.

Homologous brain structures are identified by examining their anatomical position in relation to surrounding structures, the characteristics of the cells of the region, and anatomical interconnections by neuronal pathways. Examining the embryological development of the brain is also helpful. In Figure 8-4 (Northcutt, 1969) are diagrams of cross-sections through several vertebrate forebrains, showing supposed evolutionary lines from an ancestral amphibian. In the brain, cell groups are called *gray matter* and fiber tracts are called *white matter* simply because of their appearance. Gray matter that covers the telencephalon is called *cortex*, while the deeper gray matter is called *subcortical nuclei*. The shaded areas of the diagram represent gray matter and indicate the structures believed to be homologous; that is, derived from the same structure in an ancestral amphibian.

The PI area in Figure 8–4 is called *hippocampus* and it is a cortical structure that becomes folded and pushed deeper into the brain in mammals (marsupials and monotremes, in Figure 8–4). The hemispheres become covered with the huge development of the PII*b* and PIII*a* regions in Figure 8-4. In mammals, this region is variously referred to as neopallium, or neocortex, or isocortex.

It must be emphasized that the names given to the various parts of the nonmammalian brain represent an unproven theoretical statement on the homologies of these structures to similarly named structures in mammals. Is the hippocampus of the alligator derived from the same tissue in a stemline vertebrate as a like-named structure in a rat? There are many structural similarities that suggest that it is, at least in part, but in the absence of the stem animal from which alligators and mammals developed, we can only guess that the hippocampus in these animals is related. While most observers agree on the hippocampus, there is a great deal of controversy over the homologues of other brain structures, particularly in the details of their anatomical parts.

Although these parts of the vertebrate forebrain may be structurally homologous in the sense that they have a common ancestry, they may be functionally quite different in living species because of adaptations to the particular ecological niche in which the organism currently exists. One might expect certain functional similarities, however. A good example is the amygdala, a large, complex cluster of nerve cells at the base of the forebrain in mammals (below the paleopallium in Figure 8–3F). Electrical stimulation of the amygdala in mammals often produces flight or attack behavior, and destruction of this region produces a profound reduction in aggression or flight behavior (Kaada, 1967). A structure believed to be in part homologous to the amygdala exists in the basal and caudal part of the telencephalon of reptiles (at the base of the cerebrum in Figure 8–3B). Stimulation of this structure in the Caiman (South American alligator) causes the animal to turn and run in the direction opposite to that in which it was facing at stimulus onset (Keating, Kormann, & Horel, 1970). If barriers are put in its path, it will go around them, which indicates that this is not a driven motor behavior. This behavior, elicited by electrical stimulation in the Caiman brain, looks very much like flight. Destruction in the caudal and basal parts of the forebrain in the region of the amygdala results in a drop in flight or attack behavior in situations that elicited flight or attack behavior in the normal animal. A marked drop in attack and flight behavior is usually seen when the amygdala is destroyed in mammals. Thus, there are functional as well as structural similarities between what is believed to be the amygdala in mammals and reptiles.

COMPARISON OF BRAIN SIZE

The most striking difference that can be seen by examining brains of different species is that they vary markedly in size (Figure 8-5). This difference has attracted some attention, for brain size might correlate with behavioral complexity or with information-processing capacity.

The brain, like other organs of the body, is larger in larger animals. It increases in size with the number of neurons it contains, but also with the size of the body that possesses it. This is usually expressed in the following way (von Bonin, 1937):

$$E = kS^r$$

E represents brain weight and S represents body weight. The exponent r is determined empirically and has an arithmetic value of about ⅔ (Jerison, 1961). The constant, k, is called the cephalization index and varies from species to species. For example, k is 0.04 for the rat, 0.07 for the rabbit, and 0.13 for the cat (Livesy, 1970). This means that for any given body weight, the same for all animals, the rabbit has more brain than the rat and the cat has more brain than the rabbit. Livesy presented evidence that the rabbit is better than the rat and the cat better than the rabbit in some complex tasks.

It can be shown that there is a relationship between the number of neurons and the size of the brain; as one would expect, the larger the brain, the more neurons it contains (Jerison, 1963). This relationship is suggestive of a greater complexity in larger brains. To draw an analogy, the complexity of computers is measured in terms of the number of elements they contain.

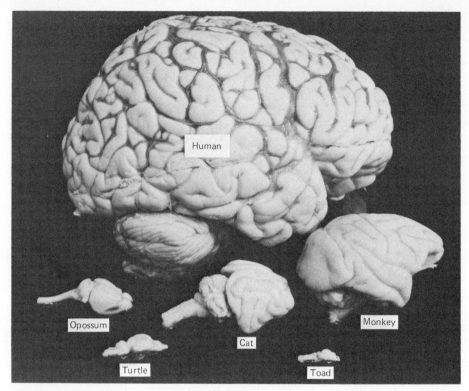

Figure 8–5.   The most striking difference between the brains of different species is that they vary markedly in size.

In Figure 8-6 (Jerison, 1969), brain weights of primates, mammals, birds, fish, and reptiles are plotted against their body weight. The figure shows that brain size is in part related to body size. The points on the graph separate into two clusters, with the mammals in one and lower vertebrates, including fish and reptiles, in the other. The sense of the graph is summarized in Figure 8-7 (Jerison, 1969). In this graph, the two clusters are enclosed in minimum convex polygons; that is, polygons of minimum areas, with vertexes on data points and no internal angle greater than 180 degrees. Using the formula: $E = k\ S^r$, with $r = \frac{2}{3}$, there is a tenfold increase in k to shift from the lower to the upper line in Figure 8-7. With the addition of estimates of dinosaur brain size made from skull casts (endocasts), the basic relationship is seen to remain the same (Figure 8-8). Dinosaurs were huge reptiles and had large brains, but their brains were much smaller than those of mammals of comparable size. The dotted lines in Figure 8–8 show the brain-body size relationship for living mammals (L), mammals of 35 million years ago (O), and mammals that lived 50 to 60 million years ago (A). The evolutionary tendency is toward a greater brain weight for a given body size in mammals. The lower vetebrates as a group appear to be fairly stable, with no apparent important changes

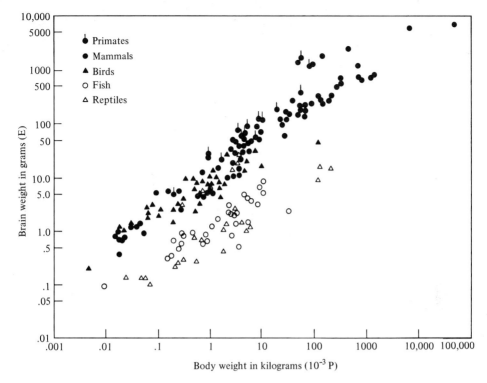

Figure 8–6. Brain and body weights of the largest specimens of 198 vertebrate species collected by Crile and Quiring (1940), graphed on log-log coordinates. Note the nonoverlapping arrays of points representing higher (birds and mammals) and lower (reptiles and fish) vertebrate classes with respect to the relative size of the brain. (After Jerison, H. Brain evolution and dinosaur brains. *American Naturalist,* 1969, **103**, 575–588 © 1969 University of Chicago Press.)

in the size of their brains relative to the size of their bodies. However, mammals show a consistent increase in brain size over geological eras, suggesting evolutionary pressures that produce a greater capacity for behavioral complexity and information processing.

Although the comparative measure of gross brain size proves to be very revealing, it is obviously a crude measure. It tells us little about the specific capacities and behavioral differences of the various animals that are compared. It has been pointed out (Holloway, 1969) that microcephalic and nannocephalic humans, who possess brains considerably smaller than that of a gorilla, remain human in their behavioral patterns while the gorilla remains nonhuman. The observation is derived from the fact that the nannocephalic humans can use language but the apes cannot (Lenneberg, 1967). Of course the gorilla may nonetheless be capable of processing sensory information of greater complexity and have a greater range of behavioral patterns exclusive of language than the deformed humans. Thus, probably neuronal organization and not neuronal

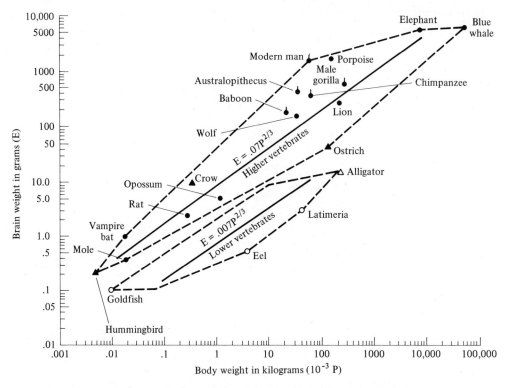

Figure 8–7.   Selected data from Fig. 8–6 to illustrate brain:body relations in familiar vertebrate species. Data on the fossil hominid, Australopithecus, and on the living coelacanth, Latimeria, are added. Minimum convex polygons are shown by dashed lines, enclosing visually fitted lines with slopes of two-thirds. (After Jerison, 1969.)

amount determines human specificity of behavior, but brain size and neuron number are probably related to capacity for behavioral complexity.

It was once believed that learning was an exclusive capacity of complex brains, specifically, a function of the neocortex. It is now known that this is not true. Quite simple organisms are capable of learning (Eisenstein, 1967, chap. 12), and fish, with no forebrain at all, can learn (Bernstein, 1961; Kaplan & Aronson, 1969). Mammals with their entire neocortex destroyed are capable of learning discriminations (Horel, Bettinger, Royce, & Meyer, 1966; Meyer, 1963), and if a learned problem is within the capacity of an animal, the amount of cortex he has does not relate to the rapidity with which he learns the task (Warren, 1965, chap. 13). Thus, learning is not something that has been added late in evolution nor is it a function of higher brain centers.

As the brain gets larger and more and more neurons are added, increasing complexity of neural interconnections occurs. There is an increased brain capacity for handling information and an increased range of things that the

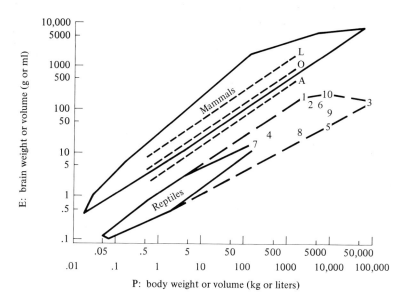

Figure 8–8. Relationship between brain size and body size in living mammals and reptiles, fossil mammals, and dinosaurs. Polygons made by solid lines are minimum convex polygons enclosing living mammalian and reptilian data reported by Crile and Quiring (1940). Reptilian polygon is extended by long-dashed lines to include dinosaurs. Data on fossil mammals in short-dashed lines are least-squares fits to living (L), Oligocone (O), and Archaic Paleocene and Eocene (A) samples, representing mammals of the present, of 35 million years ago, and of 55–60 million years ago. 1. Allosaurus; 2, Anatosaurus; 3, Brachiosaurus; 4, Camptosaurus; 5, Diplodocus; 6, Iguanodon; 7, Protoceratops; 8, Stegosaurus; 9, Triceratops; 10, Tryannosaurus. (After Jerison, 1969.)

animal can learn to do. No matter what its potential learning ability, an animal that is unable to control its digits separately would have difficulty learning to play a piano in the usual fashion. Fine motor control, such as we see in the independent finger movements of man, is made possible in part by a reduction, through evolution, in the size of the motor units. A motor unit is a single nerve cell with all its branches and the muscle cells that the branches connect. The nerve-cell axon may branch profusely and connect with many muscle fibers, and when that nerve cell is fired, all the muscle cells which receive its branches fire. If the motor units are smaller, i.e., if there are more neurons, each having fewer branches, each unit controls fewer muscle fibers and a more refined control is possible. With smaller motor units, different muscles, such as those controlling different fingers, can be doing different things rather than acting in concert. A similar distinction can be made within the senses and within the central nervous system as well. A single neuron with many branches can contact many cells, but will stimulate them all indiscriminately. More cells, each with fewer branches, provide a more refined neural control. The cost of this finer control and increased discrimination is a larger brain with more neurons. Thus, differences of overall capacity, made possible by larger brains with more units and differences in neuron organization, relate to evolutionary changes in behavior but not to neuronal plasticity as such. Plasticity per se has been clearly demonstrated in the simplest neuronal networks and is therefore not a special property of complex brains.

One would think that it would be an easy matter to compare the intellectual capacity of animals, but it is not. Some insight into the difficulties of such comparisons can be gleaned from an experience of Karl Lashley (1949), who attempted to compare the capacity of chimpanzees and rats on a white-black discrimination problem:

> I presented what seemed a very simple problem: to associate a white box with food. I placed a white and black box on a table before the cage, each box attached to a rope extending to the bars of the cage. The white box alone always contained food and if the black box were pulled in, I snatched away the other rope. When this had happened half a dozen times, my subject, Mimi, a husky female, grasped a rope in each hand, pulled one in until she could wrap it around her foot for a firm grip. She thus freed both hands to pull in one rope, while retaining complete control of the other. If the first box were empty she usually won the tug of war for the second. Her solution of the problem was better than my own, so I judge it highly intelligent. But when I finally regained control of the situation, Mimi took more than 200 trials to form the simple association between the white box and food, a task which the rat, under optimal conditions, can learn in a single trial [Lashley, 1949, p. 28].

Lashley thus made the point that the rapidity with which an animal learns a task is a poor measure of the range of his behavioral complexity.

COMPARISON OF BRAIN STRUCTURES

Some differences in behavioral organization can be related more easily to differences in circuit diagram. Such differences are discovered by experimental methods that permit the study of the neuronal wiring diagram and would not be likely to be reflected in differences in brain size. Until studies relating neural circuits to specific behaviors become informative, however, comparative studies on the relative size of different parts of the brain reveal some interesting relationships. Gross measures of overall brain size do not reveal the richness of the variations that exist in the changing brain as it develops. While it is possible to obtain information about the gross brain size from the endocranial casts, we must rely on living animals for information about relative amounts of different brain structures. This poses some problems in interpreting phylogenetic relationships. In one attempt to surmount this problem in a study of the primate brain (Stephan & Andy, 1969), comparisons were made with a group of insectivores that are least developed in those features that are found to increase in size in complex primate brains. Primates are believed to have evolved from primitive insectivores. These basal insectivores provide a baseline for examining the changes that take place in the phylogenetic development of primates. The progressive index in Figure 8-9 is the number of times the structure (neocortex and hippocampus, in this case) is larger than the same structure in a typical basal insectivore of the same body weight.

The most conspicuous change of an individual brain structure during phylogenetic development is in the neocortex. Some idea as to the reasons man has thought this structure to be so important can be gleaned from Figure 8–9A (Stephan & Andy, 1969), which illustrates how many times larger the

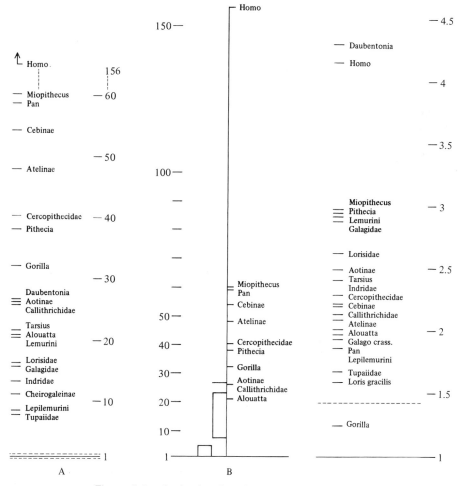

Figure 8–9. Scale showing the number of times larger the neocortex (A & B) and the hippocampus (C) are than those of a typical basal insectivore of equal body weight. (B) is a reduced scale to demonstrate the position of man. (After Stephan & Andy, 1969.)

neocortex is in these species than it is in primitive insectivores of the same body weight. In man the neocortex is more than 150 times as great, and in chimpanzee (*Pan*) it is 60 times as great as the basal insectivore brain. The graph is condensed in Figure 8–9A to include man. The numbers are the progressive indices. The graph represents an ascending primate scale, with man alone at the top, far from his nearest competitor in the amount of neocortex. We can see why man has had such an interest in this gray mantle covering the hemispheres and has looked to it as the property that has endowed him with his intelligence and his capacity to construct a civilization. If the size of a brain structure can be assumed to have some importance as an index of functional specialization, then the neocortex clearly represents an enormous contribution to what makes man unique among living things.

In all the brain areas that have been examined by Stephan and Andy's method, only olfactory structures show a reduction in development. None shows the enormous development achieved by the neocortex. The hippocampus, although representing an enlargement in development, does not develop in a consistent manner (Figure 8-9c). In some groups it is extensively enlarged, and in others it has changed very little from the primitive form. Its development seems independent from that of the neocortex. It would be interesting to see if there are differences in behavior that correlate with differences in development of the hippocampus, a structure that has been implicated in various aspects of the learning process.

Although the concept that brain size as an indicator of brain complexity and hence, behavioral complexity, has considerable face validity, there has not been complete agreement that much significance could be attached to such distinctions. The striking relationship between brain size and phylogenetic position found by Jerison (1963) and Stephan and Andy (1969) partially answers the questions raised about the importance of such measures. However, they have not always been considered to be of functional significance. For example, early in the study of brain function, it was discovered that language was largely a left-hemisphere process in most human brains, and the left hemisphere was therefore called *dominant*. It was anticipated that the left hemisphere should consequently be larger than the right hemisphere. However, little consistent difference in their size could be detected (von Bonin, 1962). Recently, Geschwind and Levitsky (1968) carefully examined the areas of the hemispheres that are particularly involved with language function in 100 normal human brains. In a region of the temporal lobe, called Wernicke's area, that is intimately involved with language function, they found the left area to be on the average one-third larger than the right. It was larger on the left in 65 percent of the brains, and on the right in only 11 percent. There thus appears to be a clear correlation between a specialization in the function of a localized brain region and its anatomical size. This demonstrates that if one is to find correlative differences between functional specializations and brain development, some information must be available on the regions of the brain most intimately involved with that specialization. No consistent differences in size between the two hemispheres of the brain as a whole are detectable (von Bonin, 1962), but Geschwind and Levitsky demonstrated that there is at least one important regional difference associated with Wernicke's area and language function.

Further evidence that brain size is of functional significance comes from experiments showing that environmental enrichment will produce enlargement of parts of the cerebral cortex (Diamond, Krech, & Rosenzweig, 1964). Rats kept in an enriched environment with toys and mazes show an increased thickness of cortex in the occipital region. The increase in thickness of the cortex was found to be due to increased amounts of glial cells and increased size of neurons (M. C. Diamond, 1967). There was also an increased branching of the dendritic processes of the neurons in the enlarged region that would permit a larger number of synaptic contacts on the cell (Holloway, 1966).

The experiments on environmental enrichment demonstrate that some of the differences in brain size may be attributable to environmental stimulation during the ontogenetic development of the animal. However, much of the difference seen in enlargement of brain areas must be due to genetic changes and phylogenetic pressures. Some of the genetic changes may originate outside the brain, however. It is known that the number of neurons associated with a structure, such as a muscle, will increase or diminish as the size of the muscle increases or diminishes. Du Brul (1967) has proposed that evolutionary changes in the brain may be started by evolution of the muscles which changes the attached neurons during development and thence the whole neural chain with which the muscles are connected.

There are several examples of correlations between behavioral specializations and enlargements of the related brain area. For example, the raccoon uses its hands much more than others of its family in the tactile exploration of the environment, and it has a disproportionately large representation of the hand area in the somatic sensory region of the brain (Welker & Seidenstein, 1959). The related coatimundi uses its snout for tactile exploration, and its forepaws with their claws to hook and scrape objects. The coatimundi has a much smaller tactile representation of the hand area than the raccoon and a much larger representation of the snout region (Welker & Campos, 1963).

Thus, it seems that the early negative results correlating increased functional capacity with increased brain size were due to the failure to examine the areas of the brain most closely related to that function. Earlier workers did not have the information on functional differentiation of the brain that Welker and his coworkers had. In addition, there were strong feelings that such functional differentiation, if it existed, was relatively unimportant in explaining behavioral differences. Total mass of tissue was thought to be a more ciritcal factor (Lashley, 1949).

THE DORSAL THALAMUS AND NEOCORTEX

There are other interesting differences in the relative development of cortical areas. The dorsal thalamus is the source of nearly all the input to the neocortex. It is divided up into many clusters of cells called nuclei, and the neurons within the nuclei send their axons to particular areas of the neocortex. The thalamic nuclei have been classified as intrinsic or extrinsic, depending upon whether or not they receive the major portion of their input from extra thalamic sources (Rose & Woolsey, 1949). Extrinsic nuclei receive most of their input, such as vision or audition, from outside the thalamus. These project to what has been called *primary receiving areas* of the neocortex, or the *extrinsic cortex,* which together with motor areas, makes up most of the cerebral mantle of primitive mammalian brains (Figure 8–10).

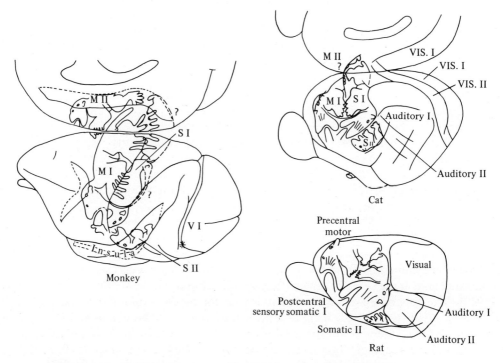

Figure 8–10.   Diagrams showing functional divisions of the neocortex as defined by electrical stimulation and recording. The regions not so defined are called association areas. MI and II, Motor area I and II. SI and II, Somatic sensory areas I and II (touch, kinesthesis, etc.). Vis I and II, Visual areas I and II. Aud I and II, Auditory areas I and II. (After Woolsey, C. N. Organization of somatic sensory and motor areas of the cerebral cortex: In H. F. Harlow & C. N. Woolsey (eds.), *biological and biochemical bases of behavior.* Madison: University of Wisconsin Press, 1958, Pp. 63–81. (© 1958 by the Regents of the University of Wisconsin.)

The intrinsic thalamic nuclei could be regarded as a higher evolutionary development, since they are removed one further step from input sources. The intrinsic nuclei are of two parts: first, those which project onto the olfactory-related cortex and are most highly developed in those animals with well-developed olfactory systems (macrosmatic); and second, those nuclei which project upon the neocortex and are poorly developed in macrosmatic mammals and most extensively developed in primates. The intrinsic thalamic nuclei project to what has been termed *secondary cortical areas,* or *association areas*, or just *intrinsic cortex*. In Figure 8-10 the areas not covered by sensory or motor areas are the association areas.

The cerebral cortex develops from almost nothing in nonmammalian brains to a structure with about 8 billion nerve cells in each hemisphere of man (Blinkov & Glezer, 1968). This tremendous increase in brain tissue can be found in both the intrinsic and extrinsic cortex, but the most characteristic feature of the human brain is the enormous development of the intrinsic cortex. Despite years of study, however, there is little that can be said unambiguously about the functions of the intrinsic cortex. It was once thought that the extrinsic cortex was the basis of sensation and was therefore *primary* cortex, and that the intrinsic cortex was involved with the perception or association of stimuli and therefore was designated *association* cortex or *secondary* cortex. It was believed that learned associations between stimuli and between stimuli and responses would occur in these association areas. Research proved disappointing in this regard and little evidence could be found for the assumption that such association occurred in the secondary cortex. Certainly, the association cortex is not necessary for the kinds of associations we call learning.

Diamond and Hall (1969) have argued that primary visual cortex (visual area I) and its adjacent association area evolve from a visual belt around the visual cortex that constitutes visual area II.

The profound deficit in visually controlled behavior that follows destruction of visual cortex in primates (Kluver, 1942), carnivores (Smith, 1938), and rodents (Horel et al., 1966; Lashley, 1931) is not apparent in some of the other sensory systems and does not occur in all mammals. Tree shrews have a primitive mammalian brain that has some of the features of the primate brain, including a prominent, highly localized primary visual cortex. Destruction of this area in the tree shrew does not produce the disruption in vision seen in other species (Diamond & Hall, 1969). Lesions of visual area II, as well as I, produce severe deficits in learning visual patterns in the tree shrew. Visual area I receives its projection from an extrinsic thalamic nucleus, the lateral geniculate body (GL), while visual area II receives its projections from the lateral posterior nucleus (LP), which is classed as an intrinsic nucleus. This nucleus gets an important input from the superior colliculus, a primitive visual center that is prominent in the early development of the vertebrate visual system (optic lobe, Figure 8-3).

The hedgehog has a very primitive mammalian brain that seems to have evolved very little from an ancestral type, and the projection of the LGB and the LP nucleus overlaps in this species. Removal of visual area I does not completely abolish pattern vision in the hedgehog, although some deficits are evident. Diamond and Hall conclude that it is actually visual area II that represents the primitive visual area, and that association cortex, as well as visual cortex, developed from this belt around the visual area. The authors' views on the evolution of the visual system are diagramed schematically in Figure 8-11. This illustrates the way in which progressive changes in neuron circuits can occur in evolution. Complexity increases as separate functional systems differentiate from a single system. We have three separable visual systems where before there was one, ostensibly increasing the animal's visual capacities while the brain increases in anatomical complexity and size.

The diagram in Figure 8-11 suggests that three separate visual systems have evolved; one by way of the superior colliculus and an extrinsic part of LP; another through an intrinsic part of LP; and a third by way of the GL and visual cortex. Several experimenters have come to the conclusion that there are at least two visual systems: one for locating and the other for identifying, visual information (Ingle, Schneider, Trevarthen, & Held, 1967–1968). Evidence for this duality of visual systems was found in the fish (Ingle, 1967), in the hamster (Schneider, 1967), in the primate (Trevarthen, 1968), and in the cat (Held, 1968). A dramatic example of the separability of the two visual functions was demonstrated by Schneider's work on hamsters. Hamsters were chosen because this animal has a substantial neocortex, including a visual cortex, but the cortex does not overlay the superior colliculus as in most mammals so endowed. This permits separate injury to the two structures, a decided advantage in attempts to compare their function. Selection of experimental animals because of some such convenience is one of the important by-products of the study of comparative neurology. Basic principles worked out in the simpler system are then tested for their generality by applying the principle to the study of other animals.

After damage to the tectum of the hamsters, Schneider found that they had no difficulty learning to discriminate visual patterns as long as the testing apparatus permitted them to follow the walls of the enclosure to the correct door. The animal with the superior colliculus missing could not guide its motor behavior by vision. It did not orient toward food held over its head. On the other hand, the animal with its visual cortex destroyed was unable to distinguish visual patterns in the same two-choice learning task, but did orient correctly to a piece of food held overhead. It could not have used odor cues because there was glass between it and the seed. Thus, it seems to Schneider as though the animal with the missing visual cortex can see *where* it is but not *what* it is, and the animal with the missing superior colliculus can see *what* but not *where*.

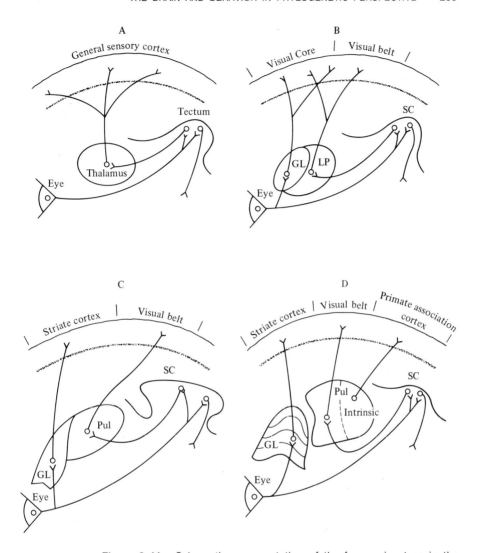

Figure 8–11. Schematic representation of the four main steps in the evolution of thalamic and cortical visual areas. (A) Reptilelike ancestral types. Visual information is projected diffusely onto the cortex via the tectum and thalamus. (B) in early mammals a more direct relay via GL is provided and there is a greater differentiation of cortical areas, but there is overlap in the projection of the two systems. This stage is approximated in the hedgehog. (C) LP nucleus in (B) develops into the thalamic structure called the pulvinar (pul) and the two systems project to separate cortical areas, an arrangement found in the tree shrew. (D) Represents the situation found in higher primates. Here there is further differentiation of the pulvinar. (After Diamond, I. T. & Hall, W. C. Evolution of neocortex. *Science,* 1969, **164,** 251–268. Copyright 1969 by the American Association for the Advancement of Science.)

Thus the brain separates visual function in ways we would not have anticipated. Presumably, these different visual functions can be carried on simultaneously in animals that possess them. Similarly, we are able to carry on many motor functions simultaneously. Consider the many separate things we do with our extremities while driving a car with a standard transmission. Compare this to the rigid way in which the frog uses its extremities in progression.

The greater range of motor capacity exhibited by mammals has been attributed in part to the addition of a corticospinal tract which originates principally in the motor cortex (MI in Figure 8-10) and descends into the spinal cord. It is present only in mammals, and it varies in its extent and distribution in different species (Kuypers, 1958). The raccoon, which uses the digits of its forepaws to grasp and hold food, has a corticospinal tract which connects more intimately with the motor cells in the region of the cord that innervates the forelimbs than does the closely related dog. The dog does not use its paws in nearly so intricate a manner (Buxton & Goodman, 1967). The dog does have a corticospinal tract, however, but its injury does not prevent the animal from normal locomotion. At first glance, the dog with the damaged corticospinal tract seems normal, but if an intricate motor behavior is required, such as walking on the edges of small boards, the injured dog does very poorly in comparison to the normal animal (Buxton & Goodman, 1967).

Thus, there are several motor and sensory mechanisms that operate simultaneously in the complex mammalian brain. These added mechanisms are reflected in the greater bulk of the mammalian brain, its increased number of neurons, and the greater range of behavior at its disposal.

PROSPECTS AND GENERALITIES

The Neuron Doctrine

We have seen that the brain has evolved from simple mechanisms of irritability and response to a complex circuit arrangement that simultaneously makes multiple decisions and coordinated complex responses and stores enormous amounts of complex information. The kinds of "decisions" and "logical functions" that are made by the brain can be accounted for by its known physiological and anatomical properties (e.g., McCulloch, 1952). The idea that these logical functions of the nervous system can be accomplished by circuits of neurons is an old but durable concept that has survived repeated heavy attack by experimenters and theorists. It is the essence of the *neuron doctrine* first formally stated by Waldeyer in 1891, but it constitutes the work of many of his contemporaries, especially Ramon y Cajal. The doctrine (or theory) states that the neuron is the genetic, structural, and functional unit of the nervous system. Neurons contact one another at synapses but there is no continuity of protoplasm. They are the only elements involved with conduction, and the nervous system is made up of billions of such units linked together in conducting systems.

Adjustments in the statement of the neuron doctrine will undoubtedly be made in the future. Glial cells, for example, which are found completely surrounding all nerve cells and are between the nerve cells and blood vessels, may play a much more important role than the nutritive and supportive functions that heretofore they have been thought to play. Also, the orderly arrangement found for synapses on cell bodies suggests that the neuron may be more complicated than is suggested by its place as a simple summating element in a huge computer (Palay, 1967). However, the basic notion that the function of the nervous system in the control and regulation of behavior can be understood in terms of neuron interrelationships—neuron circuits—seems to be more clearly underscored than ever by modern research. Modern methods, using the light and electron microscope and microelectrodes that permit recording from single cells, have revealed a high degree of precision, orderliness, and functional specialization in the nervous network (Hubel & Wiesel, 1959; Palay, 1967; Sperry, 1965). These findings tend to confirm the basic theme of the neuron doctrine that the brain functions as a huge assortment of interconnecting neurons and that its role in the control and regulation of behavior is to be sought in neuronal interrelations. It is the challenge of research to untangle and describe these relationships.

The Survival Value of Brains

In this chapter we have made much of differences in brain size and progressive changes in the structure of the brain during evolution. A caveat is in order.

Man has an understandable inclination to be self-congratulatory of his fine brain. Throughout discussions of brain evolution, we find comparisons which use "higher" and "lower" along a dimension that has man at the peak. In the light of an awakening awareness of man's destruction of his own environment through pollution, overpopulation, and war, it is worth noting that there are many animals with smaller brains that have made a better adjustment to their environment than Homo sapiens. The late Tilly Edinger, who was the leading authority on neuropaleantology (the study of the brains of extinct species), points out that rats and mice are dominant mammals in North America—they reproduce faster than man's intelligence can destroy them. She makes the timely point that neuropaleantology cannot help solve the great enigma of extinction. "Its object is collecting facts from the Past. Its literature now consists of more than 1,500 papers and books. In not one phylogeny has it been proven—can it be proven?—that survival or extinction was due to either relative or absolute brain size, or to unprogressive or progressive forebrain evolution [Edinger, 1969, pp. 160–161]."

REFERENCES

ARIËNS KAPPERS, C. U., HUBER, G. C., & CROSBY, E. C. *The comparative anatomy of the nervous system of vetebrates, including man.* New York: Macmillan, 1936.

BERNSTEIN, J. J. Brightness discrimination following forebrain ablation in fish. *Experimental Neurology*, 1961, **3**, 297–306.

BLINKOV, M., & GLEZER, I. *The human brain in figures and tables.* New York: Basic Books, 1968.

BONIN, G. VON. Brain-weight and body-weight of mammals. *Journal of General Psychology*, 1937, **16**, 379–389.

BONIN, G. VON. Anatomical asymmetries of the cerebral hemispheres. In V. B. Mountcastle (Ed.), *Interhemispheric relations and cerebral dominance.* Baltimore: Johns Hopkins, 1962. Pp. 1–6.

BUXTON, D., & GOODMAN, D. C. Motor function and the corticospinal tracts in the dog and raccoon. *Journal of Comparative Neurology*, 1967, **129**, 341–360.

DIAMOND, I. T., & HALL, W. C. Evolution of neocortex. *Science*, 1969, **164**, 251–268.

DIAMOND, M. C. Extensive cortical depth measurements and neuron size increases in the cortex of environmentally enriched rats. *Journal of Comparative Neurology*, 1967, **131**, 357–364.

DIAMOND, M. C., KRECH, D., & ROSENZWEIG, M. R. The effects of an enriched environment on the histology of the rat cerebral cortex. *Journal of Comparative Neurology*, 1964, **123**, 111–119.

DU BRUL, E. L. Pattern of genetic control of structure in the evolution of behavior. *Perspectives in Biology and Medicine*, 1967, **10**, 524–539.

EDINGER, T. Brains from forty million years of camelid history. In R. Hassler & H. Stephan (Eds.), *Evolution of the forebrain.* New York: Plenum, 1969.

EISENSTEIN, E. M. The use of invertebrate systems for studies on the basis of learning and memory. In G. C. Quarton, T. Melnechuck, & F. O. Schmitt (Eds.), *The neurosciences.* New York: Rockefeller University Press, 1967. Pp. 653–665.

GESCHWIND, N., & LEVITSKY, W. Human brain: Left-right asymmetries in temporal speech region. *Science*, 1968, **161**, 186–187.

GODDARD, G. Functions of the amygdala. *Psychological Bulletin*, 1964, **62**, 89–109.

HELD, R. Dissociation of visual functions by deprivation and rearrangement. *Psychologische Forschung*, 1968, **31**, 338–348.

HOLLOWAY, R. Dendritic branching: Preliminary results of training and complexity in rat visual cortex. *Brain Research*, 1966, **2**, 393–396.

HOLLOWAY, R. Some questions on parameters of neural evolution in primates. In J. M. Petras & C. R. Noback (Eds.), Comparative and evolutionary aspects of the vertebrate central nervous system. *Annals of the New York Academy of Sciences*, 1969, **167**, 332–340.

HOREL, J., BETTINGER, L., ROYCE, J., & MEYER, D. R. Role of neocortex in the learning and relearning of two visual habits by the rat. *Journal of Comparative and Physiological Psychology*, 1966, **61**, 66–78.

HORRIDGE, G, *Interneurons.* San Francisco: Freeman, 1968.

HUBEL, D. H., & WIESEL, T. N. Receptive fields of single neurons in the cat's striate cortex. *Journal of Physiology*, 1959, **148**, 574–591.

INGLE, D. Two visual mechanisms underlying the behavior of fish. *Psychologische Forschung*, 1967, **31**, 43–51.

INGLE, D., SCHNEIDER, G., TREVARTHEN, C., & HELD, R. Locating and identifying: Two modes of visual processing. *Psychologische Forschung*, 1967–1968, **31**, 42–348.

JERISON, H. Quantitiative analysis of evolution of the brain in mammals. *Science*, 1961, **133**, 1012–1014.

JERISON, H. Interpreting the evolution of the brain. *Human Biology*, 1963, **35**, 263–291.

JERISON, H. Brain evolution and dinosaur brains. *American Naturalist*, 1969, **103**, 575–588.

KAADA, B. Brain mechanisms related to aggressive behavior. In C. Clemente & D. Lindsley (Eds.), *Aggression and defense*. Vol. 5. *Brain Function*. Los Angeles: University of California Press, 1967. Pp. 95–133.

KAPLAN, H., & ARONSON, L. R. Function of forebrain and cerebellum in learning in the teleost *Tilapia heudelotti macrocephala*. *Bulletin of the American Museum of Natural History*, 1969, **142**, 141–208.

KEATING, E. G., KORMANN, L., & HOREL, J. The behavioral effects of stimulating and ablating the reptilian amygdala (*Caiman sklerops*). *Physiology and Behavior*, 1970, **5**, 55–59.

KENNEDY, D. Small systems of nerve cells. *Scientific American*, 1967, **216**, 44–52.

KENNEDY, D., EVOY, W. H., & HANAWALT, J. T. Release of coordinated behavior in crayfish single central neurons. *Science*, 1966, **154**, 917–919.

KLUVER, H. Functional significance of the geniculo-striate system. *Biological Symposia*, 1942, **7**, 253–299.

KUYPERS, H. G. J. M. Some projections from the pericentral cortex to the pons and lower brain stem in monkey and chimpanzee. *Journal of Comparative Neurology*, 1958, **110**, 221–255.

LASHLEY, K. S. The mechanism of vision: IV. The cerebral areas necessary for pattern vision in the rat. *Journal of Comparative Neurology*, 1931, **53**, 419–478.

LASHLEY, K. S. Persistent problems in the evolution of mind. *Quarterly Review of Biology*, 1949, **24**, 28–42.

LENNEBERG, E. *Biological foundations of language*. New York: Wiley, 1967.

LIVESY, P. J. A consideration of the neural basis of intelligent behavior: Comparative studies. *Behavioral Science*, 1970, **15**, 164–170.

MCCULLOCH, W. S. *Finality and form*. Springfield, Ill.: Charles C. Thomas, 1952.

MEYER, P. M. Analysis of visual behavior in cats with extensive neocortical ablations. *Journal of Comparative and Physiological Psychology*, 1963, **56**, 397–401.

NORTHCUTT, G. Discussion of "The organization of the avian telencephalon and some speculations on the phylogeny of the amniote telencephalon" by H. J. Karten. In J. M. Petras & C. R. Noback (Eds.), Comparative and evolutionary aspects of the vertebrate central nervous system. *Annals of the New York Academy of Sciences*, 1969, **167**, 180–185.

PALAY, S. L. Principles of cellular organization in the nervous system. In G. C. Quarton, T. Melnechuck, & F. O. Schmitt (Eds.), *The neurosciences*. New York: Rockefeller University Press, 1967. Pp. 24–31.

ROSE, J., & WOOLSEY, C. Organization of the mammalian thalamus and its relationships to the cerebral cortex. *Electroencephalography and Clinical Neurophysiology*, 1949, **1**, 391–401.

SCHAPIRO, H., & GOODMAN, D. C. Motor functions and their anatomical basis in the forebrain and tectum of the alligator. *Experimental Neurology*, 1969, **24**, 187–195.

SCHNEIDER, G. Contrasting visuomotor functions of tectum and cortex in the golden hamster. *Psychologische Forschung*, 1967, **31**, 52–62.

SMITH, K. U. Visual discrimination in the cat: VI. The relation between pattern vision and visual acuity and the optic projection centers of the nervous system. *Journal of Genetic Psychology*, 1938, **53**, 271–272.

SPERRY, R. W. Embryogenesis of behavioral nerve nets. In R. L. De'Haan & H. Ursprung (Eds.), *Organogenesis.* Holt, Rinehart and Winston, 1965. Pp. 161–186.

STEPHAN, H. & ANDY, O. J. Quantitative comparative neuroanatomy of primates: An attempt at a phylogenetic interpretation. In J. Petras & C. Noback (Eds.), Comparative and evolutionary aspects of the vertebrate central nervous system. *Annals of the New York Academy of Sciences*, 1969, **167**, 370–387.

TREVARTHEN, C. Two mechanisms of vision in primates. *Psychologische Forschung*, 1968, **31**, 299–337.

WARREN, J. M. The comparative psychology of learning. *Annual Review of Psychology*, 1965, **16**, 95–118.

WELKER, W., & CAMPOS, G. Physiological significance of sulci in somatic sensory cerebral cortex in mammals of the family *Procyonidae. Journal of Comparative Neurology*, 1963, **120**, 19–36.

WELKER, W., & SEIDENSTEIN, S. Somatic representation in the cerebral cortex of the raccoon (*Procyon lotor*). *Journal of Comparative Neurology*, 1959, **111**, 469–501.

Chapter 9

The Biopsychology of Hormones and Behavior

Norman T. Adler

THE NEUROENDOCRINE SYSTEM AND ITS STUDY

A Survey of the Endocrine System

The Mammalian Hormones   Behavior is an integrated phenomenon; it is the result of physiological processes in the organism, and it in turn influences the physiology, genetics, development, and evolution of organisms. In this chapter, we shall examine the interaction of behavior (primarily reproductive behavior) and one class of biological chemicals, the hormones; the purpose is to analyze not only the variety of interactions between hormones and behavior but also the adaptive significance of these interactions.

Let us begin with some definitions. Reproductive behavior is easy to define. The phrase refers to all activities of the organism which are related to the production and care of the young. The definition of hormone is not so simple, for almost any single definition will be found to have exceptions. Nonetheless, let us start with one definition and modify it as the data warrant. A substance is a hormone if: (1) it is a specific chemical, (2) it is secreted by a specific gland into the bloodstream, and (3) it exerts a specific influence on some organ or process at a distance from the gland (Gorbman & Bern, 1962). A hormone, in short, is an internal chemical messenger; and so the endocrine system can be classified with the nervous system as an organ system which helps to integrate the physiological processes of an organism into one functional unit.

Figure 9-1 diagrammatically represents the location of the various endo-

crine organs in the adult human; with some modifications, this figure describes
the basic mammalian pattern. Table 9-1 lists the major hormones from these
glands and gives some of their physiological effects.

Brain-Pituitary-Gonad Axis   In the present chapter, we shall be primarily concerned with the sex hormones (androgens in the male and estrogen and progesterone in the female) and with the pituitary hormones. The sex hormones
are important for behavior because they are directly involved in stimulating
reproductively important structures and behavior.

The pituitary, which sits at the base of the brain, is important because
its secretions influence the activity of such glands as the testes, the ovaries,
the adrenal gland, and the thyroid. For example, under the influence of the
pituitary gonadotrophins (literally, gonad-stimulating hormones), the ovarian
follicle matures and secretes estrogen.

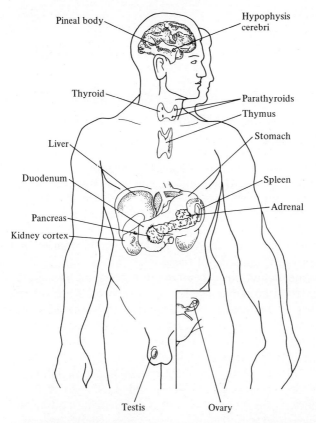

Figure 9–1.   Diagrammatic representation of the major endocrine organs
in humans and their locations in the body. [From C. D. Turner &
J. T. Bagnara, *General endocrinology.* (5th Ed.) Philadelphia: Saunders,
1971.]

Table 9–1   A Summary of the Major Hormones and Their Effects

Hormones	Principal actions
Pars distalis (anterior lobe)	
Somatotrophin (STH, growth hormone)	Growth of bone and muscle; anabolic effect on nitrogen metabolism; carbohydrate and lipid metabolism; elevates glycogen stores of skeletal and cardiac muscles.
Adrenocorticotrophin (ACTH)	Stimulates the secretion of adrenal cortical steroids by the adrenal cortex; probably exerts certain extra-adrenal actions.
Thyrotrophin (TSH)	Stimulates the thyroid gland to form and release thyroid hormones.
Prolactin (lactogenic hormone, luteotrophin)	Proliferation of mammary gland and initiation of milk secretion; prolongs the functional life of the corpus luteum—the secretion of progesterone.
Gonadotrophins	Ovary: formation of corpora lutea; secretion of progesterone; probably acts in conjunction with FSH.
(a) Luteinizing or interstitial cell-stimulating hormone (LH or ICSH)	Testis: stimulates the interstitial cells of Leydig, thus promoting the production of androgen.
(b) Follicle-stimulating hormone (FSH)	Ovary: growth of ovarian follicles; functions with LH to cause estrogen secretion and ovulation.
	Testis: Possible action on seminiferous tubules to promote spermatogenesis.
Pars intermedia (intermediate lobe)	
Melanocyte-stimulating hormone (MSH, intermedin)	Dispersion of pigment granules in the melanophores; darkening of the skin.
Neurohypophysis	
Vasopressin (antidiuretic hormone)	Elevates blood pressure through action on arterioles; promotes reabsorption of water by kidney tubules.
Oxytocin	Affects post-partum mammary gland causing ejection of milk; promotes contraction of uterine muscle; possible action in parturition and in sperm transport in female tract.
Thyroid	
Thyroxine and triiodothyronine	Accelerate metabolic rate and oxygen consumption by tissues.
Parathyroid	
Parathormone	Conditions the metabolism of calcium and phosphorus; acts on skeleton and possibly on kidney.
Pancreatic islets	
Insulin	Regulates the storage and utilization of carbohydrate; reduces blood sugar.
Glucagon (HGF)	Promotes liver glycogenolysis and causes an elevation of blood sugar.

Table 9–1   *(Continued)*

Adrenal medulla Epinephrine	Emergency functions. Actions on heart muscle, smooth muscle, and arterioles; effects on pulse rate and blood pressure. Promotes both liver and muscle glycogenolysis.
Norepinephrine	Chemical mediator at adrenergic nerve terminals. Causes contraction of arterioles and increased peripheral resistance. A pressor hormone functioning in the maintenance of blood pressure.
Adrenal cortex Aldosterone	A steroid hormone of especial importance in electrolyte and water metabolism.
Other steroid hormones	Metabolism of carbohydrates, fats, and proteins. Effects on fluid shifts; immunity and resistance to infection; inflammation and hypersensitivity.
Testis Testosterone	Maturation and functional maintenance of male reproductive tract; development of secondary sex characters; direct stimulation of the testis itself; influences sex behavior.
Ovary Estrogens (estradiol, estrone, etc.)	Maturation and cyclic functions of female reproductive tract; development of secondary sex characters; stimulates duct system of mammary gland; direct effect on ovary itself; affects sex behavior.
Progestogens (progesterone from corpus luteum)	Cooperates with estrogen in regulating the female tract; develops alveolar system of mammary gland; prepares uterus for implantation of blastocyst; maintenance of pregnancy.
Relaxin	Relaxation of pubic symphysis; cervical tone; facilitates parturition.
Placenta Estrogens Progesterone Relaxin Chorionic gonadotrophin	As for ovary. As for ovary. As for ovary. Similar to but not identical with gonadotrophins from the pars distalis.
Gastrointestinal mucosa Secretin Pancreozymin Cholecystokinin Enterogastrone Gastrin	Secretion of fluid by acinar pancreas. Enzyme secretion by acinar pancreas. Contraction and evacuation of gallbladder. Inhibits motility and acid secretion of stomach. Stimulates acid secretion by stomach.

(From Turner, C. D. & Bagnara, J. T. *General Endocrinology*, 5th edition. Philadelphia. Saunders, 1971.)

The pituitary itself is influenced by the brain. Thus, external stimulation (for example, long day-lengths) can be transmitted via neural mediation to the pituitary and can result in growth of the gonads.

The brain-pituitary-gonadal system is integrated into one functional unit because of one final link, the influence of the sex hormones on the brain. This last link permits *feedback control* of many hormones. For example, the follicle-stimulating hormone (FSH) of the pituitary stimulates the secretion of ovarian estrogen; when the level of estrogen rises to a high enough level in the bloodstream, it affects the nervous system in such a way that the release of the pituitary hormone is reduced, thus limiting the secretion of ovarian estrogen. By means of the *negative feedback* of the ovarian hormone on the brain-pituitary complex, the secretion of the ovarian hormones is regulated at a stable level.

History of Neuroendocrinology

Early Speculation and Experiments   From this brief description of endocrine function, it is apparent that any thorough consideration of hormones and behavior must involve an integration of behavioral, hormonal, and neurophysiological effects. Consequently, the history of behavioral neuroendocrinology has involved behaviorists, endocrinologists, and neurologists. The history of this field is, however, a peculiar one, combining conflicts as well as syntheses; and although there are ancient dates that one could choose as the start of endocrinology, its beginnings as an experimental science are recent.

It is true that Hippocrates (400 B.C.) developed a humoral hypothesis (postulating that health is dependent on the proper balance of humors in the body), and also true that Brown-Sequard (1875) injected himself with animal testis extracts and claimed a "rejuvenation" (Gorbman & Bern, 1962). While both these events stimulated interest in the humoral mediation of behavior, the history of experimental endocrinology really begins with A. A. Berthold in 1849 (Quiring, 1944).

In that year, Berthold performed the first endocrine experiment, which was by today's standards extremely simple in the techniques employed; yet this experiment still stands as a model of the inductive process. The purpose of Berthold's experiment was to determine the function and mode of action of the testes in cockerels. In the first part of his study, Berthold removed the testes from each of two cockerels. These animals became like capons; they were not aggressive to other cockerels, they developed a monotonic voice, and their combs and wattles were quite small. In two other birds, he removed both testes but donated one testis from each bird into the intestinal region of the other one. Each cockerel therefore had one testis, and the testis was situated in an abnormal place (the intestine). The results were clear; the birds with implanted testes crowed lustily, they battled, they showed the usual reaction to hens, and their combs and wattles developed normally. From this simple experiment, Berthold drew the following conclusions concerning the role of the testis and its secretions.

> Since ... transplanted testes are no longer connected with their original innervation, and since ... no specific secretory nerves were present, it follows that the results in question are determined by the productive function of the testes, i.e., by their action on the blood stream, and then by corresponding reaction of the blood upon the entire organism of which, it is true, the nervous system represents a considerable part [Quiring, 1944, p. 401].

Berthold was able to rule out a specific neural influence on the testis and to conclude that the testis produces a substance which satisfies the criteria for being a hormone.

Berthold's paper, which demonstrated a humoral effect independent of specific neural control, was not appreciated in its own time. It was not really until 1902 that the basis of modern endocrinology was set. In that year, two English physiologists, Bayliss and Starling, published a paper which conferred upon endocrinology the status of an independent discipline (Bayliss & Starling, 1902).

The Modern Synthesis   While investigating gastrointestinal physiology, these pioneer investigators discovered a chemical secreted by the mucosa of the upper intestine. The function of this substance, as they recognized, was to aid digestion. Since this was one of the first hormones to be systematically studied, Bayliss and Starling appropriately named it *secretin*. Attempting to proclaim a new field of endocrinology, they argued for the existence of exclusive chemical control in this physiological system. In a series of articles, the two English endocrinologists engaged in controversy with a Russian physiologist who believed that the nervous system and the endocrine system were integrated into one functional unit. Their adversary was Ivan Pavlov, who, after having completed work in digestion, was beginning his research on conditioned reflexes and cerebral function. As a consequence of the research in this period, Bayliss and Starling helped establish modern endocrinology as an independent field, and Pavlov went on to his monumental contributions in the nervous control of behavior.

Despite the early rift between endocrinology and neurology, practitioners in the two fields gradually generated the unified area of research today called neuroendocrinology. A convenient event with which to begin the history of this field is, perhaps, Carol Pfeiffer's discovery that the pituitary gland operates differently in males and females (Pfeiffer, 1936). In the female, the pituitary secretes its products cyclically, while in the male, the gland maintains a tonic secretion. Pfeiffer ascribed these differences (the cyclic female secretory pattern versus the tonic masculine pattern) to the pituitary gland itself. He thought that if the young pituitary developed under the influence of androgen (the male hormone), it would become "male" in its adult function. Later, it was discovered that the adult male and female pituitaries were bipotential: a given adult pituitary could function either cyclically or tonically, depending on whether it was controlled by a "female brain" or a "male brain" (Harris & Levine, 1965). This was an extremely important discovery, for it showed that the pituitary, and therefore the entire endocrine system, was influenced by the nervous system.

The other neuroendocrine relationship, the influence of hormones on the nervous system, was studied in the 1940s and 1950s (Kent & Liberman, 1949). In these experiments, small bits of crystalline hormone were placed in various regions of the brains of castrated animals. Although castrated animals do not ordinarily exhibit sexual behavior, this behavior did occur following administration of the hormone. Subsequently, other investigators extended this finding and began a search for the anatomical locus of hormone action in the brain (Harris, Michael, & Scott, 1958).

Another kind of experiment was also important in demonstrating hormonal influences on the brain; this type of experiment showed that hormones could alter the electrical activity of the central nervous system (Kawakami & Sawyer, 1967). As a result of this research, the modern field of neuroendocrinology developed, and with it, the interest in the relation between behavior and the neuroendocrine axis.

Principles of Hormone-Behavior Interaction

It is the variety of relations between behavior and the neuroendocrine system that is the subject of this chapter. Each of three types of relationships will be examined. The first relationship is the hormonal *arousal* of behavior. The classic experiment of Berthold on the role of testis secretions in cockerels is an example of this effect. A second major relationship is the triggering of hormonal secretion by stimuli arising from behavior. The fact that a female cat ovulates (secretes pituitary LH) only when she receives copulatory stimulation is an example of this effect (Diakow, 1971). Finally, there is the influence of one organism's chemical secretions on the behavior of another organism. Ants can locate a new food source because their comrades that have already discovered the food lay a chemical trail to it. These secretions are not, strictly speaking, hormones because they act between organisms and do not circulate within one organism. Nevertheless, these secretions (or pheromones) are a potent form of communication throughout the animal kingdom and illustrate the third type of behavior-chemical interaction in which the secretion itself is a form of behavior, or communication, that integrates the behavior of two organisms.

HORMONAL AROUSAL OF BEHAVIOR

Rodent Copulatory Behavior

In 1923, Wang made a discovery which illustrates the effect of hormones on behavior. He showed that the female rat, when in estrus, displayed very high levels of general running activity (see Figure 3–3). In fact, the word "estrus" is derived from a root meaning "gadfly"; the term originally implied that a female who was sexually receptive was in a state of frenzy.

Regardless of any value judgment implied by the early investigators who employed this term, sexual behavior intuitively appears to be the result of an aroused state in which the hormones have "turned on" the nervous system. Since it is rodent sexual behavior which has most often been invaded, observed, and quantified, a discussion of rat sexual behavior and its hormonal arousal will be useful (Beach, 1956).

A male rat begins copulation with an investigation of the female, particularly her anogenital region. He then tries to mount her. The female may respond to the male's attention in one of several ways. She may display a "courting run" in which she coquettishly darts away from the male, coming to an abrupt halt with her head pointed slightly upward. (This response usually elicits pursuit by the male.) Occasionally, she may become more active and will investigate the male. Finally, she may exhibit lordosis, the consummatory element in the female's sexual pattern; in response to the male's mount, the female's back is arched into a concave shape, the pudendal area is elevated, and the tail is deviated to one side, thus exposing her vaginal opening (Figure 9-2). During the male's mount (while she is in lordosis), his hind quarters move in and out in a series of extremely rapid pelvic thrusts. If erection occurs and the male is oriented properly, the final thrust of the mount can result

Figure 9–2. Male and female rat copulating. Female shows lordosis in response to the mount of the male. (From S. A. Barnett *The Rat: A study in behaviour.* London: Methuen, 1963.)

in an intromission of the penis into the vagina. Repeatedly the male mounts, sometimes gaining intromission, and then he dismounts. Finally, after anywhere from eight to fifteen mounts with intromissions, the male ejaculates.

Sex hormones are necessary for copulation to occur. A male without testes and a female without ovaries will not perform these patterns of behavior. The next paragraphs will deal with the mechanism by which hormones produce these behavioral effects.

Male Behavior

Neural Substrate: The Spinal Cord   Hormones act on several levels of the nervous system. There are reflexlike aspects in sex (lordosis in female rodents and the intromission and ejaculatory pattern of males). These sexual reflexes seem to be programmed by the lower brain centers and spinal cord and then modified by higher centers in the brain. In a sexually unresponsive state, higher levels of the nervous system are thought to inhibit the appearance of these sexual reflexes. Then, in the sexual state, the blood-borne hormones inhibit these higher centers, and because of the lack of inhibition from these centers, the spinal reflexes are released (Beach, 1966; Hutchison & Poynton, 1963).

To investigate the spinal control of sexual reflexes in males, Hart recently performed an extensive series of experiments on rats. He transected the spinal cord of male rats in the mid-thoracic region. After the animal recuperated from the operation, it was tested for the presence of genital reflexes. The rat was placed on its back in a restraining cylinder with the genital area outside the container. When the experimenter pulled back the preputial sheath over the glans of the penis, a series of genital responses occurred approximately every 2 or 3 minutes. The responses came in clusters, and although the specific responses that appeared in each cluster varied, there were only three or four basic patterns. A typical response cluster included three or four erections, one to three quick flips of the penis, and one to four long flips of the penis.

After the response cluster was completed, the animal remained completely quiet for at least 2 or 3 minutes even though constant pressure on the penile area was being exerted. Despite the constant stimulus to the penis and the presumably constant level of hormones circulating in the blood, the genital reflexes occurred periodically; the 2 to 3 minutes between clusters seemed programmed by the spinal cord itself (Hart, 1968).

According to the hypothesis that hormones affect higher nervous centers that normally inhibit spinal reflexes, more responses should appear in a spinally transected animal than in a nontransected animal. In a transected animal, a cut is made through the spinal cord, thus destroying the neural connection between the brain and the cord. This is precisely what happened. When the unoperated male rats were given the same kind of testing as the spinally transected animals, the former had significantly fewer genital responses and practically no long flips.

Even though hormones affect the spinal cord via their modulating effects on higher centers, they also have a direct effect on the spinal cord. To demonstrate this effect, Hart performed another experiment (see Figure 9-3). In addition to cutting the spinal cord of male rats, he castrated them, thus removing the endogenous supply of androgen. The animals were divided into two groups of six animals each, and both groups received injections of the androgen (testosterone propionate). The animals in both groups responded with erections, quick flips, and long flips in well-defined response clusters. In the second part of the experiment, animals in group A were given hormone therapy but animals in group B were not. The genital reflexes just described were produced quite frequently in the group that received the hormones, but declined in the animals that did not. The hormone treatments were reversed in the third part of the experiment; the animals in group A were taken off the hormone and the animals in group B now received the testosterone. As was expected, the animals that received the hormone showed increased sexual responsiveness while those that had no hormone showed decreased sexual responses. This experiment shows that hormones directly influence spinal reflexes (Hart, 1967).

In a third experiment, Hart demonstrated this finding in another way. In this experiment, he implanted crystals of testosterone directly into the spinal cord. The animals responded to this treatment with genital reflexes. Thus, for the full expression of copulatory behavior, the hormones not only affect the higher nervous system but also have a direct excitatory effect on the spinal cord (Hart & Haugen, 1968).

Neural Substrate: The Brain   Although the spinal cord plays a direct role in shaping sexual reflexes, and although hormones have a direct effect on the cord, it is only with the intact and functioning brain that isolated reflexes become coordinated into meaningful patterns of reproductive behavior and that hormones have their most striking effects.

Several investigators have consequently tried to determine the anatomical locus for hormone action in the brain. In order to map out the relevant areas, tiny bits of crystalline hormone are placed in various brain sites in males that have had their testes removed. If it can be shown that a male rat without its endogenous supply of androgen begins to mate following the direct chemical stimulation of a particular brain area, then there is presumptive evidence that this area is sensitive to hormones and is directly involved in controlling sexual behavior.

Davidson has shown that crystalline androgen will lead to sexual behavior in castrated males if the hormone is implanted in the preoptic-hypothalamic region of the brain. Even after careful anatomical study, he could not localize the active areas more precisely within this region, and he therefore concluded that the hormone was acting on a system which runs throughout the preoptic-hypothalamic area of the brain (Davidson, 1967).

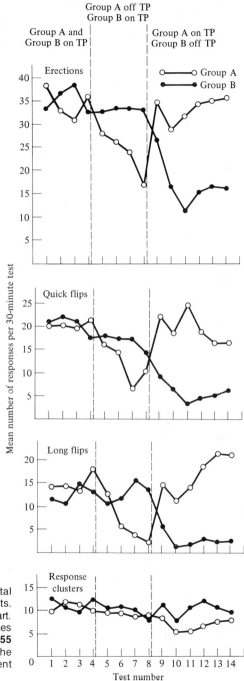

Figure 9–3. Effect of hormones on genital reflexes in spinally transected male rats. (See text for explanation.) (From B. L. Hart. Testosterone regulation of sexual reflexes in spinal male rats, *Science,* 1967, **155** (3767), 1283–1284. Copyright © 1967 by the American Association for the Advancement of Science.)

Peripheral Effects   In the studies just discussed, the investigators limited their research to the effect of hormones on the central nervous system and tried to exclude the involvement of peripheral structures. Their results, however, do not rule out the possibility that peripheral stimulation normally plays a role in hormone-dependent behavior. Hormones may, for example, have a direct effect on peripheral organs which in turn activate the central nervous system (CNS). Such an effect was found in the male rat by Beach and Levinson, who showed that after castration, male rats gradually stopped copulating (Beach & Levinson, 1950). Concurrent with the decline in mating, the penes of these rats showed very striking morphological changes. In the intact (non-castrated) rat, the penis had spines protruding around the circumference of the glans; in the area of these spines are free nerve endings. Beach and Levinson hypothesized that the spines were activated by pressure and that the spine in turn activated the nerves.

After castration, both the amount of copulation and the size of the penile spines decreased; this led the authors to postulate that the spines, which were influenced by androgen, might normally arouse the CNS. One reason that the castrated animals stopped copulating might have been that the penile spines regressed and central stimulation was reduced.

In a more recent experiment, Aronson and Cooper studied the changes in penile morphology and copulatory behavior after castration in male cats (Aronson & Cooper, 1967). They also found a decrease in copulation and in the size of the penile spines following removal of the male hormone. However, the relationship between copulatory behavior and penile morphology was, in this experiment, more variable; in some animals, the spines regressed while the animal was still copulating, and in other animals, copulation decreased while the penis was morphologically intact. Precise neurophysiological recordings are needed to clarify the relationship between these peripheral structures and activation of the central nervous system during copulation; the general correlation between hormone-dependent penile morphology and copulation, however, has been established in two species.

Exogenous and Endogenous Stimulation in Rodent Sexual Behavior

Somatic Sensory Stimulation   Hormones can influence sexual behavior by acting on various structures: the brain, the spinal cord, and the peripheral end organs. This endogenous hormonal stimulation often interacts with stimulation from exogenous sources. Sexual behavior depends on a minimal level of both types of stimulation. For example, although male and female rabbits, rats, cats, and male guinea pigs still mated following the surgical elimination of olfaction, vision, or audition, a certain amount of sensory input is necessary for the correct performance of sexual behavior (Aronson & Cooper, 1968).

A classic experiment on the role of sensory input was performed by Beach

(1942). He destroyed the olfactory bulbs, desensitized the snout, and sectioned the sensory roots of the trigeminal nerve in rats. Sexually experienced males, after being subjected to any single one of the operations, readily mated. Sexual performance decreased precipitously in animals given any two of these operations, and the one rat deprived of all three modalities ceased sexual behavior completely. It seemed that the neural mechanisms controlling sexual arousal were excited by both external stimulation and the internal hormonal condition. In this classical view, external sexual stimulation was thought to be nonspecific with respect to sensory modality, and the effects of stimulation seemed additive. (It is interesting that the concept of the additiveness and equipotentiality of stimulation necessary for sexual behavior appeared at the same time as Karl Lashley's idea of cortical equipotentiality and mass action of the brain in the control of learning.)

In recent years, however, it has been shown that there is a rather precise role for external stimulation in the control of sexual behavior of various species. For example, removing the olfactory bulbs in golden hamsters renders males totally uninterested in copulation. (This deficit is, in fact, only one part of a large behavioral syndrome in which bulbectomized males show little territorial behavior.) The hamster's entire social behavior is highly dependent on odor. Before and during mating, a male hamster sniffs and licks a highly odorous substance secreted by the female. If a male hamster is wiped with this substance and placed in the home cage of another male, he will be treated like a female; the home male will even attempt to mate with him. Thus, in this species of mammals at least, sexual behavior seems directly dependent on olfactory stimulation (Murphy & Schneider, 1970).

Penile Sensory Feedback   Olfaction is not the only sensory modality important in sexual behavior. There is another type of specific stimulation that is unique in the kind of information it provides the organism. This is sensory feedback: the stimulation derived from the animal's own behavior. It is this type of stimulation which is responsible for proper orientation and precise execution of copulatory behavior. In the sexual behavior of male mammals, sensory feedback is concentrated in one area, the penis. The role of this feedback from the penis has been investigated in several species of organisms. The results of these studies show a remarkable similarity: dependence of copulatory performance on penile stimulation (Adler & Bermant, 1966; Aronson & Cooper, 1968; Carlsson & Larsson, 1964).

The disruption of copulation following sensory deprivation in the cat has been studied in an extensive and elegant series of experiments (Aronson & Cooper, 1968). In one experiment, they found that after applying anesthetic ointment to the cat's penis, the male's mounts were disoriented; only after 26 to 30 minutes of abortive mounting did an intromission occur. These investigators also cut the dorsal nerve to the cat penis and observed the behavior of these male cats in weekly tests. The short-term changes were very similar to those following application of a local anesthetic: disorientation. In fact, the male sometimes fell on his side and thrusted when the female was not close enough for insertions (Figure 9-4). One major result of surgical or pharmacological desensitization is an amorous but inefficient male.

After continually testing the cats for several years, a second effect of penile desensitization was found. Regardless of the month of the year in which the operation was performed, sexual arousal (measured by the total amount of copulatory activity) dropped markedly every autumn and remained at a very low level until the end of each year. The seasonal variations in the desensitized male cat were parallel to morphological changes in the testis; the size of the interstitial cells of the testis and the size of the cells lining the epididymis decreased and increased cyclically. These morphological changes indicated seasonal variations in androgen secretion.

Wild felines, like most other mammals, have definite breeding seasons (Matthews, 1941). With domestication, however, these breeding seasons tend to lengthen and become less distinct (Amoroso & Marshall, 1960). Aronson and Cooper speculate that sensory input is insufficient to induce sexual behavior in wild cats during the fall when androgen levels are low. With domestication, the seasonal regression of testes is no longer as great as it is among

Figure 9–4. Disorientation of a male cat attempting copulation following desensitization of his penis. [From L. R. Aronson & M. L. Cooper, Desensitization of the glans penis and sexual behavior in cats. In M. Diamond (Ed.), *Reproduction and sexual behavior.* Bloomington: University of Indiana Press, 1968. Pp. 51–82.]

wild cats. Another effect of domestication may have been an increase in the effectiveness of sexual stimulation so that penile stimulation could compensate for fluctuating hormone levels and maintain high levels of sexual arousal throughout the year. Following penile desensitization in the domestic cat, however, the seasonal decrease in androgenic stimulation was no longer supplemented by external sexual stimulation; in the fall of the year, exogenous and endogenous stimulation were removed and sexual behavior decreased.

External stimulation over the long term is thus necessary to maintain a sexually aroused animal. General somatic stimulation, genital stimulation, and hormonal stimulation all have one common action—they *arouse* the male to perform. Penile stimulation, in addition, guides and orients the stimulated male during copulation.

Female Sexual Behavior

Cyclicity and Its Endocrine Correlates   The research discussed in the previous section treated the effects of hormones on males of several species of mammals. The effects of hormones on females are just as pervasive. In female primates, a vast number of physiological and psychological phenomena vary in a systematic way during the menstrual cycle. Mood shifts, the type and amount of dreams, the amount of water in the body, and to some extent, sexual appetites are all correlated with the menstrual cycle (Moos, Kopell, Melges, Yalom, Lunde, Clayton, & Hamburg, 1969). These phenomena comprise part of the subject matter of the rapidly developing field of human neuroendocrinology. Despite the intrinsic interest of these hormonal effects on women and the fast-growing field devoted to their study, the most analytic work on hormones and behavior in females has, to date, been performed on animals. Consequently, the present discussion will center on nonhuman species.

In female rats and guinea pigs, the cyclic variations in behavior are most striking; female rats display behavioral receptivity for only 15 hours once every four or five days. Much of the research on hormones and behavior has dealt with the mechanism by which the female's hormones induce cyclic occurrence of behavioral receptivity.

Thirty years ago Boling and Blandau (1939) demonstrated that a female guinea pig would show receptivity if she had been primed with exogenous injections of estrogen and progesterone. In this respect, she was similar to the castrated female rat which would show receptivity following injections of the same hormones (Dempsey, Hertz, & Young, 1936). In the succeeding years, the mechanism by which these hormones facilitate (and inhibit) receptivity was investigated intensively in these two species. Much of this elegant and thorough research was conducted under the supervision of, or in collaboration with, the late W. C. Young. An anatomist by training, Young was one of the first to study ovarian function in terms of its effects not only on physiology of the organism but also on its behavior.

Spinal Control of Lordosis   The first step in the study of hormonal induction of receptivity is the selection of a reliable behavioral criterion for receptivity. When a female rat is receptive, she shows lordosis, the concave curvature of the spine in response to the male's mount (Figure 9-2). Even though receptivity includes more than simple lordosis, this reflex posture has been a useful index of heat when trying to analyze the effects of hormones on behavior.

Lordosis is a spinal reflex. That is, it is a simple behavior controlled by the spinal cord and lower brain centers. The evidence for its reflexive nature was developed over several decades of research. First, Bard showed that severing the spinal cord from the brain of the female cat resulted in the facilitation of the receptive posture even when the cat was not in hormonal estrus (Bard, 1940). Recently, Hart found that lordosis can be elicited in the female rat throughout the estrous cycle if the spinal cord is freed from cerebral influence by cutting the cord (Hart, 1969).

In addition to this direct evidence, there are some indirect but sophisticated observations indicating that lordosis is not tied to a specifically sexual motivation (Beach, 1966). In adult guinea pigs, it is displayed only by females and then only at one point during their estrous cycles. Soon after birth, however, it can be elicited by mechanical stimulation of both male and female guinea pigs. The mother guinea pig is able to elicit lordosis from her pups for at least 15 days after birth by licking their anogenital region. During these 2 weeks, however, the pups become less and less responsive to stimulation from the mother; finally, they do not respond at all. This seemingly anomalous situation is really quite adaptive, for the young guinea pig is not able to eliminate feces or excrete urine by itself. Anyone who has tried to raise young rodent pups knows that he must stimulate the anus with something like a small artist's brush, or else the fecal matter becomes impacted and the young animal perishes. Neonatal lordosis, in response to the mother's licking, facilitates the pups' defecation and urination reflexes.

After approximately 2 weeks, though, the guinea pig's nervous system is sufficiently developed for internal cues from the bladder and rectum to stimulate excretion and elimination. As endogenous stimulation becomes able to initiate urination and defecation, cortical centers come to inhibit the spinal pathways, and lordosis is inhibited. The mother's licking is no longer needed for the pup's hygiene, and it can no longer stimulate lordosis. According to this hypothesis, lordosis appears in adult females because the cortical inhibition is removed by the hormones which circulate during estrus. Lordosis therefore develops as a spinal reflex early in life, independent of hormones; in adulthood, however, it can only be released under the appropriate humoral conditions. The next section deals with the nature of these conditions.

Hormonal Facilitation of Lordosis   It is clear from the early experiments that estrogen and progesterone facilitate lordosis. These two hormones act synergistically. Progesterone alone will not lead to receptivity, and estrogen alone leads to only minimal receptivity. An injection of estrogen followed by an injection of progesterone, however, produces maximal receptivity. (Typically, in these experiments, progesterone follows estrogen injection by 36 hours.)

Progesterone does not simply add to estrogen's effect. In fact, it acts biphasically: it first augments estrogen in producing receptivity, and then actually diminishes receptivity to subsequent hormonal stimulation. Goy, Phoenix, and Young (1966) showed that estrogen and progesterone did not produce receptivity if they were injected into the intact female guinea pig at a point in her cycle when she herself had been secreting large amounts of progesterone. At the time of injection, the large amounts of endogenous progesterone inhibited the normally facilitatory action of the injected hormones. Once post-estrous progesterone has set up a state of neural refractoriness, it becomes autonomous, i.e., the neural inhibition exists even without the continued presence of circulating progesterone in the body (Zucker, 1968). Inhibition later in the cycle depends on the continuing circulation of progesterone.

Because of a large number of experiments dating from the 1940s, as well as a modern reappraisal from the work of Zucker and his coworkers, the hormonal events that normally lead to receptivity in the cycling female guinea pig can be specified as follows:

1   Estrogen primes the system. This hormone alone leads to only a minimal level of sexual receptivity, but it prepares the animal for progesterone's action.
2   Progesterone acts synergistically with estrogen; their combined action leads to full sexual receptivity.
3   The second effect of the progesterone now appears; sexual receptivity is inhibited, and the female becomes refractory to estrogen's priming effect.
4   Finally, after the disappearance of the neural inhibition produced by progesterone, there is a return to a sexually neutral state. Hormones can again induce receptivity.

These experiments on sexual receptivity show that hormones activate and inhibit the neural machinery controlling mammalian sexual behavior.

The Action of Hormones on the Brain   In recent years, endocrinologists have begun the search for hormone-sensitive areas in the brain that mediate female sexual behavior (Harris, Michael, and Scott, 1958). Lisk (1962) reported that estrogen implanted in the preoptic-anterior hypothalamic area was effective in producing receptivity. In an interesting confirmatory experiment, Stumpf (1968) found that radioactive estradiol, injected systemically, was taken up in this area. This kind of anatomical investigation lays the groundwork for the eventual understanding of how the hormones affect the brain.

Recently, we have found a direct effect of hormones on the peripheral nervous system of female rats. The sensory field of the pudendal nerve lies in the perineal region of the lower abdomen. In castrate female rats receiving estrogen injections, the overall size of the sensory field was 32% larger than the field of uninjected castrate female rats. In some areas (e.g., the clitoris), the field was increased by 75% (Komisaruk, Adler, & Hutchinson, in press).

BEHAVIORAL AND NEURAL CONTROL OF HORMONAL PROCESSES

Effect of Tissue Sensitivity in Hormone-dependent Processes

Nervous systems are not equally responsive to hormonal stimulation at all times or in all species. As just described, progesterone induces a temporary state of sexual refractoriness in the brain of the female rodent. There are also long-lasting changes of hormonal responsiveness in neural tissues. Some of these modifications occur in the course of the species' evolution. The cowbird's maternal responsiveness provides an example of an evolutionary change in responsiveness to hormones (Selander & Kuich, 1963).

The members of the icterid family of birds are sensitive to prolactin; in response to this hormone, females develop brood patches and incubate their eggs. One exception to this rule is the cowbird, a parasitic species which lays its eggs in other birds' nests. For cowbirds, it is no longer adaptive to respond maternally to hormonal stimulation. Experiments have shown that the cowbird has lost its sensitivity to the maternal action of prolactin; injections of it will not make a female cowbird broody. The females of this species have not lost the hormone itself, just the neural sensitivity to it.

Neuroendocrine Reflexes

The Induction of Pregnancy in Female Rats   The change in tissue responsiveness of cowbirds, and the way this change modifies prolactin's effects, both are related to the second major paradigm to be discussed in this chapter: the behavioral and neural control of hormonal processes.

Let us look first at the copulatory behavior of the rat and the way this behavior may affect the female. Recall that the male rat, before ejaculating, mounts and dismounts from the female several times. During some of these mounts, he rapidly inserts and withdraws his penis from the vagina, and only on the final insertion of the series does he ejaculate, depositing sperm and a seminal coagulate, the vaginal plug. The stability of this behavior pattern prompted a functional question: What effect does the male's copulatory behavior, particularly the multiple intromissions, have upon the occurrence of successful pregnancy in the female rat? (Adler, 1969.) From a simple evolutionary point of view, it would seem most efficient that the male would mount, ejaculate, and dismount as quickly as possible. Why does he bother with the elaborate pre-ejaculatory behavior?

To investigate this problem, we performed the following experiments (Wilson, Adler, & Le Boeuf, 1965; Adler, 1969). We divided naturally receptive female rats into two groups. One group of females received a normal amount of copulatory stimulation from a male; that is, the male partners were allowed an uninterrupted series of intromissions. The males always intromitted at least four times before finally ejaculating. Approximately 90 percent of the female rats treated this way became pregnant.

For the other group of females in the experiment, the copulatory stimulation was reduced. The male partners were first allowed to intromit a number of times with "teaser" females. When a male was judged ready to ejaculate, the teaser female was removed and the experimental female was introduced. The females in this group received an ejaculation preceded by two or fewer intromissions, and only 20 percent of them became pregnant. Ejaculation alone is therefore not sufficient to ensure pregnancy in female rats; multiple copulatory intromissions must also occur.

Why should this be the case? The answer depends on some concepts from the endrocrinology of the rat. During its 4- to 5-day estrous cycle, the female rat secretes two gestational hormones, progesterone and 20-alpha-hydroxy-progesterone (Feder, Resko, & Goy, 1967). This estrous cycle, however, does not include a functional luteal phase, i.e., the ovary's short-lived corpora lutea do not secrete enough progesterone to permit uterine implantation of the egg. If implantation and subsequent pregnancy are to occur, some external event must stimulate the necessary progestational response. From a consideration of these endocrine events, we hypothesized that stimulation from the male's intromissions initiated a neuroendocrine reflex which resulted in pregnancy.

Like the familiar spinal reflex, the afferent segment of a neuroendocrine reflex is a neural process. The efferent segments of the two kinds of reflexes differ, however. Whereas the efferent segment of a spinal reflex is neural, in the neuroendocrine reflex the efferent limb is hormonal. The result of this particular reflex was thought to be the secretion of gestational hormones in amounts sufficient to permit implantation of the egg and subsequent pregnancy. In this system, copulatory stimulation would be relayed via the peripheral innervation from the vaginocervical area to a central nervous system mechanism, which in turn causes the release of pituitary gonadotrophin. The pituitary hormones would lead to the secretion of ovarian progesterone, which is necessary for ovum implantation and subsequent pregnancy. This neuroendocrine reflex is diagramed in the top portion of Figure 9-5.

There are several experiments which seem to verify the existence of this neuroendocrine reflex. First, the sensory receptors mediating the intromis-

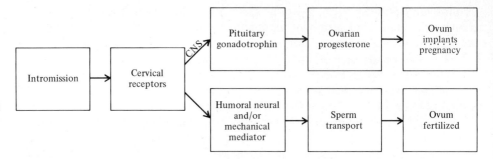

Figure 9–5. Summary diagram of the effects of the male rat's copulatory behavior on pregnancy in the female. (From N. T. Adler. Effects of the male's copulatory behavior on successful pregnancy of the female rat, *Journal of Comparative and Physiological Psychology,* 1969, **69,** 613–622. Copyright © 1969 by the American Psychological Association and reproduced by permission.)

sions' effects on pregnancy seem to lie in the vaginocervical area. Mounts without insertion are not sufficient to induce the progestational state; and as Adler (1969) found, the number of females becoming pregnant decreased if prior to copulation, a local anesthetic had been applied to the vaginocervical area.

Electrophysiological analyses have shown that some neurons in the hypothalamus respond to genital stimulation; the degree of specificity of this response, however, has not yet been determined (Barraclough & Cross, 1963; Ramirez, Komisaruk, Whitmoyer, & Sawyer, 1967). Changes in pituitary hormones are also known to occur as a consequence of genital stimulation (Taleisnik, Caligaris, & Astrada, 1966).

The last stage of the reflex is the secretion of ovarian progesterone. The idea that the male's copulatory behavior facilitates progesterone secretion is supported by the conclusions of three sets of experiments: (1) Progesterone is able to maintain pregnancy in ovariectomized females (Talwalker, Krahenbuhl, & Desaulles, 1966); (2) exogenous injections of progesterone partially compensated for the detrimental effects of reduced intromission stimulation (Adler, 1969); and (3) females receiving a large number of intromissions had significantly more progesterone in their peripheral bloodstreams than females receiving a reduced number of intromissions. This difference in progesterone levels was apparent as soon as 6 hours after mating (Adler, Resko, & Goy, 1970).

Thus, one way in which the male rat's intromissions stimulate pregnancy is by initiating the secretion of progesterone in the female. Each of the successive stages of the neuroendocrine reflex amplifies the effect of the previous stage. In the first stage, each intromission provides stimulation lasting a few hundred milliseconds (Pierce & Nuttall, 1961). The insertions lead to a central nervous system event in the next stage; the exact duration of this stage is still undetermined but it probably requires several hours or days (Barraclough & Sawyer, 1959). The next stage in which the pituitary is involved may last 12 days (Pencharz & Long, 1963). The final stage, uterine pregnancy, continues for more than 20 days.

The Effect of Male's Copulatory Behavior on Sperm Transport   In the behavioral initiation of pregnancy, the male rat's intromission triggers the tonic secretion of progesterone via the release of pituitary gonadotrophins. There is also a second set of events initiated by the intromissions (lower half of Figure 9-5); the copulatory intromissions facilitate passage of sperm through the cervix. Without this copulation-dependent transport of sperm, there can be no fertilization and no pregnancy even though progesterone is being secreted (Adler, 1969; Chester & Zucker, 1970). The intromission-dependent transport of sperm may involve a second neuroendocrine reflex, or it may reflect a purely mechanical mechanism. The intromissions are, however, necessary both for the secretion of progestational hormones and for sperm transport.

The situation is made even more complex because a male rat's intromissions, if they occur too soon after an ejaculation, *inhibit* pregnancy (Adler & Zoloth, 1970). The male rat's postejaculatory refractory period, during which he does not mount the female, may therefore provide the female with the tranquillity necessary for sperm transport to occur.

Species Differences in Pregnancy Induction   There may be an evolutionary aspect of the male rat's influence on the female's physiology. There is a relation, present in several species of rodents, between the kind of reproductive cycle exhibited by the female and the male's copulatory pattern. In the rat, the golden hamster, and several species of mice, the male delivers several intromissions prior to ejaculating (Beach & Rabedeau, 1959; Clemens, 1969; McGill, 1962). In these same species, the female displays a short estrous cycle without a true progestational phase, i.e., the amount of progesterone secreted by unstimulated females is insufficient to permit implantation. In the chinchilla and guinea pig, however, the male typically ejaculates with one intromission; the female has a long luteal phase in which she secretes functional amounts of progesterone even without copulatory stimulation (Bignami & Beach, 1968; Young & Grunt, 1951).

Pathological Induction of False Pregnancies   Behavioral effects on hormonal processes can occur in pathological, as well as normal, states. Although the male rat's behavioral "trigger" for pregnancy is a normal part of his copulatory sequence, progestational changes in humans can occur out of context.

Sometimes a woman, or even a man, may believe wholeheartedly that she or he is pregnant when there is no fetus or real pregnancy. This condition is called *pseudocyesis*. There are several exotic anecdotes of this condition occurring among royalty, as well as some rather tragic psychiatric case histories of the not-so-famous. Queen Mary Tudor of England, known as Bloody Mary, believed she was pregnant. After a number of months she learned that there was no baby in her womb; she concluded that God was punishing her for having been too easy on the heretics and consequently slaughtered many thousands of her subjects (Biven & Klinger, 1937).

Sometimes the false belief in one's pregnancy is accompanied by radical changes in hormone levels (Rakoff, 1968). Often false pregnancy is completely psychic in origin and manifestation, i.e., no detectable endocrine disturbance occurs: the progestational changes are purely psychological. Occasionally, the pseudocyetic patient's abdomen even becomes distended (Biven & Klinger, 1937).

To some extent, the physiological machinery for initiating progestational changes is common to rats and humans. In rats, prolonged secretion of progesterone is a normal consequence of the copulatory sequence; in humans, any physiological change during pseudocyesis is an example of a stress syndrome. In both cases, behavior or mental stress is the independent variable which affects physiology, the dependent variable. Even a normal pregnancy is a complex affair which encompasses psychological and physiological changes. From the biopsychological view, false pregnancy is the occurrence of one or more components out of context with the total pattern of pregnancy.

CHEMICAL SECRETIONS AS BEHAVIOR

Insect Pheromones

Ant Trail Substance   In the previous sections, the discussion centered on how hormones influence behavior and how behavior in turn influences hormonal secretions. There is a third paradigm of behavior-hormone interaction: chemicals as a form of behavior.

In some systems, chemical secretions can act as a form of communication between animals. If a colony of fire ants is given sudden access to a fresh foraging field like a clean glass platform, the workers from the colony move into the new area in large numbers. They spread across the field and thoroughly explore a few square meters during the first hour or two. After the initial surge of excitement, the number of ants in the field stabilizes at less than half the peak number (E. O. Wilson, 1962).

How does the information about food spread among the colony members? If a foraging worker finds a food source like a dead beetle, it quickly mounts the object and touches it with its antennae. After this investigation, the ant returns homeward; its behavior, however, differs from that of the ants which have found no food. It moves slowly, crouching close to the ground. The forward part of its body periodically swings back and forth. The abdomen is bent downward, and periodically the tip of the sting touches the ground.

Following this ritual, the number of colony mates rushing to the food source increases at an exponential rate; within 10 minutes after the first ant finds the food, more than 150 other ants arrive.

How do the ants communicate with one another? They communicate by chemical secretions. After an ant discovers a source of food, it leaves a chemical trail which is invisible to the human investigator but which is an extremely potent olfactory stimulus to other ants. The periodic extension of the sting and its contact with the ground constitute the behavior which is responsible for laying the trail. If the experimenter applies this trail substance in a straight line between a food source and the nest, the ants behave as if a trail had been laid by another ant. A mass of workers orient themselves along the trail and soon discover the food source. If the chemical is placed in a circle, the hapless ants will follow even this path.

The ant's trail substance is only one example of humoral communication. Chemical secretions convey information between organisms in almost every animal group investigated. These chemicals, acting between organisms, are called pheromones and were probably the first signals used in the evolution of animal communication. (Communication between protozoans was almost certainly of a chemical nature) (Haldane, 1955). Pheromones and hormones are discussed together in this chapter because, although hormones are chemicals that operate within an individual organism and pheromones act between organisms, they are both chemical messengers that integrate biological units.

Pheromones are tremendously diverse in their effects. They can be used as sex attractants which attract male to female, as trail substances in which an organism can inform its community where food has been discovered, as alarm substances which spread information about potential danger, and even as funeral substances.

An ant that has just died will be groomed by other workers as if it were still alive. It is not until it decomposes that the dead ant is removed from the nest. This removal is dependent on the process of decomposition. When an animal decomposes, its body produces a small number of fatty acids. If other subjects, including living ants, are treated with these acids, they are removed from the nest. If these "zombies" return to the nest, they are again expelled; this rejection continues until the funeral substance has worn off (E. O. Wilson, 1963).

Mechanisms of Pheromone Control   Wilson (1963) classifies pheromones into two general types. The first is the *releaser* type. This term derives from ethology, in which the control of behavior is discussed in terms of releasing and directing stimuli. The releaser triggers a nervous mechanism that leads to the performance of certain behavior patterns, e.g., the fly-catching movement of frogs' tongues and the undirected part of a young thrush's gaping response. Analogously, a releaser pheromone triggers behavior by directly affecting the nervous system.

The second type, the *primer* pheromone, has a different mechanism: it leads to a generalized physiological change. The organism's physiology is primed by the pheromone and then, upon appropriate external stimulation, the animal will react with the proper response. In the case of the primer pheromones, external (presumably nonchemical) stimuli acting upon the primed organism trigger the behavior.

In Wilson's experiments on fire ants, the animals were aroused by a releaser pheromone. The reason for the rapid buildup in the number of ants at the feeding ground was that, as new workers came to the food source, they repeated the behavior of the first successful forager; the newcomers investigated the food and then began to lay chemical trails from the food to the nest. Because many workers are attracted by a single trail and because each of them in turn lays a trail, the buildup at the bait is exponential.

The number of ants at the source, however, reaches an upper limit. This limit is determined by two major factors. First, as workers begin to crowd on the food source, the number of animals that can get to the food itself reaches a limit; and since only workers that have contacted and examined the food lay trails, the total number of trails laid reaches a limit. Second, the odor trail itself is not permanent. Trails evaporate below the behavioral threshold within a very few minutes on a clear glass surface (and within 10 to 20 minutes on absorbent paper). These two mechanisms produce a kind of negative feedback control that prevents the excessive buildup of workers at a finite food supply; as the bait becomes crowded, the number of workers laying trails stabilizes.

The fire ant trail substance is a potent releaser pheromone. In the strict ethological sense, it is both a releasing stimulus and a directing (orienting) stimulus, for it not only triggers the ants' leaving the nest but also guides the recruits to the food source. Like most stimuli controlling stereotyped animal response, it is highly species-specific (E. O. Wilson, 1963); in the species of ants studied, the molecules of the trail substance were quite different.

Mammalian Primer Pheromones

Pheromones are now known to influence reproduction in mammals as well as insects. Like many discoveries in science, however, the pheromonal control of mammalian reproduction was discovered accidentally (Parkes & Bruce, 1961). The classic view was that female rodents displayed a series of regularly occurring estrous cycles which were interrupted by periods of pregnancy. However, workers in Holland found that when female mice displaying normal estrous cycles were housed together in small groups, the number of females becoming spontaneously progestational increased; up to 25 percent of all the cycles were interrupted by periods of progestational secretion. This phenomenon is known as the Lee-Boot effect.

This was not the only anomalous result of manipulating caging conditions. If female mice were housed in large groups (e.g., thirty per box), then the estrous cycles became highly irregular. Many females became anestrous, i.e., they stopped showing estrous cycles for long periods of time.

At about the same time that these observations were made, Whitten (1956) drew attention to another unexpected effect on reproduction: Females that were caged in proximity to male mice had estrous cycles that were shorter and more regular than those of females caged without males. Moreover, when a group of anestrous or progestational females was exposed to a male, the estrous cycles became regular and synchronized; up to 50 percent of the females came into heat on the same night. Since the estrous cycle is 4 to 5 days, one would normally expect no more than 25 percent of the females to show receptivity on a given day.

In one of several experiments by which the investigators concluded that olfaction was the sensory modality involved in estrous synchronization, wire barriers were placed in the females' cages. Although physical contacts between the animals were thereby prevented, estrous synchronization still occurred.

Pregnancy Block in Mice

One of the clearest examples of the pheromonal control of reproduction in mammals is provided by the pregnancy block effect (Bruce effect). If a female mouse is mated to a male, she will normally become pregnant. If, however, a newly mated female is removed from her partner and exposed to a strange male, she will usually return to estrus within 3 to 4 days, as if coitus had not occurred. As with the other pheromonal effects on reproduction, pregnancy block occurs even if the newly mated female has no physical contact with a strange male.

Pregnancy block is strongly influenced by the quality of olfactory stimulation that the female receives. The degree of pregnancy block, for example, is proportional to the difference between the mating partner and the blocking male. If the two males are from different strains, then approximately 80 percent of the pregnancies are blocked. If the two males are from the same strain, only 30 percent of the pregnancies are inhibited, and if the mating partner and the strange male are from the same strain which has been inbred, the pregnancy block may fail altogether.

The blocking stimulation can be masked. If the initial mating partner is present when the alien male is placed with the female, pregnancy is blocked in only 20 percent of the females.

The female mouse possesses some sort of olfactory memory for the kind of stimulation she has received. If, for example, the mating partner is removed for 24 hours after copulating and then brought back, no pregnancy block occurs.

The precise chemical structure of the pregnancy block pheromone(s) has not yet been worked out. The chemical is probably related to androgen, since a castrated male mouse is no longer able to block pregnancy effectively (Bruce, 1965).

A good deal of research has been devoted to the physiological mechanisms mediating the pregnancy block effect. It seems that the odors of the strange males inhibit the release of pituitary prolactin which is necessary for the ovary to secrete progesterone. Prolactin injections, given over the 3 days during which female mice were in the presence of alien males, prevented the block of pregnancy.

Pheromonal Effects in Primates

Pheromonal control in mammals is not restricted to rodents. Female rhesus monkeys have vaginal secretions which act as pheromones (Michael, Keverne, & Bonsall, 1971). These pheromones (dubbed *copulins*) stimulate the sexual behavior of male rhesus monkeys. Even a female who had been castrated for several months became highly attractive to males after copulins had been applied to her sexual skin.

Human beings may also be influenced by pheromones. It is well known that many perfumes are based on mammalian secretions. In one study (McClintock, 1971), menstrual cycles were synchronized among college roommates and groups of close friends; preliminary investigation indicates a possible pheromonal mechanism.

The Role of Olfactory Stimuli in Mammalian Reproduction

Odor Preference in Rats   Previously, it was pointed out that no single sense was considered crucial for the expression of mammalian sex behavior. This does not mean that a specific sense plays no role at all. While rats deprived of their olfactory bulbs could still mate, chemical stimuli of an olfactory nature might normally play a role in attracting a male to a female and might provide information as to whom an appropriate mating partner would be. The olfactory guidance of mating in rats was demonstrated by Le Magnen (1952). In his experiment, Le Magnen placed an estrous female rat in one arm of a T maze and a nonestrous female in the other arm. Normal adult male rats showed a significant preference for the arm of the maze from which the odor of the receptive female emanated, but both castrated and immature male rats showed such a preference only after they were injected with testosterone. This experiment demonstrates two things. First, male rats can be directed by sex-related odors. Second, their responses to these odors depend on their own circulating hormone levels.

After demonstrating again that intact male rats preferred estrous urine while castrates did not, Carr and Caul (1962) asked in what way androgen changed the male rat's preference behavior. Possibly a male rat with no testosterone was unable to discriminate between estrous and nonestrous urine. The lack of a hormone might have been analogous to a lesion's destruction of the neural olfactory apparatus. Alternatively, it was possible that a male without hormones could still discriminate between the two types of urine but would not prefer one over the other; he was unmotivated. If there were two variables, motivational preference and sensory discrimination, there had to be some way of disassociating them experimentally. The investigators removed the possibility of a motivational factor by forcing a thirsty male rat to respond to an olfactory cue in order to get water. If a castrated male could still discriminate between the two odors, he could be trained to use urine as an olfactory discriminative stimulus.

Carr and Caul (1962) placed a male rat at the base of a Y maze. One arm of the Y contained a castrated female that was obviously not receptive; the other arm contained a female brought into receptivity by exogenous hormone injections. Air was blown over each female into the body of the maze. For half the males tested, the nonestrous female was considered the correct choice by the experimenter; for the other half, the estrous female was considered the correct choice. If the water-deprived male approached the correct arm, he would receive water; if he approached the wrong arm, he would not receive a drink.

Over the 70 days of testing, there was no significant difference between the performances of castrated males and normal males; a thirsty rat could discriminate between estrous and nonestrous odors, even if he were castrated. Since a castrated rat does not prefer estrous to nonestrous urine and an intact male rat does show a preference, the deficit in performance of the castrated male rat must have been due primarily to a loss of motivation and not to a loss of discriminatory ability.

The preference of male rats for female urine types is quite sensitive. Not only do males prefer estrous to nonestrous urine, but in some cases, they prefer odors of novel estrous females to odors of familiar females. Carr, Krames, & Costanzo (1970) have shown that male rats with polygamous mating histories prefer the odor of a new estrous female after they have finished copulating with another female. Since in seminatural conditions rats are probably not monogamous (Calhoun, 1962b), in a communal situation the preference of a polygamous male for the odor of a novel female may ensure that the male will distribute his sexual attention to several females during a single mating session. This in turn would facilitate maximal dispersion of his sperm (Carr et al., 1970).

The Neurophysiological Basis of Odor Preference   Because of the accumulated research on mammalian olfaction and sex behavior, it has become increasingly important to look for the neurophysiological basis of olfactory discrimination and the possible role of hormones. In an extensive series of experiments, Pfaff and Pfaffmann recorded both gross electroencephalograph (EEG) and single-unit activity of the brain in response to olfactory input (Pfaff & Pfaffmann, 1969a). The investigators asked two questions in their study. First, are there primarily olfactory inputs affecting the sexual areas of the brain? Second, can the response of these sexual areas be modified by circulating hormones?

The investigators began by recording from the preoptic area of the brain because this region and the surrounding structures in the basal forebrain seemed to mediate many of the hormonal effects on reproductive physiology and behavior. Lesions, implantations of steroid hormones, and electrical stimulation—all affected sexual physiology and mating behavior if the preoptic area of the brain was involved. Pfaff and Pfaffmann first investigated the extent to which specifically olfactory input affected these nerve cells.

Twenty-five out of forty-four single nerve cells in the preoptic area responded to electric shocks delivered to the olfactory bulb. These nerve cells were therefore capable of responding to olfactory input. The stimulus might not have to be specifically olfactory in nature, though; any stimulus might have affected neural activity in the area. This does not seem to be the case, for several reasons. First, many preoptic neurons responded with very short latencies when electric shock was applied to the olfactory bulb; this short-latency response indicates a close connection between olfactory and preoptic neurons. Second, the response to odors in the preoptic area stopped after the olfactory bulbs were cut. Finally, some cells which responded to odor did not respond to somatic stimuli, such as tail, foot, or nose pinches. Overall, 76 percent of the units tested responded to olfactory stimuli, whereas a significantly smaller number, 59 percent, responded to painful stimuli in the foot, nose, or tail.

Granted that olfactory stimuli in particular arouse the preoptic and related structures, these stimuli may still be evoking a general response in many areas in the brain. The preoptic area would then just be one of these regions and would not be assigned a specifically olfactory function. In fact, the preoptic area does seem to be singularly responsive. There are several records in which the preoptic area showed changes in unit firing rates even though these changes were not accompanied by a change in the gross EEG. This disassociation of single-cell firing and EEG activity contrasts with the dynamics of the reticular formation; in the general reticular area, single-cell activity always correlates quite closely with the EEG.

It is important for correct experimental methodology to monitor the gross EEG at the time that one records single-cell activity. Only in this way can an investigator be sure that hormonal or exteroceptive stimuli are not affecting the whole brain. By carefully monitoring EEG, the investigators in this study were free to examine specific hormonal influences on olfactory-dominated preoptic activity.

Testosterone, applied directly to the preoptic region, caused an increase in the resting activity and also an increased response to olfactory input. The altered response of the preoptic units seemed to be due to the direct effect of the hormone and not to some general physiological effect (like altered respiratory movement, increased passage of air through the nose, or changes in blood pressure, heart rate, body temperature, or EEG).

Even when there is a good correlation between an electrophysiological response and behavior, it may be incorrect to make a causal statement, e.g., that activity in a certain area of the brain influences or produces behavior. There may be a third system, causing both. The epistemological difficulties of such statements are illustrated by an observation often related in statistics classes. There is said to be a strong correlation between the number of babies born and the number of storks seen in a given area. This does not mean, however, that "Off the Stork" buttons should be circulated, i.e., you should not go out and destroy all the storks in order to control the population explosion. In this particular example, the relationship between babies and storks is determined by a third factor, the presence of a rural economy; in areas of farmland, there are more storks flying and also more babies born. One factor does not, however, cause the other. Great care must be exercised in synthesizing the physiological and behavioral data into a unitary description of how the system works.

The Evolution of Sensory Control   Even at this early stage of research, Pfaff and Pfaffmann (1969b) point out what seems to be an evolutionary difference between olfactory control in insects and in mammals. Sensory control in mammals seems much less specific. For example, in the moth some olfactory units respond to sex attractants but not to other types of odors (Schneider, 1963). There is no such specificity in the rat brain. There were no units in Pfaff and Pfaffmann's study that responded exclusively to one of the urine odors and to none of the others, nor were there any units that responded to only urine odors and to none of the nonurine odors. This difference between sensory function in insects and mammals seems fairly general. For most sensory systems, there seems to be greater specificity of coding in lower forms than there is in mammals. In recording from the taste receptors in the blowfly, Dethier (1968) demonstrated a greater response specificity than has been discovered at any stage of the taste pathways in the rat (Pfaffmann, Erickson, Frommer, & Halpern, 1961). The visual systems of frogs and pigeons have shown highly constrained stimulus requirements at early stages of the visual pathway; such specific stimulus requirements do not appear until higher levels in the nervous system of cats and monkeys (Lettvin, Maturana, McCulloch, & Pitts, 1959; Maturana & Frenk, 1963; Hubel & Wiesel, 1962).

INTEGRATION OF HORMONES AND BEHAVIOR

Maternal Behavior and Its Hormonal Basis

The Development of Maternal Behavior in the Rat   The underlying concept in this chapter has been that behavior and physiology interact, often in a complex manner. The nervous system not only "causes" behavior, but the stimuli arising from behavior stimulate and organize physiological processes. The emphasis on this kind of integration is seen in the kind of developmental analysis developed by Schneirla, Lehrman, and Rosenblatt (Aronson, Tobach, Lehrman, & Rosenblatt, 1970); this analysis is applicable to any cyclically varying pattern of behavior and requires consideration of events at the neurophysiological, endocrinological, and behavioral levels.

Let us analyze maternal behavior from this integrative point of view. A normal virgin rat displays an estrous cycle of 4 to 5 days; if she becomes pregnant, she stops showing estrous responses for the 22 days of pregnancy. The animal gives birth and, for the succeeding 3 to 4 weeks, she attends to her young. The maternal period can be viewed as an epoch in the life of the female rat which follows copulation and pregnancy and precedes subsequent periods of receptivity. It is a dynamic state which is influenced by the state preceding it and which influences the state following it (Rosenblatt, 1967, 1969).

Licking and the Development of Nursing   During pregnancy, the female rat is undergoing radical changes: she stops showing estrous cycles, her vaginal smear is primarily leucocytic, and specific behavior patterns (like grooming) change drastically. The changes in grooming are particularly interesting. A nonpregnant female, or a pregnant female near the beginning of pregnancy, starts a grooming episode by licking her forepaws and brushing them over her head and face. She then starts licking at the anterior part of her body, shifting from one shoulder to the other shoulder. After cleaning the anterior regions of her body, she begins licking down the rest of her body and finishes in the genital area. A nonpregnant female cleans her entire body, but spends much more time on the nongenital areas than on the genital areas. During the last week of pregnancy, the licking pattern changes: the pelvic region, the nipple line, and the genital area receive much more attention. This change is illustrated in Figure 9-6.

The increased licking of the "critical areas" has an important effect on the female's physiology. Roth and Rosenblatt (1968) have shown that pregnant females that were prevented from licking their nipple region (by placing collars around their necks) have mammary glands at the time of parturition which

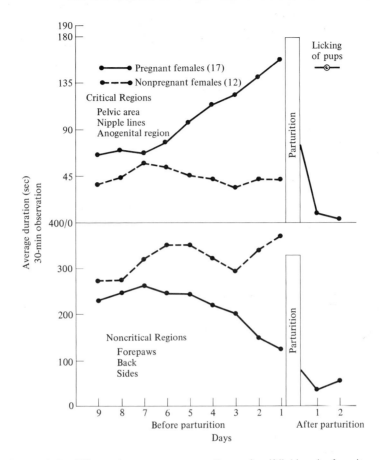

Figure 9–6. Effect of pregnancy on pattern of self-licking in female rats. (See text for explanation.) [From J. S. Rosenblatt, & D. S. Lehrman, Maternal behavior of the laboratory rat. In H. L. Rheingold (Ed.), *Maternal behavior in mammals.* New York: Wiley, 1963. Pp. 8–57.]

are significantly smaller and less secretory in appearance than females who were allowed to lick the ventral region of their bodies. Thus, the development of mammary tissue (necessary for nursing) depends on more than the endogenously controlled secretion of hormones. The female's own behavior stimulates mammary development (via hormonal secretion, probably), and the behavior was in turn stimulated by the female's prior hormonal status. This system is therefore a model of the interaction between internal and external stimulation.

The Neural Substrate of Maternal Behavior   What is the bare physiological minimum required for the appearance of maternal behavior? Rosenblatt (1967) has shown that maternal behavior may be induced in virgin females, in pregnant females, and in ovariectomized and hypophysectomized females. All these females show maternal behavior after being placed with young pups for a sufficient number of days. Maternal behavior measured by retrieval of the pups, crouching, licking, and nest-building may even be induced in castrated or intact males. It therefore seems that the neural substrate for maternal behavior is part of both the male and female rat's basic neural equipment.

However, in order to elicit maternal behavior from the animals in the experiment just described, pups had to remain with the adults for an average of 6 days before the maternal behavior appeared. This is in sharp contrast to the female who has just given birth. As soon as the pups appear, the mother devotedly performs all the responses necessary for their survival. While the neural basis of maternal behavior is always present, there may be a hormonal factor responsible for the rapid onset of maternal responsiveness.

The Hormonal Induction of Maternal Behavior   There is some direct evidence that a blood-borne hormone is involved in the elicitation of maternal behavior in the rat. First, Terkel and Rosenblatt (1968) have shown that females will exhibit maternal behavior within 48 hours if they receive intravenous injections of plasma supplied by donor females who are themselves maternal. Injections of saline or plasma from nonmaternal females were not effective. Second, properly timed injections of estrogen, progesterone, and prolactin induced maternal behavior within 40 hours in ovariectomized females (Moltz, Lubin, Leon, & Numan, 1970).

Evidence for hormonal involvement in rat maternal behavior is also provided by indirect means. The description of the normal development of maternal behavior itself indicates the general way in which hormones act in the normal life of the organism. In some of the experiments described above, maternal behavior developed as a consequence of exposure to pups. The pup-induced behavior was more easily elicited during the later stages of pregnancy. When the pups were placed with mothers on the eleventh day of pregnancy, maternal behavior did not appear for 6 days. If pups were placed with females on the seventeenth day of pregnancy, however, on the average, maternal behavior appeared in 3.63 days. There seems to be some change in the internal condition of a pregnant female that makes her more maternal later in pregnancy. Moltz, Robbins, and Parks (1966) showed that following delivery by Caesarian section on the last day of pregnancy, maternal behavior was induced after only a few hours.

Recall, however, that females normally show maternal behavior to their young almost immediately after birth while, in all the experiments just described, there was a delay of at least a few hours. This delay might be due to some technical difficulty with the experiment, but there is another possibility. The rapid onset of maternal behavior following normal birth might be triggered by the cessation of pregnancy. In the case of maternal behavior, there in fact seems to be a *termination* effect. As noted, when females are given pups on the seventeenth day of pregnancy, maternal behavior appears in 3.63 days. In another group of pregnant females, the uterus and the pups were removed on the sixteenth day. Foster pups were then given to them 24 hours later, on what would have been the seventeenth day of pregnancy. Maternal behavior appeared in these *terminated* females, on the average, in only 2.31 days. Approximately 48 hours after their natural pregnancies had been terminated, the females became maternal.

If the ovaries of these terminated females were removed at the same time that the pups and uteri were taken out, the termination effect did not appear. That is, maternal responsiveness appeared at about the same time that it would in pregnant females left completely intact. This means that the pregnancy termination effect is probably mediated by ovarian hormones. The ovarian hormones (estrogen and progesterone) normally play an important role around the time of parturition; the mother, in fact, becomes sexually receptive just a few hours after giving birth. Because of the buildup of maternal responsiveness during pregnancy and because of the pregnancy termination effect, the mother is ready to perform all the acts necessary for her pups' survival by the time the young are born.

Maintenance of Maternal Behavior   For several weeks after birth, the mother continues to care for the young. Extending the developmental analysis, the question is no longer, What prepared maternal behavior? but, What are the conditions maintaining this behavior? Rosenblatt (1969) divided the maternal period into three phases. From the first to the third day post partum, the female is in the initiation phase: nursing, retrieving the pups, licking them, and nest-building are initiated and practiced at a high intensity.

The second phase (maintenance) extends from the fourth day through the second week. During this period, the female initiates all feeding by approaching the young in the nest, licking them, and crouching over them. Gradually, the pups increase their ability to crawl and to cope with the environment independent of their mother.

The third phase of maternal behavior begins around the fifteenth or sixteenth day and extends through the third or fourth week; in this period the maternal behavior declines. Nest-building first drops out; retrieving disappears a few days later; and finally, nursing, which may continue until approximately the twenty-eighth day, declines.

It is conceivable that the changes in the mother's maternal tendencies are merely a reflection of changing stimulation from the growing pups. As the pups grow older, they would no longer elicit from their mother the same degree of maternal behavior. Conversely, it is possible that the female's motivation (e.g., the hormonal milieu) is changing and that this accounts for the changes in maternal responsiveness. Mothers rearing their own litters were tested for one hour each day from parturition to the end of the fourth week with stimulus pups (which were always five to ten days old). These pups (born to other females) were optimal stimuli that remained constant throughout the period of testing. If maternal behavior were completely controlled by the stimulus, then the maternal behavior should remain constant during this period. If, however, maternal responsiveness were determined by the female's internal motivation, there should be a variable response to these optimal stimuli. The latter is the case.

The female's response to the five- to ten-day old pups varies through the 28 days of testing in the same way that her behavior to her own young varies. A high degree of maternal responsiveness is shown for the first 2 weeks, and then there is a gradual decline. Since the test pups were providing constant stimulation, the mothers must have become unresponsive to the stimuli. Changes in the female's motivational state are thus involved in the cycle of maternal behavior.

What causes the changes in the female's maternal motivation? The answer seems to be that the pups themselves control it. This was determined by an experiment in which one group of females was allowed to give birth and keep their young with them, while another group gave birth but had their pups removed. After one week, both types of mothers were given standard test pups (five to ten days old). Four out of the six mothers who had been allowed to keep their young nursed the test pups, and all of them retrieved. Only one of the six mothers who had been without pups for a week retrieved or nursed. This study shows that maternal responsiveness depends on the stimulation from the young; without it, the maternal urge wanes and disappears within a week.

Parturition, then, is the pivotal event. The motivational changes consequent upon pregnancy and pregnancy termination lead to a female rat which is at the peak of maternal responsiveness. Her internal condition has prepared her to care for the young. Immediately after birth, the maintenance of her maternal motivation becomes dependent on stimulation from her pups. If they remain with her, the maternal responsiveness stays high. If they are removed, her motivation rapidly decreases.

Termination of Maternal Behavior: The End of the Cycle   There is one final question concerning the motivation of maternal responsiveness. Why does the maternal urge disappear? If the pups actively maintain the female's maternal motivation, then perhaps it is their growth and their independence from the mother that lead to the passive decline of her maternal motivation. Maternal behavior normally begins to decrease on the fifteenth day of maternity. In one group of females, the litters were removed on the fourteenth day, and the females were tested daily with stimulus pups. The decline of maternal behavior in these mothers was slower than the decline in females that were left with their young. The percentage of mothers without their own young that retrieved and nursed test pups on the eighteenth and twenty-first days was higher than the percentage of mothers that still cared for their own litters in this way. Whereas pups in the earlier stages of maternity maintain maternal behavior, as they grow older they seem to diminish it.

To summarize, maternal behavior in the female rat is a product of complex interactions. There is a basic neural substrate independent of the hormones. The basic ability is normally stimulated during pregnancy because of two factors: the gradual buildup of a motivational (hormonal) state, and the termination of pregnancy. The birth process is the pivotal event in the development of maternal behavior. After parturition, the control of maternal behavior shifts from the mother's internal motivational system to the pups' control. The young, at first, maintain the maternal potential of their mother, and, as they become older, they probably turn off this maternal responsiveness.

Population Dynamics and Reproduction

The final synthesis of hormones and behavior must occur on the level of population. On this level of biological function, there is also an interaction between physiology and behavior. Hormones influence the reproduction of individuals and therefore the structure of populations; population structure in turn affects the reproductive performance of individual animals. In the section that follows, it will be seen that population structure and density influence the reproductive performance of several species of organisms. Of particular interest is the periodic fluctuation in size of mammalian populations.

A word of caution should be given before the studies are discussed. This type of research is controversial primarily because laboratory studies of crowding are used as models of natural populations. Negus and his coworkers (1961) have, for example, questioned the applicability of data from caged populations because of the unnatural densities involved—approaching 1 million organisms per acre or more, in some experiments; on the basis of field studies, they maintained that the rate of social contact remains constant as density increases. Even if a physiological mechanism is well worked out on experimental animals, it is necessary to be sure that the phenomena occur in natural populations.

A Field Study   One study which applies an experimental approach to a natural phenomenon is Snyder's analysis of changes in the population of woodchucks (Snyder, 1961). There were two adjacent populations; one was left intact, and the other was periodically depleted by removing individuals. One population, therefore, had a higher density of woodchucks while the other had a reduced density.

At the end of the study, after the one population had been reduced several times, it seemed that the size of the two populations was the same. There must have been a density-sensitive response which compensated for the removal of animals in the depleted population. In general, there are three possible mechanisms by which population size is regulated: birth, death, and migration. In this experiment, all these mechanisms seemed to be involved.

Considering first the denser population, there were several changes. First, many animals emigrated from the high-density area to the depleted area. Also, there was a high death rate among the younger animals and intrauterine mortality was high (an average of 1.25 embryos and fetuses lost per pregnancy). Finally, only 20 percent of the females became pregnant. Clearly, these responses would limit population growth.

In the other (artificially depleted) population, following the elimination of a proportion of the older animals from an area, reproductive efficiency improved, more young woodchucks survived and remained in the area, and at the same time several young woodchucks migrated into the population. In turn, these responses would promote growth of the population. Responses of both these populations would tend to stablize the population size.

Laboratory Models of Natural Populations This type of field study has led behaviorally oriented ecologists into laboratory investigations of population dynamics (Calhoun, 1962a; Snyder, 1968). The first study on confined populations of mice was performed by Crew and Mirskaia in 1931. They found that as density increased, litter size dropped, incidence of pregnancy decreased, and the death rate mounted. Snyder extended this type of analysis by generating a population of mice in a 42-square-foot enclosure and examining the behavior of the group over several years. The populations were started with two males and two females of breeding age. Figure 9-7 illustrates the birth

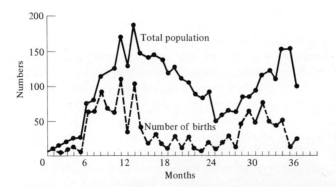

Figure 9–7. Cyclic variation in total size and birthrate of a population of confined mice. [From R. L. Snyder, Reproduction and population process. In E. Stellar & J. M. Sprague (Eds.), *Progress in physiological psychology.* New York: Academic Press, 1968. Pp. 119–160.]

rate and population size over three years. The founding females produced litters. As the young of the first two litters matured and reproduced, the number of pups born each month increased precipitously. After the population reached a peak of almost two hundred within 13 months, it ceased to grow. Numbers decreased over a period of 12 months until only fifty animals were left. At this point, a new surge of reproduction started; this growth phase lasted another 11 months, at which time the second peak started to decline. This fluctuating population in the laboratory may be a model for the cyclic variations in the natural populations.

A primary question was how the reproductive performance in the population changed as a function of the density. During the first year of population growth, the mice moved throughout the enclosure and the females established nest sites for the offspring in all parts of the cage. As these populations reached the first peak and the reproduction rate began to drop, a remarkable change took place. Several classes of mice began to appear, and these classes were spatially separated.

Considering first the males, there were what Snyder calls *dominants*—a few glassy-furred, unscarred individuals that roamed freely throughout the enclosure. There were also recluses, males which sat on the upright supports on the cage. The third group consisted of *huddlers*, a class of males that would huddle together in aggregations usually located in a corner. Occasionally, there would be a huddler group containing more than a 100 individuals. Finally, there were withdrawn individuals, partially hairless, with many wounds. Many of these animals, after autopsy, showed grossly scarred kidneys; they did not huddle and were often observed on top of a shelter box but rarely inside one.

There were several classes of females. First, there were a few large, healthy individuals restricting their movements to the first floor; these females produced young even during periods of maximum density. There was a second class of females which were capable of producing offspring, but during periods of high density, their newborn pups invariably perished, usually within 24 hours of birth. Third, there were comparatively lightweight, relatively unscarred females that joined large huddles on the second deck.

From this analysis of social class, two questions developed. First, why do some individuals belong to one class and other individuals go into another class? Why, for example, are some males dominant and some huddlers? Second, how does each class affect the changing reproductive capacity of the population as a whole?

In the case of the male mice, it was not so much size and sex that conferred dominance but rather the fortuitous circumstances of being born when population density was lowest.

The toes of newborn mice were clipped according to a number scheme so that the experimenter could determine the age at death of each mouse.

The average longevity of mice was found to be much greater if they were born during the first 5 months, when the population density was low. The first pups born to the founding female lived between 200 and 325 days; if a mouse was born after the population had been in existence for 5 or 6 months, the average longevity was less than 100 days, and more often than not, newborn mice perished within 24 to 48 hours. Thus, population density is one pervasive factor that determines both the class stratification of individuals and the reproductive performance of the entire population.

What is the mechanism for the reduced fertility in dense populations? Snyder (1966) found that following the grouping of male mice (twenty per cage), the fertility of these animals decreased, the weight of the reproductive organs decreased, and the concentration and total number of sperm in the ejaculate decreased. Eighty-nine percent of the males were proven fertile after 2 weeks of grouping; but by 50 weeks of grouping, only 21 percent of the males were fertile.

It is unlikely, though, that a reduction in male fertility was the primary cause of reproductive decline. The dominant males alone had more than enough sperm to stock the colony with young at all times during the population cycle. Snyder therefore ascribed much more importance to the female's role in regulating population structure. A certain proportion of males can be infertile without affecting the colony's productivity to any extent, but reproductive rate is directly related to the number of females that can breed; the failure of even a small proportion of the females to produce young leads to a decline of population size. Snyder cites evidence to show that females growing up in populations with low densities tend to mature sexually at an earlier age than those growing up in dense populations. Recall also that in large groups of mice, many females become anestrous (Parkes & Bruce, 1961).

In a previous section, we saw how the male's copulatory behavior may be directly responsible for evoking ovulation in the cat or for triggering the release of ovarian progesterone in the mouse and rat. Snyder (1966) found that the longer a male mouse had been in a crowded cage, the less he was able to promote ovulation and/or ovarian corpus luteum function. There was a small but consistent difference in the number of corpora lutea present at the end of pregnancy between females who had cohabited for two weeks with previously grouped males and females who had cohabited with males who had previously been uncrowded. Moreover, there was a much higher rate of embryonic absorption when females had been mated to males previously crowded together.

There is much that remains to be done in correlating changes in physiology with an individual's behavior and ultimately with population dynamics. The research on population structure and reproduction is perhaps the most complex illustration of the evolutionary paradigm basic to the study of hormones and behavior: The biological realm is integrated on all levels (physiological, behavioral, ecological) in an adaptive manner. Interference with this organization leads to pathology.

REFERENCES

ADLER, N. T. Effects of the male's copulatory behavior on successful pregnancy of the female rat. *Journal of Comparative and Physiological Psychology*, 1969 **69**(4), 613–622.

ADLER, N. T., & BERMANT, G. Sexual behavior of male rats: Effects of reduced sensory feedback. *Journal of Comparative and Physiological Psychology*, 1966, **61**(2), 240–243.

ADLER, N. T., RESKO, J. A., & GOY, R. W. The effect of copulatory behavior on hormonal change in the female rat prior to implantation. *Physiology and Behavior*, 1970, **5,** 1003–1007.

ADLER, N. T., & ZOLOTH, S. R. Copulatory behavior can inhibit pregnancy in female rats. *Science*, 1970, **168,** 1480–1482.

AMOROSO, C., & MARSHALL, F. H. A. External factors in sexual periodicity. In A. S. Parkes (Ed.), *Marshall's physiology of reproduction.* Vol. 1. London: Longmans Green, 1960. Pp. 707–831.

ARONSON, L. R., & COOPER, M. L. Penile spines of the domestic cat: Their endocrine-behavior relations. *Anatomical Record*, 1967, **157,** 71–78.

ARONSON, L. R., & COOPER, M. L. Desensitization of the glans penis and sexual behavior in cats. In M. Diamond (Ed.), *Reproduction and sexual behavior.* Bloomington: University of Indiana, 1968. Pp. 51–82.

ARONSON, L. R., TOBACH, E., LEHRMAN, D. S., & ROSENBLATT, J. S. (Eds.). Development and evolution of behavior: Essays in memory of T. C. Schneirla. San Francisco: Freeman, 1970.

BARD, P. The hypothalamus and sexual behavior. *Association of Nervous and Mental Disease, Research Publications*, 1940, **20,** 551–579.

BARRACLOUGH, C. A., & CROSS, B. A. Unit activity in the hypothalamus of the cyclic female rat: Effect of genital stimuli and progesterone. *Journal of Endocrinology*, 1963, **26,** 339–359.

BARRACLOUGH, C. A., & SAWYER, C. H. Induction of pseudopregnancy in the rat by reserpine and chlorpromazine. *Endocrinology*, 1959, **65,** 563–571.

BAYLISS, W. M., & STARLING, E. H. The mechanism of pancreatic secretion. *Journal of Physiology*, 1902, **28,** 325.

BEACH, F. A. Analysis of the stimuli adequate to elicit mating behavior in the sexually inexperienced male rat. *Journal of Comparative Psychology*, 1942, **33,** 163–207.

BEACH, F. A. Characteristics of masculine "sex-drive." In M. Jones (Ed.), *Nebraska symposium on motivation.* Lincoln: University of Nebraska Press, 1956. Pp. 1–32.

BEACH, F. A. Ontogeny of "coitus-related" reflexes in the female guinea pig. *Proceedings of the National Academy of Sciences*, 1966, **56,** 526–533.

BEACH, F. A. Cerebral and hormonal control of reflexive mechanisms involved in copulatory behavior. *Physiological Review*, 1967, **47**(2), 289–316.

BEACH, F. A., & LEVINSON, G. Effects of androgen on the glans penis and mating behavior of castrated male rats. *Journal of Experimental Zoology*, 1950, **114,** 159–168.

BEACH, F. A., & RABEDEAU, R. G. Sexual exhaustion and recovery in the male hamster. *Journal of Comparative and Physiological Psychology*, 1959, **52**(1), 56–61.

BIGNAMI, G., & BEACH, F. A. Mating behaviour in the chinchilla. *Animal Behaviour*, 1968, **16,** 45–53.

BIVEN, G. D., & KLINGER, M. P. *Pseudocyesis.* Bloomington, Indiana: Principia Press, 1937.

BOLING, J. L., & BLANDAU, R. J. The estrogen-progesterone induction of mating response in the spayed female rat. *Endocrinology*, 1939, **25,** 359–364.

BRUCE, H. M. Effect of castration on the reproductive pheromones of male mice. *Journal of Reproduction and Fertility*, 1965, **10,** 141–143.

CALHOUN, J. B. A "behavioral sink." In E. L. Bliss (Ed.), *Roots of behavior.* New York: Harper & Brothers, 1962. Pp. 295–315, (a)

CALHOUN, J. B. *The ecology and sociology of the Norway rat.* Washington: Department of Health, Education, and Welfare, 1962. (b)

CARLSSON, S. G., & LARSSON, K. Mating in male rats after local anesthetization of the glans penis. *Zeitschrift für Tierpsychologie*, 1964. **21,** 854–856.

CARR, W. J., & CAUL, W. F. The effect of castration in the rat upon discrimination of sex odours. *Animal Behaviour*, 1962, **10,** 20–27.

CARR, W. J., KRAMES, L., & COSTANZO, D. J. Previous sexual experience and olfactory preference for novel versus original sex partners in rats. *Journal of Comparative and Physiological Psychology*, 1970, **71**(2), 216–222.

CHESTER, R. V., & ZUCKER, I. Influence of male copulatory behavior on sperm transport, pregnancy, and pseudopregnancy in female rats. *Physiology and Behavior*, 1970, **5**(1), 35–43.

CLEMENS, L. G. Experimental analysis of sexual behavior of the deermouse, *Peromyscus maniculatus gambeli. Behaviour*, 1969, **34**(4), 267–285.

CREW, F. A., & MIRSKAIA, L. Effect of density on adult mouse population. *Biologia Generalis*, 1931, **7,** 239.

DAVIDSON, J. M. Hormonal control of sexual behavior in adult rats. *Advances in the bio-sciences.* 1. Schering Symposium on Endocrinology. Berlin: Pergamon Press, 1967. Pp. 119–141.

DEMPSEY, E. W., HERTZ, R., & YOUNG, W. C. The experimental induction of oestrus (sexual receptivity) in the normal and ovariectomized guinea pigs. *American Journal of Physiology*, 1936, **116**(1), 201–209.

DETHIER, V. G. Chemosensory input and taste discrimination in the blowfly. *Science*, 1968, **161,** 389–391.

DIAKOW, C. Effects of genital desensitization on mating behavior and ovulation in the female cat. *Physiology and Behavior*, 1971, **7,** 47–54.

FEDER, H. H., RESKO, J. A., & GOY, R. W. Progesterone concentrations in the peripheral plasma of cyclic rats. *Proceedings of the Physiological Society*, 1967. Pp. 50–51.

GORBMAN, A., & BERN, H. A. *A textbook of comparative endocrinology.* New York: Wiley, 1962.

GOY, R. W., PHOENIX, C. H., & YOUNG, W. C. Inhibitory action of the corpus luteum on the hormonal induction of estrous behavior in the guinea pig. *General and Comparative Endocrinology*, 1966, **6,** 267–275.

HALDANE, J. B. S. Animal communication and the origin of human language. *Scientific Progress*, 1955, **43** (171), 385–401.

HARRIS, G. W., & LEVINE, S. Sexual differentiation of the brain and its experimental control. *Journal of Physiology*, 1965, **181,** 379–400.

HARRIS, G. W., MICHAEL, R. P., & SCOTT, P, P. Neurological site of action of stilboestrol in eliciting sexual behavior. *Ciba Foundation Symposium on the Neurological Basis of Behaviour.* London: Churchill, 1958.

HART, B. L. Testosterone regulation of sexual reflexes in spinal male rats. *Science,* 1967, **155,** 1283–1284.

HART, B. L. Sexual responses and mating behavior in the male rat. *Journal of Comparative and Physiological Psychology,* 1968, **65**(3), 453–460.

HART, B. L. Gonadal hormones and sexual reflexes in the female rat. *Hormones and Behavior,* 1969, **1,** 65–71.

HART, B. L., & HAUGEN, C. M. Activation of sexual reflexes in male rats by spinal implantation of testosterone. *Physiology and Behavior,* 1968, **3,** 735–738.

HUBEL, D. H., & WIESEL, T. N. Receptive fields binocular interaction and functional architecture in the cat's visual cortex. *Journal of Physiology* (London), 1962, **160,** 106–154.

HUTCHISON, J. B., & POYNTON, J. C. A neurological study of the clasp reflex in *Xenopus laevis* (Daudin). *Behaviour,* 1963, **22,** 41–63.

KAWAKAMI, M., & SAWYER, C. H. Effects of sex hormones and anti-fertility steroids on brain thresholds in the rabbit. *Endocrinology,* 1967, **80,** 857–871.

KENT, G. C., & LIBERMAN, R. J. Induction of psychic estrus in the hamster with progesterone administered via the lateral brain ventricle. *Endocrinology,* 1949, **45,** 29–32.

KOMISARUK, B. R., ADLER, N. T., & HUTCHISON, J. B. Genital sensory field: Enlargement by estrogen treatment in female rats. *Science,* 1972, **178,** 1295–1298.

LE MAGNEN, J. Les phenomens olfacto-sexuels chez le rat blanc. *Archives des Sciences Physiologiques,* 1952, **6,** 295–332.

LETTVIN, J. Y., MATURANA, H. R., MCCULLOCH, W. S., & PITTS, W. H. What the frog's eye tells the frog's brain. *Proceedings of the Institute of Radio Engineers,* 1959, **47,** 1940–1951.

LISK, R. D. Diencephalic placement of estradiol and sexual receptivity in the female rat. *American Journal of Physiology,* 1962, **203,** 493–496.

MATTHEWS, L. H. Reproduction in the Scottish wild cat, *Felis silvestris grampia* (Miller). *Proceedings of the Zoological Society of London,* 1941, **111.** Pp. 59–77.

MATURANA, H. R., & FRENK, S. Directional movement and horizontal edge detectors in the pigeon retina. *Science,* 1963, **142,** 977–979.

MCCLINTOCK, M. K. Menstrual synchrony and suppression. *Nature,* 1971, **229**(5282), 244–245.

MCGILL, T. E. Sexual behavior in three inbred strains of mice. *Behaviour,* 1962, **29,** 341–350.

MICHAEL, R. P., KEVERNE, E. G., & BONSALL, R. W. Pheromones: Isolation of male sex attractants from a female primate. *Science,* 1971, **172,** 964–966.

MOLTZ, H., LUBIN, M., LEON, M., & NUMAN, M. Hormonal induction of maternal behavior in the ovariectomized nulliparous rat. *Physiology and Behavior,* 1970, **5,** 1373–1377.

MOLTZ, H., ROBBINS, D., & PARKS, M. Caesarian delivery and the maternal behavior of primiparous and multiparous rats. *Journal of Comparative and Physiological Psychology,* 1966, **61,** 455–460.

MOOS, R. H., KOPELL, B. S., MELGES, F. T., YALOM, I. D., LUNDE, D. R., CLAYTON, R. B., & HAMBURG, D. A. Fluctuations in symptoms and moods during the menstrual cycle. *Journal of Psychosomatic Research,* 1969, **13,** 37–44.

MURPHY, M. R., & SCHNEIDER, G. E. Olfactory bulb removal eliminates mating behavior in the male golden hamster. *Science,* 1970, **167,** 302–304.

NEGUS, N. C., GOULD, E., & CHIPMAN, K. Ecology of the rice rat, *Oryzomys palustris* (Harlan) on Breton Island, Gulf of Mexico, with a critique of the social stress theory. *Tulane Studies In Zoology,* 1961, **8,** 95–123.

PARKES, A. S., & BRUCE, H. M. Olfactory stimuli in mammalian reproduction. *Science;* 1961, **134,** 1049–1054.

PENCHARZ, R. I., & LONG, J. A. Hypophysectomy in the pregnant rat. *American Journal of Anatomy,* 1963, **53,** 117.

PFAFF, D. W., & PFAFFMANN, C. Olfactory and hormonal influences on the basal forebrain of the male rat. *Brain Research,* 1969, **15,** 137–156. (a)

PFAFF, D. W., & PFAFFMANN, C. Behavioral and electrophysiological responses of male rats to female rat urine odors. In C. Pfaffmann (Ed.), *Olfaction and taste III.* New York: Rockefeller University Press, 1969. Pp. 258–267. (b)

PFAFFMANN, C., ERICKSON, R. P., FROMMER, G. P., & HALPERN, B. P. Gustatory discharges in the rat medulla and thalamus. In W. A. Rosenblith (Ed.), *Sensory communication.* New York: Wiley, 1961. Pp. 455–473.

PFEIFFER, C. A. Sexual differences of the hypophyses and their determination by the gonads. *American Journal of Anatomy,* 1936, **58,** 195–225.

PIERCE, J. T., & NUTTALL, R. Duration of sexual contact in the rat. *Journal of Comparative and Physiological Psychology,* 1961, **54,** 584–586.

QUIRING, D. P. (Transl.) Texts and documents: The transplantation of testes, Arnold Adolph Berthold. *Bulletin of the History of Medicine,* 1944, **16,** 399–402.

RAKOFF, A. E. Endocrine mechanisms in psychogenic amenorrhoea. In R. P. Michael (Ed.), *Endocrinology and human behavior.* London: Oxford University Press, 1968. Pp. 139–160.

RAMIREZ, V. D., KOMISARUK, B. R., WHITMOYER, D. I., & SAWYER, C. H. Effects of hormones and vaginal stimulation on the EEG and hypothalamic units in rats. *American Journal of Physiology,* 1967, **212,** 1376–1384.

ROSENBLATT, J. S. Nonhormonal basis of maternal behavior in the rat. *Science,* 1967, **156,** 1512–1514.

ROSENBLATT, J. S. The development of maternal responsiveness in the rat. *American Journal of Orthopsychiatry,* 1969, **39,** 36–56.

ROTH, L. L., & ROSENBLATT, J. S. Self-licking and mammary development during pregnancy in the rat. *Journal of Endocrinology,* 1968, **42,** 363–378.

SCHNEIDER, D. Electrophysiological investigation of insect olfaction. In Y. Zotterman (Ed.), *Olfaction and taste I.* Oxford, England: Pergamon, 1963. Pp. 85–103.

SELANDER, R. K., & KUICH, L. L. Hormonal control and development of the incubation patch in icterids, with notes on behavior of cowbirds. *Condor,* 1963, **65**(2), 73–90.

SNYDER, R. L. Evolution and integration of mechanisms that regulate population growth. *Proceedings of the National Academy of Sciences,* 1961, **47**(4), 449–455.

SNYDER, R. L. Fertility and reproductive performance of grouped male mice. *Comparative Aspects of Reproductive Failure,* 1966, 458–472.

SNYDER, R. L. Reproduction and population process. In E. Stellar & J. M. Sprague (Eds.), *Progress in physiological psychology.* Vol. 2. New York: Academic Press, 1968. Pp. 119–160.

STUMPF, W. E. Estradiol-concentrating neurons: Topography in the hypothalamus by dry-mount autoradiography. *Science,* 1968, **162,** 1001–1003.

TALEISNIK, S., CALIGARIS, L., & ASTRADA, J. J. Effect of copulation on the release of pituitary gonadotrophins in male and female rats. *Endocrinology,* 1966, **79,** 49–54.

TALWALKER, P. K., KRAHENBUHL, C., & DESAULLES, P. A. Maintenance of pregnancy in spayed rats with 20-alpha-hydroxypregn-4-ene-3-one and 20-beta-hydroxypregn-4-ene-3-one. *Nature*, 1966, **209,** 86–87.

TERKEL, J., & ROSENBLATT, J. S. Maternal behavior induced by maternal blood plasma injected into virgin rats. *Journal of Comparative and Physiological Psychology*, 1968, **65**(3), 479–482.

WANG, G. H. The relation between spontaneous activity and oestrous cycle in the white rat. *Comparative Psychology Monographs*, 1923, **2**, 1–27.

WHITTEN, W. K. Modification of the estrous cycle of the mouse by external stimuli associated with the male. *Journal of Endocrinology*, 1956, **13**, 399–404.

WILSON, E. O. Chemical communication among workers of the fire ant, *Solenopsis saevissima.* 1. The organization of mass-foraging. 2. An information analysis of the odour trail. 3. The experimental induction of social responses. *Animal Behaviour*, 1962, **10**(1–2), 134–164.

WILSON, E. O. Pheromones. *Scientific American*, 1963, **208**(5), 100–106, 108, 110, 114.

WILSON, J. R., ADLER, N. T., & LE BOEUF, B. The effects of intromission frequency on successful pregnancy in the female rat. *Proceedings of the National Academy of Sciences*, 1965, **53**, 1392–1395.

YOUNG, W. C., & GRUNT, J. A. The pattern and measurement of sexual behavior in the male guinea pig. *Journal of Comparative and Physiological Psychology*, 1951, **44**, 492–501.

ZUCKER, I. Biphasic effects of progesterone on sexual receptivity in the female guinea pig. *Journal of Comparative and Physiological Psychology*, 1968, **65**(3), 472–478.

Chapter 10

Comparative Sensory Processes

Eckhard H. Hess

Comparative psychologists and ethologists investigate sensory processes, not only to determine the actual adaptive function of the sense organs and sensory cells that have been demonstrated by anatomical methods, but also to identify the kinds of physical information to which animals may be sensitive even when no obviously related sensory organ has been found. That is, the nature and range of stimuli to which an animal will respond and how it reacts to a single stimulus variable are the objects of study.

METHODS

It is obviously not feasible to use such methods as psychophysics, which involve subjective reports, to obtain this kind of information. More rigorous and objective methods in the investigation of sensory processes are necessary because of the inaccessibility of an animal's subjective experience.

There are four basic methods used as testing procedures in comparative sensory processes: (1) the measurement of the electrical activity of the neurons, called action potentials; (2) neural extirpation or interruption; (3) the measurement of learned responses; and (4) the measurement of innate, or unlearned, responses.

Measurement of Action Potentials

A major advantage of action-potential investigation is the fact that we can measure sensory processes directly. However, caution must certainly be used when evaluating experimental results obtained with this method. It is possible to record action potentials in neurons leading from sensory receptors that indicate a stimulus discrimination, although the animal is unable to give any behavioral evidence of the discrimination. In other words, it looks as though an animal may sometimes possess the requisite for discrimination of certain sensory stimuli peripherally, that is, at the sensory cell level, but does not make use of the information centrally, in the brain.

For example, an octopus is able to adjust its muscles to pick up different weights. But it does not seem able to use this proprioceptive information as a means for learning something (Wells, 1961).

In the past decade, however, single-cell recording has become increasingly important. It has been used with particular success in the area of vision, both at the retinal cell level and at the visual cortex cell level. An example of the latter is the research by Hubel and Wiesel (1963) which studied the responses of single visual cortex cells to visual stimuli presented to the eyes of very young kittens. This research showed that patterned vision is mediated by highly organized cortex cell connections which develop even in the absence of actual patterned-vision experience.

Neural Extirpation or Interruption

In order to test a hypothesis of sensory processes physiologically, it is sometimes necessary to remove a part of the central nervous system or to sever a neural pathway. It is obvious, however, that this method seldom can give sufficient information by itself and must be supplemented with either discrimination training of learned responses or testing of innate, unlearned behaviors.

Measurement of Learned Responses

This is the most common method for determining sensory processes and capacities in organisms. The method may be adapted in a variety of ways. The classical conditioning procedure uses a natural (unconditional) stimulus, such as food, to produce a natural (unconditional) response, such as salivation. Then a neutral (conditionable) stimulus, such as a tone signal, is presented immediately prior to the natural stimulus. In this example, if an animal can learn to salivate to a specific tone signal which precedes the food, then it is possible to say that the particular tone used lies within the boundaries of the animal's discrimination abilities. Many kinds of sensory discrimination have been tested in this manner.

Another variation on the same method is the one customarily called *instrumental conditioning*, where an animal has to act on the basis of a signal or cue in order to be rewarded or to escape punishment. Failure to perform correctly in the learned response method is sometimes taken as evidence that discrimination is lacking, but predictions based on such negative results are often unwarranted and sometimes incorrect. The animal may actually possess the discrimination ability in question but cannot show the ability by means of its behavior because the experimenter has chosen to condition a response that for some reason conflicts with the animal's normal behavior pattern.

Measurement of Innate or Unlearned Responses

One of the advantages of this method is the ease with which experiments are usually done with respect to both the experimental apparatus and the time required. Another advantage is the greater probability that one will be working within the actual response repertoire of the animal. A common example of this method is the optokinetic response observable in most seeing animals when a field with some sort of articulation, such as stripes, is moved past the eyes of the animal. Usually, if the animal can perceive the changes in the visual field, movements of the eye, head, or whole body may be observed. With this technique, visual acuity, brightness discrimination, color sensitivity, and other visual phenomena have been explored.

Another, and rather dramatic, example of this technique is given by Moericke's (1950) demonstration of negative-color after-image in the peach aphid. He first noted that the peach aphid would make stabbing movements to penetrate the substrate only if it were placed on a green field. So he exposed aphids for some time to a field of purple, a complementary color of green, and then placed them on a neutral gray substrate, whereupon the aphids made penetrating movements, something they would not normally do on a gray substrate.

Differential natural preferences shown by an animal also can be used to indicate the existence of some type of discrimination. For example, chicks and ducks readily peck at nonfood objects, pecking at certain colors more frequently than at others (Hess, 1956). This pecking response was also used as a means of demonstrating that chicks experience color constancy (Gogel & Hess, 1951).

EXPERIMENTAL DETERMINATION OF THE VARIABLES OF SENSORY PROCESSES

We may define stimuli as energy changes that initiate or steer activities of the organism. These energy changes, sometimes extremely small, are received by specialized receptor organs or by unspecialized cells. In single-celled animals, energy-change information goes directly to effectors; in higher animals, it is first relayed to the central nervous system and then to effectors. Reception of stimuli involves the absolute energy level, their temporal duration, and their quality.

Absolute Energy Levels

We have already said that the amount of energy needed to activate a receptor is extremely small. Some receptors have such a low absolute threshold, the energy level at which a receptor will first respond, that it is difficult to imagine how they could be more sensitive and still maintain adequate performance. The absolute threshold is about 10^{-18} watts per second for the human ear or eye (Burkhardt, Schleidt, & Altner, 1967). If they were more sensitive than this, we would have such problems as constant sound produced by Brownian movement of air molecules. The conclusion should not be drawn, however, that man has primary claim to ultimate receptor sensitivity. Some insects can perceive underground vibrations of the same 10^{-18} watts per second energy level, and greater sensitivity would subject them to the cellular vibrations of their own bodies. Butterflies need only a *few* molecules to perceive some scents.

Temporal Energy Durations

In order to say much about minimal stimulus energies, we must introduce the factor of time. A minimal stimulus must endure a certain length of time to cause a reaction. It is also necessary that stimuli endure long enough to be perceived as discrete events. The shortest times that can be perceived as time are quite long. Durations of time shorter than 1/20th of a second usually cannot be separated. For example, flashes of light appear equally long when *equal stimulus energies* are presented to the sense organs. It is impossible to distinguish between stimuli of 5 milliseconds and 40 milliseconds, in terms of duration, when the shorter one is correspondingly eight times more intense. This is a principle known as the Bunsen-Roscoe law: $I \times T = K$, where I = intensity, T = time, and K is a constant. The law does not hold under certain conditions because, while there is a lower limit for the perception of time, there is none for a short stimulus if the intensity is increased to a sufficiently high level. In other words, a flash of light which lasts only a millionth of a second can be seen easily if it is intense enough.

Quality of Energies

Sensory organs are adapted for the reception of specific kinds of energy. However, there is also an optimal range within the stimulus range that can be perceived by any given sense organ. For example, in low-illumination conditions the human eye is more sensitive to 507 millimicron (m μ) light waves than to other parts of the visible spectrum. In other words, one can detect lights of this green wavelength at lower energy levels than would be required for other frequencies of the visual spectrum.

VISION

It has been said that nearly every type of eye imaginable from the engineering viewpoint has been developed by some animal. At the higher levels of development, which include all image-forming eyes, there seems to be no particular improvement of the visual process, except possibly in the primates. Compared to man, birds have better acuity, bees and other insects, such as the Indian luna moth, can see ultraviolet wavelengths, and other insects have faster recoveries from visual stimulation. Even the lens type of eye is not confined to vertebrates but shows up in the invertebrates, although in a somewhat different form, particularly in the cephalopods. A way of demonstrating the extreme diversity of visual organs is by referring to the size of the eye lens in several animal species. In some of the smaller rodents, the lens may be as small as 0.3 millimeters in diameter, compared with the average 16.2 millimeters found in man, while the whale has perhaps the largest of mammalian eyes with a lens diameter of 40 millimeters. Nonetheless, these cannot compare with the tremendous eye of the giant squid, in which the lens has been measured at 300 millimeters, and it may be even larger in some specimens in which actual eye measurements were difficult to obtain.

Among the many different types of eyes that have developed, it is possible to find variations on a single theme. Many retinas have foveas, that is, small depressions which contain densely packed retinal cells, usually exclusively cones, as in the human fovea centralis. This type of fovea increases acuity and sensitivity. Some birds have two foveas, a temporal one that is used in binocular vision, and a central one that is used in monocular vision. While sensitivity can be enhanced through increasing the number of retinal cells, some animals achieve it by means of large pupils and large lenses. For example, the lens of the mouse and opossum fills a much greater proportion of the eye than does the lens in a man's eye. Another phylogenetic trick is the tapetum. This is a kind of reflecting substance in the back of the retina which permits the light to be reflected back through the retina and provides for reception under low-illumination conditions. Nocturnal animals often possess tapeta, and so do raccoons, frogs, and alligators; if a flashlight is shone on any of these animals at night, their eyes seem to glow. Diurnal animals, on the other hand, may have a layer of black pigment to absorb all light so as to prevent "ghost" images.

Accommodation, one of the important mechanisms for perceiving depth, is achieved in fishes, amphibians, and snakes by moving the lens toward and away from the retina; in birds, reptiles other than snakes, and mammals, the lens changes shape. The amount of accommodation varies over a wide range; in man and the domestic chicken, it is about 10 dioptres (a measure of accommodation), whereas, in the cormorant, it is up to 50 dioptres, and in the turtle, as much as 100 dioptres.

The majority of animals having eyes possess two of them. Single eyes are highly unusual in the animal kingdom, although there are two minute crustacean species, one marine and one freshwater, that have cyclopean eyes. Interestingly enough, the marine species is a staple of whale diet and its members are eaten by the millions, so that the number of individuals on the earth must be extremely high. There are several species that have multiple eyes: for example, grasshoppers have two compound eyes and one "simple" eye (ocellus) which acts as a light meter. Bees have three ocelli in addition to two compound eyes, and most spider species have eight eyes. Some spider species have six eyes and a few spider species have none at all.

The pineal body (epiphysis) has long been a mysterious organ. The philosopher Descartes suggested in the seventeenth century that it might be the seat of the soul. In some species it is a third, unpaired eye which is sometimes supplemented by a *pineal complex*. In minnows (*Phoxinus laevus*), it is an efficient eye which is maximally sensitive to 532 mμ. Trout and pike can use it to perceive light when their other eyes are sealed. Some lizards, and the New Zealand tuatara (*Sphenodon punctatum*), a lizardlike reptile closely related to the dinosaurs, also have well-developed pineal eyes with lens and retina. Frogs have a pineal eye concealed under a depigmented spot of skin on the forehead between the lateral eyes; it acts as a photoreceptor capable of discriminating wavelengths.

In lizards, the pineal eye appears to control the body's color changes which occur for camouflage purposes. In these cases, the pineal complex seems to trigger the hormonal changes. However, there are no visual cells whatever in the pineal body of mammals. Instead, it is a gland which secretes hormones. Even so, it is still very much related to light stimulation. It has been demonstrated that female rats acquire lighter epiphyses and more active ovaries under constant light conditions. Changes in the photoperiod can affect organismic rhythm, as has been shown by several investigators. The greater laying activity of hens maintained in constant light conditions is well known to farmers; the increased gonadal activity of migratory birds during the spring is still another example. Recent studies have shown that in the rat, the pineal gland is controlled by sympathetic nerves which are connected to the eye retina via the optic nerve and by basic rhythms of the central nervous system which are endogenous but also cued by changes in environmental illumination. Interestingly enough, the evidence now available indicates that the pineal gland functions to *inhibit* gonadal activity and that environmental light serves to inhibit the pineal body's inhibitory activity (Wurtman & Axelrod, 1965).

Diffuse Light Sensitivity

Many organisms possess a diffuse light sensitivity. This is apparent in a number of unicellular organisms. For example, amoebas react to shade anywhere on the cell by moving faster on their pseudopodia. When light is sufficiently intense, the amoeba stops moving. *Amoebus proteus* moves faster in red light and slower in green light. Hence, it is more sensitive to green than to red.

Other organisms which appear to have only diffuse light sensitivity are coelenterates such as hydras, the sea anemone *Actinaria*, the dahlia anemone *Tealia*, and the sea pen *Pennatula*. The last two open up in darkness and fold up in light. Plumose anemones have been induced to stay open all day by illuminating them with red light to which they are insensitive.

It has been suggested that these diffuse sensitivities, particularly in unicellular animals, are accomplished through the several photochemical processes that have been observed to be activated by light. These processes involve changes in the degree of fluidity and viscosity in the protoplasm, in cell-wall permeability, in fat saponification, in enzyme inhibition or activation, and in hormone secretion. Light-sensitive pigments localized on unicellular or multicellular organisms may intensify these photochemical reactions and may transform the light energy. For example, the unicellular flagellate *Euglena* has from forty to fifty photosensitive orange-red granules (rods) in a mass called the stigma. It is located next to the flagellum and reacts to light by swelling and then causing the flagellum to change the direction in which it beats. Multicellular animals, on the other hand, may have light-sensitive spots over their bodies. Earthworms, for example, have many light-sensitive epithelial cells, located mostly on their ends.

Eye Types

The probable evolution of eyes from simple eyespots containing photosensitive pigments can easily be estimated because such eyespot cells normally are at the surface of the body and contain otherwise transparent protoplasm. The cell membrane, in fact, usually curves outward because of the pressure of the protoplasm against it. This results in light being refracted and concentrated on the pigment. Stages in the evolution of eyes thus can be seen as involving increasing density of protoplasm, thus creating a simple lens. Then the light-sensitive cell splits up into a transparent lens cell on top of a retina cell which holds the pigment. This very simple eye can be found in the free-swimming larval stages of the tunicate sea squirts. Once this separation of lens and retina has occurred, further evolutionary stages appear to involve increasing size and differentiation of cell structure.

The mollusc phylum contains a rather wide spectrum of eye types. The limpet, a sea-dwelling gastropod, for example, has small depressions in its skin which are lined with pigment and retina cells. In more advanced development, the animal has cuplike pits which are partially closed and filled with jelly which is in contact with the water in which the limpit lives. In still further development the cup is covered with a transparent skin. In the snail, the jelly is firmer and has developed into a definite lens which lies on top of the retina cells.

Some cephalopod molluscs have simple eyes, and others, complex eyes. The nautilus has eyes similar to the limpet's, whereas the octopus and squid have highly complicated eyes whose structures have achieved, through convergent evolution, a cameral form rivaling our own. These animals have a lenses, irises, and a perfectly full-fledged retinas.

Bivalve molluscs generally have light-sensitive eyespots. Scallops, however, have about a hundred prominent eyespots on the body edge just inside the shells, each having a lens and retina. In still other mollusc species, the eyes are bunched together to form light-sensitive compound eyes. The arthropod insects often possess both *ocelli* (the "simple" eyes mentioned earlier) and compound eyes. The ocelli are called simple eyes so as to distinguish them from the compound eyes. However, their structure is usually fairly complex: Their lens is formed by either thick cuticle cells or by transparent cells derived from cuticle-forming cells, and they have photosensitive, pigmented retinas supplied with nerve endings. While some ocelli, as in grasshoppers and bees, serve only to detect light intensity, others can give a clear image from at least a short distance, as in stalking spiders.

The compound eyes, however, are constructed of many very small elongated "cameras," called *ommatidia*, which are clustered tightly together. The individual lenses are all arranged together under a hemispherical covering layer, while the ends of the ommatidial cameras are supplied with nerve fibers. Each ommatidial tube is lined with pigment cells which prevent light from passing obliquely from one tube to another. Some insects even have a fine network of air tubes which surround individual ommatidia and reflect light out of the eye. The effects of this function can be seen in moths' eyes, which glow when a light is shone on them. The ommatidia do not produce thousands of separate complete pictures as would be expected if each tube worked on the pinhole principle, nor do they result in a strictly mosaic picture as would be expected if each tube transmitted only rays which had an axis identical to its own. Microelectrode recordings have shown that individual ommatidia can respond to light rays from a 6 to 10 degree visual angle in the blowfly, depending upon the central or peripheral location of the ommatidium. In locust eyes it has been shown that the angle of acceptance depends upon light- or dark-adaptation, for it is 3.0 to 3.5 degrees and 6.0 to 6.5 degrees for the respective conditions (see Figure 10-1). In recent years, the nature of image formation by insect ommatidia has become controversial, with the suggestion that ommatidial lenses act as a diffraction-grating system receiving considerable debate. (Bernhard, 1966)

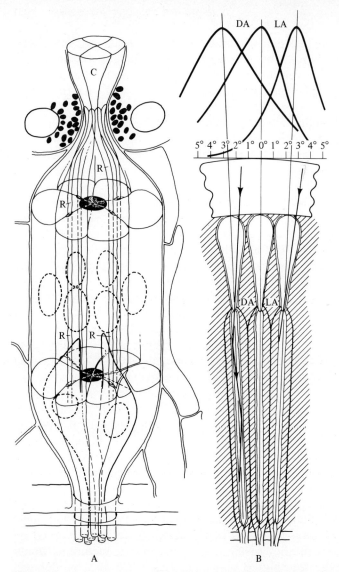

A   B

Figure 10–1. *(A)* Structure of *Locusta migratoria* ommatidia. The roots (R) of the cone (C) spread around the rhabdom. The rhabdom in this case is composed of the rhabdomeres of six retinula cells. Two basal retinula cells are shown without rhabdomeres. (B) Diagram showing the light pathways into retinula cells of adjacent ommatidia and Gaussian response curves for light rays coming from different angles, as determined by microelectrode recordings. The left half of (B) shows responses during dark adaptation while the right half of (B) shows responses during light adaptation. The retinula cells belonging to the same ommatidium usually have the same axis, presumably because rhabdomeres are fused together within the ommatidia. (From G. A. Horridge, The retina of the locust. In *The functional organization of the compound eye,* C. G. Bernhard, Ed. Oxford, England: Pergamon Press, 1966. Pp. 513–541.)

Very few animals do, in fact, use the pinhole method to form images, and the nautilus is one of the exceptions. The reason is that the images formed in this way are not very bright.

Even a camera eye can be found among arthropods: the horseshoe crab possesses, in addition to compound eyes, a third eye that consists of a pair of very closely placed, minute camera eyes that function solely for the reception of ultraviolet light.

Sensitivity to Polarized Light

Although sensitivity to polarized light is not very common, there are indications that it does exist in a number of animals, including wasps, bumblebees, ants, flies, caterpillars, beetles, water striders, water fleas, funnel-spiders, squid, and octopus. The most famous work in this area was done by von Frisch (1949), who discovered that bees could see polarized light in the sky and use it as a means of orientation. With only a patch of blue sky visible, bees can tell where the sun is by means of the polarized light from the patch. The only higher animals that have been demonstrated to have polarized light vision are some of the large wading birds, such as herons. In the latter case, the mechanisms may simply be used for killing glare on the shallow water in which they wade, thereby making it easier to see the prey in the water and to seize it. The effect is like our wearing polarizing sunglasses when we are in areas of high reflection or our using polarizing filters to photograph objects in water.

Brightness Discrimination

Brightness discrimination is probably the most universal visual response in the entire phylogenetic scale. Most organisms down to the protozoans have been found to possess it, and some quantitative work has been done, particularly with marine invertebrates, to determine its extent. One can say that there is no essential improvement in brightness discrimination as one progresses in the phylogenetic scale, and that variations in discrimination ability more likely represent inadequate measuring techniques.

Visual Acuity

Experimental investigation of visual acuity has often been carried out by means of the optomotor method, although a number of training techniques have also been used. Many animals at the higher vertebrate levels show essentially small variation in their ability to discern small stimuli (Walls, 1942). The visual angle is measured in terms of minutes and seconds of arc (60 seconds equal 1 minute, and 60 minutes equal 1 degree). The visual angle that can be discriminated by man is usually reported as about 64 seconds, by the chimpanzee as 47 seconds, and by the rhesus monkey as 67 seconds. Under higher illumination conditions, 35 to 40 seconds have been reported for man (Keesey, 1960; Shlaer, 1937). Fantz (1965) has reported that the newly born human infant can see 44 minutes; two-month-old infants, 40 minutes; four-month-old infants, 20 minutes; and six-month-old infants, 10 minutes. Actually, man is not near the peak of ability in visual acuity. Most birds have an acuity four to five times greater than that of man. On the other hand, the visual acuity of many invertebrates is rather less, due mainly to the eye types they possess. Lower vertebrates have poorer visual acuity than the higher ones, apparently because of the smaller number of sensory receptors per unit area in their eyes. Most nocturnal animals have poorer acuity. For example, the cat can see 5.5 minutes, the alligator, 11 minutes, the opossum, 11 minutes, the rat, 26 minutes, and the white rat, 52 minutes.

Form Vision

Form vision is undoubtedly absent in many of the lower invertebrates simply because their sense organs do not produce images. An exception may be the form vision possible in some insects possessing faceted eyes which appear to be capable of discriminating at least certain types of forms in the "mosaic" vision involved. For example, bees can be trained to discriminate a five-rayed star from a square or a circle. However, this may not necessarily be form vision per se but may be based on the amount of flicker produced in the faceted eye, which would be greater for the more highly articulated star. Jumping spiders, which have an intricate courtship dance, may have form vision. Among other invertebrates, probably only the octopus and squid have some degree of form vision.

The eye is relatively the same in all vertebrate species and form vision has been demonstrated from fish to primates. While some investigators have denied that form discrimination per se exists in lower vertebrates, the question may be merely a semantic one. For example, Bingham (1922) insisted that the ability to discriminate a circle from a triangle does not at all require the conclusion that an animal possesses form vision but only that it can perceive differences in detail. In other words, the animal need not have the concept of triangularity or of circularity as such to make these discriminations.

But then again, the methodology used for testing form discrimination can affect the ability of animals to make this type of discrimination. For example, many years ago it was thought that white rats could not discriminate form. But Lashley (1938), using his jumping stand technique, easily trained rats to make discriminations which were certainly in line with what is considered form vision in human discrimination experiments. The cat has also been accused of having poor form vision, but Sperry and his coworkers (Sperry, Miner, & Meyers, 1955) taught cats to discriminate between patterns which varied so slightly that the conclusion must be drawn that the cat certainly does have form vision.

Depth Perception

Stereoscopic vision can be achieved only through two eyes having overlapping fields of vision. But this is not in itself a sufficient condition for depth perception. The two eyes must focus and move in concert *and* send neural impulses which are integrated together in the brain.

The presence or absence of stereoscopic vision in a species is generally rather highly related to its life style. Predatory animals, such as man, cats, wolves, and owls, need to be able to judge distance precisely in order to catch their prey. Animals that leap or swing between tree branches—squirrels, primates—also need depth perception in order to navigate properly. Tool-using or such actions as picking food up with the paws for transport to the mouth usually involve depth perception.

But the eyes of prey animals such as rabbits, cows, deer, or other ungulates usually are set at the sides of their heads so as to provide a maximally panoramic view and thus best to warn the animal of the impending approach of a predator. Of course, many of these species also utilize an extremely strong sense of smell to detect the presence of predators. Some animals are both prey and predators and may have a small degree of stereoscopic vision as well as a relatively panoramic range. Chickens are an example of this type of arrangement: they are subject to predators such as hawks and man, and they in turn prey upon worms and insects.

Color Vision

Of all the visual processes studied in animals, color vision has attracted the most attention from investigators. Even the lay public is fascinated by the question of color vision, as demonstrated by perennial articles in hunting and fishing magazines on whether fish are color blind or whether bulls really see red. However, there is indeed a great deal of evidence that there is color vision in at least some animals throughout the animal kingdom. Training techniques have tested almost all higher vertebrates and some of the higher invertebrates, such as cephalopods, molluscs, and insects, for color vision.

In the last two decades, electrophysiological methods of studying color vision have become increasingly significant. Electroretinograms and microelectrode recordings have become extremely sophisticated, dealing even with single retinal cells. As shown by the rainbow spectrum formed by the passage of light through prisms or raindrops, light is composed of many different wavelengths from the long red ones at one end of the spectrum through the progressively shorter ones to the short violet ones at the other end. Color perception begins with the reception of the particular wavelengths out of the many that are reflected back from objects to the eye. The studies of single retinal cells have shown that throughout the animal kingdom, where there are eyes that can see color, there are usually at least three different types of visual cells maximally sensitive to different wavelengths. These visual cells thus work on a three-color principle much as a television picture tube does. However, the neural information sent from these visual cells to higher visual centers is actually a two-color system consisting of on-off signals. Figure 10-2 depicts three-pigment sensitivity in a goldfish retina.

To date, the retinal visual pigments have been found to be most sensitive to the 500- to 540-mμ region of the visible spectrum and to be secondarily sensitive to 360 mμ, ultraviolet. The retinas of diurnal vertebrates, however, do not receive the ultraviolet wavelengths because the lens and the vitreous liquid in the eye completely absorb incidental environmental ultraviolet as well as infrared wavelengths (Kennedy & Milkman, 1971; Zigman, 1971). Looking directly at the sun or prolonged exposure to intensely lit snow or an ultraviolet lamp or sunlamp, however, provides more infrared or ultraviolet rays than can be absorbed, and "snowblindness" or irreversible damage to the retina can occur. Insects (including bees), frogs, toads, and fish do see ultraviolet, however, and probably as a color. Humans who have had their eye lens removed, usually for a cataract operation, are known as *aphakics*. They can see ultraviolet radiation and are able to read an optical chart in 365 mμ illumination. Such people have helped us to understand the nature of insect color vision in the ultraviolet region. Of course, they get retinitis casily and have to wear glasses to absorb ultraviolet.

Outside of ultraviolet, humans have absorption maxima at 430, 540 and 575 mμ; rhesus monkeys at 447, 540, and 575 mμ; goldfish at 455, 530, and 625 mμ (as shown in Figure 10–2); and bees at 430, 470, and 540 mμ. Flies have a maximum at 490 mμ and a few individuals also have a maxima at 470 and 520 mμ. These retinal maxima, of course, do not necessarily mean that the animal in question sees each one of these wavelengths well enough to utilize it in a behavior-training situation. Many species see only one or two colors well enough to be useful in this kind of situation.

Many other ways of studying color vision have been used. Innate movement response is one which we have already discussed, an example being the optokinetic nystagmus reflex in the eye in response to movements. In this case, an animal is placed inside a hollow, revolving cylinder whose walls are painted in colored stripes interspaced with gray stripes; if the animal sees the color as color and different from the matched shade of gray, its eyes will make the nystagmus movements as the cylinder revolves. And, of course, the natural behavior of animals in relation to color may be used as a basis for indicating the presence of color vision. For example, if an animal changes its color to adapt to the particular background on which it is resting, as do

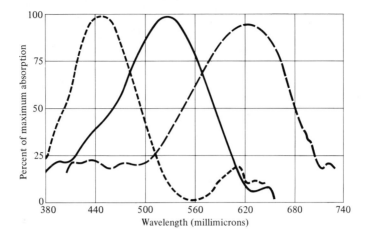

Figure 10–2. An example of the 3-pigment retinal cone sensitivity as found in a species that can see color. This graph depicts data obtained by W. B. Marks who used the method of difference spectra on goldfish. (After Edward F. MacNichol, Jr., Three-pigment color vision. *Scientific American*, 1964, *211*, No. **6**, 48–56. © 1964 by Scientific American, Inc. All rights reserved.)

certain fishes, crustaceans, and cephalopods, its color vision may be tested by systematically varying the color of the background and then observing the action of its chromatophores. Also, if the colors on an animal are used for courtship purposes, it is likely that that species possesses good color vision.

Although the biological meaning of color vision is quite clear when we consider an animal, such as the bee, which is dependent on flowers for its food supply, there is some question regarding its biological usefulness in many other species. In various flies, frogs, or turtles, it is not so easy to recognize the biological utility of a well-developed color sense. The general distribution of color vision is limited principally to vertebrates; among invertebrates, only arthropods and cephalopods seem to have a color sense.

Color Vision in Insects

Color vision in insects is very widespread, but there is no apparent correlation between the biology and behavior of the animals and the presence or absence of color vision. For instance, some insects which visit flower blossoms may be color-blind, while some insects, feeding for example on dung, may be quite capable of good color discrimination.

One of the classic arguments in the extensive literature of the past in color vision was whether color vision exists in bees. Von Frisch (1915), however, demonstrated color sense in bees beyond any doubt through the so-called checkerboard technique, which has been used since then for insects other than bees. On the whole, color vision in insects is not a matter of clearly discriminating between a number of colors but of discriminating between groups of colors. Most insects perceive two color groups, and bees discriminate four.

Some electrophysiological work has also been done in color vision of insects. Autrum and Stumpf (1953) used the method of color-flicker photometry and concluded that there were at least three different kinds of color receptors in the insect eyes investigated. Tsuneki (1953) reported that two species of ants showed discrimination, or at least relative sensitivity to various monochromatic lights, but he was unable to find any evidence of color learning in these species. He suggested that the results indicated that the ant has color vision but cannot associate color with any of the particular behaviors in which it engages. This is a problem in much of the color discrimination research involving animals.

Color Vision in Molluscs

We know almost nothing of the color senses of snails and most other molluscs, but have information regarding the color vision of cephalopods. Kühn (1950) investigated the color vision of squids by means of training techniques, using the association of color with punishment. By this means he demonstrated color vision not only in squids, but also in the cuttlefish *Sepia*, since this animal's chromatophores change color upon exposure to various substrates of different colors. However, work by other investigators with the octopus has been inconsistent (Wells, 1961).

Color Vision in Vertebrates

As we have already indicated earlier in this chapter, the vertebrate eye is characterized by two different kinds of light receptors. The more sensitive elements are the rods, while the cones are assumed to mediate color vision. Among the many vertebrate animal species, there are cone retinas, rod retinas, and mixtures of both. The mixtures are the most common. The *duplicity* theory of color vision, which was formulated by von Kries in 1896, postulated that rod retinas are used primarily by animals that are nocturnal and that cones are used for color vision; therefore, cones would be essentially the property of diurnal animals. One argument for the duplicity theory is the *Purkinje effect*, that is, the difference in the apparent brightness of the different spectral colors under conditions of bright and of dim illumination in the environment. A shift in maximal apparent brightness toward the shorter wavelength colors of the spectrum under conditions of low environmental illumination can be explained only in terms of two different receptor systems which operate under these two illumination conditions.

The Purkinje phenomenon has been demonstrated to exist not only in humans but also in a number of lower animal forms. It has been found in fish, frogs, the alligator, various birds, and a number of mammals. Where it does appear to be missing is in animal species that seem to have only one type of receptor in their visual systems. Von Frisch (1925) was able to show that, in fish, there is an actual movement or migration of some of the sensitive cells and pigment in the retina which allows for light and dark adaptation and in which conditions he could histologically recognize rods and cones. He was able to show that a color discrimination which a fish had readily learned could not be manifested by the fish when, because of a lower illumination level, its cones had moved away from the retinal plane and its rods had taken over. This is just one example of the many complexities of color vision as found in all vertebrates.

Actually, the capacity of fishes to see color had been doubted for several decades. Contributing to this belief was the general assumption that colors lost their quality in water. In other words, it was believed that fish in even a reasonably shallow depth would be unable to see color since red and yellow wavelengths are rather completely absorbed and as a result colors change into a kind of greenish monochrome. However, experimental findings show that down to a depth of 100 meters there is reasonable opportunity for the fish to discriminate color.

A number of similarities have been found between the vision of fish and of man. For example, the law of complementarity is demonstrable at the fish level and there is also simultaneous color contrast. Color vision is most highly developed in the telcost fish, and is probably absent only in those that are primarily nocturnal and depend to a greater degree on chemical sensitivity than on visual recognition of food objects. Trichromaticity is also present. For example, Yager (1967) used behavioral measures to determine that goldfish *(Carassius auratus)* are sensitive to wavelengths between 401 and 755 mμ and concluded that they have trichromatic vision. This concords with the physiological data shown in Figure 10-2.

The color vision of amphibians was early studied by Babák (1913), who investigated the changes in breathing rhythms of a frog under the influence of various color illuminations. Experimental procedures involving discrimination learning were carried out much later by a number of investigators, mainly by means of optomotor and electrophysiological techniques. These methods showed that the frog *Rana temporaria* could differentiate red from blue but not green from yellow. Granit's (1941) later results, however, indicated that the frog's color-vision system really is similar to the human's, a result which was not concordant with the earlier conclusions. Birukow (1949, 1950) has since shown that both *Rana* and *Hyla* species possess well-developed color-vision systems, and the work of Thomas (1955) has confirmed this.

Color vision seems to be present in those reptiles which have been investigated, with the exception of species that are essentially nocturnal. For example, true lizards and salamanders see color quite well, and can see at least eight hues. Chameleons and geckos can change their body color to blend in with the environment; since this response is mediated through their eyes, they obviously can see colors. Iguanas can see at least four hues.

The microelectrode technique has demonstrated retinal sensitivity for green and red wavelengths in snakes. Training techniques have been used very little (if at all) in snakes, but they have been used with turtles. Wojtusiak (1933) has shown that turtles possess good color vision, with perception of at least five discriminable hues, including infrared.

All diurnal birds seem to have a highly developed color-vision sense. In general, they are quite well endowed with retinal cones, some species having so many cones that they are nearly blind at night.

There is very little question that the color sensitivity of mammals compared with other vertebrates' is rather poor. One possible reason is that many mammals are primarily nocturnal and depend, to a greater extent than most vertebrates, on their sense of smell. A really well-developed color sense is found mostly among primates and humans. Several primate species have been studied for color vision: baboons, cebus, macaques, guenons, wooly monkeys, spider monkeys, squirrel monkeys, marmosets, sooty mangabeys, tree shrews (whose classification as a primate has been controversial), and probably several others. Platyrrhine monkeys of the *Cebus* and *Ateles* species lack red vision and are very much like human protanopes, while the Catarrhine monkeys, rhesus monkeys, baboon, and chimpanzee, though possessing a very good color vision, are slightly weak in red vision and thus are protanomalous, as some humans are. Trendelenburg and Schmidt (1930) found that the retinal wavelength sensitivity patterns of *Macacus mulatta* (rhesus) and of *Pithecus fascicularis* monkeys are almost identical with those of the normal human: the major maxima were at 589 and 490 mμ, as reported for humans, and the minor maxima were at 535 mμ, in comparison with the human's at 540 mμ.

Rodents in general are definitely deficient in color vision. This statement includes rats, mice, and rabbits. Among the sciurids, however, the retinas have been found to be composed entirely of cones that are actually modified rods. Members of this family include the gray squirrels, the suslik and antelope ground squirrels, chipmunks, prairie dogs, and tree squirrels. Electroretinograms have detected good color sensitivity in the retinas of these species. On the behavioral side, antelope ground squirrels, tree squirrels, and prairie dogs have all been trained to discriminate stimuli on a wavelength basis (Cain & Carlson, 1968; Crescitelli & Pollack, 1965; Michaels & Schumacher, 1968). In most instances the color vision of diurnal birds appears to be quite similar to that of man, although their sensitivity is less at the short-wavelength (violet and blue) end of the spectrum than it is at the long-wavelength (red) end.

Among other nonprimate mammals, horses (Grzimek, 1952), zebras (Hoffmann, 1952), and pigs (Klopfer, 1966) have shown clean-cut behavioral evidence of color vision. The pig, for example, was found to be sensitive from below 420 to 680 mμ by means of color-discrimination training techniques involving food reward (Klopfer, 1966). The photopic maximal sensitivity peak was found by these methods to be at approximately 550 to 575 mμ, with a minor peak at 465 mμ. They were slightly better in blue than humans are while their red sensitivity was found to be the same as the human's. This is somewhat similar to the sensitivity of the sooty mangabey, which has been found to be a bit better in blue than humans, but not quite so good in red as humans (Adams & Jones, 1967).

The question of color vision in cats, dogs, and guinea pigs has been conflicting and controversial. In fact, the color vision of cats is a problem that has generated a great deal of heated scientific controversy. There has been no question that the cat has perfectly good, though relatively sparsely distributed, color receptors in its retina (Glickstein & Labossiere, 1968; Ingvar, 1959; Walls, 1942). Electrophysiological techniques, furthermore, have demonstrated a clean-cut differential wavelength sensitivity at the retinal level with a maximum peak at 450 to 470 mμ, an intermediate peak at 550 mμ, and a small peak at 610 mμ (Ingvar, 1959). The cat retina, furthermore, shows the Purkinje shift, according to the electrophysiological evidence (Barlow, Fitzhugh, & Kuffler, 1957; Granit, 1943). Yet, for the first half of this century, behavioral techniques failed to show any evidence of color-discrimination ability in cats (e.g., Deross & Ganson, 1915; Gunter, 1954; Meyer, Miles, & Ratoosh, 1954). In more recent years, however, improved methodology has obtained evidence supporting the opposite conclusion. Buchholtz (1952), using the reward of allowing cats to play with a colored model which was moved by the experimenter, found that they were able to discriminate this colored model from any of a large series of neutral gray models. Behavioral data obtained from other training techniques by Sechzer and Brown (1962), Mello and Peterson (1964), Meyer and Anderson (1965) and Clayton and Kamback (1966) have shown that the cat does in fact possess color vision. The principal problem that remains is the assessment of the relative difficulty of color discrimination for cats, and this is the area in which there is still considerable controversy. Most investigators have concluded that brightness and pattern discrimination are easier for the cat than color discrimination (Bonaventure, 1962, 1964). Bonaventure (1962), for example, suggested that cats could see only red; Clayton and Kamback (1966), on the other hand, obtained evidence that cats can successfully discriminate between red, blue, green, and gray, and between yellow, blue, and gray. Mello's (1968) work has shown that cats in discrimination-learning experiments tend to treat color as an irrelevant factor in comparison with intensity unless they receive specific training to discriminate between two different wavelengths. With this kind of specific training, color-discrimination problems did not appear to be uniquely difficult for the cats to solve. This finding is extremely interesting in the light of the low number of cone receptors in their retinas.

INFRARED AND HEAT RECEPTION

Infrared radiation lies just outside the visible-light portion of the electromagnetic spectrum. The radiant heat from infrared is generally diffusely sensed all over the body by means of the warm-sensitive cells located on the surface. There are, however, two kinds of snakes that possess extremely efficient, localized, and sensitive receptors for infrared (Bullock & Cowles, 1952; Bullock & Diecke, 1956; Burkhardt, 1964). These are the *Crotalidae* (rattlesnake) and *Pytonidae* snakes, which use these receptors, called *pit organs*, to localize the position of prey. These pit organs are bilaterally placed on the snake's head and are capable of a degree of depth perception that enables the snake to strike precisely at its prey. Functioning much like eyes, each pit organ contains a richly enervated curved membrane that has a reception threshold low enough to detect a mouse 15 centimeters away involving a temperature rise of only .003°C at the membrane. The pit organs work upon thermal perception mechanisms and not through wavelength-dependent photochemical reactions (Harris & Gamow, 1971).

Night moths (Callahan, 1964) also possess efficient infrared sensitive receptors which are reportedly used by males to find females. Mosquitoes, bedbugs, and body lice are also highly sensitive to extremely small temperature changes which enable them to locate prey from a distance of several feet. Herter (1962) has reported that the mosquito is sensitive to a temperature difference of as little as .002°C. These capabilities in perceiving the source of radiant heat are truly amazing when compared with our own. We are generally limited to being able to tell which side of our bodies the sun is shining on or at which end of a drafty room a hot radiator or fire is located. Our ability to perceive radiant heat is something like the earthworm's ability to see light, and the rattlesnake's and the mosquito's ability to perceive radiant heat is about as keen as our ability to see light!

Other temperature perception appears to be based upon the heat-exchange principle. That is, when there is direct contact with another object, the flow of heat between the object and the sensor is the basis for perception. The temperature sense of fish is generally very well developed. They are able to react to .02°C water-temperature differences. Not only does this enable them to remain in waters of the proper temperature, but it apparently serves to guide some species of migratory fish.

Several animals, unlike man, possess an absolute temperature sense which is behaviorally evident. The incubator bird, also known as the Australian brush turkey (*Leopoa ocellata*), has become deservedly famous for its construction of an incubator for its eggs and its maintenance of the interior temperature of the incubator at precisely 33°C regardless of the external environmental conditions. Every few minutes the bird tests the internal temperature by taking sand from the interior and putting it in its oral cavity. After the test, the bird takes whatever action is necessary to keep the temperature at 33°C.

While the incubator bird is genetically programmed for this particular temperature, rodents, bees, and fish can be trained to pick a specific temperature, such as 19.4°C, in a choice situation, regardless of whether they have been in cold or warm adaptation previous to a specific trial. In contrast, human beings have failed to show any behavioral evidence of having an absolute temperature sense of this sort as a result of training.

Human beings, however, like most other mammals, do have a highly precise physiological response to temperature. This is the thermostat system which maintains the entire body temperature at a relatively constant temperature of 37.1°C. This thermostat system is sensitive to as little as .01°C changes in blood temperature. Cold-blooded animals, nevertheless, can construct precise and elaborate thermostat systems by means of collective effort. Bees are able to maintain the temperature of their hive at 35°C summer and winter; termites in Africa maintain their colony at 30°C by means of an elaborately constructed air-conditioning system which is constantly manipulated in order to keep the internal temperature constant.

PAIN

Although the sense of pain is universal in the human species, lacking only in very abnormal individuals, its presence in other animals is much more difficult to define clearly, since animals cannot report their subjective experiences. However, there are several species in which the behavioral reaction to a stimulus that is painful to human beings is highly similar to that given by humans, and it does not seem to be mere anthropomorphism to ascribe the sense of pain to these creatures. Dogs, cats, some ungulates, and birds make noises and motor movements which appear highly analogous, if not homologous, to those made by man. Lower vertebrates, such as fish and lizards, are normally silent creatures, so their reactions to such stimuli are confined to motor actions. In such cases it would also seem that pain perception is present. Among invertebrates, the squid shows evidence of being able to perceive and localize the application point of a painful stimulus. But among most other animals, the perception of pain appears to be lacking, since their reactions, as exemplified by insects, are very similar to those of vertebrates whose neural pathways have been severed or damaged in order to prevent the sensation of pain from being received.

TOUCH AND PROPRIOCEPTION

Proprioception and touch are senses that exist practically universally in the animal kingdom. When one-celled organisms are observed under a microscope, they can be seen to respond to a touch from a very fine wire. Colonies of one-celled animals readily spread one member's reaction to such a stimulus to all the other members. Multicellular organisms, of course, will also respond to a touch stimulus of this sort.

Many animal species use touch as a means of getting information about the environment, often with the aid of antennae or "whiskers." In addition, fine touch reactions frequently serve as a means of hunting prey or, alternately, of avoiding predation. A fly, for example, may move only one hair on our body for us to be aware of its presence. Our fingers can detect extremely small differences in size, and observations have shown that the behavior of many other animals can be governed by minute size differences or by touch from very small and lightweight particles.

Even so, and in spite of the vital importance of touch reception in the lives of many species, it has not yet been found that the tactile sense of any animal is as sensitive as are the visual and auditory senses. The minimum energy needed to excite a touch receptor is at least 100,000,000 times that needed to excite a visual or an auditory receptor.

Proprioception, important in locomotion—flying, walking, crawling, swimming, and so on, refers to the sense of gravity and balance. It is usually a form of the tactile sense. This is because a balance organ normally consists of an enclosed cavity having a number of sensory hair cells which are touched either by a small stone kept in the cavity or by the movement of fluid within the cavity. Thus, when the position of the balance organ is altered relative to the line of gravity, the small stone shifts its position and touches sensory hair cells. The pattern of tactile stimulation thus received by the sensory hair cells furnishes information regarding the organism's body position. This statocyst system is used in the vertebrate phyla and even in invertebrates such as worms, molluscs, and jellyfish. The semicircular canals of the mammalian inner ear are a highly refined version of the statocyst (see Figure 10-3).

While some arthropods, such as crayfish, also use the statocyst type of balance organ, insects have sensory hair pads on limb joints which are exposed to the air and react directly to gravity. The pattern of stimulation from the sensory hairs on the different body locations thus indicates the position in relation to the force of gravity (see Figure 10-4).

VIBRATION AND AUDITION

At one time it was the practice to attribute sound sensitivity only to animal species that had receptive structures homologous to the human ear. Actually, hearing is properly defined as the awareness of vibrations in an elastic medium, and a sound that is airborne is not qualitatively different from one that is waterborne or earthborne. Reactions to vibration are observable in a very large portion of the animal kingdom. In many cases, these reactions are rather

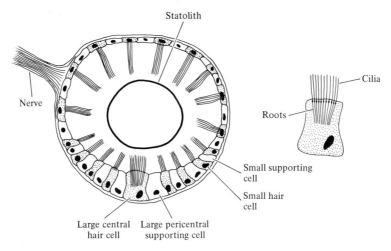

Statolith

Nerve

Cilia

Roots

Small supporting cell

Small hair cell

Large central hair cell   Large pericentral supporting cell

Figure 10–3. Simple molluscan statocyst model. When the small round stone, the statolith, rests on certain sensory hairs the nerve impulses from their cells indicate bodily balance. But when sensory hairs elsewhere are touched the cells are stimulated to transmit imbalance to the nervous system, thus causing the animal to attempt to correct its bodily imbalance. (After Sergei Tsachotin, Die Statocyste der Heteropoden. *Zeitschrift für Wissenschaftliche Zoologie,* 1908, **90**, 343–422; and V. C. Barber, The structure of mollusc statocysts, with particular reference to cephalopods. In J. D. Carthy and G. E. Newell (Eds.), *Invertebrate receptors. Symposium of the Zoological Society of London,* 1968, **23**, 37–62.

closely allied to touch receptors. Vibration is, in a sense, *repeated* touch. For example, ordinary earthworms demonstrate an extreme sensitivity to vibration transmitted by the ground. They react not only to our footsteps but also to a tuning fork held lightly against the substrate. Spiders react to the vibrations of their webs when a prey falls into them. Caterpillars respond to vibration of the plants upon which they feed. Female fiddler crabs are sensitive to the rappings of the male upon the ground. Many animals are very much more sensitive to substrate vibration than humans are, with the result that we have not been properly aware of its significance in the animal world. Folklore, however, has credited cats, dogs, and horses with being able to presage earthquakes and volcanic eruptions, and a German zoologist, Ernst Kilian (1964), believes that this may be accomplished through sensitivity to a certain vibration pattern of advance tremors. There are, of course, other things that could possibly be involved, such as magnetic changes, or barometric air pressure.

The balance organ, which we have just discussed in connection with proprioception, appears to have served, very long ago in the course of evolution, as the forerunner of the auditory organ. The oldest vertebrates, Devonian

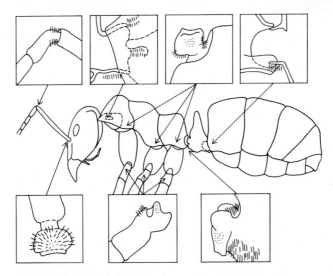

Figure 10–4. All of the red ant's joints have small sensory hair pads as shown by the enlargements of the schematic diagram. The greater the deflection of any part of its body from the normal orientation with respect to gravity, the more the hairs on the pads bend, generating signals regarding the relative position of that body part. (From Hubert Markl, Wie orientierung sich Ameisen nach der Schwerkraft? *Umschau,* 1965, **65,** 185–188.)

ostracoderms, had balance organs in the form of bone whorls which resembled semicircular canals. This early balance organ exists today in a tiny jellyfish, *Obelia*.

The early fish that possessed the ancestral balance organ could not, of course, hear with it. But later fish, as well as some species today, developed air bladders which were able to expand and contract when subjected to sound waves in the water. When the air bladders moved thusly, they in turn moved the fish's body fluids. The movement of body fluids then stimulated the fish's inner ear–balance organ. Thus the ancient air bladders, like those of today, served a function much like that of the mammalian eardrum.

When amphibians arose, the inner ear–balance organ developed a projection which enabled the animal to hear in the air, since this medium is poorer for conducting sound waves than water is. This projection became the straight lagena of reptiles, the slightly curved cochlea (also called the lagena) of birds, and the spiraled cochlea in mammals. In all these species, the inner ear serves for both balance and hearing. The middle ear, on the other hand, evolved from certain fish gill slits, and the three Weberian ossicles, the moving bones in the middle ear (malleus, incus, and stapes), evolved from the fish's jawbone. This evolutionary progression, visible in the frog, explains why contemporary fish have several jawbones while mammals have only one. The fish jawbones, furthermore, do play a role in audition. They are connected to the air bladder, from which they transmit sound waves to the inner ear–balance organ. In amphibians and birds, one of the jawbone ossicles has evolved into the *columella*, the forerunner of the mammalian stapes. In air-hearing reptiles, the columella is formed from two bones.

Interestingly, fish demonstrate still another link between the tactile sense and hearing in addition to that found in the inner ear. This is the *lateral line*, which is possessed by all fish and by many aquatic species, such as the African clawed frog (*Xenopus laevis*). The lateral line has developed from hair cells (sensilla) and nerves of the same type as found in the inner ear. The lateral line, principally a tactile organ, typically consists of a series of sensory hair cells placed in a longitudinal line along the body axis. The tactile function of the lateral line is to sense the movements of the water about the body. Thus it can serve to detect distant water disturbances made by prey, predators, or other species members. Precise formation in fish schools is possible through the lateral line organ as well as through other sensory systems.

Furthermore, the lateral line is also sensitive to lower auditory frequencies, principally in the region of 20 to 200 or 300 cycles per second (Hz). Figure 10-5 depicts the lateral line system of the killifish.

Auditory Reception in Insects

Insects have been the most investigated of the arthropods for auditory processes. Not only are they sensitive to airborne sounds, but some of them employ ultrasonic frequencies for communication.

There are two different types of receptor organs involved: one comparatively simple type for low frequencies, and another, more elaborate type for communication at high-frequency levels. The simpler organ is composed of *hair sensilla*. On the base of each hair rests a dendrite of a sense cell. The hair and the cell together form a unit that has a remarkably low threshold. Using an oscillator as a stimulus and an oscillograph to record nerve impulses, Pumphrey (1940) investigated the hair sensilla of the cricket, cockroach, and locust. He was able to show that the sensilla are so sensitive to air currents that the ever present neural activity is likely caused by excitation of the end organs by Brownian movements of molecules. Minnich (1936), by watching the innate reaction to sound, decided that the upper frequency limit for the hairy caterpillars of the *Vanessa antiopa* butterfly is about 1,000 cycles per second, while the lower limit extends below 32 cycles per second.

The second type of receptor is usually called the *tympanic organ*. Unlike the hair sensilla, it is limited to a few species. Anatomically, it may be located in different places: it may occur in the thorax, as in the grasshopper, in the legs, as in the cricket, or at wing bases, as in butterflies and moths. Whatever its location, it is essentially of the same morphological nature. Typically, there are paired slits in the exoskeleton; the cavity behind each slit forms the tympanal duct, and each cavity ends on a thin membrane which functions in much the same way as the human eardrum. On the inner side of the membrane is an air sac, with the effect that the membrane can act as a lever. One end of the membrane is anchored to the exoskeleton, and the other is fastened to the so-called chordotonal organ. The latter generally consists of a distal cell with one end attached to the tympanum and the other surrounding the

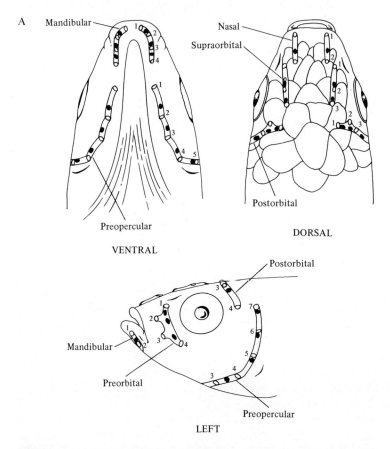

Figure 10–5. (A) Arrangement of lateral line canals on the head of the killifish, *Fundulus heteroclitus,* from three views. The black spots represent the loci of the sensory receptors within the canals. The numerals at the pore-openings indicate the overlap between the three views. (B) Cross section of supraorbital lateral line canal. The axis C-C' is the site of the section shown in (C). (C) Longitudinal section of a portion of supraorbital lateral line canal. The axis B-B' is the site of the section shown in (B). (From: Willem A. van Bergeijk and Susan Alexander, Lateral line organs on the head of *Fundulus heteroclitus. Journal of Morphology* 1962, **110,** 333–346.)

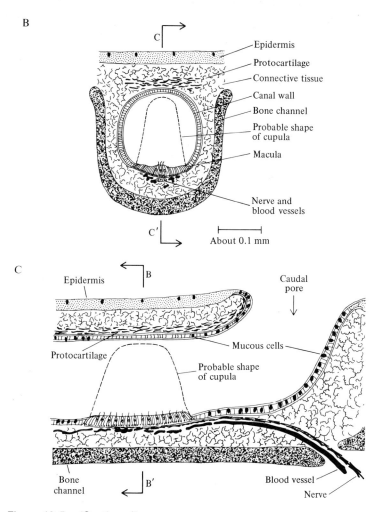

Figure 10–5. (Continued)

sense cells. Relative movements between the distal and sense cells serve to stimulate the latter. See Figure 10-6 for a typical tympanic organ.

The frequency range of tympanic organs in insects differs from species to species, but in all cases it is high and its upper limit is usually always beyond the boundaries of human hearing. Noctuidae, night-flying moths subject to predation by bats, for example, hear up to 150,000 cycles per second (Roeder & Treat, 1961). The threshold for intensity is low; in the Acridiidae it is not much higher, at 10,000 cycles per second, than it is in man. The tympanic pits act as localizers so that localization in space is also reasonably good.

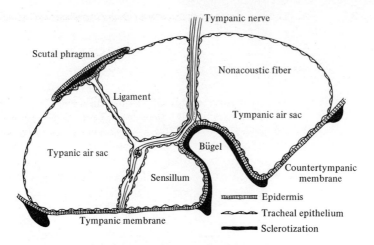

Figure 10–6. Schematic diagram of a frontal section of the left tympanic air sac and related auditory structures of a night-flying noctuid moth. The structures are located in the posterior thorax. Despite the extreme simplicity of this system in comparison with vertebrate ears, ultrasonic bat calls are heard from at least 100 feet away. Details shown in the sensillum and nerve are partly presumptive, and accessory cells, cap cells, and fibers enveloping sensory cells and scolopes in the sensillum are omitted. The nonacoustic fiber is shown on the basis of physiological evidence only. (From Kenneth D. Roeder and Asher E. Treat. Ultrasonic reception by the tympanic organ of noctuid moths. *Journal of Experimental Zoology*, 1957, **134**, 127–157.)

For quite some time, scientists were perplexed as to how the tympanic organ permits insects to distinguish calls of their own species from those of other species or from artificial sources, since the structure of the tympanic organ precludes its being anything but a poor harmonic analyzer. In addition, experimental evidence for frequency discrimination was slight. Finally, however, Pumphrey and Rawdon-Smith (1939) found that high frequencies act as carrier waves which are modulated in intensity or amplitude by lower frequencies, just as radio waves are. Hence, the high-frequency tones to which insects respond are meaningless in themselves; what is important is the detection of the lower frequencies riding the carrier frequency.

A third type of insect hearing organ is seen in mosquitoes, which use their antennae to hear. The feathery antennae vibrate in time with airborne vibrations. These vibrations thus stimulate the bulb-shaped Johnston's organ at the base of the antennae. The Johnston's organ contains a flexible membrane innervated by sense cells which register the amount of bending performed by the antennae in reaction to sound-wave displacement. These sense-cell nerves transmit their information by neural pathways to the brain.

Different insect species usually stress different frequency bands. Field crickets, for example, generally use the region of 4,000 to 5,000 cycles per second for their signals, while many grasshopper species use ultrasonic frequencies. The large green grasshopper *Tettigonia viridissima* sends out frequencies as high as 100,000 cycles per second. Autrum's (1940) grasshoppers also went up to 90,000 cycles per second, and their auditory sensitivity was found to be strongly dependent upon temperature conditions, with sensitivity being the highest at about 30°C. Many New World moths, particularly among the arctiid and ctenuchid species, produce high-pitched clicks, usually 45,000 to 85,000 cycles per second, when touched or when exposed to the cries of echolocating bats. These sounds have been found to serve to warn and repel bats in a fashion similar to warning coloration, since some of the species possess odors or tastes which are noxious to bats (Covalt-Dunning, 1968).

Hearing in Fish

Because of their pivotal role in the evolution of the vertebrate hearing organ, we have mentioned a great deal regarding the hearing organs of fish. The lateral line organ derives its usefulness from the fact that the body of a fish has the same average compressibility and density as the medium surrounding its body. An object moving close to a fish will maximally deform its body surface. The lateral line organ, capable of perceiving deformation or touch, is thus specialized in localization of distant disturbances. It is also capable of making simultaneous comparisons, as it is innervated from one source. While the lateral line is extremely sensitive, it is limited in range since it usually receives from approximately 20 to 200 cycles per second. There does not seem to be much pitch discrimination performed by the lateral line.

The fish inner ear, however, is used for the reception of higher frequencies. Goldfish, for example, are sensitive to frequencies as high as 15,000 cycles per second, as shown by classical conditioning of heart rate, whereas other behavior techniques have shown a sensitivity up to 3,000 cycles per second. The inner ear of fish is a labyrinthine structure with a utricle and a saccule. The saccule has a small evagination, the lagena. The lagena of fish, like the cochlea of mammals, is served by a separate branch of the eighth cranial nerve. The upper-frequency limit varies from species to species, although some of the variation reported is due to differences in testing techniques. Von Frisch (1936) obtained responses from minnows to 5,000 and 6,000 cycles per second, whereas some other researchers have measured up to 7,000 cycles per second. Dwarf catfish are receptive to 13,000 cycles per second. On the other hand, the ray has a rather less well-developed inner ear and can detect only up to 120 cycles per second, which is as good as a sensitive lateral line organ can do. With most fish, pitch discrimination appears to be best in the frequency range of 400 to 800 cycles per second, with all lower frequencies being heard as a uniform low sound and all higher frequencies being heard as a uniform high tone.

Hearing in Amphibians

As earlier mentioned, among amphibians one of the Weberian ossicles in the fish jawbone has turned into a bony rod called the columella. The columella connects the inner ear to the eardrum in amphibians. In the early tadpole stages, a bronchial columella bridges from the round window to a part of the lung sac, reminiscent of the air bladder connection in fish, particularly since the bronchial columella picks up underwater vibrations from the lungs. In later developmental stages, the tadpole's bronchial columella disappears, heralding the transition from a purely aquatic life to an amphibious one involving exposure to air. During metamorphosis, another columella, the tympanic, grows in the middle ear from the oval window to the eardrum, and one of the jawbones makes a radical shift in position to lie directly under the eardrum and becomes connected to the tympanic columella. Despite these extensive changes in the middle ear, the frog's inner ear is structured exactly like the tadpole's.

Field observations and conditioning techniques have indicated that frogs (*Rana pipiens*) can hear between 50 and 24,800 cycles per second (Kleerekoper & Sibabin, 1959). But techniques based upon unconditioned responses and electrophysiological indices such as the Galvanic Skin Response have obtained responses in frogs only to the range of 50 to 4,000 cycles per second (Strother, 1962), and in the tree frog (*Hyla cinerea*) up to 5,000 cycles per second (Weiss & Strother, 1965).

Hearing in Reptiles

The hearing ability of many reptilian species has frequently been doubted. For example, snakes have no external ear, no middle ear, and no tympanic membrane. The columella reaches from the oval window to a flat triangular bone, the quadrate, which rests loosely on the skull. Many workers (e.g., Manning, 1923) have concluded that snakes hear ground vibrations rather than airborne ones.

However, the snake's inner ear, as is the case with most reptiles, consists of the three semicircular canals, utricle, saccule, lagena, and a simple cochlea. Wever & Vernon (1961) obtained cochlear potentials in snakes in response to *both* airborne and bone-conducted frequencies in the range of 100 to 700 cycles per second. Hence snakes, while not deaf, are limited in their sensitive hearing range.

The investigation of hearing in turtles has also presented problems to investigators. While Wever and Bray (1930) obtained microphonic potential responses in the same turtle genus for which Andrews (1916) claimed to have found hearing by means of a training method, no other behavioral studies were able to substantiate these findings until Patterson and Gulick (1966) conditioned turtles to withdraw the head to sound signals of 20, 63, 200, 400, 640, 800, and 1,000 cycles per second.

Lizards, on the other hand, obviously have behavioral and physiological reactions to airborne sounds. Wever and Peterson (1963) and Wever, Crowley, and Peterson (1963) have tested the cochlear potentials of at least nine lizard species and have found some to respond optimally to the range of 700 to 2,000 cycles per second and others to the range of 400 to 4,000 cycles per second. The fan-toed gecko, however, has even higher cochlear potentials, up to 10,000 cycles per second (Wever & Hepp-Reymond, 1967).

Lizards in general have two columellae in the middle ear. Crocodiles and alligators, which also have a two-ossicle columella, have auditory organs that are obviously more highly developed than the amphibia. They have an external ear in the form of a fold of skin above the ear opening. The lagena of the alligator forms three ducts and a basilar membrane. The crocodile hears in the range of 20 to 6,000 cycles per second.

Evidence that reptiles possess frequency-pitch discrimination is relatively scanty, although one would be hard put to explain why those reptiles having a functionally advanced inner ear should be deficient in this sensory dimension.

Hearing in Birds

The bird's lagena has developed to the point where it is often referred to as a cochlea. Although it is long and uncoiled, its inner structure is much the same as the mammalian cochlea. Birds possess a single columella, and a tympanic membrane located deep enough in the head so that there is also an external auditory meatus. An interesting fact is that owls have asymmetrical ears which provide greater accuracy in locating the source of sound. They also have the most highly developed cochlea of all birds studied to date.

Birds often have a lower frequency-sensitivity range than man. One estimate has placed the lower limit at 40 cycles per second and the upper limit at 14,000 cycles per second for parrots and crossbills. Robins hear from 250 to 21,000 cycles per second, however. Frequency discrimination in these birds parallels that of man. Perhaps the best indication, empirically, for a higher level of frequency discrimination in some birds is the ability to mimic. Parrots, mockingbirds, and parakeets are well known in this respect, although other birds are able to mimic both animate and inanimate sounds.

Naturalists have known for some time that the tremendous range of sound emitted by birds serves a communicative function. Courtship, territory, rearing of young, alarm, all are involved in bird songs and calls. In the past decades there have been an increasing number of studies involving spectrographic analysis of bird songs, observation of their function, and the influence of experience and heredity upon the acquisition and development of specific song in different species.

There is at least one case in which birds have put their sound-producing and hearing ability to a noncommunicative purpose. This is seen in the oilbird of Venezuela, a species that is known to exist in only one cavern, now protected by the government. The oilbird is nocturnal and performs its feats of navigation in total darkness by echolocation, as do bats. Griffin (1954) electronically analyzed the emitted click sounds of this bird and found that each click had a frequency of about 7,000 cycles per second and lasted about .001 to .002 second. Since the wavelength is much longer than that of bats, it cannot reflect objects that are as small as those which bats can detect. Hence, with a lower sonar acuity, the oilbird is probably a poorer navigator than is the bat. Another cave-dwelling bird using echolocation for catching prey is the Bornean "edible-nest swiftlet" (Harrison, 1966).

Hearing in Mammals

In all mammals the cochlea is well developed. The amount of spiraling may vary from a quarter-turn to five turns, but there is no known factor that correlates with the number of turns. Terrestrial mammals, of course, have the three Weberian ossicles in the middle ear, as is well exemplified by man. The external ears, usually called pinnae, of mammals are commonly movable, but even in species, including humans, where they are not, they still serve as concentrators and channelers of sound waves to the eardrum.

Much of the experimentation on hearing in nonhuman mammals has involved dogs, cats, and various rodents, with bats and porpoises receiving a great deal of attention because of their ultrasonic hearing ability and sonar systems.

Rodents have comparatively high upper-frequency limits. The white rat and the guinea pig can hear up to about 40,000 cycles per second, and the mouse appears to be able to go as high as 95,000 cycles per second. It has been known since Galton's time that the dog is sensitive to ultrasonic sound. It has been estimated that it can hear up to about 50,000 cycles per second, while the cat's hearing range has been set from 60 to 65,000 cycles per second.

Although people often assume that some animals, including the dog, have keener hearing than man, in a certain sense this is impossible. That is because the absolute energy threshold for man's ear, 10^{-18} watts per second, is about as low as it could be without molecular actions becoming audible. Dogs, however, hear higher frequencies than humans can, and thus can pick up a greater amount of sound energy from a given source. For example, even the jingling of keys emits ultrasonic frequencies. Other factors in keenness of hearing are habit and experience. The Mabaans of eastern Africa, studied by Rosen, Bergman, Plester, El-Mofti, & Satti (1962) and by Bergman (1966), live in a remote region and are extremely quiet people having relatively sharp hearing, primarily because their high-frequency reception abilities do not deteriorate with age. Certainly it seems that the high noise level to which civilized ears are subjected has the effect of sharply reducing hearing vigilance as well as high-frequency reception, particularly during aging.

Actually, in comparison with the rest of the class Mammalia, the sensitive-frequency range of human beings is rather below average. The human range, from about 20 to 20,000 cycles per second, is exceeded in at least twenty-three other mammalian species—including bats, porpoises, seals, whales, hedgehogs, mice, rats, chinchilla, guinea pigs, opossums, raccoons, sheep, dogs, cats, lesser anteaters, two-toed sloths, armadillos, and many primates. The chimpanzee's hearing range, however, is somewhat similar to man's, since it hears up to about 26,000 or 30,000 cycles per second, while gerbils are slightly superior, with a frequency limit of about 32,000 cycles per second. Nevertheless, man can in fact hear tones up to at least 176,000 cycles per second if the transmitter has direct contact with the skull bones so that the sound is not purely airborne but also bone-conducted. On the other hand, this bone-conducted reception does not permit any frequency discrimination because all ultrasonic tones thus received are heard as being the same as the highest pitched airborne frequency that can be heard.

Without question the bat, porpoise, and seal excel in receiving high frequency sounds, and it appears certain that related whales also do. The bat was the first of these mammals to be studied for high-frequency reception. When Galambos (1942) first investigated the microphonic potential in bats, he discovered that their range was beyond that of his equipment, which ended at 98,000 cycles per second. Since then, it has been determined that bats have potentials up to 120,000 cycles per second, that porpoises can react to as high as 150,000 cycles per second (with sensitivity falling above 120,000 cycles per second), and that common seals can hear up to 180,000 cycles per second.

The story of the discovery of bat sonar is a rather interesting one. As long ago as 1793, an Italian priest and scientist, Lazara Spallanzani, discovered that bats could somehow "see" in the dark with their ears. But since humans cannot hear the bat's ultrasonic sounds, other scientists of the time could not understand how this could possibly be. So Spallanzani's work was, after heated controversy, completely disregarded and subsequently forgotten. It was not until 1938 that Pierce and Griffin discovered that bats actually emit ultrahigh-frequency sounds. Griffin then teamed up with Galambos and the many subsequent experiments by the two researchers showed how bats can avoid obstacles by means of ultrasonic echolocation, that is, by sonar (Galambos & Griffin, 1942; Griffin, 1958). Not only that, but bats also use echolocation to hunt prey in the dark (Griffin, Webster, & Michael, 1960). Several night-flying moths, in fact, have been found to be able to hear the bats' cries, and thus they have some chance of evading their predator. Mother bats and their infants communicate with ultrasonic sounds and respond to each other's calls (Gould, 1971).

The echolocation ability of bats is truly amazing, particularly in view of the fact that their ears detect echos that are usually one two-thousandth the intensity of the original cry. It has been shown that they can hear echos that are only a hundred-billionth as strong as the emitted sound. The sounds emitted by the bats are extremely intense, "hideously loud," in Griffin's words, when transposed to audible frequencies. They have been likened to a four-engine jet flying a mile overhead. Bats avoid being deafened by their own sounds by having a muscle in the inner ear that contracts just before a cry is emitted and then relaxes before the echo returns a millisecond later. When bats fly, they emit their cries in pulses which increase in rate upon approaching a small or flying target. The bat sonar system uses ultrasonic frequencies, thus utilizing the fact that sound waves, to be reflected best, should be smaller in size than the reflecting objects. For example, a sound wave of 50,000 cycles per second is ¼ inch long per cycle, good for detecting mosquitoes on small twigs.

As for porpoises, their sonar system is at least as good as the bat's if not even better, since they can use even higher frequencies. They produce sounds up to at least 170,000 cycles per second, and the many experiments of Kellogg (1961) have demonstrated that their echolocation system is extremely sophisticated and efficient. Whales, which are related to porpoises, apparently also have a similar sonar system. Seals also may use sonar actively. Poulter (1966) showed that normal California sea lions can be trained to use sonar and suggested that blind ones use sonar actively. Møhl (1968), using operant conditioning techniques, determined that common seals hear water-borne sounds up to 180,000 cycles per second and airborne sounds up to 22,000 cycles per second.

These aquatic mammals evolved from air-living ones and hence had to adapt their ears for underwater sound reception during the course of evolution. In doing so they developed their ultrahigh-frequency reception systems to a high degree. Porpoise ears, in line with this, are well developed. Like other mammalian ears, they consist of an ear canal (but not a visible pinna), a middle ear, and an inner ear. The "eardrum," however, is different in being a ligament rather than drumlike. It transmits its movements to the three middle-ear ossicles. It still is not known, however, just how the porpoise makes its ultrasonic noises.

ELECTRIC AND MAGNETIC SENSES

The unpleasant effects of coming in too close contact with electric catfish, electric eels, and electric rays have been known for centuries. It has been discovered only relatively recently, however, that there are species that generate low voltages and use these discharges as the means of perceiving the environment (Grundfest, 1960). Skates and rays possess sensory organs, called ampullae of Lorenzini, which are distributed over the body surface and which serve to detect lines of flux in the environmental space. Since they are

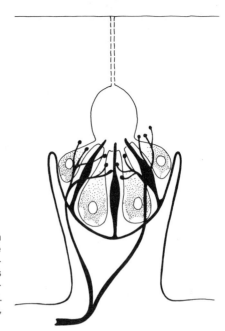

Figure 10–7. An electric sense pore in the skin of a mormyrid fish. The extremely narrow pore and the bulb cavity contain a gelatinous substance which transmits the electrical force lines to the nerve cells at the bottom. (From W. Stendell, Die Schauzenorgane der Mormyriden. *Zeitschrift für Wissenschaftliche Zoologie,* 1916, **115,** 650–669.)

specialized lateral line organs (Cahn, 1967), they were once thought to be temperature or pressure receptors. The perception of flux lines enables them to perceive the presence, location, and size of objects in the environment. This sensory method is totally unlike sonar or radar since no echos or time lags are utilized. However, feedback is involved, since it is the fish that generates the electric field and then senses the flux in that electric field.

The African knife fish (*Gymnarchus niloticus*), also called Nile fish, is a mormyrid studied by Lissmann (1958, 1963). Its electric organs discharge 3 to 7 volts at the rate of 300 impulses per second. Its electrically sensitive organs, much like the ampullae of Lorenzini, are fine sensory pores arranged in fairly regular patterns all over the body almost 2 millimeters away from each other. They are very similar to taste organs in appearance, a fact which suggests their relation to chemical receptors. African elephant-nose fish and South American knife fish also possess electrically sensitive organs. At any rate, the electrically sensitive organs of *Gymnarchus* can detect changes in electrical conductive paths (called potential gradients, in technical literature) which are as low as .03 microvolts per centimeter, the same as a current density of .04 microamperes per square centimeter. This permits the fish to detect a glass rod 2 millimeters in diameter at a distance of a few centimeters. This electric sensitivity certainly is extremely useful to *Gymnarchus*, since it lives in highly turbulent and muddy waters. The strong and rapid movement of its waters prevents it from being able to use its pressure wave-sensitive lateral line organ as there would, in effect, be far too much "noise" from the turbulence for the lateral line organ to be of any use. In addition, *Gymnarchus's* eyes are very poorly developed as visual organs and react only to rather bright light. Again, even if its eyes were good, they too would not be of much help in the muddy waters. With its electric sense, however, *Gymnarchus* is able to keep tabs on events in its environment that are as much as 6 feet away. Figure 10-7 depicts a mormyrid electric sense pore.

Some scientists have suggested that some species of electric fish use their sense to establish and maintain territories. Möhres (1961), in fact, has recorded an electric duel between two rival electric fish. However, there are also a few species of elephant fish that live together and use their electric signals as the means of maintaining school formation, particularly since, once again, they cannot use their lateral line organs for this purpose.

Most of these low-voltage electric fish would thus also be affected by the presence of magnets since they influence the lines of electric force. In fact, Lissmann (1958) discovered that *Gymnarchus* and other electric fish were positively attracted by a large magnet placed in the water. Related to this is the fact that fishermen have been luring tuna to their nets with a particular type of electric current; perhaps the electric eel also attracts its prey with low-voltage electricity and then stuns its prey with a high-voltage discharge.

In other, very different species, it has been found, both by accident and by careful experimentation, that there is a sensitivity to magnetic fields. The German zoologist Merkel (Merkel, Fromme, & Wiltschko, 1964; Merkel & Wiltschko, 1965) experimented for years with robins before he was able to demonstrate just how this species could use magnetic fields for orientation. Here, as it has been with many other senses, the experimentation was difficult and initially inconclusive simply because of our own incomprehension of how an animal's magnetic sense would work. In the first place, the robin's magnetic sense does not respond like a compass needle, able to react instantly upon any change in the magnetic field. Sometimes, however, for reasons not yet fully understood, adaptation to changed magnetic conditions took place much sooner than at other times. Also, the sense may respond more to whole-field magnetic conditions than to local disturbances such as would be engendered by magnets attached to the bird's body. Work on the magnetic sensitivity of birds is continuing and has been also undertaken by others (e.g., Eldarov & Kholodov, 1964).

As a further indication of the existence of the magnetic sense, termite queens of certain species, including the African *Macrotermes* and *Odontotermes,* have always been found to be lying either directly north-south or directly east-west when their nests are opened. Becker (1963, 1964) shook queens of these two species into the bottom of a breeding box so that they lay in random positions. Some hours later, however, they were all found to be lying in an east-west position. After a most careful 90°-degree rotation of the box, a few hours later the queens had adjusted their position back to the east-west orientation. Only when placed in a very thick steel box which considerably weakened the earth's magnetic field did they fail to maintain an east-west position. When a bar magnet was introduced into the box, the queens then took a position across the axis of the bar magnet.

At least one other termite species is very probably influenced by a magnetic sensitivity. This is the Australian compass termite which always builds its long, thin, and high (10' × 3' × 13') nest along the north-south axis. This may be useful in enabling the nest to receive an even amount of sunshine during the day, since the high noon heat would be received the least by this type of construction.

Still other species now appear to be sensitive to magnetic fields: the unicellular volvox (Palmer, 1963), the planaria *Dugesia* and the protozoan *Paramecia* (Brown, 1962); *Drosophila* fruit flies (Picton, 1964); a June bug, the cockchafer (Schneider, 1961); weevils, crickets, locusts, wasps, flies (Hüsing, Struss, & Weide, 1960); the pond snail *Nassarius obsoleta* (Brown, Barnwell, & Webb, 1964; Brown, Bennett, & Webb, 1960). It may be, since a magnetic sensitivity is possessed by such disparate species, that it is far more widespread in the animal kingdom than we now suspect.

X-RAYS

Yet another portion of the electromagnetic spectrum appears to be perceptible by some members of the animal kingdom. As with the magnetic sense, however, there is as yet little or no knowledge whether there are any sensitive receptors involved, what their nature might be, or where they might be located if they do exist. Since the late 1950s it has been known that cats, rats, mice, pigeons, and rhesus monkeys show behavioral reactions to low-level ionizing radiation (Haley & Snider, 1964; Kimeldorf & Hunt, 1965). Radiation results in the formation of aversive behavior toward stimuli presented in conjunction with the exposure, so that it acts as an unconditioned stimulus. Rats, mice, cats, and monkeys have thus been conditioned to avoid taste stimuli, and mice and rats, to avoid the visual characteristics of the exposure site. Overt behavioral arousal from sleep can be elicited reliably in rats by a dose rate of 3.2 rads per second in less than 12 seconds. (A rad is a radiation dose containing 100 ergs of energy per gram of absorbing weight.) A conditioned aversion to saccharin can be produced in rats by a .0007 rad per second exposure for a period of 4 hours. Radiation can be used as a warning stimulus to signal the occurrence of a subsequent electric shock to a rat's paw.

Some of the radiation effects appear likely to be physiological stress reactions rather than stimulus-response learning since, for example, ionizing radiation can be presented to rats at any time within 12 hours after the presentation of saccharin and 6 hours in the case of sucrose (Smith & Roll, 1967), which are rather long time periods indeed.

The only clues so far obtained as to the anatomical substrates of the sensitivity to ionizing radiation are the facts that abdominal irradiation is more effective than head irradiation in conditioning taste aversion, that head irradiation is more effective in eliciting sleep arousal, and that in three species, rats, pigeons, and monkeys, radical disruption of the olfactory system removes this sensitivity.

THE CHEMICAL SENSES

Chemical sensitivity may well be called a property of life itself. The common chemical sensitivity is possessed by the lowest animal forms, over large body areas by aquatic species, and in more clearly defined areas in higher animals, including man. In the human animal, the common chemical sense receptors are found principally on all mucous membrane surfaces of the body—nose, mouth, anal and genital apertures—although any cut or scratch on the skin exposes a chemically sensitive area. The common chemical receptors of humans usually react to ammonia or acid fumes, for example, causing the subjective feeling of irritation and often reflex actions such as tearing of the eyes or some other secretory discharge. The common chemical sense receptors possessed by various animal species consist of free nerve endings rather than some specific receptor cell. It is clear that taste and smell receptors evolved from the common chemical sense receptors, with olfactory receptors consisting of olfactory cell endings and gustatory receptors consisting of taste-bud endings. Figure 10-8 shows these relationships.

In general, the evolutionary development and phylogenetic progression of the chemical senses are highly gradual. In fact, it is difficult to say just where specialization of the chemical sense begins. Protozoa are able to distinguish between different substances, as shown by their ingestion of food particles and rejection of unsuitable matter. Coelenterates such as sea anemones show definite reactions to chemical stimuli from food items, and so do planarian flatworms which have different sensory cells for touch, temperature, and chemical stimuli.

It is to insects that we can, without hesitation, assign a strong differentiation of chemical stimuli (Dethier, 1963). They are the first invertebrates to have clearly separate organs for smell and taste, and they are generally superior to man in chemoreception ability. Their chemoreceptors, usually located on antennae or on legs, react to a wide variety of insect pheromones, among which the sex attractants are one. The amazing potency and importance of olfactory sex attractants of several species, particularly moths, have generated a tremendous amount of research work. While we humans are absolutely insensitive to moth sex attractants no matter what the concentration, they enable

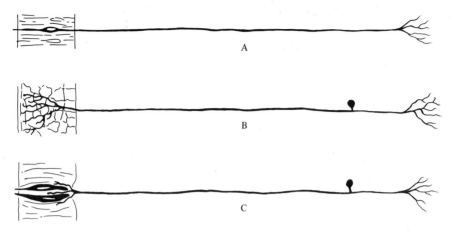

Figure 10–8. Vertebrate receptor systems of: (A) Olfactory and vomero-nasal organ, with olfactory cell. (B) Common chemical sense organ, with free nerve endings. (C) Taste organ, with taste bud. In all three cases one nerve is depicted as representative of those in each class. (From Geòrge Howard Parker, The relations of smell, taste, and the common chemical sense in vertebrates. *Journal of The Academy of Natural Sciences of Philadelphia,* 1912, **15**, 219–234.)

the males of a species like the silkworm moth *Bombyx mori* to find a female from a distance of several miles away. The male, interestingly, is 10 million times more sensitive to the sex attractant, called bombykol, than is the female which produces it. The male's antennae have at least 40,000 sensory nerve cells for olfactory reception, and it has been estimated that only two or three molecules of bombykol are sufficient to activate his search for the female that emitted it. Electrophysiological and behavior experiments have shown that the bombykol receptor reacts to a single molecule (Schneider, 1969). Figure 10-9 details the complex structure of the silkworm moth's antennal olfactory apparatus.

Other insects that have been extensively studied for chemical sensitivity, including responsiveness to food, location of prey, olfactory identification of females or of colony members, and code of chemical communication, are houseflies, fruit flies, blowflies, bees, ichneumon flies, cockroaches, and ants. Insect pheromones of all types are being studied increasingly, and in the next two decades we should acquire a much greater insight into this aspect of insect olfaction than we now have. Most known insect pheromones operate as alerting substances, trail markers, sex attractants, aphrodisiacs, aggregating substances, and controllers of development, with few pheromones functioning to promote dispersal (Butler, 1967).

Research in the chemical senses has been very difficult and our knowledge therefore relatively fragmentary and confusing despite the tremendous number

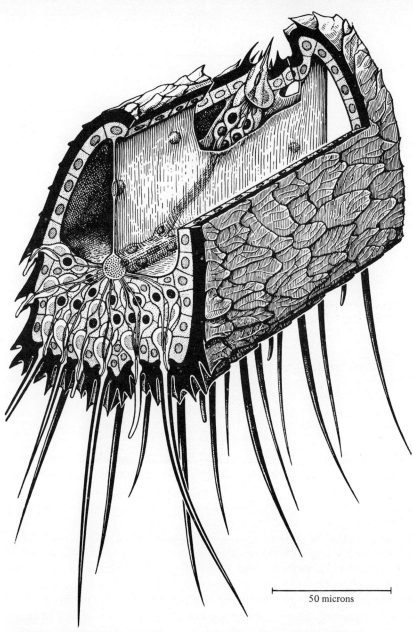

Figure 10–9. Detailed 3-dimensional representation of a section of the antennal branch of the silkworm moth, *Bombyx mori* L. Shown are the short, thin-walled sensilla basiconica and long, thick-walled sensilla trichodea (below) and one sensillum coeloconium (above). The richness of innervation for the "hairs" is readily apparent. From Dietrich Schneider and K.-E. Kaissling, Der Bau der Antenne des Seidenspinners *Bombyx mori* L. III. Das Bindegewebe und das Blutgefäss. *Zoologische Jahrbücher, Abteilung für Anatomie und Ontogenie der Tiere*, 1959, **77,** 111–132.

of research papers that have been published. The reason is that the human species is not endowed with as well-developed chemical senses as many other species have. These other species have much keener senses of smell and taste and much higher powers of discrimination. This greater sensitivity is not always simply a matter of their being tuned in, for example, to different kinds of odors from those to which we are tuned, since dogs can be trained to recognize and locate the source of many odors, such as gas or marijuana, which we can smell, but at dilutions that we are unable to perceive. For a few substances, a dog's sensitivity can be two or three thousand times more acute than our own, but for many others its sensitivity is at least a million times better. Also, it is clear that dogs are highly superior to human beings in discriminating between, and identifying, human individuals on the basis of scent alone. Dogs can possess 125 to 220 million olfactory cells, whereas humans have a mere 5 million of them. We are, in effect, nearly anosmic creatures in an extremely vast and highly differentiated olfactory world which we can barely perceive.

Even so, there are still substances which are extremely potent in activating our olfactory sense. We can detect the bad-smelling mercaptan in a threshold dilution of 1 part to 3 billion of air (on a weight per weight basis) and the more pleasant vanillin in a threshold dilution of 1 part in 300 billion of air (weight per weight), according to Bach (1937). Or, to state it in another way, Moncrieff (1967) has estimated that the human nose can detect the presence of mercaptan when it is in a concentration of only 1 molecule among 50 billion air molecules. Quantities like these are well beyond the present detection ability of laboratory balances and most microscopes. It has been estimated by de Vries and Stuiver (1961) that the threshold of one human olfactory cell is, at the most, 8 molecules for potent odorous substances, and that at least 40 molecules are necessary in order to elicit an actual sensation of odor.

Man's sense of smell, furthermore, is much more acute than either his sense of taste or his common chemical sense. For example, ethyl alcohol, which has a taste independent of its odor and an odor independent of its taste, is perceptible at the following lowest concentrations:

.44% wt./wt. in air for smell reception
14.00% wt./wt. in water for taste reception
25.00% wt./wt. in water for common chemical reception

Even if one takes into account that smell and taste organs are maximally sensitive to different kinds of substances, the sense of smell still wins out easily over the sense of taste. Strychnine hydrochloride, for example, is a very effective taste stimulus, and its threshold detection value for humans is on the order of 1 part in 400,000 on a weight per weight basis. On the other hand, a relatively common odorant, chlorphenol, can be smelled at a threshold value of 1 part in 30 million (weight per weight), according to Moncrieff (1967). Of course, the actual relative difference between smell and taste cannot be determined in an absolute sense since factors such as the volume required for a sniff versus that required for a taste, the density differences between air and water, the different methods of determining sensory threshold, and so on, complicate the whole matter.

It has been suggested that the human's highly developed visual sense is at least partially responsible for the lack of chemical sensitivity in this species. In contrast to the 5 million olfactory cells possessed, there are at least 100 million end receptors for vision (Adrian, 1947), a figure that approaches the dog's 125 to 220 million (depending on breed) olfactory cells.

The range of gustatory differences between various species is also rather great. While man certainly does better than most bird species, he is on the same level as the hare with his 9,000 taste buds and is below the pig and the goat, each of which have about 15,000 taste buds. All of these are far outclassed by the catfish with its 100,000 taste buds. The comparative study of taste is still a relatively young and unexplored area, although numerous scientific studies have been conducted (Kare & Ficken, 1963). Much research has been carried out regarding sensitivity to sugars, particularly in insects, fowl, and some mammals.

Snakes have few taste buds, but possess a Jacobson's organ, also called the vomeronasal organ. This organ exists in many vertebrates, such as the snake, cat, rat, rabbit, and several lizards. Even man has a vestigial vomeronasal organ. Embryo humans have a fairly prominent one, though it is not innervated. Human infants are born with a vomeronasal organ consisting of a pair of tubular processes about .5 to 2.5 millimeters long, opening into the nasal cavity by means of a small pore in the nasal septum (the dividing partition between the two nostrils). In some adults the vomeronasal organ disappears, but in some others it grows and may become as much as 8 millimeters long. In other animals, however, nerve fibers join the vomeronasal tube and mingle with the regular olfactory fibers. Lizards, snakes, and lower mammals such as the Australian duckbill have well-developed vomeronasal organs.

In recent years research has been carried out to investigate the olfactory discrimination powers of the Jacobson's organ of snakes. An example is the research by Burghardt (1970) which measured the incidence of tongue flicking and prey-attack response of naïve newborn snakes of three sympatric species of *Natrix* to water extracts prepared from different animal species. The response preferences shown by these three snake species toward the different extracts (including fish, earthworms, amphibians, slugs, crickets, baby mice, and crayfish) were shown to be strongly correlated with the actual natural diets of each particular species tested: *N. siphedon* newborns responded with increased tongue-flicking attack only to fish and amphibian extracts, while *N. grahamii* and *N. semptemvittata* responded only to crayfish extracts and particularly to those prepared from newly molted crayfish. Findings of species differences were also discovered for several other snake species (Burghardt, 1970).

Although it is not presently known just how the vomeronasal organ is used in species other than snakes, one certainly can assume that it should serve as an auxiliary olfactory organ.

Many fish are highly sensitive to taste stimulation, and indeed, olfaction is often important in the procuring of food. A number of species, such as the cod, have a large number of taste receptors on the body surface. It has already been mentioned that the catfish has about 100,000 of them. An instance of the extreme taste sensitivity that can be found in fish is the fact that Teichmann (1959) trained European eel fish to detect beta-phenyl ethyl alcohol at a threshold concentration of 1 part in 3×10^{18}, or 3 billion billion, of water. Fish can also detect potassium phenylacetate at dilutions of 1 part in 10^{13}, or 10 thousand billion, of water (Hasler & Wisby, 1959). This has the effect of frightening them away without poisoning them. Salmon are alarmed by a "mammalian skin factor," identified as consisting of at least 1-serine amino acid. This factor is present in the human hand, the bear paw, and the sea lion skin. The alarm reaction is elicited even by a 1-serine concentration as low as 1 part in 80 billion of water. This alarm reaction, however, is given by adult, migrating salmon and not by young fish on their way downstream to the sea.

The olfactory sense of salmon also has been implicated in the ability of the adults to migrate back to their original spawning grounds after several years' absence in the open seas. Hasler (1960) showed that blunt-nosed minnows and salmon fingerlings can be successfully trained to discriminate between water samples from different rivers, and that salmon with their nostrils blocked were unable to orient themselves to the tributary from which they had come. Therefore, it is clear that the olfactory sense permits the adults to find the home tributary when the main stream has been reached. Here again is an olfactory response possessed by adult salmon and not by the young ones on their way to the sea. Other factors, of course, appear also to be implicated in the ability to locate the main river from the open sea.

Many fish species, all belonging to the *ostariophysi* order and all swimming in schools, have developed a system of warning school members of the presence of predators: the "fright substance" (von Frisch, 1941) secreted in special club cells in the skin (Pfeiffer, 1965). It is released into the water at the slightest injury to the skin. When a fish of the same species perceives the fright substance, it immediately flees. Young minnows, *Phoxinus laevis*, do not react to the fright substance until the age of four to eight weeks. Some fish species are able to respond to the fright substance of other species. These interspecies reactions are correlated with phylogenetic relationship and hence are useful for elucidating taxonomic relationships. There are at least two nonfish species that possess a skin-fright substance: the toad tadpole (Eibl-Eibesfeldt, 1949) and the South American water snail *Helisoma nigricans*.

Finally, there is good evidence that some fish species, such as minnows, not only discriminate other species by their odor but also are able to discriminate individuals of their own species purely on the basis of smell (Göz, 1941). Olfaction has been shown to be involved in the schooling behavior of Mexican blind characins. Olfaction also plays a role in sex recognition in some species and in parental care in two cichlid fish species.

While it is known that all bird types have olfactory epithelia and olfactory bulbs, the question of bird olfaction has been as controversial as that of cat color vision. Behavioral evidence has been rather scanty, even though some species, such as the kiwi, have rather large olfactory bulbs. Electrophysiological recording of avian olfactory nerves has shown different responses to odorous stimuli from those shown to nonodorous ones (Tucker, 1965). Wenzel (1967) recorded heart rate and respiration rate changes in pigeons, shearwaters, and a parrot in response to various odorous stimuli and also obtained differential responses to air and to some odorants. The parrot, which has a small olfactory bulb, did not, however, show as much evidence of such perception as did the pigeons and shearwaters. These results are shown in Figure 10-10.

While our relative olfactory and gustatory insensitivities have hampered us in studying the chemical perception of other species, we have also erred in approaching other animals with the notion that their chemical sensations are much like ours. Concomitant with this was the once held attitude that the physiology of all animals is virtually the same. Now we know much better: there are indeed very large differences in metabolism, nutritional needs, endocrine systems, and so on. This is why, even though there is an overall continuity in the biochemistry of the animal kingdom, there is no single chemical, physical, nutritional, or physiological pattern that can presently account for the results obtained in the comparative study of the chemical reactions of different species. As Kare and Ficken (1963) have pointed out, the qualities of taste used in human work, for example, are useless where animals are concerned, since the results obtained with different kinds of sugars "support a concept of separate taste worlds for each species." Not only are there absolute differences between species in taste responses, but there are also individual differences in degree and differences dependent upon physiological state. It certainly is much the same where olfaction is concerned.

CONCLUSION

In a short review it is impossible to be completely comprehensive concerning the subject of sensory processes considered from a comparative viewpoint. Species differences can be very wide, and the insects, in particular, are usually very different from other species in their sensory physiology. We have made no attempt to give a detailed account, either anatomically or psychologically, of the human sense organs and sensory processes. Details regarding these may be found in most texts on sensory physiology. As a matter of fact, most texts in this area do little else but explain human senses.

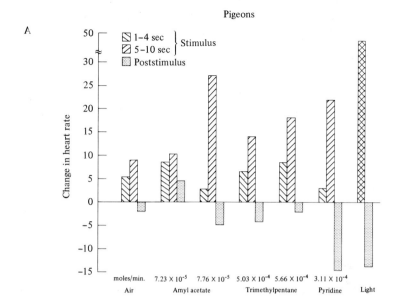

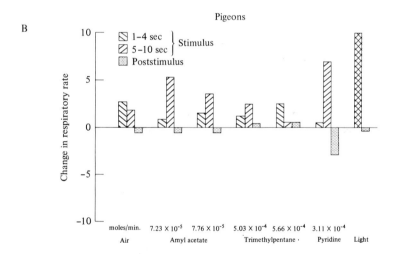

Figure 10–10.   (A) Mean changes in heart rate of pigeons to various stimuli during the first four seconds of stimulus presentation, during the succeeding six seconds, and during the first ten seconds after the cessation of the stimulus, combined with the ten-second period immediately preceding stimulus presentation. (B) Mean changes in respiratory rate of pigeons to various stimuli during the same three periods depicted in (A). (From Bernice M. Wenzel, Olfactory perception in birds. In *Olfaction and taste II*. Proceedings of the Second International Symposium held in Tokyo, September, 1965. T. Hayashi, Ed. Oxford, England: Pergamon Press, 1967. Pp. 203–217.)

Therefore, we have concentrated on giving an introduction to the means whereby living creatures receive the stimuli that guide and direct them. Our phyletic approach was aimed to give a glimpse—informative and, it is hoped, interesting—of what is actually a vast and complex field of study.

REFERENCES

The double asterisk (**) indicates a general reference book.

ADAMS, C. K., & JONES, A. E. Spectral sensitivity of the sooty mangabey. *Perception and Psychophysics*, 1967, **2**, 419–422.

ADRIAN, E. D. Rod and cone components in the electric response of the eye. *Journal of Physiology*, 1946, **105**, 24–37.

ADRIAN, E. D. *The physical background of perception*. Oxford, England: Clarendon Press, 1947.

ANDREWS, O. The ability of turtles to discriminate between sounds. *Bulletin of the Wisconsin Natural History Society*, 1916, **13**, 189–195.

AUTRUM, H. Ueber Lautausserungen und Schallwahrnehmung bei Arthropoden. II. Das Richtungshören von Locusta und Versuch einer Hörtheorie für Tympanalorgane vom Locustidentyp. *Zeitschrift für Vergleichende Physiologie*, 1940, **28**, 326–352.

AUTRUM, H., & STUMPF, H. Electrophysiologische Untersuchungen über das Farbensehen von Calliphora. *Zeitschrift für Vergleichende Physiologie*, 1953, **35**, 71–104.

BACH, H. Von der Geruchsmessung. *Gesundheits-Ingenieur, Zeitschrift für die Gesamte Städtehygiene*. 1937, **60**, 222–225.

BABAK, E. Ueber den Farbensinn des Frosches, vermittels Atemreaktion untersucht. *Zeitschrift für Sinnesphysiologie*, 1913, **47**, 331–351.

BARLOW, H. B., FITZHUGH, R., & KUFFLER, S. W. Dark adaptation, absolute threshold and Purkinje shift in single units of the cat's retina. *Journal of Physiology*, 1957, **137**, 327–337.

BECKER, G. Ein Magnetfeldorientierung bei Termiten. *Naturwissenschaften*, 1963, **50**, 455.

BECKER, G. Wirkung magnetischer Felder auf Insekten. *Zeitschrift für angewandte Entomologie*, 1964, **54**, 75–88.

BERGMAN, M. Hearing in the Mabaans. *Archives of Otolaryngology*, 1966, **84**, 411–415.

BERNHARD, C. G. (Ed.) *The functional organization of the compound eye*. Proceedings of the International Symposium on the Functional Organization of the Compound Eye, Stockholm, October 1965. Oxford, England: Pergamon, 1966.

BINGHAM, H. C. Visual perception of the chick. *Behaviour Monographs*, 1922, **4**, No. 4, 1–104 + i–vi.

BIRUKOW, G. Die Entwicklung des Tages- und des Dämmerungsehens im Auge des Grasfrosches, *Rana temporaria* L. *Zeitschrift für Vergleichende Physiologie*, 1949, **31**, 322–347.

BIRUKOW, G. Vergleichende Untersuchungen über das Helligkeits- und Farbensehen bei Amphibien. *Zeitschrift für Vergleichende Physiologie*, 1950, **32**, 348–382.

BONAVENTURE, N. Travaux et recherches á propos de la vision des couleurs. *Bulletin de Psychologie*, 1962, **16**, 83–85.

BONAVENTURE, N. La vision chromatique du chat. *Académie des Sciences, Paris. Comptes-rendus hebdomadaires des séances*, 1964, **259**, 2012–2015.

BROWN, F. A. JR. Responses of the planarian, *Dugesia*, and the protozoan, *Paramecium*, to very weak horizontal electrostatic fields. *Biological Bulletin*, 1962, **123**, 264–281.

BROWN, F. A., JR., BARNWELL, F. H., & WEBB, H. M. Adaptation of the magneto-receptive mechanism of mud-snails to geomagnetic strength. *Biological Bulletin*, 1964, **127,** 221–231.

BROWN, F. A., JR., BENNETT, M. F., & WEBB, H. M. A magnetic compass response of an organism. *Biological Bulletin*, 1960, **119,** 65–74.

BUCHHOLTZ, C. Untersuchungen über das Farbensehen der Hauskatze, *Felis domestica L.* *Zeitschrift für Tierpsychologie*, 1952, **9,** 462–470.

BULLOCK, T. H., & COWLES, R. B. Physiology of an infrared receptor. The facial pit of vipers. *Science*, 1952, **115,** 541–543.

BULLOCK, T. H., & DIECKE, F. P. J. Properties of an infrared receptor. *Journal of Physiology*, 1956, **134,** 47–48.

BURGHARDT, G. M. Chemical perception in reptiles. In J. W. Johnson, D. G. Moulton, & A. Turk (Eds.), *Advances in chemoreception. Vol. 1. Communication by chemical signals.* New York: Appleton-Century Crofts, 1970. Pp. 241–308.

BURKHARDT, D. *Sehzellen. Mikrokosmos*, 1964, **53,** 161.

**BURKHARDT, D., SCHLEIDT, W., & ALTNER, H. (Eds.). Trans. Kenneth Morgan. *Signals in the animal world.* New York: McGraw-Hill, 1967.

BURTON, R. *Animal senses.* New York: Taplinger, 1970.

BUTLER, C. G. Insect pheromones. *Cambridge Philosophical Society, Biological Reviews and Biological Proceedings.* Cambridge, England: Cambridge Philosophical Society, 1967, **42,** 42–87.

CAIN, R. E., & CARLSON, R. H. Evidence for color vision in the prairie dog (*Cynomys ludovicianus*). *Psychonomic Science*, 1968, **13,** 185–186.

CAHN, P. H. (Ed.) *Lateral line detectors.* Proceedings of a Conference held at Yeshiva University, New York, 1966. Bloomington: Indiana University Press, 1967.

CALLAHAN, P. S. Insects tuned in to infrared rays. *New Scientist*, 1964, **23**(400), 137–138.

CARTHY, J. D., & NEWELL, G. E. (Eds.). Invertebrate receptors. *Symposia of the Zoological Society of London*, 1968, **23, 1–341 + xiv.

CLAYTON, K. N., & KAMBACK, M. Successful performance by cats in several colour discrimination problems. *Canadian Journal of Psychology*, 1966, **20,** 173–182.

COVALT-DUNNING, D. Warning sounds of moths. *Zeitschrift für Tierpschologie*, 1968, **25,** 129–138.

CRESCITELLI, F., & POLLACK, J. D. Color vision in the antelope ground squirrel. *Science*, 1965, **150,** 1316–1318.

DEROSS, J. C., & GANSON, R. Color blindness in cats. *Journal of Animal Behavior*, 1915, **5,** 115–129.

DETHIER, V. G. *The physiology of insect senses.* New York: Wiley, 1963.

**DRÖSCHLER, V. B. *The magic of the senses: New discoveries in animal perception.* (Trans. U. Lehrburger & O. Coburn.) New York: Dutton, 1969.

EIBL-EIBESFELDT, I. Uber das Vorkommen von Schreckstoffen bei Erdkrötenquappen. *Experientia*, 1949, **5,** 236.

ELDAROV, A. L., & KHOLODOV, Y. A. The influence of constant magnetic field upon the motive activity of birds. *Zhurnal obschei biologii*, 1964, **25,** 224–229.

FANTZ, R. L. Ontogeny of perception. In A. M. Schrier, H. F. Harlow, & F. Stollnitz (Eds.), *Behavior of non-human primates.* Vol. 2. New York: Academic Press, 1965. Pp. 265–403.

FRISCH, K. VON. Weitere Untersuchungen über den Farbensinn der Fische. *Zoologische Jahrbücher, Abteilung für allgemeine Zoologie & Psychologie der Tiere*, 1913, **34,** 43–68.

FRISCH, K. VON. Der Farbensinn und Formensinn der Biene. *Zoologische Jahrbücher, Abteilung für Allgemeine Zoologie & Physiologie der Tiere*, 1915, **35**, 1–183.

FRISCH, K. VON. Farbensinn der Fische und Duplizitätstheorie. *Zeitschrift für Vergleichende Physiologie*, 1925, **2**, 393–452.

FRISCH, K. VON. Uber den Gehörsinn der Fische. *Cambridge Philosophical Society, Biological Reviews and Biological Proceedings.* Cambridge, England: Cambridge Philosophical Society, 1936, **11**, 210–246.

FRISCH, K. VON. Über einen Schreckstoff der Fischhaut und seine biologische Bedeutung. *Zeitschrift für Vergleichende Physiologie*, 1941, **29**, 46–145.

FRISCH, K. VON. Die Polarisation des Himmelslichtes als orientierender Faktor bei den Tanzen der Bienen. *Experientia*, 1949, **5**, 142–148.

GALAMBOS, R. Cochlear potentials elicited from bats by supersonic sounds. *Journal of the Acoustical Society of America*, 1942, **14**, 41–49.

GALAMBOS, R., & GRIFFIN, D. R. Obstacle avoidance by flying bats. *Journal of Experimental Zoology*, 1942, **89**, 475–490.

GLICKSTEIN, M., & LABOSSIERE, E. Histological technique and the comparative anatomy of the mammalian retina. *Anatomical Record*, 1968, **160**, 511–512.

GOGEL, W. C., & HESS, E. H. A study of color constancy in the newly hatched chick by means of an innate color preference. *American Psychologist*, 1951, **6**, 282. (Abstract)

GOULD, E. Studies of maternal-infant communication and development of vocalizations in the bats *Nyotis* and *Eptesicus*. *Communications in Behavioral Biology*, 1961, **5**, 263–313.

GÖZ, H. Uber den Art- und Individualgeruch bei Fischen. *Zeitschrift für Vergleichende Physiologie*, 1941, **29**, 1–45.

**GRAHAM, C. H. (Ed.). *Vision and visual perception.* New York: Wiley, 1965.

GRANIT, R. Colour receptors of the frog's retina. *Acta Physiologica Scandinavica*, 1941, **3**, 137–151.

GRANIT, R. The spectral properties of the visual receptors of the cat. *Acta Physiologica Scandinavica*, 1943, **5**, 219–229.

**GRANIT, R. *Sensory mechanisms of the retina.* London: Oxford University Press, 1947.

**GRANIT, R. *Receptors and sensory perception.* New Haven, Conn.: Yale University Press, 1955.

GRIFFIN, D. R. Bird sonar. *Scientific American*, 1954, **190**(3), 79–83.

**GRIFFIN, D. R. *Listening in the dark.* New Haven, Conn.: Yale University Press, 1958.

GRIFFIN, D. R., WEBSTER, F. A., & MICHAEL, C. R. The echolocation of flying insects by bats. *Animal Behaviour*, 1960, **8**, 141–154.

GRUNDFEST, H. Electric fishes. *Scientific American*, 1960, **203**(4), 115–124.

GRZIMEK, B. Versuche über das Farbensehen von Pflanzenessern. I. Das farbige Sehen (und die Sehschärfe) von Pferden. *Zeitschrift für Tierpsychologie*, 1952, **9**, 23–39.

GUNTER, R. The discrimination between lights of different wave lengths in the cat. *Journal of Comparative and Physiological Psychology*, 1954, **47**, 169–172.

HALEY, T. J., & SNIDER, R. S. (Eds.). *Responses of the nervous system to ionizing radiation.* Second International Symposium held at the University of California, Los Angeles, 1963. Boston: Little, Brown, 1964.

HARRIS, J. F., & GAMOW, R. I. Snake infrared receptors: Thermal or photochemical mechanism? *Science*, 1971, **172**, 1252–1253.

HARRISON, T. Onset of echo-location clicking in *Collocalia* swiftlets. *Nature*, 1966, **212**, 530–553.

HASLER, A. D. Guideposts to migrating fishes. *Science*, 1960, **132**, 785–792.

HASLER, A. D., & WISBY, W. Repelling fish by treatment with potassium phenylacetate. U. S. Patent 2,880,113, March 31, 1959.

HENNING, H. Optische Versuche an Vögeln und Schildkröten über die Bedeutung der roten Olkugeln im Auge. *Pflueger's Archiv für die Gesamte Physiologie des Menschen und der Thiere*. 1920, **178**, 91–123.

HERTER, K. *Der Temperatursinn der Tiere*. Wittenberg, Germany, Ziemsen Verlag, 1962.

HESS, E. H. Natural preferences of chicks and ducklings for objects of different colors. *Psychological Reports*, 1965, **4**, 477–483.

HOFFMAN, G. Untersuchungen über das farbensehenvermögen des Zebu. *Zeitschrift für Tierpsychologie*, 1952, **9**, 470–479.

HUBEL, D. H., & WIESEL, T. N. Receptive fields of cells in striate cortex of very young, visually inexperienced kittens. *Journal of Neurophysiology*, 1963, **26**, 994–1002.

HÜSING, J. O., STRUSS, F., & WEIDE, W. Uber Reaktionen der Honigbiene (*Apis mellifica* L.) gegenüber starken elektrischen Felden. *Naturwissenschaften*, 1960, **47**, 22–23.

INGVAR, D. H. Spectral sensitivity as measured in the cerebral visual centers. *Acta Physiologica Scandinavica Supplementum*, 1959, **159**, 1–105.

**JOHNSON, J. W., MOULTON, D. G., & TURK, A. *Advances in chemoreception*. Vol. 1. Communication by chemical signals. New York: Appleton-Century Crofts, 1970.

KARE, M., & FICKEN, M. S. Comparative studies on the sense of taste. In Y. Zotterman (Ed.), *Olfaction and taste*. Proceedings of the First International Symposium, Wenner-Gren Center, Stockholm, September 1962. Oxford, England: Pergamon, 1963.

KELLOGG, W. N. *Porpoises and sonar*. Chicago: The University of Chicago Press, 1961.

KEESEY, U. T. Effects of involuntary eye movements on visual acuity. *Journal of the Optical Society of America*, 1960, **50**, 769–774.

KENNEDY, D.. & MILKMAN, R. Ultraviolet absorption in lenses. *Science*, 1971, **173**, 654–655.

KILIAN, F. Wie verhalten sich Tiere bei Erdbeben? *Naturwissenschaftliche Rundschau*, 1964, **17**, 135–139.

KIMELDORF, D. J., & HUNT, E. L. *Ionizing radiation: Neural function and behavior*. New York: Academic Press, 1965.

KLEEREKOPER, H. *Olfaction in fishes*. Bloomington: Indiana University Press, 1969.

KLEEREKOPER, H., & SIBABIN, K. A study on hearing in frogs, *Rana pipiens* and *Rana clamitans*. *Zeitschrift für Vergleichende Physiologie*, 1959, **41**, 490–499.

KLOPFER, F. D. Visual learning in swine. In L. Bustad & R. O. McClelland (Eds.), *Swine in biomedical research*. Richland, Wash.: Battelle Memorial Institute, Northwest Laboratories, 1966. Pp. 559–574.

KRIES, J. VON. Ueber die functionellen Verschiedenheiten des Netzhaut-Centrums und der Nachbartheile. *Albrecht von Graefe's Archiv für Opthalmologie, vereinigt mit Archiv für Augenheilkunde*, 1896, **42**, 95–133.

KÜHN, A. Uber Farbwechsel und Farbensinn von Cephalopoden. *Zeitschrift für Vergleichende Physiologie*, 1950, **32**, 572–598.

LASHLEY, K. S. The mechanism of vision: XV. Preliminary studies on the rat's capacity for detail vision. *Journal of General Psychology*, 1938, **18**, 123–193.

**LEGRAND, Y. *Light, colour and vision*. London: Chapman & Hall, 1968.

LISSMANN, H. W. On the function and evolution of electric organs in fish. *Journal of Experimental Biology*, 1958, **35**, 156–191.

LISSMAN, H. W. Electric location by fishes. *Scientific American*, 1963, **208**(3), 50–59.

MANNING, F. B. Hearing in rattlesnakes. *Journal of Comparative Psychology*, 1923, **3**, 241–247.

MAST, S. O. Changes in shade, color and pattern in fishes and their bearing on certain problems of behavior and adaptation. *Proceedings of the National Academy of Sciences*, 1915, **1**, 214–219.

**MATTHEWS, L. H., & KNIGHT, M. *The senses of animals*. New York: Philosophical Library, 1963.

MELLO, N. K. Color generalization in cat following discrimination in training in achromatic intensity and on wavelength. *Neuropsychologia*, 1968, **6**, 341–254.

MELLO, N. K., & PETERSON, N. J. Behavioral evidence for color discrimination in cat. *Journal of Neurophysiology*, 1964, **27**, 323–333.

MERKEL, W. M., FROMME, H. G., & WILTSCHKO, W. Nichtvisuelles Orientierungsvermögen bei nächtliche zugunruhigen Rotkehlchen. *Vogelwarte*, 1964, **22**, 168–173.

MERKEL, W. M., & WILTSCHKO, W. Magnetismus Richtungsfinden zugunruhiger Rotkehlchen. *Vogelwarte*, 1965, **23**, 71–77.

MEYER, D. R., & ANDERSON, R. A. Color discrimination in cats. In A. V. S. de Reuck & J. Knight (Eds.), *Color Vision: Physiology and Experimental Psychology*, Ciba Foundation Symposium. Boston: Little, Brown, 1965. 325–339.

MEYER, D. R., MILES, R. C., & RATOOSH, P. Absence of color vision in the cat. *Journal of Neurophysiology*, 1954, **17**, 289–294.

MICHAELS, K. M., & SCHUMACHER, A. W. Color vision in tree squirrels. *Psychonomic Science*, 1968, **10**, 7–8.

MILNE, L. J., & MILNE, M. *The senses of animals and men*. New York: Atheneum, 1962.

MINNICH, D. W. The responses of caterpillars to sound. *Journal of Experimental Zoology*, 1936, **72**, 439–453.

MOERICKE, V. Ueber das Farbensehen der Pfirsichblattlaus. *Myxodes persical* Sulz. *Zeitschrift für Tierpsychologie*, 1950, **7**, 265–274.

MØHL, B. Auditory sensitivity of the common seal in air and water. *Journal of Auditory Research*, 1968, **8**, 27–38.

MÖHRES, F. P. Die elektrischen Fische. *Natur und Volk*, 1961, **91**, 1–13.

**MONCRIEFF, R. W. *The chemical senses*. London: Leonard Hill Books, 1967.

**MYRBERG, A. A., JR. Hearing and allied senses in fishes. Final report to National Science Foundation, Grant No. GB–8399, March 1971. Miami, Fla., No. M171023.

PALMER, J. D. Organismic spatial orientation in very weak magnetic fields. *Nature*, 1963, **198**, 1061–1062.

PARKER, G. H., & VAN HEUSEN, A. P. Mechanical stimulation of skin, lateral line organ and ears: Fish. *American Journal of Physiology*, 1917, **44**, 463–489.

PATTERSON, W. C., & GULICK, W. L. A method for measuring auditory thresholds in the turtle. *Journal of Auditory Research*, 1966, **6**, 219–227.

PFAFFMANN, C. Gustatory afferent impulses. *Journal of Cellular and Comparative Physiology*, 1941, **17**, 243–258.

**PFAFFMANN, C. (Ed.), *Olfaction and taste III*. New York: Rockefeller University Press, 1969.

PFEIFFER, W. Die Schreckreaktion der Fische. *Umschau*, 1965, **65**, 401–405.

PICTON, H. D. The responses of *Drosophila melanogaster* to weak electromagnetic fields. Unpublished doctoral thesis, Northwestern University, 1964.

PIERCE, G. W., & GRIFFIN, D. R. Experimental determination of supersonic notes emitted by bats. *Journal of Mammalogy*, 1938, **19**, 454–455.

POULTER, T. C. The use of active sonar by the California sea lion *Zalophus califorianus* (Lesson). *Journal of Auditory Research*, 1966, **6**, 165–173.

PUMPHREY, R. J. Hearing in insects. *Cambridge Philosophical Society, Biological Reviews and Biological Proceedings. Cambridge, England:* 1940, **15**, 107–132.

PUMPHREY, R. J., & RAWDON-SMITH, A. F. Frequency discrimination in insects. *Nature*, 1939, **143**, 806–807.

ROEDER, K. D., & TREAT, A. E. The detection and evasion of bats by moths. *American Scientist*, 1961, **49**, 135–148.

ROSEN, S., BERGMAN, M., PLESTER, D., EL-MOFTY, A., & SATTI, M. H. Presbycusis study of a relatively noise-free population in the Sudan. *Annals of Otology, Rhinology, and Laryngology*, 1962, **71**, 727–743.

ROSENBLITH, W. A. (Ed.). *Sensory communication*. New York: M.I.T. Press and Wiley, 1961.

SCHNEIDER, D. Insect olfaction: Deciphering system for chemical messages. *Science*, 1969, **163**, 1031–1037.

SCHNEIDER, F. Beeinflussung der Aktivität des Maikäfers durch Veränderung der gegenseitigen Lage magnetischer und elektrischer Felder. *Mittelungen der Schweizerischen Entomologischen Gesellschaft*, 1961, **33**, 232–237.

SECHZER, J. A., & BROWN, J. L. Color discrimination in the cat. *Science*, 1964, **144**, 427–429.

SHLAER, S. The relation between visual acuity and illumination. *Journal of General Physiology*, 1937, **21**, 165–188.

SMITH, J. C., & ROLL, D. L. Trace conditioning with X-rays as an aversive stimulus. *Psychonomic Science*, 1967, **9**, 11–12.

SPERRY, R. W., MINER, N., & MEYERS, R. E. Visual pattern perception following subpial slicing and tantalum wire implantations in the visual cortex. *Journal of Comparative and Physiological Psychology*, 1955, **48**, 50–58.

STEVENS, S. S., WARSHOFSKY, F., & THE EDITORS OF LIFE. *Sound and hearing*. New York: *Time*, Inc., 1965.

STROTHER, W. F. Hearing in frogs. *Journal of Auditory Research*, 1962, **2**, 279–285.

TEICHMANN, H. Uber die Leistung des Geruchssinnes beim Aal, *Anguilla anguilla L. Zeitschrift für Vergleichende Physiologie*, 1959, **42**, 206–254.

THOMAS, E. Untersuchungen über den Helligskeits-und Farbensinn der Anuren. *Zoologische Jahrbücher, Abteilung für Allgemeine Zoologie & Physiologie der Tiere*, 1955, **66**, 129–178.

TRENDELENBURG, W., & SCHMIDT, I. Untersuchungen über das Farbensystem der Affen. (Spektrale Unterschiedsempfindlichkeit und spektrale Farbenmischung bei Helladaptation.) *Zeitschrift für Vergleichende Physiologie*, 1930, **12**, 249–278.

TSUNEKI, K. On colour vision in two species of ants with special emphasis on their relative sensitivity to various monochromatic lights. *Japanese Journal of Zoology*, 1953, **11**, 187–221.

TUCKER, D. Electrophysiological evidence for olfactory function in birds. *Nature*, 1965, **207**, 34–36.

VRIES, H. DE., & STUIVER, M. The absolute sensitivity of the human sense of smell. In W. A. Rosenblith (Ed.), *Sensory communication*. New York: M.I.T. Press and Wiley, 1961. Pp. 159–167.

WALLS, G. L. *The vertebrate eye*. Bloomfield Hills, Mich.: Cranbrook Institute of Science, 1942.

WEISS, B. A., & STROTHER, W. F. Hearing in the green tree frog (*Hyla cinerea cinerea*). *Journal of Auditory Research*, 1965, **5**, 297–306.

WELLS, M. J. What the octopus makes of it: Our world from another point of view. *American Scientist*, 1961, **49**, 215–227.

WENZEL, B. Olfactory perception in birds. In T. Hayashi (Ed.), *Olfaction and taste II*. Proceedings of the Second International Symposium, Tokyo, September 1965. Oxford, England: Pergamon, 1967. Pp. 203–217.

WEVER, E. G., & BRAY, C. W. Relation between sound and impulse frequency in auditory nerve. *Journal of Experimental Psychology*, 1930, **13**, 373–387.

WEVER, E. G., CROWLEY, D. E., & PETERSON, E. A. Auditory sensitivity in four species of lizards. *Journal of Auditory Research*, 1963, **3**, 151–157.

WEVER, E. G., & HEPP-REYMOND, M. C. Auditory sensitivity in the fan-toed gecko, *Ptyodactylus hasselquistii puisuexi boutan*. *Proceedings of the National Academy of Sciences*, 1967, **57**, 681–687.

WEVER, E. G., & PETERSON, E. A. Auditory sensitivity in three iguanid lizards. *Journal of Auditory Research*, 1963, **3**, 205–212.

WEVER, E. G., & VERNON, J. A. The problem of hearing in snakes. *Journal of Auditory Research*, 1961, **1**, 77–83.

WOJTUSIAK, R. Über den Farbensinn der Schildkröten. *Zeitschrift für Vergleichenden Physiologie*, 1933, **18**, 393–436.

WOLKEN, J. J. The photoreceptors of arthropod eyes. *Symposia of the Zoological Society of London*, 1968, **23**, 113–133.

**WRIGHT, R. H. *The science of smell*. London: Allen & Unwin, 1963.

WURTMAN, R. J., & AXELROD, J. The pineal gland. *Scientific American*, 1965, **213**(1), 50–60.

YAGER, D. Behavioral measures and theoretical analysis of spectral sensitivity and spectral saturation in the goldfish *Carassius auratus*. *Vision Research*, 1967, **7**, 707–721.

ZIGMAN, S. Ultraviolet absorption in lenses. *Science*, 1971, **173**, 655.

Chapter 11

Perception in Comparative Perspective

Austin H. Riesen

When the response of an organism is determined by a unique stimulus complexity rather than by a simple change in environmental energies, such as the onset or offset of a tone or light, the behavioral outcome may be said to depend upon a perceptual process. A given perception may be primarily innate (not experience-dependent) or heavily dependent upon experience. Examples of perceptual determinations of behavior include the discrimination of depth in binocular stereopsis or depth based on motion parallax (monocular), binaural sound localization, and the recognition of a sound sequence or a visual form. Animals may show such discriminative behavior innately upon first encountering a given complexity. The ease with which a response based upon a given perceptual discrimination may be modified by experience varies enormously, whether or not it appears in some recognizable form in the repertoire of innate mechanisms of neural organization. Some initial responses are highly determined and others tend to be altered quite readily. Crucial adaptive responses in relation to the organism's particular ecological niche exhibit more rigid determination than do those not necessary for immediate survival.

Sensory capacities of a given organism as measured behaviorally or physiologically are fundamental to any perceptual activity. Perception cannot be understood without some knowledge of the sensory mechanisms underlying discriminations, but such knowledge cannot by itself predict perceptual behavior. Some sensory abilities appear to be very little utilized in perception, whereas others contribute constantly to the organism's adaptive interactions with its environment. The cat, for example, is typically unresponsive to hue differences in the visual environment (Meyer & Anderson, 1965), although both physiological and behavioral correlates of hue may be demonstrated. By contrast, this animal promptly utilizes differences in light intensities and guides much of its behavior by sound cues. Higher primates are correctly viewed as strongly *visual*. However, intriguing as are such broad categorizations of preferred modality, most vertebrate species and many invertebrates respond to specific releasers in the several sense modes.

In this chapter, the word "cue" will be used to designate a complex stimulus *pattern* or stimulus *relationship* that has a specifiable function in directing or modifying behavior. Often the pattern or constellation of stimuli will reside in a single stimulus domain, such as vision. Again, combinations of stimuli that cross modalities become involved together to constitute some of the most fascinating problems in perception.

Organismic states and developmental stages play a powerful role in cue selection. The concept of a dominant sense is therefore limited in usefulness and serves mainly to call attention to certain broad contrasts in behavioral adaptations. Thus, the porpoise may with justification be called an auditory mammal in order to emphasize perceptual abilities that contrast sharply with those of most other organisms. Man expresses no extremes of specialization, and while relatively weak in chemical responsivities, Homo sapiens is noteworthy for balanced perceptivity in visual, auditory, and somesthetic domains. The human being often expresses unique stimulus preferences as one of the more outstanding characteristics among many that mark him or her as a distinct individual. This form of individuality in behavioral traits is also revealed in other mammals, as now increasingly documented both in behavioral genetics and studies of the effects of early experience.

Cross-modal Transfer in Animals.   Only rarely do animals that have learned to respond to a pattern of stimulation in one modality, such as vision, transfer that response to the comparable pattern in another modality, such as touch or audition.

Such positive evidence as exists for cross-modal transfer in animals comes from primates. Rhythm sameness versus difference is an abstraction that has worked well. Presented with a series of clicks in a pair of short sequences, African green monkeys discriminated whether the rate was the same or different. Transfer to light-flash sequences was successful (Stepien & Cordeau, 1960). Wegener (1965) attempted and failed to find any facilitation in the learning by rhesus monkeys of a discrimination between high and low levels of illumination and high and low sound intensities. Neither was there interference when monkeys learned to make opposing right versus left responses to the higher intensity across the two sensory modes. An earlier study with monkeys utilizing other dimensions also produced only negative results (Ettlinger, 1960). Blakeslee and Gunter (1966) were able to train one of seven cebus monkeys on learning sets in the visual domain and to obtain transfer to the tactual (haptic) mode. No cebus showed transfer from tactual to visual learning sets.

The anthropoid apes, after training in the cross-modal matching task, are capable of identifying objects that are new in their experience when these are visually presented and then chosen haptically. However, two chimpanzees and an orangutan were each able to select correctly only 75 percent of forty novel objects (where 50 percent was chance). Performance increased to 90 percent when sets of objects were used repeatedly (Davenport & Rogers, 1970). Cross-modal transfer of complex-object identification, according to all available evidence, requires prior correlated sensory experience across the relevant modalities. Young chimpanzees, for example, did not identify a favorite furry toy or a cloth by vision following only diffused-light experience even when they had learned by touch that these were highly desired objects. Tactual recognition of the feeding bottle did not hasten recognition by vision (Riesen, 1958).

Little is yet known about cross-modal transfer when the questions of critical period or of species differences are asked. Only in recent years have fundamental problems in within-modality perceptual learning and critical periods yielded to carefully executed and ingenious experimental investigations.

VISUAL PERCEPTION

Developmental Studies in Comparative Perspective

Birds and mammals extract remarkably complex and crucial information from their visual environments. Homing behavior represents a class of orienting, navigating, and relocating actions that depends heavily upon visual direction-finding. Its study engages the efforts of competent behavioral investigators, several of whom have asked key questions regarding the origins of these essential perceptual capacities. Visual-depth perception is another critical discriminative ability that receives continuing attention in research. These and other categories of the integration of sensory input are to varying degrees dependent upon innate neural organization. In many species the organization is gene-determined and a manifestation of the biological intelligence of that species. The survival and continuation of each animal form depend upon the readiness of the individual to engage in behavior appropriate to the place or the season or both. Mistakes or delays can be costly or fatal.

Direction-finding by Inexperienced Birds   Migrations of birds over long distances depend most often upon visual guidance from star patterns or from visual orientation supplied by positions of the sun. Other senses sometimes contribute, and the learning of local landmarks modifies the behavior of older birds. Reviews of many studies and evaluations of the several supporting factors in this class of behavior are available (cf. Matthews, 1968).

In young storks and starlings without prior experience of migrational flights, the appropriate compass direction is followed in their initial southerly migration. If they are displaced in an easterly or westerly direction, the birds fail to compensate for such displacement, since they maintain the fixed orientation in relation to the visible sky. Adult starlings, on the other hand, will compensate by modifying their orientation as much as 60 degrees (Perdeck, 1956), presumably because of experience with their goal. Birds maintained in an aviary, as shown chiefly by studies of several species of warblers (Sauer, 1957), persistently orient during the fall migratory season in the direction of normal migration, but do so only if the central part of the night sky is visible. An artificial night sky of the planetarium is an adequate substitute for normal night star patterns. Star patterns in the area of sky surrounding Polaris, the North Star, determined a correct orientation by indigo buntings (*Passerina cyanea*) even when the planetarium positions were advanced many hours ahead of local time (Emlen, 1967). Such evidence supports the hypothesis of an innate preference for maintaining a specifiable gestalt (configuration) of stars within a particular region of the visual field.

In daytime migratory flight, a *sun-compass* reaction that includes compensation for time of day serves as the guide for the required direction of flying, and it also influences orienting on the perch within an aviary. The use of sun-compass orientation is reported in nest-finding and food-foraging by insects, amphibians (Landreth & Ferguson, 1968), fish (Winn, Salmon, & Roberts, 1964), and several species of mammals including mice (Bovet, 1962). (For a review of studies of orientation in animals, including the use of vision by insects, the reader is referred to Hinde, 1970.)

Depth Perception in Birds, Rats, Rabbits, and Other Mammals.   Birds and rats have been found in repeated studies to discriminate depth (and distance) on an innate basis, i.e., upon initial opportunity for responding under the appropriate visual conditions. It is a common observation that domestic chicks and other precocial birds will peck at small objects or spots on the day of hatching. That they will do so with appropriately controlled variations in the energy and distance of head movements was demonstrated by Hess (1956b), who further showed that the binocular cues for depth were involved in this control.

Perhaps the earliest experimental demonstration of the innate organization of distance perception in birds was that of Spalding (1873), the naturalist who also published the first account of imprinting. Spalding permitted chicks to break out of the egg at hatching into a dark flannel bag. When first released to run toward the clucking mother hen, even with hearing eliminated, the chicks avoided obstacles in their path.

When chicks are hatched in the dark and first exposed, 24 hours after hatching, to a simulated drop-off on the *visual cliff,* they promptly show avoidance for a deep area as opposed to a shallow area (Shinkman, 1963; Walk, 1965). This technique (Figure 11-1) has been used with great effectiveness in comparative studies (Gibson, 1970, Walk, 1966). Late-maturing birds, such as the ring dove, are more difficult to test. Prolonged dark-rearing results in complicating adverse effects. Pilot observations indicate that experience is not a necessary precursor to depth discriminations in these species, and that we may conclude tentatively that diurnal land birds have in common the innate ability to perceive visual depth. Nocturnal birds have not been tested on the visual cliff, whereas observations on ducklings revealed a remarkable indifference (Walk, 1962). They waddled off the cliff readily in either direction. We may conclude from this only that another test is needed to answer questions about the early appearance of depth perception in certain of the birds. Turtles have also failed to respond differentially on the visual cliff.

The innate organization of depth perception has been found in experiments with pigmented and albino rats, both under conditions that required the animals to jump across gaps, with energy of the jump as a measure (Lashley & Russell, 1934), and in a series of experiments with the visual cliff. The young of sheep

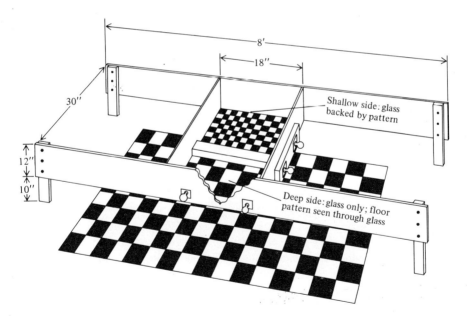

Figure 11–1. A visual cliff as designed for small animals. Glass surfaces equate sound (echolocation) and tactual stimuli from the two sides. The shallow pattern slides in grooves under the bridge to permit interchange of deep and shallow sides on successive trials. (From Walk, 1966; by permission of the Society for Research in Child Development, Inc.)

and goats are found to discriminate appropriately during the first day after birth (Walk, 1965; Walk & Gibson, 1961). The cliff-avoidance responses of wild rodents and of wild members of the cat family have been consistently found to be strong, but really vital differences among other species are correlated with survival requirements in the natural environment (Routtenberg & Glickman, 1964).

As a broad summarizing statement, experimenters working on the problem of the origins of depth perception with a sampling of vertebrate forms have concluded that animals (and human infants) exhibit discriminations on the visual cliff at approximately the same time as they begin to locomote. Thus, some succeed on the day of birth, and others shortly after their eyes open. Still other animals show delays until considerable visual experience and postural development have been achieved.

Rabbits, kittens, and a few representative higher primates have been tested on the cliff and do *not* show the discrimination at birth nor immediately after their eyes open. Must we deny the innate organization for perception of depth in these organisms? Our current knowledge of visual neurophysiological development requires us to accept a strong contribution from innate determinants. To this we must add, for some mammalian forms, the requirement of certain refinements to perceptual performance that only experience can provide. We are making progress in the specification of what these experiential requirements are.

Rearing animals in the dark or in diffused light may delay indefinitely, or in some species even permanently abolish, the capacity for visual cliff discriminations. Thus, in the albino rabbit, which under normal rearing discriminates well at four weeks of age, maintaining the animal in darkness to four weeks results in refusal by most animals to descend on either the shallow or the deep side. Among a few that do make the descent, there is a trend toward preference for the shallow (Walk, 1966), but in all cases recovery in the lighted environment is slow after 4 weeks in the dark.

Data for kittens reared in darkness or diffused light are more extensive. Without prior practice, kittens do not discriminate but respond at a chance level. Kittens reared normally develop the response slowly between twenty-two and thirty days of age, while dark-reared kittens may develop depth avoidance more rapidly after they are moved into a patterned visual environment (Walk, 1966). This would be expected from what is known about the maturation of the kitten's visual system. Following extensive growth of nerve cells and nerve processes and myelination of the optic nerve fibers between birth and four weeks, several hours of patterned visual experience adds critically to the perceptual capacity as measured in the visual cliff test, and as further documented by the appearance of visual placing (Held & Hein, 1963; Riesen, 1961). Improvement in visual cliff performance as a function of early perceptual experience has also been found in behavioral studies with infant rats (Eichengreen, Coren, & Nachmias, 1966).

A categorical answer to the question of whether *primates* exhibit innate depth perception would be premature. Early perceptual preferences are by now well documented both for the human infant and for nonhuman primates (Fantz, 1967). The newborn rhesus monkey is a relatively mature mammal, no doubt in part because of a prolonged period of gestation in relation to its life span. Emotional disturbance as well as motor responses has been used to assess depth perception in monkeys from 3 to 20 days following birth, and discrimination of depth apparently occurs as early as the third day (Rosenblum & Cross, 1963). Following 20 days or 60 days of rearing from birth in diffused light, rhesus monkeys still required a minimum of 28 hours of experience in patterned light, with freedom to be active and to interact with other animals, before showing avoidance of the deep side of the visual cliff (Wilson & Riesen, 1966). For these infants visual placing appeared shortly prior to cliff avoidance. This requirement for patterned visual experience may be compared with the 5 hours of experience found by Munro to be necessary for kittens after being reared in diffused light to 27 days (Riesen, 1961).

Upon what cues for visual depth perception do the earliest responses of infant animals depend? Binocular cues are in general not found to be necessary. Texture density does not provide the essential cue (Schiffman & Walk, 1963; Walk & Gibson, 1961). Motion parallax, sharpness of focus especially in myopic animals such as the rat, and accommodative effort are possible candidates, with the first of these three best supported by available evidence (Gibson, 1970; Palen, 1965). During body movements or even slight head movements, the rate and pattern of image displacement depend upon the distance and the slope of the patterned surface, independent of grain or texture so long as a texture is available to the visual system in question. This "shearing action" is the motion parallax cue, one of the major determinants of space perception under monocular as well as binocular viewing.

Perception of Visual Direction   Visual direction or "local sign" has immediate behavioral effects in the innate reflexes that support the eye and head orientations of most insects and vertebrates. The optomotor (also called optokinetic and opticokinetic) responses normally serve to maintain a stable relationship between the animal's eyes, often with movements that include head and body, and the environment. The projected visual field moving across the retina pulls with it the eye or eyes. When eyes are fixed or quite limited in the ability to rotate in the head, neck reflexes promptly respond to support the visual following, as seen especially in birds. With insects the entire body moves, as is true also in fish and amphibia. Man shares these powerful orienting reflexes, and for some workers this has been convincing evidence for the innateness of the perception of visual direction. Since other behavioral responses to visual direction are modifiable, and since the optomotor reflexes survive ablations of the visual cortex, we must question the validity of such a sweeping conclusion. Nevertheless, there is no denying the fundamental importance of these midbrain sensory-motor integrations in normal visual perception even in those mammalian organisms with the most elaborate and modifiable nervous systems.

Birds exhibit two clear types of response that involve orientation on an innate basis. Shortly after hatching or immediately after a day or two of dark-rearing, an appropriate small target releases the pecking response in precocial birds. Nestling altricial birds direct their gaping response to the appropriate region of the nest when the parent bird arrives, and, as shown by the use of models, toward the protrusion that extends from the model "body" if of appropriate relative size (Figure 2-3a). The elevation and opening of the bill of the nestling are both released and directed by the visual stimuli (Tinbergen & Kuenen, 1939).

The classical studies of Sperry (see Sperry & Hibbard, 1968) established, both in development and regeneration of neural structures, the orderly point-to-point projection of fibers from the retina to the brain. Precise chemical affinities are postulated to account for the anatomical growth patterns. These patterns in turn account well for the behavioral controls as seen in optokinetic responses and in appropriately directed initial feeding responses. The universality of these sensory-motor mechanisms is of utmost significance. Prey-catching movements by the proper orientation and extension of tentacles in *Sepia* (cuttlefish) when newly hatched and feeding for the first time (Wells, 1962), the many behavioral studies of amphibians by Sperry and others (cf. Lettvin, Maturana, McCulloch, & Pitts, 1959), and the behavior of newly hatched birds speak to the broadly based phylogenetic origins of visually guided behavior. But complete and rigid determination of such behavior on the basis of genetic information would prevent even the modification that is required concurrently with a change in size of an organism as it grows.

Prism adaptation studies that show modifiable direction of responding in man are well known (Held, 1961). Prisms that consistently displace the visual field laterally cause misdirected reaching initially, followed by improving compensation. Between the extremes in levels of neural complexity and presumed plasticity of the primates and of the birds and amphibians, we may expect to find a range of capacities for modification. The early dependence upon experience for the initiation of visually guided behaviors should relate to the degree of modifiability during the wearing of displacing prisms (Held & Bossom, 1961).

Birds have generally been considered to resemble amphibians in their extreme degree of innate fixity of responding to visual direction. Earlier findings (Hess, 1956) and more recent work (Rossi, 1968) agree that newly hatched domestic chicks fail to show prism adaptation when required to view the world through laterally displacing prisms during the first 4 days after hatching. Extending the exposure to 8 days sufficed to demonstrate directional compensation. Rate of adaptation is relatively slow, perhaps little more than sufficient to keep ahead of physical growth requirements (Rossi, 1969). In higher primates an exposure of less than an hour is sufficient to obtain a shift, and complete adaptation in the monkey to 13 degrees of displacement has been reported in 2 to 4 days (Bossom & Hamilton, 1963).

Guided forelimb extension of newborn monkeys and of maturing kittens requires prior visual experience conjoined with motor activity (Hein & Held, 1967; Held & Bauer, 1967). The consequences of paw extension must be observable (Figure 11-2). Earlier in this chapter we saw that initial optokinetic orienting responses did not require such experience in man, monkey, or cat. Clearly, the behavior must be specified when we draw inferences concerning the determinants of perceptual adaptations.

When the visual consequences of motor action can be correlated with that motor action (or efference), we have an example of a *closed loop* system.

Figure 11–2. A test for visually guided reaching. The forelimb may simply be extended (placing response), striking the prongs on approximately 50% of trials, or the extension may show accurate visual guidance. Kittens or monkeys reared without opportunity to see their limb movements do not show guided reaching. (From Hein & Held, *Science,* 1967, copyright 1967 by the American Association for the Advancement of Scienco.)

The visual information is designated as "reafference" (Held, 1961; von Holst, 1954), and the attendant feedback may serve two distinct functions. It will typically have an immediate effect in confirming or altering the rate of motor activity. It may also serve in a trial-and-error manner to modify future action. It is this second function that generates or modifies the direction of approach responses. In a visual rearrangement experiment, the two components of the closed loop become recorrelated.

The closed loop is required in the development of guided reaching as illustrated in Figure 11–2, in kittens and baby monkeys, and in establishing certain other kinds of visually directed responding in primates. Some early visually guided behaviors of infant monkeys are listed in Table 11–1. Living in light from birth (left column), the infants responded first with ocular pursuit and crude reaching movements on day 3 or later. Other infants were reared in diffused light from birth to 20 or 60 days of age (right column). They were then given normally patterned visual environments during 2½ hours daily (Wilson and Riesen, 1966).

These data clearly lead to the conclusion that opportunity for perceptual learning is necessary and is gradually utilized when available to the infant higher primate. It has been shown that the human adult requires continuing experience with functioning closed loops, since degrading or disarranging the consistency of feedback results in distortions of perception and losses of reaching accuracy (Freedman, 1961; Held, 1961). Such facts speak against a *critical period* or *imprinting* phenomenon. However, Fantz has shown that monkeys

Table 11–1 The Development of Visually Directed Behaviors in Infant Rhesus Monkeys

Behavior	Range, in days, of first appearance in any given animal following exposure to full patterned environment	
	Light-reared Ss	Ss reared initially in diffused light
Ocular pursuit of a moving light	3–12	1–3
Ocular pursuit of objects	4–28	4–12
Inaccurate reach toward object	3–10	6–13
Visual placing response	6–21	5–16
Accurate reach to object	14–56	12–29
Binocular convergence	21–35	7–11
Visual cliff depth avoidance	—	11–34

SOURCE: After Wilson, P. D. & Riesen, A. H. visual development in rhesus monkeys neonatally deprived of patterned light. Journal of Comparative and Physiological Psychology, 1966, **61**, 87–95. Copyright 1966 by the American Psychological Association and reproduced by permission.

do progressively less fixating of visually articulated areas the longer they continue to be deprived of visual experience (Fantz, 1967). Furthermore, the
studies of pattern deprivation in cats (Hubel & Wiesel, 1963) and in chimpanzees (Chow, Riesen, & Newell, 1957) indicate that unless demands are
made upon the integrative functions of the nervous system, their normal
development becomes more and more difficult.

The Perception of Patterns and Objects   From insects to man, looking preferences that are independent of specific experiences with the preferred visual
target support the concept of innate discriminative capacities. These preferences are also susceptible to modification. Mere exposure on repeated trials
may reduce the relative standing of a preferred visual target. Food or other
rewards may enhance the amount of looking and also such additional instrumental behavior as is followed by the reward.

Insects show spontaneous preference behaviors that strongly influence
the surfaces upon which they will settle. They do not readily learn to discriminate between geometric forms, such as circles, triangles, and rectangles.
Landing sites are favored if they are characterized by broken outlines rather
than by more gradual curves or smoother outlines. With broken outline forms
that are identical, color may quickly become the determinant of a trained
preference in experiments that provide food reward. Most insect studies of
form and color discriminations have been with bees (von Frisch, 1967, pp.
478–491; Zerrahn, 1933).

The strong preference for forms with flowerlike contours has generally
been ascribed to properties of compound eyes, many segments of which would
receive flicker stimulation as the insect flies toward or across the flower petals.
A spontaneous preference for checkerboard over solid or outline figures is
further evidence in agreement with this interpretation. Upon return to the
hive from a foraging flight, bees reverse their preference toward choice of
a simple shape. Von Frisch assigns this preference to its relation to the
entrance of the hive.

Specific dimensions of forms that insects discriminate are only recently
being investigated. Bees are capable of discriminating differences in the orientation of multiple-stripe patterns as small as 10 degrees. According to one
study, the shift from the vertical alters trained response levels more than an
equal shift from the horizontal (Wehner, 1967). Diagonals of 45 degrees and
135 degrees are readily discriminated, a behavior unlike the octopus discrimination behavior described a few lines further on.

Wasps utilize visual landmarks to return to a nesting or feeding location.
Shifting single objects (sticks, bark, stones, and so on) does not disturb the
return flight, but transposition of a group of objects to retain their pattern
results in a corresponding shift of the place of landing. Objects that reach
upward on the horizon are especially important components of such a shifted
pattern (Tinbergen & Kruyt, 1938).

The image-forming eye of the octopus has brought scientific attention to its visual capabilities. Training methods work well with this cephalopod (Sutherland, 1969). Geometric figures are readily discriminated. Oblique lines of opposite slant are generally confused although horizontal versus vertical striations are readily differentiated, just as is true for human infants. This is a special case of the more general difficulty that these and other species (including monkeys) have in confusing right-left mirror images. Up-down inversions are quite easily discriminated.

Form identification and form preferences are highly developed in birds. Round shapes and spherical objects are pecked more frequently than square or star-shaped patterns by newly hatched chicks. Chicks kept in darkness or diffused light to permit neuromuscular maturation without specific experience pecked significantly more frequently at rounded than at pointed objects of a small constant size (Fantz, 1957). Other work by Eckhard Hess and his students at the University of Chicago demonstrated size and color preferences in chicks and ducklings. Since birds have excellent color vision and since the food objects found normally by birds vary in color, shape, and size, it is not surprising that innate preferences vary with species. Our knowledge of these and other perceptual variations among birds is extremely limited. Nocturnal birds, such as owls, constitute exceptions to the rule that birds have high acuity and color vision. Some owls rely heavily on motion detection and on auditory localization since they eat prey rather than seeds. A study of form preferences, if any exist, and of the ability of owls to learn form discriminations would add much to scientific knowledge of the behavior and sensory-perceptual capacities of birds.

Fish make excellent use of form vision under natural conditions. They undoubtedly have strong innate preferences for color and form, and the two dimensions clearly interact as they do in birds, but the detailed nature of such preferences has not been systematically investigated. Fishermen's lore could serve as a starting point for work in this field. Fish have learned form discriminations in the biologist's laboratory, and have supplied valuable information regarding the organization of the vertebrate visual nervous system. Goldfish associate the "meaning" of a given form specifically with its location in space (Ingle, 1967/1968), a finding that may have some parallel with a dependence upon context and motivation, independent of sensory capacity, in other learned discrimination behaviors. This principle applies with great generality across the animal kingdom.

Objects in motion induce orienting and following behavior in the young of precocial animals, both birds and mammals, in the first day after birth. This earliest perceptual activity is discriminative in the sense that size, color, and form are significant determinants of the strength of the following responses. Animals that are less mature at birth or hatching show early alerting and orienting, although often these behaviors appear only some days after the end of gestation. In such animals, experience plays a greater part in neural and behavioral development, with looking preferences playing a fundamental role in the environment-organism interactions.

During early development, looking preferences change gradually as a function of looking. Initial preferences persist longer if opportunities to view specific targets are available but limited to a few minutes per day. A method, since used extensively in work with human infants, was first developed for work with infant chimpanzees (Fantz, 1958). Two visual viewing fields are presented above the baby lying on its back in a crib. A looking preference is shown if the baby consistently looks for longer time periods at one rather than the other target area. Reflections of the pattern or object being viewed are photographed or tabulated by an observer through a small opening directly above the face of the baby. From birth to five weeks of age, one chimpanzee was reared in darkness except during daily tests that totaled 30 minutes. During this time, a strong preference for blue over red was observed; between three and five weeks, a strong preference (90 percent versus 10 percent) for a solid model of a head over a cut-out, flat oval similar in size was recorded. Approximately equal viewing time for circle cut-outs versus cross cut-outs at the age of six weeks (and earlier) shifted after 3 weeks of unrestricted vision to a 77 percent preference (p <.01) for the cross. This type of result and many similar findings in kittens and in primates support the general conclusion that, with experience, the direction of preferences shifts to stimuli of greater complexity.

In spite of these early indicators of behavioral control by patterns and objects, the earliest recognition as defined by food-motivated or socially motivated learning may not appear until weeks later in monkeys or chimpanzees. As stated by Fantz (1958): "Tests pairing a nursing bottle with an unfamiliar but comparable object failed to show consistent differential fixation after weeks of visual and rewarding experience with the bottle [p. 65]."

The rate at which infant primates learn new approach or avoidance responses to visual patterns or visual objects is in marked contrast to that of birds. Perceptual development is rapid in birds. They learn to alter their pecking responses to objects of different color, size, or form within hours after hatching. Primates require days or weeks before such approach responses show alteration. Interaction with complex stimuli is required in either case. Primates appear to confuse patterns or objects during their earliest discrimination learning. With stimulus patterns having multiple dimensions, some of which are irrelevant, the primate has an attentional problem. In the bird this is much less in evidence. Being initially more selective in its responses to a pattern or object, the bird promptly gains reinforcement of a generally (for the bird) relevant dimension when it is able to see, seize, and swallow an object. Whereas birds modify pecking preferences within an hour or so of pecking experience, reasonably comparable observations with the rhesus monkey show that for simple black versus white, or for redundant cues from multiple horizontal versus vertical striations, the first discrimination learning on the basis of reward and nonreward requires from 6 to 20 days. Later, of course, such discriminations can be learned in one session, or even in one or two trials, by a highly experienced monkey. When a task is more complex, such as discriminating a triangle from a circle, the initial habits require from 20 to 45 days, training being given at the rate of ten trials daily (Wilson & Riesen, 1966).

Another method for assessing perceptual development involves the everyday experience of the animal and its interaction with familiar or novel objects. Well known is the speed with which birds and young mammals of certain species discriminate a familiar moving object from one which is strange. The imprinting process shows improved discriminative powers over trials or days, but the amount of learning that occurs within 10 or 15 minutes of exposure is dramatic. Avoidance of the strange and approach to the familiar is a natural discrimination behavior that confirms the previous general conclusion. This behavior develops slowly in higher primates as contrasted with birds and many mammalian forms that have been observed. Infant chimpanzees avoid strange objects and approach familiar ones during the third month of life under normal rearing conditions. The more difficult discrimination of persons develops in the fourth month. Early rearing under diffuse light conditions to allow general organismic maturation permits some saving of experiential time. But this is a relatively modest saving, reducing to about 40 days the time required to develop a fear of the strange object (Riesen, 1958). Fear of strange persons may persist in the infant chimpanzee as in the infant human from its onset at about four months of age to an age of three or four years, depending heavily upon the nature of social experiences as they affect the individual.

In birds, the basis for recognition of other individuals appears to be simple when contrasted with the complex patterns utilized in individual recognitions by the higher primates. Evidence for individual recognition focuses on such a straightforward dimension as the size of the comb in chickens or turkeys (Guhl & Ortman, 1953). Nature has clearly given many animals the advantage of simplifying the problem of attention or stimulus selection. Clearly this is a problem related to the genetic encoding of innate *releasing* stimuli.

The first learning of form and certain kinds of movement discriminations by kittens is also slow. Intensity differences (total flux rather than brightness cues) are again relatively easy. Discrimination of both a rotating versus a stationary cross (+) and the oscillation of a solid circle versus a motionless one proved to be exceedingly difficult for kittens reared in diffused light and kittens exposed to patterned light during periods of bodily restraint (Riesen, 1965; Riesen & Aarons, 1959). Redundant form differences (multiple striations oriented horizontally versus vertically) were intermediate in difficulty, just as for the monkey. The possibility that visual-acuity differences contribute to certain of these results is supported by data from the monkeys, which required several days of patterned visual experience before they resolved narrow stripes in the optokinetic drum (Riesen, Ramsey, & Wilson, 1964). The data for kittens that gained visual experience while prevented from active locomotion require a different explanation, which will be discussed in a later section.

Visually Perceived Relationships and Visual Constancies

Perception of Location   Egocentric location in space and the perception of paths and goals are studied both in the natural environment of animals and through the use of maze problems, delayed response tests, delayed alternation, and other laboratory methods. Learning a "cognitive map" requires both a background of visual experience in articulated space and the exposure to a particular spatial arrangement that forms the problem or test situation. Although other senses contribute to the animal's perception of its own locus at a given moment, vision provides a much greater amount of immediate information. We have already noted that insects locate their nests on the basis of simultaneous information about the relative positions of a cluster of landmarks. Vertebrates with good detail vision clearly do the same. Based upon observations on rats that utilized the relative location of more distant landmarks like windows in preference to certain details near at hand, Hebb (1949) developed his neuropsychological theory of space perception. The adequacy of memory for location in the solution of "place" problems depends upon the degree to which prior sequences of experience in the larger setting are available. A useful analogy may be that of two persons in the front seat of a car, one of whom actively negotiates a sequence of turns and distances with attendant perceptions of landmarks. The other is like the passive kitten in the gondola of the Held and Hein experiment (Figure 11-3). Visual exposures may be virtually the same. Which individual could more readily retrace or repeat the route? Let us proceed to the behavioral implications without concerning ourselves with the neurologizing.

Several of Hebb's students and colleagues have done animal experiments to evaluate the role of the enriched or impoverished early (spatial) environment. Many experiments have been performed in other laboratories as well. Rats, cats, and dogs reared in plain cages or barren room environments, and especially if they cannot see beyond the walls of these compartments, subsequently perform poorly on maze problems and spatial delayed-response tasks (Thompson & Heron, 1954). Enrichment of the early spatial environment results in the one-trial learning of spatial delayed-response and delayed-alternation tasks, as well as fewer errors in maze learning. There is often greater facility in the learning of other visual and even nonvisual tasks (Forgays

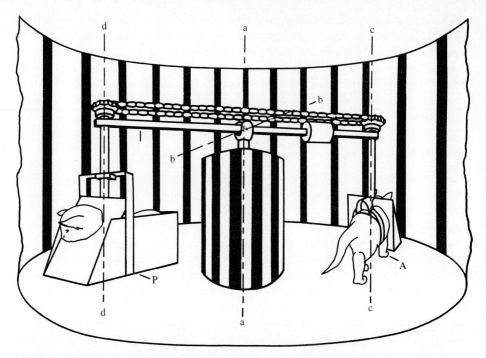

Figure 11–3. A, "active, and P, "passive" kittens in the gondola apparatus. Visual experience within the drum is equated by the chain drive and by pivots at the a—a and b—b axes. The d and c axes are 36 in. apart. (R. Held & A. Hein. Movement produced stimulation in the development of visually .guided behavior. *Journal of Comparative and Physiological Psychology,* 1963, **56,** 872–876. Copyright 1963 by the American Psychological Association and reproduced by permission.

& Forgays, 1952; Forgus, 1954; Hymovitch, 1952; Riesen, 1965; Rosenzweig, 1966). The age at which differential experience occurs is clearly an important variable (Dews & Wiesel, 1970).

Size, Distance, Shape, and Movement Constancies   Animals, like man, respond to objects in the real world, not simply to the isolated projection of such objects on the retinal mosaic. Although direct evidence for this comes only from studies of a few species, the relational properties upon which size and distance discriminations depend influence the visual behavior of invertebrates as well as birds and mammals. The constancies are a general phenomenon of object perception. If experience does anything, it enables the individual to respond more independently of the constancy relationship by permitting abstraction of component cues from their context. Animals and children have greater difficulty in escaping constancies than in responding to them. Paradoxically, constancies also improve with age up to a point. This results from such factors as improving abilities to resolve detail (an acuity factor) and learning about objects.

Little work has been done to study developmental processes in animal perceptual constancies directly. The inability of kittens to discriminate moving from nonmoving patterns after motor restriction (Riesen & Aarons, 1959) is one example of an experiential requirement, the perception of a stable visual environment being dependent during self-initiated movement upon an accurate cancellation of the efferent from the correlated reafferent neural-movement coordinates.

Retinal size of an object changes with distance. The cat has been shown to discriminate size as relatively invariant with distances up to 2 meters (Gunter, 1951). Size constancy has also been demonstrated in ducklings, monkeys, and chimpanzees.

Retinal projections of a given object vary with the angle from which it is viewed. The familiar experimental demonstration is to present a circular disc in varying degrees of slant. Judgments may then vary in describing the disc as any shape from circular to strongly elliptical. Monkeys match according to the real object. The circular cut-out is consistently chosen over the elliptical as the match for the round disc presented at various angles (Zeigler & Leibowitz, 1958).

Contrasts and Constancies in Brightness and Color   The mechanisms for simultaneous contrast effects exist in compound eyes of arthropods (Hartline & Ratliff, 1956). Similar mechanisms are found in the retinas of vertebrates. They undoubtedly form the basis of innate releasing stimuli in frogs and many other prey-catching animals since they serve to enhance the stimulating effect of a moving edge even more than they do a stationary contour. The spatial transition from one brightness level or one color to another level or color is accompanied by lateral inhibition. Thus, a ratio of two stimulus intensities or the energy ratios of complementary colors, rather than local absolute values, will determine levels of responding at more central projections of the visual nervous system. During the movement of an edge across receptors, the central projection areas of those receptors will jump suddenly from an inhibited to a facilitated level of activation or vice versa. Translating this via the motor system into a directed head-and-tongue movement of the frog or a pecking response of the chick, we begin to explain the fixed action patterns of feeding behaviors in so many representative amphibians, birds, and mammals. Assuming innately organized "signs" of sufficient accuracy, we can understand the prompt self-sufficiency of young precocial birds and other animals.

Since flicker discrimination is markedly more acute in many insects than in man, we may with some justification assume that their visual system functions to enhance contrast more efficiently than does ours or those of other mammals. At the perceptual level, the study of these effects has been limited in coverage. We know, on the one hand, that bees resolve flicker at rates more than double the critical fusion frequency for man. In one quantitative study, the chimpanzee has been demonstrated to see contrast effects in both brightness and color in the same degree as does man (Grether, 1942).

Binocular Vision   The nearer a visual target is to the viewing organism, the greater the contribution is to accurate depth perception of binocular disparity and convergence cues. The benefits are weak at distances beyond 12 meters, but for seizing of prey, brachiating, or jumping, binocular vision provides crucial information. Stereopsis is often cited as one of the advances in phylogenesis. Many animals with laterally mounted eyes possess very limited stereopsis. Animals that are hunted, such as rabbits and small birds, have vision all around the head, but only 10 to 30 degrees of binocular overlap. Man and the higher primates share the advantages of binocular vision with many other vertebrates (Walls, 1942). Even with a small arc forward of overlapping visual fields, the stereoscopic depth cues are usually of considerable adaptive significance, as in birds (Hess, 1956). The acuity provided by foveal vision and a cone retina was once associated theoretically with stereopsis, but this correlation is not high. Cats and other animals with primarily rod vision have the perceptual advantages of stereopsis.

Behavioral studies of stereo acuity in animals are almost nonexistent. Evidence that a monkey sees depth in random-dot patterns that have a central segment displaced (Julesz figures) has recently been obtained by an operant training method (Bough, 1970). A recently discovered type of *detector* cell in the primate visual cortex presumably serves as the neural integrating element for binocular disparity (Hubel & Wiesel, 1970a). Single-cell recording reveals cells that respond maximally only when both eyes are simultaneously stimulated from points on the retinas (or visual fields) that are optimally displaced from the points of exact retinal correspondence. These binocular depth detectors were first discovered in the striate cortex of cats (Barlow, Blakemore, & Pettigrew, 1967). Thus far, they have been demonstrated not in monkey striate cortex, but in the prestriate or so-called visual association areas.

Somewhat indirect behavioral evidence for the presence of stereoscopic depth perception may be seen in the convergent fixation movements of the two eyes as a target approaches a near point, beyond which one eye suddenly breaks away laterally from fixation. This can be observed in young monkeys after the age of ten days (Table 11-1). Domestic cats are variable in their response but many show excellent convergence movements. With disuse of pattern vision in one eye during a critical period in the cat between the fourth week and three months after birth, there is permanent impairment of acuity and of stereoscopic depth perception, although some behavioral recovery in the deprived eye is possible even in the absence of recovery of the cortical units (Dews & Wiesel, 1970).

Perceptual Problem Solving in Animals   Comparative studies of the solution of bent-wire and patterned-string problems have revealed differences between monkeys and apes. Analysis of a spatial pattern is required in a series of problems of varying difficulty. In the patterned-string tests, two, three, or four strings are arranged in slanting or crossing patterns, and a lure, such as a raisin or grape, is attached to the far end of one. The animal must grasp the one string that leads to the fruit. Chimpanzees, gorillas, and orangutans are individually somewhat unequal in their proportions of successes, but do not show differences from species to species. Monkeys have failed consistently on certain of the more difficult problems (for a list of references and a summary, see Riesen, 1970).

Rhesus monkeys and five adolescent and two adult chimpanzees were tested on a series of bent-wire detour problems. Lifesaver candies could be removed by appropriate threading movements from the starting point to the open end of the bent wires. The easier problems were solved by all. More difficult patterns were solved best by the adult chimpanzees. The adolescent chimpanzees were superior to the monkeys (Davis, McDowell, & Nissen, 1957). Complexity and stability of perceptual organization are shown to increase both with the level of primate and with individual experience in these and other problem-solving tests.

AUDITORY PERCEPTION

Auditory Space Perception

Localization of Sound Sources   Finding food, locating offspring or the parent animal, and avoiding predators are in many animals based largely or in part upon sound localization. Both direction and distance of sound sources are perceived by a vast range of animal species. General knowledge about these behaviors is extensive, but careful analyses of the contributions of various component cues have been done with only a few animal forms. As in vision, reflex orienting movement toward or away from a sound source is the common endowment of most organisms, invertebrates included. A startle response to loud sounds is a typical vertebrate response, and may not be followed by body-orienting movements.

Orienting depends upon differences in physical properties of sound arriving at the two sides (or two ears) of the perceiving organism. Intensity, time, phase, and spectral composition, either singly or in combinations, may contribute to the localizing of a source. Ingenious recording of the physical, electrophysiological, and behavioral correlates has gone into the better studies of animal auditory localization. One of the few investigations on insects reveals that moths may show escape orienting away from the high-frequency sounds emitted by bats. Sound shadow from the moth's body reduces intensities at the ear that is away from the source. The binaural cue, verified electrophysiologically, is a response difference between the ears (Roeder, 1964).

In mammals, the greater distance between the ears permits time differences to contribute heavily. This makes possible the localization of low-frequency sounds which are little attenuated by the head. Cats are capable of discriminating differences in the direction of two sources only 5 degrees apart (Neff & Diamond, 1958). Comparable threshold studies with other animals are not available, but man, probably because he has a larger head to aid the triangulation, is capable of resolving about 3 degrees in the same situation.

Echolocation and Echoranging   A few remarkable species of birds, some bats, and dolphins avoid obstacles and find food without vision by emitting sounds and receiving reflected sounds through exceptionally sensitive auditory systems. At much more crude levels, rats and even human beings can utilize some echo cues. So-called facial vision of the blind is based on improved skills of this kind, but human hearing has too restricted a range to be highly effective.

The oilbird of South America negotiates the complete darkness of caves and locates objects by emitting clicks of about 7,000 cycles per second. Its speed and precision of localization do not compare favorably with those of bats and dolphin. Ultrasonic (as defined for man) vibrations in extremely short pulses are emitted by bats and by dolphins (*Delphinus* and *Tursiops*). Reflected sounds at 50,000 cycles per second and above return sound spectra to ears that are sensitive to 90,000 cycles per second. These echoes carry much information about the nature of the echoing material and its location in space. Bats catch moths and other insects, and dolphins discriminate between fish in accordance with feeding preferences (Griffin, Webster, & Michael, 1960; Kellogg, 1961).

Identification of Auditory Patterns

In the cat and the rhesus monkey, the learned identification of three-tone pitch sequences requires functional contributions from the temporal cortex. The component tones can themselves be discriminated without cortical participation. The role of the cortex appears to be that of holding component tones in short-term memory until they can be combined into a distinctive temporal pattern (Neff & Diamond, 1958).

Certain species of birds are notable for their powers of sound reproduction (mimicry). Some develop song patterns from basic components, or subsongs, each of which can be babbled by the inexperienced young bird. Combining these into a full song that may last several seconds requires that young birds hear such a tonal sequence either from other birds or from recordings. Auditory pattern perception is clearly implicated in the song development of chaffinches and other passerine birds. (For a review of work on innate subsongs, song learning, and effects of early isolation or deafening in passerine birds, consult Hinde, 1970, pp. 451-462).

Recognition of the voice of an individual organism is for some species crucial for survival. Parent and offspring recognition may be the most significant example. While this is common in human experience, we have few certain instances in studies with animals. Surprisingly, most evidence that other higher primates discriminate individual vocalizations is anecdotal. Territories are maintained by howler monkeys on this basis, and the young of apes and monkeys appear generally to respond selectively to their own parents' voices. A study utilizing careful experimental controls has demonstrated that chicks of the laughing gull, *Larus atricilla,* which breed and hatch under colony conditions, can identify the calls of their parents as early as 6 days post hatching. They turn away from comparable calls of other adult gulls (Beer, 1969).

The perceptual basis for auditory communication in the social behavior of animals is greatly in need of investigation. Examples of responses to emotional cries are common. Many of these calls are innate releasers. The extent to which experience may alter individual responses is only beginning to be understood, and only in a very few species. Studies of this broad category of perceptual learning are needed in order to bring about advances in the science of behavior.

SOMATOSENSORY PERCEPTION

Tactual Discriminations

Stimuli applied to the skin surface or made available to manipulation are necessarily multisensory. They exert pressure, have temperature characteristics, and have both a location and a spatial pattern. Roughness versus smoothness is a tactual discrimination frequently used in animal studies of the neurophysiology of skin sensitivities. Higher mammals succeed in this discrimination by utilization of input to the temporo-parietal region of the cortex (Mountcastle & Darian-Smith, 1968).

Many animals, especially those with nocturnal rather than diurnal activity cycles, show response preferences to tactual information. When rats are given conflicting tactual information (from contact to the vibrissae) and visual information, the tactual information wins out over the visual in the depth avoidance on the visual cliff.

The recognition of solid objects can be difficult for man and chimpanzee. With practice there is much improvement. Few nonprimate animals have been tested for this ability. The generous endowment of "arms" and contact points of octopus makes this organism a promising subject. Does the octopus have the somesthetic integrating nervous system necessary for stereognosis? A series of ingenious experiments has shown that it fails to recognize the shape of larger objects unless local distortions of its sucker organs, as at sharp corners or curvatures, are available as differential cues. Local texture, rather than outline shape, must be the distinguishing feature to which the animal responds. There is no evidence that proprioceptive cues concerning the bending of its arms are available for this animal's discriminative learning (Wells, 1962). Consistent with this general finding is the further observation that one cylinder carrying grooves around the cylinder cannot be discriminated from another cylinder carrying longitudinal grooves when the total lengths of the grooves are approximately equated. This task would seem appropriate for comparative studies but has thus far received surprisingly little use.

Discrimination of Verticality and Slant

Animals, like man, obviously depend constantly upon gravity-sensitive receptors. Most of our behavioral observations are predicated upon this assumption, but knowledge about mechanisms is largely limited to studies of the gravity reflexes. To make quick adjustments in space, higher primates obviously use visual information extensively when it is available. This information is integrated with joint, muscle, and skin senses as well as with the statoreceptors' inputs from the semicircular canals. The visual frame of reference contributes strongly to perception of the vertical in man. Individual development factors contribute to an improving ability to respond discriminatively to verticality in spite of misleading visual cues (Witkin, Lewis, Hertzman, Machover, Meissner, & Wapner, 1954). Comparative studies are needed before much can be said concerning individual and species characteristics in this perceptual-adaptive sphere. A preliminary report of species differences among related macaque monkeys supports the expectation that information imbedded in a complex visual context is readily extracted by some members of the primate order. Others are much less successful (Rosenblum, Witkin, Kaufman, & Brosgole, 1965). A highly plausible suggestion that arboreal and ground-dwelling species may differ in this respect has been advanced (Rumbaugh & McCormack, 1969). Horizontal and vertical lines in a visual frame of reference may be expected to influence perception of the true gravity-vertical direction to a greater degree in ground-dwelling than in arboreal animals. Tree-living animals (especially primates) would be expected to perceive the true gravity-vertical more consistently than those living on flat surfaces. The expectation is in some degree confirmed in the human sex difference since males, who climb and tumble more than do females, respond more accurately to true vertical in the rod-and-frame test. Genetic factors may interact with experience in early ontogeny in this and other areas of space perception. Unfortunately, much of the research in spatial learning by animals has involved only discriminations of places and pathways in the horizontal plane. The vertical dimension is somewhat less convenient for man, and this fact has resulted in its neglect in the comparative psychophysics of spatial adjustments.

OLFACTORY AND TASTE PERCEPTION

General Chemical Responsivities

All organisms respond to chemicals. Again, there is no sharp line separating perceptual from sensory mechanisms. Injurious chemicals induce quick-acting escape responses or reflexes whose function is often to dilute the injurious substance, as in tear gland and salivary gland secretion. Social behavior, broadly defined, and more specific sexual responses often depend upon exocrine gland secretions that induce changes in the behavior of other members of the species. The study of these hormonelike substances (pheromones) and their contributions to social behavior is a relatively recent development (Wilson, 1965). (Pheromones were introduced in Chapters 5 and 9.) Much insect social behavior is supported or even critically determined by chemicals released into the local environment by one organism to be received by another either as olfactory, gustatory, or general chemical stimuli. Effects on the nervous system of the receiving organism are rapid or more gradual, in either case resembling the direct action of hormones. As a *microsmatic* organism, man has been slow to appreciate and study the significant chemical signals that govern other mammalian behavior as well as the behavior of insects and of nonmammalian vertebrates. Man is discovering chemical influences in his own life processes as a consequence of new knowledge about animals.

Pheromones in Insect Communication

No fewer than eleven exocrine glands have been identified in bees. Their secretions serve individually or in combination in the control of other bees in a hive. Ants and termites are similarly endowed. Odor trails serve to lead additional workers to food. Disturbance of a hive or nest results in alarm secretions. These are volatile and of simple molecular structure, with rapid fading time. In some species, the alarm substance is secreted by the mandibular gland; in others, by Dufour's gland (Figure 11-4).

The behavioral effects and the chemical composition of many of the pheromones of social insects have not been identified. Soldier ants respond strongly to formic acid secretion. This material is thus classified as a *defense* secretion, although it is also considered to be a secondary alarm substance for worker ants.

The "meaning" or behavioral outcome of the release of a given pheromone depends sometimes on the context, often also on the concentration, and occasionally on the concurrent release of another pheromone (Wilson, 1965, p. 1070).

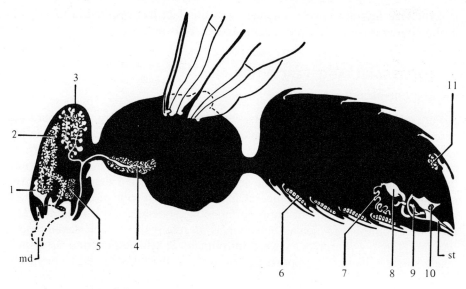

Figure 11–4. The exocrine glands of the honey bee worker. 1. mandibular gland; 2, hypopharyngeal (= maxillary) gland; 3, head labial gland; 4, thorax labial gland; 5, postgenal gland; 6, wax glands; 7, poison glands; 8, vesicle of poison gland; 9, Dufour's gland; 10, Koschevnikov's gland; 11, Nasanoff's gland. (From Wilson 1965, Copyright 1965 by the American Association for the Advancement of Science.)

Pheromones in Mammalian Behavior

Birds probably do not utilize chemical communication. The evidence is lacking, if they do. The older view that they lack olfactory sense organs, however, is clearly wrong.

Salmon locate the home river and even specific streams in the watershed by chemical sensitivity and memory based on early imprinting (Hasler, 1957). The approach to the spawning season predisposes the salmon to behavioral preference for swimming toward the stream's source. The schooling of fishes is also dependent upon chemical as well as visual information.

In mammals the significance of chemical senses ranges from modest to exceptionally strong. Rooting animals, such as pigs, various rodents, and dogs, perform remarkable olfactory feats of discrimination and recognition. The marking of home territories by dogs, wild Canidae, and some species of lemurs is well documented. Rodents are reported to be capable of choosing correct or incorrect alleys in a maze if the "frustration" odor remains following an error by a previous animal. In a Y maze, mice are capable of discriminating moving air laden with odors from two different species of mice, and also between the odors from two male mice of the same inbred strain (Bowers & Alexander, 1967). Whether such biochemical individuality is expressed through pheromone secretion or incidental to sweat gland or other skin exudates remains uncertain.

Primates are now claimed to possess pheromone mediators of sexual behavior. Clearest evidence for this comes from studies of rhesus monkeys. Male rhesus will do mechanical work in order to gain access to a female if she has estrogen odor in the vaginal area, but the male interest ceases following blockage of his nasal passages (Michael & Keverne, 1968). Progesterone or testosterone injections of the female reduce her attractiveness to the male to low levels. The full behavioral response to the female is dependent upon combined visual, olfactory, and somatosensory perceptual integration.

Recognition of Individuals by Odor

Recognition of individual persons by dogs is normally a multisensory perceptual integration. At a distance and from upwind, vision, and particularly the visual recognition of characteristic gait and other movement patterns, serves as the primary basis of perception. Auditory cues from gait and voice contribute strongly when available. Odor is sufficient for person perception by dogs, and according to one study, the odor of an individual human being is difficult to mask either by mixing in odors of other persons or by using other chemicals that have strong olfactory-stimulating properties (Kalmus, 1955).

PERCEIVING AND PERCEPTUAL LEARNING

In the development of perceptual behavior, the contributions of gene-determined neural systems cannot be overemphasized, *except* by denial of their continuing dependence upon confirming and modifying processes. Perceiving requires the early use, sometimes even prenatal, of innate neural integrating (detecting) circuits. These circuits are afferent information extractors. Edge and movement detectors that provide for convergence of information from a mosaic of retinal cells to single cells of the visual cortex are notable examples (Hubel & Wiesel, 1965). In the refinement of such basic convergence systems and in the extension of them to even more unique detection and recognition mechanisms, new afferent organizations may be developed through sensory (S-S) learning. This class of perceptual learning requires "rich" as opposed to impoverished environments. Recurrent regularities, not chaotic sensory overloads, are the essential environmental requirements. The same rich environments will support sensory-motor and motor-sensory learning. We have examined, earlier in this chapter, a few of a larger number of experiments that demonstrate the requirement for an active organism. Sensory enrichment during motor restriction is inadequate. In order to understand the nature of each of several simultaneously improving perceptual systems, we will do well to isolate them for discussion in the following sections.

Associations within and between Sensory Modalities

When the identity of an individual organism is perceived on the basis of stimuli from several modalities in varying combinations, is this due to prior associative learning? Theorists dispute the question. Perceptual learning may include a process of associating more than one afferent process directly. "Seeing" a familiar face when only the voice is coming over the telephone or from around a corner is dependent upon stimulus associations. Evidence that dogs, primates, or any other animals develop such cross-modal or within-modality associations has been difficult to secure. Are there clear examples of perceptual development through "enrichment," as contrasted with "differentiation"? Based on a fundamental tenet of gestalt theory that wholes are not built from parts, some current authorities maintain an exclusive emphasis on perceptual differentiation (Gibson, 1969; Gibson & Gibson, 1955). They say that details or subunits are perceived only after the larger "natural" gestalt has been broken apart by progressive differentiation. Experience provides repeated opportunities for isolating certain cues from others, as in the disembedding of figures and the isolation of gravitational from visual cues.

Development through differentiation need not exclude development through combination. With animals, experimenters have shown that sensory preconditioning may endow one sensory event previously paired with another with the power to elicit behavior previously conditioned only to the other. This occurs between stimuli across modalities (Seidel, 1959) and within a modality (Kendall & Thompson, 1960). Within-modality and cross-modal stimulus combinations occur frequently in the environments of animals. Imprinting involves the development of attachment behaviors to a set of cues that normally include more than one sensory modality. A complex visual figure and sound patterns come to develop unity through sense associations. This is a combinatorial gestalt that elicits following behavior. Individual organisms may show stronger following to some components than to others. Thus, within the breed of domestic duckling (*Anas platyrhinchos*), some birds imprint more strongly to the visual model and others to the intermittent auditory cue when both are available (Klopfer & Gottlieb, 1962). A general finding of imprinting studies is that the combined visual and auditory patterns are more effective than either one alone.

The imprinting process is perceptual learning in animals in its most dramatic manifestation. Starting as an orienting and following response to a relatively broad class (stimulus generalization) of multimodal stimuli, the discrimination process narrows down the range of effective cues. Distinctions are learned so that stimulus generalization is reduced. Precise components of visual forms and sound cues are *both* differentiated from similar but not identical ones, and at the same time are associated with one another.

Turning to the perceptual learning of particular locations in space, we must assume that a comparable twofold process is going on. The cognitive map (Tolman, 1948) that a rodent or a primate develops in learning to recognize and to find a place in three-dimensional space is acquired both by dissecting elements out of global areas like a room, a maze, or a cage and by combining sights, echoes, smells, and somesthetic information. Without severely disrupting the acquisition of recognition for such learned places, one sense modality at a time may be eliminated from the complete pattern (Honzik, 1936). Some of the missing information is presumably redintegrated, i.e., supplied by associational processes, just as a person remembers something he will see around the next corner before actually arriving at where that something becomes visible.

Perceiving and Responding

Sensory-motor adjustments of organisms are both innate and learned. Precision of innate responses typically leaves room for improvement. Initial paw-placing responses, for example, exhibit low precision. With behavior in the appropriate, or ecologically normal, environment, guided reaching emerges as an improving perceptual-motor integration. Held and his coinvestigators have contributed the essential experimental studies to support their recorrelation model of a two-way stimulus-response (S-R) and response-stimulus (R-S) behavioral adaptation process. According to their explanatory model, a response (or motor action self-initiated) occurs in a stimulus context. The action is registered in the organism's nervous system and is followed by sensory change. The R-S event may conform (correlate well) with previously learned or innate R-S "memories," or it may deviate in some degree and thereby initiate recorrelation. A revised perceptual memory develops only if the recorrelation event is repeated over a series of actions, for many minutes or for days, depending both on species and on response rates (trials).

The development of perception may be conceptualized as a three-phase process, the phases going on both successively and simultaneously. A primitive unity of organization selects sensory inputs and is represented by behavioral preferences within and among modalities. Differentiation of this unity and the combining of recurring component sensory and motor processes provide a continuing modification of earlier perceptual preferences. An essential aspect of this series of modifications is what we may call *learning to attend.* Motor behavior supports and responds to the perceptual modifications. Behavior of the individual organism remains unified to the degree that current perceptions are supported by previous perceptual-motor behavior. A progression of changing responses results when behavior is constantly adjusting (as in any improving skill) to recurrent and new combinations of cues from both the internal and the external environments. Phylogenetic advancement is related to the range of combinations and differentiations that an organism may achieve in its innate and learned utilization of cues.

REFERENCES

BARLOW, H. B., BLAKEMORE, C., & PETTIGREW, J. D. The neural mechanism of binocular depth discrimination. *Journal of Physiology*, 1967, **193,** 327–342.

BEER, C. G. Laughing gull chicks: Recognition of their parents' voices. *Science*, 1969, **166,** 1030–1032.

BLAKESLEE, P., & GUNTER, R. Cross-modal transfer of discrimination learning in Cebus monkeys. *Behaviour*, 1966, **26,** 76–90.

BOSSOM, J., & HAMILTON, C. R. Interocular transfer of prism-altered coordinations in split-brain monkeys. *Journal of Comparative and Physiological Psychology*, 1963, **56,** 769–774.

BOUGH, E. W. Stereoscopic vision in the macaque monkey: A behavioral demonstration. *Nature* (London), 1970, **225,** 42–44.

BOWERS, J. M., & ALEXANDER, B. K. Mice: Individual recognition by olfactory cues. *Science*, 1967, **158,** 1208–1210.

BOVET, J. Influence d'un effet directionnel sur le rétour au gîte des Mulots fauve et sylvestre (*Apodemus flavicollis Melch.* et *A. Sylvaticus* L.) *et du Campagnol roux (Cletheiononmys glareolus* Schr.). *Zeitschrift für Tierpsychologie*, 1962, **19,** 472–488.

CHOW, K. L., RIESEN, A. H., & NEWELL, F. W. Degeneration of retinal ganglion cells in infant chimpanzees reared in darkness. *Journal of Comparative Neurology*, 1957, **107,** 27–42.

DAVENPORT, R. K., & ROGERS, C. M. Intermodal equivalence of stimuli in apes. *Science*, 1970, **168,** 279–280.

DAVIS, R. T., MCDOWELL, A. A., & NISSEN, H. W. Solution of bent-wire problems by monkeys and chimpanzees. *Journal of Comparative and Physiological Psychology*, 1957, **50,** 441–444.

DEWS, P. B. The effect of multiple Ss periods on responding on a fixed-interval schedule. *Journal of the Experimental Analysis of Behavior*, 1962, **5,** 369–374.

DEWS, P. B., & WIESEL, T. N. Consequences of monocular deprivation on visual behavior in kittens. *Journal of Physiology*, 1970, **206,** 437–455.

EICHENGREEN, J. M., COREN, S., & NACHMIAS, J. Visual-cliff preference by infant rats: Effects of rearing and test conditions. *Science*, 1966, **151,** 830–831.

EMLEN, S. T. Migratory orientation in the indigo bunting, *Passerina cyanea.* I and II. *Auk,* 1967, **84,** 309–342, 463–489.

ETTLINGER, G. Cross-modal transfer of training in monkeys. *Behaviour*, 1960, **16,** 56–65.

FANTZ, R. L. Form preferences in newly hatched chicks. *Journal of Comparative and Physiological Psychology*, 1957, **50,** 422–430.

FANTZ, R. L. Visual discrimination in a neonate chimpanzee. *Perceptual and Motor Skills,* 1958, **8,** 59–66.

FANTZ, R. L. Visual perception and experience in early infancy. In H, W, Stevenson, E. H. Hess, & H. L. Rheingold (Eds.), *Early Behavior: Comparative and Developmental Approaches*, 1967. New York: Wiley, 1967. Pp. 181–224.

FORGAYS, D. G., & FORGAYS, J. W. The nature of the effect of free-environmental experience in the rat. *Journal of Comparative and Physiological Psychology*, 1952, **45,** 322–328.

FORGUS, R. H. The effect of early perceptual learning on the behavior organization of adult rats. *Journal of Comparative and Physiological Psychology*, 1954, **55,** 816–818.

FREEDMAN, D. G. The infant's fear of strangers and the flight response. *Journal of Child Psychiatry*, 1961, **2,** 242–248.

FRISCH, K. VON. *The dance language and orientation of bees.* Trans. L. E. Chadwick, Cambridge, Mass: Harvard, The Belknap Press, 1967.

GIBSON, E. J. *Principles of perceptual learning and development.* New York: Appleton-Century-Crofts, 1969.

GIBSON, J. J., & GIBSON, E. J. Perceptual learning: differentiation or enrichment? *Psychological Review*, 1955, **62**, 32–41.

GRETHER, W. F. The magnitude of simultaneous color contrast and simultaneous brightness contrast for chimpanzee and man. *Journal of Experimental Psychology*, 1942, **30**, 69–83.

GRIFFIN, D. R., WEBSTER, F. A., & MICHAEL, C. R. The echolocation of flying insects by bats. *Animal Behaviour*, 1960, **8**, 141–154.

GUHL, A. M., & ORTMAN, L. L. Visual patterns in the recognition of individuals among chickens. *Condor*, 1953, **55**, 287–289.

GUNTER, R. Visual size constancy in the rat. *British Journal of Psychology*, 1951, **42**, 288–293.

HARTLINE, H. K., & RATLIFF, F. Inhibitory interaction of receptor units in the eye of Limulus. *Journal of General Physiology*, 1957, **40**, 357–376.

HASLER, A. D. Olfactory and gustatory senses of fishes. In M. E. Brown (Ed.), *The physiology of fishes*, Vol. 2. New York: Academic Press, 1957. Pp. 187–209.

HEBB, D. O. *The organization of behavior: A neuropsychological theory.* New York: Wiley, 1949.

HEIN, A., & HELD, R. Dissociation of the visual placing response into elicited and guided components. *Science*, 1967, **158**, 390–391.

HELD, R. Exposure history as a factor in maintaining stability of perception and coordination. *Journal of Nervous and Mental Disease*, 1961, **132**, 26–32.

HELD, R., & BAUER, J. A. Visually guided reaching in infant monkeys after restricted rearing. *Science*, 1967, **155**, 718–720.

HELD, R., & BOSSOM, J. Neonatal deprivation and adult rearrangement: Complementary techniques for analyzing plastic sensori-motor coordinations. *Journal of Comparative and Physiological Psychology*, 1961, **54**, 33–37.

HELD, R., & HEIN, A. Movement produced stimulation in the development of visually guided behavior. *Journal of Comparative and Physiological Psychology*, 1963, **56**, 872–876.

HESS, E. H. Natural preferences of chicks and ducklings for objects of different colours. *Psychological Reports*, 1956, **2**, 477–483. (a)

HESS, E. H. Space perception in the chick. *Scientific American*, 1956, **195**, 71–80. (b)

HINDE, R. A. *Animal Behaviour.* (2nd ed.) New York: McGraw-Hill, 1970.

HOLST, E. VON. Relations between the central nervous system and the peripheral organs. *British Journal of Animal Behaviour*, 1954, **2**, 89–94.

HONZIK, C. H. The sensory basis of maze learning in rats. *Comparative Psychology Monographs*, 1936, No. 64.

HUBEL, D. H., & WIESEL, T. N. Receptive fields of cells in striate cortex of very young, visually inexperienced kittens. *Journal of Neurophysiology*, 1963, **26**, 994–1002.

HUBEL, D. H., & WIESEL, T. N. Receptive fields and functional architecture in two nonstriate visual areas (18 and 19) of the cat. *Journal of Neurophysiology*, 1965, **27**, 229–289. (a)

HUBEL, D. H., & WIESEL, T. N. Binocular interaction in striate cortex of kittens reared with artificial squint. *Journal of Neurophysiology*, 1965, **28**, 1041–1059. (b)

HUBEL, D. H., & WIESEL, T. N. Stereoscopic vision in macaque monkey. *Nature*, 1970, **225,** 41–42. (a)

HUBEL, D. H., & WIESEL, T. N. The period of susceptibility to the physiological effects of unilateral eye closure in kittens. *Journal of Physiology*, 1970, **206,** 419–436. (b)

HYMOVITCH, B. The effects of experimental variations on problem solving in the rat. *Journal of Comparative and Physiological Psychology*, 1952, **45,** 313–321.

INGLE, D. Two visual mechanisms underlying the behavior of fish. *Psychologische Forschung*, 1967/1968, **31,** 44–51.

KALMUS, H. The discrimination by the nose of the dog of individual human odours and in particular of the odours of twins. *British Journal of Animal Behaviour*, 1955, **5,** 25–31.

KELLOGG, W. N. *Porpoises and sonar.* Chicago: The University of Chicago Press, 1961.

KENDALL, S. B., & THOMPSON, R. F. Effect of stimulus similarity on sensory preconditioning within a single stimulus dimension. *Journal of Comparative and Physiological Psychology*, 1960, **53,** pp. 439–442.

KLOPFER, P. H., & GOTTLIEB, G. Imprinting and behavioral polymorphism: Auditory and visual imprinting in domestic ducks (*Anas platyrhinchos*) and the involvement of the critical period. *Journal of Comparative and Physiological Psychology*, 1962, **55,** 126–130.

LANDRETH, H. F., & FERGUSON, D. E. The sun compass of Fowler's toad *Bufo woodhousei* Fowleri. *Behaviour*, 1968, **30,** 27–43.

LASHLEY, K. S., & RUSSELL, J. T. The mechanism of vision: XI. A preliminary test of innate organization. *Journal of Genetic Psychology*, 1934, **45,** 136–144.

LETTVIN, J. Y., MATURANA, H. R., MCCULLOCH, W. S., & PITTS, W. H. What the frog's eye tells the frog's brain. *Proceedings of the Institute of Radio Engineers*, 1959, **47.** Pp. 1940–1951.

MATTHEWS, G. V. T. *Bird navigation.* New York: Cambridge University Press, 1968.

MEYER, D. R., & ANDERSON, R. A. Color discrimination in cats. In A. V. S. de Reuck and J. Knight (Eds.), *Color vision: Physiology and experimental psychology*, Ciba Foundation Symposium. Boston: Little, Brown, 1965. Pp. 325–339.

MICHAEL, R. P., & KEVERNE, E. B. Pheromones in the communication of sexual status in primates. *Nature*, 1968, **218,** 746–749.

MOUNTCASTLE, V. B., & DARIAN-SMITH, I. Neural mechanisms in somesthesia. In V. B. Mountcastle (Ed.), *Medical physiology.* Vol. 2. St. Louis: Mosby, 1968. Pp. 1372–1423.

NEFF, W. D., & DIAMOND, I. T. The neural basis of auditory discrimination. In H. F. Harlow & C. N. Woolsey (Eds.), *Biological and biochemical bases of behavior.* Madison: The University of Wisconsin Press, 1958. Pp. 101–126.

PALEN, G. F. Focusing cues in the visual cliff behavior of day-old chicks. *Journal of Comparative and Physiological Psychology*, 1965, **59,** 452–454.

PERDECK, A. C. Vogeltrekstation (Texel). *Jaarsverlag*, 1956, 66–74.

RIESEN, A. H. Plasticity of behavior: Psychological aspects. In H. F. Harlow & C. N. Woolsey (Eds.), *Biological and biochemical bases of behavior.* Madison: The University of Wisconsin Press, 1958. Pp. 425–450.

RIESEN, A. H. Stimulation as a requirement for growth and function in behavioral development. In D. W. Fiske & S. R. Maddi (Eds.), *Functions of varied experience.* Homewood, Ill.: Dorsey Press, 1961. Pp. 57–80.

RIESEN, A. H. Effects of early deprivation of photic stimulation. In S. F. Osler and R. E. Cooke (Eds.), *The biosocial basis of mental retardation.* Baltimore: Johns Hopkins, 1965. Pp. 61–85.

RIESEN, A. H. Chimpanzee visual perception. In G. Bourne (Ed.), *The chimpanzee*. Vol. 2. Basel/New York: Karger, 1970. Pp. 1–15.

RIESEN, A. H., & AARONS, L. Visual movement and intensity discrimination in cats after early deprivation of pattern vision. *Journal of Comparative and Physiological Psychology*, 1959, **52**, 142–149.

RIESEN, A. H., RAMSEY, R. L., & WILSON, P. D. Development of visual acuity in rhesus monkeys deprived of patterned light during early infancy. *Psychonomic Science*, 1964, **1**, 33–34.

ROEDER, K. D. Aspects of the noctuid tympanic nerve response having significance in the avoidance of bats. *Journal of Insect Physiology*, 1964, **10**, 529–546.

ROSENBLUM, L. A., & CROSS, H. A. Performance of neonatal monkeys on the visual cliff-situation. *American Journal of Psychology*, 1963, **76**, 318–320.

ROSENBLUM, L. A., WITKIN, H. A., KAUFMAN, I. C., & BROSGOLE, L. Perceptual disembedding in monkeys: Note on method and preliminary findings. *Perceptual and Motor Skills*, 1965, **20**, 729–736.

ROSENZWEIG, M. R. Environmental complexity, cerebral change, and behavior. *American Psychologist*, 1966, **21**, 321–332.

ROSSI, P. J. Adaptation and negative aftereffect to lateral optical displacement in newly hatched chicks. *Science*, 1968, **160**, 430–432.

ROSSI, P. J. Primacy of the negative aftereffect over positive adaptation with newly hatched chicks. *Developmental Psychology*, 1969, **2**, 43–53.

ROUTTENBERG, A., & GLICKMAN, S. E. Visual cliff behavior in undomesticated rodents, land and acquatic turtles, and cats (*Panthera*). *Journal of Comparative and Physiological Psychology*, 1964, **58**, 143–146.

RUMBAUGH, D. M., & MCCORMACK, C. Attentional skills of great apes compared with those of gibbons and squirrel monkeys. *Proceedings of the 2nd International Congress of Primatology*. Vol. 1. Basel/New York: Karger, 1969. Pp. 167–172.

SAUER, F. (Die Sternenorientierung nächtlich ziehender Grasmücken) (*Sylvia atricapilla, bovin und curruca*). *Zeitschrift für Tierpsychologie*, 1957, **14**, 29–70.

SCHIFFMAN, H. R., & WALK, R. D. Behavior on the visual cliff of monocular as compared to binocular chicks. *Journal of Comparative and Physiological Psychology*, 1963, **56**, 1064–1068.

SEIDEL, R. J. A review of sensory preconditioning. *Psychological Bulletin*, 1959, **56**, 58–73.

SHINKMAN, P. G. Visual depth-discrimination in day-old chicks. *Journal of Comparative and Physiological Psychology*, 1963, **56**, 410–414.

SPALDING, D. A. Instinct with original observations on young animals. *British Journal of Animal Behaviour*, 1954, **2**, 2–11. (Originally published: *MacMillan's Magazine*, 1873, **27**, 282–293.)

SPERRY, R. W., & HIBBARD, E. Regulative factors in the orderly growth of retino-tectal connexions. In G. E. W. Wolstenholme & M. O'Connor (Eds.), *Growth of the nervous system*. London: Churchill, 1968.

STEPIEN, L., & CORDEAU, J. P. Memory in monkeys for compound stimuli. *American Journal of Psychology*, 1960, **73**, 388–395.

SUTHERLAND, N. S. Shape discrimination in rat, octopus and goldfish. *Journal of Comparative and Physiological Psychology*, 1969, **67**, 160–176.

THOMPSON, W. R., & HERON, W. The effects of restricting early experience on the problem-solving capacity of dogs. *Canadian Journal of Psychology*, 1954, **8**, 17–31.

TINBERGEN, N., & KRUYT, W. Uber die Orientierung des Bienenwolfes (*Philanthus triangulum* Fabr.): Die Bervorzugung bestimmter Wegmarken. *Zeitschrift für Vergleichende Physiologie*, 1938, **25**, 292–334.

TINBERGEN, N., & KUENEN, D. J. Uber die auslösenden und die richtunggebeden Reizsituationen der Sperrbewegung von jungen Drosseln (*Turdus m. merula* L. *und T. e. ericetorum* Turton). *Zeitschrift für Tierpsychologie*, 1939, **3**, 37–60.

TOLMAN, E. C. Cognitive maps in rats and men. *Psychological Review*, 1948, **55**, 189–208.

WALK, R. D. Can the duckling respond adequately to depth? Paper presented at the 33rd meeting of the Eastern Psychological Association, Atlantic City, April, 1962.

WALK, R. D. The study of visual depth and distance perception in animals. In D. S. Lehrmann, R. A. Hinde, & E. Shaw (Eds.), *Advances in the study of behavior*. New York: Academic Press, 1965. Pp. 99–154.

WALK, R. D. The development of depth perception in animals and human infants. *Monographs of the Society for Research in Child Development*, 1966, **31**, 82–108.

WALK, R. D., & GIBSON, E. J. A comparative and analytical study of visual depth perception. *Psychological Monographs*, 1961, **75,** No. 15.

WALLS, G. L. *The vertebrate eye*. New York: Hafner, 1963. (Originally published: Bloomfield Hills, Mich.: Cranbrook Institute of Science, 1942.)

WEGENER, J. Cross-modal transfer in monkeys. *Journal of Comparative and Physiological Psychology*, 1965, **59**, 450–452.

WEHNER, R. Zur Physiologie des Formensehens bei der Honigbiene. *Zeitschrift für Verhleichende Physiologie*, 1967, **55**, 145–166.

WELLS, M. J. *Brain and behavior in cephalopods*. London: Heinemann; Stanford, Calif.: Stanford University Press, 1962.

WILSON, E. O. Chemical communication in the social insects. *Science*, 1965, **149**, 1064–1071.

WILSON, P. D., & RIESEN, A. H. Visual development in rhesus monkeys neonatally deprived of patterned light. *Journal of Comparative and Physiological Psychology*, 1966, **61**, 87–95.

WINN, H. E., SALMON, M., & ROBERTS, N. Sun-compass orientation by parrot fishes. *Zeitschrift für Tierpsychologie*, 1964, **21**, 798–812.

WITKIN, H. A., LEWIS, H. B., HERTZMAN, M., MACHOVER, K., MEISSNER, P. B., & WAPNER, S. *Personality through perception*. New York: Harper, 1954.

ZEIGLER, H. P., & LEIBOWITZ, H. A methodological study of "shape constancy" in the rhesus monkey. *Journal of Comparative and Physiological Psychology*, 1958, **51**, 155–160.

ZERRAHN, G. Formdressur und Formunterscheidung bei der Honigbiene. *Zeitschrift für Vergleichende Physiologie*, 1933, **20**, 117–161.

PART FOUR

MODIFICATION OF BEHAVIOR

All organisms possess some degree of plasticity. Their structure and future behavior are altered by their experiences. Most organisms can learn. It is this modification of behavior as a function of experience that has fascinated men for so long and which has become the major focus in the study of animal psychology. As so much of human behavior appears learned, it is easy to understand the interest and significance of research on learning.

The ability to modify response tendencies as a function of experience is of obvious adaptive value as it permits the individual to "learn by experience." The analogies between the processes through which natural selection shapes the evolution of behavior and those through which the contingencies of reinforcement shape the ontogeny of behavior have been pointed out by B. F. Skinner and others. Yet, learning is much faster than evolution and it permits modification of behavior within a single individual quite rapidly and in contrast to the slow but steady changes produced by evolution. The ability or abilities to learn thus confer a considerable selective advantage on the individual.

The learning capacities of animals with relatively simple nervous systems have fascinated scientists. How plastic is a nervous system with relatively few cells? Can an animal with few or no synapses learn? Just how much tissue is necessary for adaptive modifications of behavior? The experimenters' biases regarding whether a simple organism should be able to learn, and the difficulty inherent in working with organisms with sensory and behavioral capacities so different from our own, have combined to produce much controversy in this area. The current status of research on learning in invertebrates is the topic of Chapter 12.

In studying the evolution of learning in vertebrates, the topic of Chapter 13, men have long sought to place extant species along a continuous scale of learning ability. Are cats smarter than dogs? Which is the most intelligent species? The notion is that there is a single capacity termed learning ability, and that different species have different amounts of it. The species with more learning ability should be those with the most complex nervous systems. Presumably man should be at the top of such a scale, with simpler organisms at the bottom. Although Aristotle looked for Indian elephants to rank just below man, most men would expect to find primates, carnivores, rodents, reptiles, amphibians, and so on, to rank in that order. The fallacies involved in posing such questions are discussed in Chapter 13. The importance of considering learning abilities, the difficulties in comparisons across species, and the probable course of evolution all are stressed. The study of the manner in which performance in laboratory tasks is a reflection of the mode of adaption of the organism to its habitat is providing a new look to the comparative psychology of learning in vertebrates.

The occurrence of complex behavior is of particular interest to us. As many people virtually define themselves in terms of the complexity of their behavior, humans are fascinated when they observe complex behaviors in other species. Anecdotes of remarkable feats by animals are well known. The status of scientific research on complex processes is discussed in Chapter 14.

These three chapters present a broad treatment of the manner in which the behavior of a great variety of organisms is modifiable. Together, they give a comprehensive and varied picture of the ways in which experiences with the environment alter the behavior of the individual.

Chapter 12

Learning in Invertebrates

James V. McConnell and Allan L. Jacobson*

An unbiased observer—perhaps an alien psychologist on a field trip from another planet—might well conclude that there is a conspiracy against terrestrial invertebrates. If we took a census of every living animal on earth, the vertebrates would come to less than 1 percent of the total. There are probably more invertebrate organisms within a mile of you than there are people on the entire globe. If we count the number of different species, we find there are a hundred or more without vertebrae for each species blessed with a backbone. The invertebrates were the first animals on earth and predate the vertebrates by billions of years. They range in size from single-celled organisms so tiny you need a microscope to see them to squid whose two tentacles may stretch 200 feet from tip to tip. Invertebrates are found everywhere—from the bottom of the ocean to as far up on Mt. Everest as any life endures. And yet, most of these millions of fascinating creatures have been totally ignored by comparative psychologists. Over the years, less than 5 percent of the animal studies published in the scientific journals by experimental psychologists have had invertebrates as subjects. We know a great deal more about the behavior of the white rat—a creature of little economic importance —than about the reactions of the earthworms that make our farms productive or about the psychology of the worms, insects, and protozoans that occasion-

*The sections on Annelids, Mollusks, and Arthropods were prepared by Allan L. Jacobson, and all other sections by James V. McConnell.

ally inhabit our own bodies. Psychologists—who, more than anyone else, should know and control their biases—are obviously prejudiced toward the "higher" organisms. We are all anthropocentric—interested more in man and manlike creatures than in any other species. And so the complex and captivating world of the "lower" organisms has largely gone uncharted. In this chapter we shall map one small part of that world—learning in invertebrates—as best we can.

Considering the odd unpopularity of these animals, why would anyone bother to investigate their behavior at all? As was said in an earlier publication, for several reasons:

First, invertebrates are obviously less complex in structure than, say, the mammals; one might expect them therefore to be less complex in behavior too. The innate response patterns might well be stronger and hence more visible in invertebrates than in vertebrates, in which case the genetic substrata of behavior would be more available to experimental manipulation. Second, the invertebrate nervous system is in many instances much more available to scalpel, electrode, and cannula than is the vertebrate central nervous system, an ideal situation for someone interested in correlating nerve activity with behavioral changes. Third, many of the animals have rather special talents: for instance, the facts that one can graft parts of one animal to another, that even very small portions of whole organisms can be kept alive and functioning fairly normally for long periods of time, that invertebrates can often regenerate lost sections of their bodies, and that they often reproduce asexually as well as sexually, make them valuable subjects for all sorts of "odd" (i.e., nonanthropocentric) experiments. Fourth the invertebrates offer fertile testing grounds for any psychological theory that claims broad phylogenetic generality. And, at last, there are those scientists who pick the invertebrates because so little is known about them, and, like Mt. Everest, "they're there." [McConnell, 1966, pp. 107–108]

As intriguing as invertebrates can be as experimental subjects, however, large groups of them have never once been subjected to a maze, jump stand, or Skinner box. In this chapter we shall cover only a few of the millions of species and genera of the phyla, a limitation that stems from the fact that almost no work has been published on learning in the rest of the invertebrates. A more complete summary of research on invertebrate learning appears in a new book by Corning, Dyal, and Willows (In press).

THE PROTOZOANS

During the late 1950s and early 1960s, one of the hottest issues in comparative psychology was whether or not invertebrates could learn. Prior to this period, most psychologists had followed the lead of Maier and Schneirla (1935), Jennings (1906), and many others in accepting invertebrates into the camp, as it were. In those days, *learning* was typically defined *behaviorally*—a more or less enduring (and usually adaptive) change in an organism's behavior due to experience or practice and not due to "mere" maturation or physical injury. But in the early 1950s, psychologists discovered the neuron. Hebb's physiologically oriented learning theory appeared in 1949. According to Hebb, the physical correlate of learning was some kind of structural or functional change at the synapse—that junction point between the axon of one neuron and the dendrites (or soma) of another (Hebb, 1949). In the post-Hebbian era, psychologists continued to define learning primarily in behavioral terms, but underlying many such definitions was the unspoken belief that nerve cells were somehow necessarily involved in mediating the learned response. As stimulating as Hebb's theory was, it discriminated against those millions of organisms that lacked the neural hardware thought to be necessary for "true" learning to occur. Thus some psychologists—almost without understanding why—began to question the prior assumption that learning in invertebrates had been amply demonstrated in the laboratory. Learning, if it did occur in brainless invertebrates, would apparently have to be mediated by different mechanisms than those that mediate learning in mammals; how easy, then, to assume that the learning would have to be *qualitatively* different as well.

Contributing to the controversy as well was the rise of the so-called *chemical theory of learning,* in which it was postulated that the physical change by which memories were stored in an organism was primarily a molecular alternation of some kind, probably intracellular rather than between cells (as in the synaptic space). Invertebrates may lack the complex neural structures found in higher organisms—indeed, they may be totally without neurons at all—but even the amoeba is packed with a large number of exceedingly complex molecules (DNA, RNA, and proteins). Since many of the most visible experimental studies supporting the molecular approach to memory had planarians and paramecia as their subjects, the neurologically oriented psychologists had a double reason for their disbelief that learning could occur in such lowly organisms.

Has the issue been resolved? Each person must view the data and decide for himself. Our unbiased alien might well venture the opinion that reactions that appear to meet the *behavioral* criteria of learning have been more than amply demonstrated in many invertebrates (such as the octopus, various insects, and perhaps some of the worms). As the chemical explanation of learning and memory gains strength at the mammalian level—and as it becomes clear that the molecular theory supplements rather than supplants the synaptic theory—the earlier studies become less important (and hence less disturbing to neurologically oriented psychologists).

From the point of view of logic (as opposed to empirical data), however, it would be extremely surprising if learning of some kind did not occur even in the simplest animals, the protozoans. After all, these tiny beasts had several billion years of development prior to the appearance of the vertebrates. If, during these millenia, even one organism had accidentally acquired the ability to shift its behavior in response to environmental demand, surely the mutation would have become dominant. Can you imagine any characteristic that would have greater survival value than the ability to learn, to adapt to the world around you?

The protozoans have a number of interesting characteristics which might make them of interest to the comparative psychologist. To begin with, they range in size from less than 1/25,000th of an inch (an African parasite called *Leishmania donovani* that causes swollen spleens and causes a mortality rate of 80 to 90 percent in man) to several feet (*Mycetozoida plasmodia,* an odd, almost funguslike organism that, during one stage of its development, crawls over rotting logs and looks much like a huge amoeba). Their reproductive cycles are often highly complex. Many protozoans are colonial—that is, they live attached to one another in huge groups, the groups constituting something like a superorganism, but the social psychology of these animals has been almost completely neglected.

The protozoans are often described as being *unicellular,* which is to say that they have but one major nucleus per organism and each individual cell (for the most part) does all its own metabolic work without depending on the specialized organ systems of the multicellular organisms. However, many of the protozoans have such complex inner structures that it is customary to refer to them as being *acellular.* For example, some species have developed light-sensitive areas within their single cell that appear to be the prototype of the multicellular eye found in higher organisms. Other species, such as the ciliates, have developed complex motor systems that apparently demand rather a high level of coordination of movements in fairly distant parts of the animal's body. How this coordination occurs in an animal that not only lacks a brain, but has no nerve tissue at all, is still something that zoologists debate hotly.

The behavior of protozoans was studied fairly intensively (by zoologists) even before the turn of the century, and many of these early scientists demonstrated that something akin to learning could be achieved in protozoans before Pavlov began his famous work on conditioning in dogs. Surprisingly enough, many of these early experiments were fairly well controlled, although latter-day critics have not always given them their due.

One of the most interesting of the pre-1950 experiments on protozoans was performed by a Russian zoologist named N. N. Plavilstchikov (1928), who used as his subjects a bell-shaped, colonial ciliate, *Carchesium lachmanni.* These organisms attach themselves to the colony by means of a long, slender stalk that contains a single, musclelike fiber. When *C. lachmanni* is disturbed, the stalk contracts quickly, giving the organism a popping sort of movement. Plavilstchikov used the onset of a light as his conditioning stimulus (CS) and stimulated the colony, using a rod with glass fibers on it as his unconditioned stimulus (UCS). The CS was turned on for 1 to 2 seconds prior to the onset of the UCS (which lasted for about a minute). Each colony received twenty trials per day, with an intertrial interval of 15 to 20 minutes. After they had been given 100 to 200 training trials, the colonies began to contract to the onset of the light even when the UCS was not presented. Once training was completed, Plavilstchnikov transplanted parts of trained colonies on to host colonies that had previously not been disturbed at all. After the transplants had been given a few days to "take," Plavilstchnikov gave the first conditioning trials to the hosts. To his surprise, the host ciliate colonies began contracting during the first few trials. After giving the hosts a day's conditioning trials, Plavilstchnikov removed the transplants (leaving only the original, untrained ciliates in the colonies) and subsequently retested the hosts. Again to his surprise, the hosts continued to contract to the onset of the UCS. Although Plavilstchnikov did not run additional groups to control for the effects of sensitization, it does seem as if he achieved the transmission of some kind of behavioral tendency from one colony to another via transplantation (Corning, 1971).

Spontaneous Alternation

If an animal is forced to make several right turns in a complex maze, it usually tends to turn left at the first choice point in the maze at which it is given freedom of choice. This tendency toward *spontaneous alternation* in mazes has been reported in animals ranging from protozoans through man (in a finger maze). In 1952, Lepley and Rice reported evidence for the existence of spontaneous alternation in paramecia (Figure 12-1). Their subjects were run in a series of narrow-channel T mazes (Figure 12–2a) and were forced to make zero, one, or two forced turns prior to entering the free-choice point. A decade later, Lachman and Havlena (1962) attempted to replicate the Lepley and Rice study, but failed to achieve the same results. Running their subjects in a series of wide-channel Y mazes (Figure 12–2b) with from zero to nine forced turns prior to the choice point, Lachman and Havlena found no evidence at all for spontaneous alternation. It is over such failures to replicate that most of the battles involving learning in invertebrates have been fought—and fought needlessly. Notice that Lepley and Rice used narrow-channel T mazes while Lachman and Havlena used wide-channel Y mazes. It apparently did not occur to these latter authors that their equipment differed considerably from that used in the experiment they thought they were replicating. Paramecia are tiny animals—one needs to watch their behavior with a microscope or large magnifying glass in order to see what they are doing. They move through the water they live in by making rather wild, corkscrew movements that propel them along until they hit an obstacle. Then they back up a short distance, turn slightly, and try again. They keep trying until they find a channel that takes them away from whatever is barricading their forward movement. In a narrow-channel T maze, the paramecia would all strike the top of the maze and have to keep backing and turning until they found a way into the next arm. In a wide-channel Y maze, on the other hand, the animals might well get most of the way through the apparatus without ever once having their forward movement impeded. Under these conditions, it is little wonder that Lachman and Havlena failed to find any evidence for spontaneous alternation, although it is clear from their paper that they consider that their research cast grave doubts on the accuracy of the earlier report. Luckily for all concerned, Rabin and Hertzler (1965) later repeated both experiments exactly. As you might expect, they found evidence for spontaneous alternation when they ran their animals in the Lepley and Rice T maze and no evidence for spontaneous alternation when they ran their animals in the Lachman and Havlena Y maze.

Conditioning

Most of the articles on learning in protozoans published since 1950 have borne the name either of Beatrice Gelber or of Donald Jensen. In general, Gelber has reported a long series of experiments that seem to demonstrate that paramecia (one of the most highly developed of the protozoans) were capable of learning simple associations, while Jensen has mounted what was chiefly a highly theoretical and not always clearly formulated series of attacks on invertebrate learning studies in general and Gelber's work in particular.

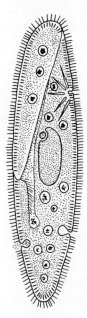

Figure 12–1. *Paramecium caudatum,* a protozoan about 200 microns in length. (From T. L. Jahn, *How to know the protozoa.* Dubuque: W. C. Brown, 1949.)

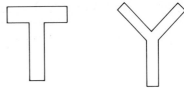

Figure 12–2. (A) A simple T Maze. (B) A simple Y Maze.   A.   B.

In 1952, Gelber published what was to be a prototype of most of her later studies. Three isolated cultures of paramecia were used as subjects: an experimental, a trained-control, and an untrained-control culture. At the beginning of the experiment, a clean platinum wire was dipped into all three groups for 3 minutes and the number of animals that clung to the wire was recorded. Gelber then dipped the wire forty times more into the experimental and the trained-control cultures (but not into the water containing the untrained-control animals). On every third trial, Gelber baited the experimental culture's wire lightly with a type of bacteria that the paramecia devour with gusto, hoping that the experimental animals would learn to associate the presence of the wire with the food she was giving them. The wire was never baited for either of the other groups. At the end of forty trials, she again dipped the bare wire into all three cultures. The number of "wire clingers" increased steadily and significantly during training in the experimental group, but not in the other two groups (Gelber, 1952).

Jensen (1957a, 1957b) correctly criticized this and some later studies because Gelber failed to run one additional control group, that is, a culture of paramecia that was given exposure to the wire *and* was given bacteria, but in such a way that the wire and the bacteria could not be associated in any way. (In one of her later studies, Gelber did in fact successfully use such a control group, a fact that Jensen apparently never has acknowledged in print). Jensen's criticism of Gelber's first experiment was indeed a valid one on the face of it, for it was quite possible that when the baited wire was immersed in the culture, the paramecia were attracted to it and simply remained in the vicinity of the food for a period of time. The animals would then, so Jensen reasoned, be much more likely to cling to the bare wire the next time it was inserted. As proof of this contention, Jensen dumped large numbers of bacteria into a culture, then inserted a wire. He found that the paramecia tended to clump together at the bottom of the culture near the wire. Gelber's rejoinder was as follows: To begin with, she used but a tiny fraction of the food that Jensen had used, believing that it would all be consumed in a matter of seconds, yet she found her experimental animals would approach and cling to the wire even if she inserted it 19 hours after the final training. It is hard to imagine paramecia hanging around a spot devoid of food for that long a time, just waiting for the next meal to come along. Second, Jensen counted the number of animals that clumped together at the bottom of the culture, while Gelber counted the number of animals that clung to the wire (quite a different response). Apparently few if any of Jensen's control animals did in fact show wire-clinging behavior, a critical point in Gelber's favor.

In her most devastating rebuttal to Jensen's criticisms, however, Gelber took a culture of "trained" paramecia and flooded the culture (after training) with a mass of bacteria, so many that all the paramecia underwent division and cast off daughter cells. Yet when she tested this (now twice as large) culture several hours later, they showed significantly greater wire-clinging behavior than did appropriate control groups.

In 1958, Katz and Deterline repeated Gelber's 1952 experiment more or less exactly, adding a control group that was not given the forty training exposures to the wire but that was, just prior to the final posttraining count, given a dose of bacteria to eat. Katz and Deterline (1958) counted all the animals in the region near the wire rather than those clinging to it, a questionable variation from Gelber's procedure, but they did find that the experimental culture was significantly superior to all the control cultures. At this point, they stirred all cultures vigorously by blowing a jet of air on them in order to circulate the water and destroy any food-rich zone that might be created by dipping the baited wire into the cultures. Immediately after this vigorous stirring, they once more dipped the wire into all four cultures for a 3-minute period. The number of paramecia in the vicinity of the wire dropped significantly in all cultures, although there were still more animals near the wire in the experimental culture than in any other. Whether this difference was statistically significant is a point that Gelber (1965) has debated vigorously with Katz and Deterline (see also Poskocil, 1966).

But we need not concern ourselves with statistical problems, since the Katz and Deterline experiment is absurd on the face of it. The vigorous stirring that these authors employed to dissipate any concentration of bacteria surely would have either seriously injured many of the animals or disoriented them considerably. If one "vigorously stirred" a rat in a maze immediately after it had learned the maze, then *at once* put the rat back at the starting point, might one not readily demonstrate that rats are incapable of learning? And, since Gelber had shown that the effects of her training procedure lasted for many hours, one wonders why Katz and Deterline did not wait a decent period of time after the stirring before testing the animals.

The experiments attempting to show that protozoans can learn embody, in a way, all the good and bad points of comparative psychology itself. Those experimenters have prospered who have first of all attempted to get to know their animals by spending countless hours simply observing the animals. These men and women have typically designed experiments that took into account their subjects' unique capacities and limitations. One does not expect the same behavior from a paramecium as from a professor; experiments performed on humans and other vertebrates simply do not translate readily into the miniature world of water-dwelling but evolutionary ancient protozoans. Those experimenters who believe on theoretical grounds that all invertebrates should or should not be incapable of learning despite the fact that they lack the complex neural structures found in the vertebrates have tended, in general, to perform research that proved their prior hypotheses. It is not easy to empathize with an amoeba, a worm, or a cockroach; but unless the scientist knows and appreciates his subjects well enough to understand their own special way of life, he is very likely to undertake investigations that appear to show that the invertebrates are impoverished in their behavioral repertoires. In such cases, it is the scientist's creativity, not the behavior of the invertebrate, that is surely impoverished.

In recent years, the use of the electron microscope has given us a tool to investigate the structure of the protozoans that we never had before. Under the electron microscope, these primitive acellular organisms display an order of internal complexity that could hardly be dreamed of just a few short years ago. Studies on the electrical properties of the cell membranes of the ciliates, in particular, have revealed that they have many similarities to those of nerve cells, including potential changes associated with activity and a threshold current for just perceptible changes in ciliary beat (Bullock & Horridge, 1965). The biochemical nature of these animals has barely been examined, but they are surely more complex internally than any given single cell in the vertebrate body. Whatever the physiological/biochemical mechanisms underlying learning turn out to be, it is likely that these mechanisms already existed in the protozoans (at least in prototype) hundreds of millions of years before the first vertebrate developed a backbone.

In the final analysis, of course, the question, Can protozoans learn? will be settled on the basis of well-controlled behavioral studies, not on the basis of what today's anatomists, physiologists, and biochemists can find within the animals' bodies. If Gelber's work—and that of workers like Rabin and Hertzler—holds up under replication, it will be up to the protozoologists to discover the internal mechanisms (including the necessary receptor systems) by which these behavioral alternations are mediated.

COELENTERATES

Any serious student of comparative psychology will have asked himself, at one time or another, "Why do we study animals instead of plants?" The answer to this unusual question seems to be, "Because animals move around a lot, while plants are stick-in-the-muds." It is the *behavior* of an organism that attracts a psychologist's notice, and with the notable exception of some mobile single-celled plants and a few odd species that close or contract when touched (such as the mimosa and the Venus flytrap), plants are essentially motionless. Some attempts have been made to condition the mimosa, the most recent reports being both well-controlled and positive, but a "comparative psychology of flora" remains to be written.

The coelenterates come about as close to looking and acting like plants as do any members of the animal kingdom. Although when young they are primarily free-swimming, as they approach maturity many of them (such as the corals) tend to find a comfortable resting place and attach themselves for long periods of time. These are, in short, *sessile* or stationary in their habits. Other members of this phylum—such as the jellyfish—remain free-swimming all their lives. Many coelenterates—such as the sea anemone and the sea fan (Figure 12–3)—take their names from plants that they resemble. For all their immobility, however, these animals do move occasionally, they often have tentacles around their mouths to aid in food-getting, and it is at this level of the phylogenetic scale that primitive nerve networks first make their appearance. In these primitive animals, however, nerve conduction is a two-way affair; that is, unlike the unipolar neurons found in higher organisms, electrical activity in the coelenterate nerve cell can move from back to front

Figure 12–3.   A sea fan. (Picture by the American Museum of Natural History from R. D. Barnes, *Invertebrate zoology,* Philadelphia: Saunders, 1963.)

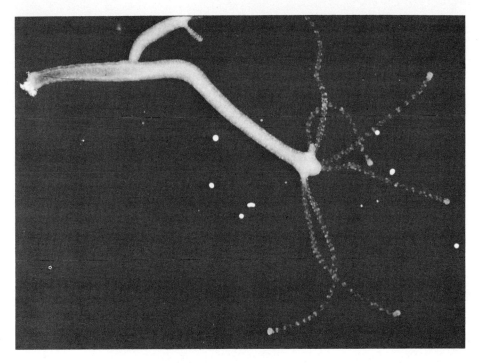

Figure 12–4.   Hydra (Photograph by Dr. J. A. L. Cooke. Courtesy of the American Museum of Natural History.)

as well as from front to back. The coelenterate nervous system is a meshwork or network of neurons that appear to be connected with minimal synapses or perhaps none at all. There are no neural centers or ganglia so common in the nervous systems of higher organisms. Excitation of any one spot in the network rapidly spreads to all other points. As in all other organisms, the purpose of neural activity in these animals seems to be the control of motor systems; differentiation of motor responses in these animals seems to be a matter of which of several nerve networks gets excited and how long (or how intense) the excitation is.

The evidence for associative learning, such as classical or operant conditioning in coelenterates, is sketchy at best. However, there is no question that habituation (which, according to some theorists, is a primitive form of associative learning) does occur in these organisms. Rushforth and his associates (1963, 1964, 1965) have studied habituation to mechanical stimulation in hydra (Figure 12–4). If *Hydra piradi* is jiggled for 2.5 seconds every 16 seconds, the usual contraction the animals show to shaking habituates almost completely in a matter of 2 to 3 hours. That this habituation is stimulus-specific and not due to mere muscular fatigue is shown by the fact that, once habituation to mechanical stimulation has reached its zenith, the animals will still show a complete and vigorous response to the onset of light. The effects of the habituation linger for several hours after the jiggling has stopped. A related species of hydra is relatively insensitive to mechanical stimulation; interestingly enough, however, animals formed from grafts between hydra of the two species have behavior patterns intermediate between those of the parent species.

Sea anemones are preyed upon by certain species of starfish and have developed rather vigorous escape reactions to the smell or taste of these predators. If ground-up starfish material is applied to the tentacles of the sessile anemone *Stomphia coccinea,* it rapidly detaches itself from its resting place and makes violent if rather clumsy swimming movements until it is out of danger. This anemone has an antagonistic response—if you press firmly on the animal's base (by which it attaches itself to the bottom), it closes down and hugs the bottom. Ross (1965) delivered starfish material to the tentacles of the animals and then, two seconds later, pressed on their bases. The closure response inhibited the swimming response. Ross continued to pair the starfish juice (the CS, in a rough sort of way) with pressure to the base (a rough sort of UCS) for many trials. Then he presented the starfish juice alone, without the base pressure. All the animals showed the closure response instead of the swimming response. As he continued to apply the CS without the UCS, the swimming response reappeared; however, the more CS-UCS pairings he had made prior to this extinction procedure, the longer it took before the swimming response came back. Although Ross did not run sufficient pseudoconditioning controls (in which the CS and the UCS would be presented but not paired), his results suggest that conditioned inhibition and perhaps classical conditioning can be demonstrated in coelenterates.

One of the difficulties in dealing with reactions such as the closure response in anemones is that the reaction lasts so long (up to several hours) that the intertrial interval must perforce also be quite long. In light of several studies (to be mentioned later) in headless annelid worms that suggest that conditioning may occur when the interval between trials is very short but does not occur at longer intervals, one might suspect that more clear-cut results with the "brainless" coelenterates might be obtained if an unconditioned response that had a very short recovery time were chosen.

PLANARIANS

The planarian flatworm is found in both fresh and salt water and is widely distributed throughout the world (Figure 12–5). Most of the animals are less than an inch in length even when full-grown, but the few terrestrial species may reach several feet in length. The flatworm occupies a unique niche in comparative zoology and psychology. It is the simplest animal to have true

Figure 12–5. Planarian, *Dugesia dorotocephala,* taken from Buckhorn Springs, Oklahoma.

bilateral symmetry, to have true synapses and a brain. In many ways, the vertebrate nervous system is little more than an elaboration of that found in the planarian flatworm. Furthermore, the animal is capable of incredible feats of regeneration. One may cut a large flatworm of the species *Dugesia dorotocephala* into 50 to 100 pieces and, under the best of circumstances, each piece will regrow an entire organism that, within weeks, will be as large as the original worm from which the pieces were taken. Some species are, in addition, capable of reproducing sexually. Such planarians are hermaphrodites—that is, each animal contains functional testes and ovaries. When they mate, each animal fertilizes the other, and each then lays a cocoon that contains six to twenty or more eggs. (Some species are capable of self-fertilization.) When the young hatch, they are fully formed although rather tiny. Within 4 to 6 months, they reach sexual maturity and mate for a period of several years. Then they grow old and misshapened, and often die. In a few species (such as *D. dorotocephala*), however, these senile animals break in two and each half regenerates its missing parts. When the worms reach their normal size, they again begin the mating cycle, since the regeneration process has rejuvenated them as well.

The behavior patterns of the free-living flatworms are considerably more complex than those of the simple coelenterates. The first, and still one of the most convincing studies on planarian learning, was reported more than 50 years ago by a Dutch scientist named P. van Oye (1920). Van Oye began by attaching a piece of meat to the end of a wire and then immersing it into a bowl containing a number of planarians. The water level in the bowl was 7 centimeters high, the meat being immersed 3.5 centimeters deep and to one side of the bowl. To get to the meat, the worms had to crawl up the side of the container, then crawl out on the undersurface of the water (the meniscus) until they found the wire, then crawl down the wire to the meat. Although many worms did indeed get to the surface (they have excellent, bilaterally arranged chemoreceptors on their auricles, the earlike protrusions at the side of their heads), none of them found the wire and crawled down it. Van Oye then raised the meat to the surface for several trials, letting those animals that reached the meat feed on it briefly. After the planarians were accustomed to reaching the meat on the surface, van Oye began lowering it back toward the center a few millimeters at each trial. Eventually this *shaping* procedure resulted in his animals' being able to find and crawl down the wire even when the meat was again suspended halfway between the top of the water and the bottom of the container. Unfortunately for later planarianologists, van Oye's interesting experiment was published in Dutch in a little-known European journal and languished in obscurity until it was rediscovered a decade or so ago.

As interesting and as pioneering as van Oye's experiment was, it did lack one important control group—one in which the meat was continuously presented at a depth of 3.5 centimeters for the same number of trials as were given during the shaping of the experimental group. We utilized this control group in experiments performed in our laboratory in 1964. Although animals in this additional control group did occasionally find the meat, they did so significantly less often than did animals given the shaping procedure in the experimental group. We also found that learning in this situation was affected by a number of factors, including the length of time the worms were allowed to feed when they reached the meat, how hungry they were, and most important of all, the number of trials given in any unit of time. Massed practice (more than one or two trials in a day, and more than two or three training sessions per week) appeared to slow down the learning considerably (Austad, 1965).

In 1955, Thompson and McConnell reported that they had been able to train planarians *(D. dorotocephala)* in a classical conditioning paradigm in which the conditioned stimulus was the onset of light and the unconditioned stimulus was electric shock. The apparatus used in this experiment was quite similar to that shown in Figure 12–6. The worms were put (one at a time) in a water-filled groove in a block of plastic about a foot in length and were given a few minutes to habituate to the apparatus. Two electric light bulbs suspended over the trough supplied the CS, while shock, passed through the water from electrodes at either end of the trough, served as the UCS. After the worm had habituated, it was given 150 light-shock trials in which the light was turned on by itself for 2 seconds, then the shock came on for 1 second, then both CS and UCS were shut off. Another trial was begun 20 to 30 seconds later, whenever the worm was behaving normally again. The experimenters watched the animals closely and recorded any responses the worms made during the 2-second period when the light was on prior to the onset of the shock. Over the course of the 2-hour, massed-training session, this group of experimental planarians showed a slight but statistically significant increase

Figure 12–6.   An apparatus for training planarians. The animal crawls in the water-filled trough. Electrical current passed through the water in the unconditioned stimulus (UCS), while the onset of the lights above the trough is the conditioning stimulus (CR).

in their response rate to the onset of the CS, the electric light. Three control groups were run, one in which the animals were given 150 trials of light without shock, another in which the worms were presented with 150 trials of shock (with a test trial of light alone given after each five shock trials), and a group that was given neither light nor shock. All the animals in the control groups showed decreased responsivity to the light during training, a finding which suggested to Thompson and McConnell (1955) that the increased responsivity shown by the experimental animals was indeed classical conditioning.

The Thompson-McConnell experiment served as a prototype for hundreds which followed it and was justly criticized on a number of points. To begin with, planarians tire rather easily—particularly when given electric shock—so that the massing of the 150 training trials within a space of 2 hours was not a particularly good idea. In later experiments in our laboratory, we showed that flatworms could easily be trained to very high and persisting response rates to light as a CS when no more than twenty-five trials per day were given the animals (Humphries & McConnell, 1964; McConnell, Jacobson, & Kimble, 1959). The second problem was that Thompson and McConnell did not measure how long the learning lasted after the training; in our later work, we showed that animals retained significant amounts of the original conditioning even when allowed to sit for a period of several months without further training (McConnell, 1967).

But most crucial of all, Thompson and McConnell failed to control adequately for pseudoconditioning effects—that is, changes in behavior due not to the *pairing* or *association* of the CS and the UCS, but merely to the fact that the worms were stimulated (and hence presumably sensitized or excited) by the occurrence of so much light and shock. This issue was settled fairly conclusively by studies from a number of laboratories in which several types of pseudoconditioning control groups were employed, none of which showed any evidence of learning (Jacobson, Horowitz, & Fried, 1967). Griffard and Peirce (1964) trained their worms to turn left in an open field when one stimulus was presented and to turn right to a different stimulus, an experiment that we have successfully replicated. But perhaps the most telling series of studies involved a *double discrimination* on the part of the planarians. In these experiments, the worms were presented with two different CSs, one being light, the other being weak vibration. Each animal was put through four stages of training. During stage 1, CS_1 was paired with the shock (UCS) while CS_2 was presented an equal number of times but never associated with the UCS. During the second stage, both CSs were presented without the shock (extinction training). During the third stage, the previously neutral CS_2 was paired with the UCS while CS_1 was presented an equal number of times but not associated with the shock. Stage four again constituted extinction training in which neither CS was paired with the UCS. For half the animals, CS_1 was light and CS_2 was weak vibration, while for the rest of the worms, the stimuli were reversed.

The results of one of several similar double-discrimination experiments are presented in Figures 12–7 and 12–8 (Block & McConnell, 1967). Figure 12–7 shows that the animals given light (CS_1) paired with shock in stage 1 showed a rapid increase in their response rate to light but no increase at all to the neutral CS_2 (in this case, weak vibration). During extinction training in stage 2, the light-shock conditioning disappeared (although there was significant saving on the first day of extinction training). During stage 3, the worms responded appropriately to CS_2 (now paired with shock for the first time) but did not respond to CS_1, while extinction again occurred during stage 4. Figure 12–8 shows similar curves for the animals given weak vibration as CS_1 and light as CS_2. As one might expect if this were true classical conditioning, the learning curves during stage 3 (for both groups) were considerably

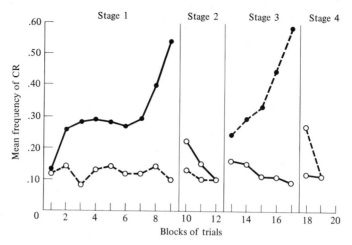

Figure 12–7. Response curves for Group LV in the "double discrimination" experiment of Block & McConnell. There were twenty-five trials in each block. N=8. ●————●, Conditioning Stimulus 1 (light) paired with shock; ●— — — —●, Conditioning stimulus 2 (vibration) paired with shock; 0————0, Conditioning stimulus 1 (light) not paired with shock; 0— — — —0, Conditioning stimulus 2 (vibration) not paired with shock. (From Block & McConnell, 1967.)

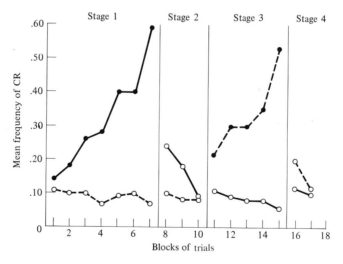

Figure 12–8. Response curves for group VL in the "double discrimination" experiments of Block & McConnell. There were twenty-five trials in each block. N=8. ●————●, Conditioning stimulus 1 (vibration) paired with shock; ●————●, Conditioning stimulus 2 (light) paired with shock; 0————0, Conditioning stimulus 1 (vibration) not paired with shock; 0— — — —0, Conditioning stimulus 2 (light) not paired with shock. (From Block & McConnell, 1967.)

steeper than during stage 1, while extinction proceeded faster during stage 4 than during stage 2.

Other investigators have shown that planarians can be trained in a variety of mazes using either reward or punishment to motivate the animals (Jacobson, 1963, 1965; McConnell, 1967). Best (1963) and Lee (1963) were able to train planarians to perform an operant task similar to lever-pressing in rats. To date, more than forty laboratories in a dozen different countries have reported successful training paradigms with planarians as subjects (Corning and Riccio, 1970).

During the first part of the 1960s, a storm of controversy raged over a series of experiments that seemed to show that memories could be transferred from one planarian to another. The storm clouds first appeared on the horizon when McConnell, Jacobson, and Kimble (1959) reported the results of their first regeneration study. Using spaced trials in the Thompson-McConnell light-shock apparatus, we trained the five planarians in our experimental group until these flatworms were responding to the onset of the light (prior to the onset of the shock) at least 92 percent of the time. We then cut the animals in half and let them rest for a month (during which the head sections grew new tails and the tail sections grew new heads). At the end of the month, both head and tail regenerates were retrained to the 92 percent response rate. As Table 12–1 shows, the original flatworms had taken 134 trials to reach criterion; after regeneration, the heads took but 40 trials and the tails but 43 trials to reach the same criterion. Since the minimum number of trials in which the regenerates could reach criterion was 23, the means of 40 and 43 trials to criterion show highly significant savings. Indeed, two of the tail sections demonstrated almost perfect retention of the training given the original, intact animals a month earlier.

Whenever you learn something—that is, whenever your body stores away a bit of information that you will wish to recall later on—there must be a

Table 12–1   Number of Conditioned Responses Made by Experimental Flatworms in Training and after Regeneration following Cutting of Head and Tail Sections

S	Original training	Retest head	Retest tail
E-1	99	50	51
E-2	191	37	24
E-3	97	48	72
E-4	83	35	44
E-5	200	30	25
M	134	40	43.2

SOURCE: J. V. McConnell, A. L. Jacobson, & D. P. Kimble. The effects of regeneration upon retention of a conditioned response in the planarian. *Journal of Comparative and Physiological Psychology*, 1959, **52**, 1–5. Copyright 1959 by the American Psychological Association and reproduced by permission.

physical change of some kind involved in the storage process. The physical representation of a memory inside your body is called an *engram*. For more than a hundred years, physiologists and psychologists have engaged in an almost frantic search for the engram, that is, they have spent hundreds of thousands of laboratory hours attempting to locate and define the memory mechanism. Until fairly recently, most scientists assumed that memory storage involved some kind of functional and/or structural change at the synapse; indeed, this assumption was so strong that it led many scientists to reject the notion of learning in lower animals, since many of the simplest invertebrates do not have synapses at all. By 1950, however, a small group of scientists began to speculate seriously that the formation of an engram might involve specific chemical changes in the organism's body rather than merely some fairly nonspecific structural reshuffling of axonic fibers at the synapse. Although the details of the chemical theory of memory have by no means been worked out, theorists who hold this view usually assume that when an organism learns, the nervous system produces new and unique molecules (probably RNA and protein) that either act directly on nerve cells to change their firing patterns or act indirectly by affecting transmission of electrical impulses across the synapses.

As bizarre as the chemical theory seemed at first, there were many scattered bits of data to support this view. By the mid-1950s, the geneticists had begun to unravel the mysteries of the genetic code. Since instinctual behavior patterns are inherited, they must somehow be coded for in the DNA molecules present in the sperm and the egg. Indeed, the whole blueprint for an organism's brain must be present in the DNA, which somehow arranges for all normal members of a given animal species to behave in the same way (in certain situations, such as mating and migration). In a very real sense, the genetic code is a *memory* code, the memories in this case being the species-specific behavior patterns that one generation passes along to another. About the same time, a Swedish biologist named Holger Hydén began reporting evidence (now confirmed many times over in other laboratories) that highly specific chemical changes seemed to occur in the brains of trained rats, rabbits, and fish that did not occur in control animals given similar experiences where no learning was involved (Hydén, 1963). Other supporting evidence came from studies which showed that injecting animals with chemicals that sped up metabolism (including DNA, RNA, and protein synthesis) seemed to facilitate learning and memory, while chemicals that interfered with metabolism seemed to retard or even abolish memory formation and storage.

By far the strongest support for the chemical theory of memory, however, came from the still controversial *memory transfer* experiments that began with our work on planarians. The structural theory of memory seemed to predict that the engram would be stored at a very limited number of synapses in an animal's brain. The first regeneration study (McConnell, Jacobson, & Kimble, 1959) suggested that, in planarians at least, the engram was stored throughout the animal's body. The fact that the tail of a trained planarian had to regrow an entirely new brain (complete with new synapses), yet remembered as well as, or even better than, did the head section (which retained the brain of the original worm), was a proposal that many structural theorists simply could not accept. Further experiments showed that trained worms could be cut in several pieces, all of which apparently "remembered" the original training after regeneration. Worse than this, McConnell, R. Jacobson, and Maynard (1959) showed that completely regenerated animals retained some part of the original learning. They cut off and discarded the tails of trained animals, then let the trained heads grow new tails. Once regeneration was complete, they again cut their animals in half (without giving them additional training) and discarded the heads, letting the re-formed tails now regenerate new heads and brains. These completely regrown animals still demonstrated savings when given conditioning trials, an experiment that suggested that the engram "migrated" from one part of the worms' bodies to another during regeneration. Since it was difficult to imagine a structure such as a synapse migrating, but since chemicals from the trained head obviously did find their way into the regenerating tail, these experiments were often cited as evidence that memories must somehow have a molecular component to them.

Hydén had speculated that the "memory molecule" might well be RNA, and his experiments showed that following training, measurable changes in brain RNA did occur in many organisms. Shortly after the first regeneration studies on planarians were published, Corning and John (1961) trained flatworms, cut them in half, and let some of the animals regenerate normally while others regenerated in a weak solution of ribonuclease (an enzyme that destroys RNA). Corning and John reported that the ribonuclease not only attacked the RNA in their regenerating worms, but wiped out the memory in the tail regenerates as well. Animals that regrew their missing parts in ordinary water showed the retention first reported by McConnell, Jacobson, and Kimble. Thereafter, a number of other investigators, both here and abroad, were able to confirm not only the retention of a variety of learned tasks in pieces of regenerating, trained planarians, but also the destructive effects of ribonuclease on learning and memory even in intact flatworms.

The major support for the chemical theory, however, came from the *cannibalism* experiments. When some species of planarians (such as *D. dorotocephala,* used in so many studies) are starved, they turn cannibalistic. We took advantage of this fact to perform the first of the so-called *memory transfer* experiments.

Let us assume for the moment that the chemical theory of memory storage is correct, that when an organism learns something, a unique (and task-specific) molecule is somehow synthesized in the organism's body. Now, the interesting question is this: If two animals learn exactly the same response pattern under identical training conditions, will their bodies synthesize identical memory molecules? We assumed the answer to this question would be Yes, that if two animals had exactly the same memory, they would have somehow manufactured internally exactly the same chemical engram. Planarians are famous in zoological circles because one can graft any part of one animal onto another and the graft will usually take. For example, one may cut off the heads of several worms and graft them all onto the body of one otherwise intact planarian, and (under the best of surgical conditions) all the grafted heads will become functional and send out neural connections to the nervous system of the host worm. If it is possible to graft new heads on old worms, we reasoned, shouldn't it be likewise possible to graft new memories onto an old planarian? That is, if molecule X is the engram for a conditioned response in all planarians, shouldn't it be possible to create molecule X in one worm by giving it training and then somehow to extract this molecule from the trained animal and insert it into the body of an untrained worm, thereby transferring the first worm's memories to the second?

To test this rather peculiar hypothesis, we trained donor worms using the (by then) standard light-shock classical conditioning paradigm. Once the donors had reached the 92 percent response rate, they were chopped in small pieces and fed to hungry, untrained, cannibalistic planarians. The cannibals were given one to two days to digest their meals, then were given their first training trials in the conditioning apparatus. Other cannibals were given a meal of untrained worms and were then also given light-shock training. The experiment was repeated several times and was performed blind (that is, the person testing the cannibals did not know what the animal had eaten prior to training). As one of us reported in 1962 (McConnell, 1962), from the first block of training trials it was clear that the cannibals that had eaten educated "victims" were significantly superior to the cannibals that had eaten untrained donors. The memory transfer hypothesis seemed to have some validity.

Other laboratories soon confirmed the original cannibalism findings and were able to show that habituation and a variety of maze habits also could be transferred from one planarian to another via cannibalistic ingestion (for a review of this literature, see McConnell, 1967b). Although some experimenters argued that it was not learning that was being transferred but rather, an increased activity level or sensitization (Hartry, Keith-Lee, & Morton, 1964), several later studies indicated that both sensitization *and* associative learning could be transferred, depending on how the study was performed (McConnell & Shelby, 1970). Perhaps the most interesting fact of all was this—even those experimenters who argued that it was activity level that was transferred showed that *some* behavioral tendency was passed cannibalistically from one animal to another, a most startling finding in and of itself.

Arguments about the specificity of the transfer effect raged hot and heavy during the early 1960s. Some theorists (such as Jensen) who refused to believe that any invertebrate could learn anything under any circumstances took comfort from the fact that a relatively few experimenters who tried were unable to train their planarians at all. Since a majority of the scientists who made the attempt (and who followed closely the established training paradigms) reported consistent success, these objections seemed untenable. Furthermore, every experimenter who was able to achieve training in his or her animals and who then attempted a transfer experiment of some kind reported success (although, as we have noted, a few of these experimenters believed it was sensitization and not learning that was passed on to their cannibals). Arguments concerning the specificity of the memory transfer seemed to be answered by a study by McConnell and Shelby (1970). They trained their planarians (*D. dorotocephala*) in a simple T maze, one arm of which was light gray, the other dark gray. Since the worms showed no initial preference for either arm, half their donors were trained to go to the light arm, the rest to the dark arm. Criterion of learning was nine correct responses out of ten training trials achieved 2 days in a row. The donor animals took about 200 trials to reach this criterion. They were then cut in small pieces and fed to untrained cannibals. Other cannibals were fed pieces of untrained donors.

In the McConnell and Shelby experiment, group I cannibals were trained to go to the same color arm of the maze as had been the donors they ate (the "positive" or + transfer group). Group II cannibals were trained to go to the opposite color arm of the maze as had been the donors they ate (the negative or − transfer group). The cannibals in group III were given rather a special feeding. Each cannibal in this group was fed both a donor trained to the light arm and one trained to the dark arm. The group III animals comprised the "conflicting instructions" or ± group. The worms in group IV were fed untrained donors (the "no instructions" or zero group). Half the cannibals in each group were trained to the dark gray and half to the light gray arm. Testing of the cannibals was performed blind.

The results of the McConnell and Shelby experiment are shown in Table 12–2. The group I animals reached criterion significantly sooner than all other groups. The group II animals reached criterion significantly sooner than groups III and IV. The group III and group IV animals were not significantly different, although the difference did approach significance (P = .10). Additionally, the group III animals showed significantly more vacillation at the choice point in the maze than did the animals in the other three groups.

Table 12–2 Mean Trials to Criterion in a T Maze for Four Groups of Planarians Fed Different Types of Donor Animals

	Group I (+ Group)	Group II (− Group)	Group III (± Group)	Group IV (0 Group)
Mean trials to criterion	113.8	166.3	263.8	228.8

SOURCE: From McConnell and Shelby, 1970.

It is difficult to explain the results of this experiment except in terms of actual transfer, from one organism to another, of rather specific behavioral tendencies. The fact that the group I animals were significantly superior to all other groups, but particularly to the group III animals, suggests that the transfer effect is stimulus-specific. The finding that the group II animals were significantly superior to those in group IV suggests that nonspecific as well as specific learning factors can be transferred, but that with the proper experimental paradigm we can differentiate between these two types of transfer. That the group III animals were significantly inferior to the animals in groups I and II shows that conflicting tendencies can be transferred. The fact that the group III animals showed more vicarious trial-and-error behavior at the choice point gives additional support to this conclusion.

The biochemical mechanism by which cannibalistic transfer takes place is still unknown, but certain data do appear to be pertinent. To begin with, it should be noted that one would not expect to achieve memory transfer through cannibalism in most species higher on the phylogenetic scale than the planarian. The flatworm lacks a true digestive system. According to Hyman (1951), digestion in the planarian is largely intracellular. Food taken in through the pharynx fills the large intestinal cavity or lumen but is not digested there. Rather, the phagocytic cells lining the intestinal walls take in food particles in amoeboid fashion by putting out pseudopods. Digestion subsequently occurs in these cells, so the complex molecules thought to code memories in this animal would reach cells throughout the cannibals' bodies intact. In higher organisms, digestion typically takes place prior to the incorporation of the material into the body cells; thus the coded molecules would most likely be broken into subunits by enzymic action and the memory presumably would be lost.

Assuming that the cannibalism studies are valid and do give support to the chemical theory of memory storage, what chemicals are involved? In 1962, several of us attempted to answer this question (Zelman, Kabat, Jacobson, & McConnell, 1963). Several groups of donor planarians were given light-shock training, or equal numbers of trials of light and/or unpaired shock, or no experience at all. These animals were then ground up and a cold phenol technique was used to extract RNA from the donor tissue (Davis, 1967). The RNA-rich extract was then injected into untrained animals, a micropipet and syringe being used for the injections. The injectees were subsequently assigned code numbers randomly and then were given light-shock conditioning trials. Statistically significant differences obtained between those recipients injected with the RNA-rich extract taken from conditioned donors and (A) those recipients injected with an RNA-rich extract from animals given unpaired trials of light and shock or trials of light only (or shock only), and (B) animals injected with an equal amount of aquarium water. To the best of our knowledge, this is the first experiment reported anywhere suggesting that acquired behavioral tendencies could be transferred from one organism to another by means of purely chemical extracts, and also the first such experiment to suggest that RNA might be capable of mediating this type of transfer. It should be noted, however, that this study was far from being conclusive. To begin with, the extract contained measurable amounts of protein in addition to the RNA (recent experiments with rats and mice by Ungar and his associates suggest that the active ingredient in the memory transfer experiments may be a protein that is tied to, or associated with, an RNA molecule). Much more convincing experiments involving RNA extracts with planarians were soon reported, the best being by Fried and Horowitz (1964) and Jacobson, Fried, and Horowitz (1966a, 1966b). Coward et al. (1970) subsequently reported a transfer of behavioral tendencies between two species of crab, *Uca pugnax* and *U. pugilator,* using RNA extract not from the brain of the crabs but rather from their hepatopancreas, a most provocative (and as yet unconfirmed) report indeed.

By the mid-1960s, reports of successful chemical transfer studies in rats and mice came from several laboratories, and most of the experimenters who had been using planarians as subjects turned their attention to rodents. A running battle soon erupted between those scientists who were able to achieve the effect with some regularity and those scientists who could not do so, but as of 1970, the bulk of the studies had yielded positive transfer effects and many of the investigators who at first had reported negative results had corrected their techniques and were achieving success (Dyal, 1970). By the spring of 1971, Ungar (one of the original scientists to report success with rats and mice) had not only characterized the structure of a protein molecule that appeared to mediate the transfer of dark avoidance in rats, but had been able to synthesize the protein as well. Zippcl and Domagk (1971) in Germany and Braud and Braud (1972) in the United States had demonstrated that the effect in goldfish was so highly stimulus-specific that they could transfer responses to very specific colors or even to inverted versus upright triangles. Despite the fact that several hundred successful chemical transfer experiments now appear in the literature, it is probably too soon to accept the effect as having been established beyond reasonable doubt. If memory transfer via chemical injection is eventually accepted as a valid phenomenon, however, it will be because early investigators seized upon the unusual physiological characteristics of the planarian and exploited these characteristics in rather novel fashion.

ANNELIDS

The phylum Annelida includes all the segmented worms, such as the earthworms and leeches you are probably familiar with, as well as a great number of oceanic and freshwater species that few people have seen or heard of. The marine species are by far the most numerous. In spring in the northern American states, when the ground is moist and soft, the earthworm is abundant near the surface, as gardeners know only too well. But even a shovelful of the richest soil would not yield the diversity of annelids as would an equal amount of muddy coastal sand turned over on a beach at low tide. The most distinguishing feature of the annelids is the division of their bodies into segments which are arranged linearly like beads on a string from front to back. Although the front and rear segments are usually specialized, each of the middle sections typically contains (in replicate) almost all the organs and parts that an intact organism would need. Two massive ganglia—one located just above the esophagus (the supraesophageal ganglion) and one below (the subesophageal ganglion)—constitute the brain in most annelids. Each segment, however, contains minor ganglia of its own.

Annelids are divided into three classes. Polychaeta, usually considered the most primitive, is made up of the marine annelids. The terrestrial earthworms and the freshwater annelids make up the class Oligochaeta, while the leeches belong to the class Hirudinea and are usually considered the most advanced of the three classes.

Jacobson (1963) reviewed studies of annelid learning rather comprehensively to that date. More recently, Ratner (1967) has provided a critical review of literature on this subject, with special attention to the adequacy of control procedures. The present discussion will attempt to characterize the learning literature, give the flavor of common methodological problems, and describe some of the most recent research reports.

Earthworms (oligochaetes) have most typically been studied in mazes and in classical conditioning situations, with scattered references on habituation, straight alleys, and the usual assortment of peculiar paradigms. Polychaetes, usually *Nereis,* have been tested in habituation, tube-crawling, and more recently, maze and classical conditioning situations. Only occasional reports appear on sedentary polychaetes—e.g., Krasne's (1965) study of habituation to touch in the sabellid worm *Branchiomma vesiculosum.* All these situations involve serious problems of interpretation in that adequate control procedures have often not been employed. Of all this work, the most solidly established, other than habituation, would appear to us to be the classical conditioning of earthworms. Two laboratories, those of Ratner and Wyers and their associates, have reported experiments involving careful controls for pseudoconditioning, sensitization, and the like (for a critical discussion of classical conditioning and appropriate control procedures, see Jacobson, 1967). For example, Peeke, Herz, and Wyers (1967), using weak vibration as the conditioned stimulus and bright light as the unconditioned stimulus, found significant increments in the anterior contraction response during acquisition and decreases during extinction for a forward-conditioning group of earthworms. No such changes were observed in backward- or pseudo-conditioning control groups. A similar differentiation between experimental and control groups occurred in another experiment (Wyers, Peeke, & Herz,

1964) in which a partially reinforced group was found to exhibit greater resistance to extinction than a consistently reinforced group. And again, when anterior extension rather than contraction was employed as the UCR, response increments occurred only in the forward-conditioning group (Herz, Peek, & Wyers, 1967). The paradigm used by Wyers's group was originally developed by Ratner (see Ratner, 1965), whose findings support those consistently obtained by Wyers and his colleagues.

Probably the most famous earthworm of all was the sole subject of Robert Yerkes's famous 1912 report. This worm not only learned to turn correctly in a T maze, but also continued to perform the response after the first five segments, containing the pharyngeal ganglia, had been removed. Further studies of maze learning in earthworms are described in Jacobson (1963). Ratner (1967) has criticized many of these studies on the grounds that "defensive responses" are typically elicited by shock for incorrect turns and by prodding for inactivity in the stem of the maze. Ratner points out that when such stimulation is omitted, as in Datta's (1962) excellent effort, learning still occurs, but apparently reaches a lower asymptote of correct responding. The Yerkes apparatus, which has been adopted by most subsequent investigators, involves shock for incorrect turns as well as reward (darkness and moisture) for correct turns. While this paradigm is certainly more complex than a reward-only situation (such as Datta's) and does confuse the question of exactly what is learned, it is not invalid as a learning situation. Prodding the animal is certainly an inelegant procedure at best but need not introduce bias if the experimenter is careful. Ratner (1964) suggested the use of a straight alley to avoid the difficulties supposedly inherent in the use of mazes for earthworms; but this apparatus, too, clearly has its own problems as a device for assessing learning (Reynierse, Halliday, & Nelson, 1968).

We may conclude this section on maze learning in earthworms by reference to two recent studies concerned with the role of the pharyngeal ganglia in learning and memory. Zellner (1966) compared the effects of the removal of the suprapharyngeal ganglion on maze performance with the effects of sham operation. We may summarize his major results as follows: (1) learning rate was not affected by pretraining removal of the suprapharyngeal ganglion; (2) retention was not affected by ganglion removal *or* by subsequent regeneration (Yerkes had found habit loss as the new tissue grew, but Zellner's results suggest this was a time effect); (3) extinction responding was prolonged by ganglion removal after training. Another group of researchers (Aranda, Fernandez, Celome, & Luco, 1968) obtained roughly confirmatory findings, in that posttraining removal of the anterior 4½ segments produced no decline in T-maze performance. This operation removed the subpharyngeal ganglion, plus the fourth and fifth ganglia, hence was more extensive than Zellner's lesions; but retention was apparently good, nonetheless.

A final study on earthworms concerns the interesting phenomenon of habituation. Kuenzer (1958) earlier provided extensive observations about habituation in 1958. A more recent contribution compares the relative habituation rates of two component responses. Earthworms subjected to vibration show (1) anterior withdrawal, and (2) hooking of the posterior end. Gardner (1968) found that the two responses habituate at quite different rates—the former disappearing after some fourteen trials, on the average, and the latter only after some seventy-five trials. Overhabituation produced no significant effect on recovery. Gardner also confirmed Kuenzer's finding that significant retention of habituation is observed 24 hours later—in fact, as much as 4 days later.

In the last few years, more attention has been paid to the learning abilities of nereid polychaetes (Figure 12–9). Earlier, poorly controlled demonstrations of learning have been supplanted by studies involving more careful consideration of control procedures. An excellent example of this trend is the work

Figure 12–9.   A male Nereis polychaet, *Nereis irrorata*. (From R. D. Barnes, *Invertebrate zoology*, 2nd Ed. Philadelphia: Saunders, 1968.)

of Evans (1966a, 1966b, 1966c) on what he calls "non-associative behavioral modifications" in nereid polychaetes. Some years ago, Copeland (1930) followed light changes (or touch) to nereids by the presentation of food, and found an increasing tendency by the animals to advance to the food end of the tube when light (or touch) was presented. Evans has found that light and food need not be paired for this behavioral change to occur. Similarly, supposed demonstrations of classical conditioning in nereids are invalidated by Evans's findings of comparable changes when CS and UCS are presented in unpaired fashion. Evans himself had shown that if nereids are shocked at the end of a plastic channel, they avoid punishment by reversing direction or not moving. In later work, Evans (1966b) has shown that the shock need not be given at the end of the channel—i.e., punishments given before entering the apparatus or after leaving it are just as effective as punishment at the exit.

What is left, then, of nereid learning? First, there are Clark's (1960a, 1960b) interesting studies of habituation to various stimuli in *Nereis pelagica*. Clark reported observations on parameters (e.g., intertrial interval) and properties (e.g., interactions between stimuli) of the habituation process. Evans (1969a, 1969b) has examined habituation of the withdrawal response to tactile and mechanical stimuli and changes in illumination in several species of nereids. He reports, among these things, that decerebrate worms respond to the same stimuli as intact ones, and also show habituation to the stimuli.

Research on the maze-learning capacities of nereids is also worthy of attention. Clark (1965) has reviewed studies of nereid learning and the role of the supraesophageal ganglion, and we can draw upon his discussion here. Evans (1963) succeeded in training several species of nereids in a T maze by punishing with shock in one arm and rewarding with darkness in the other. Omission of shock apparently precludes learning. If worms are decerebrated after training, they revert to random responding. Also, decerebrated worms fail to learn the maze. Clark points out that decerebration abolishes input from anterior sense organs and hence interferes with the sensory discriminations the animal must make to pick the correct alley. In confirmation of Clark's view, Flint (1965) found that following an operation that disconnects the supraesophageal ganglion from the rest of the nervous system but that still allows sensory input to the subesophageal ganglion and the ventral nerve cord, at least half the trained animals showed retention of a previously learned maze habit. Naïve animals subjected to this operation prior to training were unable to learn the maze, however. Clark concludes that the supraesophageal ganglion "does not serve as a unique memory storage center"; indeed that "to search for a single, discrete morphological memory store is perhaps to hunt the chimaera [Clark, 1965, p. 98]." The same conclusion might apply equally well to the search for the engram in higher organisms.

THE MOLLUSKS

About the only types of invertebrates to generate much interest among laymen are the mollusks, that phylum that contains such familiar animals as clams, oysters, snails, squids, and octopuses. The mollusks are widely distributed both on land and in the water, and are valued not only for their shells but as delicacies for the table (although, as fiction writer Anthony Boucher once said, the bravest person in the history of the human race was probably the first man or woman to eat an oyster). In diversity, the mollusks (with more than 80,000 living and 35,000 fossil species known) rank second only to the arthropods. The relationship between the snail and a squid is often hard for the layman to see, yet they are all possessed of similar anatomical blueprints and most of them (including the squid, but not the octopus) have at least a rudimentary shell.

The mollusk nervous system is, along with that of some insects and spiders, the most highly developed of any invertebrate. In the cephalopods (the squid and octopus), for example, a large number of ganglia have fused to form a brain that encircles the esophagus, each ganglion being so well differentiated that it has recently become possible experimentally to determine which ganglia (or parts of ganglia) control the various parts and functions of the body. The sense receptors are also highly developed, particularly the eye, which, in the cephalopods, is surprisingly close in structure and function to the vertebrate eye.

Most of the research on learning in this group has been concerned with the octopus. A few reports have appeared of efforts to train snails, and recently some attention has been devoted to aplysia. Evidence concerning the learning capacities of other mollusks is largely preliminary—for example, Thorpe (1963) points out that limpets are reputed to recognize their home territory and to return there after being experimentally displaced (p. 212). We shall discuss the work on snails, aplysia, and octopus, in that order.

Several different forms of behavioral modification have been tested in snails. Humphrey (1930) subjected snails to a repeated jerking of the platform they were on. Initially, the jerking elicited antenna withdrawal, but this response declined with further trials. Other observations suggested that fatigue could not account for the decline and that this was a case of habituation. Thompson (1917) reported a phenomenon like classical conditioning in a freshwater snail. Lettuce in the animal's mouth elicits chewing; pressure on the foot elicits foot contraction but not chewing. When the two stimuli were presented simultaneously, no chewing movements occurred for a number of trials—pressure apparently inhibiting the chewing response to lettuce. After some 60 to 110 trials, chewing reactions were reinstated. This is a peculiar form of training; perhaps the most significant finding was that pressure alone elicited chewing responses some 48 hours after the completion of training, and that this response ceased suddenly and finally after several trials.

Thompson also attempted to train snails in a maze but was unsuccessful in this effort. Garth and Mitchell (1926) obtained positive results in a maze study on land snails. They record very vividly their difficulties in maintaining and running the subjects. The snails were required to turn to one side of the maze to escape a bright light and reach darkness. The major evidence for learning comes from one star pupil, called snail XX. Snail XX would only run two trials on most days, and sometimes took as long as a half-hour or more to complete a trial; but over the course of 100 trials, his correct choices increased distinctly: on the first 50 trials he made twenty errors, on the last 50 trials, only two. During this progression, the average running time per trial dropped roughly from 15 to roughly 4 minutes, and, according to the experimenters, the path taken became more direct.

Several recent studies of aplysia suggest that this organism, which has a relatively simple nervous system, might be useful for studying neuronal mechanisms of learning. Bruner and Tauc (1966) applied drops of water to special preparations of aplysia and observed what appeared to be a habituatory decrement in both motor and neural responses. They infer that these changes may be due to long-lasting changes occurring at synapses. Lickey (1968) established a response in aplysia which appears analogous to a passive avoidance response in higher organisms. He presented the seaweed ulva, a natural food for aplysia, to the animal's lip. On other trials, a forceps was presented, or a combination of forceps and ulva. Initially, the animals ingested and chewed the forceps as they did the ulva; but with continued practice, they rejected the forceps more frequently by withdrawing the mouth parts, while still (on other trials) consistently ingesting the ulva. This response, Lickey reports, was retained for 4 days without practice.

More recently, a concerted attack on the neural basis of habituation in aplysia has been reported by Costelluici, Pinsker, Kupferman, and Kandel (1970); Kupferman, Costelluici, Pinsker, and Kandel (1970); and Pinsker, Kupferman, Costelluici, and Kandel (1970). Habituation occurred when the gill-withdrawal reflex was repeatedly elicited by a tactile stimulus applied to the siphon or mantle shelf. Dishabituation could be produced by a strong tactile stimulus to another part of the animal; and other parametric characteristics of habituation, as seen in more complex organisms, were also observed (Pinsker et al., 1970, p. 1742). The gill-withdrawal reflex is controlled by the abdominal ganglion, which contains a small number of nerve cells and has been well mapped. These investigators proceeded to study neural correlates of the habituation and dishabituation processes. Intracellular recordings showed that these behaviorial changes were not due to peripheral changes, either sensory or motor, but were caused by alterations of excitatory synaptic potentials at gill motor neurons (habituation involving a decrease, dishabituation an increase, in these potentials). Further efforts by this team of researchers were directed at analyzing the changes in potential. A special preparation was used, consisting of an isolated abdominal ganglion connected to a piece of skin from the tactile receptive field of the gill-withdrawal reflex. Intracellular recordings were taken simultaneously from both sensory neurons and one of the main identified motor neurons. The data led Costelluici et al. (1970) to conclude that most of the behavioral changes can be explained by changes in the efficacy of specific excitatory synapses between the sensory and motor neurons, due perhaps to changes in the release of excitatory transmitter from the presynaptic terminal.

In contrast to the limited references on gastropods, the literature on learning in cephalopods, primarily octopus, is enormous. The octopus has been a favorite subject particularly with British ethologists and psychologists. At least two books have been based on research on octopus learning and behavior (Wells, 1962; Young, 1964). Much research is directed at understanding the physiological basis of the octopus's memory system (see, for example, Young, 1965). A number of experiments have attempted to assess the role of the vertical lobe system in octopus learning and memory. A summary of much of this work can be found in Young's (1961) review, and a relevant discussion in Thorpe (1963). In addition to studies involving lesions, numerous papers have been concerned with various properties of octopus learning as such. The best we can do here is characterize this vast body of research by describing a few typical studies, and refer the reader to more comprehensive reviews (Sutherland, 1963; Wells, 1962, 1965; Young, 1961, 1964). Wells's (1965) presentation at a conference on invertebrate behavior in Cambridge, England, nicely exemplifies much of his work. He begins by reviewing the work of several investigators, showing that octopuses can be trained to make a variety of tactile, chemotactile, and visual discriminations. Most of these studies have required the animal to discriminate between pairs of patterns of objects, seizing food (a crab or a piece of fish) only when a particular member of the pair accompanies it. Shock is typically administered for errors. Wells reports that octopuses fail to make discriminations when they must integrate information about the parts of their own bodies when they learn. For example, blinded animals cannot distinguish between objects differing in shape nor between objects differing in weight; removal of the statocysts in visually intact animals upsets recognition of figure orientation since the animal then has no means of discriminating its own bodily orientation in space. Wells also discusses in this paper the results of training experiments in relation to work on brain lesions in octopuses.

Wells and Young (1966) have reported findings on "split-brain" octopuses. Blinded octopuses were trained on a tactile discrimination, using the arms of one side of their body only. When the brain was split before training, no side-to-side transfer occurred. In a more recent paper, the same authors (Wells

& Young, 1969) reported that octopuses without vertical lobes or lacking one-half brain learned more slowly than normals when trials were massed. These differences did not occur when fewer trials were given per session.

Sutherland and Mackintosh have found the octopus useful in their comparative approach to learning. They have been particularly concerned with discriminative processes, and the properties of these processes in various species. They have in general found what they consider striking similarities between rats and octopuses in comparable learning situations: "Neither species attends equally to all features of the stimulus input; both show the phenomenon of transfer along a continuum; both learn reversals faster after overtraining on the original problem; both learn later reversals faster than earlier reversals in a series; both learn a non-reversal shift more slowly after prior overtraining [Mackintosh, 1965, p. 133]." Mackintosh notes that some of these phenomena are difficult to demonstrate in other animal groups, and suggests that these similarities in behavior between rat and octopus may imply similar underlying learning mechanisms.

THE ARTHROPODS

For the most part, the invertebrates are water dwellers. Only the arthropods have established themselves firmly and diversely on land, which they also used as a stepping-stone to their conquest of the air. All winged invertebrates belong to this phylum as do most of the land dwellers. Probably this invasion of the three possible biospheres is the reason the arthropods are so numerous; more than 800,000 different species have been described, and they compose at least 80 percent of all the known animal species. The phylum includes the extinct trilobites (that show up so often in fossil records), the horseshoe crab (that looks as if it should be a fossil), the arachnids (scorpions, spiders, ticks, and mites), the crustaceans (shrimp, crabs, lobsters, and crayfish), the insects, the centipedes, the millipedes, and countless others too numerous to mention. The nervous system in many arthropods has reached a very high level of development. Their brains are probably the largest and the most complex of all invertebrates, this encephalization being matched or correlated with the occurrence of highly specialized and refined sensory equipment. The behavior patterns of the arthropods are also probably the most complex of any of the invertebrate groups.

Since this phylum includes more species than all the other animal phyla combined, and since the learning capacities of a number of these species have been rather extensively studied, our review of learning in arthropods must be sketchy and illustrative. Included in this literature are a number of fascinating preparations and experimental approaches. Maze learning in ants and honey finding in bees are classical topics in comparative psychology. A more recent development is the use of special preparations of both crustaceans (crayfish, crabs) and insects (cockroaches, locusts) to investigate electrophysiological and chemical events correlated with learning. Several recent articles are devoted to this topic (Bullock & Quarton, 1966; Eisenstein, 1967; Kandel & Spencer, 1968). In recent years also, improved behavioral techniques have been applied to the study of the learning capacities of various arthropod groups, including crabs, bees, and fruit flies. Finally, in this preface, we should mention the scattered and often fascinating reports on learning in such creatures as mayfly nymphs, sow bugs (also called wood lice or pill bugs), dragonfly larvae, mealworms, caterpillars, jumping spiders, moths, blowflies, daphnids, and water mites. The earlier literature, in particular, contains many such reports (see Thorpe, 1943/1944, 1963).

Among the crustaceans, lobsters, crabs, and crayfish have all been subjected to learning experiments, and one even finds an occasional reference to daphnids (Blees, 1919). Schone (1965) reviewed some of the research on learning in crustaceans with reference to its relevance to the animals' natural functions (feeding, social behavior, and so on). He reported (Schone, 1961) that spiny lobsters learn to select the side of a maze that leads to a water tank, either on the basis of position or brightness discrimination. Few, if any, other such studies have been performed on lobsters. Crabs, on the other hand, have received more attention. Several early studies appeared on such varieties as fiddler crabs (Schwartz & Safir, 1915), hermit crabs (Spaulding, 1904), and green crabs (Yerkes, 1902). Two investigations, reported in 1960, seem well controlled and present positive evidence of learning. In one of these (Smith & Baker, 1960), light and shock were paired to classically condition tail movement in horseshoe crabs. Acquisition and extinction effects were shown which did not occur in groups that received light alone or shock alone. Catta, Milstein, & Bitterman (1960) found that Bermuda land crabs could improve significantly in performance in a two-choice spatial situation, with escape from water as reinforcement, but that the asymptotic level was relatively low. No progressive improvement was found with repeated reversals. More recently, Makons (1969) reported that his attempts to train horseshoe crabs in several different situations were largely unsuccessful. He achieved only limited success with classical conditioning (replicating Smith and Baker) and shuttle-box avoidance, and none with operant conditioning. Wasserman and Patton (1969), however, also using the horseshoe crab, established avoidance conditioning, when tail movement was the effective response. They report that the type of tail harness employed is critical for successful conditioning. A final paper on crabs that deserves mention describes techniques of permanent electrode implantation and cannulation of the horseshoe crab (Corning, Feinstein, & Haight, 1965). These preparations might be useful for the study of physiological correlates of learning in this animal.

Maze learning and habituation have been studied in crayfish. Both Yerkes and Huggins (1903) and, many years later, Capretta and Rea (1967) reported that these animals can learn to select the side of a maze that leads to water. The latter investigators also looked for improvement with successive reversals, but found none. Krasne has been concerned with the neural correlates of habituation in crayfish. The response studied was a tail-flip escape reflex which occurs when the abdomen is pinched with a forceps. Rapid habituation and slow recovery were observed (Krasne & Woodsmall, 1969). Further studies (Krasne, 1969; Krasne & Roberts, 1967) have examined the relationship of changes in potentials from lateral giant fibers to the occurrence and waning of the escape response.

As we turn our attention now to insects, perhaps a good starting point is Schneirla's extensive analysis of maze learning in ants. This work is described in Thorpe's (1963) book, and references are given there. We may simply say here that these investigations viewed the maze as, in a sense, a duplicate of the natural foraging situation, and that ants proved capable of mastering some rather complex problems—e.g., mazes with six choice points.

Vowles (1967) has performed a series of studies on maze learning in ants, which are designed to investigate the role of the mushroom bodies of the ant brain in such learning. Interocular transfer and the effects of brain lesions were studied in visual-discrimination tasks.

The study of learning and memory in bees has largely been conducted in the context of the question of social communication in these animals. Von Frisch, who spent a lifetime studying honeybees, is the discoverer of the "waggle dance," which was described in Chapters 4 and 5. Adrian Wenner and his colleagues in California place much greater emphasis on the role of learning in *recruitment*. They found that many foragers did not bother to dance once they returned to the hive and that the bees that surrounded the dancer during its dance were often not the animals that were recruited. Instead, the recruits seemed to consist of animals that had already been to the feeding station many times when it contained food (on prior occasions). As Wenner and Johnson wrote recently:

> Bees experienced at visiting a given source can rely upon their memory of the location and can be recruited by means of a conditioned response to either food odor or location odor brought back into the hive by hive mates. . . . Thus we conclude that the experienced bees, which require no language for re-recruitment, are basically responsible for providing food for their colony [1967, p. 1067].

Other experiments by these investigators (Johnson & Wenner, 1966; Wenner & Johnson, 1966) show that bees can learn to approach a food dish when an originally neutral or even aversive stimulus (light or smoke) is presented. That bees are capable of learning is not, of course, new information: von Frisch showed in his earlier work that bees can learn to respond selectively to a particular odor or color. What is novel is the importance that Wenner and Johnson attribute to this process in the explanation of communication and recruitment. Von Frisch, of course, has his own views about this, and the interested reader will want to consult his reply to this argument (1967). In another study of bee learning, Bermant and Gary (1966) have shown that bees can make a simultaneous discrimination between yellow and blue cards, when food is used as reward. And Thorpe (1963, pp. 250–251) refers to a study by Weiss (1953), in which bees and wasps were reportedly taught to master mazes with from eight to eleven choice points. Frings (1944) and Takeda (1961), in a classical conditioning situation, trained bees to extend the proboscis when neutral aromas were presented.

Fruit flies, so popular in work on behavioral genetics, have not often been tested in learning situations. Hershberger and Smith (1967) found that "imagoes reared on a peppermint-scented food medium subsequently selected the peppermint-scented arm of an insect olfactmeter more often than did controls reared on a non-scented medium [p. 261]." They interpret this as a conditioning process. A less questionable demonstration of learning is the recent work of Murphey (1967, 1969) on maze learning in fruit flies. The subjects had been selected for negative geotaxis, and reward for choosing the correct arm of the maze was opportunity to ascend a vertical tube. Shock for incorrect choices apparently improved performance but was not necessary for learning to occur.

In the last decade, the work of Horridge on headless cockroaches and locusts has been extended by a number of investigators. Earlier learning research on cockroaches had largely been concerned with mazes: Turner (1913) and Eldering (1919) used complex mazes, and Minami and Dallenbach (1946) studied the effects of activity and inactivity on retention of a maze habit. A more recent study of maze learning in cockroaches is that of Longo (1964).

Avoidance conditioning has been the type of learning used in the research of Horridge (1962, 1965) and others on headless cockroaches and locusts. The animal is suspended in such a way that one leg receives regularly repeated shock whenever the experimental animal does. In this situation, the latter soon learns to hold the leg in an elevated position, thus avoiding shock. This preparation has proved useful for investigations of neurophysiological, electrophysiological, and biochemical correlates of learning. Eisenstein and Cohen (1965) showed that the same type of learning could be achieved in the prothoracic ganglion after it had been removed from the rest of the ventral cord. Hoyle (1965) has also confirmed and extended Horridge's basic observations. We might add here the observations of one group of investigators (Disterhoft, Nurnberger, & Corning, 1968): Although experimental animals did better than controls on the day of testing and 24 hours later, a reversal, if anything, was observed when testing was postponed for 48 hours. Disterhoft et al. suggest close attention to behavioral control problems in this preparation.

CONCLUSIONS

Can invertebrates learn? Considering the hundreds of experiments reporting success in training these organisms, the answer would seem to be, "Yes, if you treat them right and train them properly." But honeybees are not white rats with stingers and a fondness for pollen and sugar water; they are organisms with their own unique capacities and liabilities as experimental subjects. There are many tasks that a bee, or a worm, or a squid, can learn better and faster than a rat or mouse, and there is no reason to believe that the invertebrates—in their own ways—are less intelligent than many of the vertebrate species. The ants and termites, for instance, have survived for many millions of years longer than any of the vertebrate species have been on earth. And is not survival one of the ultimate criteria of what intelligence is all about?

Invertebrates—like their distant cousins with backbones—solve their own day-to-day problems with the physiological and behavioral equipment they have available to them. There are thousands of different ways in which an organism may obtain and digest its food, all of which can be successful as far as the animal itself is concerned. No one physiological mechanism underlies food-getting, digestion, locomotion, or reproduction in all the thousands of different animal species. Why then should we expect that learning should be the same in all organisms or be mediated by the same underlying mechanism or mechanisms?

The invertebrates offer the scientist a rich and challenging experience that most psychologists have so far chosen to ignore. But if comparative psychology is to become truly *comparative,* these fascinating animals must soon take their rightful place in experimental laboratories.

REFERENCES

ARANDA, L. C., FERNANDEZ, O. P., CELOME, E. S., & LUCO, J. V. The influence of the first four anterior ganglia on learned behavior in *Lumbricus terrestris. Physiology and Behavior*, 1968, **3**, 753–756.

AUSTAD, E. A preliminary attempt at food-rewarding conditioning in planarians. *Worm Runner's Digest*, 1965, **7**(2), 41–45.

BERMANT, G., & GARY, N. E. Discrimination training and reversal in groups of honey bees. *Psychonomic Science*, 1966, **5**, 179–180.

BEST, J. B. Protopsychology. *Scientific American*, 1963, **208**(2), 54–62.

BLEES, G. H. J. Phototropiame et experience chez la daphnie. *Archives Neerlandaises de Physiologie de l'Homme et des Animaux*, 1919, **3**, 279–306.

BLOCK, R., & MCCONNELL, J. V. Classically conditioned discrimination in the planarian, *Dugesia dorotocephala. Nature*, 1967, **215**, 1465–1466.

BRAUD, L. W., & BRAUD, W. G. Biochemical transfer of relational responding (transposition). *Science*, 1972, **176**, 942–943.

BRUNER, J., & TAUC, L. Habituation at the synoptic level in Aplysia. *Nature*, 1966, **210**, 37–39.

BULLOCK, T. H., & HORRIDGE, G. A. *Structure and function in the nervous systems of invertebrates.* San Francisco: Freeman, 1965.

BULLOCK, T. H., & QUARTON, G. C. Simple systems for the study of learning mechanisms. *Neurosciences Research Bulletin*, 1966, **4**(2), 105–233.

CAPRETTA, P. J., & REA, R. Discrimination reversal learning in the crayfish. *Animal Behaviour*, 1967, **15**, 6–7.

CATTA, L. E. G., MILSTEIN, S., & BITTERMAN, M. E. Habit reversal in the crab. *Journal of Comparative and Physiological Psychology*, 1960, **53**, 275–278.

CLARK, R. B. Habituation of the polychaete *Nereis* to sudden stimuli: Part 1. General properties of the habituation process. *Animal Behaviour*, 1960, **8**, 82–91. (a)

CLARK, R. B. Habituation of the polychaete *Nereis* to sudden stimuli: Part 2. Biological significance of habituation. *Animal Behaviour*, 1960, **8**, 92–103. (b)

CLARK, R. B. The learning abilities of nereid polychaetes and the role of the supra-oesophageal ganglion. *Animal Behaviour, Suppl.*, 1965, 89–100.

COPELAND, M. An apparent conditioned response in *Nereis virens*. *Journal of Comparative Psychology*, 1930, **10**, 339–354.

CORNING, W. C. Conditioning and "transfer of training" in a colonial ciliate: A summary of the work of N. N. Plavilstchikov. *Journal of Biological Psychology*, 1971, **13**(1), 39–41.

CORNING, W. C., DYAL, J. A., & WILLOWS, A. O. D. (Eds.). (In press). *Invertebrate learning.* New York: Plenum.

CORNING, W. C., FEINSTEIN, D. A., & HAIGHT, J. R. Arthropod preparation for behavioral, electrophysiological, and biochemical studies. *Science*, 1965, **148**, 394–395.

CORNING, W. C., & JOHN, E. R. Effect of ribonuclease on retention of conditioned response in regenerated planarians. *Science*, 1961, **134**, 1363–1364.

CORNING, W. C., & RICCIO, D. The planarian controversy. In W. L. Byrne (Ed.), *Molecular approaches to learning and memory.* New York: Academic Press, 1970.

COSTELLUICI, V., PINKSER, H., KUPFERMANN, I., & KANDEL, E. Neuronal mechanisms of habituation and dishabituation of the gill-withdrawal reflex in *Aplysia*. *Science*, 1970, **167**, 1745–1748.

COWARD, S. J., GERHARDT, H. C., & CROCKETT, D. T. Behavioral variation in natural populations of two species of fiddler crabs (*Uca*) and some preliminary observations on directed modifications. *Journal of Biological Psychology*, 1970 **12**(1), 24–31.

DATTA, L. E. Learning in the earthworm, *Lumbricus terrestris*. *American Journal of Psychology*, 1962, **75**, 531–553.

DAVIS, G. The extraction of ribonucleic acid from the planarian. *Cura foremanii*. In J. V. McConnell (Ed.), *A manual of psychological experimentation on planarians*. Ann Arbor, Mich.: Planarian Press, 1967, 63–64.

DISTERHOFT, J., NURNBERGER, J., & CORNING, W. C. "P-R" differences in intact cockroaches as a function of testing interval. *Psychonomic Science*, 1968, **12**, 265–266.

DYAL, J. A. Transfer of behavioral bias: Reality and specificity. In E. J. Fjerdingstad (Ed.), *Chemical transfer of learned information.* Amsterdam: North-Holland Publishing Company, 1970, 219–263.

EISENSTEIN, E. M. The use of invertebrate systems for studies on the basis of learning and memory. In G. C. Quarton, T. Melnechuk, & F. O. Schmitt (Eds.), *The neurosciences.* New York: Rockefeller University Press, 1967, 653–665.

EISENSTEIN, E. M., & COHEN, M. J. Learning in an isolated prothoracic insect ganglion. *Animal Behaviour*, 1965, **13**, 104–108.

ELDERING, F. J. Acquisition d'havitudes par les insectes. *Archives Neerlandaises de Physiologie de l'Homme et des Animaux*, 1919, **3**, 468–490.

EVANS, S. M. Behaviour of the polychaete *Nereis* in T-mazes. *Animal Behaviour*, 1963, **11**, 379–392.

EVANS, S. M. Non-associative avoidance learning in nereid polychaetes. *Animal Behaviour*, 1966, **14**, 107–119 (a).

EVANS, S. M. Non-associative behavioral modifications in the polychaete *Nereis diversicolor*. *Animal Behaviour*, 1966, **14**, 102–106 (b).

EVANS, S. M. Non-associative behavioral modifications in nereid polychaetes. *Nature*, 1966, **211**, 945–948. (c)

EVANS, S. M. Habituation of the withdrawal response in nereid polychaetes. I. The habituation process in *Nereis diversicolor*. *Biological Bulletin*, 1969, **137**, 95–104. (a)

EVANS, S. M. Habituation of the withdrawal response in nereid polychaetes. 2. Rates of habituation in intact and decerebrate worms. *Biological Bulletin*, 1969, **137**, 105–117. (b)

FLINT, P. The effect of sensory deprivation on the behavior of the polychaete *Nereis* in T-mazes. *Animal Behaviour*, 1965, **13**, 187–193.

FRIED, C., & HOROWITZ, S. Contraction—a leaRNAble response? *Worm Runner's Digest*, 1964, **6**(2), 3–6.

FRINGS, H. The loci of olfactory end-organs in the honeybee. *Journal of Experimental Zoology*, 1944, **97**, 123–134.

FRISCH, K. VON. Honeybees: Do they use direction and distance information provided by their dancers? *Science*, 1967, **158**, 1072–1076.

GARDNER, L. E. Retention and overhabituation of a dual-component response in *Lumbricus terrestris*. *Journal of Comparative and Physiological Psychology*, 1968, **66**, 315–318.

GARTH, T. R., & MITCHELL, M. P. The learning curve of a land snail. *Journal of Comparative Psychology*, 1926, **6**, 103–113.

GELBER, B. Investigations of the behavior of *Paramecium aurelia:* I. Modification of behavior after training with reinforcement. *Journal of Comparative and Physiological Psychology*, 1952, **45**, 58–65.

GELBER, B. Studies of the behaviour of *Paramecium aurelia*. *Animal Behaviour, Suppl.* 1, 1965, **13**, 21–29.

GRIFFARD, C. D., & PEIRCE, J. T. Conditioned discrimination in the planarian. *Science*, 1964, **144**, 1472–1473.

HARTRY, A. L., KEITH-LEE, P., & MORTON, W. D. Planaria: Memory transfer through cannibalism re-examined. *Science*, 1964, **146**, 274–275.

HEBB, D. O. *Organization of behavior; a neuropsychological theory*. New York: Wiley, 1949.

HERSHBERGER, W. A., & SMITH, M. P. Conditioning in *Drosophila melangaster*. *Animal Behaviour*, 1967, **15**, 259–262.

HERZ, M. J., PEEKE, H. V. S., & WYERS, E. J. Classical conditioning of the extension response in the earthworm. *Physiology and Behavior*, 1967, **2**, 409–411.

HORRIDGE, G. A. Learning of leg position by the ventral nerve cord in headless insects. *Proceedings of the Royal Society of London*, Series B, 1962, **152**, Pp. 33–52.

HORRIDGE, G. A. The electrophysiological approach to learning in isolatable ganglia. *Animal Behaviour, Suppl.*, 1965, **1**, 163–182.

HOYLE, G. Neurophysiological studies on "learning" in headless insects. In J. E. Treherne & J. W. L. Beament (Eds.), *The physiology of the insect central nervous system*. New York: Academic Press, 1965, 203–232.

HUMPHREY, G. Le Chatelier's rule and the problem of habituation and dehabituation in *Helix albolobria. Psychologische Forschung*, 1930, 113–127.

HUMPHRIES, B., & MCCONNELL, J. V. Factors affecting maze learning in planarians. *Worm Runner's Digest*, 1964, **6**, 52–59.

HYDÉN, H., & EGYHÁZI, E. Glial RNA changes during a learning experiment in rats. *Proceedings of the National Academy of Sciences*, 1963, **49**, 618–624.

HYMAN, L. H. *The invertebrates.* Vol. II: *Platyhelminthes and Rhynchocoela.* New York: McGraw-Hill, 1951.

JACOBSON, A. L. Learning in flatworms and annelids. *Psychological Bulletin*, 1963, **60**, 74–94.

JACOBSON, A. L. Learning in planarians: Current status. *Animal Behaviour, Suppl.* **1**, 1965, 76–81.

JACOBSON, A. L. Classical conditioning and the planarian. In W. C. Corning & S. C. Ratner (Eds.), *Chemistry of learning.* New York: Plenum, 1967, 195–216.

JACOBSON, A. L., FRIED, C., & HOROWITZ, S. D. Planarians and memory: I. Transfer of learning by injection of ribonucleic acid. *Nature*, 1966, **209** (5023), 599–601. (a)

JACOBSON, A. L., FRIED, C., & HOROWITZ, S. D. Planarians and memory: II. The influence of prior extinction on the RNA transfer effect. *Nature*, 1966, **209**, 601. (b)

JACOBSON, A. L., HOROWITZ, S. D., & FRIED, C. Classical conditioning, pseudoconditioning, or sensitization in the planarian. *Journal of Comparative and Physiological Psychology*, 1967, **64**(1), 73–79.

JENNINGS, H. S. *The behavior of lower organisms.* New York: Columbia University Press, 1906.

JENSEN, D. D. Experiments on "learning" in paramecia. *Science*, 1957, **125**, 191–192. (a)

JENSEN, D. D. More on "learning" in paramecia. *Science*, 1957, **126**, 1341–1342. (b)

JOHNSON, D. L., & WENNER, A. M. A relationship between conditioning and communication in honey bees. *Animal Behaviour*, 1966, **14**, 261–265.

KANDEL, E. R., & SPENCER, W. A. Cellular neurophysiological approaches to learning. *Physiological Review*, 1968, **48**, 65–134.

KATZ, M., & DETERLINE, W. A. Apparent learning in the paramecium. *Journal of Comparative and Physiological Psychology*, 1958, **51**, 243–247.

KRASNE, F. B. Escape from recurring tactile stimulation in *Branchiomma vesiculosum. Journal of Experimental Biology*, 1965, **42**, 307–322.

KRASNE, F. B. Excitation and habituation of the crayfish escape reflex: The depolarizing response in lateral giant fibers of the isolated abdomen. *Journal of Experimental Biology*, 1969, **50**, 29–46.

KRASNE, F. B., & ROBERTS, A. Habituation of the crayfish escape response during release from inhibition induced by picrotoxin. *Nature*, 1967, **215**, 769–770.

KRASNE, F. B., & WOODSMALL, K. S. Waning of the crayfish escape response as a result of repeated stimulation. *Animal Behaviour*, 1969, **17**, 416–424.

KUENZER, P. P. *Verhaltenphysiologische Untersuchungen über das Zucken des Regenwurms. Zeitschrift für Tierpsychologie*, 1958, **15**, 31–49.

KUPFERMAN, I., COSTELLUICI, V., PINSKER, H., & KANDEL, E. Neuronal correlates of habituation and dishabituation of the gill-withdrawal reflex in *Aplysia. Science*, 1970, **167**, 1743–1745.

LACHMAN, S. J., & HAVLENA, J. M. Reactive inhibition in the paramecium. *Journal of Comparative and Physiological Psychology*, 1962, **55**, 972–973.

LEE, R. M. Conditioning of a free operant response in planaria. *Science*, 1963, **139**, 1048–1049.

LEPLEY, W., & RICE, G. E. Behavior variability in paramecia as a function of guided act sequences. *Journal of Comparative and Physiological Psychology*, 1952, **45,** 283–286.

LICKEY, M. E. Learned behavior in *Aplysia vaccaris*. *Journal of Comparative and Physiological Psychology*, 1968, **66,** 712–718.

LONGO, N. Probability-learning and habit-reversal in the cockroach. *American Journal of Psychology*, 1964, **77,** 29–41.

MACKINTOSH, N. J. Discrimination learning in the octopus. *Animal Behaviour, Suppl.* 1, 1965, 129–134.

MAIER, B. R. F., & SCHNEIRLA, T. C. *Principles of animal psychology*. New York: McGraw-Hill, 1935.

MAKONS, W. L. Conditioning in the horseshoe crab. *Psychonomic Science*, 1969, **14,** 4–6.

MCCONNELL, J. V. Memory transfer through cannibalism in planarians. *Journal of Neuropsychiatry, Suppl.* 1, 1962, **3,** S42–48.

MCCONNELL, J. V. Comparative physiology: Learning in invertebrates. *Annual Review of Physiology* (Palo Alto, Calif.: Annual Reviews, Inc.) 1966, **28,** 107–136.

MCCONNELL, J. V. (Ed.), *A manual of psychological experimentation on planarians*. (2nd ed.) Ann Arbor, Mich.: *Journal of Biological Psychology*, special publication, 1967.

MCCONNELL, J. V., JACOBSON, A. L., & KIMBLE, D. P. The effects of regeneration upon retention of a conditioned response in the planarian. *Journal of Comparative and Physiological Psychology*, 1959, **52,** 1–5.

MCCONNELL, J. V., JACOBSON, R., & MAYNARD, D. M. Apparent retention of a conditioned response following total regeneration in the planarian. *American Psychologist*, 1959, **14,** 410.

MCCONNELL, J. V., & SHELBY, J. Memory transfer in invertebrates. In G. Ungar (Ed.), *Molecular mechanisms in memory and learning*. New York: Plenum, 1970. Pp. 71–101.

MINAMI, H., DALLENBACH, K. M. The effect of activity upon learning and retention in the cockroach (*P. amerians*). *American Journal of Psychology*, 1946, **59,** 1–58.

MURPHEY, R. M. Instrumental conditioning of the fruit fly, *Drosophila melanogaster*. *Animal Behaviour*, 1967, **15,** 153–161.

MURPHEY, R. M. Spatial discrimination performance of *Drosophila melanogaster*: Some controlled and uncontrolled correlates. *Animal Behaviour*, 1969, **17,** 43–46.

OYE, P. VAN. Over het geheugen bij de Platwormen en andere Biologische waarnemingen bij deze dieren. *Natuurwetenschappelijik Tijdschrift*, 1920, **2,** 1–9.

PEEKE, H. V. S., HERZ, M. J., & WYERS, E. J. Forward conditioning, backward conditioning, and pseudoconditioning sensitization in the earthworm (*Lumbricus terrestris*). *Journal of Comparative and Physiological Psychology*, 1967, **64,** 534–536.

PINSKER, H., KUPFERMANN, I., COSTELLUICI, V., & KANDEL, E. Habituation and dishabituation of the gill-withdrawal reflex in *Aplysia*. *Science*, 1970, **167,** 1740–1742.

PLAVILSTSHIKOV, N. N. Observations sur l'excitabilité des Infusories. *Russkii Arkhiv Protistologii*, 1928, **7,** 1–24.

POSKOCIL, A. If you're a paramecium, can you learn? A query. *Worm Runner's Digest*, 1966, **8**(1), 31–42.

RABIN, B. M., & HERTZLER, D. R. Replications of two experiments on reactive inhibition in paramecia. *Worm Runner's Digest*, 1965, **7,** 46–50.

RATNER, S. C. Worms in a straight alley: Acquisition and extinction or phototaxis. *Psychological Record*, 1964, **14,** 31–36.

RATNER, S. C. Research and theory on conditioning of annelids. *Animal Behaviour, Suppl.* 1, 1965, 101–108.

RATNER, S. C. Annelids and learning: A critical review. In W. C. Corning and S. C. Ratner (Eds.), *Chemistry of learning*, New York: Plenum, 1967. Pp. 391–406.

REYNIERSE, J. H., HALLIDAY, R. A., & NELSON, M. R. Nonassociative factors inhibiting earthworm straight-alley performance. *Journal of Comparative and Physiological Psychology*, 1968, **65**, 160–163.

ROSS, D. M. Behavior of sessile coelentrates in relation to some conditioning experiments. *Animal Behaviour, Suppl.*, 1965, **1**, 43–53.

RUSHFORTH, N. B. Behavioral studies of the coelenterate *Hydra pirardi* Brien. *Animal Behaviour, Suppl.*, 1965, **1**, 30–42.

RUSHFORTH, N. B., BURNETT, A. L., & MAYNARD, R. Behavior in hydra: Contraction responses of *hydra pirardi* to mechanical and light stimuli. *Science*, 1963, **139**, 760–761.

RUSHFORTH, N. B., KROHN, I. T., & BROWN, L. K. Behavior in hydra: Inhibition of the contraction responses of *hydra pirardi*. *Science*, 1964, **145**, 602–604.

SCHONE, H. Learning in the spiny lobster *Panulirus argus*. *Biological Bulletin*, 1961, **121**, 354–365.

SCHONE, H. Release and orientation of behavior and the role of learning as demonstrated in crustacea. *Animal Behaviour, Suppl.* 1, 1965, 135–143.

SCHWARTZ, B., & SAFIR, S. R. Habit formation in the fiddler crab. *Journal of Animal Behaviour*, 1915, **5**, 226–239.

SMITH, J. C., & BAKER, H. D. Conditioning in the horseshoe crab. *Journal of Comparative and Physiological Psychology*, 1960, **53**, 279–281.

SPAULDING, E. G. An establishment of association in hermit crabs, *Eupagurus longicarpus*. *Journal of Comparative and Neurological Psychology*, 1904, **14**, 41–61.

SUTHERLAND, N. S. Shape discrimination and receptive fields. *Nature*, 1963, **197**, 118–122.

TAKEDA, K. Classical conditioned response in the honeybee. *Journal of Insect Physiology*, 1961, **6**, 168–179.

THOMPSON, E. L. An analysis of the learning process in the snail *Physic Gyrina Say*. *Behaviour Monographs*, 1917, **3**, 1–97.

THOMPSON, R., & McCONNELL, J. V. Classical conditioning in the planarian, *Dugesia dorotocephala*. *Journal of Comparative and Physiological Psychology*, 1955, **48**, 65–68.

THORPE, W. H. Types of learning in insects and other arthropods. *British Journal of Psychology*, 1943/1944: **33**, 220–234; **34**, 20–31, 66–76.

THORPE, W. H. *Learning and instinct in animals*. Cambridge, Mass.: Harvard University Press, 1963.

TURNER, C. H. Behavior of the common roach (*Periplaneta orientalis*) in an open maze. *Biological Bulletin, Woods Hole*, 1913, **25**, 348–365.

VOWLES, D. M. Interocular transfer, brain lesions, and maze learning in the wood ant, *Formica rufa*. In W. C. Corning & S. C. Ratner (Eds.), *Chemistry of learning*. New York: Plenum, 1967, 425–447.

WASSERMAN, G. S., PATTON, D. G. Avoidance conditioning in Limulus. *Psychonomic Science*, 1969, **15**, 143.

WEISS, K. Versuche mit Biener und Vesper in farbigenlabyrinthen. *Zeitschrift für Tierpsychologie*, 1953, **10**, 29–44.

WELLS, M. J. *Brain and behavior in cephalpods*. London: Heinemann; Stanford, Calif.: Stantord, 1962.

WELLS, M. J. Learning and movement in octopuses. *Animal Behaviour, Suppl.*, 1965, **1,** 115–128.

WELLS, M. J., & YOUNG, J. Z. Lateral interaction and transfer in the tactile memory of the octopus. *Journal of Experimental Biology*, 1966, **45,** 383–400.

WELLS, M. J., & YOUNG, J. Z. Learning at different rates of training in the octopus. *Animal Behaviour*, 1969, **17,** 406–415.

WENNER, A. M., & JOHNSON, D. L. Simple conditioning in honey bees. *Animal Behaviour*, 1966, **14,** 149–155.

WENNER, A. M., & JOHNSON, D. L. Honeybees: Do they use direction and distance information provided by their dancers? *Science*, 1967, **158,** 1076–1077.

WYERS, E. J., PEEKE, H. V. S., & HERZ, M. J. Partial reinforcement and resistance to extinction in the earthworm. *Journal of Comparative and Physiological Psychology*, 1964, **57,** 113–116.

YERKES, R. M. Habit formation in the green crab, *Carcinus granulatus. Biological Bulletin*, 1902, **3,** 241–244.

YERKES, R. M. The intelligence of earthworms. *Journal of Animal Behavior*, 1912, **2,** 332–352.

YERKES, R. M., & HUGGINS, G. E. Habit formation in the crawfish, *Cambarus affinis. Harvard Psychology Studies*, 1903, **1,** 565–577.

YOUNG, J. Z. Learning and discrimination in the octopus. *Biological Review*, 1961, **36,** 32–96.

YOUNG, J. Z. *A model of the brain.* Oxford: Clarendon Press, 1964.

YOUNG, J. Z. The organization of memory system. *Proceedings of the Royal Society of London*, Series B, 1965, **163,** 285–320.

ZELLNER, D. K. Effects of removal and regeneration of the suprpharyngeal ganglion on learning, retention, and negative movements in the earthworm, *Lumbricus terrestris. Physiology and Behavior*, 1966, **1,** 151–159.

ZELMAN, A., KABAT, L., JACOBSON, R., & MCCONNELL, J. V. Transfer of training through injection of "conditioned" RNA into untrained planarians. *Worm Runner's Digest*, 1963, **5**(1), 14–21.

ZIPPEL, H. P., & DOMAGK, G. F. Transfer of color and taste preference from double-trained goldfish (*carassius auratus*) into untrained recipients. *Journal of Biological Psychology*, 1971, **13**(1), pp. 27–32.

Chapter 13

Learning in Vertebrates

J. M. Warren

Comparative psychologists have traditionally studied the evolution of intelligence by comparing the performance of different species on standard learning tests (Boring, 1950). Their research has been strongly influenced by two, frequently tacit, assumptions: (1) Animals possess a unitary trait of intelligence or general ability to learn, and (2) the capacity for learning increases progressively in vertebrate phylogeny. This chapter is a selective review of the comparative psychology of learning by vertebrates. Its aim is to assess the validity of these traditional beliefs regarding the phylogeny of learning.

SINGLE-PROBLEM LEARNING

Classical and Instrumental Conditioning

It is generally agreed that there is no relationship between taxonomic status and the rate with which representatives of the different vertebrate classes form classical conditioned responses or solve instrumental learning problems. Brookshire (1970) compared many of the recent studies of classical conditioning in animals along several dimensions and failed to discern any suggestion of consistent differences among vertebrates. Thus, for example, the number of times a light and shock must be paired before the appearance of conditioned responses to the onset of light is about the same in fish, pigs, and rhesus monkeys, with monkeys requiring a few more trials than either pigs or fish (Noble & Harding, 1963).

In passive avoidance training, animals learn to withhold responses that are followed by shock or some other aversive event. Monkeys learn to distinguish between quinine-flavored and unadulterated pieces of bread on the basis of color cues in one or very few trials (Schuckman, Kling, & Orbach, 1969). Cats and rats learn in one or two trials not to eat or drink in situations where these responses are followed by shock (J. M. Warren, 1965b). Blue jays learn very quickly to avoid emetic butterflies (L. P. Brower, 1969), and many toads learn not to eat bees after being stung only once or twice (Brower, Brower, & Westcott, 1960; Cott, 1936). Perch and pike, after very few painful contacts, stop trying to feed on three-spined sticklebacks which are protected by sharp spines (Hoogland, Morris, & Tinbergen, 1957). The available data thus indicate that vertebrates generally are capable of rapid, passive avoidance learning in respect to feeding responses.

Similar findings characterize the experiments dealing with other forms of instrumental learning. Careful, detailed analyses of the acquisition of active avoidance learning by 246 rabbits, 282 cats, and 46 dogs reveal a high degree of similarity in the learning functions and no significant differences among species (Brogden, 1969). Rats learn complex mazes about as quickly as humans (Skard, 1950), and, as may be seen in Figure 13–1, they surpass rhesus monkeys and squirrel monkeys in learning a simple Y-maze problem (Rumbaugh, 1968). Paradise fish, goldfish, chickens, cats, horses, and rhesus monkeys all learn a formally identical discrimination task at roughly the same rate (J. M. Warren, 1965a). Chimpanzees frequently learn simple visual discriminations so much more slowly than rats that Hebb (1958) speculated that a "large brain like a large government may not be able to do simple things in a simple way [p. 454]."

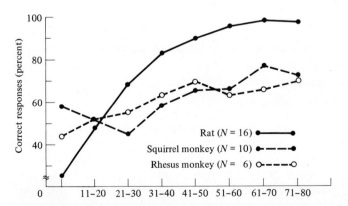

Figure 13–1. Learning curves for rats and for rhesus and squirrel monkeys in a Y maze. By permission from D. M. Rumbaugh in L. A. Rosenblum and R. W. Cooper, *The Squirrel Monkey,* Academic Press, New York, 1968.

Complex Problems

From about 1900 to 1920, comparative psychologists devised a number of complex learning tasks like delayed response, multiple choice, double alternation, and various instrumentation or tool-using problems in order to demonstrate "ideational" behavior in animals. It is doubtful that success on such tasks implies the presence of any processes beyond those involved in simpler learning situations (Maier & Schneirla, 1935; Schiller, 1952). It is clear that the performances of vertebrate species on these complex problems are not highly correlated with taxonomic status (J. M. Warren, 1965a, 1965b). Rhesus monkeys, for example, learn the double-alternation problem at about the same rate as rats and more slowly than cats or rabbits (Livesey, 1969). The length of the delay that animals of the same species can manage in delayed-response tasks varies from a few seconds to many hours, depending upon the experimental circumstances (Maier & Schneirla, 1935). The range of individual scores for a sample of 102 cats on a multiple-choice problem was so wide as to include the mean for almost every species that has been tested on this task (Warren & Warren, 1966). Tool-using performances in animals have been regarded as important indicators of relative intelligence. It is now generally conceded, however, that the occurrence of tool-using behavior in a given species tells very little about its general capacity to learn. Field observations on birds and mammals that use tools in their natural environments suggest that tool-using is often a species-typical behavior pattern which is little affected by experience (Hall, 1963, 1965; Morse, 1968; van Lawick-Goodall & van Lawick, 1966).

INTERGROUP DIFFERENCES IN LEARNING

The rate with which animals solve single problems varies greatly, within and between species, as a consequence of variations in the conditions under which the subjects are tested. This circumstance makes it impossible to sustain any claim that the ability to learn single problems is highly correlated with phylogenetic status in vertebrates. It does not, however, imply that the pattern of intraspecific and interspecific variation in learning is chaotic. The experimental literature indicates that much of the variation in the efficiency of learning by animals can be attributed to the following factors, independent of the classification of the species in question: (1) response availability; (2) sensory dominance; (3) preparedness to associate particular stimuli and responses.

Response Availability

Species are adapted to survive in particular environments by means of a characteristic and limited number of fixed action patterns (see Chapters 2 and 3); even closely related species may differ greatly in respect to the presence or absence of particular motor responses and in their readiness to execute particular actions. The strong influence that the relative availability of responses may have on learning of various tasks by members of several vertebrate classes is illustrated in the following examples.

Goldfish and Siamese fighting fish were trained to make an active avoidance response in a shuttle box, i.e., to swim from one of two compartments in the apparatus to the other in response to a light cue in order to avoid shock. The goldfish learned significantly more rapidly than the Siamese fighting fish (Otis & Cerf, 1963), and, indeed, more rapidly than most mammals trained in similar two-way avoidance situations. The discrepancy in the learning performance of the goldfish and the Siamese fighting fish reflected species differences in adaptation and characteristic responses to aversive stimuli. Goldfish are bottom-feeding scavengers, and flight is their typical reaction to the abrupt onset of an intense stimulus. Siamese fighting fish, in contrast, are active predators that capture live prey, and are so aggressive as to be used in public competitions for sports fans and gamblers. The most probable response of the fighting fish to abrupt stimulation is immobility or aggression. Potent flight responses facilitate active avoidance, whereas predominant tendencies to immobility or attack retard such learning. Hence the difference in the rate of active avoidance learning between these species.

Boice (1970) tested the hypothesis that differences in active avoidance learning among four species of anuran amphibians could be predicted from knowledge of the characteristic level of spontaneous activity in each species. The animals were required to avoid shock signaled by raising a door between the two chambers in a one-way shuttle box. Markedly passive toads (*Scaphiopus hammondi*) and frogs *(Rana pipiens)* failed to make any avoidance responses in 200 trials. Moderately active frogs *(Rana clamitans)* showed marginal avoidance, and toads *(Bufo woodhousei),* which are active hunters in the wild, showed significant evidence of learning, eventually making about 50 percent avoidance responses. One wonders, however, whether raising the door in a shuttle box is an optimal conditioned stimulus for avoidance learning by toads. Toads trained with olfactory cues (Martof, 1962) learned to a higher level and in fewer trials than the subjects in Boice's experiment. It is also likely that frogs and toads would learn more quickly if the signal for avoidance were an ecologically significant stimulus like a moving shadow.

Operant Conditioning in Dolphins and Monkeys   Response availability affects the performance of advanced mammals on complex learning tasks as strongly as it does the performance of nonmammalian organisms on simple problems. Dolphins quickly learn to emit vocalizations of a specified duration, amplitude, and intensity when rewarded by stimulation of positive reinforcement sites within the brain. Rhesus monkeys could not be trained to do so in similar experiments (Lilly & Miller, 1962). In experiments with food reinforcement, dolphins learn with reasonable facility to mimic certain features of human vocal utterances, to emit, for example, a number of sonic bursts that matches the number of syllables spoken by a human (Lilley, Miller, & Truby, 1968). Dolphins have also been trained to use vocal responses in cooperative problem solving (Bastian, 1967). A male and a female were first taught individually to strike the right or left of two targets depending upon whether a signal light was steady or flashing. The male was then prevented from seeing either the female or the signal lamp and both animals were required to make the correct choice on every trial, the male first and the female second. As long as the female was in acoustic contact with the male, the pair of dolphins were able to discriminate successfully. Although the code the dolphins used to transmit the information necessary for success in this task is not known, Bastian's experiment leaves no room for doubt concerning the essential role of vocal communication in this situation.

It is quite difficult to train monkeys to vocalize for food rewards. Cebus monkeys learn much more slowly to make vocal operant responses than they learn to press a lever, and performance of the vocal operant is easily disrupted (Leander, Milan, Jasper, & Heaton, 1972; Myers, Horel, & Pennypacker, 1965). Yamaguchi and R. E. Meyers (1972) compared the rate with which rhesus monkeys learned to make three different kinds of discriminated operants. Their subjects learned in ten to twenty sessions to press a lever in the presence of a red light (S+) and not to press in its absence (S−), when responses were not reinforced. If required to make an arbitrary "head up" response, the monkeys clearly discriminated S+ and S−, although they failed to reach a criterion of 90 percent discrimination in forty sessions. One of four monkeys required to make a vocal response failed to reach even a pretraining criterion, and the remaining three failed to manifest any discrimination between S+ and S− in forty to fifty sessions. These findings show that it is harder to achieve stimulus control over a vocal operant than even a completely arbitrary postural response in rhesus monkeys.

There are two obvious interpretations of the discrepancy between the performance of dolphins and monkeys in these experiments. Dolphins may be generally more intelligent than monkeys, or dolphins may excel monkeys specifically on those tasks which depend upon the refined control of vocalization and the utilization of auditory cues. The second interpretation seems more plausible. Dolphins find food and avoid obstacles by means of echolocation which demands precise control of vocal activity and refined use of acoustic information, often in circumstances which provide little useful visual stimulation, in turbid water or at sea in the night. They have thus been subjected to intense selection for efficient use of audition but to less severe selection for efficiency in processing visual information. It is not surprising that dolphins learn some visual discrimination tasks (Kellogg & Rice, 1964) in much the same way as most birds and mammals, and are distinctly inferior to birds and mammals on more demanding visual discrimination learning problems (Herman, Beach, Pepper, & Stalling, 1969). On the other hand, rhesus monkeys have successfully been trained to communicate information concerning the location of food in a situation where one animal can see the reward and must induce a partner that can see him but not the food to select the correct one of four response alternatives (Mason & Hollis, 1962).

The superiority of dolphins over monkeys is restricted, therefore, to situations in which the animals are obliged to emit vocal operants. In view of the information concerning the ecological adaptations and ethology of these animals, we should be surprised only if this were not so.

Tool-using   The extreme importance of familiarity with the spontaneous motor patterns of species for a proper understanding of their performance on learning tests is forcefully illustrated by Schiller's (1952) classic work with monkeys and chimpanzees. Köhler (1925) observed that chimpanzees would stack boxes to obtain food suspended from a string and join two sticks together to make one long enough to rake in otherwise inaccessible rewards, and he interpreted these findings as evidence for "insight" in chimpanzees. Schiller found that both these motor patterns occurred spontaneously in chimpanzees given boxes or sticks, and in the absence of any external incentive like food. He also observed that the chimpanzees were slow to associate these acts with food and argued that, given the presence of the responses in the animals' repertoire, their application in a problem-solving context need imply no principles beyond those of operant conditioning.

Schiller also observed the duration and quality of spontaneous play with sticks and the rate and level of performance attained on a graded series of instrumentation tests by rhesus monkeys and spider monkeys, and by immature and adult chimpanzees. The two measures were perfectly correlated. Again the results indicated that success in using sticks as tools could be accurately described in terms of operant-conditioning principles, and that only those animals which exhibited sustained and complex responses with sticks in spontaneous play made a sufficient number of responses in the tests with food to be adequately reinforced.

Observations of birds in a situation where they can obtain food suspended from a string in a test tube by pulling up the string (Thorpe, 1963) provide additional evidence for the importance of response availability as a determinant of learning. Some species, like robins and wrens which do not use the feet in feeding, are evidently incapable of learning this task, while individuals of species like the great tit and the blue tit which feed with coordinated beak and foot movements, often learn quite quickly.

Sensory Dominance

Sensory dominance denotes the fact that animals of a given species pay more attention to cues in one sensory modality than to cues in other modalities while solving learning problems. Rhesus monkeys appear to be particularly attentive to visual cues. They consistently learn to discriminate visual stimuli more rapidly than auditory stimuli when trained with food reinforcement (Wegener, 1964).

Cats, in contrast, are more responsive to auditory than to visual stimuli. Diamond (1967) trained cats to approach a box signaled by a buzzer and a flashing light, rather than a silent, unlighted box, for food rewards. After the cats mastered this task, they were given test trials with light alone, buzzer alone, and light and buzzer in conflict, with one stimulus on each of the boxes. Five of five cats responded almost as accurately with buzzer alone as with light-buzzer compound. All the animals performed more poorly with the light alone than with the buzzer alone, and they all chose the buzzer in preference to the light when the cues were opposed in conflict tests.

Wegener (1964) trained cats and rhesus monkeys to discriminate two boxes, separated by 180 degrees and distinguished by the presence or absence of sound from a buzzer, for food reinforcement. The monkeys required 437 trials to learn to approach the silent box, and more than twice as many trials to learn to approach the box signaled by the buzzer. All his cats learned to approach the sound source and averaged 33 trials to criterion.

The inferior learning performance of the rhesus monkeys on this auditory localization task cannot be attributed to insensitivity to the relevant stimulus cues. The available data indicate that the absolute and relative thresholds for auditory stimuli are similar in cats and monkeys, and monkeys learn avoidance responses to auditory signals as quickly as cats (Wegener, 1964).

The inferiority of rhesus monkeys to cats in learning an instrumental food-getting response on auditory cues implies that cats are more attentive to auditory stimuli than monkeys in this situation. This is what might be expected in view of these species' characteristic adaptations. Monkeys are diurnal vegetarians. Cats are nocturnal predators and rely on auditory cues to locate their prey. In addition, anatomical studies indicate that the cortical auditory system is relatively more highly elaborated in cats than in monkeys (Diamond, 1967).

Some evidence suggests, however, that more than simple inattention to auditory cues is involved in the dismal performance of rhesus monkeys on food-reinforced auditory learning tasks. When trained with visual cues in the Wisconsin General Test Apparatus (WGTA), monkeys learn delayed response somewhat more quickly than cats (J. M. Warren, 1965a). When trained in the Nencki Testing Situation (NTS), which requires them to make delayed responses to one of two automatic feeders signaled by a buzzer, monkeys (Divac & Warren, 1971) learn much more slowly, and more frequently fail to learn at all, than cats (Divac, 1968, 1969), even though the monkeys were provided with a salient visual cue, a flashing light, that was not present in the experiments with cats. Observations of the subjects indicated that the sound stimulus was attractive to the cats, but aversive for the monkeys. It will be recalled that Wegener's (1964) monkeys took many more trials to learn to approach than to avoid the source of sound in his auditory localization task, as one would expect on the assumption that monkeys, unlike cats, are reluctant to approach the source of a brief arbitrary sound. The paradoxical finding that monkeys learn delayed response on combined visual and auditory cues more slowly than cats learn on auditory cues only may well have resulted from the aversive auditory component suppressing the monkeys' otherwise efficient learning based on visual cues. The suggestion that species may vary greatly in their ability to associate particular responses with specific sorts of stimuli is considered more fully in the next section.

Preparedness to Associate Stimuli and Responses

Seligman (1970) has introduced the term *preparedness* to describe the wide variations in the rate with which animals learn to associate different stimuli and responses. Animals form some associations very quickly and others slowly or not at all, indicating that they are prepared to learn some associations but contraprepared to learn others. Often there is some evidence to suggest that prepared associations are those which might favor survival in the natural environment of the species concerned, and that contraprepared associations would be inappropriate or positively antagonistic to survival. There is a large third class of unprepared associations, like lever pressing for food by rats, that are more or less neutral in respect to apparent survival value and are learned more slowly than prepared associations but faster than contraprepared associations.

Seligman's distinction between prepared and contraprepared associations is clearly illustrated by an experiment carried out by Garcia and Koelling (1966). Thirsty rats were required to drink "bright-noisy" saccharin-flavored water in a situation where a light and a noise come on every time the rat took saccharin solution from a drinking tube. Some animals were later subjected to X-radiation in the experimental situation, and exhibited radiation sickness about an hour after exposure. These rats subsequently avoided saccharin-flavored water but accepted water accompanied by the light and noise, indicating that they associated the radiation-induced illness with the taste cue but not with the auditory and visual cues. Another group of rats was given shocks to the feet in the same situation, and these subjects later avoided water accompanied by noise and light but not the taste of saccharin.

These results indicate that rats are prepared to associate taste cues with gastric disturbances and contraprepared to associate light and noise with malaise, and also that rats are contraprepared to associate taste stimuli with foot shock. These findings are quite consistent with observations on wild rats that survive eating poisoned food. Such animals avoid eating the bait in which the poison was given, but not the place where it was provided (Barnett, 1963).

Readiness to learn an association is not necessarily dependent upon the spontaneous (operant) frequency of the required response. Self-scratching and licking are common responses in cats. Yet, if escape from confinement is made contingent upon scratching or licking, cats learn the required response much more slowly than they learn to pull strings, press levers, or execute other initially improbable responses (Thorndike, 1911). Cats are thus contraprepared to associate licking and scratching with escape from confinement. Licking is motivationally inappropriate to the task in hand.

Pigeons are highly prepared to associate key-pecking with food reinforcement (Brown & Jenkins, 1968). When exposed to paired presentations of a lighted key and food in the magazine of a Skinner box, they increase markedly the frequency with which they peck the key, even though the presentation of food is in no way contingent upon pecking. In contrast to the ease of autoshaping in training with food rewards, it is extremely difficult and frequently impossible to train pigeons to avoid shock by key-pecking. Pigeons are prepared to fly away from noxious stimuli and peck to eat. The severe difficulties encountered in teaching pigeons to peck as an avoidance response reflect the inappropriateness of the response to the birds' motivation state.

Bolles (1970) has used a concept much like preparedness in his attempt to account for the extremely wide variation in the rate with which rats learn active avoidance responses. If one puts a rat in a box and shocks it, it usually learns in one trial to jump out of the box. If the rat is required to run down an alley to avoid shock in a one-way avoidance situation, it learns the avoidance response in about half a dozen trials. Approximately forty trials are needed for rats to learn to avoid shock by running in an activity wheel. Rats tested in a two-way avoidance apparatus, where both compartments of the shuttle box alternate as the safe and shocked loci, require about 100 trials to learn, and some animals never acquire the response. Rats that are obliged to press a bar or turn a wheel with their forepaws to avoid shock learn even more slowly, and failures are frequent (Bolles, 1970). If we accept Bolles's eminently reasonable argument that severe aversive stimulation restricts the rat's response repertoire to a narrow class of species-typical defense reactions, the relative ranking of avoidance tasks in difficulty of learning for rats is about what one would expect. The species-typical defense reactions of rats are fleeing, freezing, and fighting. Thus active avoidance learning proceeds more rapidly when the animal responds by running away than when it must remain in one place and make a manipulatory response, and one-way avoidance is learned more quickly than two-way avoidance, since the subject is not required to approach an area where it has been previously shocked in the one-way situation. With rats confined to a chamber from which no physical escape is possible, animals that can avoid shock by freezing learn much more rapidly than rats that must avoid shock by making overt responses (Brener & Goesling, 1970).

Somewhat different patterns of results have been obtained from rodents other than rats, however. Hamsters and guinea pigs learn much more readily than rats to avoid shock by lever pressing; this may reflect the higher operant level of lever pressing by hamsters and guinea pigs compared with rats (Pearl, 1963). Gerbils are also more proficient in learning bar-press avoidance responses than rats (Walters, Pearl, & Rogers, 1963). On the other hand, hansters and guinea pigs are inferior to rats in learning avoidance responses in shuttle boxes (Babbini & Davis, 1967; Lin & Mogenson, 1968). It is not presently possible to state conclusively that these interspecies differences between rodents are correlated with differences in their repertoires of species-typical defense reactions, but the existence of these different patterns of learning provides a good opportunity for testing the generality of Bolles's analysis of avoidance learning.

This discussion of species differences in learning single problems can be summarized briefly. Under the pressure of natural selection, animals have elaborated a diversity of adaptive specializations to fit them for survival in many different environmental niches. This has entailed the development of unique, species-specific repertoires of motor patterns, of selective responsiveness to sensory cues, and of readiness to associate particular stimuli and responses. Any single learning task is differentially biased, for members of different taxa, according to the degree of compatibility between the specific demands of the learning problem and the characteristics of the species involved. We should, on these grounds, anticipate that performances on such tests fail to correlate with taxonomic status.

Alternatively, the results surveyed in this section may be regarded as providing extensive documentation in support of Tinbergen's classical critique of the early comparative studies of delayed response:

> The "delayed response" (Carr-Hunter) was originally used to test an animal's ability to retain an "idea." It is now considered to be one of a number of methods to study memory. The experimental set-up is nearly always the same. In a multiple-choice apparatus one door is indicated by a stimulus (either conditioned or unconditioned). The animal is not allowed to react while the stimulus is present but only a certain time after the stimulus has disappeared. The maximum delay allowed by the animal is a measure of its memory,
>
> The value of the method has often been doubted, for instance by Maier (Maier & Schneirla, 1935), who pointed out the remarkable disparity between the values found for the gorilla (48 hours) and for the orangutan (5 minutes).
>
> Criticism of a more fundamental nature has been given by Baerends (1941) on the basis of his study of the digger wasp, *Ammophila campestris*. A female of this species, when about to lay an egg, digs a hole, kills or paralyzes a caterpillar, and carries it to the hole, where she stows it away after depositing an egg on it (phase *a*). This done, she digs another hole, in which an egg is laid on a new caterpillar. In the meantime, the first egg has hatched and the larva has begun to consume its store of food. The mother wasp now turns her attention to the

first hole (phase *b*), to which she brings some more moth larvae, then she does the same thing in the second hole. She returns to the first hole for the third time to bring a final batch of six or seven caterpillars (phase *c*), after which she closes the hole and leaves it forever. In this way she works in turn at two or even three holes, each in a different phase of development. . . . Baerends investigated the means by which the wasp brought the right amount of food to each hole. He found that the wasp visited all the holes each morning before leaving for the hunting grounds. By changing the contents of the hole and watching the subsequent behaviour of the wasp, he found that (1) by robbing a hole he could force the wasp to bring far more food than usual; and (2) by adding larvae to the hole's contents he could force her to bring less food than usual. But these changes influenced the wasp only when they were made before the first visit. Any later change had not the slightest effect. The situation in the hole at the time of the first visit determined the wasp's behavior for the whole day. On the basis of the situation she found in the three holes she was attending, the wasp chose the one she supplied during the rest of the day. In this way Baerends proved that the response of the wasp could be delayed as long as fifteen hours.

Apart from the amazing length of the delay, this fact demonstrates the importance of carefully selecting that part of normal behaviour in which a delayed reaction normally plays a part. It is highly probable that a delayed-reaction test carried out in the conventional way, for example with a foraging wasp, would not have the slightest result. Thanks to the preparatory survey of the whole behaviour pattern of the species, Baerends was able to find out where a delayed reaction played a part. This peculiar "localization" of higher processes to certain phases of behaviour is by no means rare [Tinbergen, 1951, pp. 9–10].

The amazing achievement of *Ammophila campestris* in delaying a reaction throws another sidelight on the problem of experimental procedure: it shows that "standardization" of method has to be based on a knowledge of the behaviour pattern as a whole. To put different species in exactly the same experimental situation is an anthropomorphic kind of standardization. As I have already said, there is little doubt that *A. campestris* would fail entirely in the conventional delayed-reaction test. In view of the differences between one species and another, the only thing that can be said for certain is that one should *not* use identical experimental techniques to compare two species, because they would almost certainly not be the same to *them* [Tinbergen, 1951, p. 12].

LEARNING SETS

The term *learning set* denotes *interproblem learning,* the cumulative improvement in performance which occurs when an animal is trained upon many different problems of the same general class. This type of multiple-problem learning was first clearly recognized and described by Harlow (1949).

The apparatus used in Harlow's (1949) original studies of learning set formation in rhesus monkeys, and in most of the subsequent investigations with other species, is the Wisconsin General Test Apparatus, shown in Figure 13–2. The monkey, confined in the restraining cage, responds by displacing

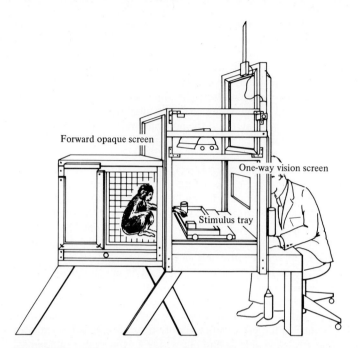

Forward opaque screen

One-way vision screen

Stimulus tray

Figure 13–2.   Wisconsin General Test Apparatus. From H. F. Harlow. The formation of learning sets. *Psychological Review*, 1949, **56**, 51–65. By Permission from the American Psychological Association.

one of the stimulus objects covering food-wells on the test tray. An opaque screen is lowered in front of the animal between trials to prevent its seeing which stimulus is associated with the reinforcement, and a one-way vision screen prevents the animal from seeing the experimenter during trials. The most common sort of stimuli used in learning set experiments are junk objects, made in the laboratory or obtained from variety and hardware stores. They characteristically vary in multiple visual and tactual cues, such as brightness, hue, saturation, shape, area, thickness, weight, and texture. The subject is required to choose the rewarded one of two objects independent of predetermined shifts in the right-left position of the objects. A different pair of stimulus objects is used in each discrimination problem within the learning set series.

A representative experiment (Harlow, 1949) is summarized in Figure 13–3. Eight monkeys were trained on 344 problems with 344 different pairs of objects. The first 32 problems were tested for fifty trials each; the next 200 for six trials each; and the last 112 for an average of nine trials. Figure 13–3 shows the percentage of correct responses on the first six trials of these discrimination problems, and demonstrates that the monkeys progressively improve in their ability to learn discrimination tasks, manifesting a gradual transition from slow and inefficient (trial-and-error) learning on problems 1 through 8 to rapid and highly efficient (insightful) solution on problems 257 to 312.

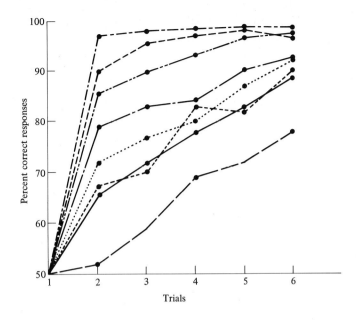

Figure 13-3. Discrimination learning curves for rhesus monkeys on successive blocks of problems. From H. F. Harlow. The formation of learning sets. *Psychological Review,* 1949, **56,** 51–65. By permission from the American Psychological Association.

Early Interspecies Comparisons

Two important kinds of observations suggested that learning set experiments measure a form of learning which is different and perhaps more relevant for interspecies comparisons than the learning involved in the solution of single discrimination tasks: (1) The capacity for solving isolated discriminations at a rate comparable to naïve adults matures much sooner in the infant rhesus monkey than the ability to form learning sets. (2) Ablations of the temporal association cortex in monkeys may severely impair proficiency on multiple visual discrimination tasks without producing equivalent deficits in the learning or retention of single visual discrimination habits (Harlow, 1959a, 1959b).

These considerations, together with the "almost human" quality of the one-trial learning by experienced monkeys, led to studies of learning set formation in a variety of species. Some of the results obtained in these experiments are presented in Figures 13–4 and 13–5, which show the number of correct responses made on trial 2 as a function of successive blocks of problems for several species. On the basis of such data, Harlow (1959a) concluded:

> By and large the phylogenetic data demonstrates that LS (learning set) formation is closely related to evolutionary position, as conventionally described, and to cortical complexity in so far as this characteristic has been effectively measured. These data contrast with the little that is known about single-problem discrimination learning, for at present there is no evidence to indicate that single problems are learned more rapidly by members of one genus, family, or order than another within the class of mammals....[p. 508]

More recently, it was possible to argue that "Old World primates are *quantitatively* superior to nonprimate mammals in the speed with which they form learning sets, and in the asymptotic level of performance attained on learning-set problems (no nonprimate animal has yet shown one-trial solution of visual discrimination problems) [J. M. Warren, 1965a, p. 274]."

Individual Differences in Learning Set Performance

These conclusions concerning learning sets can no longer be defended. The curves presented in Figures 13–4 and 13–5 are based on samples of three to six animals, far too few to provide a realistic estimate of the variance within species to test adequately the significance of the differences between species.

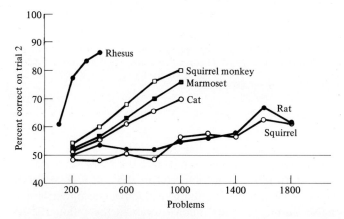

Figure 13–4. Learning set formation by primates, carnivores, and rodents. By permission from Warren in A. M. Schrier, H. F. Harlow, and F. Stollnitz, *Behavior of Nonhuman Primates: Modern Research Trends.* Academic Press, New York, 1965.

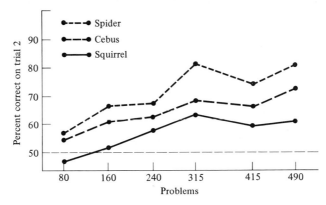

Figure 13–5. Learning set formation by squirrel, cebus, and spider monkeys. By permission from H. F. Harlow in S. Koch, *Psychology: A Study of a Science,* McGraw-Hill, 1959. Vol. 2, 507.

More extensive recent work shows that the variation in learning set performance among individuals of the same species is wide indeed. Rumbaugh (1968) has described the magnitude of the differences among squirrel monkeys *(Saimiri spp)* as follows:

> *Saimiri* specimens vary widely in their basic learning-set skills, to the extent that if one used trial 2 performance as the criterion, equivalent training conditions will net essentially perfect and efficient performance on the part of a few (better than 90% correct—as good as the best macaques and apes) and equally impressive and inefficient performance on the part of others (to the extent that they remain "learning-setless") [p. 309].

The range of individual differences among cats is almost as great as in squirrel monkeys. Warren and Baron (1956) trained four cats on 340 object discriminations. The cats were trained to a criterion on the first four problems and were tested for fifty trials on problems 5 through 80, and twenty-five trials on problems 81 through 140; the last 200 were ten-trial problems. The performances of the most and least successful cats are compared in Figure 13–6, which shows the percentage of correct responses over trials 1 through 10 for each animal at three stages of training. Cat 1 averaged 84 percent correct responses on trial 2 over problems 141 through 340; this subject's performance exceeds the mean for every species shown in Figures 13–4 and 13–5 except rhesus monkeys. Note that cat 3's performance suggests "learning not to learn." Although it was not grossly inferior to cat 1 on problems 81 through 140, cat 3 regressed to a level which was little better than chance when tested on ten-trial problems (141 to 340).

A similarly wide range of individual differences is characteristic of learning

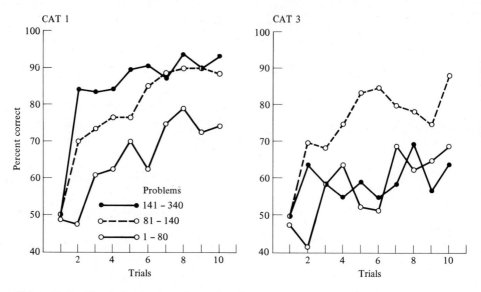

Figure 13–6. Discrimination learning curves for two cats on successive blocks of problems.

set performance in rhesus monkeys; the magnitude of intraspecific variation in discrimination learning by rhesus macaques is suggested in Table 13–1.

Recent Interspecies Comparisons

In addition to the evidence for a very substantial degree of overlap in learning set proficiency among mammals of different taxa, group differences have been reported recently which cannot be reconciled with the idea that quantitative indices of learning set formation are related to phylogenetic status or cortical complexity. Doty, Jones, and Doty (1967) tested groups of mink, ferrets, skunks, and cats on a series of 600 object-discrimination problems. The percentage of correct responses on trial 2 of the last 500 problems for these groups is presented in Figure 13–7. These learning set curves indicate that performance of mink and ferrets on trial 2 of sequential problem blocks is superior to some primates, namely, marmosets and platyrrhine monkeys. The curve for mink resembles that for rhesus monkeys and chimpanzees, although the rate of improvement is somewhat slower in mink. Mink and ferrets also showed one-trial learning of problems after extended learning set training, a phenomenon usually observed only among primates.

Plotnik and Tallarico (1966) trained four White Plymouth chicks to discriminate fifty pairs of junk objects to a criterion of eight out of ten consecutive correct responses. The mean percentage of correct responses on trial 2 for these birds is plotted as a function of successive blocks of five problems in

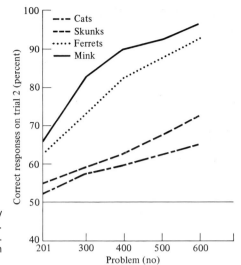

Figure 13–7. Learning set formation by mink, ferrets, skunks, and cats. From B. A. Doty, C. N. Jones, and L. A. Doty (1967). Copyright 1967 by the American Association for the Advancement of Science.

Figure 13–8, which shows that the birds made approximately 70 percent correct responses on problems 20 through 50. The learning set performance of these chickens is roughly equal to that observed in raccoons, cats, and marmosets. Some further deviations from expectancies based on the notion that learning set proficiency is related to taxonomic status or complexity of the cortex may be noted briefly. Langurs greatly surpass rhesus monkeys in the rate of learning set acquisition, although these species enjoy roughly the same standing in taxonomy (Manocha, 1967). Gerbils form learning sets more slowly than cats but eventually attain the same average asymptote of accuracy in performance on trial 2 (Blass & Rollin, 1969). Dolphins perform less adequately on learning set problems than chickens and most mammals (Herman, 1969). Galagos, lorises and lemurs seem only marginally apt at solving learning set problems (Jolly, 1964a). In the face of these data, it is clearly impossible to maintain that

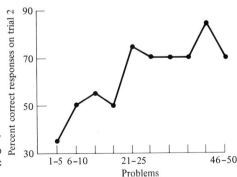

Figure 13–8. Learning set formation by chickens. From R. J. Plotnik & R. B. Tallarico (1966). By permission from Psychonomic Journals, Inc.

performance on learning set problems varies systematically with evolutionary position or with cortical complexity.

Critique of the Learning Set Method

The apparent correlation between phyletic status and learning set performance suggested by the early experiments summarized in Figures 13–4 and 13–5 led previous reviewers to overlook a critical weakness inherent in the learning set comparisons. Quantitative learning scores never yield uncontaminated measures of learning capacity, since they are affected by so many variables that cannot be equated for different species. The experimental literature provides evidence that the results of learning set experiments with different kinds of animals are strongly influenced by two other sorts of interspecies differences in addition to differences in learning ability per se.

Species Differences in the Number of Effective Visual Cues   The rate and final level of performance in visual discrimination learning by primates are strongly affected by the number and conspicuity of the differential cues available to the subjects (Meyer, Treichler, & Meyer, 1965). A typical experiment upon which this generalization is based was a comparison of color, form, and size as cues for visual pattern discrimination learning (J. M. Warren, 1953). Eight experienced rhesus monkeys were trained to discriminate cardboard squares which differed in the color, form, or size of central patches of construction paper and were tested on 30 ten-trial problems with each type of cue. The percentage of correct responses on trials 2 through 10 on four classes of problems by the most and least efficient subjects and the median monkey is given in Table 13–1. The range of individual differences is fairly wide, but both the best and worst monkeys, and the group as a whole, performed much more adequately when tested on color problems than on form or size problems, and discriminated stimuli which differed in both form and size more accurately than stimuli that differed only in form or only in size.

Similar relations obtain for object discrimination learning by rhesus monkeys (Meyer et al., 1965; Zimmermann & Torrey, 1965). Objects that differ

Table 13–1   Percentage of Correct Responses on Four Types of Visual Discrimination Problems by Rhesus Monkeys

Subject	Cues			
	Color	Form	Size	Form and size
Best	98	85	83	90
Median	96	80	74	81
Worst	82	61	61	63

only in color or only in form are less readily discriminated than objects differing in multiple visual dimensions, and colored objects are usually more easily discriminated than objects that differ only in form.

Similar comparisons of the effectiveness of different sorts of visual cues in multiple-problem learning situations are not available for nonprimate animals. Cats have been trained, however, to discriminate objects differing in multiple dimensions and objects differing only in form under otherwise very similar conditions (J. M. Warren, 1966, 1969). Figure 13–9 shows that cats tested on the form discriminations make a dramatic improvement in the rate of problem solution with practice, but even after training on almost 100 problems, they still commit more errors in learning form discriminations than naïve cats do in discriminating objects that differ in multiple dimensions. These findings suggest that multiple-problem learning in nonprimates is as strongly influenced by the number of relevant cues available as is the case with primates. This conclusion is also quite compatible with the results of single-problem learning experiments with rats and cats, which indicate that the larger the number of relevant cues, the more rapid the course of problem solution (Warren & McGonigle, 1969).

Cats, unlike monkeys, are not highly responsive to color cues. Although they can be trained to discriminate colors when rigorous precautions are taken to extinguish responses to irrelevant cues like brightness and position, they are so reluctant to do so that only recently have experimenters been able to demonstrate differential responses to color cues by cats (Clayton & Kamback, 1966; Mello, 1968; Sechzer & Brown, 1964). The typical junk objects

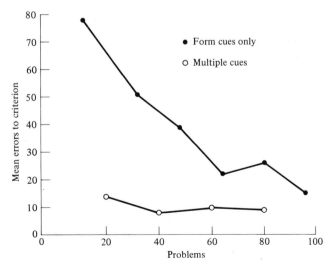

Figure 13–9. Learning set formation by cats tested with single and multiple object-cues.

used in learning set experiments provide differences in color to which primates are highly responsive and to which cats and most other nonprimate mammals are not. At least part of the difference in learning set scores between primate and nonprimate mammals may, therefore, be attributed to the fact that primates have more salient relevant cues available to differentiate the objects. The rather rapid formation of learning sets by chickens probably reflects the fact that chickens have good color vision and are quite responsive to color cues.

Species Differences in Responsiveness to Visual and Nonvisual Cues   If differences in responsiveness to color cues were the only variable confounded with species differences in the comparative work on learning sets, one could eliminate this source of confusion by testing all species with objects that did not differ in color. But this is not the case.

Successful performance on learning set problems is contingent upon the subject's responding consistently to the visual characteristics of the stimulus objects, and upon inhibiting responses to position cues since the spatial location of the stimuli is irrelevant in visual discrimination learning tasks. Species vary greatly in their relative responsiveness to visual and spatial cues. Cats (J. M. Warren, 1966), rats, and skunks (Doty & Combs, 1969), for example, learn spatial discrimination tasks more quickly than visual discriminations. Rhesus monkeys (J. M. Warren, 1966), chickens (Mackintosh, 1965), mink, and ferrets (Doty & Combs, 1969) solve visual problems faster than spatial problems. It is interesting to note that the species whose learning set performance exceeds the levels which would be anticipated from their evolutionary position, namely mink, ferrets, and chickens, are those which manifest superior learning performance on visual rather than spatial cues. It is therefore possible to argue that relative facility in forming learning sets is more highly correlated with responsiveness to visual cues than with phyletic status or cortical complexity.

Until now, the only comparative data on the formation of learning sets have been obtained in experiments that required visual discrimination. In view of the large differences in responsiveness to the sensory modes, within and between species, it is impossible not to speculate that rats might be markedly superior to monkeys in forming *olfactory* learning sets. Many rats do in fact manifest rather rapid interproblem learning when tested on multiple olfactory discrimination problems (Jennings & Keefer, 1969). No one has trained monkeys on multiple olfactory discrimination problems, but they learn single discriminations on odor cues more slowly than rats (Brown, Rosvold, & Mishkin, 1963; Santibañez & Pinto-Hamuy, 1957; Schuckman, Kling, & Orbach 1969).

This discussion of the ambiguities involved in efforts to interpret quantitative differences in learning set scores has emphasized species differences in sensory and perceptual processes because some data regarding these processes have been obtained in multiple-problem learning situations. The reader should recognize that similar arguments could be based upon the impossibility of testing animals under equivalent conditions of deprivation or the impossibility of equating the amount and quality of incentives for different species. The basic point is this: Performance on learning tests is necessarily influenced by many factors in the experimental situation. One cannot assess the contribution of these situational variables to the final resultant, the quantitative measures of interproblem learning in a single experiment. One can therefore never safely conclude that any quantitative difference in learning set performance, however large, is a valid indication of a difference in learning capacity, rather than a reflection of species differences in adaptation to the arbitrary demands of the test situation.

FUNCTIONAL COMPARISONS

Interspecies comparisons of numerical learning scores are intrinsically ambiguous because experimental conditions cannot be equated for different species. Bitterman (1960, 1965a, 1965b) has proposed a strategy for comparative learning research which recognizes and seeks to avoid this basic weakness of the traditional method for comparing learning in different species. He advocates species comparisons in terms of *functional relations* rather than numerical scores, and *control by systematic variations* rather than control by equation. These terms are defined in the following description of Bitterman's research on reversal learning and probability learning by representatives of the major vertebrate classes.

Serial Reversal Learning

Goldfish and African mouthbreeder fish have been trained on reversal and probability learning problems in the apparatus illustrated in Figure 13–10. The animals respond by striking or biting the Plexiglas panels and are reinforced for correct responses by a worm dropped into the opposite end of the tank.

Pigeons have been tested in the experimental chamber shown in Figure 13–11, where they respond by pecking the Plexiglas panels and are rewarded with grain presented in the central hopper adjacent to the panels.

Rats and turtles are required to displace panels with the head or forefoot in the apparatus shown in Figure 13–12 during training on reversal problems. The reward for turtles is a piece of fish, and for rats, a sugar pellet. Turtles have been tested in the same apparatus on probability learning tasks, and rats have been trained on probability learning problems in a modified Lashley jump stand or in mazes. Monkeys have been tested in the WGTA. The general aim is to adapt the testing equipment to the response capabilities of each species and to provide each type of animal with an appropriate reward while keeping the essential features of the apparatus and test procedure constant across species.

Automatic reward device

Response circuitry

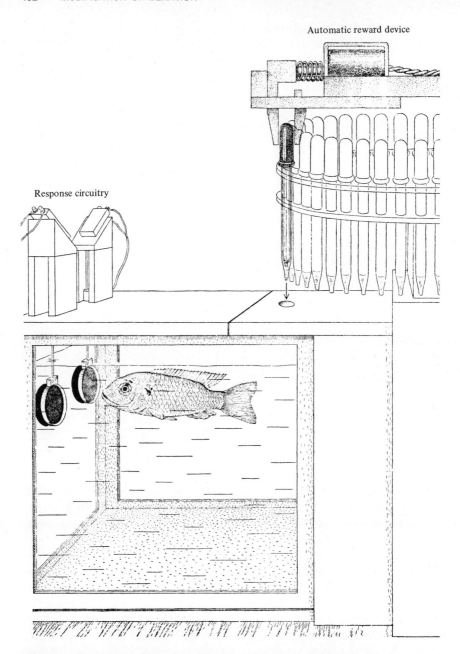

Figure 13–10. Fish in a discrimination tank is presented with a visual problem in which the lights projected on two stimulus disks are differently colored. By pressing its head against the proper disk the fish triggers an automatic reward device; the pincers above the eye-dropper close, squirting a *Tubifex* worm into the tank. From *The Evolution of Intelligence* by M. E. Bitterman. Copyright © 1965 by Scientific American. All rights reserved.

Figure 13–11. Pigeon making a choice is offered two visually distinct stimuli. (The center light is used in another type of test.) If the correct choice is made, some grain is presented in the rectangular opening. The experimental sequence is programmed by relay circuitry. From *The Evolution of Intelligence* by M. E. Bitterman. Copyright © 1965 by Scientific American, Inc. All rights reserved.

In reversal learning experiments, the subject is trained to choose consistently one stimulus, *A,* and to refrain from responding to a second stimulus, *B*. After a fixed number of trials or when the animal satisfies a criterion, *B* becomes correct, and *A* incorrect. This sequence can be extended indefinitely by alternately rewarding the two members of a single pair.

When tested on serial reversals of a spatial or visual discrimination, mammals generate a typical reversal learning curve of the sort presented in the upper panel of Figure 13–13. It is characterized by an initial increase in errors on the first or first few reversals, followed by a progressive decline in errors, so that reversals late in the series are learned more quickly than the initial discrimination.

The lower panel of Figure 13–13 is representative of the results obtained in experiments on reversal learning by mouthbreeders and goldfish. Neither species of fish shows an improvement in reversal performance, and there is a suggestion that reversal performance in these fish deteriorates during extended training. Bitterman (1965a) reports having trained some fish on more than 150 reversals without detecting any sign of improvement in reversal learning.

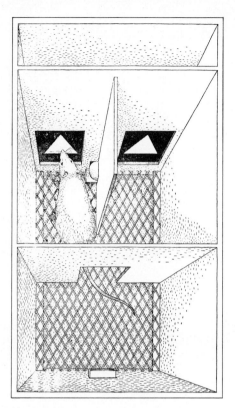

Figure 13–12. Rat solving a spatial problem is confronted by two visually identical stimuli. The rewarded alternative is determined by its position. When the animal chooses correctly, a sucrose pellet drops in the cup between the panels. The rat then initiates the next trial by going into the other section of the box and pulling a lever on the wall (bottom). From *The Evolution of Intelligence* by M. E. Bitterman. Copyright © 1965 by Scientific American, Inc. All rights reserved.

The difference between reversal learning in rats and in goldfish and mouthbreeders exemplifies a difference in a functional relation. The performance of the rats and of these two species of fish is differentially affected by the same variable. Practice in reversal learning improves performance in rats, but not in goldfish or mouthbreeders. Note that this qualitative comparison can be made without reference to absolute numerical scores and that it could be made even if the rats made more errors than mouthbreeders or goldfish.

Functional differences could result from testing rats and mouthbreeders under grossly different levels of motivation. There is no way known to render rats and mouthbreeders equally hungry, but the general validity of the difference in reversal learning by the two species may be assessed by use of the method of control by systematic variation. If the difference between mouthbreeders and rats shown in Figure 13–13 were due simply to differences in degree of motivation, there should be a level of hunger at which fish will show improvement in reversal learning. If it is found that, under the widest possible variation in hunger, mouthbreeders fail to manifest progressive improvement in reversal learning, it is unlikely that differences in motivation

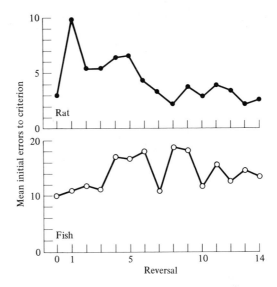

Figure 13–13.   Spatial reversal learning by fish and rats. From M. E. Bitterman. Phyletic differences in learning. *American Psychologist*, 1965, **20**, 396–410. By permission from the American Psychological Association.

produced the qualitative difference between mouthbreeders and rats. The importance of other potentially significant variables in the experimental context can be tested in the same way, by systematic variation over a wide range of values. Bitterman and his colleagues have not discovered any set of circumstances under which goldfish or mouthbreeders learn to solve reversals with progressively fewer errors.

Probability Learning

Probability learning problems are discrimination problems in which both stimulus alternatives are associated with partial reinforcement. This reinforcement is either differential, as when one stimulus is reinforced on 70 percent of the trials and the other on 30 percent of the trials in a session, or nondifferential, when both alternatives are reinforced on a random 50 percent of the trials in a session. Probability learning tasks are described in terms of the reinforcement ratio, which indicates the proportion of trials that the more and less frequently rewarded stimuli are rewarded (e.g., 80:20, 70:30, 50:50).

As in ordinary discrimination learning, training trials may be presented under three different conditions. Under the noncorrection procedure, the subject is permitted only a single response on each presentation of the stimuli, and the experimenter proceeds to the next trial or stimulus presentation in the balanced, irregular sequence regardless of whether the subject has made a correct or an incorrect response. This is the technique used in learning set experiments.

A single response terminates a noncorrection trial. Correction and guidance trials end only when the subject chooses the correct stimulus and receives a reinforcement; these procedures entail repeated presentations of the stimuli if the animal does not make an initial correct response. When the correction procedure is used, the same configuration of the stimuli is presented over and over again until the subject responds correctly; this method is frequently used to break up persistent position habits in ordinary visual discrimination learning experiments, and in probability learning studies, to ensure that the animal is exposed to the probabilities of reinforcement associated with both stimulus alternatives. This latter purpose can also be realized by the guidance procedure. Say that an animal chooses the nonrewarded stimulus on the first presentation of a particular configuration. One may then force the animal to correct its error by presenting only the rewarded stimulus after a brief delay or time out. This is more economical of time than the unlimited-rerun correction method. Limited correction plus guidance and simple guidance are the procedures generally used in Bitterman's experiments.

Bitterman maintains that vertebrates, when tested with noncorrection, *maximize* the number of reinforcements they receive by always choosing the more frequently rewarded alternative. However, when the experimenter controls the distribution of reinforcements associated with each alternative by use of correction or guidance procedures, mouthbreeders and goldfish choose the stimulus alternatives with frequencies that approximate the likelihood of their being reinforced. This is described as *matching* behavior. Rats, in contrast to goldfish and mouthbreeders, usually maximize when tested with correction. Sometimes rats display a sequential pattern of responding by reward following, choosing on each trial the stimulus that has been reinforced on the preceding trial. Monkeys may tend systematically to avoid the stimulus rewarded on the preceding trial when tested with correction. In both cases, the proportion of choices to the alternatives corresponds to, or matches, the probability of reinforcement associated with each, but the matching seen in rats and monkeys, differs significantly from that in mouthbreeders and goldfish. Clear sequential dependencies can be demonstrated over series of responses in mammals, but matching in mouthbreeders and goldfish is unsystematic in the sense that no clear temporal ordering of responses to the two stimuli can be shown. These patterns are designated as *nonrandom* and *random* matching, respectively. Both random and nonrandom matching result in a lower payoff than maximizing. On a 70:30 problem, for example, consistent choice of the more frequently rewarded alternative leads to reinforcement on 70 percent of the trials, but matching produces only 58 percent ($.7 \times .7 + .3 \times .3$). Systematic matching is, however, the typical response of human subjects on probability learning problems, and may be regarded as reflecting "an emerging hypothetical or strategic capability," an attempt to find a pattern that leads to 100 percent reinforcement, which is qualitatively superior to random matching.

The results obtained in experiments on probability and reversal learning in six vertebrate species are summarized in Table 13–2. The findings of experiments in which spatial and visual cues were used are shown in separate columns since "as we ascend the phyletic scale new modes of adjustment appear earlier in spatial than in visual contexts [Bitterman, 1965, p. 408]."

In this table, *F* indicates "fish-like behavior," random probability matching, and failure of improvement in serial reversal learning, while *R* indicates "rat-like behavior," maximizing or nonrandom probability matching, and progressive improvement in serial reversal learning. Horizontal lines emphasize the level at which the transition from *F* to *R* type behavior occurs on each task; inspection of the table reveals that pigeons and turtles can be differentiated both from the pairs of fish and of mammals, and from one another, in terms of the pattern of their performance on the four tasks.

My aim to this point in the discussion has been to present a nonevaluative summary of Bitterman's 1965 papers. Subsequent developments are outlined in the next two sections.

Recent Research on Reversal Learning

The view that birds and mammals show a progressive improvement in the rate of learning visual and spatial reversals has been consistently confirmed (Doty & Combs, 1969; Fuller, 1966; Gossette, 1967; Gossette & Kraus, 1968; Gossette, Kraus, & Speiss, 1968; King, 1965; Schusterman, 1966). There are now, however, substantial grounds for doubt that mammals and birds differ fundamentally from reptiles and fish in this respect. Holmes and Bitterman (1966) have demonstrated that turtles show a significant improvement in visual reversal learning when tested to criterion on each problem in the series of reversals. Other investigators have succeeded in demonstrating interreversal improvement in performance by fish tested on both spatial (Setterington &

Table 13–2 Bitterman's Categorization of Behavior on Four Classes of Problems

Animal	Spatial problems		Visual problems	
	Reversal	Probability	Reversal	Probability
Monkey	R	R	R	R
Rat	R	R	R	R
Pigeon	R	R	R	F
Turtle	R	R	F	F
Mouthbreeders	F	F	F	F
Goldfish	F	F	F	F

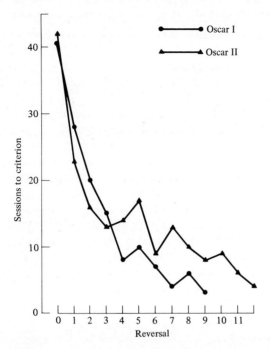

Figure 13–14. Number of sessions required to reach criterion (48 correct responses in 50 trials) on successive reversals by two Oscars. From L. H. Squier (1969). By permission from Psychonomic Journals, Inc.

Bishop, 1967) and visual (Squier, 1969) problems. Reversal learning curves for two fish of the species *Astronotus ocellatus* (Oscars), trained on serial reversals of a discrimination between a white cross on a green background and a white triangle on a red background, are presented in Figure 13–14. The improvement in the rate of reversal learning is striking and convincing. It is impossible to specify why Squier's (1969) Oscars differed from Bitterman's goldfish and mouthbreeders. Oscars may be more responsive to visual cues and may have profited from the provision of two redundant relevant cues (shape and color). The fact that the fish in Squier's experiment were reinforced in close proximity to the place where they responded may be critical; the reinforcement in Bitterman's apparatus for fish is delivered at some distance from the response panel, as may be seen in Figure 13–10. Relatively small deviations from strict contiguity in the stimulus-responsive-reinforcement sequence may severely retard the rate of discrimination learning. Pigeons that must peck a key and then take food from a nearby food magazine to learn to reverse color-discrimination habits much more slowly than birds that respond by putting their heads into magazines illuminated by different-colored lights, even though the difference in the interval between response and reward is only about a half-second for the two groups (Gonzalez, Berger, & Bitterman, 1966).

Recent Research on Probability Learning

Birds, like mammals, can learn to maximize on visual probability learning problems. Thousands of trials must be presented before maximizing is stable in pigeons tested in a Skinner box (Shimp, 1966), but young chickens quickly learn to maximize in the Grice box, a discrimination apparatus essentially like that shown in Figure 13–12. The performance of ten rats and ten chicks on 75:25 visual and spatial problems is compared in Figure 13–15, which shows that the chicks learned to choose the more frequently rewarded visual stimulus just as quickly as rats (Mackintosh, 1969).

The performance of rats on probability learning tasks also varies markedly in different testing situations. Rats often fail to maximize or to match systematically when tested in automated operant conditioning chambers (Johnson & Levy, 1969; Longo & Beideman, 1966; Treichler & Homick, 1966; Treichler & Marsalla, 1965; Uhl, 1963; Weitzman, 1967; Weitzman & Guthrie, 1968).

Rats maximize when tested with discrete trials in Grice boxes, modified Lashley jumping stands or mazes (Bitterman, Wodinsky, & Candland, 1958; Gonzalez, Roberts, & Bitterman, 1964; Mackintosh, 1969; Mackintosh & Holgate, 1967; Mackintosh, McGonigle, Holgate, & Vanderver, 1968; Roberts, 1966).

Obviously, then, little significance can be given to the findings that fish match in operant apparatus and rats maximize in discrimination boxes or mazes. The difference may be entirely due to the difference in testing apparatus, since rats, too, fail to maximize in operant training situations.

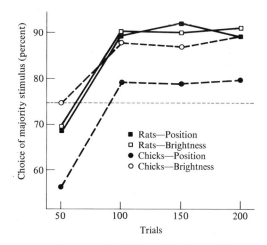

Figure 13–15. Performance of rats and chicks trained on either a brightness or a spatial 75:25 probability learning problem. By permission from N. J. Mackintosh in R. M. Gilbert and N. S. Sutherland, *Animal Discrimination Learning,* Academic Press, London, 1969.

Thus, the attempt to establish species differences in functional relations which are correlated with the taxonomic status of vertebrates has not been conspicuously more successful than earlier efforts to rank species in terms of absolute scores on standard learning tasks. Control by systematic variation is impractical. There are too many contextual variables that are likely to influence the results of learning experiments for one experimenter to vary each systematically and to investigate interactions among them, as is evident from the great rapidity with which Bitterman's (1965) claims have been disconfirmed by experimenters who changed the "standard" apparatus and procedures.

CONCLUSIONS

Comparisons of vertebrate species in terms of their performances on standard laboratory tests of learning yield no convincing support for the notions that animals can be characterized in terms of a general ability to learn and that the distribution of this trait is correlated with taxonomic rank. A given species may learn as well as, or better or worse than, a second species, depending upon the nature of the task and the conditions of testing. Studies of intraspecific variations in learning by dogs (Scott & Fuller, 1965) and by rats (Searle, 1949) have been equally unproductive of evidence for a general learning ability in animals. A given breed of dogs or strain of rats may rank high in one test situation and quite low in another.

The classical approach to the comparative psychology of learning was based on oversimplified and obsolete ideas concerning natural selection and phylogeny. Animal species are subjected to selection for survival and success in reproduction, not for the degree to which they manifest progressively more humanlike capacities for learning and problem solving in the Skinner box or WGTA. Natural selection has produced species adapted for survival in unique ecological niches by a great diversity of species-typical adaptations. Learning ability may help a species to adapt to its environment, but learning is only one of many alternate modes of adaptation. The survival of a species may be served as well by its ability to fly or to swim fast, high fertility, the capacity to metabolize a new type of food, or by other adaptations which permit it to exploit an unoccupied niche. Thus, Professor Heinroth, a distinguished student of avian behavior, once commented that birds are stupid because they can fly.

Again, the ability to learn avoidance responses may enable some potential prey species to escape predators, but relative freedom from predation can be achieved by several other adaptations: an unpleasant flavor, cryptic coloration, poison glands, armor plates or sharp spines, and appropriate unconditioned responses to warning signals and stimuli associated with common predators.

The basic point of this discussion is that each surviving species has become adapted to survive as a species in a particular niche by whatever means that responded most adequately to selection pressures. Specific learning capacities must have been subjected to the same kind and degree of selection as any other trait of the organism, and therefore, specific learning capacities are no more likely to vary with ~~taxonomic~~ status than any other functional or morphologic trait. *phylogenetic ?*

The literature on the evolution of intelligence often suggests that evolution produced a linear series of species, neatly ranked in learning ability; see Table 13–2 and Warden's (1951) Figure 3. The notion that living animals can be arranged along a continuous phylogenetic scale with man at the top is inconsistent with contemporary models of animal evolution (Hodos & Campbell, 1969). Evolution is currently pictured as a complex, continuing process of divergence, convergence, and specialization within independent lines of descent (Diamond & Hall, 1969), as is illustrated in Figure 13–16.

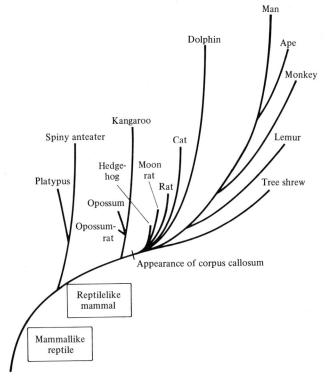

Figure 13–16. Phyletic relations in a few mammalian species. The height of the various lines of descent attempts to suggest the expansion of neocortex relative to old cortex. By permission from I. T. Diamond in W. D. Neff, *Contributions to Sensory Psychology,* Vol. 2, Academic Press, New York, 1967.

This chart, however, also illustrates that the neocortex has repeatedly expanded in separate lines of mammalian descent, suggesting that an enlarged neocortex does indeed contribute to survival. The frequency with which this increase in the size of the neocortex has occurred in different lines of mammalian phylogeny implies that it might be silly to conclude, from the failure of traditional approaches to the evolution of learning capacity, that brains have nothing to do with learning. Perhaps new and more appropriate methods for comparing learning in different species will enable us better to identify the reasons for the increases in neural complexity that have occurred in vertebrate phylogeny. These methods must necessarily be based upon contemporary concepts of natural selection and phylogenesis, facts from ethology, and recognition of the fact that in comparative, as in physiological, psychology, the results of a single test tell us very little (Weiskrantz, 1968). One can only speculate as to what specific methods may prove profitable in future research, and very tentatively indicate a few approaches that seem worthwhile at this writing.

The argument regarding the relation between species-typical characteristics and performance on single-problem learning tasks (pages 471 to 481) consists largely of plausible but *post hoc* interpretations and correlations between separate experiments carried out for diverse reasons. The general view advocated in this chapter stands badly in need of validation by experiments expressly designed to test specific predictions made before, rather than after, the data are collected.

Hodos and Campbell (1969) have suggested that many of the difficulties inherent in comparing species from unrelated taxa may be avoided or attenuated by comparing species within the same line of descent. Glickman and Sroges's (1966) investigation of curiosity in zoo animals appears to be the most adequate published study of behavioral differences within orders (Figure 3–7). They found little evidence that the strength of curiosity in various species of primates and carnivores was correlated with the species' taxonomic standing within its order. Curiosity seemed instead to be related to feeding habits and species-typical patterns of evading predators. In general, their findings were compatible with the hypothesis

> that feeding patterns which required extensive manipulation of the environment, coupled with moderate metabolic requirements, would favor the development of sustained investigatory activity. On the other hand, the very ready availability of food, which required only the simplest kind of stereotyped manipulatory responses for its acquisition; or unusual metabolic requirements which necessitated constant attention to consuming *per se* (or severely limited the necessary consumption), would not favor intensive manipulation of the environment in a particular species. Investigatory activities also necessarily imply attention to objects, often in exposed places, and a consequent reduction in the vigilance to attack. Any factor which reduced predator danger would permit the expansion of investigatory

activities. Effective defensive weapons, organized social structures, low incidence of predators in the biotype, or an environment offering good protective "cover," would all favor a high quantity of reactivity. As to the form of the reactivity, we might expect that this would frequently coincide with the living patterns of the animals, i.e., with the sequences of motor actions or postures that appear in the normal course of eating, catching prey, or construction of a dwelling [Glickman & Sroges, 1966, pp. 176–177].

Further studies of behavior and learning by "primitive" and "advanced" members of the same orders should contribute materially to the definition of the relative roles of ecological and taxonomic factors in interspecific differences. Glickman and Sroges's position suggests, for example, that animals from oceanic islands that are immune to predation should be much more inquisitive than members of closely related continental species that are liable to predation, even though they differ very little in taxonomic rank.

More diverse taxa can be compared in respect to the importance of learning in the development and modification of species-typical behavior patterns. Ewer (1969) has observed, for example, that the development of hunting behavior is more dependent upon learning in placental than in marsupial predators. The capacity to learn to respond appropriately to social releasers from different but related species by members of diverse taxa might also yield valuable information concerning the relative modifiability of behavior in animals.

Still other methods might be developed to exploit what is known about the specificity of species-typical adaptations. Do species differ in ability to learn responses to modalities that are low in attention value? Are monkeys, for example, able to form sets which will eventually enable them to solve auditory or olfactory discrimination problems as quickly as they learn visual discriminations, and do different species vary in this respect? Do species differ in the capacity to learn contraprepared responses? Schiller (1952) found that chimpanzees could be trained with food rewards to approach a dead snake which initially aroused intense fear. Little is known about the ability of other animals to suppress similar species-typical aversions.

In addition, many questions remain unanswered regarding ecotypes in the same and different lines of descent. Do rodents with well-developed visual systems like the squirrel's learn visual discrimination tasks in the same way as nocturnal rodents like rats do? Can one identify common characteristics in the behavior of successful species, i.e., those which are very numerous and occupy a wide geographical range, and less successful, related species in different lines of descent?

These speculative questions clearly differ in generality and theoretical importance. They are an idiosyncratic and impressionistic sample, designed primarily to show that good reasons remain for studying interspecies differences in learning after we abandon the oversimplified and overly optimistic assumptions of the traditional approach of comparative psychologists.

   In any event, the wide variation in learning particular tasks by different species of vertebrates that has been documented in this chapter has two important implications for the study of learning as a process, independent of phylogenetic problems. It is no longer possible to accept the classical proposition of learning theorists that all stimuli and all responses are equally associable. It is also evident that it is unwise to concentrate research on learning upon any small sample of species. Only by studying learning in a variety of species can we detect and discount the unavoidable contribution of particular species-typical characteristics in experiments that purport to demonstrate general laws of learning. "Rat laws" do not always hold for cats and monkeys (Warren & McGonigle, 1969). There is no sound reason to expect that they should do so in detail, in view of the material summarized here.

REFERENCES

BABBINI, M., & DAVIS, W. M. Active avoidance learning in hamsters. *Psychonomic Science*, 1967, **9**, 149–150.

BAERENDS, G. P. Fortpflanzungsverhalten und Orientierung der Grabwespe *Ammophila campestris Jur. Tijdschrift voor Entomologie*, 1941, **84**, 68–275.

BARNETT, S. A. *A study in behaviour*. London: Methuen, 1963.

BASTIAN, J. The transmission of arbitrary environmental information between bottlenose dolphins. In R. G. Busnel (Ed.), Les systèmes sonars animaux, biologie et bionique. Jouy-en-Josas, France: Laboratoire de Physiologie Acoustique., INRA-CNRZ, 1967. Pp. 803–873.

BITTERMAN, M. E. Toward a comparative psychology of learning. *American Psychologist*, 1960, **15**, 704–712.

BITTERMAN, M. E. Phyletic differences in learning. *American Psychologist*, 1965, **20**, 396–410. (a)

BITTERMAN, M. E. The evolution of intelligence. *Scientific American*, 1965, **212**(1), 92–100. (b)

BITTERMAN, M. E., WODINSKY, J., & CANDLAND, D. K. Some comparative psychology. *American Journal of Psychology*, 1958, **71**, 94–110.

BLASS, E. M., & ROLLIN, A. R. Formation of object-discrimination learning sets by Mongolian gerbils *(Meriones unguiculates)*. *Journal of Comparative and Physiological Psychology*, 1969, **69**, 519–521.

BOICE, R. Avoidance learning in active and passive frogs and toads. *Journal of Comparative and Physiological Psychology*, 1970, **70**, 154–156.

BOLLES, R. C. Species-specific defense reactions and avoidance learning. *Psychological Review*, 1970, **77**, 32–48.

BORING, E. G. *A history of experimental psychology*. New York: Appleton-Century-Crofts, 1950.

BRENER, J., & GOESLING, W. J. Avoidance conditioning of activity and immobility in rats. *Journal of Comparative and Physiological Psychology*, 1970, **70**, 276–280.

BROGDEN, W. J. Acquisition of a conditioned avoidance response by cats, dogs and rabbits. *Journal of Comparative and Physiological Psychology*, 1969, **68**, 343–347.

BROOKSHIRE, K. H. Comparative psychology of learning. In M. H. Marx (Ed.), *Learning: Interactions*. New York: Macmillan, 1970. Pp. 289–364.

BROWER, L. P. Ecological chemistry. *Scientific American*, 1969, **220**(2), 22–29.

BROWER, L. P., BROWER, J. V. Z., & WESTCOTT, P. W. Experimental studies of mimicry. 5. The reactions of toads *(Bufo terrestris)* to bumblebees *(Bombus americanorum)* and their robberfly mimics *(Mallophora bomboides)* with a discussion of aggressive mimicry. *American Naturalist*, 1960, **94**, 343–355.

BROWN, P., & JENKINS, H. Autoshaping of the pigeon's key-peck. *Journal of the Experimental Analysis of Behavior*, 1968, **11**, 1–8.

BROWN, T. S., ROSVOLD, II. E., & MISHKIN, M. Olfactory discrimination after temporal lobe lesions in monkeys. *Journal of Comparative and Physiological Psychology*, 1963, **56**, 190–195.

CLAYTON, K. N., & KAMBACK, M. Successful performance by cats on several colour discrimination problems. *Canadian Journal of Psychology*, 1966, **20**, 173–182.

COTT, H. B. The effectiveness of protective adaptations in the hive-bee, illustrated by experiments on the feeding reactions, habit formation, and memory of the common toad *(Bufo bufo bufo)*. *Proceedings of the Zoological Society of London*, 1936. Pp. 111–133.

DIAMOND, I. T. The sensory neocortex. In W. D. Neff (Ed.), *Contributions to sensory physiology*. Vol. 2. New York: Academic Press, 1967. Pp. 51–100.

DIAMOND, I. T., & HALL, W. C. Evolution of neocortex. *Science*, 1969, **164**, 251–262.

DIVAC, I. Effects of prefrontal and caudate lesions on delayed response in cats. *Acta Biologiciae Experimentalis (Warsaw)*, 1968, **28**, 149–167.

DIVAC, I. Delayed response in blind cats before and after prefrontal ablation. *Physiology and Behavior*, 1969, **4**, 795–799.

DIVAC, I., & WARREN, J. M. Delayed response by frontal monkeys in the Nencki Testing Situation. *Neuropsychologia*, 1971, **9**, 209–217.

DOTY, B. A., & COMBS, W. C. Reversal learning of object and positional discriminations by mink, ferrets and skunks. *Quarterly Journal of Experimental Psychology*, 1969, **21**, 58–62.

DOTY, B. A., JONES, C. N., & DOTY, L. A. Learning-set formation by mink, ferrets, skunks, and cats. *Science*, 1967, **155**, 1579–1580.

EWER, R. F. Some observations on the killing and eating of prey by two dasyurid marsupials: The mulgara, *Dasycercus cristicauda*, and the Tasmanian devil, *Sarcophilus harrisi*. *Zeitschrift für Tierpsychologie*, 1969, **26**, 23–38.

FULLER, J. L. Transitory effects of experimental deprivation upon reversal learning in dogs. *Psychonomic Science*, 1966, **4**, 273–274.

GARCIA, J., & KOELLING, R. A. Relation of cue to consequence in avoidance learning. *Psychonomic Science*, 1966, **4**, 123–124.

GLICKMAN, S. E., & SROGES, R. W. Curiousity in zoo animals. *Behaviour*, 1966, **26**, 151–188.

GONZALEZ, R. C., BERGER, B. D., & BITTERMAN, M. E. A further comparison of key-pecking with an ingestive technique for the study of discriminative learning in pigeons. *American Journal of Psychology*, 1966, **79**, 217–225.

GONZALES, R. C., ROBERTS, W. A., & BITTERMAN, M. E. Learning in adult rats with extensive cortical lesions made in infancy. *American Journal of Psychology*, 1964, **77**, 547–562.

GOSSETTE, R. L. Successive discrimination reversal (SDR) performances of four avian species on a brightness discrimination task. *Psychonomic Science*, 1967, **8**, 17–18.

GOSSETTE, R. L., & KRAUS, G. Successive discrimination reversal performance of mammalian species on a brightness task. *Perceptual and Motor Skills*, 1968, **27**, 675–678.

GOSSETTE, R. L., KRAUS, G., & SPEISS, J. Comparison of successive discrimination reversal

(SDR) performances of seven mammalian species on a spatial task. *Psychonomic Science*, 1968, **12**, 193–194.

HALL, K. R. L. Tool-using performances as indicators of behavioral adaptability. *Current Anthropology*, 1963, **4**, 479–494.

HALL, K. R. L. Animals that use tools. *Animals*, 1965, **7**, 16–21.

HARLOW, H. F. The formation of learning sets. *Psychological Review*, 1949, **56**, 51–65.

HARLOW, H. F. Primate learning. In C. P. Stone (Ed.)., *Comparative Psychology*. (3d ed.) New York: Prentice-Hall, 1951. Pp. 183–238.

HARLOW, H. F. Learning set and error factor theory. In S. Koch (Ed.), *Psychology: A study of a science*. Vol. 2. New York: McGraw-Hill, 1959. Pp. 492–537. (a)

HARLOW, H. F. The development of learning in the rhesus monkey. *American Scientist*, 1959, **47**, 459–479. (b)

HEBB, D. O. Alice in wonderland or psychology among the biological sciences. In H. F. Harlow and C. N. Woolsey (Eds.), *Biological and biochemical bases of behavior*. Madison: The University of Wisconsin Press, 1958. Pp. 451–467.

HERMAN, L. M., BEACH, F. A. III, PEPPER, R. L., & STALLING, R. B. Learning-set formation in the bottlenose dolphin. *Psychonomic Science*, 1969, **14**, 98–99.

HINDE, R. A. *Animal behaviour*. (2d ed.) New York: McGraw-Hill, 1970.

HODOS, W., & CAMPBELL, C. B. G. *Scala naturae:* Why there is no theory in comparative psychology. *Psychological Review*, 1969, **76**, 337–350.

HOLMES, P. A., & BITTERMAN, M. E. Spatial and visual habit reversal in the turtle. *Journal of Comparative and Physiological Psychology*, 1966, **62**, 328–331.

HOOGLAND, R., MORRIS, D., & TINBERGEN, N. The spines of sticklebacks *(Gasterosteus and Pygosteus)* as means of defence against predators *(Perca and Esox)*. *Behaviour*, 1957, **10**, 205–236.

JENNINGS, J. W., & KEEFER, L. H. Olfactory learning set in two varieties of domestic rat. *Psychological Reports*, 1969, **24**, 3–15.

JOHNSON, R. N., & LEVY, R. S. Probability learning in rats reinforced with brain stimulation. *Psychonomic Science*, 1969, **14**, 27–28.

JOLLY, A. Choice of cue in prosimian learning. *Animal Behaviour*, 1964, **12**, 571–577. (a)

JOLLY, A. Prosimians' manipulation of simple object problems. *Animal Behaviour*, 1964, **12**, 560–570. (b)

KELLOGG, W. N., & RICE, C. E. Visual problem-solving in a bottlenose dolphin. *Science*, 1964, **143**, 1052–1055.

KING, J. E. Discrimination and reversal learning in the rock squirrel. *Perceptual and Motor Skills*, 1965, **20**, 271–276.

KÖHLER, W. *The mentality of apes*. New York: Harcourt, Brace, 1925.

LAWICK-GOODALL, J. VAN, & LAWICK, H. VAN. Use of tools by the Egyptian vulture, *Neophron percnopterus*. *Nature*, 1966, **212**, 1468–1469.

LEANDER, J. D., MILAN, M. A., JASPER, K. B., & HEATON, K. L. Schedule control of the vocal behavior of *Cebus* monkeys. *Journal of the Experimental Analysis of Behavior*, 1972, **17**, 229–235.

LEONARD, C., SCHNEIDER, G. E., & GROSS, C. G. Performance on learning set and delayed-response tasks by tree shrews *(Tupaia glis)*. *Journal of Comparative and Physiological Psychology*, 1966, **62**, 501–504.

LILLY, J. C., & MILLER, A. M. Operant conditioning of the bottlenose dolphin with electrical stimulation of the brain. *Journal of Comparative and Physiological Psychology*, 1962, **55**, 73–79.

LILLY, J. C., MILLER, A. M., & TRUBY, H. M. Reprogramming of the sonic output of the dolphin: Sonic burst count matching. *Journal of the Acoustical Society of America*, 1968, **43,** 1412–1424.

LIN, J. J., & MOGENSON, G. J. Avoidance learning in the guinea pig, hamster, and rat. *Psychological Reports*, 1968, **22,** 431–439.

LIVESEY, P. J. Double- and single-alternation learning by rhesus monkeys. *Journal of Comparative and Physiological Psychology*, 1969, **67,** 526–530.

LONGO, N., & BEIDEMAN, L. R. Probability learning in immature and adult rats. *Psychonomic Science*, 1966, **5,** 291–292.

MACKINTOSH, N. J. Overtraining, reversal and extinction in rats and chicks. *Journal of Comparative and Physiological Psychology*, 1965, **59,** 31–36.

MACKINTOSH, N. J. Comparative studies of reversal and probability learning: rats, birds and fish. In R. M. Gilbert and N. S. Sutherland (Eds.), *Animal discrimination learning.* London: Academic Press, 1969. Pp. 137–162.

MACKINTOSH, N. J., & HOLGATE, V. Effects of several pretraining procedures on brightness probability learning. *Perceptual and Motor Skills*, 1967, **25,** 629–637.

MACKINTOSH, N. J., MCGONIGLE, B., HOLGATE, V., & VANDERVER, V. Factors underlying improvement in serial reversal learning. *Canadian Journal of Psychology*, 1968, **22,** 85–95.

MAIER, N. R. F., & SCHNEIRLA, T. C. *Principles of animal psychology.* New York: McGraw-Hill, 1935.

MANOCHA, S. N. Discrimination learning in langurs and rhesus monkeys. *Perceptual and Motor Skills*, 1967, **24,** 805–806.

MARTOF, B. S. Some observations on the role of olfaction among salientian amphibia. *Physiological Zoology*, 1962, **35,** 270–272.

MASON, W. A., & HOLLIS, J. H. Communication between young rhesus monkeys. *Animal Behaviour*, 1962, **10,** 211–221.

MELLO, N. K. Color generalization in cat following discrimination training on achromatic intensity and on wavelength. *Neuropsychologia*, 1968, **6,** 341–354.

MEYER, D. R., TREICHLER, F. R., & MEYER, P. M. Discrete-trial training techniques and stimulus variables. In A. M. Schrier, H. F. Harlow, & F. Stollnitz (Eds.), *Behavior of nonhuman primates: Modern research trends.* Vol. 1. New York: Academic Press, 1965. Pp. 1–49.

MORSE, D. H. The use of tools by brown-headed nuthatches. *Wilson Bulletin*, 1968, **80,** 220–223.

MYERS, S. A., HOREL, J. A., & PENNYPACKER, H. S. Operant control of vocal behavior in the monkey, *Cebus albifrons. Psychonomic Science*, 1965, **3,** 389–390.

NOBLE, M., & HARDING, G. E. Conditioning in rhesus monkeys as a function of the interval between CS and US. *Journal of Comparative and Physiological Psychology*, 1963, **56,** 220–224.

OTIS, L. S., & CERF, J. A. Conditioned avoidance learning in two fish species. *Psychological Reports*, 1963, **12,** 679–682.

PEARL, J. Avoidance learning in rodents: A comparative study. *Psychological Reports*, 1963, **12,** 139–145.

PLOTNIK, R. J., & TALLARICO, R. B. Object-quality learning-set formation in the young chicken. *Psychonomic Science*, 1966, **5,** 195–196.

ROBERTS, W. A. Learning and motivation in the immature rat. *American Journal of Psychology*, 1966, **79,** 3–23.

RUMBAUGH, D. M. The learning and sensory capacities of the squirrel monkey in phylogenetic perspective. In L. A. Rosenblum & R. W. Cooper (Eds.), *The squirrel monkey*. New York: Academic Press, 1968. Pp. 255–317.

SANTIBAÑEZ, G., & PINTO-HAMUY, T. Olfactory discrimination deficits in monkeys with temporal lobe ablations. *Journal of Comparative and Physiological Psychology*, 1957, **50**, 472–474.

SCHILLER, P. H. Innate constituents of complex responses in primates. *Psychological Review*, 1952, **59**, 177–191.

SCHUCKMAN, H., KLING, A., & ORBACH, J. Olfactory discrimination in monkeys with lesions in the amygdala. *Journal of Comparative and Physiological Psychology*, 1969, **67**, 212–215.

SCHUSTERMAN, R. J. Serial discrimination-reversal learning with and without errors by the California sea lion. *Journal of the Experimental Analysis of Behavior*, 1966, **9**, 593–600.

SCOTT, J. P., & FULLER, J. F. *Genetics and the social behavior of the dog.* Chicago: The University of Chicago Press, 1965.

SEARLE, L. V. The organization of hereditary maze-brightness and maze-dullness. *Genetic Psychology Monographs*, 1949, **39**, 279–325.

SECHZER, J. A. & BROWN, J. L. Color discrimination in the cat. *Science*, 1964, **144**, 427–429.

SELIGMAN, M. E. P. On the generality of the laws of learning. *Psychological Review*, 1970, **77**, 406–418.

SETTERINGTON, R. G., & BISHOP, H. E. Habit reversal improvement in the fish. *Psychonomic Science*, 1967, **7**, 41–42.

SHIMP, C. P. Probabilistically reinforced choice behavior in pigeons. *Journal of the Experimental Analysis of Behavior*, 1966, **9**, 443–455.

SKARD, O. A comparison of human and animal learning in the Stone multiple T-maze. *Acta Psychologia*, 1950, **7**, 89–109.

SQUIER, L. H. Reversal learning improvement in the fish *Astronotus ocellatus* (Oscar). *Psychonomic Science*, 1969, **14**, 143–144.

THORNDIKE, E. L., *Animal intelligence.* New York: Macmillan, 1911.

THORPE, W. H. *Learning and instinct in animals.* London: Methuen, 1963.

TINBERGEN, N. *The study of instinct.* Oxford, England: Clarendon Press, 1951.

TREICHLER, F. R., & HOMICK, J. L. Pretraining influence on relationship between extent of deprivation and probability learning performance. *Psychological Reports*, 1966, **18**, 689–690.

TREICHLER, F. R., & MARSELLA, A. J. Extent of deprivation and probability learning performance. *Psychological Reports*, 1965, **16**, 915–916.

UHL, C. N. Two-choice probability learning in the rat as a function of incentive, probability of reinforcement and training procedure. *Journal of Experimental Psychology*, 1963, **66**, 443–449.

WALTERS, G. C., PEARL, J., & ROGERS, J. V. The gerbil as a subject in behavioral research. *Psychological Reports*, 1963, **12**, 315–318.

WARDEN, C. J. Animal intelligence. *Scientific American*, 1951, **184**(6), 64–68.

WARREN, J. M. Additivity of cues in visual pattern discriminations by monkeys. *Journal of Comparative and Physiological Psychology*, 1953, **46**, 484–486.

WARREN, J. M. Primate learning in comparative perspective. In A. M. Schrier, H. F. Harlow, & F. Stollnitz (Eds.), *Behavior of nonhuman primates: Modern research trends.* New York: Academic Press, 1965. Pp. 249–281. (a)

WARREN, J. M. The comparative psychology of learning. *Annual Review of Psychology*, 1965, **16**, 95–118. (b)

WARREN, J. M. Reversal learning and the formation of learning sets by cats and rhesus monkeys. *Journal of Comparative and Physiological Psychology*, 1966, **61**, 421–428.

WARREN, J. M. Retention of discrimination learning sets by cats. *Psychonomic Science*, 1969, **17**, 170–171.

WARREN, J. M., & BARON, A. The formation of learning sets by cats. *Journal of Comparative and Physiological Psychology*, 1956, **49**, 227–231.

WARREN, J. M., & MCGONIGLE, B. Attention theory and discrimination learning. In R. M. Gilbert & N. S. Sutherland (Eds.), *Animal discrimination learning*. London: Academic Press, 1969. Pp. 113–136.

WARREN, J. M., & WARREN, H. B. Performance of immature and adult cats on the Hamilton search test. *Psychonomic Science*, 1966, **6**, 5–6.

WEGENER, J. G. Auditory discrimination behavior of normal monkeys. *Journal of Auditory Research*, 1964, **4**, 81–106.

WEISKRANTZ, L. *Analysis of behavioral change*. New York: Harper & Row, 1968.

WEITZMAN, R. A. Positional matching in rats and fish. *Journal of Comparative and Physiological Psychology*, 1967, **63**, 54–59.

WEITZMAN, R. A., & GUTHRIE, P. M. Matching as a group phenomenon. *Psychonomic Science*, 1968, **10**, 311–312.

YAMAGUCHI, S., & MEYERS, R. E. Failure of discriminative vocal conditioning in rhesus monkey. *Brain Research*, 1972, **37**, 109–114.

ZIMMERMANN, R. R., & TORREY, C. C. Ontogeny of learning. In A. M. Schrier, H. F. Harlow, & F. Stollnitz (Eds.), *Behavior of nonhuman primates: Modern research trends*. Vol. 2. New York: Academic Press, 1965. Pp. 405–447.

Chapter 14

Complex Processes

A. J. Riopelle and C. W. Hill

HISTORICAL INTRODUCTION

A little over a hundred years ago, Darwin's publications *On the Origin of Species* and *The Descent of Man* started a furor, remnants of which remain today. His bold, but now widely accepted, proposition that man shares ancestry with some of the modern animals, and that all the present widely diversified species may be traced to one or a few very simple animal forms, ran counter to the prevailing theological dogma, the theory of special creation. The storm would never have risen to more than teapot-tempest proportions had evolutionary theory been restricted to man's bodily structure. When it was also proposed that man's emotions, his drives, and his motor and intellectual capacities were also shared by lower animals, his special position at the pinnacle of the animal kingdom was seriously questioned. Thus comparative psychology became central to the study of mental evolution. The facts as we find them do not detract from the nobility of man; instead, they enrich our appreciation for our animal relatives.

Soon after Darwin's publications appeared, it became evident that detailed analysis and description of the intellectual capabilities of different animal genera were needed in order to demonstrate the extent to which animals display behavior that any human would call intelligent. To many, this meant that terms descriptive of human behavior would be applied directly to other animals, and their task was to see how far down the phyletic tree one had to go still to find ancestors of man that were also ancestral to the animals showing the intelligent behavior.

Descriptions of amazing behavior in lower animals and reports of their incredible powers appeared in both the scientific and the popular press. Reporters described their findings with enthusiasm that surpassed objectivity. And when multiple reports of similar behaviors by different observers appeared, confirmation of results, a touchstone of science, lent credence and universality to these anecdotes. We must remember that more objective methods were not to enter scientific psychology until the twentieth century.

Romanes (1888) expressed the rules of the game:

> The criterion of mind, therefore, which I propose, and to which I shall adhere throughout the present volume, is as follows: Does the organism learn to make new adjustments, or to modify old ones in accordance with results of its own individual experience? (p. 4)... Here I desire only to make it plain that the mind of animals must be placed in the same category with reference to this problem as the mind of man: and that we cannot without gross inconsistency ignore or question the evidence of mind in the former while we accept precisely the same kind of evidence as sufficient proof of mind in the latter.
>
>   ... And this proof, as I have endeavored to show, is in all cases and in its last analysis the fact of a living organism showing itself able to learn by its own individual experience. Wherever we find an animal able to do this we have the same right to predicate mind as existing in such an animal that we have to predicate as existing in any human being other than ourselves.
>
>   ... More correctly, the word reason is used to signify the power of perceiving analogies or ratios, and is in this sense equivalent to the term "ratiocination," or the faculty of deducing inferences from a preconceived equivalency of relations. (p. 14)
>
>   ... considering it desirable to cast as wide a net as possible, I have fished the seas of popular literature as well as the rivers of scientific writing. (p. viii)... The first and most obvious principle that occurred to me was to regard only those facts which stood upon the authority of observers well known as competent; but I soon found that this principle constituted much too close a mesh. Where one of my objects was to determine the upper limit of intelligence reached by this and that class, order, or species of animals, I usually found that the most remarkable instances of the display of intelligence were recorded by persons wearing names more or less unknown to fame. (p. viii)

By the end of the first decade of the twentieth century, the limitations of this anecdotal method became obvious, especially since the capabilities of the objective methods of laboratory experimentation were beginning to be known. C. Lloyd Morgan (1909) criticized observations by untrained persons:

> There are, I am well aware, many people that fancy that by the objective study of animal life they can pass by direct induction to conclusions regarding the psychical faculties of animals. But this is, I think, through ignorance of the methods

of psychology, or perhaps one might say, without injustice, through ignorance of the method that they themselves unconsciously adopt.... (p. 50)

For the practical man accuracy of the observation and careful induction therefrom are of primary importance, validity of psychological interpretation being for him altogether subsidiary. For the scientific investigator, thorough and accurate knowledge of and training in psychology is of at least coordinative importance with accuracy of objective observation.... (p. 52)

There is one basal principle, however, that brief exposition of which may fitly bring to a close this chapter. It may be thus stated: *In no case may we interpret an action as the outcome of the exercise of a higher psychical faculty if it can be interpreted as the outcome of the exercise of one which stands lower in the psychological scale.... (p. 53)*

The impact of this rule on subsequent thought was so great that it is often called Morgan's canon.

We should recognize that, despite their differences, both Romanes and Morgan agreed on the domain of behavior to be observed and the character of the explanations to be employed. Basically, both sides are saying that the analysis should be in terms of psychological concepts which can be generalized across many species, including man. They emphasized the promulgation of sets of behavioral laws which apply, but for quantitative differences, to broad ranges of the animal kingdom.

Instead of concentrating on species-typical behavior as modern-day ethologists do, eschewing the easy flow of concept and data between animal and man, they borrowed freely from the human data for information unattainable with animal experiments. Accordingly, the psychological study of animal behavior throughout its history has been intimately correlated with the studies of human perception, learning, and problem solving. Indeed, much of what we have learned about animal behavior came both from experiments conducted specifically to apply the results to the understanding of man's behavior and from others that are analogies of human experiments.

Another vocal critic of the anecdotal method was Thorndike (1898). In his view, most books of animal behavior were merely eulogies of the animals they purported to study. They were biased in their selection of material in that they gave no descriptions of the stupidities of animals, only their great successes. Secondly, the facts were derived from anecdotes which led to observer bias. Thirdly, usually only a single case was studied, the observations were not repeated, and the animals' history was unknown; thus it was impossible to know whether the particular intelligent behavior was a product of cumulative past experience or was, indeed, a novel solution to a problem.

Thorndike invented the *problem box*. This device was essentially a cage into which the animal was put. Located somewhere within or about the cage was a device which, if manipulated properly, released a spring-loaded door, allowing the animal to escape. Thorndike was impressed by the slow, gradual improvement in learning displayed by the animals he observed. Rarely, if ever, did he note any signs of insight, those flashes of reason that allow the animal to solve the problem instantly; instead, most learning occurred through trial and error. Hobhouse (1901), an early critic of Thorndike's problem box, noted that it obscured the relations among the elements essential for solving the problem, and he devised a number of problem situations which he believed could make it possible to demonstrate relational perceptions in nonhuman forms. Among the problems were the patterned-string test (in which the animal has to select the one string, among several crossing strings, that leads to food), the multiple-stick test (the animal manipulates a short stick nearby to reach a longer stick with which it can obtain a distant food), the rod-and-tube test (food in a tube must be pushed out by a rod if it is to be gotten), and the box-climbing test (a box must be pushed under a food suspended from the ceiling to enable the animal to reach it).

Köhler, a founder of the gestalt school, also criticized Thorndike, his emphasis on trial-and-error learning, and his dependence on the problem-box method (1925). Köhler argued that inasmuch as animals in the problem box could not survey and analyze the whole situation, they could not perceive all its components and their interrelationships. Hence the animals did the only thing they could do, namely, start off blindly manipulating whatever they could, with skill developing mechanically through a process off instrumental conditioning.

Köhler refined the Hobhouse methods and brought them into the framework of gestalt psychology. He emphasized the roundabout or *detour* principle in animal intelligence: Basically, the experimenter sets up a situation in which the direct path to the objective is blocked but a roundabout way is left open. The animal is introduced into the situation, which can, potentially, be wholly surveyed. It displays intelligent behavior when it takes the round-about way suddenly and deliberately, more or less after a pause filled with nonproductive activity. Köhler, through a quirk of fate, was interned on the island of Tenerife during World War I. He believed that the animals had to restructure the situation before they could display intelligent behavior, and he devised a number of situations in which chimpanzees clearly showed behavior that he accepted as intelligent and insightful. More recent research by Birch (1945) demonstrated that the stick-using performance of chimpanzees whose prior experience included extensive play with sticks was superior to that of naïve animals. His research emphasized that the opportunity to survey the structure of the problem situation is far from sufficient to generate an insightful solution; past experience was also important. Of course, we don't know exactly what is learned during stick play, but surely the animal becomes familiar with its physical properties (hardness, weight, length) and its behavior when he holds it (length, strength, size of arc when swung). The chimpanzee also satisfies its investigative tendencies or overcomes its fear during this experience. The animal also learns what *it* can do with a stick. Birch concludes that insightful problem solution represents the integration into new patterns of activity of previously learned part processes that were developed in the course of the animal's earlier activities.

Thus the comparative psychology of problem solving became intimately related to the psychology of learning and perception, and attempts were made to analyze problem solving using learning concepts. Accordingly, much of the subsequent information gained about problem-solving abilities of different species was obtained in experimental programs directed toward the elaboration of theoretical concepts of learning and perception.

COMPLEX PROCESSES

The term *complex processes* implies the prior occurrence of complex stimulus conditions and the subsequent occurrence of complex behavioral responses. An analysis of these processes should therefore be directed toward situations and behaviors of appropriate complexity. Before this can be done, however, an operational definition of complexity must be provided, and finding an acceptable one has proved to be difficult. At best, we can only outline some of the commonly found stimulus and response characteristics of complex behavior and the problems that are widely accepted as being complex.

Stimulus complexity arises out of the multiplicity or variety of relevant discriminanda and the relationships among them. Relevant discriminanda are those whose uniqueness can be employed in the learning of a task or in the solution of a problem. In the first and simplest case, complex perceptual processes may be invoked when the sheer number of varied stimuli are to be discriminated, especially when interdiscriminanda thresholds are small and figural stability is low. Additional processing complexity may be induced when there is a large ratio of irrelevant to relevant discriminanda, or when they are spatially or temporally separated. Relationships among discriminanda on different dimensions or stimulating different modalities should also increase the amount and variety of perceptual and cognitive activity. Finally, within a single task, the appearance or disappearance of stimuli, or changes in their spatial or temporal arrangement, will produce additional processing complexity.

Indicators of the second type of complexity, response complexity, include (1) the coordinated employment of multiple muscle systems, especially when such responses are different in pattern or timing; (2) extended series of response sequences, particularly when the time intervals are extremely short; and (3) within-task changes in behavioral patterns, in either timing, sequence, or transfers among muscle systems. It can be readily seen that the characteristics of manipulanda and their interrelations which are most effective in the production of motor system complexity are quite similar to those features of the discriminative situation which might be expected to create perceptual and cognitive complexity.

A third source of complexity in the central processes may be found in the relation between discriminanda and manipulanda. It is possible for either situation to be relatively simple in itself, but their interaction may vary in irregular, novel, or unpredictable ways. For instance, the cue-values of the discriminanda or the response outcomes of the manipulanda may change through alternation or reversal from time to time, or the stimulus arrangements may induce response biases in the subject.

We now see that it is unrealistic to attempt a complete yet simple definition of complex problems and processes; the numbers of ways they can be both produced and observed are simply too great to allow any such definition. Different authors emphasize different aspects of complexity, and new facts are yet to be discovered. Instead of trying to describe complex processes further, we shall summarize the facts and theoretical formulations which have been developed under this rubric in the past. When we are finished, we shall see that, in accordance with Morgan's canon, much complex human behavior can be plausibly accounted for by nonverbal mechanisms revealed by animal studies. Similarly, we shall have a better appreciation than we had before of the roles played by perception, motivation, and memory as they interact with complex learning behavior.

PERCEPTION, MOTIVATION, AND MEMORY

There is a growing realization that successful performance in learning complex tasks and in solving complex problems depends upon many more capacities and abilities than were subsumed under the so-called intellectual processes of the past. The importance of perceptual, motivational, and memory skills, together with integrative processes essential to their coordination, must be acknowledged. The implications of this expanded domain have been extended further into the problems of interspecies comparisons, for they represent three important axes by which species can differ.

The first prerequisite for the efficient extraction of relevant information from a complex environment is the capability for *versatile selective attention*. Total sensory input is achieved, of course, via multiple sensory systems responding to diverse stimulus parameters. The central processing of the resulting flood of afferent activity, however, keeps pace by means of central and peripheral mechanisms for rapid scanning, flexible shifting, and selective inhibition. Furthermore, the different sensory systems vary greatly in the capability for registering the scope and range of the surrounding stimulus-objects, and species differ, even within the class of mammals, in the functional importance of their sensory systems. In terms of the simultaneous reception of stimuli emanating from multiple sources, the visual system is far superior to any other, and as Warren points out in Chapter 13, the human investigator, in assessing complex processes, favors those other animals, e.g., birds and primates, which share with him a dominant visual system.

Secondly, neither general activity levels nor specific motivational drives have often been the concern of investigators in the area of complex learning and problem solving. Yet no one was surprised by the findings of Glickman and Sroges (1966) which arranged a number of animal orders rather nicely along a continuum of general responsiveness. Primate investigative drives, like those producing exploration and manipulation, add further bases for species differences in the processing of complex data (Butler, 1965). The combination of multiple sensory receptors and multiple arousal states greatly increases the susceptibility of sophisticated mammals to motivated problem-solving activity in many kinds of environmental conditions.

A third category of biological development contributing to complex processing capability is that of memory storage, or the capacity for retaining the behavior modifications acquired over a succession of learning experiences. The possibilities for alternative action provided by the diversity of afferent input are supplemented by the accumulated learning from earlier experiences. And again a complementary capability for selective inhibition is essential in order that the central processing may eventuate in a single response.

DISCRIMINATION LEARNING

By discrimination learning we mean the formation of a differential (selective) response to temporally proximate stimulus differences presented through the sensory channels: auditory, visual, tactual, and so on. Notice that there are two factors in this definition: (1) the detection of the difference, and (2) the development of a consistent response relative to the differing stimuli. Variables affecting the former concern intensity levels, wavelengths, sensory modalities involved, spatial and temporal contiguities of the relevant stimuli, and other alterable conditions. The fact that we are at present unable to measure independently the contributions of these two factors to performance on a single problem has forced the experimental psychologist to investigate the problem by manipulating the variables of one type while deliberately holding the others constant.

Methods of Investigating Visual Discrimination Learning

Several methods are used for testing visual discrimination. The most common one is the *simultaneous discrimination method,* in which the animal is presented with two or more stimuli at the same time, response to one of which is rewarded. Its most important characteristic is that the animal is able to compare the stimuli many times before a choice is made (Figure 13–2).

Other procedures have been developed which do not permit this comparing behavior. They are classed as *successive discrimination methods*. In one variation, sometimes called the *differentiation* method or the *yes-no* method, only one stimulus, positive or negative (i.e., rewarded or unrewarded), is presented on a single trial. In this method, the animal is trained to respond rapidly to the rewarded stimulus object and to inhibit response (for, say, 10 seconds) when the negative stimulus is presented. Typically, two or more identical stimuli are presented on each trial. When all are of one type, the reward is found at the left position; when they are of the other type, reward is found at the right position. In one variation, only one stimulus, *A* or *B,* is used to indicate whether the reward is on the left or the right.

Two different reward procedures have been used. In the *correction procedure,* the animal, after responding to the negative stimulus, either reruns the trial until it is rewarded or it responds to the remaining objects in turn until it obtains reward. In the *noncorrection procedure,* the animal is permitted only a single choice on each trial. The most important difference between the correction and the noncorrection procedures is in the bookkeeping; it is impossible to translate one scoring system into the other. With the correction method, twenty-five trials may mean twenty-five, fifty, or even more responses. On the other hand, with the noncorrection method, twenty-five trials mean only twenty-five responses.

Various kinds of apparatus have been used, most of which have been employed with slight modification for both simultaneous and successive discrimination. We shall describe their use for simultaneous discrimination only; you will have little difficulty envisaging their use in successive discrimination.

For small animals, such as rats, a Y maze or a T maze is frequently used. The stimuli, usually freely mounted cards, are presented at the yoke of the Y. The rat executes its choice by nudging the chosen card out of its way with its nose. Because the rat must continue to run to the end of the alley where the reward is, several seconds may elapse before it gets the reward even though it selects the correct card. To avoid this delay, which produces inefficient learning, Lashley, a pioneer in this field, developed the jumping stand (1930). This device contains a platform and two adjacent windows several inches from the platform. The rat jumps directly from the platform to one of the stimulus cards, behind which the food is located. Fields (1953) increased the number of stimuli present at one time and placed four of these modified jumping stands in tandem. He obtained very efficient learning in the rat.

For animals with good manual dexterity, a pull-in technique developed by Klüver (1933) can be used. The stimuli often are cards fixed to little boxes attached to strings that can be pulled in by the animal. Figure 14–1 shows a variation of this technique. With Klüver's form-board, the stimuli are presented on a tray containing food wells under the stimuli. In this case, the animal displaces a stimulus from its food well to get the hidden reward. A

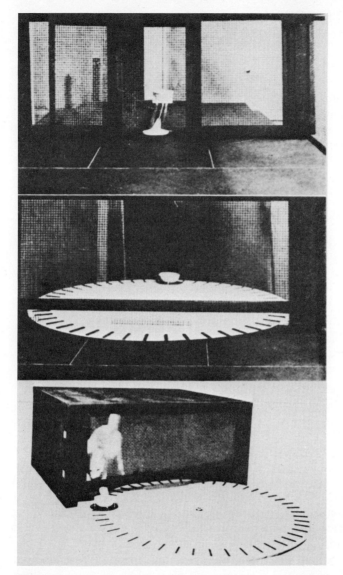

Figure 14–1. Tests used by Herbert and Harsh to study observational learning. Animals were tested after they had observed another perform the task. (After M. S. Herbert & C. M. Harsh. Observational learning by cats. *Journal of Comparative and Physiological Psychology,* 1944, **37,** 81–95. Copyright 1944 by the American Psychological Association and reproduced by permission.

procedure suitable for large animals involves placing the reward in a box with a hinged lid. The animal must learn to open the box having the correct pattern on its lid.

Comparisons among Species in Visual Discrimination Learning

A few studies throw some light upon the capacities of different animal species in visual discrimination. Gardner trained horses, cows, sheep, and human aments (mental defectives—idiots, and imbeciles) to obtain food from one of three boxes. The correct box was covered by a black cloth. In a subsequent study Gardner and Nissen (1948) tested ten chimpanzees and then summarized the entire set of data, all gathered under conditions as comparable as possible. In terms of making the correct response, the domestic animals had the best scores, followed by aments, and finally by the chimpanzees. Data for dogs, raccoons, and cats, all carnivores, show performance equivalent to that of the animals of the Gardner study. Under appropriate testing conditions, even doves can learn simple discriminations at speeds comparable to those for mammals. The rate of formation of a simple discrimination habit does not correlate well with neural complexity.

ATTENTIONAL FACTORS AND CAPACITIES

A basic consideration in assessing the problem-solving capacities of animals is their ability to survey and extract the relevant aspects of the environment which, if properly rearranged or utilized, would enable them to solve the problem. If we obscure the essential relations by improper stimulus presentation, the animals will be unable to solve the problems and we, as experimenters, will underestimate their problem-solving capacity. Certain factors have proven to be significantly related to ease of discrimination. They are not only important in a technical way in that they determine the clarity of the problem for the animal; they also reveal which aspects of the presentation determine the animal's perception of it. In addition, tests have been developed that are based primarily on obscured stimulus relations. Thus perceptual prowess may itself be an important component or dimension of problem-solving ability. We shall see that those factors which are important in discrimination learning are also meaningful dimensions for comparing different species.

Attentional factors, as such, have not received much emphasis in the studies of complex processes. This is not to say, however, that the differential learning of cues and their interrelations has been ignored, but that their perceptual nature has not been emphasized. Instead, emphasis has been placed on factors in the stimulus presentation such as color, size, and form, objects versus patterns, contiguity of stimulus, reward, and response, all of which affect discrimination performance.

Animals innately possess, or they acquire, observing responses that are very important for discrimination-learning performances. They selectively respond to certain aspects or dimensions of the stimuli, such as color, form, and slant, and they ignore others. This selectivity for one rather than another stimulus aspect is one of the important component skills in complex problem solving as well as in simple associative learning.

We might attempt to construct different profiles of stimulus discriminability based on various physical characteristics of the stimuli and so specify differences among species. For example, most primates possess color vision; most carnivores do not. There is the possibility, as we shall see, that the rules of gestalt organization might apply for many species. Recent data from ethological investigations suggest that components in the natural life experience of a species might also be greatly salient in a complex cluster of stimuli. Rhesus monkeys prefer to look at other rhesus monkeys, frogs are neurophysiologically equipped to respond quickly to movements of small objects in space that are similar to those of their ordinary flying prey, and some brain cells of monkeys respond differentially to the cry of another monkey or other meaningful sound (Szirtes, 1970). Only a beginning has been made in understanding the structure of the domain of naturally distinctive stimuli. Nevertheless, the possibility exists for discovering new insights into the attention processes of animals by further research along these lines.

An important property of salient stimulus characteristics is their tenacity. Fidura (1969) found that Japanese quail learned a red-green discrimination faster than a discrimination between a horizontal versus a vertical line or a triangle versus a circle. Furthermore, the color cues were just as effective when they were embedded among irrelevant cues as they were when presented alone. Moreover, prior experience with them as irrelevant stimuli added nothing to their effectiveness when presented alone. The less salient cues, on the other hand, were less effective when compounded with irrelevant stimuli, and their effectiveness as simple discriminanda was increased by prior experience with them as irrelevant variables. Apparently, salient cues remain salient among competing stimuli, but the distinctiveness of the less salient cues fades in competition.

Training can modify salience but not without limit. Stollnitz (1969) trained rhesus monkeys to attend selectively to the brightness dimension and to ignore orientation, but he could not teach them the converse. He also demonstrated that two color dimensions, hue and brightness, were inextricably related insofar as perceptual learning was concerned. It is evident that potential stimuli are not equally effective. Some are more commanding than others by virtue of the subject's innate perceptual mechanisms or its past experience.

Color, Size, and Form

In any visual discrimination problem, the stimuli presented may differ in color (including differences in hue, brightness, and saturation) as well as in size, form, or any combination of these dimensions. Does the animal learn to respond to most or all such possible differences, or does it isolate a single difference and respond accordingly? For example, if both color and size of the stimulus pattern *could* be cues to the reward, which would the animal use, or would it employ both?

Lashley (1938) trained rats to discriminate stimuli different in multiple dimensions and found, in subsequent critical tests designed to determine the basis of the discriminative response, that the animals had been responding to differences in a single dominant dimension. To see if these findings held for monkeys, Warren (1954) trained four rhesus monkeys on ninety-six problems. During the first six trials of each problem, the stimuli differed in three aspects: color, form, and size. On trials 7 to 15, new stimuli, differing in only one or two of these aspects, were introduced.

The results are shown in Figure 14–2. The curve on the left shows performance when the stimuli differed in color, size, and form, whereas data for the trials when one or two of the possible cues were eliminated are on the right. The top curve on the right denotes performance on the tests for discrimination when the stimuli presented differed in color and form, color and size, or only color. (All results from these tests were combined into one curve because the separate curves were practically superimposable.) When the test problems involved stimuli that varied only in size, performance was poorest. Color, in this investigation, was the most helpful cue. Chimpanzees also respond more predominantly on the basis of color than of size (Nissen & Jenkins, 1943).

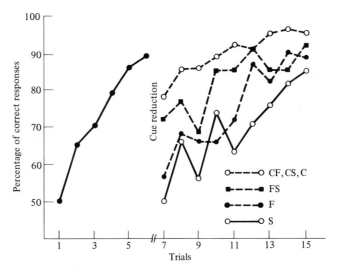

Figure 14–2. The effects of cue reduction on discrimination learning. Monkeys were given 6 trials on stimulus objects differing in color (c), form (F), and size (s). On subsequent trials the stimuli differed in fewer ways, for example in color and form only. (After J. M. Warren. Perceptual dominance in discrimination learning by monkeys. *Journal of Comparative and Physiological Psychology,* 1954, **47,** 290–292. Copyright, 1954 by the American Psychological Association and reproduced by permission.

The relative efficacy of one cue or the other probably depended on the absolute size difference and the magnitude of the color difference. It is possible that by magnifying the size and form differences and reducing the color differences between the stimuli, trends might be reversed. An intermediate position is probably the most defensible one: animals generally depend more on one type of cue than another, but not exclusively on a single cue.

The study of the salience of different cue dimensions in learning has been extended to members of a Stone Age human culture whose language did not initially have hue or geometric-form concepts. Heidler (1971) found that members of the Dani people of New Guinea tend to use color categories more readily than form categories when they classify groups of objects.

Contiguity of Stimulus, Response, and Reward

In general, contiguity of stimuli, responses, and rewards aids learning. Gellermann (1933) trained chimpanzees to discriminate between two stimuli pasted on the front of food boxes, the lids of which had to be raised to secure food. Efforts to learn were fruitless in the first 500 trials, apparently because the necessary stimulus cues were hidden by the raised lids when the responses were made. At this point, the stimuli were moved to a position adjacent to, and on the same plane with, the box lids. Under these conditions, the apes learned to respond correctly in about fifty trials each. The same results are obtained with monkeys. The closer the stimuli to be discriminated and the response, the better the performance (McClearn & Harlow, 1954).

Rats trained to jump through the stimuli in a Lashley jumping apparatus learn discriminations faster than they do if they jump through nondifferentiated cards located adjacent to the cue cards (Wodinsky, Varley, & Bitterman, 1954). Apparently the effectiveness of contiguity of stimulus and response is not restricted to primates.

Using monkeys and chimpanzees, Jarvik (1953) placed the discriminable cues (colors) in close association with the reward and the punishment. On the first day, small pieces of bread were colored red or green and were sweetened or made distasteful. The colored breads were offered in pairs. Learning was practically instantaneous. The next day, the animals were tested with red and green plaques covering food wells, with a peanut for reward to see if they would learn as rapidly as they did on day 1. On day 3, squares of uncolored bread, flavored like the original colored breads, were placed in the food wells and covered by red and green transparent celluloid. Of course, the bread *looked* red or green. Next, bread-size red and green squares of celluloid were pasted on the bread in the fourth day of testing. Finally, these celluloid squares were laid about one millimeter in front of the bread on the fifth day. The same color was consistently correct for a given animal throughout the five days of testing. The results for three naïve rhesus monkeys are

Table 14–1   Percentage Errors in 25 Discrimination Learning Trials for Three
Rhesus Monkeys

Day	1	2	3	4	5
Subject 1	0	56	44	0	44
Subject 2	0	52	36	0	40
Subject 2	4	60	48	0	48

SOURCE: M. E. Jarvik. Discrimination of colored food and food signs by primates. *Journal of Comparative and Physiological Psychology*, 1953, **46**, 390–392. Copyright 1953 by the American Psychological Association and reproduced by permission.

shown in Table 14–1. The animals performed errorlessly on day 1, but they did not transfer to day 2 or day 3. Performance was again errorless on day 4 but back to practically chance level on day 5. Clearly, the manner in which the stimuli were presented was very important in determining the monkeys' proficiency.

Multiple Negative Stimuli

In the simultaneous discrimination method as it's usually practiced, we present one positive and one negative stimulus. There is reason to believe, however, that discrimination may be better when there are many identical negative stimuli rather than only one. Results with cats (Smith, 1936) and with chimpanzees (Nissen & McCulloch, 1937) indicate that more efficient learning occurs when several identical negative stimuli are used. Pastore (1954) taught canaries to select the odd one out of three stimuli. Although the birds initially had little preference for the odd stimulus, they learned to respond to it. Performance improved substantially when the number of negatives were increased to eight rather than only two. Apparently, when many stimuli of one kind and only one of another kind are present, the single one stands out as different from the others, as gestalt principles would suggest.

Similarity and Difference

If the odd stimulus stands out perceptually from the others, it means that probably similarity and diversity can themselves be cues for discrimination. Perhaps, then, an animal can directly distinguish a homogeneous from a heterogeneous stimulus array. J. S. Robinson (1955) trained chimpanzees to respond to compound objects with two dissimilar components. Furthermore, the chimpanzees generalized their response to new problems even on their first trial, thus showing that they were able to use the sameness-difference relation as an essential cue irrespective of the particular stimuli used. Robinson later identified the specific relevant cues that were functional within this problem. For chimpanzees, the difference in identical elements between the positive and negative object-pairs was most critical, the difference in dissimilar elements was next in importance, and the twin-component nature of the positive stimulus apparently contributed nothing to the successful performance of these animals (J. S. Robinson, 1960).

In a modified version of the sameness-difference task, developed by Konorski (1959), the two object-compounds of a pair are presented successively, with a short period of time intervening. Memory and recall thus become emphasized. When this test was given to African green monkeys (*Cercopithecus aethiops*) by Stepien and Cordeau (1960) using auditory clicks, these animals gradually achieved 95 percent correct responses.

Oddity

The oddity problem requires the learning of a "double sign," for the correctness of a given stimulus is dependent on whether or not another like it is also presented. Several versions of this problem are used; they differ principally in the extent to which other bases for solution have been eliminated. The simplest type of oddity learning is required in the "one-odd" problem (Levinson, 1958), in which a single set of three discriminanda, two alike and the third different, is presented for a number of trials. It is obvious that this is no more than a simultaneous discrimination problem with multiple negative alternatives. The concept of oddity becomes more essential in the "two-odd" problem as first developed by E. W. Robinson (1933). Two pairs of identical stimuli are used in this problem. Only three of the four objects are presented on a single trial; two are alike and the third is different. As in the one-odd problem, the animal is required to select that object which differs from the other two. The difference to be noted, however, is that on successive trials one stimulus may be positive or negative. It is apparent that the two-odd problem can be solved through the learning of specific responses to each of the various configurations of stimuli as if they were separate problems, and without learning the concept of oddity. On the other hand, that is not the sole basis of solution, for Levine and Harlow (1959) demonstrated that rhesus monkeys solved each of a series of oddity problems as well on the first trial as they did on later trials. Performance improved from problem to problem but not within problems.

Probably the most complex version of the oddity task is the dimension-abstracted problem developed by Bernstein (1961). Basically, instead of remaining constant, the stimulus objects vary along a number of dimensions with only the relevant dimension dichotomized into odd and non-odd categories. Strong, Drash, & Hedges (1968) confirmed Bernstein's findings that this task is more difficult than other kinds of oddity tasks, and he demonstrated that it can be learned by several species of monkeys in addition to apes and humans, once they have gained experience with simpler learning tasks.

Matching

Logically complementary to the oddity problem is the matching problem. In the first form of the test, as devised by Kohts (1928), several objects were held in a tray and a sample object was held in the experimenter's hand. Her chimpanzee subject successfully learned to select that object on the tray which was identical with that held in her hand.

Nissen, Blum, and Blum (1949) have discussed a variety of ways that the matching problem can be solved, and the student interested in this aspect of the problem should consult their work. More to our purpose is the conclusion they drew from a comparison of their work with other work involving chimpanzees and rhesus monkeys. Both species learn matching in 1,000 to 1,500 trials, with chimpanzees probably learning the problem faster.

Conditional Discrimination

One way of further complicating a discrimination task is to require the animal to respond to two dimensions in order to find the correct object. For example, we might first demand that the animal select one object of a pair when the problem is presented on a light background and the other object when on a dark background. The animal must then respond to two cues: nature of the object and color of the test board. The reward values of the stimuli change from trial to trial whenever the tray color changes. The response may generalize to new objects and to new tray colors (Riopelle & Copelan, 1954). Not only stimuli but also dimensions can be made conditional on tray color. For example, the animal may be required to select the larger stimulus when the tray is light and the smaller when the tray is dark. Even the instructions to the animal may be made contingent on the tray color. Animals can be trained to select the lateral object that matches a central object on a light tray and to choose the nonmatching object on a dark tray. There is nothing sacred about tray color as a cue; the objects themselves may carry the conditional cue.

Complexity can also be increased by increasing the number of contingencies. Two-cue problems are not beyond the capabilities of some non-primate mammals. Because of the wide differences in procedures, direct comparisons among experiments are not possible; however, most of the data obtained thus far are in agreement with the usual ordering of species in terms of neural complexity. When we come to three-cue and four-cue problems, we are most likely to exclude nonprimates from the list of animals capable of solving them. The differentiation is likely to be even sharper and wider when generalization tests are conducted, for it is in a generalization test that we can be more nearly sure that the animal is solving the problem on an "if then" basis rather than on the basis of learning several different problems under conditions of high negative transfer.

Animals that can be trained to do either the matching or the oddity problem can also be trained to do the other, since both are two-cue problems. If a third cue is introduced, the animal may be able to do both, each in turn, as denoted by this cue. Nissen (1951a) attempted to determine whether there was a quantitative limit to the number of cues to which the chimpanzee can respond. Thirty-two stimulus objects were constructed, representing all possible combinations of five two-valued dimensions: size, color, form, margin, and presence or absence of a peg. In the first problem, only size was the relevant cue; the second problem involved both color and size. Simultaneous mastery of the sixteen pairs of habits involved all five dimensions. Training was spread over a 3-year period and involved a total of 17,740 trials. During the last fifteen sessions, the chimpanzee made 71 to 100 percent correct solutions on the individual problems. Nissen believed it to be highly unlikely that the chimpanzee simply learned sixteen independent configurations, for he found evidence, though unimpressive, that the animal transferred successfully to new problems when they were introduced.

Discrimination Reversal

The cue-values in a simple discrimination task may be reversed after a predetermined number of trials or some performance criterion has been attained. If the shift occurs without warning, the subject primarily derives its cue from the information obtained on the first trial after the shift in reward. A single reversal may be introduced into each of a series of discrimination problems, or several reversals may be presented in a single problem. Using the former technique, Harlow (1950) trained seven rhesus monkeys and one mangabey on 112 discrimination-reversal problems after they had been trained on 232 discrimination problems. The shift in reward occurred after the seventh, ninth, or eleventh trials. At first the animals continued to choose the originally rewarded object for several trials even though it no longer brought reward. By the time the monkeys had completed the 112 problems, they were reversing their preferences in only one trial.

The successive discrimination-reversal task has been applied probably to a greater variety of species than any other learning task. Primates, carnivores, rodents, birds, fish, amphibians, reptiles, insects, and isopods have all been subjected to successive reversals of either position or visual cues. The extent of this effort may be ascribed to the initial promise of the technique for the phylogenetic ordering of the species (Gossette, 1970) and its apparent susceptibility to theoretical analysis. The gradual improvement in performance over successive reversals can be explained in terms of increasing retention decrement, growing differential extinction, or altered attentional factors. Since the discrimination must first be learned before it can be reversed, the amount of original learning determines in part the speed of reversal. Hence, interspecies comparisons on reversal performance are complicated by differences in original learning. To avoid the complication, some authors (Rumbaugh, 1970) calculate the percentage of correct responses in the first ten trials of the reversed problem divided by the percentage correct in the trials required to achieve a given criterion during acquisition. This ratio, called the *transfer index,* showed the great apes to be superior either to gibbons or to two species of African cercopithecid monkeys.

Response Alternation

This task requires the subject to make a series of alternating responses, usually four in number, without external cues. In the simple case, responses must alternate after each trial; in double alternation, a response change is required between the second and third trials only. Responses may be differential in terms of position (spatial), or they may be directed toward different objects (nonspatial). A number of species, including rats, rabbits, raccoons, cats, rhesus monkeys, and gibbons, have been given this task with varied results. In general, there has been no relation obtained between performance efficiency and phylogenetic status.

Intermodal Transfer and Equivalence

Much of poetry's lyricism is based on the use of words in one situation that ordinarily are appropriate to another. Many poetic metaphors depend on intersensory similarity: the cold blue, the heavy cold, a sharp, dense sound, and so on. To what extent does intersensory similarity exist in animals, and to what extent does it depend on verbal processes? What is the role of learning and transfer?

Take first the simple classical conditioning situation. If a series of fairly strong unconditioned stimuli (e.g., mild shock) is presented alone and if that series is followed by a previously neutral stimulus, such as a light, the previous stimulus now evokes a response similar to the one given to the unconditioned stimulus *even though the two stimuli have never been paired.* The phenomenon is called pseudoconditioning, and it is an important (although seldom used) control in conditioning studies. Obviously, a stimulus in the visual modality (light) has the ability to acquire the response-provoking characteristic of an event in the cutaneous modality (shock) without any apparent opportunity for learning to occur.

Did the shock training transfer to the visual modality, and if so, how? A number of hypotheses have been advanced to explain pseudoconditioning, some based on supposed neural mechanisms, and others based on the idea that the subject expects to respond, and because of the expectancy, responds to even an "inappropriate" stimulus. Wickens and Wickens (1942) proposed that the conditioning might in fact be true conditioning by virtue of the fact that light, the pseudostimulus, actually had some characteristics in common with the shock, one of which became a sufficient conditioned stimulus. One such characteristic might be *suddenness of onset,* since both the shock and the light can be turned on rapidly or slowly.

They gave thirty-five training trials in which only shock was presented to rats in a two-compartment shuttle box. Usually, the animals quickly ran to the other compartment to escape the shock when it was presented. After several trials, the rats were tested for response to a light in place of the shock. Four groups were used. The two experimental (E) groups had similar rates of onset for both training and test and the two control (C) groups had dissimilar rates. If the animals respond to the common element, the experimental groups should respond to the test stimulus (light) more frequently than the control groups do. Table 14–2 shows exactly this result.

Table 14-2 Number of Animals Responding to Pseudoconditioned Stimulus

Groups	Total	Responding	Not Responding
1. Sudden-sudden (E)	9	7	2
2. Gradual-gradual (E)	10	8	2
3. Sudden-gradual (C)	9	1	8
4. Gradual-sudden (C)	9	2	7

SOURCE: D. D. Wickens & C. D. Wickens. Some factors related to pseudoconditioning. *Journal of Experimental Psychology,* 1942, **31,** 518–526. Copyright 1942 by the American Psychological Association and reproduced by permission.

The conclusion, therefore, is that response occurred to an *amodal* relation between the light and shock based on rate of onset. At best, this is an inferior or primitive form of intermodal equivalence.

Cross-modal transfer implies that a discrimination acquired in one modality will transfer to another modality without specific practice. The number of demonstrations of this phenomenon in nonhuman animals are indeed few. Verbal mediation should help; nevertheless, even in humans the demonstrations do not always succeed outstandingly. For example, Gebhard and Mowbray (1959) asked subjects to match rates of flicker (interrupted white light) and auditory flutter (interrupted "white" noise). Cross-sensory matching was less accurate than intrasensory matching. Identical temporal patterns are apparently not identical to the eye and the ear even when the subjects are concentrating on finding similarities and differences.

Earlier evidence for the gradual improvement in intermodal integration in children from three to twelve years of age (Abravanal, 1968) has shown that it is attributable to increased performance within a single modality (Bryant, 1968; Milner & Bryant, 1970).

Burton and Ettlinger (1960) studied whether macaque monkeys that were trained to discriminate between two rates of light interruption would maintain their accuracy when a sound was interrupted at comparable rates, and they found no evidence of any transfer. A similar experiment in which the stimuli were first two light intensities and then two sound intensities also failed (Wegener, 1965).

In another experiment (Stepien & Cordeau, 1960), African green monkeys *(Cercopithecus aethiops)* were trained to discriminate between two compound signals, each of which was composed of two bursts of either sound or light separated by a short interval. An auditory signal with two identical bursts was positive (followed by food) and the signal with dissimilar components was negative (unrewarded). In other words, Sx-Sx and Sy-Sy were positive and Sx-Sy was negative. In one example S_5-S_{20} (negative), the first burst had 5 clicks per second and the second had 20 per second. After the animals had learned this discrimination, they were presented with visual compounds made up of bursts of light flashes given at the same rates as those used with the clicks. Whereas the original auditory training required many sessions, learning the subsequent visual discrimination was very rapid, criterion being achieved in one session. Stepien and Cordeau interpret the results in terms of which the rhythm, an amodal stimulus characteristic, is abstracted from the other characteristics of the stimuli, and it serves as a discriminative stimulus. Ten years later, Ward, Yehle, and Doerflein (1970) demonstrated positive transfer effects from the visual to the auditory modality in bush babies *(Galago senegalensis)* when the stimuli were flashes or clicks of different frequencies.

A more direct and general kind of equivalence is that between objects presented visually and the same ones presented tactually. Here the amodal temporal events like rate of onset or rhythm no longer apply. Ettlinger (1960) trained rhesus monkeys *(Macaca mulata)* to distinguish a solid triangle from a solid disk visually. He then tested them on the same discrimination, but this time allowing examination only by active touch (haptic sense). The result was utter failure of transfer.

Blakeslee and Gunter (1966) also had a go at it, this time with white-fronted organ-grinder monkeys from the New World, *Cebus albifrons*. In their first experiment, they trained seven animals on multiple problems using either the visual or the haptic modality. Later, using new stimuli, they tested for transfer in the alternate modality. The investigators wanted to see if a learning set that was developed in one modality transferred to another. One monkey showed significant positive transfer. In a second experiment, eight Cebus (including the seven of experiment 1) were tested, using the same stimuli in both modalities. Extremely little transfer could be demonstrated. It is likely that what little improvement occurred on the transfer problems might have resulted from continued adaptation to the overall test situation and not to the specific preliminary training.

Up to this time, we have no evidence that monkeys or "lower" animals can unequivocally recognize tactually what they see, or vice versa. Is the situation equally gloomy for the great apes? The answer to this question is clearly *no*. Davenport and Rogers (1970) tested three chimpanzees and two orangutans, presenting each with three objects on every trial, one of which (the sample) it could see but not touch and two others which it could touch but not see (the haptic objects). One of the two haptic objects was identical with the sample and the other was quite different. The arrangement was as shown in Figure 14–3. The ape had to look at the sample, then feel the two dissimilar haptic objects and select the one that matched the sample. If it matched, the animal was rewarded. No reward was given if it erred.

Initially, the subjects matched objects at about chance level but they improved rapidly, so that by the end of the first 500 trials, four of the animals were performing at better than 90 percent accuracy and the remaining subject at better than 80 percent. Recombination of problems had virtually no detrimental effect on performance. Problems involving new sets of stimuli were solved also at better-than-chance accuracy, showing that chimpanzees and orangutans are able to generalize to new stimuli. They also were able to respond at equivalent above-chance levels to problems in which the sample visual stimuli were photographic representations rather than real objects.

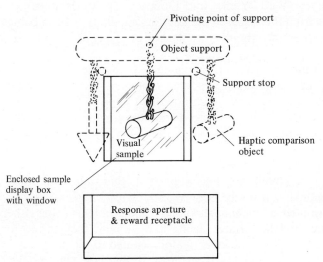

Figure 14–3. Cross-modal matching to sample apparatus. The parts depicted by dashed lines are not visible to the subject. The visual sample is suspended from the center of the object support, enclosed in a box behind the plexiglass window so that it may bee seen but not touched by the subject. Conversely, the haptic objects, suspended at each end of the support, may be felt but not seen. The response aperture is about 40 cm wide. (From Davenport and Rogers, *Science*, 1970, **168**, 279–280, Copyright 1970 by the American Association for the Advancement of Science.)

Moreover, performance at first-sight presentation of new problems was equally good.

Great apes can translate a visual scene into its kinesthetic counterpart, and they can do so to problems never seen before. This skill so far appears to be beyond the capabilities of any other species except man. Now that apes have been shown to solve these problems, perhaps investigators who work with monkeys will eventually discover technical modifications that will allow some species of monkeys to show that they, too, can solve problems of this type.

OBSERVATIONAL LEARNING AND IMITATION

The behavior of any member of a species is similar to that of other members of the same species. Some of this behavioral similarity is due to common innate factors and some to experiences shared by all animals. Perhaps the rest is due to one animal's learning from another by observation and imitation. Kawamura (1963), for example, watched when a Japanese macaque first washed a potato in a lagoon before eating it. Shortly afterward, he noted that many of the monkeys in the troop also adopted the practice. He assumed the spread was due to observation and imitation.

In some situations, the observing animal (the *observer*) can perceive the significant relationships among certain salient aspects of the environment, the responses made by the *demonstrator,* and their consequences to the demonstrator as seen from its behavior. The observer thus has the opportunity to infer that similar consequences would follow to it if it responded in a similar manner. But can animals in fact profit from observing the rewarded, the nonrewarded, or the punished responses of other animals? That an observing animal might make such an inference seems reasonable if it displays one-trial learning after being given an opportunity to use the *information* gained during the observation period.

In the typical laboratory learning experiment, only one animal is involved. It learns by receiving reward or punishment for its own responses. In laboratory studies of observational learning, the observer does not get immediate reward for observing the demonstrator's response. The animal's reward comes from faster learning made possible by observation. Two different procedures have been used in studying such observational learning. In one procedure, an animal known as a demonstrator executes a response in some kind of apparatus and thereby conveys information to a second animal, the observer, that, when tested later, shows whether it has learned from its observation. In the second procedure, an animal, while or after observing another animal perform an act, attempts to duplicate (copy) that act. In the former case, there is no necessity for formal similarity of the responses of the two animals, whereas, in the second case, similarity of the act is crucial. Simple direct influences of one or more animals upon another, such as (1) the starting or stopping of a behavioral act by a vocalization or a gesture, (2) the concomitant following of one animal by another, and (3) the participation of an animal in the presentation of a stimulus cue, do not involve complex processes and are not considered here.

Unfortunately, in few investigations have the above distinctions been maintained. The same descriptive terms have been used for a variety of acts, the most common of which is *imitation*. A few decades ago, imitation was thought to be an instinct characteristic of many species. The comparative psychologist attempted to determine the lowest phylogenetic level in which this instinct appeared. Today, it is recognized that imitation includes several kinds of behavior, each of which is a function of different factors. The present aims are to differentiate, analyze, and explain the various kinds of behavior that one animal displays when it observes another, regardless of its phyletic status.

In an early study, Thorndike devised a special test situation in which one bird, the observer, had an opportunity to imitate a skilled demonstrator. In these first experiments on imitation, Thorndike used the problem-box method. The bird had to escape from an enclosure by performing some act. An illustration follows for chicks: "No. 64 learned to get out of a pen by crowding under the wire screen at a certain point. There was also a chance to get out by walking up an inclined plane and then jumping down. No. 66 was put in with 64. After 9 minutes 20 seconds, 66 went out by the inclined plane, although 64 had in the meantime crawled out under the screen 9 times [Thorndike, 1898, p. 51]." Thorndike also tested dogs, cats, and monkeys and found no evidence for imitation.

However, other investigators have found it. Kinnaman (1902) stated that a female rhesus monkey imitated a male monkey in opening the catch on a door of a puzzle box. Results supporting imitation in problem-box learning were also obtained from cats (Herbert & Harsh, 1944). Five problems were used, in each of which one animal performed on the problem while another observed. The simplest problem involved a turntable bearing food which had to be rotated by the cat to secure the food (Figure 14–1). The most difficult was a pedal-door arrangement. Some animals observed during the entire learning period of the demonstrator, and other animals observed only their last and most skillful trials. In general, scores for observers were consistently better than those for nonobservers. Also, animals that observed for all trials solved the problems faster than those observing only for the skilled performances. The investigators concluded that either prolonged observation or observation of errors was beneficial to learning.

Warden and Jackson (1935) introduced the *duplicate-cage* method to test for imitation. Two problem boxes, side by side, were used. One contained the demonstrator, the other the observer. As soon as the demonstrator solved its problem, an identical problem was revealed in the observer's cage, enabling the observer to begin immediately. This apparatus produced imitative responses in 46 percent of the tests used.

How did imitation occur? Crawford and Spence (1939) argued that " . . . in the problem-box test the activity of the demonstrator simply enhances certain aspects of the stimulus situation which the imitator later attacks in his own way. Since discovery of the locus of attack is usually the most difficult part of a problem-box test, the imitator often meets with quick success without need of specific copy, after beginning to manipulate the part last manipulated by the demonstrator [p.133]."

Scientists investigating behavior of primates in the wild have emphasized the importance of a natural propensity for young animals to be attracted to the objects their mothers manipulate. Hall (1963), for example, concluded, primarily from informal developmental and field studies, that young monkeys and apes acquire basic feeding and avoidance habits chiefly by applying their exploratory tendencies to places and objects indicated in the behavior of their mothers or of others in the group. There is no doubt in his mind that the affectional situation of the participants is crucial as to whether a demonstrator is approached, attended to, and imitated or not. The idea that this kind of innate stimulus enhancement, which occurs if the demonstrator is the right animal, is in sharp contrast to the notion that the youngster learns that the mother is a good demonstrator, and that therefore she is a useful guide and so behooves watching. In the latter case, the young animal has learned something about the mother's behavior that is useful to it and has put it to work in the acquisition of new behavior.

Consider this specific example. Menzel (1967) put a plastic orange on the ground in full view of a troop of wild rhesus. Immediately, the animals, accustomed to being provisioned by human caretakers, sounded the food cry that is characteristic of the species. Several animals raced toward the orange at the same time, but a dominant female got to it first. As she reached for it, she jerked back her hand, peered closely, and gave an avoidance bark. The others immediately stopped vocalizing, and they avoided further contact with the orange. Only later did some young animals cautiously peer at the object to investigate it. Obviously the remaining animals, regardless of their affectional relation to the female, drew significant inferences from her actions and behaved accordingly.

In a further study, Menzel (1971) provides additional evidence that animals may use information about the behavior of other animals to achieve a desired end: This is not merely the result of cumulative rewarding of a natural propensity; it is itself a kind of problem solution, this time in a social context. Animals use other animals' behavior as a source of cues for learning about the environment. A group of young chimpanzees, each of which was intimately acquainted with the others, was held in a release cage while a member of the group was taken on a tour of a 1-acre test field and shown the location of a cache of fruit. Then the "leader" was returned to the cage and the whole group released simultaneously. The leader, remembering the cache, started out in its direction, followed by the others. Leaders were dependent on their followers, and seldom traveled far unaccompanied. Although various signals, such as gestures, glances, and whimperings, were used to recruit recalcitrant individuals, the most effective cue or signal was simply to start running independently and with resolution. Leadership was not related to dominance status, but it was positively related to the length of time that leaders and particular followers had known each other.

Studies on factors affecting ease of discrimination learning showed one-trial learning in monkeys could be made the rule rather than the exception by means of learning set procedures. With this in mind, Darby and Riopelle (1959) adapted these procedures to the study of primate observation learning. Two monkeys faced each other across a test board containing a pair of stimulus objects. The demonstrator was allowed one trial on the problem. This demonstration was observed by the second animal, which was then tested. The animals, naïve at the beginning of the experiment, acquired much skill in discrimi-

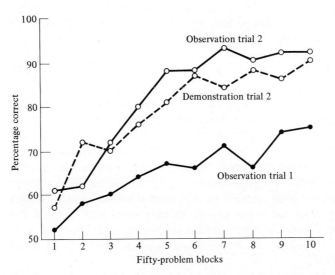

Figure 14–4. Acquisition of observational-learning performance by monkeys. The line with filled circles denotes performance on the first test trial of the animal that had an opportunity to observe one demonstration trial. Performance by the demonstrator on that one trial was exactly 50 percent correct. Curves with open circles refer to second trial performance of the demonstrator and the observer. (After C. L. Darby & A. J. Riopelle. Observational learning in the rhesus monkey. *Journal of Comparative and Physiological Psychology,* 1959, **52,** 94–98. Copyright 1959 by the American Psychological Association and reproduced by permission.)

nation learning during the series of 500 problems, as is shown in Figure 14–4. The observer's first-trial performance improved throughout the entire 500 problems until it attained 75 percent correct. Both the demonstrator and the observer were given second trials. Performance on these trials is also shown in Figure 14–4. The difference in favor of the observer during the latter part of the training is small though consistent. The difference favoring the observer's second test trial suggests that learning is better when observation precedes the tests rather than the other way around. Darby and Riopelle further analyzed their data to determine whether the observer went to the object first selected by the demonstrator (as expected from *stimulus enhancement*) or whether it went to the rewarded object irrespective of the demonstrator's choice. The results showed that the animals had no significant tendency to select the object first chosen by the demonstrator; instead, they selected the correct object, thereby showing that they made use of the information concerning the food-object relationship gained during the demonstration.

In a subsequent study on observational learning with experienced monkeys, Michels (1955) trained the observers to choose (1) the object selected by the demonstrator, (2) the object not selected by the demonstrator, or (3) the correct object as defined in the preceding experiment. First-trial performance significantly exceeded chance in every case. Thus, rhesus monkeys in an object-quality discrimination situation can profit from the successes and the failures of the demonstrator under differing rules of the game.

The demonstrator need not be of the same genus as the observer. One can train monkeys for zero-trial discrimination by presenting the discriminanda with an accompanying sign stimulus (showing food over the correct object or merely tapping it), although this test, called a *nonspatial delayed reaction,* is very difficult. If monkeys need only go to the place where the demonstrator deposits food, the task, called a *spatial delayed reaction,* is very easy.

In the above discussion, the emphasis was on those studies in which a demonstrator's behavior was directed toward obtaining a reward. It would seem more crucial for an animal to avoid a dangerous situation without having to experience it directly. To get an idea of the possibilities, we shall bring the problem to the laboratory and ask: Can an observer watching a trained animal solve a problem to avoid harm benefit from its observational experience? Brogden (1942) provided an opportunity for dogs to imitate in an avoidance-conditioning situation. A pair of animals was taken to the conditioning room. Both members of the pair were restrained in conditioning frames in such a way that one animal could see the other. The demonstration animal was then conditioned to withdraw its leg from a metal plate to avoid shock. Brogden found that not only did the observing dog fail to imitate the conditioned animal, but that it also failed to learn more rapidly when conditioned later. However, monkeys can learn something of an avoidance situation by watching another animal learn (Presley & Riopelle, 1959). Monkeys that had observed another learn to leap over a barrier in a double-compartment box whenever a light came on subsequently learned the same avoidance response faster than did control animals.

Some evidence for intergeneric differences in capacity for this kind of complex behavior has been produced within the operant-conditioning situation. Powell (1968) found that rats learned an instrumental response in fewer trials with shaping procedures than by observation. On the other hand, observer cats learned both approach and avoidance operants faster than those trained by conventional shaping methods (John, Chesler, Bartlett, & Victor, 1968). Also, macaque monkeys were able to show some improvement in acquiring an operant schedule when they could only observe an accomplished demonstrator but could not perform, and were not reinforced, during the observation period (Myers, 1970).

The Hayeses (1952) raised a chimpanzee, Viki, in their home. They investigated her imitative ability along with that of a cage-reared animal and that of four children under three years of age. They observed many instances of imitation while Viki played. At about sixteen months of age, Viki imitated a number of household tasks as performed by Mrs. Hayes. A fairly complete act of putting on lipstick was observed. Many of Viki's imitations occurred some time after the original demonstration.

Subsequently, the Hayeses tried to establish a *set* to imitate. That is, they wanted her to learn to imitate a response on the command, "Do this." Seventy items were tried, of which many were too difficult for her to execute. For example, Viki would not close her eyes but did adopt the pseudosolution of putting her finger to her eye, which caused it to close. Figure 14–5 shows Viki imitating a photograph of herself. Viki was also given a series of problems to solve, such as the stick-and-tunnel problem. She solved this problem in about 30 seconds after the second demonstration. The children performed about as well as Viki did, whereas the cage-reared chimpanzee was decidedly inferior.

It is abundantly clear that chimpanzees can and do imitate, immediately and after a lapse of time, in the widest sense of the term. Furthermore, they can learn to perform new copying responses upon command.

In a previous section, we discussed discrimination learning and the factors upon which performance depends. Performance on any trial can be directly related to the animal's prior experience with reward. Thus the response on trial 2 of a problem is determined to a great extent on whether or not the animal obtained reward on trial 1. In the observational learning problems discussed in the present section, no such simple relationship can be found, for under these circumstances, learning takes place even when the demonstrator doesn't get the reward. Although it is not known whether or not rodents and carnivores can make systematic corrections for the erroneous responses of the demonstrator, it is clearly established that monkeys can do so if the problem is presented in such a way as to make use of the principles discussed

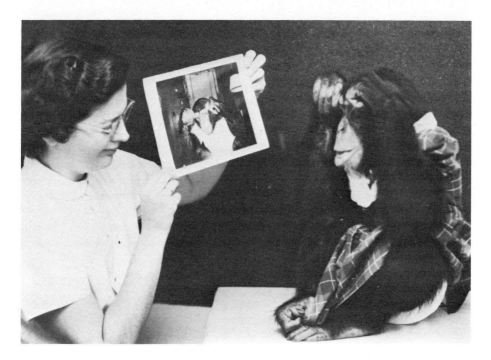

Figure 14-5. Viki imitating a photograph of herself.

in the early part of this chapter. Not only is there a decreased dependence on reward for learning in these animals, but evidence is at hand which points to the role of inference in determining the monkey's response.

Inferential imitation is to be distinguished from imitative copying behavior, in which emphasis is placed on duplicating an act in its form if not in its aim. Gradations in complexity of behavior are evident also, and it is likely that the fundamental behavioral mechanisms differ too. Consider that kind of (imitative) behavior exhibited by birds when they repeat in their songs phrases from tunes whistled by the milkman. Thorndike (1898) wrote, "... now if a bird really gets a sound in his mind from hearing it and sets out forthwith to imitate it as mockingbirds are said at times to do, it is a mystery and deserves closest study. If a bird, out of a lot of random noises that it makes, chooses those for repetition which are like sounds he had heard, it is a mystery why, though not as in the previous case a mystery how, he does it [p. 47]." The kind of imitation described by the Hayeses for chimpanzees is clearly of the first sort, whereas the kind in which one rat tracks another down a runway or the kind in which birds are trained to "talk" represent Thorndike's second type of imitation.

In summary, it can be said that there are several ways by which a demonstrator serves the observer or learner. First, the action of the demonstrator may be merely a sign or cue to which a rewarded response (by the learner) is associated. Second, the demonstrator may serve the learner by permitting the latter to observe the place or locus in the external field where the correct responses must be made. The demonstrator may simply enhance certain places, or aspects of the stimuli, which later the learner responds to in his own way, often by trial and error. Since the determination of the locus of attack (place to respond) is often the most difficult to achieve, such a service by a demonstrator may lead to very quick learning. A third way by which a demonstrator may serve the observer is by performing the rewarded response. In general, the demonstrator's behavior permits the learner to perceive the relations between certain stimuli and the consequences of its responses. The observer can then profit immediately from the consequences of its responses. How this occurs is not known, but it's possible that there is an inference by the observer, used later in its performance. The degree of previous experience of the observer in solving problems is significant in the use that the animal can make of demonstrations.

TOOL-USING

When an animal seizes a stick, rock, or other object and manipulates it as a means of achieving a goal, comparative psychologists usually regard the act as an indicator of intelligent, adaptive behavior. The use of the instrument extends the animal's range of movement or increases its efficiency. It is no simple matter to determine whether any given instance of tool-using behavior should be classified as intelligent and adaptive or merely as a species-typical or learned response. The solitary wasp holds a small pebble in its mandibles, using it as a hammer to pound dirt into the next burrow. The Egyptian vulture throws stones at ostrich eggs to break them (van Lawick-Goodall, 1968b). Are these activities complex processes? The woodpecker finch of the Galapagos Islands provides another example. This bird resembles the woodpecker in that it climbs vertical trunks in search of food. Unlike the woodpecker, which, having tapped a hole in the trunk with its beak, inserts its tongue into the hole to remove the insect, the finch finds a cactus spine, holds it lengthwise in its beak, and pokes it into the hole. When the irritated insect emerges, the finch drops the spine and seizes the insect. The finch can modify the behavior to fit the situation; for example, it rejects spines that are too short for the hole.

These three examples, although surely tool-using, must be disqualified as adaptive, intelligent responses for our purposes, since they are acts that are characteristic of the species as a whole and not of individual animals. Moreover, they are the responses that are always used in these situations.

Considerably more complex types of tool-using behavior are seen in primates. Not only are sticks used to obtain food, they are used to ward off enemies or strangers (agonistic behavior). Before describing some examples of primate behavior, we should note two points made by Hall (1963), who observed primates in the wild and worked with them in the laboratory. "Not a single authenticated instance of tool-using as an element in agonistic behavior is known in animals other than that of the monkeys and apes [p. 480].... There is an extensive experimental literature, many observations on animals in captivity, and extremely few field data that provide evidence for analysis [p. 483]."

The sea otter's behavior, described by Fisher (1939), is a rare example of tool using by a wild nonprimate mammal. The otter feeds by swimming along the Pacific Coast and diving to the sea bed to obtain crabs, urchins, mussels, or an abalone. After surfacing, it then floats on its back, placing the food on its chest. When it feeds on mussels, it comes to the surface with a flat stone, 5 inches in diameter, and places it on its chest; then it dashes the mussel against the stone until its shell is broken enough for the otter to extract the contents.

Only the chimpanzees observed by Jane van Lawick-Goodall (1968a) use tools to obtain food in the wild.

> Typically, a chimpanzee first scrapes away the thin layer of soil from the entrance of one of the passages with its index, second finger, or thumb, and then picks a grass stalk, thin twig or piece of vine, which it pokes carefully down the hole. After a momentary pause it withdraws the tool, the end of which is coated with soldier and worker termites hanging on by their mandibles (provided the hole is "working"). These insects the chimpanzee then picks off with its lips and teeth. Termites that fall to the surface of the heap are picked up with the lips, between thumb and forefinger, or by a characteristic "mopping" movement with the back of the hand or wrist [p. 188].

Agonistic tool-using also occurs. Gorillas, orangutans, and gibbons among the apes, and howlers, red spider monkeys, and Cebus among the New World monkeys, break off branches or nuts and throw them down at intruders. Kortlandt and his colleagues (1965) have photographed wild chimpanzees which, surprised at the sudden appearance of an experimentally contrived mechanical leopard whose head moved from side to side, flailed it with sticks and branches. Baboons, macaques, and patas monkeys seem to be addicted to throwing or rolling stones or rocks down hills at intruders below.

Tool-using behavior in the wild, Hall (1963) believes, results from reinforcement of natural propensities (including emotional responses) in situations where the appropriate elements are immediately available and the response yields reward. Culture can also play a role in the learning of tool-using, since through observational learning a response can perpetuate within a group of animals. Lest the concept of culture prove embarrassing, consider a finding by Nissen (1944). He found at the Yerkes laboratories that captive chimpanzees born in Africa, when tested with "suitable" materials, built nests, whereas laboratory-born animals typically played with the materials instead (see Figure 3–5). Since the African-born chimpanzees were imported as infants long before they themselves built nests, they obviously had acquired the rudiments of nest-building through observation of their elders, as doubtless their parents before them had done. This transgenerational passage of information is what we mean by culture. It should be noted also that the nests were built in cages (the wrong place!) and with materials obviously different from those used by their mothers in Africa, indicating that the infants generalized greatly from the information they gained while observing their mothers.

Although it is tempting to speculate on the evolutionary significance of behavior observed in the field, it is clear that the origins of behavior in the wild are obscure indeed and sometimes beyond observation. For that reason, laboratory studies of primate tool-using may be more revealing for the solution of certain problems.

A basic difference between restricted laboratory-reared and wild-born chimpanzees on a new stick-using test was reported by Menzel, Davenport, and Rogers (1970). Even though both groups of animals had lived together for several years, during which they played with many kinds of objects, the wild-born chimps at six to eight years of age far surpassed their restricted-reared (for the first 2 years) companions in learning how to roll in bananas with a stick. From their accompanying observations, Menzel et al. were able to attribute the superior performance to adaptability, i.e., a "predisposition to continously expand upon and refine whatever spatial skills and object skills are ... available in the repertoire [1970, p. 282]."

Menzel (1972) has observed the spontaneous invention of ladders in a group of young chimpanzees. He studied the behavior of eight wild-born chimpanzees in a 1-acre field cage. During the first few years, the animals acquired much information about the physical and reactive properties of twigs, sticks, and trees through play. They learned about the hardness, frangibility, and weight of the objects, and they learned that they did not fly, jump, or bite. Yet for many months the chimpanzee did not use sticks or branches to climb when they were already in an appropriate position. The first stage in the development of ladders is the intrinsically motivated *standing up and vaulting*. Here a pole is first stood on end in a vertical position. Then the chimpanzee hurls itself upward or climbs the pole rapidly before it topples. The animal does this for the sheer pleasure it derives from the game. The second stage is an extension of the first, and involves *extrinsically motivated pole climbing*. The activity itself is not the reward; instead, pole climbing is used to get to a particular location. Menzel discovered this behavior when he found that during the night all his chimps had climbed into the observation booth that jutted into the field cage. In the last stage the animals *combined pole-ladders with other vertical extensions.* An elevated runway located near some trees (that had been wired to prevent their being climbed) had served as an intermediate staging area, for the chimps had hauled the pole onto the runway and had leaned the pole against the nearby tree, successfully bridging the wires. From Menzel's observations, we gain the clear impression that although familiarity with the objects is an essential component of complex tool-using, there is no automatic consequence that follows from that familiarity. It is indeed intelligence that transforms a plaything into a means to an end. Simple reinforcement, whether it be physical or social, is inadequate to account for the enormous changes that result in behavior potential when the animals perceive the environment in new ways.

OVERVIEW

The material discussed in the present chapter does not exhaust the work that has been done in the area of complex processes. Many other problems have been employed in the study of cognition, reason, and judgment, and excellent treatments of these topics can be found in the writings of Maier and Schneirla (1935), Nissen (1951b), and Rumbaugh (1970). The works of these authors and the volumes on primate behavior edited by Schrier, Harlow, and Stollnitz (1965) are well worth consulting.

Restricting our interpretation of phylogenetic comparisons to the data of the present chapter, we can state a few general themes which run through the entire set of data. First, not every test which ostensibly measures intelligence will neatly arrange the species on a ladder. There are several important reasons for this, one of which is simply that evolution did not yield such a stratification of the animals by any scale. Instead, we see parallel evolution of several genera. The Old World monkeys, for example, have not been evolving any longer than those of the New World. Both groups form independent radiations from ancestral stock. The same phenomenon occurs at most phyla. On the psychological side, also, the concept of intelligence, none too clear when applied to the measurement of human abilities, is not so definite as we would like it to be when applied to lower animals. Human intelligence includes the operation of several factors or abilities: spatial, numerical, verbal, and so forth, each of which contributes only partially to the overall index. No unitary trait of intelligence has been successfully proposed. Similarly, no single trait will suffice for defining animal intelligence. Thus, ability to shift set is doubtless a component of intelligence; nevertheless, it is not the sole component, and a "pure" test of this ability will not arrange individuals or species in a descending order that will necessarily coincide with measures of other components of intelligence.

Another factor which enters to upset the psychologists' preconceived superiority of the higher animals is the restricted range of animals for which the test is optimally discriminative. Let us return to another analogy with mental measurement of humans to see this point more clearly. Arithmetic manipulations are undoubtedly components of intelligence, but a set of problems as simple as $2 + 2 = ?$ would not separate the bright from the dull, except at the lower levels of development. Errors on such items if committed by, say, high school students, would not reflect lack of intelligence. Perhaps some of the tests which purportedly measure animal intelligence do so only at restricted phyletic levels. Some tasks which fail to differentiate the primates from lower animals are precisely those which elicit frustration in these higher animals. The range and diversity of situations which provoke emotion are probably greater in these higher animals, and the lability of their emotions is greater. "Dogged persistence" in overcoming an obstacle is not a characteristic virtue of primates.

Another conclusion to be drawn from the data of this chapter is the continuity of the simpler and more complex processes, functions, and tasks. Psychologists who have devised tests to measure these functions tend to classify them in terms that are readily verbalized by humans. Thus, formal relations among the supposedly significant elements are presumably emphasized in these tests. As an illustration, the human concept of triangularity isolates the significant elements from the contextual through verbal cues. The more extensive the educational background of the highly sophisticated experimenter, the farther do his own perceptual processes deviate from those of the animal subject and the more difficult it is for the experimenter to appreciate the significance of supposedly irrelevant details. It may be that the perceptual processes of the uncivilized savage may be more similar to those of lower animals than to those of civilized, cultured persons. Triangularity in patterns is unchanged for the verbal human being, whether the stimuli are objects or patterns, large or small, or whether the goal is attached or separated from the stimuli. However, as we have seen, factors such as these are not irrelevant for the nonverbal animal whose success or failure is certain to depend on them. Furthermore, the acquisition and skillful, facile manipulation of these simpler skills may permit a functional isolation and emphasis of the relevant aspects of the problem. These factors, then, must be taken into account in any adequate definition of animal intelligence.

REFERENCES

ABRAVANEL, E. The development of intersensory patterning. *Monographs of the Society for Research in Child Development*, 1968, **38** (Whole No. 118).

BERNSTEIN, I. S. The utilization of visual cues in dimension-abstracted oddity by primates. *Journal of Comparative and Physiological Psychology*, 1961, **54,** 243–247.

BIRCH, H. G. The relation of previous experience to insightful problem solving. *Journal of Comparative Psychology*, 1945, **38,** 367–383.

BLAKESLEE, P., & GUNTER, R. Cross-modal transfer of discrimination learning in Cebus monkeys. *Behaviour*, 1966, **26,** 76–90.

BRODGEN, W. J. Imitation of social facilitation in the social conditioning of forelimb-flexion in dogs. *American Journal of Psychology*, 1942, **55,** 77–83.

BRYANT, P. E. Comments on the design of developmental studies of cross-modal matching and cross-modal transfer. *Cortex*, 1968, **2,** 127–137.

BURTON, D., & ETTLINGER, G. Cross-modal transfer of training in monkeys. *Nature*, 1960, **186,** 1071–1072.

BUTLER, R. A. Investigative behavior. In A. M. Schrier, H. F. Harlow, & F. Stollnitz, (Eds.), *Behavior of nonhuman primates*. New York: Academic Press, 1965. Chap. 13, pp. 463–493.

CRAWFORD, M. P., & SPENCE, K. W. Observational learning of discrimination problems by chimpanzees. *Journal of Comparative Psychology*, 1939, **27,** 133–147.

DARBY, C. L., & RIOPELLE, A. J. Observational learning in the rhesus monkey. *Journal of Comparative and Physiological Psychology*, 1959, **52,** 94–98.

DAVENPORT, R. K., & ROGERS, C. M. Intermodal equivalence of stimuli in apes. *Science*, 1970, **168,** 279–280.

ETTLINGER, G. Cross-modal transfer of training in monkeys. *Behaviour*, 1960, **16,** 56–65.

FIDURA, F. G. Selective attention and complex discrimination learning in the Japanese quail *(Coturnix coturnix japonica)*. *Psychonomic Science*, 1969, **15,** 167–168.

FIELDS, P. E. The efficiency of the serial multiple discrimination apparatus and method with white rats. *Journal of Comparative and Physiological Psychology*, 1953, **45,** 69–76.

FISHER, E. M. Habits of the southern sea otter. *Journal of Mammalogy*, 1939, **20,** 21–36.

GARDNER, L. P., & NISSEN, H. W. Simple discrimination behavior of young chimpanzees: Comparisons with human aments and domestic animals. *Journal of Genetic Psychology*, 1948, **72,** 145–164.

GEBHARD, J. W., & MOWBRAY, G. H. On discriminating the rate of visual flicker and auditory flutter. *American Journal of Psychology*, 1959, **72,** 521–529.

GELLERMANN, L. W. Form discrimination in chimpanzees and two year old children: Form *per se*. *Journal of Genetic Psychology*, 1933, **42,** 3–27.

GLICKMAN, S. E., & SROGES, R. W. Curiosity in zoo animals. *Behaviour*, 1966, **26,** 151–188.

GOSSETTE, R. L. Comparisons of SDR performance of gibbons and three species of New World Monkeys on a spatial task. *Psychonomic Science*, 1970, **19,** 301–303.

HALL, K. R. L. Tool-using performances as indicators of behavioral adaptability. *Current Anthropology*, 1963, **4,** 479–494.

HARLOW, H. F. Performance of catarrhine monkeys on a series of discrimination reversal problems. *Journal of Comparative and Physiological Psychology*, 1950, **43,** 231–239.

HAYES, K. J., & HAYES, C. Imitation in a home-raised chimpanzee. *Journal of Comparative and Physiological Psychology*, 1952, **45,** 450–459.

HEIDLER, E. R. *Natural categories*. Paper presented at the annual meeting of the American Psychological Association, 1971.

HERBERT, M. J., & HARSH, C. M. Observational learning by cats. *Journal of Comparative and Physiological Psychology*, 1944, **37,** 81–95.

HOBHOUSE, L. T. *Mind in evolution*. New York: Macmillan, 1901.

JARVIK, M. E. Discrimination of colored food and food signs by primates. *Journal of Comparative and Physiological Psychology*, 1953, **46,** 390–392.

JOHN, E. R., CHESLER, P., BARTLETT, F., & VICTOR, I. Observation learning in cats. *Science*, 1968, **159,** 1489–1490.

KAWAMURA, S. The process of subculture propagation among Japanese macaques. In C. H. Southwick (Ed.), *Primate Social Behavior*. New York: Van Nostrand, 1963. Pp. 82–90.

KINNAMAN, A. J. Mental life of two Macacus Rhesus monkeys in captivity. *American Journal of Psychology*, 1902, **13,** 98–148.

KLÜVER, H. *Behavior mechanisms in monkeys*. Chicago: The University of Chicago Press, 1933.

KÖHLER, W. *The mentality of apes*. New York: Harcourt, Brace, 1925.

KOHTS, N. Récherches sur l'intelligence du chimpanzee par la methode de "choix d'apré model." *Journal du Psychologie Normale et Pathologique*, 1928, **41,** 62–74.

KONORSKI, J. A new method of physiological investigation of recent memory in animals. *Bulletin de l'Académie Polonaise des Sciences: Serie des Sciences Biologiques*, 1959, **7,** 115.

KORTLANDT, A. How do chimpanzees use weapons when fighting leopards? *Yearbook of the American Philosophical Society*, 1965. Pp. 327–332.

LASHLEY, K. S. The mechanism of vision. I. A method for rapid analysis of pattern vision in the rat. *Journal of Genetic Psychology*, 1930, **37,** 453–460.

LASHLEY, K. S. The mechanism of vision. IV. Preliminary studies of the rat's capacity for detail vision. *Journal of General Psychology*, 1938, **18,** 123–193.

LAWICK-GOODALL, J. VAN. *My friends the wild chimpanzees*. Washington: National Geographic Society, 1968, 1–204. (a)

LAWICK-GOODALL, J. VAN. Tool-using bird: The Egyptian vulture. *National Geographic Magazine*, 1968, **133,** 630–641 (b).

LEVINE, M., & HARLOW, H. F. Analysis of oddity learning by rhesus monkeys. *Journal of Comparative and Physiological Psychology*, 1959, **72,** 253–257.

LEVINSON, B. Oddity learning set and its relation to discrimination learning set. Unpublished doctoral dissertation, University of Wisconsin, 1958.

MAIER, N. R. F., & SCHNIERLA, T. C. *Principles of animal psychology*. New York: McGraw-Hill, 1935.

MCCLEARN, G. E., & HARLOW, H. F. The effect of spatial contiguity on discrimination learning by rhesus monkeys. *Journal of Comparative and Physiological Psychology*, 1954, **47,** 391–394.

MENZEL, E. W. Naturalistic and experimental research on primates. *Human Development*, 1967, **10,** 170–186.

MENZEL, E. W. Communication about the environment in a group of young chimpanzees. *Folia Primatologia*, 1971, **15,** 220–232.

MENZEL, E. W. Spontaneous invention of ladders in a group of young chimpanzees. *Folia Primatologia*, 1972, **17,** 87–106.

MENZEL, E. W., DAVENPORT, R. K., & ROGERS, C. M. The development of tool-using in wild-born and restriction-reared chimpanzees. *Folia Primatologia*, 1970, **12,** 273–283.

MICHAELS, K. M. Paper read at Midwestern Psychological Association, Chicago, May, 1955.

MILNER, A. D., & BRYANT, P. E. Cross-modal matching by young children. *Journal of Comparative and Physiological Psychology*. 1970, **71,** 453–458.

MORGAN, C. L. *Animal behaviour*. (2nd Ed.). New York: Charles Scribner's Sons, 1900.

MYERS, W. A. Observational learning in monkeys. *Journal of the Experimental Analysis of Behavior*, 1970, **14,** 225–235.

NISSEN, H. W. The ape colony in Florida. *Animal Kingdom*, 1944, **47**(6).

NISSEN, H. W. Analysis of a complex conditional reaction in monkeys. *Journal of Comparative and Physiological Psychology*, 1951, **44**, 9–16. (a)

NISSEN, H. W. Phylogenetic comparisons. In S. S. Stevens (Ed.), *Handbook of experimental psychology*. New York: Wiley, 1951. Pp. 347–386. (b)

NISSEN, H. W., BLUM, J. S., & BLUM, N. A. Conditional matching behavior in chimpanzee: Implications for the comparative study of intelligence. *Journal of Comparative and Physiological Psychology*, 1949, **42**, 339–356.

NISSEN, H. W., & JENKINS, W. O. Reduction and rivalry of cues in the discrimination behavior of chimpanzees. *Journal of Comparative Psychology*, 1943, **35**, 85–95.

NISSEN, H. W., & MCCULLOCH, T. L. Equated and non-equated stimulus situations in discrimination learning by chimpanzees. 1. Comparisons with unlimited responses. *Journal of Comparative Psychology*, 1937, **23**, 165–189.

PASTORE, N. Discrimination learning in the canary. *Journal of Comparative and Physiological Psychology*, 1954, **47**, 389–390.

POWELL, R. W. Observational learning versus shaping: A replication. *Psychonomic Science*, 1968, **10**, 263–264.

PRESLEY, W. J., & RIOPELLE, A. J. Observational avoidance behavior in monkeys. *Journal of Genetic Psychology*, 1959, **95**, 251–254.

RIOPELLE, A. J., & COPELAN, E. L. Discrimination reversal to a sign. *Journal of Experimental Psychology*, 1954, **48**, 143–145.

ROBINSON, E. W. A preliminary experiment on abstraction in a monkey. *Journal of Comparative Psychology*, 1933, **16**, 231–236.

ROBINSON, J. S. The sameness-difference discrimination problem in chimpanzees. *Journal of Comparative and Physiological Psychology*, 1955, **48**, 195–197.

ROBINSON, J. S. The conceptual basis of the chimpanzee's performance on the sameness-difference discrimination problem. *Journal of Comparative and Physiological Psychology*, 1960, **53**, 368–370.

ROMANES, G. J. *Animal intelligence*. New York: D. Appleton, 1888.

RUMBAUGH, D. M. Learning skills of anthropoids. In L. A. Rosenblum (Ed.), *Primate behavior; developments in field and laboratory research*. New York: Academic Press, 1970. Pp. 1–70.

SCHRIER, A. M., HARLOW, H. F., & STOLLNITZ, F. *Behavior of nonhuman primates: Modern research trends*. Vols. 1 & 2. New York: Academic Press, 1965.

SHUCK, J. R., POLIDORA, V. J., MCCONNELL, D. G., & MEYER, D. R. Response location as a factor in primate pattern discrimination. *Journal of Comparative and Physiological Psychology*, 1961, **54**, 543–545.

SMITH, K. U. Visual discrimination in the cat. III. The relative effect of paired and unpaired stimuli in the discriminative behavior of the cat. *Journal of Genetic Psychology*, 1936, **48**, 29–57.

STEPIEN, L. S., & CORDEAU, J. P. Memory in monkeys for compound stimuli. *American Journal of Psychology*, 1960, **73**, 388–395.

STOLLNITZ, F. Can monkeys attend selectively to dimensions of color? *Psychonomic Science*, 1969, **17**, 50. (Abstract)

STRONG, P. N., JR., DRASH, P., & HEDGES, N. Solution of dimension-abstracted oddity as a function of species, experience, and intelligence. *Psychonomic Science*, 1968, **11**, 337–338.

SZIRTES, J. Evoked potentials to meaningful self-produced sounds in rhesus monkeys. Paper read at the International Primatological Society meeting, Zurich, Switzerland, August, 1970.

THORNDIKE, E. L. Animal intelligence: An experimental study of the associative processes in animals. *Psychological Review Monograph Suppl.*, 1898, **2**(4, Whole No. 8).

WARD, J. P., YEHLE, A. L., & DOERFLEIN, R. S. Cross-modal transfer of a specific discrimination in the bushbaby *(Galago senegalensis)*. *Journal of Comparative and Physiological Psychology*, 1970, **73**, 74–77.

WARDEN, C. J., & JACKSON, T. A. Imitative behavior in the rhesus monkey. *Journal of Genetic Psychology*, 1935, **46**, 103–125.

WARREN, J. M. Perceptual dominance in discrimination learning by monkeys. *Journal of Comparative and Physiological Psychology*, 1954, **47**, 290–292.

WEGENER, J. G. Cross-modal transfer in monkeys. *Journal of Comparative and Physiological Psychology*, 1965, **59**, 450–452.

WICKENS, D. D., & WICKENS, C. D. Some factors related to pseudoconditioning. *Journal of Experimental Psychology*, 1942, **31**, 518–526.

WODINSKY, J., VARLEY, M. A., & BITTERMAN, M. E. Situational determinants of the relative difficulty of simultaneous and successive discrimination. *Journal of Comparative and Physiological Psychology*, 1954, **47**, 337–340.

PART FIVE

EVOLUTION
OF BEHAVIOR

It was stated in Chapter 1 that basic description of behavioral patterns can be followed by analyses of the ontogeny of behavior, the mechanisms controlling behavior, the adaptive significance of behavior, and the evolutionary history of behavior. Historically, psychologists have devoted most of their efforts to studying ontogeny and mechanisms. These approaches are illustrated repeatedly in every chapter of this book. Yet, psychologists are showing increased appreciation of the importance of studying evolutionary history and adaptive significance. Knowledge of evolution and adaptation can add depth to our understanding of behavior and promote a more comprehensive appreciation of its biological importance.

Study of the evolutionary aspects of behavior may provide a considerable service to comparative psychology. It sometimes is hard for scientist and student alike to grasp the definition, direction, and scope of comparative psychology. There sometimes appears to be no unifying theory in comparative psychology. The reasons for this are quite apparent. The task of trying to study everything every species does is too great for the small circle of comparative psychologists. Therefore, efforts appear fragmented. One investigator may provide a synthesis of differences in courtship patterns in different species of ducks, while another may provide insight into the neural mechanisms which enable a chimpanzee to solve delayed-response problems. But where is the total picture? How do we tie the many fragments of information together?

Where is there a broad conceptual framework that can enable us to interrelate the developments on different research frontiers? In biology this task has been largely accomplished by the modern synthetic theory of evolution. It is through understanding the principles underlying the evolution and adaptation of various species that biologists have been able to unify their discipline. Increasingly, comparative psychologists believe that evolutionary theory may possess equal potential for synthesis in their discipline. Is not behavior an important part of the biology of any species? Has not behavior been subjected to the same processes of evolution as have other aspects of organisms? Thus, the modern synthetic theory of evolution may enable us to get beyond fragmented experiments and to obtain an overview of behavior in comprehensible perspective.

In the one chapter in this final section, the evolution of behavior, a subject broached to some degree in all previous chapters, will be the primary topic. It is hoped that not only will the chapter serve to explicate some principles related to the evolution of behavior, but that some synthesis of material discussed in the other chapters can be achieved. Thus, the final chapter is designed not only to discuss evolution, but to restate and summarize some important points made in earlier chapters.

Chapter 15

Evolution and Behavior: A Reprise

Donald A. Dewsbury

This chapter is designed both to explicate some basic principles regarding evolution and behavior, and to relate some of the research discussed in the first fourteen chapters to those principles. The chapter begins with a discussion of the process of evolution. This is followed by discussions of the two major approaches toward relating behavior and evolution: evolution as history, and the adaptedness of behavior. In each discussion, a section dealing with methodology is followed by a review of literature regarding a variety of behavioral patterns as related to that approach toward evolution. This material is organized in a manner parallel to the organization of the book. The chapter concludes with a section dealing with three remaining evolution-related topics: reproductive isolating mechanisms, domestication, and behavior and systematics; and a discussion of man in comparative psychology.

EVOLUTION AS A PROCESS

Following the publication of the works of Darwin and others, the study of evolution entered a phase of much controversy. As the study of genetics was still limited and still separated from the study of evolution, no general synthesis could be attained. Finally, in this century, the modern synthetic theory of evolution has been developed in such a form that its major tenets now are accepted by the vast majority of biologists (e.g., Mayr, 1963; Simpson, 1958; Williams, 1966).

The fundamental principles of the modern synthetic theory of evolution are exquisitely simple. In any population there exist individuals bearing a variety of phenotypes and genotypes (see Chapter 6). There are both phenotypic variability (that in morphology and behavior) and genetic variability (that in genotype). Phenotypic variability comes about through the interaction of the genotype and the environment. Genotypic variability comes about through such random processes as mutation, recombination, and crossing over. Mutation is the primary source of new genetic material. It is natural selection which acts to shape systematic changes in the genetic structure of the population out of the random changes produced by mutation. Some individuals will be better able than others to survive in a particular environment and to produce viable, fertile offspring. This may be because they are better able to find food or avoid predators. It may be that they are better able to reproduce because they excel at finding members of the opposite sex and same species, or in providing better parental care. Natural selection acts upon phenotypes. Its effect is to alter the gene pool of the subsequent generations. Natural selection results in a relative increase in the frequency of genes which produce phenotypes of greater reproductive fitness and a relative decrease in the frequency of genes producing lesser reproductive fitness in a particular habitat. Natural selection is thus a process whereby some individuals are able to exert a disproportionate influence on the genetic characteristics of subsequent generations. Random processes create variability; natural selection shapes the result.

Gradual accumulation of small genetic changes can produce the substantial differences seen across different species. Such accumulation requires an extraordinarily large number of generations and usually is not perceptible in a single generation.

Individual Selection, Group Selection, and Altruism

Selective pressures act on individual phenotypes, but the result is to affect gene frequencies. One of the remaining sources of disagreement concerning evolutionary theory is the issue of individual versus group selection. Many species exhibit behavioral patterns which appear to facilitate the survival of their group at the expense of the individual. Wynne-Edwards (1962) proposed that selection operates at the group level in addition to the individual level. Thus, for example, if individuals in one group lower their reproductive rate in times of limited resources, survival of that group may be facilitated in comparison with that of a group which did not lower its rate. The limited resources may support the smaller population where they would not have supported a larger population, had the group continued to reproduce. From a large body of such evidence, Wynne-Edwards infers that natural selection can act on different groups just as it does on different individuals. This is an extremely important notion when one considers the evolution of social organization and of altruistic behavior.

The majority of biologists appear to reject the notion of group selection. Rather, it seems that selection almost always works on individuals as the primary focus. For example, Lack (1954) has marshaled convincing arguments in favor of the notion that animals have evolved reproductive rates that ensure the maximal number of surviving offspring. If a bird lays more eggs than is typical of its species, it may actually produce fewer, rather than more, viable offspring. This may be due to an inability to care for the larger number. It may be advantageous for an animal not to breed in a given season. Breeding entails expenditure of considerable resources and frequently an increased risk of predation. Most biologists believe that animals will cease breeding for a season only under conditions where this cessation increases the probability of successful breeding in a subsequent season. Thus, we again reach a point where the individual organism must leave a maximal number of viable, fertile offspring.

There are some special cases where "altruistic" behavior occurs, as when an animal appears to risk its life to save another. However, most of these cases can be explained in terms of selection for the individual genotype. The most striking example is that of kin selection. An individual may sacrifice itself if its action facilitates survival of several kin. As the individual and its kin share many genes, this behavior may have been selected because the individual's genes are best represented in the future through the kin. In many species of social insects, the majority of members of a colony do not reproduce. However, as they have highly similar genotypes, survival of the genotype is facilitated by their nonreproduction. Trivers (1971) has proposed a model whereby reciprocal or mutual altruism between two or more individuals can be selected for in other species. For an excellent discussion of these and related issues, the reader is referred to Williams (1966).

EVOLUTION AS HISTORY

One approach to the study of evolution and behavior involves consideration of evolution as history. In a sense, this is a rather static approach, as interest is concentrated on the results of evolution rather than on the processes which produce evolutionary change.

Methods

Studies of evolution as history can be divided into two broad types. In one, an attempt is made to trace the broad sweep of evolutionary history with comparisons across a wide range of diverse species. Alternatively, a small group of more closely related species may be selected for intensive study.

Many scientists have attempted to practice comparative psychology by working with a wide range of families, orders, classes, or even phyla. Indeed, this phyletic approach sometimes is mistakenly regarded as the only true comparative psychology. It reveals little about the genetic mechanisms or evolutionary processes underlying behavior, but can produce insight into general behavioral patterns and capacities associated with given physiological mechanisms and anatomical structures (J. A. King, 1963, 1970). Interpretation of observed behavioral differences must be conducted with much care. It must be remembered that one works with very different organisms which are adapted for life in very different habitats. An apparent difference can be observed between species merely because some seemingly trivial procedural detail produced difficulties for one species but not for another. Rarely is it possible either to equate motivational level, sensory demand, and so forth, across a wide range of species, or to conduct the parametric investigations required to bypass these problems (Bitterman, 1960). Although some very interesting generalizations may come from the broad comparative approach, great caution is required.

Many of the problems inherent in work with widely different taxa are minimized in work within more restricted taxonomic units. The history of the evolution of a pattern of behavior is more easily reconstructed within a genus or family than across orders. This method is particularly useful when a good sample of the species comprising the genus or family is available for study.

Analysis of behavioral evolution within restricted taxa has been a major approach used by the classical ethologists (see Chapter 2). The best examples come from studies of the social displays of birds, particularly those related to courtship and aggressive behavior. Ethologists propose that displays can evolve from behavioral patterns which they would classify as intention movements, displacement activities, redirection activities, and autonomic responses. Displays can become elaborated through (1) development of conspicuous morphological structures; (2) schematization of a movement (e.g., through exaggeration of certain components of the movement, changes in coordination of the movement, or changes in absolute and relative thresholds of the components); and (3) emancipation of a movement from its original context (Hinde & Tingergen, 1958; Chapter 2).

Central to this whole approach is the concept of homology. Homologous structures are those which are derived from a common ancestor. The wing of a bat, foreleg of a horse, and forearm of a primate are recognizable as homologous. The ethologists apply the concept of homology to animal behavior. Not all biologists agree that the concept is applicable in this way (Atz, 1970). The difficulties of application were discussed in Chapters 2 and 8. A major difficulty in interpreting similarities in behavior as homologous is caused by the remarkable similarity of structure and behavior that can be produced by similar selective pressures acting independently. It is easy to mistake the products of parallel and convergent evolution for homologues. The differences among these three are portrayed in Figure 15–1. An example of the problems caused by parallel and convergent evolution is found in the evolution of electric organs. These organs appear to have evolved independently in fish at least six different times (Dewsbury, 1965; Keynes, 1957). Unless one is familiar with a wide range of species and the full taxonomy of fishes, it would be easy to mistake these products of parallel and convergent evolution for homologues. Similar errors are even easier to make when dealing with behavior.

Mimicry is another potential source of confusion. An example appears in the interactions of toads and insects. Although many animals require a large number of trials to learn most tasks, toads learn not to eat honeybees in very few trials. Just a few stings are sufficient to inhibit feeding responses. Droneflies feed like honeybees, look like honeybees, and make buzzing sounds like honeybees. Toads that have been stung by honeybees also avoid striking at droneflies (Brower & Brower, 1962) even through droneflies are harmless. Evolution of honeybeelike characteristics by droneflies is an example of mimicry. Animals that are palatable and devoid of protective devices may evolve the characteristics of a species that has such protection. Thus they gain protection from predators which avoid both species. Palatable butterflies mimic others that are not palatable. These and other spectacular examples of mimicry are portrayed in an excellent film made by the Browers. An additional example appears in Figure 2–7. One must be careful not to consider similarities which are attributable to mimicry as homologous.

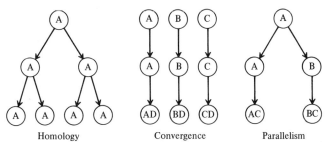

Homology   Convergence   Parallelism

Figure 15–1. A diagrammatic representation of homology, convergence, and parallelism. Each circle represents a species bearing the trait indicated by a capital letter. In *homology,* the trait is passed from the common ancestor to all derived species. In *convergence,* each ancestor contributes its homologous traits, but a new trait (D) arises in later species. This trait may obscure the homologous traits and make the three species bearing trait (D) superficially resemble each other. In *parallelism,* one species replaces the homologous trait (A) with the new trait (B) and both lines evolve under similar circumstances where trait C arises. Trait (C) may also obscure the homologous traits (A) and (B) by superficial resemblances. (From King and Nichols, 1960.)

Application of the concept of homology to behavior probably should be restricted to cases where one works within a highly restricted taxonomic unit, and with a fairly complete sample of the species which comprise that unit. In situations where it is applicable, the concept of homology can be of considerable use in understanding evolution and behavior.

Representative Examples

A variety of behavioral patterns has been studied in attempts to understand the historical evolution of behavior. Such studies have included both broad comparisons and comparisons within restricted taxonomic groups. Representative examples will be cited within an organization which parallels that of the first four parts of this book.

Patterns of Behavior   Examples of attempts to trace the evolutionary history of behavioral patterns have included studies of sleep, investigation, language, and social displays. The attempts of Allison & Van Twyver (1970) to reconstruct the evolution of sleep were discussed in Chapter 3. Fish and amphibians appear never to sleep, and reptiles have but the rudiments of sleep if they sleep at all. Interestingly, all birds and higher mammals that have been studied display both stages of sleep—slow wave and paradoxical (see Chapters 3 and 7). All therian mammalian species (marsupials and placentals) show both slow-wave and paradoxical sleep. The echidna is the only mammalian species to be studied that displays only slow-wave sleep. The echidna and platypus are the only living nontherian (egg-laying) species of mammals. The platypus has not been studied. Allison and Van Twyver suggest that slow-wave sleep must have been present in the first true mammals and therefore evolved in its present form about 180 million years ago. Paradoxical sleep probably appeared in an early therian ancestor of both marsupial and placental mammals. It is likely that paradoxical sleep evolved about 130 million years ago—or 50 million years after the evolution of slow-wave sleep. Also interesting is the proposal that birds and mammals appear to have evolved both stages of sleep independently, just as they independently evolved a four-chambered heart from the reptilian three-chambered form. A transitional avian species displaying just one form of sleep is yet to be found.

The results of a study of investigatory behavior were presented in Figure 3–7. It appears that mammals with more complex nervous systems investigate objects more readily than do older forms. Thus, reptiles showed the least investigative behavior of any group studied, while primates and carnivores showed the most. Edentates, Marsupials, Insectivores, and Rodents were intermediate.

Problems inherent in understanding the historical evolution of language were discussed in Chapter 5. It is likely that human language evolved from the apparently simpler communication systems of nonhuman species. The current wave of research on primate behavior appears to be producing considerable insight into the evolution of language.

Excellent examples of studies of the evolutionary history of behavior within restricted taxonomic groups were provided in the discussion of ritualization in Chapter 2. Thus, the various "inciting" movements of various species of ducks are seen as evolving from "intention" movements via a process of ritualization; the threat display of the Manchurian crane is seen not as a ritualized preening movement, but as a part of a continuous series of variations on unritualized displacement preening in related species. Homologous patterns in gulls are portrayed in Figure 2–8.

Origins of Behavior   Studies of the precise evolution of the manner in which the genome and the environment interact in the development of behavior have been rare. In general, however, the development of behavior in more recent species appears less channelized and more susceptible to environmental influences than that of older forms. Thus, it seems likely that the environment plays a greater role in shaping specific behavioral patterns in complex vertebrates than in most invertebrate species. Similar trends may be evident within more restricted groupings. For example, it has been proposed that the development of hunting is more dependent on learning in placental than in marsupial mammals (Chapter 13).

Correlates of Behavior   Questions of evolutionary history frequently have been studied in regard to the physiological and sensory-perceptual correlates of behavior. These were particularly evident in Chapter 8. The first question posed was that of the very evolutionary origin of nervous systems themselves. The proposal of Horridge that nervous systems may have evolved from epithelium tissue was described (Figure 8–1). Evolutionary trends in neural development show a change from primitive and diffuse neural nets to complex clumps of nerves near the anterior end of the body. The evolution of the vertebrate forebrain was reviewed (Figures 8–3 and 8–4), as were the difficulties in applying the concept of homology to the nervous system. As we move from lower to higher vertebrates, there is a progressive increase in brain size (Figures 8–6, 8–7, and 8–8). Within the probable line of evolution from insectivores to primates, the neocortex and hippocampus have shown particularly marked development. The neocortex of man is the equivalent of 150 times as large, and the chimpanzee 60 times as large, as the basal insectivore brain. The probable evolution of primary visual cortex and its adjacent association area from a visual belt was portrayed in Figure 8–11. One task that remains is better to determine the behavioral correlates of these impressive data regarding the evolution of the nervous system. Beach (1947) has proposed, for example, that sexual behavior may be more dependent upon the cortex and less directly dependent on hormones in complex primates than in relatively simpler vertebrates, such as fish and reptiles (see also Aronson, 1959).

Beach (1958) reviewed literature on behavioral endocrinology in a wide range of species. He noted that there are only minor species differences in the pituitary and gonadal hormones characteristic of various vertebrate classes, but rather large differences in the behavioral end-products which they control. Beach concluded that the data tend to support the conclusion of Medewar (1953) that "'endocrine evolution' is not an evolution of hormones but an evolution of the uses to which they are put; an evolution not, to put it crudely, of chemical formulae but of reactivities, reaction patterns, and tissue competences [p. 334]." Thus, while evolution has produced substantial species differences in reproductive cycles and behavior, the hormones involved are substantially the same from species to species.

Considerations of evolutionary history were emphasized in the review of sensory systems in Chapter 10. For example, the probable evolution of complex eyes from simple eyespots was portrayed. Eyespot cells normally are at the surface of the body and contain transparent protoplasm. Increasing density of protoplasm is seen as creating a simple lens. Once the separation of lens and retina occurred, further evolutionary stages appear to involve increasing size and differentiation. The balance organ which functioned in proprioception in early vertebrates seems to have evolved into vertebrate hearing organs. Chemical sensitivity is possessed by the simplest forms of life. In the course of evolution, the portions of the body sensitive to many forms of chemical stimulation appear to become more restricted and clearly defined.

One interesting attempt to reconstruct evolutionary changes in sensory systems was conducted by Heffner, Ravizza, and Masterton (1969). They studied hearing in a series of contemporary species ranging from marsupial to man. They found an increase in sensitivity to tones, particularly of low frequency, as they moved from the opossums through hedgehogs, tree shrews, bush babies, and man. It was proposed that "man's ancestral lineage must have been exposed to strong and persistent selective pressure for low-frequency sensitivity [Heffner et al., 1969, p. 21]".

Similar studies have been conducted in relation to perception. For example, apes appear better than monkeys in perceptual problem-solving tasks that require analysis of a spatial pattern (Chapter 11).

Modification of Behavior   Substantial evidence was marshalled in Chapter 12 to support the view that, like vertebrates, invertebrates are able to learn. However, an additional important point emerged: Although widely divergent species all may learn, they need not all learn in precisely the same way. Thus, the "laws of learning" which emerge from invertebrate studies may be quite different from those which emerge from studies of vertebrates. It should not be surprising that a complex primate learns differently from an animal comprised of very few cells. However, repeated attempts have been made to force principles applicable within one taxonomic level onto another level. Very often this results in unproductive confusion. The possibility that different principles may be applicable at different taxonomic levels is a point repeatedly and eloquently made by the late T. C. Schneirla (e.g., Schneirla, 1949; 1959).

The dangers and difficulties inherent in work on the historical evolution of behavior across a wide range of species became most evident in the discussion of attempts to understand the evolution of learning in vertebrates (Chapter 13). It is very difficult to provide testing conditions that do not bias the situation for or against one group of well-differentiated species. Most comparative psychologists are no longer optimistic about the possibility of developing an understanding of the "evolution of intelligence." Perhaps the main reason the problems in this kind of research were most evident in work on the evolution of learning is that it is there that the questions and proposed schemata have been most clearly formulated. It is more difficult to disprove a hypothesis that is stated vaguely and imprecisely. Nevertheless, it seems likely that future researchers will concentrate on better-defined learning abilities and on more closely related groups of species than has traditionally been the case in the study of the evolution of learning. This approach appears to hold more promise of generating meaningful principles.

Similar problems were encountered in the related chapter on complex processes (Chapter 14). It is clear that primates have been shown to learn problems that other species seem unable to master. For example, while some nonprimate species can learn two-cue problems, few have been shown to solve three-cue and four-cue problems. Whether this is the result of a general learning ability, a specific learning ability, a sensory capacity, a predisposition to investigate, or some other characteristic remains to be determined. Even primates have problems with some tasks, such as those which require dogged persistence.

General Approaches   Approaches which focus on general patterns of evolution are more difficult than those which focus on a single behavioral pattern. The ethology of a variety of species must be fully understood. Perhaps the best example of this approach lies in the work of Dilger (1960, 1962) on lovebirds of the genus *Agapornis*. This genus is comprised of nine forms which may be classified along a continuum as relatively primitive or highly evolved. The more primitive forms are solitary nesters and are sexually dichromatic (with differential coloration of the sexes). The more highly evolved forms are colonial nesters and lack sexual dichromatism. Because he knew the probable course of evolution and had access to almost all forms within the genus, Dilger was able to trace the evolution of many behavioral patterns in great detail. The development of highly ritualized displays from precursors with little signal function was apparent. One such interesting display that has undergone evolutionary change is "squeak-twittering." The females of primitive forms occasionally thwart the male by retreating to the nest cavity. At such times, the male utters a series of high-pitched vocalizations which are variable in pitch and tone purity, with no recognizable rhythm. In more highly evolved forms, the sound is rhythmic, more pure in tone, and less variable in pitch. The male displays squeak-twittering even when the female is present and not thwarting him. Thus, this display has become more ritualized and its functional context has undergone change.

Agonistic behavior in the more primitive species is associated with elaborate threat and appeasement displays, but there is little inhibition of actual fighting if the interaction goes that far. The results might be disastrous. In the more highly evolved species, there is little ritualization associated with threat. However, fighting itself is highly ritualized. This has the advantage of minimizing damage to the combatants—an obvious benefit in colonial nesters. This information also helps make the point that "display extinction must be as normal as display evolution [Dilger, 1960, p. 682]."

These are just a few examples of the kind of information that Dilger was able to obtain through comprehensive study of a variety of behavioral patterns in all available forms within a quite restricted taxonomic group. The value of this approach should be apparent.

Conclusions Work on evolutionary history is very difficult. Species critical to a true evolutionary continuum frequently are extinct. The extant species of an older phylogenetic status may not be representative of the stem species. Many have evolved their own way in the course of millions of years. Behavioral tasks are hard to equate or control. Nevertheless, if the behavioral pattern under study is clearly defined and the group of species intelligently selected, some understanding of evolutionary histories frequently is possible. These questions are so important to the understanding of behavior that such work must be continued.

THE ADAPTEDNESS OF BEHAVIOR

The adaptedness of behavior has been stressed repeatedly throughout this book. Many behavioral patterns discussed in Chapter 3 were related to their adaptive functions. In Chapter 4, behavioral patterns were defined as segments of behavior having particular adaptive functions. The importance of teleonomic considerations was noted in Chapter 1. The life style of an organism (i.e., its social organization, feeding habits, reproductive patterns, defense against predators, and so forth) is adapted to a particular niche. As was pointed out in Chapter 6, there is no single, most adapted pattern, but rather, a particular pattern that may be maximally effective in a particular environment.

Understanding adaptive significance is important in gaining a comprehensive understanding of behavior. Often, knowledge of the mode of adaptation of an organism can be a great aid in understanding its behavior in the laboratory.

Methods

How are we to go about studying the adaptiveness of behavior? What kinds of things can we hope to find? Behavior is adaptive in that it both serves an immediate function and has long-term survival value. The distinction between the two ends of this continuum was made in Chapter 2. Also made was a distinction between experimentation and adaptive correlation as methods of studying the adaptiveness of behavior.

Experiments furnish the most conclusive evidence of the survival value of a behavioral pattern. Such experiments have been rare in classical ethology, and almost nonexistent in classical comparative psychology. The ethological experiments of de Ruiter on countershading in caterpillar, of Blest on eyelike markings in moths, and of Tinbergen on shell removal in gulls, all cited in Chapter 2, are excellent examples of this approach. It is to be hoped that such experimentation will increase in the future.

In the absence of experimentation, one frequently is left with the method of adaptive correlation as a way of understanding how behavior is adapted. The best one can hope for with this method are general "best fit" relationships between the behavior of a variety of species and other factors. Precise, statistically supported conclusions, such as those which characterize many other endeavors in the experimentally oriented areas of psychology, are impossible here. One can produce reasonable relationships between variations in behavior and variations in other factors. Resultant correlations can be tested by studying additional, previously unstudied species. One should be able to predict the behavior of the unstudied species if the correlations are valid. However, adaptive correlations must be treated as what they are—somewhat speculative attempts to relate behavior to selective pressures. Such data are not the results of precise, controlled laboratory experiments and cannot be evaluated as such. The questions they are designed to answer are of such importance that some tolerance of ambiguity may be appropriate.

As with the study of evolution as history, comparative studies of adaptive significance can be made at either the broad phyletic level or the more restricted species level (J. A. King, 1963, 1970). For example, the sleep patterns, copulatory patterns, and maternal behavior patterns of a wide variety of mammals have been studied in relation to such factors as habitat, food, and predation pressure. Such comparative studies can be very valuable in understanding adaptive significance. However, the same difficulties of equating testing conditions and interpreting observations arise that were discussed in relation to the application of this method in the study of evolution as history.

Though it produces a more limited breadth of understanding, use of the comparative method within restricted taxonomic units can produce a great depth of understanding. In this way, the principles which act repeatedly in shaping the evolution of behavior can be elaborated and applied to other groups. The method of adaptive correlation is particularly applicable where, within a restricted taxonomic unit, there has been great radiation into a variety of ecological adaptations. As with any correlational method, this one must work with variability, so differences in behavior must be found before it can be used.

A third level of comparative analysis, the genetic level, also may produce information valuable in understanding the adaptedness of behavior. At this level, individuals of the same species, but of differing genotypes, are the subjects of study. An example of the application of information from such studies to the problem of adaptation was provided by Bruell (1967). He proposed that the pattern of inheritance in a series of genetic crosses will be intermediate if the pattern under study either has not been subjected to selection or is most adaptive at intermediate levels. Where there is a benefit to more extreme values, a tendency toward directional dominance should be evident in the F_1 crosses.

Representative Examples

A variety of behavioral patterns which have been studied in relation to adaptation will be considered with an organization which again parallels the organization of the Parts of this book.

Patterns of Behavior   Much attention has been given to the study of the adaptive significance of variations in patterns of sleep, investigatory behavior, and reproductive behavior. The proposals of Allison and Van Twyver regarding the functional significance of sleep patterns were summarized in Table 3–1. "Good sleepers" are species which either are predators or are prey but have a safe sleeping place. "Poor sleepers" tend to be species which are subject to predation throughout the day.

The importance of knowing the mode of adaptation of a species in its natural habitat for understanding its pattern of investigatory behavior in the laboratory was underscored by Glickman and Sroges (1966). Small myomorph rodents were less bold in approaching novel objects than were the larger hystricomorphs, which are less susceptible to predation. Those species of primates adapted to a greater variety of habitats explored more than did leaf-eating, tree-dwelling colobus monkeys. The considerable visual exploration in the latter appears adapted for arboreal life. Carnivores made vigorous approaches. These differences can be understood only in relation to the adaptations of each group of species for life in their natural habitat.

The study of reproductive behavior also is replete with examples of adaptive correlations. Work with birds has been particularly enlightening (see Chapter 2). For example, Cullen found that the breeding behavior of cliff-dwelling kittiwakes could be differentiated from that of ground-nesting gulls with respect to thirty-two characteristics, each apparently associated with the cliff location. Similar adaptations were found in gannets, which also are cliff dwellers although not closely related to kittiwakes. Special characteristics of breeding behavior in black-billed gulls were related to their habit of breeding on river-beds which are subject to floating.

In what is perhaps the most definitive experimental study of the adaptive significance of a behavioral pattern, Tinbergen demonstrated that the black-headed gull pattern of removing eggshells from the nest reduced predation on the young, apparently by removing the obvious bright stimulus that can be seen by predators. Those nests with remaining eggshells were shown to be more susceptible. Such behavior obviously is related to survival of the genes.

An important prerequisite to the study of evolutionary aspects of behavior became evident in attempts to elaborate adaptive correlates of patterns of copulatory behavior. Copulatory patterns provide excellent material for analysis because they are highly stereotyped within species but quite varied across species. The problem lay in the lack of an adequate taxonomy of behavior or method of classifying the patterns observed. Until a viable classification system is developed, descriptions of behavior tend to be unsystematic and somewhat imprecise. Such a system for classifying copulatory patterns has been proposed by Dewsbury (1972) and is summarized in Figure 15–2. According to this scheme, a pattern of copulatory behavior may be defined in terms of four attributes. Thus, there are 2^4, or 16, possible patterns. Some species, including dogs and short-tailed shrews, display a lock (i.e., a mechanical tie between the vagina and penis which holds the animals together during copulation). (See Table 3–2). Some species, such as laboratory rats and rabbits, cease thrusting upon gaining vaginal penetration, whereas others, such as rhesus macaques, continue thrusting intravaginally. Some species, such as cats, ejaculate on a single vaginal insertion; others, such as laboratory rats, require multiple intromissions before ejaculation is attained. Finally, some species, such as American bison, appear to terminate copulation after a single ejaculation, and others, such as rats and cats, continue for several ejaculations.

Hediger (1965) compared the copulatory behavior of carnivores and ungulates. Most ungulates, such as antelopes, are prey species which live in herds and are constantly exposed to predation. Carnivores are predators and are themselves less susceptible to predation. Hediger cites evidence to suggest that slow and prolonged copulatory patterns can occur in carnivores, but that very short copulations, perhaps with ejaculation on a single insertion and with no lock, may characterize ungulates. Hediger attempted to relate

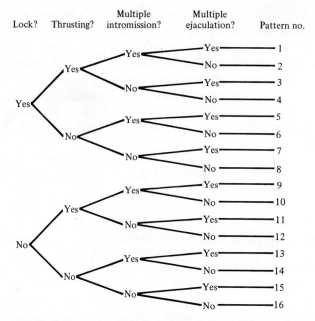

Lock?	Thrusting?	Multiple intromission?	Multiple ejaculation?	Pattern no.

Figure 15–2. A classification scheme for patterns of copulatory behavior in male mammals. See text for explanation. (From Dewsbury, 1972, p.3)

these behavioral patterns to additional characteristics of these species. He contrasted the behavior of carnivores, such as bears and lions, in which copulation may last a mattter of hours, sleep is long and deep, drinking is slow, a nest is built for parturition, and the development of young is extremely slow, with the behavior of ungulates, such as antelopes, in which copulation is quite rapid, sleep is minimal, drinking entails a quick filling of a subdivided stomach, there is no nest whatever, and the young are ambulatory within 30 minutes of birth.

An attempt to find similar correlations within the muroid rodents is being made in my own laboratory, where twenty species have been observed (e.g., Dewsbury, 1971). Several species, including grasshopper mice *(Onychomys torridus)*, golden mice *(Ochrotomys nuttalli)*, and wood rats *(Neotoma albigula)*, have locks. Other species may require single or multiple intromissions and show or lack intravaginal thrusting. Most attain multiple ejaculations. The challenge lies in attempting to relate these behavioral patterns to other characteristics within this restricted taxonomic group. At the least, these patterns may be effective reproductive isolating mechanisms in that they are likely to have differential effects in inducing neuroendocrine reflexes in the female. The manner in which apparently small variations in the copulatory pattern of the male can affect pregnancy in the female was discussed in Chapter 9.

Copulatory patterns appear critical for the initiation of neuroendocrine reflexes and sperm transport, both of which may be essential for successful reproduction in some species.

A great diversity of behavioral and morphological adaptations were discussed in Chapter 3. Bipedalism in species such as man and kangaroo rats was related to leaving the forelimbs free for purposes other than locomotion. Fossorial mammals show a variety of morphological and behavioral adaptations, as do those mammals with adaptations for aquatic life and for flight. Photoperiod appears to have been seized upon as a reliable cue for seasonal cycles in a variety of species because other possible indicants of seasonal change (e.g., temperature, rainfall, and so forth) can be so variable. A great array of behavioral patterns help mammals achieve thermoregulation appropriate for the species and habitat. The adaptive significance of hoarding (for assuring a food supply), exploration (for locating refuge spots in times of danger), and play (for permitting young animals to practice movements and learn about their environments) all received consideration. Feeding patterns were related to the type of food (animal or vegetable material). In herbivores, eating patterns can be related to the distribution of food and the pressure from predators. In carnivores, hunting patterns are adapted to the size, speed, and density of the prey. Each of these adaptive characteristics applies to a variety of species and was discussed in Chapter 3.

Much attention has been given the determinants of social organization (e.g., Ito, 1970). Some of these determinants were discussed in Chapter 4. In herd mammals, such as ungulates, food is plentiful and therefore dominance hierarchies and elaborate care-dependency relationships are rare. Among carnivores, which depend upon a more scattered food supply, learning is more important to patterns of food getting. Thus, prolonged periods of dependency are common. Dominance is the rule rather than the exception. Primates face even more complex problems and tend to develop more complex patterns of social organization.

Fisler (1969) listed eleven factors influencing social organization: basic morphology, level of aggressive tendency, level of site attachment, habitat occupied, surrounding mammalian populations, availability of den, nest, and refuge sites, availability and kinds of food, reproductive requirements, differential niche utilization by the sexes, population density, and climate.

Crook (1970) has integrated much information relating to the determinants of social organization. He stresses the importance of a social ethology in which teleonomic questions are studied with respect to populations of animals. In effect, this is a plea for the branching off of an animal sociology to go with the animal psychology as practiced by many classical ethologists and comparative psychologists. Crook proposes that among primates, populations consisting of one-male groups or "harems," along with peripheral males and all-male groups, tend to occur in areas where food supply is unstable and predation is low. Multimale troops are common where both predation and stable food supply abound. It is argued that where food is at a premium, reduction of the group to a single male leaves a maximum proportion of the available resources for the females which are frequently pregnant or lactating. Considerable data from ungulates and primates, especially baboons, appear to support these generalizations.

The value of territoriality was discussed in Chapter 4 as a function of the habitat of the species. Territoriality provides an effective basis for social organization only where boundaries can be effectively patrolled. Thus, territories generally are found among species requiring small living spaces, living in open rather than wooded areas, and having a diurnal activity pattern. The lack of generality of territory should be a warning against overgeneralizing on the basis of a few species.

In Chapter 4, it was proposed that agonistic behavior is most likely to develop from defensive fighting. Agonistic behavior tends to evolve toward harmless forms which may serve any of a variety of functions. Usually sufficient restraint patterns are developed so that destructive violence involving serious injury or death is rare in naturally occurring, stable populations.

The adaptive significance of patterns of animal communication was discussed in Chapter 5. Signals can serve any of a variety of functions in the lives of animals; each signal appears adapted for the function it serves. Signals which transmit over long distances generally are visual, auditory, or both, but contain little redundancy. Signals used when animals are in close proximity frequently involve the tactile or olfactory modalities, and are likely to be composite signals with considerable redundancy (Marler, 1965). The relationship between form and function in bird vocalizations was illustrated in Figure 2–6. The ease of localization of the signal source is related to various properties of the signal. These properties in turn appear adapted to the function of the signal and to the need for camouflage.

Origins of Behavior   Genetic factors obviously are an important determinant of adaptive behavior. Many adaptive behavioral patterns are strongly determined by the genes. These genes have been favored in the course of natural selection, probably because they play a role in the development of adaptive behavior. As cited above, Bruell (1967) has proposed that traits that have been subjected to selection pressure tend to show unidirectional dominance when studied by means of genetic analysis such as is used with inbred strains. The direction of the dominance is believed to be an indicator of the optimum value for the characteristic under study. In mice, wheel running and exploration in the open field (see Chapter 3) tend to show directional dominance, whereas alcohol preference shows intermediate inheritance. Thus, high levels of running and exploration may be related to survival in mice, whereas alcohol preference probably has not undergone substantial selection.

That the most active mice are not always the best fit to survive was demonstrated by Glickman (1971). Mice that explored the most in a laboratory test of exploratory behavior were the ones most likely to be eaten when groups of mice were caged with a barred owl.

Another trait that has been shown to display directional dominance is brain weight. It will be recalled from Chapter 7 that rats reared in complex environments tend to have greater cortical weights, different enzyme ratios related to neurotransmission, and altered neuroanatomical patterns when compared with rats reared in isolation. Henderson (1970) studied brain weights in 544 mice, including inbred animals, F_1 crosses from inbred animals, and F_2 four-way crosses. His results are portrayed in Figure 15–3. First, it is apparent that the F_1 and F_2 progeny had larger brains than the parental animals. Thus, there appears to be a directional dominance for brain size. In addition, environmental enrichment produced increases in brain size in both the F_1 and F_2 groups, but not in the inbred parents. Thus, there is directional dominance for a response of brain weight increase to increases in environmental complexity. These data and the hypothesis described above suggest that there may be a selective advantage not only to increased brain weight, but to the mouse's ability to respond to increased environmental complexity with an increase in brain weight. This study is an excellent example of the importance of considering both genetic and experiential variables when either is under study. Either variable, studied alone, can yield a distorted picture of behavioral development (Henderson, 1968; Chapter 6).

In general, developmental rates of different behavioral patterns in different species appear adapted to the ecological adaptations of the species. For exam-

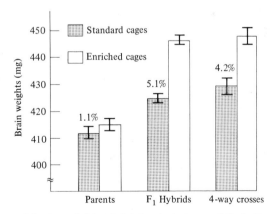

Figure 15–3. Averaged brain weights of 6 inbred strains and their F_1 and F_2 hybrid progeny reared in either standard cages or enriched environments. Small bars indicate standard errors of each mean. (From N. D. Henderson, *Science*, 1970, **169**, 776–778. Copyright 1970 by the American Association for the Advancement of Science.)

ple, the young of most plains-dwelling ungulates are highly precocial and ready to flee from danger with the herd. Many carnivores, which have stable home sites, show a much longer period of dependency (Chapter 4). In general, developmental rates appear to have evolved so that responses critical to the survival of the young are ready at the appropriate age.

A behavioral pattern may appear in one functional context in the neonate, disappear in development, and reappear at a later time and in a different functional context. The lordosis pattern of guinea pigs, discussed in Chapter 9, provides such an example. The posture is adopted by neonatal males and females in response to stimulation and appears functional in permitting the mother to stimulate urination and defecation by licking the pups. This pattern disappears in development. Later, it reappears in females under hormonal regulation as a part of the mating pattern.

The adaptive function of the high levels of paradoxical sleep characteristic of neonates was discussed in Chapter 7. It is likely that paradoxical sleep plays a role in facilitating the rate of development of the nervous systems of young animals.

Correlates of Behavior A variety of instances of adaptive correlation between the demands for appropriate behavior and characteristics of the nervous system were described in Chapter 8. It was pointed out that complex brains are a necessity where organisms are complex and their bodies are in need of elaborate regulation and control. The reduction in size of the olfactory portion of the brain in men and apes, described in the work of Stephan and Andy, was seen as correlated with the reduced olfactory sensitivity of these species. This in turn appears correlated with their particular mode of adaptation. The parallel elaboration of neocortex from insectivores to man appears correlated with a mode of adaptation in which behavioral plasticity assumes greater importance. Welker and his associates found a disproportionately large representation of somatic cortex related to the hands in raccoons and the snouts in coatimundis. These modifications are related to relatively increased use of these structures in these species. Buxton and Goodman found analogous differences in the motor systems of raccoons and dogs—also related to behavioral adaptations. Geschwind and Levitsky found increases in those unilateral structures in man that were related to language function. Thus, a mapping of the functions of the brain can produce considerable insight into the behavioral adaptations of the species under study.

One of the important functions of hormones is that of regulating the timing of behavior. For example, many species breed seasonally. Often this ensures that critical stages of the reproductive process (such as birth) take place at a time of the year when resources are maximally able to support development. Endocrine changes controlled by recurrent environmental events, such as changes in photoperiod, may regulate the timing of behavior. Both male and female must become reproductively active at the appropriate time for reproduction to be successful. The process frequently depends on mutual interaction of the male and the female. In ring doves, for example, the male and the female engage in a series of interactions which produce dramatic alterations in their behavior and endocrine systems (Lehrman, 1965). Both auditory signals, such as cooing, and visual signals, such as bowing, when emitted in the male, produce substantial endocrine changes in the female. These in turn stimulate alterations of behavior and growth in the oviduct. Such events feed back to alter the behavior and physiology of both partners in a continuing chainlike reciprocal interaction. The result is that the partners are ready to emit appropriate reproductive behavior at the appropriate stage of their reproductive cycle. The process is integrated by the mutual interaction and stimulation of the behavior and physiology in the two partners.

The *Whitten effect,* in which female rodents housed near males are more likely than controls to become sexually receptive (see Chapter 9), has a similar function. It is more advantageous to have the female receptive when the males are present than when they are absent. The Whitten effect seems to function to bring females into estrus when chances for mating are maximal. In species where ovulation is contingent upon mating, receptivity may be quite prolonged and may be terminated by mating. This, too, is a means of maximizing reproduction by tying critical endocrine events to the presence and behavior of the male.

Virgin female rats, and even males, can be made to show maternal behavior if exposed to pups for a long enough time (Chapter 9). The critical aspect of hormonal control of maternal behavior is not that a new pattern is developed, but rather that it is exquisitely timed. The new mother displays maternal behavior when she has to—as soon as the pups are born. Hormonal changes ensure that behavior, which otherwise would take days to develop, is available immediately. This is indicative of the functions of hormones in timing critical events in the reproductive cycle.

The postcopulatory preference of polygamous male rats for the odors of novel female rats (Chapter 9) was seen as permitting the male to mate with several females and thus to maximize dispersal of his sperm.

The adrenals are a part of a system precisely adapted to ensure appropriate physiological and behavioral responses to the presence or absence of stress; they also are important in metabolism (Gorbman & Bern, 1962; Selye, 1956; Shapiro, 1968). Other endocrine systems are of equal importance to the survival of the organisms, although they have received less attention from comparative psychologists.

The sensory and perceptual capacities and predispositions of different species are easily correlated with the mode of adaptation of that species. Various examples of such adaptive correlations in sensory systems were presented in Chapter 10. Visual sensitivity in some nocturnal species was seen to be enhanced through the evolution of eyes with particularly large pupils and lenses. The tapetum, which reflects light back through the retina, is found in a variety of nocturnal species and increases sensitivity. Diurnal species frequently have a layer of black pigment to absorb light and prevent ghost images. Diurnal species tend to have better visual acuity than nocturnal species—a characteristic quite useful in daytime living. Some large wading birds have polarized light vision. This helps them to see and to seize prey in the water—just as humans are aided by wearing polarized sunglasses. The presense or absence of stereoscopic vision appears related to the life style of the organism. Predators and arboreal species tend to have eyes located near the front of the head, maximizing stereoscopic vision and improving depth perception. Prey species, on the other hand, tend to have eyes set in the side of the head to provide a panoramic view with reduced depth perception. This helps them detect predators.

The efficient infrared receptors of snakes help to locate prey. Active sensory systems generally evolve where use of other senses is restricted, as in nocturnal species. The electrical senses of electric fish enable them to navigate in muddy waters and to adopt a nocturnal mode of life in waters, such as those of South America, which may be filled with diurnal predators. Many electric fish make poor aquarium pets primarily because they spend their daytime periods absolutely still on the substrate, though they are active nearly continuously in the dark. Bats have evolved a system of echolocation whereby they are able to detect flying insects (Chapter 10). This is an excellent solution to the considerable problem of locating rapidly moving, small objects in darkness. However, moths have evolved an effective system in response. Auditory stimuli in the frequency range of bat ultrasonic cries trigger changes in moths' flight patterns, including erratic evasion patterns (Roeder & Treat, 1961). The authors noted that not all animals showed evasive behavior, but those which did were the more likely to survive. In one set of observations, for every 100 reacting moths that survived, just 60 nonreacting moths survived—a selective advantage of 40 per cent.

Chapter 11 contained a variety of adaptive correlations related to perception. A major theme of the chapter was the importance of considering behavior in the natural habitat when attempting to understand perceptual phenomena demonstrated in the laboratory. The behavior that is measured with "brass instruments" in the laboratory was shaped by selection in the natural habitat. Nocturnal species tend to be more responsive than diurnal species to tactile stimulation when such stimulation is placed in competition with other modalities. Arboreal and ground-dwelling primates appear to differ in regard to their discrimination of verticality and slant. Horizontal and vertical lines in a frame of reference may affect perception of the true vertical to a greater extent in ground-dwelling species. This is consistent with the need of arboreal species to perceive the vertical independent of orientation. Performance of vertebrates on the visual cliff appears correlated with the ontogeny of locomotor activity. Some species seem to perceive depth at birth; others do not. By the time they begin to locomote, however, most species appear capable of perceiving depth. Visual preferences in insects are related to the kinds of surfaces upon which they settle. Perceptual preferences in newly hatched birds appear related to the food they will peck.

Ability to recognize individual differences in auditory signals related to reproductive behavior appears correlated with breeding structure. Thus, laughing gulls, which breed and hatch under colony conditions, can identify the specific calls of their parents as early as 6 days post hatching. They do not respond to comparable calls from other adult gulls of the species. The cues underlying individual recognition in chickens were studied, using operant techniques by Candland (1969). Recognition of individuals is critical to much social behavior (e.g., dominance hierarchies) and worthy of further study.

Modification of Behavior   As was pointed out in Chapter 12, there can be little question that invertebrates are capable of the modifications of behavior we label "learning." In a few tasks, the performance of invertebrates may exceed that of vertebrates. The delayed response of digger wasps provides an excellent example (Chapter 13). While the plasticity of invertebrate behavior appears somewhat less than that of vertebrate behavior, invertebrates have been remarkably successful—if survival is used as the criterion of success. Ants and termites have survived for millions of years longer than vertebrates. This again brings home the point that there are many ways to adapt, and the primate mode, of which we tend to be fond, is only one of them.

The tendency of comparative psychologists to stress adaptation in studying behavior is nowhere more evident than in the discussion of learning in vertebrates in Chapter 13. Classically, it was assumed that a unidimensional trait, *learning ability,* could be isolated. It was believed that increasing doses of this trait would be found as one "ascends the phylogenetic scale" to man. Currently, there is an emphasis on adaptive correlation. The earlier emphasis on learning ability has shifted to one on learning abilit*ies*. Performance in learning tasks is seen as related to adaptations in the natural habitat. This view has been summarized by Rozin and Kalat (1971) as follows:

> It is argued that the laws or mechanisms of learning are adapted to deal with particular types of problems and can be fully understood only in a naturalistic context. The "laws of learning" in the feeding system need not be the same as those in other systems; manifestation of a learning capacity in one area of behavior does not imply that it will be accessible in other areas [p. 459].

Numerous examples of the advantages of considering learning in relation to ecology were provided in Chapter 13. One was the *Garcia effect*. In most learning problems, reinforcement must occur soon after a response if it is to be effective. However, rats associate illness with taste cues even after very long delays. Equally important, other stimuli are not associated in this manner. The adaptive value of this system is evident. It enables the animal which consumes sublethal amounts of poison to avoid consuming poison in the future. This is consistent with the behavior of wild rats, which are difficult to poison if they are not killed on the first attempt. Similar adaptations may or may not appear in other response systems and in other species.

A review of literature on learning in vertebrates in Chapter 13 suggested that many species differences in learning performance could be understood as related to response availability, sensory dominance, and preparedness, independent of the classification of the species. The discrepancy in avoidance-learning performance between goldfish and Siamese fighting fish was related to species differences in adaptation and characteristic responses to aversive stimuli. Differences between dolphins and monkeys in learning to emit vocalizations in an operant-conditioning situation were related to response availability. Bolles's argument associating performance in avoidance tasks with species-typical defense responses was related to preparedness and served to integrate a variety of diverse data. As the species-typical defense reactions of rats are fleeing, freezing, and fighting, tasks in which such behavior is demanded are learned readily. Other tasks are not. Learning sets were seen to depend more on the sensory capacities of different species than on learning ability per se.

The importance of adaptation was cited again in Chapter 14 as a means of understanding the stimuli to which species are particularly responsive in the laboratory. The single units in the frog retina which respond maximally to small convex objects moving toward the center of the visual field ("bug perceivers") (Lettvin, Maturana, McCulloch, & Pitts, 1959) and the cells in monkey brains which respond differentially to the cry of another monkey and to other meaningful sounds are cited as examples. Each response is complex and adaptive. The importance of recognizing instances of parallel evolution and of remembering that no unitary trait of so-called intelligence has yet been proposed again was emphasized.

General Approaches A number of attempts have been made to study the whole life of a species rather than to concentrate on a single behavioral pattern. The beginnings of such an approach already have been discussed in relation to the work of Crook and Hediger.

Examples of work within restricted taxonomic units include much work on the rodent genus *Peromyscus* (e.g., J. A. King, 1963, 1968; Layne, 1969, 1970; Layne & Ehrhart, 1970). The approach here has been to attempt to relate behavioral patterns testable in the laboratory, such as drinking, climbing, digging, and nest-building, to ecological variables. For example, *P. gossypinus*, the cotton mouse, is widely distributed over much of the southeastern United States, whereas the Florida mouse, *P. floridanus*, lives in a much more restricted habitat. Layne (1970) found that cotton mice are better climbers than Florida mice. This is in keeping with field observations, and may serve to facilitate their wide range and broad habitat tolerance, and to reduce competition for resources where the species overlap. Digging behavior in *Peromyscus* appeared to be correlated with nesting habits. Florida mice were poorer nest-builders than were cotton mice (Chapter 3). As Florida mice are burrow dwellers, selective pressures for nest-building probably are not so great as those in the cotton mice who nest in a greater variety of situations. In this series of studies, Layne included animals representing different populations of the same species, animals that were either wild-trapped or laboratory-reared, and two species not mentioned in the present summary. This kind of comprehensive approach within a restricted taxonomic unit, utilizing a variety of species and behavioral patterns in the laboratory, may present the greatest hope for success with the method of adaptive correlation. The importance of studying animals drawn from different naturally occurring populations has been stressed by Bruell (1970). He has suggested that there may be no such thing as species-typical behavior, but, rather, behavior which is typical of a given restricted population unit of a species. It must be remembered that a pattern may be population-typical, genus-typical, or order-typical—as well as species-typical.

The importance of considering animals as total adapted units rather than as clusters of isolated traits was illustrated in Chapter 3 with a detailed description of the adaptations of kangaroo rats. The animal is relatively safe in the burrow, but subject to predation outside. Cheek pouches enable the animal to carry considerable food in a single trip, thus minimizing time outside the burrow. The eyes are located so as to be useful in predator detection. The forepaws are freed for a variety of uses. Certain mechanisms are adaptive in water conservation, an important characteristic in desert dwellers. Unpredictable saltatorial locomotion makes these animals difficult for predators to catch. Kangaroo rats thus are totally adapted animals, specialized for life in a particular habitat.

Etkin (1964) has summarized much information about the life styles of a variety of vertebrates. Song birds are portrayed as highly mobile, diurnal animals, dominated by audition and vision, feeding on insects and plant products, and subject to predation from airborne and some ground predators. They tend to be monomorphic and territorial. A mated pair occupies a territory, sharing parental duties. This integrated system of behavior can be seen as permitting both efficient use of limited resources and maximal rates of reproduction, within the limits set by the need for camouflage.

Marine birds feed in flocks which may range over long distances in search of food. Since they generally are large and strong, the major predation danger is on eggs and young. These birds tend to breed as territorial pairs within breeding colonies, as exemplified by gulls and penguins. They are monomorphic, share parental duties, and defend their territory fiercely. Nest-relief ceremonies provide some of their most spectacular behavioral patterns. Their ability to recognize a single mate in a large colony is remarkable and poorly understood.

Flock-living, surface-dwelling birds such as fowl and pheasants tend to range over large areas. Although females and the young are protectively colored, males may be brightly colored. Young are precocious. Typically, the only territoriality centers about mating, with territories held relatively briefly. Parental care is left to the female. It is in these birds that imprinting and dominance hierarchies are most evident.

In each of these bird societies, a variety of behavioral patterns interact to maximize survival. Precocial young and stable social relationships are needed in a mobile flock, whereas vigorous defense of the nest is appropriate for marine birds. Flock-living birds and marine species can "afford" to be conspicuous, whereas song birds cannot. A variety of behavioral patterns and morphological characteristics interact to make each life style viable.

Etkin also described a variety of social organization among mammals. Rats are scavengers whose primary protection lies in their ability to find cover quickly. Therefore they are nocturnal and occupy a small home range. An important adaptation is their ability to reproduce rapidly.

The mating structure of red deer involves a harem maintained by a single male. Yet, the primary social organization is a matriarchy with the older females controlling other females and the young, while males live apart in loosely organized herds. The sensory acuity and storage of learned material in the adult female serve to protect the young in this prey species.

Wolf social organization was described in Chapter 4. The pack-hunting, cooperative type of organization appears adaptive in bringing down difficult prey. Food sharing, site attachment, and stable dominance hierarchies enable the female to remain in the den with the young. Thus, the young have a prolonged dependence upon adults. This relationship permits a great flexibility of behavior from generation to generation since much of the development of behavior can depend upon learning.

Primates such as macaques tend to live in larger groups and to range in forests or semiopen areas. They are vegetarians, and usually on the move. A few dominant males tend to monopolize breeding and resources. Sexual dimorphism is apparent. Visual signals are important to the coordination of behavior in this habitat. Females usually have primary responsibility for rearing the young, although males will defend the group. The young remain close to the mother but must be prepared to move with the group. Once nursing is completed, food sharing is rare.

It has been suggested that the social organization of protocultural man, a cooperative hunter, must have been more like that of wolves than that of extant primates (Etkin, 1964).

Thus, each life style is seen as composed of a variety of elements which interact to make it a success. Dominance tends to appear where there is sexual dimorphism, polygyny, harem formation, and minimal male participation in parental care. Individual recognition of parent and young is important where many similar animals live in a group. Prolonged dependency permits considerable reliance on learning during development. Different factors interact to make the total pattern viable.

Conclusions   Psychologists increasingly are recognizing the importance of studying behavior in relation to ecological adaptation. The method of adaptive correlation provides excellent insight into the manner in which the behavior of a species is adapted to its particular ecological niche. Many of these correlations are obvious. Some appear strained. The primary need in this area of research is experimentation. Experimental demonstration of the adaptive function of a behavioral pattern, in the manner of Tinbergen's demonstration of the function of eggshell removal, will provide the most convincing demonstrations of adaptive function. The remaining need is for research and thought about adaptation to continue to filter through various areas of psychology and to increase the reliance of psychologists on the principles of evolution as a means of integrating diverse material.

EVOLUTION-RELATED TOPICS

Three topics related to evolution merit some comment in this chapter. They are reproductive isolating mechanisms, domestication, and behavior and systematics.

Reproductive Isolating Mechanisms

In order for an individual of a sexually reproducing species to ensure maximal chances for the survival of its genes, it generally must seek out and mate with a member of the opposite sex. Usually, it is important that the individual mate with a member of its own species, as such mating increases the chances of viable, fertile offspring being produced. In the course of evolution, a number of mechanisms may evolve which function to ensure that mating takes place within, rather than between, species. Reproductive isolating mechanisms are defined as "biological properties of individuals that prevent the interbreeding of populations that are actually or potentially sympatric [Mayr, 1963, p. 91]." Mayr (1963) regards these reproductive isolating mechanisms as perhaps the most important set of attributes possessed by an organism because they are almost, by definition, the species criteria (see Chapter 1). A classification of the various possible reproductive isolating mechanisms is presented in Table 15–1. Some mechanisms prevent interspecific matings. Separation by different breeding seasons and by occupation of different habitats obviously tends to

Table 15–1 A Classification of Reproductive Isolating Mechanisms

1. Mechanisms that prevent interspecific crosses (premating mechanisms):
    a. Potential mates do not meet (seasonal and habitat isolation).
    b. Potential mates meet but do not mate (ethological isolation).
    c. Copulation is attempted but no transfer of sperm takes place (mechanical isolation).
2. Mechanisms that reduce full success of interspecific crosses (postmating mechanisms):
    a. Sperm transfer takes place but egg is not fertilized (gametic mortality).
    b. Egg is fertilized but zygote dies (zygote mortality).
    c. Zygote produces an F_1 hybrid of reduced viability (hybrid inviability).
    d. F_1 hybrid zygote is fully viable but partially or completely sterile, or produces deficient F_2 (hybrid sterility).

SOURCE: From Mayr, 1963, p. 92.

prevent interbreeding. A wide variety of courtship patterns, a favorite topic of the classical ethologists, functions to ensure that individuals mate only with conspecifics displaying the appropriate behavior during courtship. In some instances, the genitals of different species simply do not fit together properly, thus producing a mechanically mediated isolation.

A number of postmating isolating mechanisms are summarized in the second part of Table 15–1. Reproduction can fail because of a failure of fertilization of the ovum, death of the zygote, reduced viability of the hybrid, or reduced fertility of the hybrid. It will be recalled that a specific number or rate of copulation-related vaginal stimulations must be given female rodents during copulation in order that neuroendocrine responses essential for pregnancy will be elicited (see Chapter 9). Diamond (1970) has termed such a system a "vaginal code." This behavioral interaction may function as such a postmating isolation mechanism.

The earlier in the chain of reproductive behavior that a potentially suboptimal mating is terminated, the less energy will have been "wasted." Therefore, there appears to be a trend toward the evolution of premating isolating mechanisms. Behavioral isolating mechanisms seem to be the most important of the isolating mechanisms that have been described. Thus mating behavior may be one of the most significant defining characteristics of a species.

Assessment of actual isolating mechanisms is difficult. Because many isolating mechanisms break down in the laboratory, it is necessary to study them in the field. Strictly speaking, one needs to observe the beginning of a reproductive sequence and see it terminated by the appropriate mechanisms. As this is rarely possible, individual mechanisms usually should be referred to as *potential* reproductive isolating mechanisms.

Selection A number of studies of selection were cited in Chapter 6 (e.g., Figures 6–7, 6–8, and 6–9). In these cases, the experimenter selected individuals scoring high or low on some test and permitted them to mate. If the scores of the

offspring change in the predicted direction over the course of several generations, one can conclude that there is a genetic component to the behavioral
pattern. However, this tells us little of how such processes act in nature.

A different kind of selection was designed by Crossley (Tinbergen, 1965)
to study the way natural selection works. It involved exerting a selective pressure on a known population. Fruit flies of the genus *Drosophila,* popular animals for this kind of study (Spieth, 1958), were used. Crossley studied the
interactions of ebony and vestigial *Drosophila melanogaster*. She selected
against heterogametic matings by not permitting hybrid offspring to mate. Over
the course of forty generations, the percentage of homogametic matings (ebony
females by ebony males and vestigial females by vestigial males) increased,
while the percentage of heterogametic matings decreased. By careful
controls, she was able to rule out such factors as habitat preference, differential rearing of progeny, and random genetic drift. Somehow, males and
females became differentially responsive to partners of their own species. How
had this change in mating patterns been brought about? As frequently is the
case, behavior played an important role. Crossley observed that both vestigial
and ebony females gave more repelling movements to heterogametic males
at the end of her experiment than at the beginning. Furthermore, the males
terminated copulation attempts in response to such repelling movements more
rapidly near the end of the experiment. Thus, selection against hybrid offspring, not against any particular behavioral pattern, produced a change in
behavior that functioned to increase the reproductive isolation between these
two populations. It is likely that this process is very much like the one that
takes place in the evolution of isolating mechanisms in the wild. Studies of
this type, in which the experimenter selects against individuals mating outside
their own population, may mimic processes occurring in nature, and may therefore lead to a better understanding of the evolution of reproductive isolating
mechanisms.

Domestication

Much research by comparative psychologists is performed on domesticated
species such as laboratory rats, mice, hamsters, gerbils, cats, and dogs.
Because domestication produces dramatic chages in the morphological characteristics and behavior of a species, its effects merit special consideration.
Psychologists interested in the evolution of behavior, and in the relationship
between behavior in the laboratory and that in the natural environment, must
examine the effects of the domestication process on behavior.

Lockard (1968) summarized much of the information regarding the effects
of domestication in the albino rat. Wild rats tend to fight more, vocalize more,
kill more mice, and behave more cautiously in the presence of novel objects

than do their domesticated conspecifics. In one attempt to reenact the domestication of rats, it was found that the rats became fatter, less vicious, more fertile, and smaller-brained as domestication progressed (H. D. King, 1939; King & Donaldson, 1929). Similar changes in fertility have been seen already in the 17 years since initial domestication of the deermouse, *Peromyscus maniculatus bairdii* (Price, 1967). Although there has been no intentional selection, it is likely that more healthy and fertile animals have been selected more frequently by man for breeding than their less fortunate counterparts. As a result, there has been a differential selection for certain genes.

On the other hand, it frequently is assumed that differences in the behavior of various inbred strains of mice have arisen since the animals have been brought into the laboratory. It is believed that different genes have become fixed in different lines as a course of inbreeding and in an essentially random manner. Van Oortmerssen (1970) has suggested that behavioral differences in nest-building, exploratory behavior, and agonistic behavior may have arisen before the progenitors of the different inbred strains were brought into the laboratory. If this is true, these differences would have to be viewed as specific adaptations to particular ecological environments rather than as arbitrary products of fixation of single genes in an inbred strain.

The behavior of dogs and their supposed wild ancestors, wolves, was compared in Chapter 4. Many of the behavioral patterns of dogs are identical with those of wolves, virtually unchanged in some 12,000 years of domestication. Many of the reactions of dogs to humans are the same as those of subordinate dogs or wolves to dominant conspecifics. The social patterns of wolves are somewhat more distinct and stereotyped than those of dogs. There have been some alterations, as, for example, in the seasonal cycle of sexual activity. Although the behavior of dogs and wolves differs in many ways, the basic functions are identical. Understanding of the functional significance of many behavioral patterns in dogs is improved through study of their function in wolf packs in the natural environment.

A loss of distinct seasonality of breeding similar to that in dogs was described for felines in Chapter 9. Following penile desensitization in domesticated cats, the ancestral seasonality became apparent.

Great care must be exercised in generalizing back and forth between wild animals and their conspecifics that have undergone domestication in the hands of man. An understanding of the process of domestication should help in evaluating such problems.

Behavior and Systematics

Many behavioral patterns are highly stereotyped and occur in virtually all appropriate members of the species. Such behavioral patterns frequently are minimally altered by experience and sometimes are termed *instinctive*. Behavioral patterns which are highly stereotyped and under substantial genetic control may be as characteristic of a species as is a morphological structure. Therefore, behavioral data can be quite useful in reconstructing probable phylogenetic histories.

Mayr (1958) cites numerous examples in which behavioral studies produced substantial clarifications or revisions of the accepted taxonomic structure of a group of species. Among birds, for example, crag martins *(Ptyonoprogne)* had traditionally been placed near bank swallows *(Riparia)*. On the basis of differences in nesting habits, it was suggested that they should be classified nearer to barn swallows *(Hirundo)*. Subsequent information has borne out this reclassification. Mayr (1958) also describes the work of Adriaanse on wasps of the genus *Ammophila*. Many wasps of what was thought to be a single species filled their nest holes with material from a quarry, ate sawflies, laid their eggs before provisioning the nest, and bred early in the summer. However, other animals filled their nest holes with material which was flown in, ate caterpillars, provisioned the nest before laying the eggs, and bred later in summer. These two groups of animals turned out to be two different "good species" (see Chapter 1).

Working with fireflies, Barber (1951) and Lloyd (1969) have relied extensively on behavioral criteria. In the mating patterns of most species of fireflies, the male flies above the ground emitting flashes in a particular pattern. The female remains near the ground and answers the male with a species-typical flash pattern after a set interval following the flash of the male. This pattern varies with the species and with temperature. The male then approaches the female as they continue to exchange flashes. A skilled observer can mimic the replies of the female, and thus attract the male to within a distance where he can be caught. Indeed, several predatory species have developed just such a mimicry. There are several species of fireflies which cannot be separated on the basis of morphology, but which display different mating patterns and thus are good species according to the definitions discussed in Chapter 1.

One of the most complete behavioral ethograms is that resulting from Lorenz's (1941) study of ducks and geese. This "shaving brush" diagram is shown in Figure 15-4. The vertical lines represent species, and the horizontal lines represent characters. Some species share a large number of behavioral patterns, whereas others share just a few. Pattern EPV is shared by all species, whereas pattern PiH is shared by just two species. Still other patterns differentiate ducks from geese. This analysis led to the reassessment of the taxonomic location of several of the species (Johnsgard, 1961).

The work of the behaviorist can make a substantial contribution to systematics just as a firm working knowledge of systematics is critical to good comparative behavioral work.

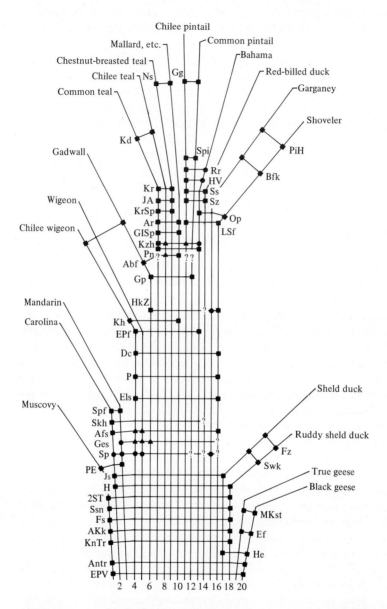

Figure 15–4. A taxonomy of Anatinae based on behavioral character-istics. Vertical and oblique lines represent species; each horizontal line signifies the presence of a character in the species whose lines it crossed. (From K. Lorenz, *Journal für Ornithologie Supplement,* 1941, **89,** 194–294.)

MAN IN COMPARATIVE PSYCHOLOGY

To what extent are studies of our own species a part of comparative psychology? There have been numerous places in this book where human behavior has been considered in relation to the behavior of other species. Yet, these instances probably will be regarded as too few by many students. Many comparative psychologists, however, feel they have enough to do to understand the behavior of non-human species without adding the additional set of problems associated with studying humans. At this point in the development of a technology of behavior, the study of human behavior frequently requires different methods from those used in the study of the behavior of other animals. Therefore, scientists trained in the study of animal behavior sometimes are reluctant to extend themselves to the study of humans. As comparative psychology matures, its contribution to an understanding of human behavior will very likely increase.

Man in Series of Comparisons

Numerous attempts have been made in this book to include the study of man as part of comparative psychology by including data from humans in a series of comparisons. In Chapter 4, the processes regulating the developmental socialization of young humans were compared with those of dogs. Although there are obvious differences in the socialization of the two species, the basic processes were found to be quite similar, albeit differently ordered and differentially emphasized. Also discussed were the interaction of man and dog and the apparent similarity between man-dog interactions and dominance interactions in dogs and wolves.

The difficulties and importance of behavior-genetic analysis in human behavior were discussed in Chapter 6. There is good evidence for a substantial contribution of genotype to differences in measured intelligence in humans (Erlenmeyer-Kimling & Jarvik, 1963). Other characteristics that are believed to be correlated with genotypic variation include personality characteristics, mental retardation, and various psychopathologies including schizophrenia (see Manosevitz, Lindzey, & Thiessen, 1969).

The sensory and perceptual capacities of man and other species were repeatedly compared in Chapters 10 and 11. Research on sensory and perceptual processes provides a good example of the way in which man can be included in a series of comparisons. Man was seen to possess a relatively balanced set of sensory-perceptual sensitivities, with olfaction his apparent weak suit.

As discussed in Chapter 1, inclusion of man in comparisons of different species may, in the long run, be the most productive method of understanding man, his uniqueness, and his place in nature.

Generalizations of Nonhuman Data to Man

One of the major reasons behind support of nonhuman research is the belief that results gathered on nonhuman subjects will be generalizable to humans. There is firm foundation for this belief. For example, many of man's most important medical advances were developed and tested on nonhuman species before application to man. Basic research on nerve cells and their interactions has been conducted on such species as squid and lobsters and has found excellent generalizability to the human nervous system. It is clear that behavioral data can be similarly generalized on some occasions. However, care must be exercised because complex behavior and social interactions are susceptible to oversimplified generalizations which may cloud issues rather than clarify them.

In Chapter 7, the behavioral and morphological anomalies created in laboratory animals by manipulating hormone levels at critical times in development were related to human pathology. Many principles appear common to the two sets of data. Although the dependent variables often are quite different, similarities are so great that nonhuman research can be fairly valuable in understanding human psychosexual development.

The debate over the usefulness of information gathered regarding nonhuman communication for understanding human language was discussed in some detail in Chapter 5. Some scientists believe that language is so deep-rooted a species-specific behavior in humans that its basic principles differ from those controlling communication in other species. Others believe that study of communication, and particularly language acquisition, in nonhumans can aid in understanding human language. The usefulness of these data for understanding human language will be evaluated in the future. Research such as Premack's, discussed in Chapter 5, appears to go far in working toward a unification of the study of communication in all species.

A number of authors have attempted to generalize rather directly from research on nonhuman social behavior to comparatively complex human social behavior, including the roots of love and war (e.g., Ardrey, 1966; Lorenz, 1966; Morris, 1967, 1969). Even when this is done without factual error, it is a risky enterprise (Crook, 1968). The complexity of the process of generalizing such data to the human situation was stressed in the conclusion to Chapter 2. It was pointed out that interpretations of the behavior of geese, for example, even if factually correct, may have little relevance to the human situation. Indeed, too early generalization may hinder, rather than help, understanding of very pressing problems. In Chapter 4, the dangers of overapplication of the principles of nonhuman territoriality to human behavior were cited.

Information gathered on nonhuman subjects frequently can be generalized to humans. However, given the present status of knowledge, this may best be restricted to relatively simple behavioral patterns. Considerations of the implications of data on more complex behavior in nonhuman species provide a very important source of hypotheses about human behavior. One must be careful to treat them as hypotheses rather than as conclusions.

Generalization of Methodology to Man

A fruitful approach to generalizing to humans from studies on nonhumans may be to generalize the methods of study rather than the results of studies (Tinbergen, 1968). There are a number of areas where this can be, and is being, done at present. The behavior of neonates provides an excellent locus for study in that they possess simpler behavioral repertoires and are less influenced by complicating cultural factors than are adults. Work of Prechtl (1965) on the significance of various neonatal reflexes and neurological development provides a case in point. Freedman (1965) has uttered a plea for use of ethological methods in human behavior genetics. He studied two biologically important behavioral patterns, smiling and fear of strangers in twins. An appreciable role of genetic influences in the development of these behavioral patterns was found. Freedman speculates that both smiling and fear of strangers in neonates may function to reinforce the bond between parent and child. An adaptive function may thus be served. Freedman suggests several ways in which such an hypothesis might be tested experimentally. Selection of discrete, biologically significant behavioral patterns may facilitate the enormous task of studying human behavior.

The highly refined behavioral technology that has been developed in work on learned behavior in nonhumans is being profitably applied to human behavior. The operant methodology (e.g., Honig, 1966) is being applied with great success in a variety of areas (see, for example, the *Journal of Applied Behavior Analysis*). An assortment of techniques can be used with infants where competing responses and complex cognitive processes are minimized and direct comparisons are simplified (e.g., Lipsitt, 1967; Papoušek, 1967).

Perhaps the major topic of human ethology is that of nonverbal communication in humans. The study of gestures, facial expressions, and so on, provides a frutiful locus for application of the methods of ethology to the study of humans. Duncan (1969) listed six forms of nonverbal communication in humans:

1   Body motion or kinesic behavior—including body movements such as gestures, postures, facial expressions, and eye movements

2   Paralanguage—voice quality, nuances of speech, and such sounds as grunting, laughing, and yawning

3   Proxemics—the use of space, both personal and social, and man's perception of it

4   Olfaction—signals transmitted via olfactory channels, including pheromonal communication

5 Skin sensitivity to touch and temperature—tactile and related communication between humans

6 Use of artifacts, such as dress and cosmetics—alteration of body appearance by application of various foreign substances

Each of these forms of communication has an analogue in nonhuman species.

Particular interest has been focused on kinesics, or *body language*. Many facial expressions in humans resemble those of nonhuman species; sometimes they appear to have analogous functions (Darwin, 1872; Eibl-Eibesfeldt, 1970). The studies of Birdwhistell (1952) and Scheflen (1964, 1969) are indicative of the considerable advances being made in understanding nonverbal communication studied as a signal.

Conclusion

In the twentieth century, it is difficult to believe that one could gain a complete understanding of man and his behavior without an understanding of evolution and man's place in it. "Evolution is no longer the property of a small group of biologists: to understand it thoroughly has become the responsibility of every person with a potential role for man's future [Alexander, 1971, p. 117]."

The pressing problems of our times often appear to require drastic actions. This may be true. However, thorough understanding of human behavior will require the slow and steady progress of scientific research. Simple answers seldom are correct answers. It is to be hoped that we can work to gain the time needed to approach a better understanding of human behavior.

As was discussed in Chapter 1 and in the conclusion to Chapter 8, man tends to think very highly of his own importance in the scheme of the universe. He forgets that rats and mice appear to be the dominant mammals in our time, while some authorities believe we are living in an Age of Insects. For all his complex brain and behavior, man is a part of nature. By learning about both his own behavior and that of his biological cousins, he may learn to live within his niche, to cease fouling the environment, and to prolong the lives of all species, including his own. The study of evolution may provide the framework for this understanding.

REFERENCES

ALEXANDER, R. D. The search for an evolutionary philosophy of man. *Proceedings of the Royal Society of Victoria*, 1971, **84,** 99–120.

ALLISON, T., & VAN TWYVER, H. B. The evolution of sleep. *Natural History*, 1970, **79**(2), 56–65.

ARDREY, R. *The territorial imperative*. New York: Atheneum, 1966.

ARONSON, L. R. Hormones and reproductive behavior: Some phylogenetic considerations. In A. Gorbman (Ed.), *Comparative Endocrinology*. New York: Wiley, 1959. Pp. 98–120.

ATZ, J. W. The application of the idea of homology to behavior. In L. R. Aronson, E. Tobach, D. S. Lehrman, & J. S. Rosenblatt (Eds.), *Development and evolution of behavior.* San Francisco: Freeman, 1970. Pp. 53–74.

BARBER, H. S. North American fireflies of the genus *Photuris. Smithsonian Institution Miscellaneous Collections,* 1951, **117,** 1–58.

BEACH, F. A. Evolutionary changes in the physiological control of mating behavior in mammals. *Psychological Review,* 1947, **54,** 297–315.

BEACH, F. A. Evolutionary aspects of psychoendocrinology. In A. Roe & G. G. Simpson (Eds.), *Behavior and evolution.* New Haven, Conn.: Yale University Press, 1958. Pp. 81–102.

BIRDWHISTELL, R. L. *Introduction to kinesics.* Louisville, Ky.: University of Louisville Press, 1952.

BITTERMAN, M. E. Toward a comparative psychology of learning. *American Psychologist,* 1960, **15,** 704–712.

BROWER, L. P., & BROWER, J. V. Z. Investigations into mimicry. *Natural History,* 1962(4), **71,** 8–19.

BRUELL, J. H. Behavioral heterosis. In J. Hirsch (Ed.), *Behavior-genetic analysis.* New York: McGraw-Hill, 1967. Pp. 270–286.

BRUELL, J. H. Behavioral population genetics and wild *Mus musculus.* In G. Lindzey & D. D. Thiessen (Eds.), *Contributions to behavior-genetic analysis: The mouse as a prototype.* New York: Appleton-Century-Crofts, 1970. Pp. 261–291.

CANDLAND, D. K. Discriminability of facial regions used by the domestic chicken in maintaining the social dominance order. *Journal of Comparative and Physiological Psychology,* 1969, **69,** 281–285.

CROOK, J. H. The nature and function of territorial aggression. In M. F. A. Montagu (Ed.), *Man and aggression.* London: Oxford University Press, 1968. Pp. 141–178.

CROOK, J. H. Social organization and the environment: Aspects of contemporary social ethology. *Animal Behaviour,* 1970, **18,** 197–209.

DARWIN, C. *The expression of the emotions in man and animals.* London: Appleton, 1872.

DEWSBURY, D. A. Electric fishes and their potential as subjects for psychological research. *Worm Runner's Digest,* 1965, **7,** 54–66.

DEWSBURY, D. A. Copulatory behavior of old-field mice. *Peromyscus polionotus subgriseus. Animal Behaviour,* 1971, **19,** 192–209.

DEWSBURY, D. A. Patterns of mammalian copulatory behavior. *Quarterly Review of Biology,* 1972, **47,** 1–33.

DIAMOND, M. Intromission pattern and species vaginal code in relation to induction of pseudopregnancy. *Science,* 1970, **169,** 995–997.

DILGER, W. C. The comparative ethology of the African parrot genus *Agapornis. Zeitschrift für Tierpsychologie,* 1960, **17,** 649–685.

DILGER, W. C. The behavior of lovebirds. *Scientific American,* 1962, **208**(1), 88–98.

DUNCAN, S. Nonverbal communication. *Psychological Bulletin,* 1969, **72,** 118–137.

EIBL-EIBESFELDT, I. *Ethology, the biology of behavior.* New York: Holt, Rinehart and Winston, 1970.

ERLENMEYER-KIMLING, L., & JARVIK, L. F. Genetics and intelligence: A review. *Science,* 1963, **142,** 1477–1479.

ETKIN, W. Types of social organization in birds and mammals. In W. Etkin (Ed.), *Social behavior and organization among vertebrates.* Chicago: The University of Chicago Press, 1964. Pp. 256–297.

FISLER, G. F. Mammalian organizational systems. *Los Angeles County Museum Contributions in Science*, 1969, **167,** 1–32.

FREEDMAN, D. G. An ethological approach to the genetic study of human behavior. In S. G. Vandenberg (Ed.), *Methods and goals in human behavior genetics*. New York: Academic Press, 1965. Pp. 141–161.

GLICKMAN, S. E. Curiosity has killed more mice than cats. *Psychology Today*, 1971, **5**(5), 54–56; 86.

GLICKMAN, S. E., & SROGES, R. W. Curiosity in zoo animals. *Behaviour*, 1966, **26,** 151–188.

GORBMAN, A., & BERN, H. A. *A textbook of comparative endocrinology*. New York: Wiley, 1962.

HEDIGER, H. Environmental factors influencing the reproduction of zoo animals. In F. A. Beach (Ed.), *Sex and behavior*. New York: Wiley, 1965. Pp. 319–354.

HEFFNER, H. E., RAVIZZA, R. J., & MASTERTON, B. Hearing in primitive mammals, IV: Bushbaby *(Galago senegalensis)*. *Journal of Auditory Research*, 1969, **9,** 19–23.

HENDERSON, N. D. The confounding effects of genetic variables in early experience research: Can we ignore them? *Developmental Psychobiology*, 1968, **1,** 146–152.

HENDERSON, N. D. Brain weight increases resulting from environmental enrichment: A directional dominance in mice. *Science*, 1970, **169,** 776–778.

HINDE, R. A., & TINBERGEN, N. The comparative study of species-specific behavior. In A. Roe & G. G. Simpson (Eds.), *Behavior and evolution*. New Haven, Conn.: Yale University Press, 1958. Pp. 251–268.

HONIG, W. K. *Operant behavior: Areas of research and applications*. New York: Appleton-Century-Crofts, 1966.

ITO, Y. Group and family bonds in animals in relation to their habitats. In L. R. Aronson, E. Tobach, D. S. Lehrman, & J. S. Rosenblatt (Eds.), *Development and evolution of behavior*. San Francisco: Freeman, 1970. Pp. 389–415.

JOHNSGARD, P. A. The taxonomy of the Anatidae—a behavioural analysis. *Ibis*, 1961, **103,** 71–85.

KEYNES, R. D. Electric organs. In M. E. Brown (Ed.), *The physiology of fishes*. New York: Academic Press, 1957. Pp. 323–343.

KING, H. D. Life processes in gray Norway rats during fourteen years in captivity. *American Anatomical Memoirs*, 1939, No. 17.

KING, H. D., & DONALDSON, H. H. Life processes and size of the body and organs of the gray Norway rat during ten generations in captivity. *American Anatomical Memoirs*, 1929, No. 14.

KING, J. A. Maternal behavior in *Peromyscus*. In H. L. Rheingold (Ed.), *Maternal behavior in mammals*. New York: Wiley, 1963. Pp. 58–93.

KING, J. A. Psychology. In J. A. King (Ed.), *Biology of Peromyscus (Rodentia)*. Lawrence, Kans.: American Society of Mammalogists, 1968. Pp. 496–542.

KING, J. A. Ecological psychology: An approach to motivation. *Nebraska Symposium on Motivation*, 1970, **18.** Pp. 1–33.

KING, J. A., & NICHOLS, J. W. Problems of classification. In R. H. Waters, D. A. Rethling-shafer, & W. E. Caldwell (Eds.), *Principles of comparative psychology*. New York: McGraw-Hill, 1960. Pp. 18–42.

LACK, D. The evolution of reproductive rates. In J. Huxley, A. C. Hardy, & E. B. Ford (Eds.), *Evolution as a process*. London: Allen & Unwin, 1954. Pp. 143–156.

LAYNE, J. N. Nest-building behavior in three species of deer mice, *Peromyscus*. *Behaviour*, 1969, **35,** 288–303.

LAYNE, J. N. Climbing behavior of *Peromyscus floridanus* and *Peromyscus gossypinus*. *Journal of Mammalogy*, 1970, **51**, 580–591.

LAYNE, J. N., & EHRHART, L. M. Digging behavior of four species of deer mice *(Peromyscus)*. *American Museum Novitates*, 1970, No. 2429. Pp. 1–16.

LEHRMAN, D. S. Interaction between internal and external environments in the regulation of the reproductive cycle of the ring dove. In F. A. Beach (Ed.), *Sex and behavior*. New York: Wiley, 1965. Pp. 355–380.

LETTVIN, J. Y., MATURANA, H. R., MC CULLOCH, W. S., & PITTS, W. H. What the frog's eye tells the frog's brain. *Proceedings of the Institute of Radio Engineers*, 1959, **47**. Pp. 1940–1951.

LIPSITT, L. P. Learning in the human infant. In H. W. Stevenson, E. H. Hess, & H. L. Rheingold (Eds.), *Early behavior: Comparative and developmental approaches*. New York: Wiley, 1967. Pp. 225–247.

LLOYD, J. E. Flashes of *Photuris* fireflies: Their value and use in recognizing species. *Florida Entomologist*, 1969, **52**, 29–35.

LOCKARD, R. B. The albino rat: A defensible choice or a bad habit? *American Psychologist*, 1968, **23**, 734–742.

LORENZ, K. Vergleichende Bewegungsstudien bei Anatiden. *Journal für Ornithologie, Suppl.*, 1941, **89**, 194–294.

LORENZ, K. *On aggression*. New York: Harcourt, Brace & World, 1966.

MANOSEVITZ, M., LINDZEY, G., & THIESSEN, D. D. *Behavioral genetics: Method and research*. New York: Appleton-Century-Crofts, 1969.

MARLER, P. Communication in monkeys and apes. In I. DeVore (Ed.), *Primate behavior*. New York: Holt, Rinehart & Winston, 1965. Pp. 544–584.

MAYR, E. Behavior and systematics. In A. Roe & G. G. Simpson (Eds.), *Behavior and evolution*. New Haven, Conn.: Yale University Press, 1958. Pp. 341–362.

MAYR, E. *Animal species and evolution*. Cambridge, Mass.: Harvard University Press, 1963.

MEDEWAR, P. B. Some immunological and endocrinological problems raised by the evolution of viviparity in vertebrates. *Symposium of the Society for Experimental Biology*, 1953, **7**, 320–338.

MORRIS, D. *The naked ape*. New York: McGraw-Hill, 1967.

MORRIS, D. *The human zoo*. New York: McGraw-Hill, 1969.

OORTMERSSEN, G. A. VAN. Biological significance, genetics and evolutionary origin of variability in behavior within and between inbred strains of mice *(Mus musculus)*. *Behaviour*, 1970, **38**, 1–92.

PAPOUŠEK, H. Experimental studies of appetitional behavior in human newborns and infants. In H. W. Stevenson, E. H. Hess, & H. L. Rheingold (Eds.), *Early behavior: Comparative and developmental approaches*. New York: Wiley, 1967. Pp. 249–277.

PRECHTL, H. F. R. Problems of behavioral studies in the newborn infant. *Advances in the Study of Behavior*, 1965, **1**, 75–98.

PRICE, E. The effect of reproductive performance on the domestication of the prairie deermouse, *Peromyscus manicalatus bairdii*. *Evolution*, 1967, **21**, 762–770.

ROEDER, K. D., & TREAT, A. E. The detection and evasion of bats by moths. *American Scientist*, 1961, **49**, 135–148.

ROZIN, P., & KALAT, J. W. Specific hungers and poison avoidance as adaptive specializations of learning. *Psychological Review*, 1971, **78**, 458–486.

SCHEFLEN, A. E. The significance of posture in communication systems. *Psychiatry*, 1964, **27**, 316–331.

SCHEFLEN, A. E. *Stream and structure of communicational behavior*. Bloomington: University of Indiana Press, 1969.

SCHNEIRLA, T. C. Levels in the psychological capacities of animals. In R. W. Sellars, V. J. McGill, & M. Farber (Eds.), *Philosophy for the future*. New York: Macmillan, 1949. Pp. 243–286.

SCHNEIRLA, T. C. An evolutionary and developmental theory of biphasic processes underlying approach and withdrawal. *Nebraska Symposium on Motivation*, 1959, **7,** 1–41.

SELYE, H. *The stress of life*. New York: McGraw-Hill, 1956.

SHAPIRO, S. Maturation of the neuroendocrine response to stress in the rat. In G. Newton & S. Levine (Eds.), *Early experience and development*. Springfield, Ill.: C. C Thomas, 1968. Pp. 198–257.

SIMPSON, G. G. The study of evolution: Methods and present status of theory. In A. Roe & G. G. Simpson (Eds.), *Behavior and evolution*. New Haven, Conn.: Yale University Press, 1958. Pp. 7–26.

SPIETH, H. T. Behavior and isolating mechanisms. In A. Roe & G. G. Simpson (Eds.), *Behavior and evolution*. New Haven, Conn.: Yale University Press, 1958. Pp. 363–389.

TINBERGEN, N. Some recent studies of the evolution of sexual behavior. In F. A. Beach (Ed.), *Sex and behavior*. New York: Wiley, 1965. Pp. 1–33.

TINBERGEN, N. On war and peace in animals and man. *Science*, 1968, **160,** 1411–1418.

TRIVERS, R. L. The evolution of reciprocal altruism. *Quarterly Review of Biology*, 1971, **46,** 35–57.

WILLIAMS, G. C. *Adaptation and natural selection*. Princeton, N. J.: Princeton University Press, 1966.

WYNNE-EDWARDS, V. C. *Animal dispersion in relation to social behaviour*. New York: Hafner, 1962.

Name Index

Subject Index

Investigation of objects:
  and manipulability, 113
  and neophobia, 113
  and neural complexity, 112, 516
  and novelty, 113
  and predation, 113, 502–503, 560
  as social behavior, 125
Isolating mechanisms (*see* Reproductive isolating mechanisms)
Isolation experiments, 50–56, 134, 254, 400–401

Jacobson's organ, 384
Johnston's organ, 370
Jumping stand, 354, 499, 517
Juvenile period, 132

Killing, 97–100
  and movement, 99
  ontogeny of, 99, 116–117
  (*See also* Hunting; Predation)
Kinesic behavior, 581

Laboratory research versus field work, 162, 335
Ladder use by chimpanzees, 540–541
Lagena, 366, 371–373
Language:
  conditioned in animals, 172–177
  development, 136, 165, 251
  evolution of, 166, 554–555, 580
  as level of communication, 164
  neural localization of, 290–291, 566
Language Acquisition Device, 164–165
Language Acquisition Gremlin, 165
Language learning potential, 171, 172–186
Larder hoarding, 100–101
Lashley jumping stand, 354, 499, 517
Lateral geniculate, 293–295
Lateral giant fibers of crayfish, 462
Lateral line organs, 367–369, 377
Laterality of language and brain structures, 290–291
Law of effect, 10
Law of parsimony, 9, 165, 512
Laws of learning, 556
Laws of psychology and genetics, 196, 230–232
Leader-follower relationships, 138
Leadership:
  in dog-human relationship, 135
  in goats, 140
  in wolves, 127
Learnability in communication, 171
Learning:
  abilities, 569
  in annelids, 452–456
  in arthropods, 460–463
  to attend, 421
  in bird embryo, 241
  and brain chemistry, 225–226, 250
  and brain structures, 286–288
  in coelenterates, 437–440
  comparisons among vertebrates, 288
  definitions of, 431
  and development, 573
  double discrimination, 444–446
  evolution of, 427–546, 557
  and food location in bees, 462
  in invertebrates, 429–464
  in mammalian fetus, 241
  in molluscs, 457–460
  and natural selection, 480
  neural bases in ants, 462
  in neonatal dogs, 131
  in nereids, 455–456
  observational, 531–538
  in paramecia, 435–436
  in PKU mice, 213
  in planarians, 440–452
  in protozoans, 430–437
  role in honeybee communication, 163, 463
  and sleep, 243–244
  and synapses, 431
  in vertebrates, 471–504
  (*See also* Avoidance learning; Classical conditioning; Discrimination learning; Escape learning; Instrumental conditioning; Learning sets; Maze learning; Operant conditioning)

Learning sets, 481–491
  in carnivores, 484–491
  in chickens, 486–487
  and cortex, 483, 487
  critique of method, 489–491
  development of, 483
  in dolphins, 487
  early interspecies comparisons, 483–484
  individual differences, 484–486
  number of effective cues, 488–490
  and olfaction, 490
  in primates, 483–491
  recent interspecies comparisons, 486–488
  in rodents, 487
  and sensory dominance, 490
Learning theory, 10
Lee-Boot effect, 324
Lens, 348
Licking, as a learned response, 479
Linkage:
  described, 200–201
  group and seizures in mice, 214
Lloyd Morgan's canon, 9, 512
Local sign, 401
Locality attachment (localization), 143
Localization auditory, 413–414, 477–478
Location, perception of, 409–410
Locomotion, 81–85
  in amphibians, 81
  in arboreal mammals, 83–84
  in bipedal mammals, 82–83
  brachiation, 83–84
  and depth perception, 400
  development in dogs, 131
  in flying mammals, 85–86
  in fossorial mammals, 84
  gallop, 82
  gliding, 85
  in marsupials, 81
  in monotremes, 81
  in paramecia, 433–434
  in reptiles, 81
  saltatory in kangaroo rats, 80
  saltatory in mammals, 82–83, 571
  swimming and diving in mammals, 84
  trot, 82
  in ungulates, 81
  and visual cliff, 569
  walking, 81–82
Locus of genes, 199
Long flips, 309–311
Longevity and population density, 336–338
Lordosis:
  and early androgens, 256–261
  and elimination, 316
  and estrous cycle, 85
  in hamsters, 110, 255–256
  and hormones, 257, 317
  in rats, 308, 316
  as spinal reflex, 309, 316
Loss of reflexes in development, 249–250

Mabaans, 374
Macrosmatic animals, 293
Magnetic senses, 378–379
Maintenance phase, 333
Mammalian skin factor, 385
Mammary glands in pregnancy, 330
Mand, 173–174
Manipulation and care-dependency relationships, 139
Man's future and evolution, 582
Mapping of genes, 214
Mass action, 291, 313
Massed versus distributed practice and genetics, 230–231
Matching:
  behavior, 496–497
  problem, 525
  to sample, 529–531
Maternal behavior, 330–335
  Caesarian section, 332
  hormonal basis, 332–333
  licking, 330
  maintenance, 333–334
  maternal calls in ducks, 241

Species Index

Species cited in this book are indexed according to their taxonomic classification. Common names are used throughout. Technical names are added for clarity where necessary. Species are arranged according to their phylum, class, or order, as appropriate for the number of citations for that group. Within each taxon an alphabetic list of general and specific categories is given. An attempt has been made to retain names used in the text; thus information on a single species may be cited under more than one heading. In the listing that follows, species, grouped by phylum, class, and order, are given numbers corresponding to the order of their appearance in this Index.

1.7 ECHINODERM PHYLUM

1.8 CHORDATE PHYLUM

2 SUBPHYLA WITHIN THE CHORDATE PHYLUM

2.1 UROCHORDATE SUBPHYLUM

2.2 VERTEBRATE SUBPHYLUM

3 CLASSES WITHIN THE VERTEBRATE SUBPHYLUM

3.1 AGNATHA CLASS (JAWLESS VERTEBRATES)

3.2 CHONDRICHTHYES CLASS (CARTILAGINOUS FISHES)

3.3 OSTEICHTHYES CLASS (BONY FISHES)

3.4 AMPHIBIAN CLASS

4.8 EDENTATE ORDER

4.12 CETACEAN ORDER

4.13 CARNIVORE ORDER